# A MODEL CIVIL PROCEDURE CODE FOR ENGLAND AND WALES

# A MODEL CIVIL PROCEDURE CODE FOR ENGLAND AND WALES

JOHN SORABJI

OXFORD
UNIVERSITY PRESS

OXFORD
UNIVERSITY PRESS

Great Clarendon Street, Oxford, OX2 6DP,
United Kingdom

Oxford University Press is a department of the University of Oxford.
It furthers the University's objective of excellence in research, scholarship,
and education by publishing worldwide. Oxford is a registered trade mark of
Oxford University Press in the UK and in certain other countries



Published in the United States of America by Oxford University Press
198 Madison Avenue, New York, NY 10016, United States of America

British Library Cataloguing in Publication Data
Data available

Library of Congress Control Number: 2024942312

ISBN 978–0–19–284868–0

DOI: 10.1093/oso/9780192848680.001.0001

Printed and bound by
CPI Group (UK) Ltd, Croydon, CR0 4YY

MIX
Paper | Supporting
responsible forestry
FSC® C013604

*For Clare and Helena*

# FOREWORD

I yield to no man (or woman) in my enthusiasm for civil procedure. I spent six years as the then Queen's Bench Division representative on the Civil Procedure Rule Committee, and a further period of more than three years chairing the same committee as the Deputy Head of Civil Justice. It was hard work and good fun and, in the words of one senior official who had never attended one of its meetings before, 'strangely compelling'.

However, I think even I would baulk at the prospect of sitting down and preparing a new model civil procedure code. Indeed, had anyone suggested to me that such a book might be written, I would have concluded that the author was either a madman or a genius. Happily, in John Sorabji, OUP have found the necessary genius. He is well-known in the Court of Appeal as a highly respected and sensible legal adviser, but I confess that I had no real idea of the depth and breadth of his knowledge of civil procedure until I read the draft of his book.

His proposed civil code is not only interesting and provocative in itself, but it helps to illuminate various aspects of the existing procedure under the CPR in a way which can only enhance the existing rules. So for example, his 'economy, efficiency and proportionality principles', and the emphasis on multi-dimensional justice, restates some aspects of the CPR but also, when expressly considering questions of timeliness, goes further (although those of us familiar with the truncated timetables of construction adjudication will be big supporters of his emphasis on speed over minutiae).

Numerous other aspects of this book also deserve comment. Putting costs and funding so high up the agenda is novel but, in my view, entirely realistic. A presumption in favour of digital procedure (Part 11 Rule 2) ought to be uncontroversial, but as HMCTS continues to drag its feet over the reform of the civil justice system, it appears to remain a distant dream.

One last point. I take a certain amount of pleasure in noting that, even in the hands of such an experienced and knowledgeable author, the model code is not short. In the modern age, no cogent set of civil procedure rules can be, because any gaps or generalities simply create more disputes. This is an argument which I find myself repeatedly having to deploy when defending the size of the current White Book.

I commend this book. I challenge anyone with any serious interest in civil procedure not to find it helpful, thought-provoking and usually right. I wish it every possible success.

Lord Justice Coulson<br>
Editor in Chief of the White Book and<br>
Former Deputy Head of Civil Justice<br>
Royal Courts of Justice<br>
January 2024

# PREFACE

*'The process of civil litigation serves purposes other than that of doing justice to those who appear before the courts, and the achievement of those purposes must be an objective of procedural law.'*[1]

Civil procedure law has often been characterised in England and Wales as a Cinderella subject; one simply for use in the courts and not worthy of serious study. Pioneering work by JA Jolowicz, Sir Jack Jacob, Cyril Glasser, Ian Scott, Adrian Zuckerman, Hazel Genn, and Neil Andrews has over the last forty years changed that view. It is now, quite properly, studied and debated not only as a subject of serious academic merit but as an integral part of our understanding of access to justice, of dispute resolution in its many varieties, and ultimately of the rule of law.

My aim in writing this book is not to provide a restatement of the law of civil procedure in England and Wales. On the contrary, it proposes a new model code. It does so against a rapidly changing backdrop, which sees the spirit of the age as one that increasingly, and rightly, sees dispute resolution as not focused on courts and judgments, but, as Hodges has put it, on the promotion of different pathways to justice whether they be litigation, negotiation, mediation, arbitration, Ombudsman schemes or regulatory forms of redress.[2] That spirit is also one that is, inevitably, while we live through the fourth industrial revolution, shaped by the increasing digitisation of society. Both these influences are already having a profound influence on the reform of the civil justice system and civil procedure. The incorporation and promotion of mediation and early neutral evaluation into civil procedure, and the move towards providing the civil courts with power to mandate the former, evidence the shift away from the courts focusing on managing disputes to judgment. The development of e-filing, e-case management, and the use of digital platforms to conduct hearings equally points to digitisation's influence, as does the idea that rules of court will be replaced in the future by instructions on court and other websites that will guide parties to complete various steps in the dispute resolution process.

These various influences suggest that English and Welsh civil justice is at a turning point. It, and the way in which civil justice is delivered, is undergoing and will continue to undergo its most significant change since the Judicature Act reforms of the late 19th century. The current phase of development is likely to fundamentally reshape our courts, civil procedure, and approach to civil dispute resolution in ways not seen since the late 1800s. It will continue to do so over the next century.

It is with that in mind that I have built on the work of the ALI/UNIDROIT Principles of Transnational Civil Procedure and, particularly on, the ELI-UNIDROIT Model European Rules of Civil Procedure (which inspired this work) to set out a model civil procedural code for England and Wales. The model code is set out in seventeen Parts (plus a preliminary Part concerning the overall regulatory architecture), rather than the currently eighty-nine Parts of the CPR, retained parts of its predecessors the RSC and CCR, its associated Practice Directions, Practice Statements, Notes, Guidance, and Court Guides. It is intended

[1] J Jolowicz, 'On the nature and purposes of civil procedural law', in J Jolowicz, *On Civil Procedure* (CUP, 2000) at 80.

[2] C Hodges, *Delivering Dispute Resolution* (Hart, 2019).

to set out the key elements of any civil procedural code. It is also intended to set out one possible way in which digitisation and preventive and consensual forms of justice could be introduced effectively and in a coherent way into such a code. In doing so, it seeks to highlight how justice is not a cloistered virtue residing solely within the walls,[3] whether physical or digital, of a court and the judgments it can deliver.

The Code's main aim can perhaps best be summed up by the words of the Australian Access to Justice Taskforce. It is to promote a view of civil justice that is focused on '*giving people choice and providing the appropriate forum for each dispute, but also facilitating a culture in which fewer disputes need to be resolved*'. It is an approach which, while it sets out model rules of court, is intended to highlight how the civil courts are one part of a wider justice ecosystem, one that needs to be co-ordinated coherently and effectively. It presents one model. There are others, and there will be others still. The idea is to stimulate debate, not least where consideration of the principles underpinning the design, operation, and funding of civil dispute resolution and, particularly, rules of court are concerned. If, as Storme suggested, the designers of any procedural code are like cathedral builders, then it can properly be said that any procedural code, model or otherwise, is more akin to Barcelona's Sagrada Família than it is to Madrid's Almudena Cathedral. It is always evolving; a work of constant progress. This model code is but one iteration of that process.

The model code has a further aim. It is intended to highlight what is likely to amount to a shift in the purpose of procedural codes as digitisation continues to take effect. Historically, procedural rules guided judges and parties through the litigation process from commencement to judgment and enforcement. This code maintains that role. Significant aspects of future procedure will, however, be instantiated in the digital processes set out in court websites. These will guide the litigation process, and will in many ways replace technical detail that was in rules of court.[4] This points to a new, and wider, role for written codes. They will become the means by which the design and implementation of digital procedures will be guided and tested against. They will form a necessary accountability mechanism. Digital procedures will, for instance, need to be consistent with the general principles underpinning procedure, such as those set out in Part 1 of the Code. They will need to make provision for the specific requirements and tests contained within the specific Parts of the Code. Procedural codes will thus not only guide, as they do now, the process of litigation, but they will guide those who design digital procedures and those who test the propriety of those latter procedures.

Finally, no book is truly the product of one person's efforts, although its missteps and errors are. I have been very fortunate to have had the great assistance, and patience, of Oxford University Press. I have also benefited greatly from insights and discussions with a wide range of people, including: Masood Ahmed; Sam Allan; Natalie Byrom; Hazel Genn; Chris Hodges; Amy Shaw; and Richard Susskind. For that I am truly grateful. Finally, I owe a great debt of thanks to all those who I have learnt from, not least: Masood Ahmed; Neil Andrews; Natalie Byrom; Hazel Genn; Robin Jacob; Ian Scott; Rolf Stürner; Adrian Zuckerman; and all my students.

[3] *Ambard v Attorney General for Trinidad and Tobago* [1936] AC 322 at 335.
[4] C Birss, *The Online Future of Civil Justice* (Fordham, 2021).

# CONTENTS

# TABLE OF CASES

**United Kingdom**

**European Commission and Court of Human Rights**

**European Court of Justice**



**Australia**



**Canada**



**New Zealand**



**United States**

# TABLE OF LEGISLATION

**United Kingdom**

*Statutes*

**International Instruments**

**European Union**



**Council of Europe**



**National Legislation**

*Australia*



*Brazil*

*Canada*

Code of Civil Procedure, Book 1, Title 1 (Quebec)
r 1 . . . 15, 15n.36
Criminal Evidence Act 1985
s 5(1) . . . 361n.268
s 5(2) . . . 361n.268
Rules of Civil Procedure (Ontario) (RRO 1990, Reg 194)
r 1.04(1) . . . 9n.4
r 49 . . . 253n.75

*Germany*

Code of Civil Procedure
s 78 . . . 35n.159
s 139 . . . 310n.2, 319, 320n.60
s 383 . . . 367n.298
s 384 . . . 360n.261
s 578 . . . 513n.130

*France*

Code of Civil Procedure
Art 57 . . . 159, 183
Art 973 . . . 35n.159
Penal Code
Art 226-13 . . . 367n.298

*New Zealand*

Urewera Act 2014 . . . 144n.5
Te Awa Tupua (Whanganui River Claims Settlement) Act 2017 . . . 144n.5

*United States*

Federal Rules of Civil Procedure . . . 329n.99
r 1 . . . 9n.2
r 23(a) . . . 269n.122

# TABLE OF INSTRUMENTS

**Practice Directions and Guidance**

# ABBREVIATIONS

| | |
|---|---|
| ADR | Alternative Dispute Resolution |
| AI | Artificial Intelligence |
| ATE | after-the-event |
| BTE | before-the-event |
| CAT | Competition Appeal Tribunal |
| CDRC | Civil Dispute Resolution Council |
| CEPEJ | Council of Europe European Commission for the efficiency of justice |
| CFA | conditional fee agreement |
| chap | chapter |
| CPR | Civil Procedure Rules |
| DBA | damages-based agreement |
| EC | European Community |
| ENE | early neutral evaluation |
| GHRs | Guideline Hourly Rates for the Summary Assessment of Costs |
| HMCTS | His Majesty's Courts and Tribunals Service |
| NCMG | Negotiation and Conflict Management Group |
| ODR | Online Dispute Resolution |
| PAPs | Pre-Action Protocols |
| PD | Practice Direction |
| RSC | Rules of the Supreme Court |

# I

# PRELIMINARY TO THE CODE

*'A procedure cannot, any more than a constitution, be born full grown ...'*[1]

[1] Solicitor's Journal (1875) cited in S Rosenbaum, *The Rule-making Authority in the English Supreme Court* (Boston, 1917), frontispiece.

# GOVERNANCE OF THE CIVIL DISPUTE RESOLUTION SYSTEM

1. This Part concerns governance of the system put in place to prevent and resolve civil disputes. Historically, that system has been divided into discrete parts: the formal civil justice system, constituted of the civil courts and judges, rules of procedure, and lawyers; and the informal justice system, which variously encompassed a range of consensual forms of dispute resolution. The premise on which this Code is based is that the historic dichotomy between these two 'systems'[2] is and should be replaced by a single, integrated dispute resolution system. An integrated approach is not a novel concept. It has been developed by, for instance, Susskind and Briggs.[3] To a limited degree it is being implemented in England and Wales through the digitisation of the civil courts.[4] The most detailed account of this idea, and the one which informs the approach taken in this Code, is that developed by Hodges, who proposes the creation of an holistic approach to dispute resolution that integrates multi-pathways to dispute prevention and resolution into a coherent whole. It requires the civil justice system to apply the right process to the right dispute at the right time.[5]
2. This Code only deals with one aspect of that integrated system; the civil court's role in it. It does so by setting out the approach to the rules of civil procedure. In doing so, it goes beyond matters that are dealt with in the current approach to civil procedure rules. It, for instance, sets out: the guiding principles that ought to underpin both the operation of the system, generally, and this Code in particular (Part 1); how dispute resolution in all its forms could be funded (Part 4); the basis on which pre-action dispute prevention and resolution is to be carried out (Part 5); and how adjudicative and consensual resolution are to be co-ordinated once litigation has been commenced (Part 11). And, throughout, it also codifies various judicial approaches to the application of current rules. The Code does so reflective of the fact that the civil courts, and their procedure, form part of a wider ecosystem, which is intended to secure effective and practical access to justice.

[2] L Nader, 'The Recurrent Dialectic Between Legality and its Alternatives: The Limitations of Binary Thinking' (1984) 132 University of Penn Law Review 621.

[3] R Susskind, *Online Courts and the Future of Justice* (OUP, 2019); M Briggs, *Civil Courts Structure Review—Interim Report* (December 2015); M Briggs, *Civil Courts Structure Review—Final Report* (July 2016).

[4] T Etherton, *The Civil Court of the Future* (Judicial Office, 2017); G Vos, *Mediated Interventions Within the Court Dispute Resolution Process* (Judicial Office, 2021).

[5] C Hodges, *Delivering Dispute Resolution* (Hart, 2019) at 553–554; F Sander, 'Varieties of Dispute Processing' (1976) 70 FRD 79, 111.

*A Model Civil Procedure Code for England and Wales*. John Sorabji, Oxford University Press. © John Sorabji 2024.
DOI: 10.1093/oso/9780192848680.003.0001

3. This Part, the Preliminary to the Code, provides the overarching mechanism intended to secure the effective integration and co-ordination of the various parts of the civil justice system. It also makes provision for ongoing systemic review and improvement. For these reasons it focuses on the governance bodies responsible for the integrated system and this Code.

## RULE 1.—CIVIL DISPUTE RESOLUTION COUNCIL

**(1) There shall be a Civil Dispute Resolution Council. Its membership shall include representatives of the government, the judiciary, ombudsman services, the legal profession, civil society, and those with an interest in the effective resolution of civil disputes.**

**(2) The Council shall be responsible for the co-ordination of the civil dispute resolution system, which shall comprise of the civil courts, public and private ombudsman schemes, legal aid, advice and representation services, and other approved dispute resolution bodies or services. It shall also be responsible for keeping the system, including issues of cost and funding, under continuous review and for recommending and implementing reforms to it.**

**(3) The Council shall carry out its responsibilities to ensure that the civil dispute resolution system is simple, fair, accessible, properly co-ordinated, makes appropriate use of technology, and is able to deliver practical and effective means to achieve dispute prevention and resolution.**

## COMMENTARY

1. This rule establishes and makes provision for the responsibilities of the Civil Dispute Resolution Council (CDRC); the body to be responsible for oversight of the civil dispute resolution system. Such a body has antecedents in the Civil Justice Council,[6] Administrative Justice and Tribunals Council,[7] the Civil Procedure Rule Committee,[8] and the Online Procedure Rule Committee.[9]

2. The rationale for its establishment is straightforward. The development and operation of civil dispute resolution has, historically, been evolutionary.[10] The starting point for this Code is that if England and Wales is to devise a fully effective dispute resolution system that is fit for the 21st century the civil justice system has to be subject to coherent, conscious design that properly integrates the variety of dispute resolution methods into a fully integrated whole, even if it does so incrementally by building on the HMCTS modernisation programme. The CDRC's role is to achieve this by ensuring that the civil dispute resolution system is designed and operated consistently with the overarching aims of promoting dispute prevention, early conflict resolution, and, where necessary, matching each dispute with the right dispute resolution method.[11] It is intended to ensure dispute resolution is

[6] Civil Procedure Act 1997, s 6.

[7] Tribunals and Inquiries Act 1992, s 1; Tribunals, Courts and Enforcement Act 2007, s 44.

[8] Civil Procedure Act 1997, s 2.

[9] Judicial Review and Courts Act 2022, s 22.

[10] Civil Justice Council, *Review of Pre-Action Protocols—Interim Report* (CJC, 2021); All Party Parliamentary Group on Consumer Protection, *Report from the Ombudsman Inquiry*, Vol 1 (2019) at 14.

[11] C Hodges (2019) at 566.

not court or litigation-centric,[12] nor that it favours any one specific form of dispute resolution.

## RULE 2.—SPECIALIST SUB-COMMITTEES OF THE CIVIL DISPUTE RESOLUTION COUNCIL

**(1) The Civil Dispute Resolution Council shall be constituted of standing sub-committees, which must include:**
  **(a) a Civil Courts Rule Committee;**
  **(b) a Costs and Funding Council;**
  **(c) a Preventive Justice Council;**
  **(d) a Consensual Justice Council; and**
  **(e) Civil Justice and Administrative Justice Councils.**

**(2) Other standing sub-committees and time and/or subject-specific working groups may be established by the Civil Dispute Resolution Council as necessary to facilitate the carrying out of its functions.**

*Sources: Civil Procedure Act 1997, ss 2, 6; Scottish Civil Justice Council and Criminal Legal Assistance Act 2013, Pt 1.*

## COMMENTARY

1. To work effectively, the CDRC ought to have standing, specialist committees. Their membership should draw upon the widest range of knowledge and expertise. This model operates well in Scotland, where its Civil Justice Council has several standing committees, including a rule committee and committees focused on discrete areas of Scottish civil and family litigation. Flexibility should also be provided to enable the CDRC to establish subject-specific or time-limited working parties, which could deal with specific issues as and when they arose.
2. The standing committees are intended to provide the CDRC with a focus on several areas of importance to the operation of the system as a whole. They may also have other, specific functions, which are set out in the Code itself. By developing the various standing sub-committees, the CDRC would subject each area of the civil dispute resolution system to effective scrutiny, while providing an overall co-ordination role.
3. The Civil Courts Rule Committee, a successor to the current Civil and Online Procedure Rule Committees, would take responsibility for devising and revising this Code. The Costs and Funding Council would be responsible for the development and promotion of funding methods. It would also be responsible for the costs regime. Responsibility for both would ensure that the two regimes were and remain consistent with each other.
4. Oversight of the provision of legal advice and assistance, public legal education and its delivery, as well as steps to reduce the incidence of individual disputes would be the responsibility of the Preventive Justice Council. This would focus on the provision of advice to enable individuals and businesses to avoid disputes arising.[13] It would also provide oversight of the role played by Ombudsman and regulators to identify systemic social, economic, and regulatory problems that give rise to legal

[12] T Sourdin, *Judges, Technology and Artificial Intelligence* (Elgar, 2021) at 171.

[13] L Brown, *Preventive Law* (Praeger, 1970); R Hardaway, 'Teaching Preventive Law' (1997) 16 Preventive L Rep 3; R Susskind, *The Future of Law* (OUP, 1998) at 2; R Susskind (2019).

disputes so that reform aimed at reducing the possibility that future disputes would arise was promoted effectively.[14] The Consensual Justice Council would then have oversight of the promotion and integration of public and private consent-based forms of dispute resolution (including arbitration) in the system. Finally, scrutiny of the operation of civil and administrative justice within the civil courts would fall to the final two subcommittees, which would take the role currently played by the Civil Justice Council and Administrative Justice Council, respectively.

[14] C Gill, 'The Evolving Role of the Ombudsman: A Conceptual and Constitutional Analysis of the "Scottish Solution" to Administrative Justice' (2014) (Oct) Public Law 662.

# II

# A MODEL CIVIL PROCEDURE CODE

# PART 1
# GENERAL PRINCIPLES

## SECTION 1: GENERAL

1. English and Welsh civil procedure has, historically, shied away from general principles. Fox summed up the position well when he noted how our civil procedure systems were like the common law in the 19th century: made up of a group of disparate remedies in search of principles. For him it was strange that, by the turn of the 21st century, no one had seen fit to furnish civil procedure with a set of overarching principles.[1] In one sense he overstated his case. US civil procedure had, since the late 1930s, provided a single overarching principle for its Federal Rules of Procedure.[2] And as he was writing, the Woolf reforms introduced a similar type of overarching principle in England and Wales,[3] just as similar provision had been and would be introduced in Australia and Canada.[4] In another sense, he was absolutely correct. While there are many principles that underpin civil procedure, they were and are not fully or explicitly articulated in our procedural rules or codes.[5]
2. This Part of the Code is intended to fill that historic gap and articulate the general principles that underpin civil procedure. In taking this approach it is consistent with the approach adopted as procedural best practice by the ELI-UNIDROIT Model European Rules of Civil Procedure.[6] By setting out such principles, as well as defining the scope and application of the Code, this Part serves several purposes. Narrowly, it is intended to guide the interpretation and application of the specific rules in each of the Parts of the Code. In this it mirrors the CPR, where its overriding objective operates as an interpretative, purposive rule.[7] By setting out all relevant procedural principles rather than just the overriding one, it goes wider than the CPR as it articulates the principles that underpin each of the specific Parts of the Code. The intention here is to make clear the full extent of the spirit in which the rules are to be applied.
3. Articulation of the general principles also serves a broader and novel purpose. They make clear to those responsible for the design and reform of any of the rules, the principles, and purposes that underpin them. This will become increasingly important as more of the civil court's practices and procedures are digitised. Clarity of purpose

[1] R Fox, *Justice in the Twenty-First Century* (Cavendish, 2000) at vii.

[2] Federal Rules of Procedure (US) r 1 (as originally drafted); R Bone, 'Improving Rule 1: A Master Rule for the Federal Rules' (2010) 87 Denver University Law Review 287 at 288–289.

[3] CPR r 1.1.

[4] Supreme Court Rules 1987, r 2.01 (South Australia); Supreme Court Civil Rules 2006, r 3 (South Australia); Rules of Civil Procedure (RRO 1990, Reg 194, r 1.04(1) (Ontario, Canada)).

[5] N Andrews, *Andrews on Civil Processes* (Intersentia, 2019) chap 23.

[6] ELI-UNIDROIT Model European Rules of Civil Procedure (OUP, 2021) (ELI-UNIDROIT Model Rules) at 6–7.

[7] H Woolf, *Access to Justice: Final Report to the Lord Chancellor on the Civil Justice System in England and Wales* (HMSO) (1996) at 274; *Swain v Hillman* [2000] 1 All ER 91 at 92–94.

*A Model Civil Procedure Code for England and Wales*. John Sorabji, Oxford University Press. © John Sorabji 2024.
DOI: 10.1093/oso/9780192848680.003.0002

and of these principles will be necessary for the Civil Courts Rule Committee to instruct those who will design the digital code that underpins new digital procedures effectively. They are also necessary to inform that body and Parliament whether the digital code and procedures can properly be approved.

4. A wider purpose yet is that express clarity in respect of these principles will also help secure democratic accountability of the future civil, and particularly digital, procedure. They will be a means by which the media and public can hold procedural, particularly digital, design to account.
5. This Part thus serves four functions. As with the CPR, it serves to guide the operation of the Code. It guides procedural design and also sets the general drafting style of the Code, which is intended to operate at a higher level of generality and be less technical than past civil procedural codes.[8] And, finally, it provides an accountability function.

## RULE 1.—SCOPE AND PURPOSE

**(1) This Code governs the procedure to be used in all civil disputes in the courts in England and Wales, except where a specialist Code applies. It also governs the procedure for the prevention and consensual settlement of civil disputes before legal proceedings commence where that is facilitated via the civil dispute prevention and resolution portal (the digital portal).**
**(2) A civil dispute is one that concerns either or both public and private civil law rights or obligations.**
**(3) This Code may apply to disputes that would otherwise be governed by a specialist procedural Code to the extent authorised by that Code.**
**(4) The Code and any Practice Direction and digital procedure made under it have the status of secondary legislation.**

*Sources: ALI/UNIDROIT Principles, Scope and Implementation; ELI-UNIDROIT Model Rules, r 1; CPR rr 2.1, 2.3.*

## COMMENTARY

1. This Code is concerned with civil procedural law applicable in England and Wales. It is not a restatement of the law. It is a proposed model for the design of a future code to govern civil dispute resolution in England and Wales. It is intended to apply to all disputes concerning substantive administrative and public law as well as substantive civil private law, including commercial law. It is not intended to apply to criminal matters or family law disputes, or as noted below to some specialist forms of civil dispute.[9]
2. English and Welsh civil procedure has since the Judicature Acts 1873–1875 adopted a trans-substantive approach.[10] The same rules apply to all civil disputes irrespective

[8] H Woolf, *Access to Justice: Interim Report to the Lord Chancellor on the Civil Justice System in England and Wales* (HMSO) (1995) at 215; *Ndole Assets Ltd v Designer M&E Services* [2017] REHC 1148 (TCC); [2017] 1 WLR 4367 at [32].

[9] RSC Ord 1 (SI 1962/2145); RSC Ord 2 (SI 1965/1776); CPR r 2.1.

[10] Schedule 1 of the Supreme Court of Judicature Act 1875; F W Maitland, *The Forms of Action at Common Law* (CUP, 1965) at 9.

of the substantive nature of the dispute.[11] More specifically it has adopted case-size trans-substantivity, ie the same procedure applies to all claims irrespective of the substantive nature of the dispute, albeit that procedure differed depending on the value of the claim as different procedures applied in the High and County Courts.[12] With the CPR's introduction and the use of procedural case tracks to match procedure to the nature and value of claims, proportionate case-size trans-substantivity has specifically been in place. This Code maintains this approach. It does so as it inherently promotes procedural simplicity rather than complexity, and is thus apt to promote procedural economy and efficiency. Equally, by providing a generalist, trans-substantive approach to procedural rule design it promotes procedural equality, as well as a more consistent application of the substantive law than would otherwise be the case were subject-specific procedure to be applied.[13] In this way it also promotes procedural proportionality.

3. Notwithstanding its commitment to trans-substantivity, the Code maintains the established approach that certain types of civil dispute are, exceptionally, matters for subject-specific procedural codes. Insolvency disputes thus remain a matter for the Insolvency Rules.[14] As with the CPR, the Code is designed to be applied to disputes that fall under such Codes should that be necessary or desirable. It does, however, differ from the historic approach to civil procedural law in one significant way. It articulates a procedure that not only governs the steps the court and parties take to resolve disputes adjudicatively through a court judgment, but also those that prevent disputes arising and those that help resolve them consensually. In that way it provides a complete code for preventive, consensual, and adjudicative civil dispute resolution.[15]

## RULE 2.—APPLICATION OF THE GENERAL AND ACCESS TO JUSTICE PRINCIPLES

**(1) The Civil Courts Rule Committee shall ensure that this Code, including any procedure and practice made under it, is intelligible and accessible. It shall do so consistently with any guidance issued by the Civil Dispute Resolution Council.**
**(2) The Committee shall approve the Code, keep it under continuous review, and make any necessary revisions to it. In particular, it must ensure that the General and Access to Justice Principles are pervasive principles underpinning this Code.**
**(3) Civil courts and parties must give effect to the General and Access to Justice principles when taking any step in matters governed by this Code.**

*Sources: ELI-UNIDROIT Model Rules, r 2; Civil Procedure Act 1997, ss 1(3); CPR r 1.2.*

[11] C Crifo, 'Does Procedural Mean Trans-substantive? A Historical and Normative Analysis of English Civil Procedure Rules', in R Assy and A Higgins, *Principles, Procedure, Justice—Essays in Honour of Adrian Zuckerman* (OUP, 2020).

[12] S Subrin, 'The Limitations of Transsubstantive Procedure: An Essay on Adjusting the "One Size Fits All" Assumption' (2010) 87(2) Denver University Law Review 377 at 378.

[13] S Subrin, 'The 50th Anniversary of the Federal Rules of Civil Procedure 1938–1988' (1988–1989) 137 U Pa L Rev 1998 at 2047.

[14] The Insolvency (England and Wales) Rules 2016 (SI 2016/1024).

[15] Civil Justice Council, *Review of Pre-Action Protocols, Interim Report* (November 2021) Appendix 3.

## COMMENTARY

1. This rule adapts and expands the approach taken in CPR r 1.2,[16] which requires the court to give effect to the CPR's overriding objective when exercising powers under its rules.
2. Rule 2(1) directs the Civil Courts Rule Committee to ensure the Code and any practice or procedure made under it, whether paper-based or digital, is both intelligible and accessible. Intelligibility is a necessary condition for accessibility. An intelligible Code or practice is not, however, necessarily accessible. It may be intelligible and complex, which would render it inaccessible to all but sophisticated parties. Complexity might also reduce accessibility through creating an expensive system that would place dispute resolution outside the financial reach of certain parties. The Code may also be intelligible, but it may use artificial intelligence that discriminates, either intentionally or unintentionally, against particular parties, hence rendering it inaccessible to them. Hence, the Rule Committee must ensure that the Code and its procedures are as accessible as they are intelligible.[17] Accessibility here is necessarily linked to the procedural equality, digital procedure, digital access, and Artificial Intelligence (AI) principles.
3. Rule 2(2) directs the Rule Committee to ensure that the Code gives effect to the General and Access to Justice Principles. This will require careful judgment. Principles are capable of coming into conflict with each other and may need to be balanced against each other.[18] A speedy trial process, consistent with the efficiency principle, may well undermine procedural equality and/or accuracy. It may unfairly favour one party over another by undermining their ability to obtain probative evidence. A balance therefore would need to be struck between efficiency and accuracy in the rules and their application. It is for the Rule Committee to ensure that an effective balance, where necessary is struck, in any rule or procedure to ensure that the overall process is, as required by the purposive principle, fair.
4. Rule 2(3) is closer to CPR r 1.2 in its function, which requires parties to assist the court in giving effect to its overriding objective.[19] The present rule directs the courts to give effect to the General and Access to Justice Principles when taking any step in matters governed by the Code. It goes further than CPR r 1.2 by placing the same obligation on parties. It thus foreshadows the co-operation principle, which emphasises the adoption of a partnership model of civil procedure, ie that the court and litigants are required to work together to secure the purposive principle. That model is well-known in other civil procedural systems, such as Austria and Germany,[20] and is endorsed by the ELI-UNIDROIT Model Rules as best practice.[21]
5. Taken together rule 2 is intended to ensure, as far as possible, that civil disputes are capable of being resolved consistently with the General and Access to Justice Principles. It also forms part of the Code's accountability function. The duties placed on the Rule Committee are the means by which it can be held accountable

[16] SI 3132/1998.
[17] M Bayles, 'Principles for Legal Procedure' (1986) 5(1) Law and Philosophy 33 at 55.
[18] M Bayles (1986) at 35.
[19] CPR r 1.3.
[20] S Frodl, 'The Heritage of the Franz Klein Reform of Austrian Civil Procedure in 1895–1896' (2012) 31(1) CJQ 43.
[21] ELI-UNIDROIT Model Rules, r 2 commentary.

by Parliament, and hence the public. As with the CPR and its predecessors, the Code is intended to be approved by Parliament as a statutory instrument further to rule 1(4). Parliamentary scrutiny of it, as part of the statutory instrument approval process, ought to provide the means by which Parliament can assess whether the Rule Committee has fulfilled its duties under this rule. Additional accountability may also arise as any breach of the duties imposed by this rule on the part of the Rule Committee ought to be capable of forming the basis of a challenge via judicial review.

## RULE 3.—PRACTICE DIRECTIONS AND COURT GUIDES

**(1) Practice Directions may only be issued under this rule. They may only supplement this Code. They may only be issued by, or with, the approval of the Head of Civil Justice. They may only be temporary and**

**(a) deal with matters not otherwise provided for in the Code;**

**(b) make provision for pilot schemes, which test new procedures or practices; or**

**(c) make provision to deal with matters arising from a novel or emergency situation.**

**(2) Where Practice Directions make provision for pilot schemes or to deal with emergency situations, they may vary or disapply any rule in this Code other than those in this Part.**

**(3) Court Guides and Practice Guidance may be issued by, or with the approval of the Head of Civil Justice. They may only be issued in order to explain the operation of this Code and any Practice Direction. No other form of guidance may be issued.**

**(4) The Head of Civil Justice may authorise the deputy Head of Civil Justice to carry out their functions under this rule.**

*Sources: Civil Procedure Act 1997, s 5; CPR rr 51.2, 51.3.*

## COMMENTARY

1. The Code is intended to be a complete code of procedure. Inevitably, situations will arise that the rules have not anticipated. Historically, the courts have dealt with such situations in either of two ways. First, they have created new rules of procedure—common law rules of court—through giving general directions in a judgment.[22] Secondly, senior judges have issued, administratively, Practice Directions, which operate in either of two ways.[23] They either supplement, as a form of additional common law rule, specific Parts of the CPR, or they explain the nature and operation of specific Parts of it.[24] None of these types of direction can overrule rules of court.[25]

2. The CPR's approach has, however, led to unnecessary complexity. It has been further exacerbated by the widespread use of informal Practice Guidance, Practice Notes,

[22] *R (Buglife: The Invertebrate Conservation Trust) v Thurrock Thames Gateway Development Corp* [2008] EWCA Civ 1209.

[23] A Zuckerman, *Zuckerman on Civil Procedure—Principles of Practice* (Sweet & Maxwell, 2021) chap 2; Civil Procedure Act 1997, s 5; *Re C (Legal Aid: Preparation of Bill of Costs)* [2001] Fam Law 620; *Bovale v Secretary of State for Communities and Local Government* [2009] EWCA Civ 171.

[24] A Zuckerman (2021) at 68.

[25] *Godwin v Swindon BC* [2001] EWCA Civ 993; [2002] 1 WLR 997; *Cameron v Liverpool Victoria Insurance Co Ltd* [2019] UKSC 6; [2019] 1 WLR 1471 at [12].

Practice Statements, and general Court Guides; each of which variously explain the operation of the CPR or best practice under it, or supplement it. In parts they also contain imprecations wrongly suggesting they are mandatory.[26] Only rules of court and Practice Directions make mandatory provision.[27]

3. This rule is intended to both clarify and simplify the approach to Practice Directions and informal guidance. It does so by codifying the court's inherent jurisdiction as well as replacing the current statutory scheme for issuing Practice Directions.[28] In future both Directions and guidance should only be made under this rule. Where a gap in the rules is identified in a judgment, this ought to be, via that judgment, brought to the attention of the Head of Civil Justice and the Rule Committee for provision to be made through either a Practice Direction or a rule change.
4. This rule also emphasises the temporary nature of any Practice Direction. It thus ensures that they cannot be used to side-step the Code's democratic accountability.[29] It thereby also eliminates their use as permanent supplements to the rules of court, ensuring that they cannot in future become a source of unnecessary procedural complexity as they are under the CPR.
5. To enable the Code to deal effectively with novel or emergency situations and also to promote necessary experimentation, it adapts the approach provided for in CPR Pt 51, which enables Practice Directions to be made for pilot schemes and to deal with emergency situations. This will be increasingly important with the further development of digital technology.
6. Further clarity and simplicity are provided for by introducing a novel rule governing the use of Court Guides and Practice Guidance. It clarifies that such guidance is explanatory only. Thus, it obviates the problem of guidance being used or being seen to be used as a means to introduce quasi-mandatory provision outside the formal rule-making process.
7. In all cases, Practice Directions and guidance may only be issued by or with the approval of the Head of Civil Justice or their deputy. This gives effect to the Woolf Reform's intention that the overall direction and co-ordination of civil justice should be in the hands of a single senior judge.[30] In this way consistency across Practice Directions and guidance is maintained, while the Head of Civil Justice can also ensure that they are intelligible and accessible. This approach also maintains the current delegation of the Lord Chief Justice's statutory authority to issue Practice Directions for civil proceedings to the Master of the Rolls as Head of Civil Justice.[31] It does so, however, by codifying the Head of Civil Justice's role.
8. Finally, this rule removes the current requirement that the Lord Chancellor concur in the making of Practice Directions, which was introduced by the Constitutional Reform Act 2005. As Practice Directions are an exercise of the court's inherent

[26] A Zuckerman (2021) at 76; N Andrews, *English Civil Procedure: Fundamentals of the New Civil Justice System* (OUP, 2003) at 16.

[27] *Mount Cook Land Ltd v Westminster City Council* [2003] EWCA Civ 1346; *Godwin v Swindon BC* [2001] EWCA Civ 993; [2002] 1 WLR 997 at [11].

[28] *Cocker v Tempest* (1841) 7 M&W 501 at 503–504; J Jacob, 'The Inherent Jurisdiction of the Court' (1970) 23 CLP 23; M Dockray, 'The Inherent Jurisdiction to Regulate Civil Proceedings' (1997) 113 LQR 120; *Grobbelaar v News Group Newspapers Ltd* [2002] 4 All ER 732 at [25].

[29] A Zuckerman (2021) at 69.

[30] H Woolf (1995) at 59; H Woolf (1996) at 69.

[31] Courts Act 2003, s 62; Lord Chief Justice's Statutory Delegations No 1 of 2020 (Judicial Office, 2020) at 17.

common law jurisdiction, whether codified—as here—or otherwise, it is constitutionally inappropriate for a member of the Executive to have a role in how it is exercised.

## SECTION 2: GENERAL PRINCIPLES

### RULE 4.—THE PURPOSIVE PRINCIPLE

**The purpose of this Code is to secure a fair procedure for the just prevention or consensual or adjudicative resolution of civil disputes, including the enforcement of any such resolution. This Code, any Practice Direction, procedural discretion, and any court order are to be interpreted and applied, in so far as practical, consistently with this purpose.**

*Sources: Code of Civil Procedure (Quebec), Book 1, Title 1, r 1; Supreme Court Civil Rules 2006, r 3 (South Australia); CPR r 1.1.*

### COMMENTARY

1. All civil procedural codes serve a purpose. Historically, it was implicit. Occasionally, it was stated in reform reports that gave birth to new procedural rules or in legislation that underpinned procedural reform.[32] The historic approach taken in England and Wales was that the purpose of the rules of procedure was implicit. That purpose was to secure what was variously known as substantive justice, justice on the merits, or complete justice, ie the achievement of justice according to law through the finding of right fact and the application of right law in each individual proceeding (adjudicative justice).[33] This approach changed with the Woolf reforms, which brought about the introduction of the first explicit purposive rule in English and Welsh civil procedure: the CPR's overriding objective.[34] Like that overriding objective this rule sets the Code's purpose and is intended to guide how specific rules are to be interpreted and applied. It also makes clear that it is to guide the exercise of the court's discretion generally.
2. Rule 4 specifically provides that the purpose of the Code is to secure a fair procedure for the just prevention or resolution of civil disputes either consensually or adjudicatively.[35] What is a fair procedure is neither solely determined by, nor is a function of, the achievement of adjudicative justice. It is determined by reference to the preventive, consensual settlement, or accuracy principles[36] as well as by reference to wider principles, such as proportionality, which take account of the need to ensure that all parties who pursue dispute resolution through the civil courts are

[32] *The First Report of the Royal Commission to inquire into the Operation and Constitution of the High Court of Chancery, Courts of Common Law, Central Criminal Court, High Court of Admiralty, and other Courts in England, and into the Operation and Effect of the Present Separation and Division of Jurisdiction between the Courts (No 4130; 1868–1869) (The First Judicature Report); Common Law Procedure Act 1852, preamble.*

[33] *Cropper v Smith* (1884) 26 ChD 700 at 710–711; A Zuckerman (2021) at 8–12; J Sorabji, *English Civil Justice after Woolf and Jackson* (CUP, 2014) chap 2.

[34] H Woolf (1996) at 274; CPR r 1; J Sorabji (2014) at 135–137.

[35] Practice Direction 31, para 1 (Hong Kong).

[36] Both the Code of Civil Procedure, Book 1, Title 1, r 1 (Quebec) and Supreme Court Civil Rules 2006, r 3 (South Australia) make these different purposes explicit. They are made explicit in this Code in r 8.

afforded access to a fair process.[37] It is important to bear in mind then that a fair procedure is one that may prevent a dispute from arising, or may see it resolved consensually or adjudicatively by a court judgment. It is also one that may, due to the application of the economy, efficiency, and proportionality principles, see the resolution process come to an end without the dispute being resolved by the courts. It may also see it resolved via a truncated process that calls into question adjudicative accuracy.

## RULE 5.—THE ECONOMY, EFFICIENCY, AND PROPORTIONALITY PRINCIPLES

**(1) A fair procedure is one that achieves the purposive principle consistently with the other rules in this Part and does so economically, efficiently, and proportionately both by reference to individual disputes and the administration of justice as a whole.**

**(2) In determining whether procedure is fair the nature of the dispute, any relevant characteristics of the parties, and the need to ensure that no single proceeding is, without good reason, afforded more than an equitable share of court time and resources, must be considered.**

*Sources: ALI/UNIDROIT Principles, principle 7; ELI-UNIDROIT Model Rules, rr 2, 5, 7, 8; Supreme Court Civil Rules 2006, r 3 (South Australia); CPR rr 1.1, 1.6.*

## COMMENTARY

1. This rule gives effect to what Zuckerman has described as multi-dimensional justice. This is the idea that in assessing whether litigants have been afforded a fair process it is necessary to consider more than whether they have been provided with adjudicative justice. It also requires questions of timeliness and cost to be considered.[38] This approach was given effect in the CPR through its overriding objective.[39] The rationale for its maintenance here is twofold.

2. First, it is intended to ensure that individual proceedings are conducted economically, efficiently, and proportionately (individual proportionality). Individual disputes should be managed to ensure that they are resolved within a minimum necessary timeframe[40] and at minimum necessary cost to the parties,[41] where both time and cost are proportionate to the nature, value, and importance etc of the dispute.[42]

[37] J Sorabji (2014) chaps 5–7; J Dyson, 'The Application of the Amendments to the Civil Procedure Rules' (2014) 33 CJQ 124; *Mitchell v News Group Newspapers Ltd* [2013] EWCA Civ 1537; [2014] 1 WLR 795; *Denton v TH White Ltd* [2014] EWCA Civ 906; [2014] 1 WLR 3926.

[38] A Zuckerman, 'Quality and Economy in Civil Procedure—A Case for Commuting Correct Judgments for Timely Judgments' (1994) 14 Oxford J Legal Stud 353; A Zuckerman, 'A Reform of Civil Procedure—Rationing Procedure rather than Access to Justice' (1995) 22 J L & Society 155 at 167; A Zuckerman (2021) at 29–36. The idea was not new. It was developed by Bentham in the 19th century: J Sorabji (2014), chap 3.

[39] CPR r 1.1; J Sorabji (2014); chaps 5–7; J Dyson (2014).

[40] A Zuckerman (2021) at 31.

[41] A A Matić, *Just Words—The Effectiveness of Civil Justice in European Human Rights Jurisprudence* (CUP, 2020).

[42] W Martin cited in J Dyson, *Justice: Continuity and Change* (Hart, 2018) at 291: *AON v Australian National University* [2009] HCA 27; (2009) 239 CLR 175 at [98].

3. The second rationale goes beyond the parties to any individual dispute. It is focused on an acceptance that the civil justice system, while incorporating the civil courts which are a branch of the State, is a public service. As any public service, and that includes Government and Parliament, it has limited resources available to it. Those resources must be used for the public good, which requires difficult choices to be made as to their allocation. Where dispute resolution is concerned resource allocation needs to be spread across the prevention of disputes, conflict resolution as well as adjudicative dispute resolution. It must also be allocated across society as a whole. In blunter terms access to dispute prevention, conflict and dispute resolution must be rationed. The question is how to ration or allocate the State's resources to them fairly, ie it is how to secure effective distributive justice where access to justice is concerned.[43] The second rationale, through the proportionality principle, is the means by which fair resource allocation is achieved.[44]
4. Proportionality as a procedural principle is thus not simply focused on the determination of what is a fair and proportionate procedure for individual parties: individual proportionality, which is dealt with above. It is also, and more importantly, focused on ensuring a fair procedure, and particularly fair access to the dispute resolution system for all members of society, ie it is focused on systemic proportionality.[45] Assessing proportionality thus not only requires parties and the court to consider what steps are proportionate by reference to the nature of their own dispute, ie by reference to individual proportionality, but also by reference to the overall need to secure a fair procedure, and access to it, for other parties to other disputes, ie by reference to systemic proportionality. Hence this rule requires, as does CPR r 1.1(2)(e), proportionality to be considered by reference to the needs of parties to all disputes, as much as it does to the needs of parties to specific disputes.
5. Systemic proportionality has an important consequence where the application of the accuracy principle is concerned. It provides a particular limit to its application. An overarching commitment to the accuracy principle, or its expression in securing a judgment on the substantive merits, might be taken to trump questions of economy and efficiency in litigation, as was the case under the RSC and, to a certain extent, the CPR. If procedure's sole or overriding purpose was to secure adjudicative accuracy then other principles and considerations would be subverted by it and set aside when they came into conflict with it. Systemic proportionality, and particularly its inherent link to the dispute management and compliance principles, is the key means by which such a consequence is to be avoided under this Code, just as it ought to be under the CPR.[46] This is particularly pertinent where decisions are taken, consistently with the need to secure systemic proportionality, to limit party access to evidence as this could reduce the court's ability to give effect to the accuracy principle by reducing the amount of relevant evidence before the court. It is also pertinent where the court, for the same reason, refuses to grant relief from the adverse consequences of non-compliance with procedural obligations. Such a refusal could, for instance,

[43] A point only made explicit in the commentary to the overriding objective of the civil procedure rules of Vanuatu: A Jensel, *Jensel's Civil Court's Practice* (AusAID, 2010) at 28.

[44] H Woolf (1996) at 24.

[45] The distinction between individual and systemic proportionality has previously been referred to as individual and collective proportionality: J Sorabji (2014) at 167–169; *Re L (a child)* [2013] EWCA Civ 1778. The term systemic proportionality is derived from J Dyson (2014) at 130–131.

[46] J Dyson (2014); *Mitchell v News Group Newspapers Ltd* [2013] EWCA Civ 1537; [2014] 1 WLR 795; *Denton v TH White Ltd* [2014] EWCA Civ 906; [2014] 1 WLR 3926.

mean a procedural strike out remains in place and thus the non-compliant party is denied a hearing and thus the opportunity to secure a judgment on the substantive merits of the dispute.[47] Where such consequences are looked at in the context of an individual dispute, they may appear unjust, notwithstanding the fact that the non-compliant party will have brought them on themselves by failing to comply with reasonable and proportionate directions or court orders. However, because the court is required to give effect to systemic proportionality, and parties are required to co-operate with the court in this respect, such consequences can be seen as, and are, properly just. They are so because the civil justice system must operate in order to do justice, provide a fair process and a fair result, for all parties who need to call on its limited resources. As the High Court of Australia put it, when discussing this approach, what may appear to be unjust by reference to its effect on an individual dispute is just when looked at in the broader context of delivering a public justice system that is accessible to all litigants.[48]

6. Giving effect to rule 5 requires careful consideration by parties of appropriate steps, which they need to take pre-action. It also requires careful consideration by both parties and the court to the approach to be taken to the management of disputes when proceedings commence, as provided for in Part 11.
7. Rule 5(2) makes provision for a factor that must be considered in the assessment of economy, efficiency, and proportionality that was only introduced into the CPR in 2021: party characteristics.[49] Under the CPR this is specifically focused on the need for consideration to be given to how its overriding objective is given effect for vulnerable parties.[50] This rule maintains that requirement. It does so in the broader context of the need to ensure that equal treatment is afforded to all parties consistently with the procedural equality principle.

## RULE 6.—THE AUTONOMY PRINCIPLE

**(1) Only a party to a dispute may initiate steps to resolve it. The court has no power to, and therefore must not, initiate proceedings.**
**(2) Parties, not the court, determine**
- **(a) the nature and scope of proceedings;**
- **(b) whether and how they wish to be represented;**
- **(c) whether to admit or contest matters in dispute;**
- **(d) whether to adduce evidence in support of claims or defences;**
- **(e) whether to withdraw or settle proceedings;**
- **(f) whether to challenge or appeal from judgments or orders or seek to have them upheld on appeal; and**
- **(g) whether to enforce any settlement, judgment, or court order.**

**(3) To give effect to the general or access to justice principles, party autonomy may be subject to the requirements of dispute management.**
**(4) Parties may agree, in advance of a dispute, on the approach they will take to resolve any dispute that may arise between them, including**
- **(a) pre-issue settlement procedures;**

[47] *Flaxman-Binns v Lincolnshire County Council* [2004] 1 WLR 2232 at [41].
[48] *AON v Australian National University* [2009] HCA 27; (2009) 239 CLR 175 at [23]–[26].
[49] Civil Procedure (Amendment) Rules 2021 (SI 2021/117).
[50] CPR r 1.6; CPR PD1A.

**(b) matters relating to the management of proceedings, including the conduct of hearings.**

**(5) Any agreement between the parties concerning the management of proceedings is, after they commence, subject to court approval.**

*Sources: ALI/UNIDROIT Principles, principle 10; ELI-UNIDROIT Model Rules, r 21.*

## COMMENTARY

1. Party autonomy, or the dispositive principle,[51] is a fundamental element of civil procedure. It has several elements.
2. Its most important aspect is that it means that it is not for courts to initiate proceedings to resolve private or public law civil disputes. Parties have a fundamental right to choose whether to take steps to resolve a dispute or to do nothing. It is thus not for the court to exercise any inquisitorial power to commence proceedings.
3. Party autonomy goes beyond the right to commence, or not, proceedings. It further finds expression in the parties' right to choose their own legal representation or to represent themselves, to withdraw or settle proceedings, to challenge or appeal from decisions, and whether to enforce any settlement, judgment, or court order. It is therefore intrinsically linked with a number of other procedural principles, eg the consensual settlement, adjudicative, reasonable assistance and representation, adversarial, effective enforcement, and appellate review principles. Arguably its other most important aspect is that it encompasses the parties' right to determine the nature and scope of proceedings and their right to contest or not specific issues.[52] It also places a limit upon the court's adjudicative role. Civil courts, when determining disputes adjudicatively, are only required to find the truth based on the parties' legal submissions and the evidence they have submitted.[53] They have no power to investigate evidential matters independently of the parties in order to find an 'independent truth'.[54] As such they have, for instance, no power to cross-examine witnesses independently of the parties.[55] Consequently, a court may adjudicate in the knowledge that the parties have not put before it relevant evidence or have agreed between themselves the 'facts',[56] or other matters, including the court's jurisdiction.[57] A court cannot go behind such matters, even if it means it reaches a decision that it suspects might be unsustainable if all the evidence were before it. Thus, the court's adjudicative role is significantly limited by party autonomy.[58]
4. Party autonomy is not, however, entirely free of constraint.[59] To give proper effect to the economy, efficiency, and proportionality principles, it is subject to limits. For instance, the parties' right to determine the nature and scope of proceedings

[51] J Jolowicz (2000) at 78; ELI-UNIDROIT Model Rules, r 21 commentary.

[52] *Loveridge & Loveridge v Healey* [2004] EWCA Civ 173; *Khaiban v Beard* [2003] EWCA Civ 358.

[53] *Briscoe v Briscoe* [1968] P 501.

[54] *Harmony Shipping Co SA v Davies* [1979] 3 All ER 177 at 181; *Air Canada v Secretary of State for Trade* [1983] 2 AC 394 at 410–411.

[55] *Southwark London Borough Council v Kofi-Adu* [2006] EWCA Civ 281; [2006] HLR 33.

[56] *Air Canada v Secretary of State for Trade* [1983] 2 AC 394; *Balchin v Chief Constable of Hampshire Constabulary* [2001] EWCA Civ 538; *Al-Medenni v Mars UK Ltd* [2005] EWCA Civ 1041.

[57] *Loveridge & Loveridge v Healey* [2004] EWCA Civ 173.

[58] *Official Solicitor v K* [1965] AC 201; *Harmony Shipping Co SA v Davies* [1979] 3 All ER 177 at 181.

[59] Compare with Arbitration Act 1996, s 1(b) and (c).

is limited by those principles where amendment is concerned. A late amendment of case statements could, on the one hand, alter the nature and scope of proceedings. It could also have a significant adverse effect on the effective operation of the court system, such that it hampered other parties' ability to resolve their dispute in an economical, efficient, and proportionate manner. It could also render the immediate dispute disproportionately costly and time consuming for the parties themselves by opening up new lines of evidential enquiry or legal controversy. A similar need to give effect to the principle of finality justifies the imposition of limits, via the permission to appeal requirement, on a party's right to challenge a judgment or order. To give effect to such constraints generally, party autonomy is limited by the dispute management principle,[60] which gives the court responsibility for the effective management of proceedings to achieve the purposive principle, and through that give effect to economy, efficiency, proportionality, and finality.[61]

5. Inherent in party autonomy is the right of parties to take steps to agree, in advance of any dispute, the means by which they are to try to resolve it. Such agreement may take the form of an arbitration clause in a commercial contract, or a valid multi-tier dispute resolution clause.[62] It may also take the form of what is increasingly becoming known as '*contract procedure*'.[63] That is to say, parties may agree on the extent to which civil procedure rules are to apply to their dispute should proceedings commence, eg they may agree on the nature and extent of evidence subject to disclosure, or on the length of any trial. The aim here, from a dispute resolution perspective, is to further the economy, efficiency, and proportionality principle, but also to promote effective dispute management both before and after proceedings commence. From the parties' perspective, such agreements may equally form part of the contract price where they are entered into as part of commercial relations. Any agreed approach to dispute resolution may favour one party or another or may simply reduce the potential quality of any adjudicative resolution. It may have a value accordingly, which can factor into the contract price. Any such agreements, as they may impinge upon effective dispute management once proceedings commence, are subject to court approval. This is necessary as proceedings must be managed in the public interest, and particularly proportionality. They cannot simply give effect to the private interests of the parties.

## RULE 7.—THE CONCENTRATION PRINCIPLE

**All matters in dispute between the parties should be pursued in a single set of proceedings.**

*Sources: Council of Europe Rec R (84) 5, principle 5; ELI-UNIDROIT Model Rules, r 22; Common Law Procedure Act 1852, s 41; Senior Courts Act 1981, s 49(2); CPR rr 1.4(2)(i), 3.1(2)(g), (h).*

[60] CPR rr 1.4, 3.

[61] N Andrews, 'A New Civil Procedural Code for England: Party-control Going, Going, Gone' (2000) 19 CJQ 19.

[62] E Lein, 'Multi-tier Dispute Resolution Clauses—An English Perspective', in A Reyes and W Gu, *Multi-Tier Approaches to the Resolution of International Disputes—A Global and Comparative Study* (CUP, 2021); *Ohpen Operations UL Ltd v Invesco Fund Managers Ltd* [2019] EWHC 2466 (TC); [2020] 1 All ER (Comm) 786.

[63] Code of Civil Procedure (Brazil) (16 March 2015, via Act No 13,105/2015), arts 190, 191, 200.

## COMMENTARY

1. Were parties to disputes able to bring separate proceedings for each matter or issue that arose from the same dispute, there would be a real risk that the same factual and legal issues would be adjudicated on several occasions. Thus, finality in litigation would be undermined; rights would never be certain as matters could always be subject to further litigation. Such an approach would result in needlessly costly and time-consuming litigation for the parties. It would also see parties waste a disproportionate amount of the court's resources, which could properly be expended on other disputes. The cost and time associated with the multiplication of proceedings could equally act as a barrier to access to justice, disincentivising parties from bringing or pursuing disputes. Any such adverse effects are likely to have a discriminatory effect on parties, adversely affecting to a greater degree those who could not afford either the time and cost of such litigation to a greater degree than other time or resource rich parties. In this way, multiplication of proceedings would also undermine procedural equality.
2. Permitting parties to bring multiple proceedings concerning matters related to the same dispute would also raise further problems, as has been repeatedly demonstrated historically and more recently. During the 19th century the ability for parties to bring claims concerning the same cause of action in both the common law and equity courts led to the unnecessary duplication of cost and time to judgment. It also led to different courts issuing conflicting judgments on the same issues. Such a situation necessarily undermines confidence in the courts and judiciary, while undermining judicial legitimacy and the rule of law. Inevitably the cost and time involved also led to increased litigation cost and time, and thus also acted as a barrier to access to justice. That problem was cured in the 19th century by consolidating the various courts into a single High Court of Justice. A similar problem has, however, arisen again in the early 21st century through the establishment of partial jurisdictions across the Tribunals justice system and the civil justice system, particularly where housing disputes are concerned. Different legal matters can and need to be litigated in such disputes across the two systems meaning, as in the 19th century, that parties must expend unnecessary time and resources to fully determine their dispute. The risk of inconsistent judgments, again, also exists. Attempts have been made to cure this problem through, for instance, authorising judges to sit simultaneously in the First-tier Tribunal and County Court so that they can deal with all claims arising from the same dispute. Those attempts have, however, only mitigated the problems to a limited extent. Parties still need to navigate two sets of procedural rules, secure such joint hearings, and then navigate different appeal processes from the two jurisdictions.[64]
3. This rule is intended to obviate the problems of multiple proceedings either in the civil courts or across jurisdictions. It does so by giving effect to the longstanding concentration principle, which requires parties to pursue all matters arising from their dispute in a single set of proceedings.[65] As such it is also a means to promote and support several other procedural principles, not least finality in litigation, while

[64] G Vos, *Professionalism in Property Conference* (2018); Civil Justice Council, *Report on Property Chamber Deployment Project for Civil Justice Council Meeting 26th October 2018* (CJC, 2018); *Avon Ground Rents Ltd v Child* [2018] UKUT 204 (LC).

[65] Common Law Procedure Act 1852, s 41; *The First Judicature Report* at 10–12; RSC (1875) Ord 17.

increasing access to justice through promoting procedural economy, efficiency, and proportionality. Its implementation is not simply a matter for the civil courts and the parties. It ought also to be implemented by the Civil Dispute Resolution Council. It ought to give effect to it, first, through securing the merger of the Tribunals into the civil courts and, secondly, through providing guidance to promote digital integration so that dispute prevention, conflict and dispute resolution mechanisms are integrated holistically and operate effectively via the digital portal. In this way the portal would be able to ensure that all aspects of a dispute, or potential dispute, could be avoided or resolved in the most time and cost-effective manner. If that is achieved the concentration principle could properly help secure a contemporary version of what, in the 19th century, was referred to as complete justice.[66]

## RULE 8.—THE PREVENTION, CONSENSUAL SETTLEMENT, AND ACCURACY PRINCIPLES

**(1) The Code shall give effect to preventive, consensual and adjudicative justice.**
**(2) Preventive justice shall be promoted through the digital procedure.**
**(3) Resolving a dispute justly means that a dispute concludes either**
  **(a) by consensual settlement, or**
  **(b) by a court judgment given or issued by the judge who tried the issue or dispute.**
**(4) Consensual settlement, as the means to achieve consensual justice, is reached by party agreement, whether facilitated or not by the court or an independent third party.**
**(5) Resolution by court judgment, as the means to achieve adjudicative justice, may be given on the dispute's substantive merits based on the application of the right substantive law to the right facts. Such a judgment gives effect to the accuracy principle.**
**(6) A court judgment may also be given on procedural grounds, including on the basis of non-compliance with the purposive or compliance principles. Such a judgment does not give effect to the accuracy principle. It gives effect to the purposive principle.**

*Sources: Council of Europe Rec R (84) 5, principle 8; ALI/UNIDROIT Principles, principles 22, 24; ELI-UNIDROIT Model Rules, r 9; CPR r 1.1.*

### COMMENTARY

1. This rule gives effect to three forms of justice: preventive, consensual, and adjudicative.
2. Preventive justice refers to the provision of measures that either help individuals or businesses to plan their affairs so as to minimise the risk that conflicts and disputes will arise. It generally falls outside the constitutional role of courts, as it is not directly related to the resolution of disputes. Where the courts have historically played a role in its promotion, that has arisen through what is referred to as the shadow of law.[67] That refers to the availability of court judgments and access to the court, which play a role in educating individuals as to their obligations, how the law is applied, and how it can be enforced. These factors play a central role in dispute formation or

[66] *The First Judicature Report* at 6–12; J Sorabji (2014), chap 2.

[67] *R (UNISON) v Lord Chancellor* [2017] UKSC 51; [2017] 3 WLR 409 at [66]; R Mnookin and L Kornhauser, 'Bargaining in the Shadow of the Law' (1978–1979) 88 Yale LJ 950.

its prevention through parties ordering their affairs to minimise the prospect that conflicts and thereafter disputes will arise. They also play a central role in promoting consensual settlement through negotiation, mediation, etc. The shadow of the law is given effect here not only through the publication of reasoned judgments and access to the court, but also through the novel provision of information to Ombudsman schemes and regulators for the promotion of law reform via the digital procedure, as detailed in Part 5. In this way this Code promotes preventive justice in two significant ways. The incorporation of this principle into the Code is a novel development in England and Wales.

3. Consensual justice and adjudicative justice refer to the two fundamental principles that determine the nature of just dispute resolution, ie they refer to the consensual settlement and accuracy principles, both of which are established principles of English and Welsh civil procedure.[68]
4. Rule 8(3)(a) gives precedence to the consensual settlement over the accuracy principle. This is reflective of the fact that resolution via court judgment, adjudicative justice, is very much the exception and, equally, that even where the litigation process is concerned it has long been acknowledged that settlement is an intrinsic element of it.[69]
5. The consensual settlement principle specifically refers to where parties resolve their dispute by consent. It thus encompasses resolution via negotiation, mediation, and other processes where parties agree upon the nature and form of resolution, eg by what has traditionally been known as alternative dispute resolution. It also encompasses arbitration and other processes where parties agree to be bound by a resolution determined by a third party. That third party can include the court or a judge where the resolution does not arise from the application of the judicial power of the State. Precedence is given to it within this rule to emphasise that consensual settlement is an inherent part of this Code and that it ought to be considered and utilised prior to parties resorting to resolution via judgment. This principle is given effect within the Code generally, and specifically by Parts 5 and 11.[70] Its achievement not only supports parties' private interest in resolving their disputes efficiently, economically, and proportionately to their satisfaction, it also supports the public interest in promoting systemic proportionality and the proper administration of justice.[71]
6. Resolution reached by a judge who has tried the dispute has historically been viewed as the court's primary if not exclusive focus; its constitutional role.[72] Civil justice systems and rules of court have generally taken as their primary purpose the objective of resolving disputes via judgments and doing so through achieving what Bentham famously described as rectitude of decision.[73] In other words by achieving justice on the merits,[74] as Zuckerman refers to it, or substantive justice,[75] as Genn has it. That

[68] *Collins v The Vestry of Paddington* (1879–80) LR 5 QBD 368 at 380; *D v National Society for the Prevention of Cruelty to Children* [1978] AC 171 at 232.

[69] M Galanter, 'Worlds of Deals: Using Negotiation to Teach About Legal Process' (1984) 34 J Legal Education 268.

[70] *Naylor v Preston Area Health Authority* [1987] 1 WLR 958 at 967–968.

[71] *Mionis v Democratic Press SA* [2017] EWCA Civ 1194; [2018] QB 662 at [88].

[72] ELI-UNIDROIT Model Rules, commentary to r 64(2).

[73] J Bentham, 'Principles of Judicial Procedure, with the outlines of a Procedure Code', in *The Works of Jeremy Bentham* (ed Bowring) (William Tait, 1843) Vol 2 (J Bentham, Principles) at 29 and following, 174, and 178.

[74] A Zuckerman (2021) at 8.

[75] H Genn, *Judging Civil Justice* (CUP, 2010).

is to say resolution is achieved through a court determining the dispute accurately by reference to the application of substantive legal principles to the true facts.[76] In this way the accuracy principle is given effect. Rule 8(1) and (5) make clear that resolution by court judgment encompasses this form of accuracy as it refers explicitly to resolution on the substantive merits. Such a resolution and the achievement of accuracy can, however, only be achieved through the application of the purposive principle, and hence it is balanced by and subject to limits imposed by the economy, efficiency, and proportionality principles.[77]

7. Rule 8(6) acknowledges that resolution via court judgment can arise in other ways than those that give effect to the accuracy principle. They can also arise on procedural grounds, albeit the rule does not incorporate a commitment to resolution by reference to what could be called procedural accuracy, ie resolution on the basis of compliance with procedural rules and obligations.[78] By referring to resolution on procedural grounds, it includes judgment in default of a defence. By referring to judgment arising through non-compliance with the purposive or compliance principles, it includes judgments that strike out claims for non-compliance with procedural obligations. Where this is the case, proceedings conclude by reference to the fact that the parties have, nevertheless been afforded a fair process, ie on the basis of procedural justice.

## RULE 9.—THE DISPUTE MANAGEMENT PRINCIPLE

**(1) The court must manage disputes, including any hearing or trial, actively. It must do so to give effect to the purposive principle. It shall do so once proceedings commence. It will also do so where a pre-commencement application is made by the parties.**

**(2) Parties, including their lawyers, must manage their dispute both before and after proceedings commence to give effect to the purposive principle.**

**(3) The management of proceedings to settlement is a judicial function.**

*Sources: Council of Europe Rec R (84) 5, principles 3, 4; ALI/UNIDROIT Principles, principle 14; ELI-UNIDROIT Model Rules, rr 3, 4, 9, 10; CPR r 1.4.*

## COMMENTARY

1. Active case or dispute management lies at the heart of modern civil procedure codes. It has been an integral element of English and Welsh civil procedure since the CPR was introduced in 1999,[79] albeit attempts had been made previously to introduce it in different forms.[80] It is equally integral to other national

[76] H Genn (2010) at 14.

[77] J Dyson (2014).

[78] J Sorabji (2014) at 34–38.

[79] R Turner, '"Actively": The Word that Changed the Civil Courts', in D Dwyer (ed), *The Civil Procedure Rules Ten Years On* (OUP 2009); A Zuckerman (2021) chap 11.

[80] Queen's Bench Division Judges' Notice as to Commercial Causes (February 1895) in A Colman, *The Practice and Procedure of the Commercial Court* (1983) at 7–8 and 47; RSC (1965) Ord 72, r 2(3); A Diamond, 'The Summons for Directions' (1959) 75 LQR 43; *Practice Direction (Case Management)* [1995] 1 WLR 262; H Heilbron and H Hodge, *Civil Justice on Trial—A Case for Change* (1993) (Joint report of The Bar Council

systems,[81] where it is variously a tool to manage proceedings to judgment and to consensual settlement.[82] At the international level, case management is acknowledged as a fundamental principle of civil procedure in the ALI/UNIDROIT Transnational Principles[83] and is a central aspect of European procedural best practice in the ELI-UNIDROIT Model Rules.

2. Two different approaches, common in some European jurisdictions,[84] can be taken to case, or as it is referred to here, dispute management.[85] A court could manage a dispute substantively (substantive or material case management) or simply procedurally (procedural case management). The former refers to the court having the jurisdiction and power to take steps on its own initiative to determine right fact and right law. Such a power could, for instance, provide the court with the ability to identify what it believed to be relevant evidence and require it to be submitted to the court. Neither English and Welsh civil procedure under the CPR nor under this Code has such a power or jurisdiction, except in limited circumstances, eg the power, subject to party agreement, to call witnesses. Such a power is not adopted given its general inconsistency with the party autonomy and adversarial principles.
3. The general approach in England and Wales is that management is procedural dispute management. It is given specific effect in this Code through Parts 5, 11, and 12. Consistently with the co-operation principle, it is to be given effect by both the parties and the court working together. The primary management obligation is, however, placed on the court. Experience has shown that where management powers are given, but their use depends on the parties to invoke them, the nature of the adversarial imperative combined with party autonomy renders the powers nugatory. Parties rarely invoke them when given the primary responsibility to do so. For active dispute management to be effective therefore it must, as it does under the CPR and here,[86] form an exception to the party autonomy principle.[87] While the primary obligation thus rests on the court, parties are also placed under an obligation to manage disputes effectively. For them, this obligation applies both before and after proceedings are commenced.
4. As both the court and party obligation is to manage disputes to give effect to the purposive principle, management must be carried out to give effect to the principles contained in this Part. It is thus the key means by which parties are afforded a fair process and through which a just resolution is achieved efficiently, economically, and proportionately. Most notably dispute management requires parties to give effect to the consensual settlement principle, as much as the accuracy principle. The former is in this way made an integral part of every set of proceedings.[88] Settlement processes

and Law Society) at 5 and Appendix 1 at [25]; Civil Justice Review Body, *Civil Justice Review 1988* (Cmd 394, 1988) at 154–162.

[81] S Frodl, 'The Heritage of the Franz Klein Reform of Austrian Civil Procedure' (2012) 31(1) CJQ 43, 54.

[82] J Resnik, 'Managerial Judges' (1982) 96 Harv L Rev 374; E Jeuland, *Introduction to French Business Litigation* (Joly, 2016) at 55; R Stürner and P Murphy, *German Civil Justice* (Carolina, 2004) chap 6.

[83] ALI/UNIDROIT Principles of Transnational Civil Procedure (CUP, 2004) (ALI/UNIDROIT Principles), Principle 14; ELI-UNIDROIT Model Rules, rr 4, 48–50.

[84] S Nieuwendijk et al, 'The Paradox of Access to Justice—Empirical Research Into The Attitude Of The Cantonal Judge Towards Unrepresented Parties In Dutch Civil Procedure', in A Uzelac and CH van Rhee, *Revisiting Procedural Human Rights* (Intersentia) (2017).

[85] Cases focus the mind on court cases. Disputes focus the mind on the substantive matter to be resolved.

[86] CPR Pt 3.

[87] N Andrews (2000).

[88] M Briggs, *Chancery Modernisation Review—Final Report* (Judicial Office, December 2013) at 67–68.

are not an optional extra, as stressed by rule 9(3) making explicit how the management of proceedings to settlement is a judicial process.[89]

## RULE 10.—THE CO-OPERATION PRINCIPLE

**(1) Parties, including their lawyers, must, in so far as possible, co-operate with each other in the proper management of their dispute consistently with the purposive principle both before and after proceedings commence.**
**(2) Parties, including their lawyers, non-parties (including lay and expert witnesses), and the court must co-operate with each other once proceedings have commenced to further the purposive principle.**

*Sources: Council of Europe Rec R (84) 5, principle 2.1; ALI/UNIDROIT Principles, principle 7; ELI-UNIDROIT Model Rules, rr 2, 3, 6; CPR r 1.3.*

## COMMENTARY

1. It has been argued that the primary objective of lawyers—and parties to proceedings—is '*to win if possible without violating the law*'.[90] Within an adversarial system and one that places significant weight on the principle of party autonomy, such an objective tends to shape the use to which parties put procedural rules. This can be seen through the use and misuse of disclosure. Its ostensible aim is to facilitate truth-finding.[91] Its implementation in practice has been another story.[92] An astute party can seek to narrow disclosure to reduce the prospect that the truth will come out. They could equally provide excessive and unnecessary disclosure thus seeking to hide the truth amongst a welter of materials. And they could, through tactical satellite litigation increase the cost and time to be expended on it, which would place a less financially secure party at a disadvantage. The use or misuse of process can thus be used to secure victory even if it is not victory on the substantive merits of the dispute. It is, perhaps, unsurprising then that tactical, adversarial approaches to litigation have dominated the history of civil procedure; a history which in the 19th century led to the party-autonomy dominated adversarial model of procedure being compared to '*a battle between the parties without the Red Cross*'.[93] It was an approach equally identified at the end of the 20th century as a key problem underpinning English and Welsh civil procedure.[94]
2. There are other approaches. Party autonomy could be placed in a broader context of court control of the dispute resolution process. The adversarial imperative can be influenced and operated by reference to a broader explicit purposive principle.[95] Additionally, as this principle does, parties can be required to co-operate with each

[89] Implicit in CPR r 3.1(2)(m).

[90] M Frankel, 'The Search for Truth: An Umpireal View' (1975) 123 U Pa L Rev 1031 at 1037; W Brazil, 'The Adversary Character of Civil Discovery' (1978) 31 Vand LR 1296 at 1311–1315.

[91] *Tweed v Parades Commission for Northern Ireland* [2006] UKHL 53; [2007] 1 AC 650 at [2].

[92] Part 12, r 14.

[93] Franz Klein cited by R H (Remco) van Rhee, 'Obligations of the Parties and their Lawyers in Civil Litigation: The ALI/UNIDROIT Principles of Transnational Civil Procedure', in J Adolphsen et al, *Festschrift für Peter Gottwald zum 70* (Beck, 2014) at 669.

[94] H Woolf (1995) at 7.

[95] CPR rr 1.1 to 1.4.

other and the court to secure procedure's purpose. The imperative to win at all costs within the law can in this way be tempered. This principle seeks to achieve that objective. It does so by going beyond the approach taken in the CPR, which only requires parties to '*help*'[96] the court to give effect to its overriding objective.[97]

3. This rule requires parties, their lawyers, and non-parties to co-operate with each other and the court actively to further the purposive principle. It thus imposes a co-operation duty on them. In doing so it adopts the best practice approach identified in the ELI-UNIDROIT Model Rules, which itself incorporated an innovative duty on the parties and the court to co-operate with each other '*to promote proportionate dispute resolution . . .*'.[98] The present principle, for instance, thus requires parties, when they become aware of procedural mistakes or errors made by their opponents at a time when they can be rectified without recourse to the court for relief from sanction or regularisation via court order, to inform them of the mistake or error. Under the CPR, they were not required to do so; they could remain silent and take advantage of the error. In so far as this principle applies to a party's lawyers, it overrides their duty to their client, just as it overrides party autonomy in the management of their dispute. It does so because the civil justice system and particularly the civil courts, forms part of a public service, one that delivers a public good, but which must be delivered and be deliverable in as efficient a way as possible so as to benefit society as a whole. This requires a pro-active approach by parties and their lawyers to minimise resource use by themselves and the court system. Co-operation and its consequences are one way to help promote the achievement of this aim. This principle is also justified as it focuses the parties on the substantive nature of their dispute and its resolution by reference to that rather than by reference to how well they play the game. It is thus also justified as it is a means to embed an approach that does not see dispute resolution as a 'war' between parties, but rather as a problem to be solved via a variety of processes, preventive, consensual, and adjudicative, which are made available to them.
4. The co-operation principle is given specific expression in this Code in several ways. At the most basic level it is intended to promote a culture of rule compliance, so as to promote effective and particularly efficient, economical, and proportionate dispute resolution.[99] It is thus intended to support the implementation of the compliance principle. Specifically, it is intended to promote co-operation between parties during the pre-action phase of dispute resolution; effective co-operation at that early stage of a conflict or dispute underpins effective consensual resolution processes. This is particularly important where negotiation, mediation, and collaborative law are being used as methods to promote consensual settlement; effective co-operation between the parties, their lawyers, and, where relevant, a mediator or other facilitators (tax specialists, therapists etc) is essential if they are to have any prospect of promoting a satisfactory resolution.[100] It is also intended to underpin specific rules governing

[96] *Hallam Estates Ltd v Baker* [2014] EWCA Civ 661; [2014] CP Rep 38 at [12]; *McCann v Bisping* [2017] EWHC 2951 (Comm) at [23].

[97] *OMV Petrom SA v Glencore International AG* [2017] EWCA Civ 195; [2017] WLR 3465 at [39].

[98] ELI-UNIDROIT Model Rules, r 6.

[99] *Denton v TH White Ltd* [2014] EWCA Civ 906; [2014] WLR 3926 at [40]; *UTB LLC v Sheffield United Ltd* [2019] EWHC 914 (Ch); [2019] 3 All ER 698 at [75]; *McParland & Partners Ltd v Whitehead* [2020] EWHC 298 (Ch) at [4], [53]–[58].

[100] S Diacoff, 'Collaborative Law: A New Tool for the Lawyer's Toolkit' (2009) 20 University of Florida Journal of Law & Public Policy 130.

post-issue dispute and evidence management. Its promotion is further supported by the imposition of sanctions for non-compliance with both this general duty and specific applications of it. As under the CPR, where a party fails to comply with the co-operation principle, the most common form of sanction should be the imposition of cost sanctions.[101]

## RULE 11.—THE COMPLIANCE PRINCIPLE

**(1) Parties and their lawyers shall ensure they comply with this Code and any relevant Practice Direction or court order.**

**(2) The court shall take steps to secure compliance with this Code, any relevant Practice Direction or court order.**

*Sources: Council of Europe Rec R (84) 5, principles, 1.2, 1.3, 1.4, 2, 7; ALI/UNIDROIT Principles, principle 17; ELI-UNIDROIT Model Rules, rr 27, 28.*

## COMMENTARY

1. English and Welsh civil procedure has taken several approaches to compliance with procedural obligations, whether contained in rules of court, court orders, or directions. Common law courts adopted a strict approach to rule compliance with no real power to grant relief from the adverse consequences of non-compliance. Equity courts adopted a more flexible approach, tending to grant relief from the adverse consequences of non-compliance. Equity's approach was cemented as the default approach following the Judicature Act reforms of 1873–1875. Thereafter a liberal approach to rule compliance was in place.[102] Consequently, rules, orders and directions were, in practice, treated by parties as guidelines. This approach stemmed from the tacit understanding that the overriding objective of the RSC (albeit not put in those terms) was to secure substantive justice or justice on the merits.[103] Parties were not to be blocked from achieving that through procedural non-compliance.[104] Where the two came into conflict, non-compliance was to be, in most cases, forgiven.
2. This liberal approach to rule compliance created several significant adverse consequences. It undermined procedural equality. Non-compliant parties would be treated differently from compliant parties. They would have access to more court time than was necessary and was afforded to their rule-compliant opponent. They would be afforded a greater share of the court's resources that ought reasonably to be allocated to them, which was to the detriment of their opponent and parties to other proceedings. This approach also undermined procedural economy and efficiency. Non-compliance meant that procedural timetables, which sought to secure such aims, were not adhered to, thus unnecessarily increasing the time and cost of litigation. That whether a non-compliant party would be granted relief from the adverse consequences of non-compliance was discretionary, even if the discretion

[101] *Emmanuel v Revenue & Customs* [2018] EWHC 1253 (Ch); [2017] Costs LR 515.

[102] A Zuckerman, 'Compliance with Process Obligations and Fair Trial', in M Andenas, N Andrews, and R Nazzini, *The Future of Transnational Civil Litigation* (BICCL, 2004).

[103] *Cropper v Smith* (1883) 32 WR 262 at 263; *Coles v Ravenshear* [1907] 1 KB 1 at 4.

[104] J Sorabji (2014) chap 2; R Jackson, *Review of Civil Litigation Costs: Final Report* (December 2009) at 391.

was heavily weighted in favour of relief, also meant that satellite litigation over the grant of such relief was a growth industry. It was one that further increased the cost and time of litigation significantly both for the immediate parties, and for parties to other proceedings whose claims were delayed due to court time being expended on such procedural matters. Consequently, it not only increased the cost and time of litigation generally but also, due to that, acted as a barrier to access to justice.[105]

3. The CPR was intended to move away from the historically lax approach to rule-compliance.[106] That intention was not, however, realised until after the Jackson Cost Review when a concerted attempt was made to eradicate it and implement a culture of rule-compliance.[107] That review first saw the introduction of a specific sub-rule within the CPR's overriding objective identifying rule compliance as an express aspect of the CPR's purpose.[108] It also, and more importantly, saw the Court of Appeal explain the rationale behind the increased emphasis on rule-compliance and the concomitant stress on a stricter, more restrictive approach to relief from the adverse consequences of non-compliance.[109] It explained that as a public service, the civil justice system's limited resources had to be fairly accessible by all court users. Rule-compliance was intended to ensure that this was the case in practice, and that all parties had access to a proportionate share of those resources. Promoting compliance and taking a strict line to relief from the adverse consequences of non-compliance was a means by which this was achieved.[110] It was intended to ensure that parties prosecuted their disputes economically, efficiently, and proportionately. More broadly, it was intended to enable the court to secure a fair distribution of its resources, and hence fair and equitable access, to other court users consistently with systemic proportionality.[111]
4. To ensure that this approach is maintained, this rule gives effect to what can properly be described as the compliance principle: that to give effect to the other principles in this Code, and particularly to secure the purposive, economy, efficiency, and proportionality principles, parties and their lawyers are required to comply with procedural obligations. The court must also ensure that its approach to rule-compliance maintains the normative force of those obligations. That it does so does not require a 'Stalinist' approach to compliance,[112] as is evident from the three stage test applicable to relief from the adverse consequences of non-compliance.[113]
5. Notwithstanding this principle, it remains open to parties to elect not to comply with procedural obligations. Where they choose not to comply, just as where they fail to do so through inadvertence, error, or negligence, they may seek relief from the consequences of their non-compliance. If they choose not to apply for such relief they

[105] A Zuckerman (2021) at 20.

[106] *Thomson v O'Connor* [2005] EWCA Civ 1533 at [17].

[107] *Fred Perry (Holdings) Ltd v Brands Plaza Trading Ltd* [2012] EWCA 224 at [1]; *Mannion v Ginty* [2012] EWCA Civ 1667 at [18]; R Jackson (December 2009); J Dyson (2014); *Mitchell v News Group Newspapers Ltd* [2013] EWCA Civ 1537; [2014] 1 WLR 795; *Denton v TH White Ltd* [2014] EWCA Civ 906; [2014] 1 WLR 3926.

[108] CPR r 1.1(2)(f).

[109] *Mitchell v News Group Newspapers Ltd* [2013] EWCA Civ 1537; [2014] 1 WLR 795; *Denton v TH White Ltd* [2014] EWCA Civ 906; [2014] 1 WLR 3926.

[110] *Scopelliti v Italy* (1993) 17 EHRR 493 at [25].

[111] J Sorabji (2014) chaps 5 to 7; J Dyson (2014); *Aon Risk Services Australia Ltd v Australian National University* [2009] HCA 27; (2009) 239 CLR 175, esp at [26] and [95].

[112] N Andrews (2019) at 706.

[113] Part 11, rr 33 and 34.

must simply accept the adverse consequences that flow from their non-compliance, just as they must if an application for relief is refused.

# SECTION 3: ACCESS TO JUSTICE PRINCIPLES

## RULE 12.—THE GENERAL ACCESS PRINCIPLE

**(1) Parties are entitled to practical and effective access to a court and to consensual settlement processes to resolve their civil disputes.**

**(2) Practical and effective access includes a right to an amount of public funding necessary to secure it. It also includes a right to receive private funding. It also includes a right to be compensated in costs where a dispute is resolved through adjudication.**

**(3) Access may be limited or restricted to give effect to**

**(a) the purposive principle; or**

**(b) a specific provision of this Code.**

**(4) Limitations and restrictions must be no more than proportionate.**

*Sources: European Convention on Human Rights, art 6(1).*

## COMMENTARY

1. Access to justice, as Lord Reed identified in *R (UNISON) v Lord Chancellor (2017)* is '*inherent in the rule of law*'.[114] Without it, substantive legal rights are incapable of vindication, interpretation, or clarification. Of the three, the first is the most important as it can properly be said that the existence of substantive rights (and obligations) necessarily implies the existence of both the right of access to a court and judgment.[115] Moreover, this right is of fundamental importance given the role judgments play in providing the shadow of the law, the framework for dispute prevention and consensual resolution.[116]

2. This rule restates the right of access to justice as a procedural principle.[117] It is a right that is recognised as a common law constitutional right.[118] It is equally affirmed by article 10 of the Universal Declaration of Human Rights and article 6 of the European Convention on Human Rights.[119] Without this right, the other principles set out in this Part would be no more than words written on water. Of all the rules, this one is the one upon which all the others rest and through which they are given their normative force. It does, however, go beyond the established right, by providing that there should also be practical and effective access to consensual settlement processes.

114 *R (UNISON) v Lord Chancellor* [2017] UKSC 51; [2017] 3 WLR 409 at [66]–[68].

115 *Matthews v Ministry of Defence* [2003] UKHL 4; [2003] 1 AC 1163; L Alexander, 'Are Procedural Rights Derivative Substantive Rights?' (1998) 17 Law and Philosophy 19.

116 *R (UNISON) v Lord Chancellor* [2017] UKSC 51; [2017] 3 WLR 409 at [66] and following; R Mnookin and L Kornhauser (1978–1979).

117 *Airey v Ireland* (1979) 2 EHRR 305; *Tolstoy-Miloslavksy v The United Kingdom* (1995) 20 EHRR 442 at [59]; *R (Gudanaviciene) v The Director of Legal Aid Casework and The Lord* Chancellor [2014] EWCA Civ 1622 at [72]; *Children's Rights Alliance for England v Secretary of State for Justice* [2013] EWCA Civ 34; [2013] HRLR 17 at [38].

118 *Bremer Vulcan Schiffbau und Maschinenfabrik v South India Shipping Corp Ltd* [1981] AC 909 at 979.

119 *Golder v The United Kingdom* (1975) 1 EHRR 524 at [35]–[36].

3. The right of access necessarily implies a right to dispute resolution funding. A party's financial means ought not to bar them from effective and practical access to justice. Consistently with procedural equality, the Code makes explicit, as part of this principle, that there is a right to receive such funding as is necessary. That may be funds provided privately, or exceptionally where that is not available, through public, legal aid funding.[120] It also, as individuals who bring proceedings to vindicate their rights successfully via a judgment ought not to be out of pocket for doing so, provides an entitlement to recover their costs from the losing party.
4. Access is not, however, absolute. It can properly be subject to limitations where they serve a legitimate purpose that is achieved through means that are proportionate.[121] On this basis, it is permissible for the court to require parties to resort to a process aimed at promoting consensual settlement.[122] Equally, the right to receive costs if you are the successful party is limited by reference to the need to ensure that the level of costs is not so high as to impair effective and practical access for the other party. It can thus be limited by measures, such as the introduction of a scheme of fixed recoverable costs or by reference to the proportionality principle.[123] Most significantly, limitations imposed by and through the application of rules in this Code, where they are proportionate, can be relied upon to restrict access to the court or deny it entirely. This is most pertinent where a party fails to comply with procedural obligations that are designed to secure practical and effective access generally. As with the proportionality and compliance principles, access to justice must be looked at in a broad sense, ie what may appear unjust in the instant case by limiting or denying access to justice for a specific individual may be just when considered by reference to the overall operation of the civil justice system and the need to secure systemic proportionality and fair access for all.

## RULE 13.—THE INDEPENDENCE AND IMPARTIALITY PRINCIPLES

**(1) The court, which includes the judiciary and its administrative staff, must be independent of the parties to a civil dispute. Independence includes both institutional and decisional independence. The court must also have no interest in the proceedings and be impartial.**

**(2) A court will not be independent, either structurally or decisionally, where constitutional, statutory, or common law guarantees of its independence are improperly undermined. It will also not be independent where an individual judge has an interest in the outcome of proceedings over which they are presiding.**

**(3) A court will not be impartial where the judge dealing with proceedings has been influenced by actual bias or a fair-minded and informed observer would conclude that there was a real possibility that the judge was biased.**

[120] *Airey v Ireland* (1979) 2 EHRR 305; *R (Gudanaviciene) v The Director of Legal Aid Casework and The Lord Chancellor* [2014] EWCA Civ 1622 at [72].

[121] *Lupeni Greek Catholic Parish v Romania* [2016] ECHR 1061; *Alassini (Environment and consumers)* [2010] 3 CMLR 17 at [64]–[65]; *Menini and Rampanelli (Approximation of laws Consumer protection: Judgment)* [2017] EUECJ C-75/16 at [61].

[122] *Momcilovic v Croatia* (2019) 69 EHRR 14; *Churchill v Merthyr Tydfil County Borough Council* [2023] EWCA Civ 1416 at [74].

[123] *Tolstoy-Miloslavksy v The United Kingdom* (1995) 20 EHRR 442.

(4) **Actual bias arises where a judge's conduct in dealing with the proceedings is prejudiced or motivated by prejudice or partiality.**
(5) **Parties may waive the right to impartiality. Waiver must be freely made, fully-informed, express, and prospective.**

*Sources: ALI/UNIDROIT Principles, principle 1; Universal Declaration of Human Rights, art 10; Commonwealth Parliamentary Association, Commonwealth (Latimer House) Principles on the Three Branches of Government, principle IV.*

## COMMENTARY

1. Judicial independence, both institutional and decisional,[124] the absence of interest and impartiality are integral and closely connected[125] aspects of any properly functioning justice system.[126] They form an inherent aspect of the proper administration of justice and the constitutional principle of the rule of law.[127] Institutional independence requires the courts and judiciary to be independent of both the Government and Parliament, ie there must be separation of powers.[128] They must also be independent of the parties.[129] Decisional independence requires judges to be able to exercise the judicial power of the State in individual proceedings autonomously.[130] It is thus a means by which a fair process is secured. Neither independence nor impartiality exist for the benefit of the judiciary.[131]They exist to secure the rule of law.
2. The centrality of independence, the absence of interest, and impartiality to English and Welsh civil justice has long been understood and guaranteed.[132] This rule restates this principle, and in doing so makes explicit that judicial independence also extends to the court's administration.[133] That is an aspect of institutional independence, not least because it promotes institutional impartiality.[134] While this aspect of judicial

[124] Promissory Oaths Act 1868, s 4; S Shetreet and S Turenne, *Judges on Trial* (CUP, 2013); J Beatson, *The Rule of Law and The Separation of Powers* (Hart, 2021) chap 7; S Levinson, 'Identifying "Independence"' (2006) 86 Boston University Law Review 1297; M McConville and L Marsh, *The Myth of Judicial Independence* (OUP, 2020); *R v Valente* [1985] 2 SCR 673, esp at [15] and following; M Redish and L Marshall, 'Adjudicatory Independence and the Values of Procedural Due Process' (1986) 95 Yale LJ 455.

[125] *Porter v Magill* [2001] UKHL 6; [2002] 2 AC 357 at [88].

[126] *Bryan v United Kingdom* (1995) 21 EHRR 342.

[127] UN Congress, *Basic Principles on the Independence of the Judiciary*, Seventh United Nations Congress on the Prevention of Crime and the Treatment of Offenders (Milan, 1985), principle 1; Latimer House Principles, principle 1; Mount Scopus International Standards of Judicial Independence (2008, as amended 2012), principle 1.1; Bangalore Principles of Judicial Conduct (2006), principle 1.1; Council of Europe, Recommendation (2010)12 on Judges, Independence, Efficiency and Responsibilities, at [3]–[5]; Constitutional Reform Act 2005, ss 1, 3; *Suratt v Attorney-General of Trinidad & Tobago* [2007] UKPC 655.

[128] *R v Valente* [1985] 2 SCR 673 at [18]. The principle of finality also supports judicial independence as it stops judicial decisions being interfered with by the Government or Parliament, as well as by other judges acting outside of a valid review or appellate process: K Clermont, 'Res Judicata as Requisite for Justice' (2016) 68(3) Rutgers University Law Review 1067 at 1077; *Sovtransavto Holding v Ukraine* [2002] ECHR 626 at [80].

[129] *Ringeisen v Austria* [1971] ECHR 2 at [95]; *Forrester Ketley & Co v Brent* [2005] EWCA Civ 562 at [3].

[130] *Associação Sindical dos Juízes Portugueses* ECLI:EU:C:2018:117 at [36]–[44].

[131] Council of Europe, *Recommendation (2010)12 on Judges, Independence, Efficiency and Responsibilities*, chaps 2 and 3.

[132] Magna Carta (2015) chap 40; Act of Settlement 1701; S Shetreet and S Turenne (2013) chap 2.

[133] *R v Valente* [1985] 2 SCR 673 at [47].

[134] J McIntyre, *The Judicial Function—Fundamental Principles of Contemporary Judging* (Springer, 2019) at 166–168.

independence is accepted as being compatible with the partnership model of court administration adopted in England and Wales since 2007,[135] greater effect could be given to institutional independence if a judicial model of court administration was adopted.[136] That is, if overall control of the court administration was placed in the hands of the judiciary with court staff becoming employees of the court rather than, as at present, the court staff being civil servants who owe a statutory duty of loyalty to the government, ie to a party to a significant number of civil disputes.[137]

3. Judicial independence is an absolute principle. It cannot be waived. It requires, amongst other things, the application of a fair and transparent judicial appointment process, security of tenure and remuneration, effective protection, including immunity from suit in respect of the exercise of judicial functions,[138] from external, improper pressure from Government, Parliament, the media, as well as private individuals and organisations.[139] It also requires judges to abstain from party political matters as that may raise questions concerning separation of powers.[140] Engagement in party political activity may also raise questions concerning judicial impartiality.[141]
4. In the future design of civil procedure systems, judicial independence will become all-the-more important. The design of any digital procedure could, for instance, undermine both aspects of judicial independence if it were carried out under the authority of Government rather than that of an independent body, which was required to ensure that the practice and procedure of the courts was consistent with judicial independence. The use of AI, whether through its design, implementation, or operation could undermine judicial independence were it to infringe upon a judge's sphere of autonomy in decision-making, particularly where that concerned adjudication. The use of AI could, particularly, undermine judicial independence were it to be used to determine dispute management directions or to give judgments or orders in particular proceedings. In such cases, judicial autonomy would have been set aside, and the judiciary would no longer be exercising the judicial power of the State. Its use could also undermine individual independence less obviously. Its use may, for instance, have an adverse impact on judicial skills: reliance on AI, particularly for research and analysis, could reduce the skill levels of individual judges thus reducing their ability to make effective judgments.[142] Care will therefore, particularly, need to be taken to ensure that any such procedures, the coding that underpins them, and the use of AI to assist or augment judicial decision-making is consistent with, amongst other things,[143] judicial independence.
5. Judicial independence may be at risk where any of the guarantees of its independence, noted above, are undermined.[144] It may also be undermined where a judge deals with proceedings in which they have a specific interest, such as a financial interest in the outcome.[145] In such a situation a judge is a judge in their own cause and

[135] HMCTS Framework Document (July 2014).

[136] Part 2, r 5.

[137] Canadian Justice Council, *Alternative Models of Court Administration* (2006) at 65.

[138] Senior Courts Act 1981, ss 11, 12; *Hamond v Howell* (1677) 2 Mod 218; *Sirros v Moore* [1975] QB 118.

[139] *Findlay v UK* (1997) 24 EHRR 221 at [74].

[140] House of Commons (Disqualification) Act 1975, ss 1(1)(a), 1(2) and Sch 1; Constitutional Reform Act 2005, s 137.

[141] Guide to Judicial Conduct 2020 (Judicial Office, 2020).

[142] Rule 25.

[143] It would also need to be consistent with, for instance, sustainability, procedural equality, and publicity.

[144] *R v Valente* [1985] 2 SCR 673.

[145] *Dimes v Properties of the Grand Central Canal* (1852) 10 ER 301.

hence not independent of the parties.[146] In such a case the judge is properly subject to automatic disqualification. Following *Ex p Pinochet Ugarte (No 2)* (1999), this rule also applies where a judge has a non-financial interest in a dispute where it is shown that the judge has another form of actual interest in the outcome of the proceedings.[147]

6. Impartiality is also as fundamental, albeit not as absolute,[148] a principle as that of independence, with which it is intrinsically linked. Independence is a key means by which impartiality is secured,[149] as is the absence of interest in the outcome of proceedings.[150] Impartiality requires judges, when exercising judicial functions, to have neither an actual nor an apparent bias or prejudice concerning the parties to the immediate proceedings.[151] It is thus intrinsically linked to the procedural equality principle, as it is intended to ensure that all parties to a dispute are afforded the same treatment in the management, adjudication or promotion of settlement of their dispute.
7. Actual bias arises where a judge is prejudiced in favour of or against a specific party to proceedings. This may arise because the judge has and has demonstrated favour or, conversely, animus towards one party or to witnesses for that party. Proof of actual bias is difficult to establish. This is due to the limits placed on parties' ability to cross-examine a judge or require disclosure from them concerning the matter said to give rise to the bias.[152] Such limits are themselves a means to protect judicial independence, as they are intended to ensure that the potential for cross-examination or disclosure does not have a chilling effect on the judicial decision-making process, ie it is intended to protect individual independence and judicial autonomy in decision-making.
8. Apparent bias is a broader means to protect impartiality as it focuses on the perception of bias. The approach to it is now well-established.[153] It is restated here, and focuses on the perception of a fair-minded and informed observer and whether they would conclude from the circumstances of the case that there was a real possibility of bias. It thus does not require proof of actual bias nor does it raise the potential for cross-examination of judges or disclosure of judicial notes. It thus both protects against impartiality, while also preserving individual independence.
9. Parties may, consistently with party autonomy, waive bias. They may, however, only do so on an informed basis. Waiver must be freely given, express, and prospective.[154] Waiver of bias has an important consequence for settlement processes.

[146] *Dr Bonham's Case* (1610) 8 Co Rep 113(b) at 118a.

[147] *R v Bow Street Metropolitan Stipendiary Magistrate, Ex p Pinochet Ugarte (No 2)* [1999] 2 WLR 272; M Groves, 'The Rule Against Bias' [2009] U Monash LRS 10.

[148] It may be waived. Equally, an impartial judge must favour the party on whose side the merits lie when determining a dispute on its merits.

[149] J McIntyre (2019) chaps 10–11.

[150] *R v Sussex Justices, ex p McCarthy* [1924] 1 KB 256; *Kyprianou v Cyprus* [2005] ECHR 873 at [118]; *Piersack v Belgium* [1982] ECHR 6 at [30]; *Sramek v Austria* [1984] ECHR 12 at [42]; *Kyprianou v Cyprus* [2005] ECHR 873 at [121].

[151] *Director General of Fair Trading v Proprietary Association of Great Britain* [2001] 1 WLR 700.

[152] *Locabail (UK) Ltd v Bayfield Properties Ltd* [2000] QB 451 at [19].

[153] *Porter v Macgill* [2001] UKHL 67; [2002] 2 AC 357; *Halliburton Co v Chubb Bermuda Insurance Ltd* [2020] UKSC 48; [2020] 3 WLR 1474 at [52]–[53].

[154] *Pfeifer & Plankl v Austria* (1992) 14 EHRR 692 at [38]; *Smith v Kvaerner Cementation Foundations Ltd* [2006] EWCA Civ 242; [2007] 1 WLR 370.

The promotion of judge-led mediation and judge-led early neutral evaluation (ENE) under the CPR has raised concerns about bias.[155] Judges who engage in such activities, as part of settlement management gain information or draw conclusions, which could, in principle, prejudice their approach to determining proceedings adjudicatively. Such concerns have led to judges who engage in such activities having to recuse themselves from further dealings with the proceedings should a dispute not settle after such processes. Given the established approach to waiver such an approach is both unjustified and too rigid and is not followed under this Code. Where waiver is given consistently with this rule a judge who has dealt with mediation or ENE may continue to deal with proceedings should the dispute not settle.

## RULE 14.—THE SELF-REPRESENTATION PRINCIPLE

**Parties may represent themselves in proceedings to which this Code applies.**

*Sources: ELI-UNIDROIT Model Rules, r 14; CPR r 39.6.*

## COMMENTARY

1. This principle codifies the position at common law, which is acknowledged by the Legal Services Act 2007, that parties have a non-delegable right to represent themselves in legal proceedings.[156] They are not required to be represented by lawyers.[157] While this means that natural persons may represent themselves, for legal persons it means they must be represented by, for instance, a suitably senior, responsible director, trustee, or employee.[158]
2. This principle is a specific application of the party autonomy principle. Some jurisdictions limit its application by requiring parties to be represented in certain types of proceedings, particularly appellate proceedings.[159] The rationale for such an inroad into party autonomy is that certain proceedings require a party's case to be advanced by an individual who is trained in advocacy and is able to deal effectively with legal issues. This rests on the assumption that only lawyers are fully able to assist the court with submissions on the law, something which is important in appellate proceedings.[160]
3. The approach adopted does not limit party autonomy as the rationales underpinning mandatory representation can be and are met in other ways. Where the court needs assistance with submissions on points of law, it may seek the appointment of an advocate to the court who could supplement whatever submissions an unrepresented party has made. Where a party needs assistance in advocacy, the court may provide that assistance under Part 12, rules 8 and 20 or the party may obtain reasonable assistance under rule 15, below.

[155] D Foskett et al (ed), *Foskett on Compromise* (Sweet & Maxwell, 2024) at 585.

[156] *Gregory v Turner* [2003] EWCA Civ 183; [2003] 1 WLR 1149 at [75] and [78]; *Owen v Black Horse Ltd* [2023] EWCA Civ 325; *Ndole Assets Ltd v Designer M & E Services UK* Ltd [2018] EWCA Civ 2865; Legal Services Act 2007, Sch 3, Part 1, para 6, Part 2, para 4.

[157] *R v Woodward* [1944] KB 118.

[158] CPR r 39.6.

[159] Code of Civil Procedure (Germany), s 78; Code of Civil Procedure (France) art 973.

[160] ELI-UNIDROIT Model Rules, r 164 and commentary.

## RULE 15.—THE REASONABLE ASSISTANCE AND REPRESENTATION PRINCIPLE

**(1) Parties are entitled to receive reasonable assistance from a non-party in any proceeding. This includes access to an interpreter or translator where that is reasonably necessary to secure procedural equality and effective access.**

**(2) The provision of reasonable assistance may be restricted where it is provided in a manner that undermines the purposive principle.**

**(3) Parties may be represented in any proceeding by a lawyer or, where permitted by the court, an authorised legal representative of their choice.**

**(4) An individual is**

**(a) a lawyer if they are a member of a regulated legal profession and authorised by a professional body to act in legal proceedings or is exempt from such authorisation;**

**(b) an authorised legal representative if they are a member of the public specifically authorised by the court, where it is just to do so, to act as a party's legal representative in specified proceedings. Authorisation may be subject to such limitations as are just in the circumstances and which will promote the proper administration of justice.**

**(5) Where necessary to give effect to the general access principle, the court may inform the Legal Services Commission that a party ought to be represented by a member of a regulated legal profession, who shall be paid for out of public funds.**

*Sources: ALI/UNIDROIT Principles, principle 4; ELI-UNIDROIT Model Rules, rr 14, 15; Legal Services Act 2007, ss 12–21; Practice Guidance (McKenzie Friends: Civil and Family Courts) [2010] 1 WLR 1881.*

## COMMENTARY

1. This rule provides a further basis on which parties can secure their effective participation in the dispute resolution process. It does so where they do not exercise the right to represent themselves, as it enables them to secure reasonable assistance from a non-party of their own choice.
2. The basis of the right to receive reasonable assistance stems from the common law.[161] It can be exercised through the provision by a non-party of: help in preparing papers for the proceedings; moral support and the giving of quiet advice in court hearings; help in identifying questions the party may wish to put to witnesses in a court hearing; help in preparing submissions the party may wish to put to the court; and, note-taking in court hearings for the assisted party.[162] This right, which is a right of the party and not of the person providing assistance, is not absolute. Rule 15(2) codifies the court's inherent jurisdiction to control its own processes and protect them from abuse where the right to receive reasonable assistance is concerned.[163] Where, for instance, the provision of assistance is unreasonable due to its cost, the time it is taking to be given, or where it is being provided in a disruptive manner, the court may limit or prohibit its provision.

[161] *R v Leicester City Justices, ex p Barrow* [1991] 2 QB 260 at 289.

[162] *Practice Guidance (McKenzie Friends: Civil and Family Courts)* [2010] 1 WLR 1881 at [3].

[163] *R v Leicester City Justices, ex parte Barrow* [1991] 2 QB 260 at 285; *Paragon Finance plc v Noueiri* [2001] EWCA Civ 1402; [2001] 1 WLR 2357 at [56].

Such restrictions are justifiable by reference to the need to secure a proportionate process for all parties.

3. Under the CPR, a distinction is drawn between the provision of reasonable assistance where proceedings are held in open court and when they are held in private where there is an applicable exception to the publicity principle. Where they are held in private, the approach taken is that rather than a right to reasonable assistance, the court has a discretion to permit a party to receive it.[164] The rationale behind the distinction is primarily to protect the privacy and confidentiality of matters discussed at a private hearing. That can, however, be protected in ways that do not call for the right to assistance to be transformed into a discretion. Privacy and confidentiality can, for instance, be protected through the application of the court's jurisdiction to protect its processes from abuse. This Code therefore does not incorporate this distinction.
4. Rules 15(3) and (4) go further than the right to reasonable assistance. They codify the right of a party to be represented by a lawyer or an authorised legal representative of their own choice.[165] The former refers to individuals who are authorised to conduct litigation and have rights of audience under the Legal Services Act 2007, eg solicitors and barristers.[166] The latter refers to individuals who are not lawyers and who are authorised by the court, exercising its inherent jurisdiction, to conduct litigation or exercise a right of audience in specified proceedings. (In this Code where lawyers are referred to, that term includes for brevity reference to authorised legal representatives.)[167] Authorisation may only be granted where it is just to do so and it may be limited where that is necessary to protect the administration of justice.[168] Historically, this latter form of authorised individual has been known as a '*McKenzie Friend*'. The use of such terminology, which provides no explanation as to its meaning is not continued here.[169] Hence this rule adopts a neutral, functional term: authorised legal representative.
5. The right to representation may also require the court to take positive steps to assist a party to obtain representation. While the court is not afforded a jurisdiction to direct the provision of legal representation, eg either free of charge or through directing the government to pay for it, it may inform the Legal Services Commission that in its view a party needs to be represented by a lawyer and that such representation should be paid for out of public funds. The court may only exercise this power to give effect to the general access principle, ie it must be sure that absent such representation the party would not have practical and effective access to the court.[170] Under the scheme

[164] *McKenzie v McKenzie* [1970] 3 WLR 472; *R v Leicester City Justices, ex parte Barrow* [1991] 2 QB 260; *Re G (A Minor) (Chambers Hearing: Assistance)* (1991) Note [1999] 1 WLR 1828; *Re O (Children) (Hearing in Private: Assistance)* [2005] EWCA Civ 759; [2006] Fam 1; *Re F (Children)* [2013] EWCA Civ 726.

[165] *Re Maguire* [2018] UKSC 17; [2018] 1 WLR 1412 at [29]–[38]; *Navigator Equities Ltd v Deripaska* [2022] EWHC 457 (Comm); *Owen v Black Horse Ltd* [2023] EWCA Civ 325.

[166] Legal Services Act 2007, s 19.

[167] *Collier v Hicks* (1831) 2 B & Ad 669; *Paragon Finance plc v Noueiri* [2001] 1 WLR 2357 at 2368; Legal Services Act 2007, Sch 3, para 1(2).

[168] *Practice Guidance (McKenzie Friends: Civil and Family Courts)* [2010] 1 WLR 1881 at [23]; *Clarkson v Gilbert (Rights of Audience)* [2000] CP Rep 58; *Re N (A Child) (McKenzie Friend: Rights of Audience)* [2008] EWHC 2042 (Fam); [2008] 1 WLR 2743 at [38]–[41].

[169] *McKenzie v McKenzie* [1970] 3 WLR 472; Civil Justice Council, *Access to Justice for Litigants in Person* (November 2011) at [141]; Lord Chief Justice of England and Wales, *Reforming the Courts' Approach to McKenzie Friends—A Consultation* (Judicial Office, 2016) [4.1]–[4.7].

[170] *Perotti v Collyer-Bristow (a firm)* [2003] EWCA Civ 1521; [2004] 2 ALL ER 189 at [32].

for funding dispute resolution set out in Part 4, the exercise of this power will be rare due to the general availability of mandatory legal expenses insurance. Part 4, rule 8, however, makes provision for public funding to be available where, amongst other things, the court exercises this power.

6. This rule also provides the basis on which a party can secure the assistance of an interpreter or translator to enable them to fully understand the proceedings and communicate with the court and other parties effectively. Such access is, however, limited to where it is reasonably necessary to promote procedural equality and effective access.[171] An unfettered right of access to an interpreter or translator would give rise to unnecessary expense and delay in the conduct of proceedings and particularly hearings, and would hence be disproportionate.[172]

## RULE 16.—THE PROCEDURAL EQUALITY PRINCIPLE

**The court must ensure that parties are treated equally except where differential treatment is in the interests of justice. Justified differential treatment must be no more than necessary and proportionate to achieve its objective.**

*Sources: ALI/UNIDROIT Principles, principle 3; CPR r 1.1(2)(a).*

## COMMENTARY

1. The requirement that parties to proceedings are treated equally, that there is equality before the law,[173] is a fundamental principle of a fair process.[174] This rule gives effect to that principle.

2. This principle is intrinsically linked to several other procedural principles. Given those links it can properly be described as '*an independent source of regulation governing the entire civil process*'.[175] Procedural equality is, for instance, inherent in due notice and evidential access, ie both parties should know the case put against them and have access, on equal terms, to relevant evidence. It is inherent in the impartiality principle, ie the judge managing and determining a dispute should be even-handed and not biased against or in favour of one party. Hence it is also a means to secure adjudicative accuracy as that is secured through due notice, equal access to evidence, and an impartial decision-maker. It also underpins the compliance principle. Compliance with procedural obligations, and the court's attitude to securing it for all parties equally, is essential for there to be a fair process. If the court adopted a more lenient approach to compliance for one party, it would afford it an unfair

[171] *Re Trepca Mines Ltd* [1960] 1 WLR 24; *Re Fuld* [1965] 1 WLR 1336; *Shuker v Inspecs Ltd (Rev1)* [2022] EWHC 2668 (Ch) at [5]–[14].

[172] Part 12, r 11.

[173] M Bayles (1986) at 54–55; M Zander, *The State of Justice* (CUP, 2000) at 5; A Zuckerman (2021) at 161.

[174] W Rubenstein, 'The Concept of Equality in Civil Procedure' (2002) 23 Cardozo Law Review 1865; *Tariq v The Home Office* [2011] UKSC 35; [2012] 1 AC 452 at [108]; *Al-Rawi v The Security Services* [2011] UKSC 34; [2012] 1 AC 531; *Delcourt v Belgium* (1969) 1 EHRR 355; *Ruiz-Mateos v Spain* (1993) 16 EHRR 505; *Dombo Beheer BV v Netherlands* (1994) 18 EHRR 213; *Nideröst-Huber v Switzerland* (1998) 25 EHRR 709; *De Haes & Gijsels v Belgium* (1997) 25 EHRR 1; CPR r 1.1(2)(a).

[175] N Andrews (2019) at 689.

procedural advantage over the opposing party. The equality principle's importance cannot be underestimated.

3. The equality principle is also intrinsically linked with the general access principle. It requires access to justice to be secured on a non-discriminatory basis.[176] This will be increasingly important in future given the development of digital procedures and the use of AI.[177] The application of this principle to such developments, and the need to ensure that the digital procedure and AI principles are both implemented consistently with it, will be pivotal in ensuring that any future civil process does not discriminate unfairly against parties depending on their '*sex, race, colour, language, religion, political or other opinion, national or social origin, association with a national minority, property, birth or status*'.[178] Its application will be a guarantee of fair access to a fair process, howsoever that process is configured or delivered.[179]
4. Procedural equality also underpins the novel development in this Code concerning dispute resolution funding. Since the 1940s and the development of civil legal aid there have been attempts to ensure that an individual's financial status has not had a differential impact on their ability to access the court process and other forms of dispute resolution in comparison with other parties to their dispute.[180] Similarly, and particularly since the 1990s, there have been attempts to level the financial playing field by promoting forms of private litigation funding and by reducing the cost of litigation.[181] Each of these processes can be seen as attempts to promote procedural equality, not least as a means to promote effective and practical access. Part 4 through mandating legal expenses insurance as the default basis on which dispute resolution funding is to be provided aims to secure that all individuals within society are placed on an equal financial footing. In that way, it is intended to ensure that access to justice is not improperly affected.[182]
5. Procedural equality is not, however, an absolute right. There may be situations that justify differential treatment.[183] There may, for instance, be reasons justifying the withholding of certain types of evidence from a party, eg where that is necessary to protect confidentiality or it is in the interests of national security to do so.[184] Specific rules and their application within this Code may thus justifiably deviate from the general approach required by this principle. They may do so for a legitimate aim and where the means used to achieve that aim are necessary and proportionate.[185]

[176] *Nasser v United Bank of Kuwait* [2001] EWCA Civ 556; [2002] WLR 1868.

[177] European Commission for the Efficiency of Justice (CEPEJ), *European Ethical Charter on the Use of Artificial Intelligence in Judicial Systems and their Environment* (COE, 2018) at 47.

[178] European Convention on Human Rights, art 14 taken in conjunction with art 6; N Andrews (2019) at 690.

[179] Procedural equality does not, however, impinge upon or limit the right of a party to have a lawyer of their own choice, see *Maltez v Lewis* (2000) 16 Const LJ 655.

[180] A Zuckerman (2021) at 163; M Cappelletti, 'Alternative Dispute Resolution Processes within the Framework of the World-Wide Access-to-Justice Movement' (1993) 56 The Modern Law Review 282; M Cappelletti and B Garth, 'Access to Justice: The Newest Wave in the Worldwide Movement to Make Rights Effective' (1978) 27 Buff L Rev 181, 228–239.

[181] Promoting compliance with the economy, efficiency, and proportionality principles is also a means to promote procedural equality in so far as it reduces the cost of dispute resolution; A Zuckerman (2021) at 163.

[182] N Andrews (2019) at 690.

[183] A Zuckerman (2021) at 162 and 167; M Bayles (1986) at 47–48, 55.

[184] Part 12, rr 35 and 36; *Promontoria (Oak) Ltd v Emanuel* [2021] EWCA Civ 1682; [2022] WLR 2004.

[185] *Jasper v UK* (2000) 30 EHRR 441 at [52].

## RULE 17.—THE DUE NOTICE AND EVIDENTIAL ACCESS PRINCIPLES

**(1) The court must take steps to bring the fact that proceedings have commenced to the parties' attention.**
**(2) Parties must be given a reasonable and practical opportunity to know and respond to the case made against them.**
**(3) A reasonable and practical opportunity to know and respond includes**
  **(a) the right to provide the court and other parties with relevant evidence; and**
  **(b) the right to access relevant evidence and information.**
**(4) Access to evidence and information may be restricted where necessary to give effect to an applicable immunity or privilege from disclosure.**

*Sources: ALI/UNIDROIT Principles, principles 5, 8, 16, 18; ELI-UNIDROIT Model Rules, r 11.*

## COMMENTARY

1. The common law, as a feature of natural justice, and article 6 of the European Convention on Human Rights both acknowledge the right to due notice and the right to receive relevant evidence and information.[186] They make up the right to be heard.[187]
2. Both rights are intrinsically linked to effective participation and procedural equality. A party cannot participate effectively or equally in proceedings absent reasonable advance notice of the claim being made against them or defence to it.[188] Moreover, were parties able to keep evidence or relevant information from their opponent either entirely or until the last minute, their opponent would not be in a position to consider and prepare their response properly. Such an approach would have a negative impact on the prospects of the court reaching an accurate decision, as that rests on both parties having proper notice of the dispute and time to prepare and assess evidence. It would also adversely affect the prospect of settlement as parties would not be in a position to assess the issues in dispute properly. Moreover, it would unnecessarily increase the cost, time, and disproportionality of dispute resolution.
3. A fair process may, in certain circumstances, require the evidential access principle to be subject to limitations that give effect to other public interests. This may arise where evidence and information are, for instance, subject to an immunity from compulsory disclosure.

## RULE 18.—THE ADVERSARIAL AND FLEXIBLE PROCESS PRINCIPLES

**(1) The process applied to resolve a dispute on its substantive merits shall be adversarial.**
**(2) The process applied to resolve a dispute consensually shall be flexible.**

*Sources: Council of Europe Rec R (84) 5, principle 8; ALI/UNIDROIT Principles, principles 5, 16.*

186 *Hadmor Productions Ltd v Hamilton* [1983] 1 AC 191 at 233; *Re D (minors) (adoption reports: confidentiality)* [1996] AC 593 at 603–604; *Tariq v The Home Office* [2011] UKSC 35; [2012] 1 AC 452 at [70], [102], [107], [118]–[124]; *Al-Rawi v The Security Services* [2011] UKSC 34; [2012] 1 AC 531 at 572, 591; *Feldbrugge v The Netherlands* (1986) 8 EHRR 425.

187 *Cameron v Liverpool Victoria Insurance Co Ltd* [2019] UKSC 6; [2019] 1 WLR 1471 at [17].

188 *R v London Quarter Sessions Appeal Committee, ex parte Rossi* [1956] 1 QB 682.

## COMMENTARY

1. Rule 18(1) gives effect to the right to an adversarial process.[189] It is linked to the participatory principle. Effective participation in an adjudicative process requires there to be an adversarial process through which the parties can set out their formal arguments and evidence and test those of their opponent.[190] It is also linked to the accuracy principle, as that is achieved through the provision of an effective adversarial process. It is additionally linked to the due notice principle. For there to be an effective adversarial process parties need to be given reasonable notice of their opponent's arguments and evidence and reasonable time to challenge them effectively.[191] The adversarial principle is thus the means by which parties' cases can be tested forensically and not decided in the abstract.[192] This is the base line for a fair adjudicative process.[193]
2. Rule 18(2) provides differently for consensual settlement processes. Where they are concerned, the aim and intention of the parties is the primary consideration in terms of process design. It is for the parties to together determine the appropriate manner in which any such process operates.[194] Where, for instance, arbitration is chosen, it is for the parties to determine which arbitral rules should apply (albeit subject to the facilitative and supportive framework provided by the Arbitration Act 1996). Where mediation is chosen or mandated by the court, it remains for the parties to determine how the mediation process should operate, eg whether the mediator's role should include an evaluative function or not. Party autonomy is thus the paramount consideration in the design and operation of such processes. This rule gives effect to this approach by providing for consensual settlement processes to be flexible. One consequence of this is that they may be adversarial, as is the case in arbitration, Early Neutral Evaluation[195] (ENE) or some forms of mediation.[196] They can equally be co-operative or collaborative,[197] eg where a principled approach to negotiation is adopted or a collaborative or co-operative law[198] approach is taken. They may equally involve a mixed approach, eg

[189] *Board of Education v Rice* [1911] AC 179 at 183; *Kanda v Government of Malaya* [1962] AC 322 at 337; *O'Reilly v Mackman* [1983] 2 AC 237 at 276; *Brandstetter v Austria* (1993) 15 EHRR 378; *Ruiz-Mateos v Spain* (1993) 16 EHRR 505; *Mantovanelli v France* (1997) 24 EHRR 370; J Jolowicz, *Adversarial and inquisitorial approaches to civil litigation*, in J Jolowicz (2000).

[190] *Griffiths v TUI UK Ltd* [2023] UKSC 48; [2023] 3 WLR 1204 at [70] restating the general rule, and exceptions to it, that evidence must be challenged if a party does not wish the court to accept it. On the importance of testing evidence as an aspect of securing a fair process, see *Tariq v The Home Office* [2011] UKSC 35; [2012] 1 AC 452 at [119]; *Al-Rawi v The Security Services* [2011] UKSC 34; [2012] 1 AC 531 at [107].

[191] *Re D (minors) (adoption reports: confidentiality)* [1996] AC 593 at 603.

[192] O J Settem, *Applications of the 'Fair Hearing' Norm in ECHR Article 6(1) to Civil Proceedings* (Springer, 2016) at 99–111 citing *Vermeulen v Belgium* [1996] ECHR 7 at [33]; *Galich v Russia* [2008] ECHR 381 at [23]–[25]; P Hirvelä and S Heikkilä, *Right to a Fair Trial* (Intersentia, 2022) at 100–104.

[193] *Tariq v The Home Office* [2011] UKSC 35; [2012] 1 AC 452 at [119], [124]; *Al-Rawi v The Security Services* [2011] UKSC 34; [2012] 1 AC 531 at [10]–[12], [30], [89]–[90].

[194] F Steffek and H Unberath (eds), *Regulating Dispute Resolution* (Hart, 2013) at 15.

[195] W Brazil, *Early Neutral Evaluation* (ABA, 2012).

[196] L Fuller, 'Mediation—Its Forms and Functions' (1971) 44 Southern California Law Review 305.

[197] J Lande and G Herman, 'Fitting the Forum to the Family Fuss. Choosing Mediation, Collaborative Law, or Cooperative Law for Negotiating Divorce Cases' (2004) 42(2) Family Court Review 280; P Tesler, 'Collaborative Family Law' (2004) 4(3) Pepperdine Dispute Resolution Law Journal 317; C Healy, *Collaborative Practice* (Routledge, 2018).

[198] R Fisher and W Ury, *Getting to Yes: Negotiating Agreement without Giving in* (RH, 2012).

through Med-Arb or Arb-Med,[199] which apply both adversarial and co-operative approaches, or they may be tiered in approach, as is the case through the use of multi-tier dispute resolution clauses[200] or the use of tiered dispute resolution design as is currently adopted by some Ombudsman schemes.[201]

3. While the design architecture of consensual settlement processes ultimately lies in the hands of the parties to the dispute, a positive role remains for the court. One consequence of its duty to manage disputes and of the co-operation principle is that the court is required to assist the parties in the design and, where necessary, operation of consensual settlement processes.[202] This manifests itself in two ways. First, through the provision of court-designed and operated settlement processes at both the pre-action and post-issue stages of dispute management. This is intended to provide a proportionate means by which parties can access such processes through obviating the cost and time of their having to design and agree upon a specific process design for their chosen dispute resolution method; it is a guided form of flexibility. Secondly, where the parties opt for their own design or for a non-court-based process, their access to such methods should be assisted, where possible, through the digital procedure. This could be through the provision of information about and access to non-court-based consensual settlement processes via the digital portal. It could also be provided by the judge managing a dispute, who could help the parties to consider which process options might best suit their dispute. Such assistance could be augmented by the use of artificial intelligence, where it is designed and is capable of analysing the nature of the dispute and identifying a recommended dispute resolution method for it. This latter approach could be applied at either the pre-action and post-issue phases of the dispute.

## RULE 19.—THE PARTICIPATORY PRINCIPLE

**The court shall ensure that parties can participate in proceedings effectively.**

*Sources: ALI/UNIDROIT Principles, principles 5, 8; CPR r 1.1(2)(e), (f).*

## COMMENTARY

1. Effective participation is a basic aspect of procedural fairness. It is inherent in and supports the right to be heard that lives in the due notice and adversarial principles. It depends particularly upon the former and is given expression by the latter.[203] Without due notice, a party cannot participate in proceedings either at all or effectively.[204] Without an effective adversarial process, adjudication cannot be reached through the formal testing of evidence and argument presented by the parties.[205] Effective participation is equally important where consensual resolution is

[199] S Shipman, B Waters, and W Brown QC, *Brown & Marriot's ADR Principles and Practice* (Sweet & Maxwell, 2019).

[200] A Reyes and W Gu (2022).

[201] W Ury, J Brett, and S Goldberg, *Getting Disputes Resolved* (PON, 1993) chap 3; C Gill, J Williams, C Brennan, and C Hirst, *Models of Alternative Dispute Resolution (ADR)* (QMU Consumer Insight Centre, 2014).

[202] It is for the court to help the parties 'fit the fuss to the forum', F Sander and S Goldberg, 'Fitting the Forum to the Fuss: A User-Friendly Guide to Selecting an ADR Procedure' (1994) 10 Negot J 49.

[203] A Zuckerman (2021) at 173.

[204] M Bayles (1986) at 54.

[205] L Fuller, 'The Forms and Limits of Adjudication' (1978) 92 Harvard Law Review 353.

concerned. Parties must be able to explain the nature of their grievance and the ways in which it could be resolved. They must equally be able to listen effectively to their opponent, and thereby analyse effectively what they are told. Effective participation is also inherent in both the impartiality and procedural equality principles. Both promote effective participation through ensuring that all parties have equal access to justice. It also supports the general access principle as it requires procedure to be economical. Costs must not act as a barrier to effective participation. Equally, the need to secure it supports the establishment of mechanisms for the provision of litigation funding.

2. Effective participation goes further than its links to other procedural principles. It has a value and importance of its own as it gives effect to human dignity.[206] It demonstrates the value, and respect for that value, which we place (or should) place on each other. It is the means by which we demonstrate that we as a society and, particularly, the justice system, as Bayles has it, takes people—and their rights and obligations—seriously.[207] This has an intrinsic value that must be reflected in our approach to the delivery of dispute resolution. It also has an important consequence for the justice system. Taking people seriously, affording them the right to be heard through due notice and an adversarial process or through effective participation in consensual settlement processes, is one of the means by which parties, and particularly losing parties, are able to gain confidence in the means by which their dispute was resolved, not least where they disagree with the outcome. The better and more effective participation is, the more likely parties are to accept and abide by decisions, which in turn promotes effective enforcement.[208] Equally, the better and more effective participation is, the more likely parties are to feel respected and in turn respect and place confidence in the justice system.
3. This rule gives effect to the participation principle by placing a positive duty on the court to secure the effective participation of parties in the dispute resolution process. A necessary prerequisite of this duty is that the Code itself, and this will be particularly important where the development and use of digital procedures and AI is concerned, must be capable of facilitating effective participation. It thus also places a prior duty on the Civil Dispute Resolution Council and the Civil Courts Rule Committee to ensure the civil justice system as a whole is able to deliver effective participation.[209]

## RULE 20.—THE PUBLICITY PRINCIPLE

**(1) The adjudication of civil disputes is inherently public. They must, as a general rule, therefore be open to the public.**

**(2) Limitations may be imposed on publicity where they are strictly necessary to protect the proper administration of justice or a relevant public interest. Any such restriction must itself be no more than strictly necessary to achieve its aim.**

206 L Solum, 'Procedural Justice' (2004) 78 Southern California Law Review 181; J Mashaw, 'Administrative Due Process: The Quest for a Dignitary Theory' (1981) 61 Boston University Law Review 885; R Summers, 'Evaluating and Improving Legal Processes – a Plea for "Process Values"' (1974) 60 Cornell Law Review 1.

207 M Bayles (1986) at 54.

208 J Thibaut and L Walker, 'A Theory of Procedure' (1978) 66 California Law Review 541.

209 A Zuckerman (2021) at 173.

**(3) Any person seeking a limitation must satisfy the court that it is strictly necessary, and of the extent to which it is strictly necessary, by clear and cogent evidence.**

**(4) Settlement processes are inherently private processes. They shall only be public to the extent agreed by the parties or to the extent that the process is sufficiently anonymised so as to prelude party identification.**

*Sources: Council of Europe Rec R (84) 5, principle 6; ALI/UNIDROIT Principles, principle 20; ELI/UNIDROIT Model Rules, r 17; Senior Courts Act 1981, s 67; Courts Act 2003, s 85A; Remote Observation and Recording (Courts and Tribunals) Regulations 2022; CPR r 39.2; Practice Guidance: Open Justice—Remote Observation of Hearings—New Powers.*

## COMMENTARY

1. The publicity principle or, as it is also known, the principle of open justice, is a fundamental principle of any civil procedural code.[210] It is an integral aspect of a fair process. It is '*the very soul of justice*'[211] and is recognised as a common law constitutional principle.[212] It also forms part of the right to fair trial guaranteed by article 6 of the European Convention on Human Rights.[213] The principle, which is intrinsically linked with the reasoned decision principle, serves several purposes.[214]

2. First, it secures the democratic accountability of the judiciary.[215] Consistently with the independence and impartiality principles, judges cannot be subject to sacrificial accountability, ie they cannot be at risk of being removed from office as a consequence of the decisions they make. However, this cannot mean that they are wholly insulated from scrutiny by the public, Government, and Parliament. Publicity means that what goes on in the civil courts and what decisions are made in proceedings are open to such scrutiny and accountability;[216] an issue which is and will be all the more important in the 21st century with its increasing focus on the need for public officials and the exercise of State power to be accountable.[217] One consequence of this aspect of the principle is that where judicial decisions interpret, apply, or develop the law in ways that are unacceptable politically, the law may be revised or corrected by Parliament. Accountability through publicity thus ensures that the law does not develop in ways that are out-of-kilter with society.

3. Linked to this, the publicity principle plays a positive role in the development and reform of the law. Through the provision of publicly available reasoned judgments society as a whole may debate issues raised in proceedings. Controversial issues, moral and social issues, changing values or approaches to them can form the focus

[210] J Jaconelli, *Open Justice* (OUP, 2002); G Nettheim, 'The Principle of Open Justice' (1984) University of Tasmania Law Review 25; *Cape v Dring* [2019] UKSC 38; [2019] 3 WLR 429.

[211] J Bentham cited in *Home Office v Harman* [1982] 1 All ER 532 at 537.

[212] *Scott v Scott* [1913] AC 417, esp at 473; *R v Sussex Justices Ex p McCarthy* [1924] 1 KB 256; *Al-Rawi v The Security Services* [2011] UKSC 34; [2012] 1 AC 531 at 572; *R (Guardian News and Media Ltd v City of Westminster Magistrates' Court* [2012] EWCA Civ 420; [2013] QB 618 at [3].

[213] *Pretto v Italy* (1984) 6 EHRR 182; *Diennet v France* (1995) 21 EHRR 554.

[214] J Jaconelli (2002) at 3 and following.

[215] *Attorney-General v Leveller Magazine Ltd* [1979] AC 440 at 450; *R (Binyam Mohamed) v Secretary of State for Foreign and Commonwealth Affairs* [2010] EWCA Civ 65; [2011] QB 218 at [38]–[41]; *Al-Rawi v The Security Services* [2011] UKSC 34; [2012] 1 AC 531 at 543.

[216] *Ambard v Attorney General for Trinidad and Tobago* [1936] AC 322 at 335; *R (Binyam Mohamed) v Secretary of State for Foreign and Commonwealth Affairs* [2010] EWCA Civ 65; [2011] QB 218 at [40].

[217] *Khuja v Times Newspapers Ltd* [2017] UKSC 49; [2017] 3 WLR 351 at [13].

of disputes. Through the application of the common law method,[218] such judgments may develop the law in the light of such matters, or they may not. Either way, by proceedings and judgments being public they may spur public debate and Parliamentary intervention. In this way the publicity principle plays a fundamental role in the promotion of democratic discourse, and helps to ensure that the law keeps pace with and may itself spur societal change.[219]

4. In turn by ensuring that issues raised in disputes and judgments are made public, the publicity principle has a therapeutic or cathartic function. It does so as it enables parties to proceedings to bring to light their grievances and see that they are heard and understood not just by the court but by the wider public.[220]
5. Additionally, the publicity principle also helps to secure high standards in adjudication. That the public, media, and Parliamentarians are able to scrutinise what goes on in courts is a spur to judicial discipline. It helps ensure judges exercise the judicial power of the State diligently, competently, and fairly. In effect, through open access to judicial proceedings and open, reasoned judgments, judges are on trial when they are presiding over proceedings.[221] Such scrutiny militates against the possibility that a judge may adopt an arbitrary procedure, may treat parties, witnesses, or lawyers in an abusive way, or depart from the proper application of the law when adjudicating. The publicity principle is, consequently, also then a means to promote confidence in the judiciary.
6. The principle also serves three other purposes. It helps protect the liberty of the person.[222] This is particularly important where contempt of court proceedings are concerned. Individuals may be imprisoned if found to be in contempt of court. That proceedings are held in public ensures that they are not imprisoned in secret. It thus helps secure their access to legal representation, to the Official Solicitor and, if necessary, the media and public may raise their imprisonment with Parliament. It also plays an educative role. It does this through making available to the public information about what goes on in court, and particularly what judgments decide. In this way it promotes the rule of law through enabling individuals and businesses to order their affairs within the law: thus it promotes preventive justice. Finally, it plays an investigative role, which helps promote both adjudicative and consensual justice. Proceedings being public means that parties and the media can make them known. This can help facilitate the production of evidence, eg it may bring the dispute to the attention of potential witnesses who could then come forward. Evidence provided by those witnesses could assist the court in reaching a substantively accurate decision. It could equally assist the parties in assessing the strengths and weaknesses of their respective cases, thus facilitating settlement.
7. Publicity may be subject to restrictions where they are necessary to secure the proper administration of justice, ie because publicity would frustrate the court's ability to

[218] J Laws, *The Common Law Constitution* (CUP, 2014) at 6–10.

[219] *Al-Rawi v The Security Services* [2011] UKSC 34; [2012] 1 AC 531 at 543, 572.

[220] J Resnik, 'The Democracy in Courts: Jeremy Bentham, "Publicity" and the Privatization of Process in the Twenty-first Century' (2013) 10 Interdisciplinary Journal of Law and Justice 84.

[221] *R v Socialist Worker Printers and Publishers Ltd, ex parte Attorney-General* [1975] QB 637 at 651; *R (Binyam Mohamed) v Secretary of State for Foreign and Commonwealth Affairs* [2010] EWCA Civ 65; [2011] QB 218 at [38]; *Al-Rawi v The Security Services* [2011] UKSC 34; [2012] 1 AC 531 at 593. In practical terms the publicity principle is given effect by the presence of lawyers in courts as the public and media are rarely present to fulfil this function.

[222] *Scott v Scott* [1913] AC 413 at 475.

do justice.[223] Such restrictions may, on the same basis, be imposed to protect other comparable public interests from being harmed, eg where they protect confidentiality, trade or business secrets, national security, or the rights of children.[224]

8. Restrictions can properly include anonymising parties and witnesses,[225] providing that hearings are held in private, and issuing judgments in private. Where a restriction is justified, given the fundamental importance and purposes of the publicity principle, it must go no further than is strictly necessary to give effect to its aim.[226] To ensure this is the case any person seeking a limitation is required to establish by clear and cogent evidence that the limitation is needed.[227] They must also establish that the sought for limitation is no more than strictly necessary.[228] Thus they must ensure that the publicity principle remains practical and effective.[229] Rules 20(1) to (3) are intended to ensure, consistently with the approach under the CPR, that any limitations and exceptions to the publicity principle are kept to an absolute minimum so as not to undermine the principle's purposes.
9. Rule 20(3) draws an important distinction between adjudicative and consensual justice. While the former is inherently public as it involves the determination and vindication of rights, the latter is inherently private.[230] Consensual settlement does not involve the determination or application of rights by a court. It rests on party consent to resolution not the exercise of State power. Resolution may involve some consideration by the parties of the law and its application, but it need not. Even where it does, such consideration is based on the parties' understanding rather than the imposition by the court of its interpretation of the law and its application. Moreover, consensual resolution rests on a party-controlled process. There is thus no requirement for publicity to apply as a means of securing accountability, to impose a disciplinary function on any third-party neutral engaged in facilitating settlement, whether they are a judge or mediator, or to secure the other rationale applicable, bar one noted below, to the principle's application to adjudicative justice.
10. Parties may, further to party autonomy, agree to consensual settlement processes being held in public, albeit that would be unusual. More significantly, and to give effect to the AI and digital integration principles, anonymised information drawn from settlement processes may be made public. This is particularly important for the facilitation of preventive justice (see, particularly, Part 5, rule 5). It is also important, as the absence of publicity may enable defendants to hide illegal or otherwise improper conduct from public scrutiny. By making anonymised information available, the law reform rationale that underpins the publicity principle's application to adjudicative justice can be applied effectively to consensual settlement. It thus helps

[223] *R v Legal Aid Board, ex parte Kaim Todner (A Firm)* [1999] QB 966 at 978; *Khuja v Times Newspapers Ltd* [2017] UKSC 49; [2017] 3 WLR 351 at [29]–[30].

[224] CPR r 39.2(3).

[225] *JIH v News Group Newspapers Ltd* [2011] EWCA Civ 42; [2011] 1 WLR 1645 at [21].

[226] *R v Chief Registrar of Friendly Societies, ex parte New Cross Building Society* [1984] QB 227 at 235; *Ntuli v Donald* [2010] EWCA Civ 1276; [2011] 1 WLR 294 at [52]–[53].

[227] *Practice Guidance—Interim Non-Disclosure Orders* [2012] 1 WLR 1003 at [12]; *Scott v Scott* [1913] AC 417 at 438–439, 463, and 477; *Various Claimants v Independent Parliamentary Standards Authority* [2021] EWHC 2020 (QB); [2022] EMLR 4.

[228] D Neuberger et al, *Report of the Committee on Super-Injunctions: Super-Injunctions, Anonymised Injunctions and Open Justice* (Judicial Office, 2011).

[229] *Riepan v Austria* [2000] ECHR 575 at [29].

[230] *Zenith Logistics Services (UK) Ltd v Coury* [2020] EWHC 774 (QB) at [65]–[66].

avoid one of the criticisms of settlement's promotion; that it has historically been a means to hide matters of public interest from public scrutiny.

## RULE 21.—THE REASONED DECISION PRINCIPLE

**Parties shall be provided with a reasoned decision where proceedings are determined adjudicatively on their substantive merits. Decisions should be given within a reasonable time.**

*Sources: Council of Europe Rec R (84) 5, principle 6; ALI/UNIDROIT Principles, principles 20.4, 23; ALI/UNIDROIT Reporters' Study, r 18.5; ELI-UNIDROIT Model Rules, rr 131(f), 132.*

## COMMENTARY

1. English and Welsh civil procedure does not regulate the substantive content of court judgments. It is, however, well-established both at common law and further to article 6 of the European Convention on Human Rights that judges must give sufficient reasons for their decisions.[231] This rule codifies that principle. It is given specific effect through Part 15. This rule, when taken together with rule 20, requires reasoned judgments to be made public, except where an exception to the publicity principle applies. This is primarily given effect through Part 15, rule 3.
2. This principle requires judgments to contain sufficient details concerning the nature of the matter it deals with, the decision, and the reasons for the court's decision. This is an aspect of fair process. It demonstrates that justice has been done. For the parties, and particularly the losing party, the giving of reasons is an essential means by which they can understand why the matter before the judge was determined the way it was. Consistently with the publicity principle, giving reasons for decisions secures a form of explanatory accountability on the court's part, both to the parties and the public. By explaining why judges reach the decisions they make, reasoned judgments also form the basis of democratic accountability under the publicity principle. Such explanations also give effect to the publicity principle's educative role.
3. The provision of reasons by promoting the prospect that court decisions are '*acceptable to the parties and to members of the public*'[232] also helps secure confidence in the judiciary. Linked to this, reasoned judgments also demonstrate that the court's decision is the product of rational argument through the identification of relevant fact and its application to right law that has been taken account of properly by judges.[233] They are thus, like the application of the publicity principle, a constraint on judicial power: reasoned judgments helps minimise the risk that judges will exercise power arbitrarily.[234] They therefore help ensure that judges exercise power legitimately according to law, including any applicable procedural principle.[235]

[231] *Hadjianastassiou v Greece* (1992) 16 EHRR 219; *Ruiz Torija v Spain* (1994) 19 EHRR 553 at [29]; *Van de Hurk v The Netherlands* (1994) 18 EHRR 481 at [59]; *Ruiz-Mateos v Spain* [1999] EHRLR 344; *Tolstoy Miloslavsky v UK* (1995) 20 EHRR 442; *English v Emery Reimbold & Strick Ltd* [2002] EWCA Civ 605; [2002] 1 WLR 2409; *North Range Shipping Ltd v Seatrans Shipping Corp* [2002] EWCA Civ 405; [2002] 1 WLR 2397; J Jolowicz, 'A Duty to Give Reasons' (2000) 59 CJQ 265.

[232] *English v Emery Reimbold & Strick Ltd* [2002] EWCA Civ 605; [2002] 1 WLR 2409 at [15].

[233] O Settem (2016) at 68.

[234] D Shapiro, 'In Defence of Judicial Candor' (1987) 100 Harv L Rev 731 at 737.

[235] *Flannery v Halifax Estate Agencies Ltd* [2000] 1 WLR 377 at 377; O Settem (2016) at 68–69.

4. What is sufficient where the giving of reasons is concerned is context specific. It depends on the proceedings and the nature of the matter before the court.[236] What is sufficient is what is necessary, in the context, to explain to the parties and the public what the decision concerned, how the court reached the decision it did,[237] and what its actual decision was.[238] As this is context-specific, the provision of sufficient reasons does not require every issue raised by the parties to be considered and set out in a judgment:[239] the giving of reasons is itself subject to the proportionality principle. Only those reasons necessary to the '*judge's conclusion (need) be identified and the manner in which (the judge) resolved them explained*':[240] judgments must thus only contain the '*building blocks of the reasoned judicial process*'.[241] An application for an interim injunction, contested dispute management application, a trial of proceedings classified as low value, or an application for permission to appeal would therefore not require the same level of detailed reasoning in a judgment as that required for a judgment in a trial of proceedings of intermediate or high value.
5. By setting out a reasoned decision, judgments also play a wider public role; again, in a way intrinsically linked to the publicity principle. They ensure that the court plays its proper role in articulating, clarifying, and developing the law.[242] And, importantly, they are the means by which issues concerning the law's development are brought to public and Parliamentary awareness.[243] Here the link with the role played by the publicity principle in promoting debate and law reform and securing the democratic accountability of the judiciary is patent.[244] This arises not only through the giving of reasoned decisions itself, but also because such decisions promote appellate accountability, as a properly reasoned judgment provides the basis for parties to determine whether they have arguable grounds for appeal.[245] Where an appeal takes place the law can be developed. The promotion of appeals, and the giving of reasoned appellate judgments, particularly provides the materials through which public debate can be stimulated and potential law reform promoted.
6. Publicly available reasoned judgments also form part of the framework within which consensual settlement takes place. This is because assessing the prospects of successfully litigating a dispute by reference to previously decided disputes is often a necessary part of a negotiation or mediation process.[246] Equally, it is the fact that it is reasoned judgments that are publicly available that enables the publicity principle to promote preventive justice. As Genn puts it, making reasoned judgments available to the public enables the courts to '*reaffirm norms and behavioural standards for private citizens, business and public bodies*'.[247] Their availability therefore provides a guide to, for instance, individuals

[236] *English v Emery Reimbold & Strick Ltd* [2002] EWCA Civ 605; [2002] 1 WLR 2409 at [14]–[15] gives the example that judgments on costs are often no more than summary in nature.

[237] *Flannery v Halifax Estate Agencies Ltd* [2000] 1 WLR 377 at 377–378.

[238] *English v Emery Reimbold & Strick Ltd* [2002] EWCA Civ 605; [2002] 1 WLR 2409 at [16].

[239] *Hiro Balani v Spain* (1994) 19 EHRR 566 at [27]; *Helle v Finland* (1998) 26 EHRR 159; *North Range Shipping Ltd v Seatrans Shipping Corp* [2002] EWCA Civ 405; [2002] 1 WLR 2397 at [20].

[240] *English v Emery Reimbold & Strick Ltd* [2002] EWCA Civ 605; [2002] 1 WLR 2409 at [19].

[241] *Glicksman v Redbridge Healthcare NHS Trust* [2001] EWCA Civ 1097; (2002) 63 BMLR 109 at [10]–[11].

[242] *National Westminster v Spectrum Plus* [2005] UKHL 41; [2005] 2 AC 680 at [32].

[243] L Fuller (1978); O Fiss, 'Against Settlement' (1984) 93 Yale LJ 1073.

[244] *R (Nicklinson) v Ministry of Justice* [2014] UKSC 38; [2015] AC 657; *Al-Rawi v The Security Services* [2011] UKSC 34; [2012] 1 AC 531 at 543, 572.

[245] *English v Emery Reimbold & Strick Ltd* [2002] EWCA Civ 605; [2002] 1 WLR 2409 at [15].

[246] R Mnookin and L Kornhauser (1978–1979).

[247] H Genn, *Judging Civil Justice* (CUP, 2009) at 3.

and businesses, either through legal advice or due to the influence they have on business practices generally, negotiate contracts, order and run businesses and their personal affairs in ways that minimise the prospect that disputes will arise.[248]

7. Reasoned judgments, and their public availability, thus lie at the heart of an open, democratic process that goes beyond the court's application of law to fact, and through their interaction with public and Parliamentary debate they help to maintain and foster the development of liberal democracy and economic development.[249]
8. Consistently with the efficiency and effective enforcement principles, a reasoned judgment must be given within a reasonable time.[250] What is reasonable will necessarily be context-dependent, ie the more complex the matter to be determined, the greater the delay between the hearing and judgment being given may reasonably be expected.[251] The judgment should, at a bare minimum, be given within a time frame that enables the parties to give effect to their rights, whether procedural or substantive, as determined in the judgment.
9. Where a judgment is unreasonably delayed, the parties may be denied a fair process. Delay may result in the judgment being flawed due to the judge being unable to recall key issues that were argued before them; even judicial memory can fade over time. This is particularly relevant where the judgment depends upon an assessment of witness evidence and credibility. While audio or video recordings, digital and written transcripts of hearings, and detailed contemporaneous notes may be capable of refreshing a judge's memory as to what was said, they would not necessarily place a judge back in the position they were in during a hearing to assess a witness's demeanour or credibility. Thus, their ability to make findings of fact at a distance from the hearing may be diminished, which could result in flawed findings, which might render the judgment unsafe and subject to a successful appeal.[252] Delay may also result in judgment, and its enforcement, coming too late for the successful party's rights to be vindicated effectively. An injunction granted too late may be redundant, if the harm it was to protect against has been carried into effect. The same can be said for a delayed declaratory judgment or money judgment, where it comes too late to provide effective vindication of the successful party's substantive rights. Delay may thus consequently also undermine the parties and public's confidence in the administration of justice.[253] As Gladstone is believed to have said, '*justice delayed is justice denied*'. Care must therefore be taken to secure compliance with this principle.

## RULE 22.—THE EFFECTIVE ENFORCEMENT PRINCIPLE

**Court judgments and orders should be capable of effective enforcement within a reasonable time.**

*Sources: Council of Europe Rec R (84) 5, principle 7; ALI/UNIDROIT Principles, principles 8, 26, 29; ALI/UNIDROIT Reporters' Study, r 35.*

[248] *R (UNISON) v Lord Chancellor* [2017] UKSC 51; [2017] 3 WLR 409 at [68]–[72].

[249] *D v National Society for the Prevention of Cruelty to Children* [1978] AC 171 at 232.

[250] *Unión Alimentaria Sanders SA v Spain* (1990) 12 EHRR 24; *Scopelliti v Italy* (1994) 17 EHRR 493.

[251] *Bank St Petersburg PJSC v Arkhangelsky* [2020] EWCA Civ 408; [2020] 4 WLR 55 at [78]. The greater the complexity the more time a judge will need to consider the matter properly.

[252] *Rolled Steel Ltd v British Steel Corporation* [1986] Ch 246 at 310; *Bond v Dunster Properties Ltd* [2011] EWCA 455; *Bank St Petersburg PJSC v Arkhangelsky* [2020] EWCA Civ 408; [2020] 4 WLR 55 at [79]–[83].

[253] *Goose v Wilson Sandford* [1998] TLR 85 at [112].

## COMMENTARY

1. The need for judgments and orders to be executed within a reasonable time of their being given has long been recognised as an essential element of a fair process. Writing in the 19th century, Bentham considered it to be as important a feature of an effective civil justice system as adjudicative accuracy.[254] As with unreasonable delay in the delivery of reasoned judgments, delay may frustrate the proper administration of justice and undermine confidence in the judiciary. Just as a delayed judgment may frustrate the vindication of rights so might delay in enforcement; the latter rendering any judgment given pyrrhic. Again, the maxim justice delayed is justice denied applies. Effective enforcement must be understood as an integral aspect of the trial process. Without it the right to fair trial would be illusory.[255]
2. This principle is specifically given effect through Part 16, which sets out the rules concerning enforcement. More generally, it is given effect through effective dispute management and the co-operation principle, which require the court and parties to ensure that disputes, including their enforcement, are managed consistently with the economy, efficiency, and proportionality principles. It is also to be given effect through the use of digital procedure, which should itself be designed to facilitate the speedy enforcement of judgments.

## RULE 23.—THE FINALITY AND APPELLATE REVIEW PRINCIPLES

**(1) The conclusion of proceedings whether through a court judgment or consensual settlement shall, as a general rule, be final.**

**(2) The public interest in promoting finality may be limited or set aside where**

**(a) it is necessary to secure the just resolution of the dispute, in which case finality may be set aside in respect of both judgments and consensual settlements; or**

**(b) it is outweighed by either the public or the private interest in appellate review of a judgment.**

*Sources: Council of Europe Rec R (84) 5, principle 5; ALI/UNIDROIT Principles, principles 23, 27, 28.*

## COMMENTARY

1. Disputes cannot be without end. Finality in litigation has always been a fundamental principle of English and Welsh civil procedure.[256] It is given expression in several ways. It underpins both claim and issue estoppel, ie the doctrine of res judicata, and the doctrine of merger, which preclude the same cause of action or issue being litigated in more than one set of proceedings.[257] It is also expressed in the requirement that parties should bring all their claims and defences relating to a dispute in a single set of proceedings, ie it is inherently linked to the concentration principle. It can also

[254] J Bentham, *Principles* at 6, 8; J Bentham in *The Works of Jeremy Bentham* (ed Bowring) (1843) (William Tait, Edinburgh) (1843) Vol 9, *The Constitutional Code* at 25–26.

[255] *Hornsby v Greece* (1997) 24 EHRR 250 at [40].

[256] *The Ampthill Peerage* [1977] AC 547 at 569; *Smith v Brough* [2005] EWCA Civ 261 at [54].

[257] Part 15, r 14.

be seen as underpinning statutory and equitable limitation periods, which ensure that the possibility of litigation over a dispute cannot endure indefinitely.[258] Finality thus requires that not only must disputes come to an end, but that they must be brought within a specified time period and must only be brought once.

2. Several rationales justify the application of the principle. Parties to a dispute have a legitimate, private, interest in their dispute being brought to an end after trial. The same is true where it is resolved through a consensual process. Once the dispute is resolved they have a legitimate expectation that that is '*the end of the matter*'[259] and their rights have been finally determined. Linked to this it promotes effective enforcement by providing a sound basis for it to take place, where necessary.[260]
3. Looking to the public interest, the principle supports the rule of law. As neither individuals nor companies are able to properly enjoy their rights if they are uncertain, the principle helps promote legal certainty. It does so by ensuring that rights cannot be called into question after the expiry of a limitation period. It also does so by ensuring that rights, as determined by a judgment or through the effect of a settlement, cannot be subject to challenge in future litigation. By promoting such certainty, it also promotes the public interest in socio-economic activity: legal certainty enables individuals and companies to enter into contracts, buy and sell property, develop their individual personality, etc.[261]
4. The principle also supports the promotion of, and is therefore also intrinsically linked with, several other procedural principles, not least the purposive principle.[262] It promotes economy, efficiency, and proportionality in litigation. Were parties able to re-open disputes after they have been resolved or were they able to raise causes of action or issues in multiple sets of proceedings, they would not only be put to the expense and time of litigating those issues time and again, they would also draw on the limited resources made available by the State for dispute resolution more than is fair. In this way finality promotes systemic proportionality as it ensures that the civil justice system is able to distribute its resources equitably, rather than enabling some parties to make multiple, unnecessary, claims on them. A necessary corollary of this is that it helps give effect to the general access principle. Were parties able to make multiple claims concerning the same dispute, that would tend to limit the ability of parties to other disputes to secure effective access due to delays caused by multiple proceedings over the same issue or re-opened disputes taking up court time. It thus, as Andrews states, promotes effective justice.[263] Equally, if parties were to delay pursuing a dispute indefinitely, they would also undermine the court's ability to properly manage disputes so as to secure adjudicative accuracy. Delay can, for instance, see documentary evidence lost or witness memory degrade. In all such cases, the court's ability to reach a substantively accurate decision would be reduced. Finally, the principle supports the public interest in procedural equality. If a party could, for instance, go on to trouble an opposing party by repeated challenges, eg through appeals or applications to vary or set aside orders, the likelihood would be that some parties would be able to, for instance, overbear less wealthy, less risk

[258] A Zuckerman (2021) at 1343.
[259] *Smith v Brough* [2005] EWCA Civ 261 at [35].
[260] N Andrews (2019) at 461.
[261] J Waldron, *The Rule of Law and the Measure of Property* (CUP, 2012) at 52.
[262] *Sainsbury's Supermarkets Ltd v Visa Europe Services LLC* [2020] UKSC 24; [2020] Bus LR 1196 at [238]–[239]; *AIC Ltd v Federal Airports Authority of Nigeria* [2022] UKSC 16; [2022] 1 WLR 3223 at [30]–[31].
[263] N Andrews (2019) at 460.

averse parties or parties for whom delay was particularly problematic. This could lead to the overborne party under-settling the dispute or withdrawing their claim if they were the claimant. Finality by limiting the prospect that a party could take such action thus also helps create and maintain a level playing field between such parties, ie procedural equality.[264]

5. The principle of finality is, as with many procedural principles, not absolute. Limitation periods can be extended.[265] The doctrine of res judicata is subject to exceptions where, for instance, a judgment has been procured by fraud.[266] Final appeals can be re-opened where it comes to light that an appeal court's decision was tainted by, for instance, corruption on the part of the court.[267] Consensual settlements can be set aside where they were procured on the basis of misrepresentation or fraud. Rule 23(2)(a) makes provision for these specific exceptions.
6. The most significant exception to the finality principle is, however, provided by the appellate principle. This Code differs from both the common law and article 6 of the European Convention on Human Rights in this regard. It views the appellate principle as an integral and necessary civil procedural principle, whereas neither the common law nor the Convention view it to be so. For both it is an optional extra. This Code thus follows the approach taken by the ALI/UNIDROIT Principles and the ELI-UNIDROIT Model Rules.[268] It does so for several reasons,[269] which can be categorised as either giving effect to the parties' private interest or to the public interest.[270]
7. First, rule 23 sees the appellate principle as a necessary feature of the procedural code for the same reason Bentham argued that there ought to be a right to appeal: that it promotes adjudicative accuracy. This serves both the private and the public interest. Appeals provide the means to correct first instance errors of law or fact. This is not to say that the appellate process is guaranteed to secure a correct decision. Appeal judges are fallible, just as judges are at first instance. The issue here is not to provide a guarantee of accuracy, but a means to overturn error and, just as importantly, a means through which parties can have reasonably justifiable fears that a judgment is tainted by substantive or procedural error scrutinised. The ability to correct adjudicative error also serves the public interest. The ability to scrutinise judgments that are reasonably likely to be incorrect and to correct them serves to promote confidence in the judiciary, and as a consequence the rule of law. Rule 23 thus rejects Lord Donaldson's cynical suggestion that appellate process was, at best, of questionable value as disputes have no right answer and therefore a mechanism to correct judicial error was unnecessary.[271]
8. An appellate process also serves to minimise the prospect of adjudicative error in another way; again, serving both the private and public interest. Just as the publicity and reasoned judgment principles help to ensure that judges are on trial while they are dealing with proceedings, so does the appellate principle. While those other

[264] R Sharpe, 'The Application and Impact of Judicial Discretion in Commercial Litigation' (1998) 17(1) Advocates' Society Journal 4 at 8.

[265] Limitation Act 1980, Part II.

[266] Part 15, rr 12(3), 13(2), and 13(3).

[267] Part 17, r 20.

[268] ALI/UNIDROIT Principles, principle 27; ELI-UNIDROIT Model Rules, Part IX, Introduction.

[269] N Andrews (2003) at 411.

[270] A Zuckerman (2021) at 121.

[271] J Donaldson, 'The Court of Appeal' (1985) 53 Medico-Legal Journal 148 at 153.

principles provide the basis for explanatory and democratic accountability, the appellate principle provides the basis for appellate accountability. That adjudicative decisions can be subject to an appeal is not only a corrective mechanism, but also a prophylactic one. That a judge can be subject to an appeal, and is thus accountable for their conduct at first instance and their decisions, is a means by which high standards in adjudication are promoted and maintained. A judge who is susceptible to appellate scrutiny is one who is less likely to act in an arbitrary manner, to act unfairly or abusively, to act incompetently, or simply be lazy.

9. Further rationales that stem from the public interest focus on the wider effect that appeals provide. Public, reasoned appellate judgments provide the means by which the civil courts are able to articulate, clarify, and develop the law. Equally, they promote the consistent application of the law.[272] Taken together, these two rationales, which are intrinsically related to the doctrine of precedent, also support the development and operation of the shadow of the law, supporting its role in preventive and consensual justice.

10. Taken together the various rationales provide strong support for the inclusion of the appellate principle as a fundamental procedural principle, one that provides a general exception to the finality principle. A balance must, however, be struck. The right to appeal that flows from the appellate principle is not incorporated here in an unrestricted form. It is made subject to a principled limitation: parties are only able to appeal where principled criteria, which are intended to promote economy, efficiency, proportionality, and finality are satisfied. Thus, it is subject to a permission to appeal requirement.

## SECTION 4: THE DIGITAL PROCEDURE PRINCIPLES

### RULE 24.—THE DIGITAL PROCEDURE AND ACCOUNTABILITY PRINCIPLE

**(1) This Code shall be given effect by and through a procedure, which shall be presumptively digital.**

**(2) The digital procedure shall be managed for each dispute through a digital dispute management file and digital dispute management account, which are to be accessible via the digital portal authorised by the Civil Dispute Resolution Council and operated by the digital dispute resolution service.**

**(3) The digital procedure shall provide the means to record and analyse, including analysis carried out through the use of artificial intelligence, case data from all proceedings to the keep the Code's operation under ongoing scrutiny. Such analysis is to form the basis of ongoing innovation and improvement to the Code. It may also be utilised by the judiciary to inform judicial training.**

**(4) To ensure the digital procedure gives proper effect to this Code, it shall be designed under the authority of the Civil Courts Rule Committee and shall be subject to the approval process applicable to this Code. The manner in which it gives effect to this**

[272] T Bingham, 'The Judge as Lawmaker', in T Bingham, *The Business of Judging* (OUP, 2000) Vol 1 at 25 and following.

**Code shall be made public. This latter obligation is subject to any necessary steps necessary to maintain the security of the procedure.**

**(5) A non-digital procedure, which shall be analogous to the digital procedure, shall be available where its application would further the purposive principle.**

*Sources: Council of Europe Rec R (84) 5, principle 9; ALI/UNIDROIT Principles, principle 19; ELI-UNIDROIT Model Rules, r 18; Judicial Review and Courts Act 2022, s 19(6).*

## COMMENTARY

1. The presumption is that civil dispute resolution in future will be digital by design and default.[273] This reflects a general trend across civil justice systems, not least in England and Wales.[274]
2. This principle places responsibility for the digital procedure's design and operation with the Civil Courts Rule Committee, which is under a duty to ensure that it gives effect to the Code and, hence, the principles set out in this Part (rule 2). To facilitate democratic accountability of the digital procedure, its code must be made public. In that way, both the procedure and the Rule Committee's approval of it can be held to account by Government, through the approval process applicable to the Code itself, and the public. To protect the digital procedure's security, the publicly available material should be redacted accordingly.
3. The digital procedure shall have several features. First, it will be provided via the digital portal, which is to be accessible via the Internet. The portal will not be operated by the civil courts. It will rather be provided by a digital dispute resolution service, which will need to be properly and securely funded so that it can maintain, update, and operate all aspects of the portal. This will be required for the service to be consistent with the general access principle. The rationale for the portal not being operated by the civil courts is that this will ensure that it is not '*court-centric*'.[275] It will not be an online multi-door courthouse, but rather a digital dispute resolution centre.[276] It will not provide an extended court,[277] but the digital court will form one part of a wider, integrated whole. This is the case because dispute prevention and resolution are not and should not primarily be delivered by the civil courts.[278] By taking this approach the digital portal will, it is anticipated, not have as its primary focus access to the court. It will rather be designed and operated with a primary focus on dispute

[273] M Briggs (2015) at 4, 77, 85; Judicial Review and Courts Act 2022, s 19(7); CEPEJ, *Guidelines on electronic court filing (e-filing) and digitalisation of courts* (2021) [] at [22].

[274] M Evers and P Ryan, 'Exploring eCourt Innovations in New South Wales Civil Courts' (2016) 5(1) Journal of Civil Litigation and Practice 65; S Salter and D Thompson, 'Public-Centred Civil Justice Redesign: A Case Study of the British Columbia Civil Resolution Tribunal' (2016) 3 McGill J Disp Resol 113; D Himonas, 'Utah's Online Dispute Resolution Program' (2018) 122 Dick L Rev 875; C Grayling MP LC, *Reform of the Courts and Tribunals* (Ministry of Justice, 28 March 2014); Joint Statement of Lord Chief Justice, Senior President of Tribunals and the Lord Chancellor, *Reforming HM Courts and Tribunals Service* (25 July 2013); M Briggs (2015); M Briggs (2016); House of Commons Committee of Public Accounts, *Transforming Courts and Tribunals—Progress Review* (HC27, 2019).

[275] T Sourdin, *Judges, Technology and Artificial Intelligence* (Elgar, 2021) at 171.

[276] F Sander, 'A Dialogue Between Professors Frank Sander and Mariana Hernandez Crespo: Exploring the Evolution of the Multi-Door Courthouse' (2008) 5(3) Article 4 University of St Thomas Law Journal 665 at 670; F Sander, 'The Multi-door Court House—Settling Disputes in 2000' (1976) 3 Barrister 18 at 20.

[277] R Susskind, *Online Courts and the Future of Justice* (OUP, 2019) at 60–63.

[278] T Sourdin (2021) at 28, chap 6.

prevention, a secondary focus on conflict and dispute resolution, and only then, as a tertiary focus, will it be concerned with access to the court and its ability to deliver both consensual and adjudicative justice.[279] This approach is intrinsically linked to the digital integration principle.

4. Secondly, the digital procedure will provide a digital one-stop-shop for parties.[280] As it will provide access to a broad range of services, users will not only be able to easily access any of those services, they will also be able to do so efficiently and economically. They will do so through the procedure providing and managing a digital dispute management file and a digital dispute management account. Each user will be able to create their own management account, through which they will be able to upload to a single digital management file all relevant information and documents.[281] This will facilitate easy provision of such material to any conflict or dispute resolution process they use. It will also, if they have to resort to commencing proceedings, form the file through which the court manages the dispute. The use of a single digital file to facilitate this will reduce the time and cost to parties of uploading information and documents, which they would have to do multiple times, if each conflict and dispute resolution process required, as they do currently, parties to upload such material.[282]
5. Thirdly, parties, when they commence proceedings must have such an account, if they have not created one during pre-action dispute management. Lawyers must have such an account through which they can manage each of the proceedings that they are engaged in. This approach while not only facilitating efficient and economical dispute management, will also enable digital service of documents, including case statements through which the court's jurisdiction is established when proceedings are commenced. It will thus facilitate the movement from paper-based service of case statements and other documents to digital service as the default approach.
6. Fourthly, the digital procedure should support both the artificial intelligence and digital integration principles. This should facilitate easy access to information and guidance, not least through the use of generative AI, eg by way of a dispute resolution chatbot.
7. Finally, case information ought to be capable of being recorded by the digital procedure. Hence information and documents uploaded to it should, wherever possible, be machine readable or transformed into machine readable form. That information should then be capable of being extracted, in anonymised form, and analysed. Such analysis may then be used to promote preventive justice. It should also be a means to promote improvements to the Code and its operation. Information extracted from digital dispute management files may, for instance, demonstrate aspects of the Code that are not operating economically and efficiently or where there are problems relating to equal access. Analysis of case data, including judgments, may also bring to light bias in the Code's design and operation, which can then be rectified through revision. Such improvements should be carried out on a continuing basis

[279] H Woolf (1996) at 4–8.

[280] CEPEJ, *Guidelines on electronic court filing (e-filing) and digitalisation of courts* (Council of Europe, 2021) [] at [45].

[281] CPR PD 51O and 51R; A Cordella and F Contini, *Digital Technologies for Better Justice—A Toolkit for Action* (Inter-American Development Bank, 2020); CEPEJ, *Guidelines on Electronic Court Filing (e-filing) and Digitalisation of Courts* (Council of Europe, 2021); Z Loebl, *Designing Online Courts—The Future of Justice is Open to All* (Wolters Kluwer, 2019) at 38, 87.

[282] G Vos, *Leading the Charge—Our international position* (Annual Bar and Young Bar Conference 2020) [] at [16].

and should thus enable the Code to be improved on a more regular basis than has traditionally been the case with rules of court. Analysis may also bring to light training gaps or needs where the judiciary is concerned. It may, for instance, identify areas of both procedural and substantive law where the judiciary needs to be provided with refresher training. Such analysis may therefore be provided to the judiciary to inform training programmes provided by the Judicial College. More controversially perhaps, analysis may also bring to light any systemic bias in judgments. Where that is the case, and subject to any such analysis not infringing judicial independence, it too could be used by the Judicial College to form the basis of unconscious bias training.[283]

8. To protect the ability of those who are unable to access the digital procedure effectively, a non-digital procedure should be maintained. This should only be used where it would further the purposive principle and, hence, secure a fair process for both parties. This does not necessarily mean that where its use is justifiable for one party to a dispute it must be used by all parties. It should be possible for one party to use the non-digital procedure while other parties use the digital procedure. This requires the system to provide for documents uploaded to the digital system or generated by the court to be provided to the non-digital party in hard copy. It would also require any documents provided to the court via the non-digital procedure to be uploaded by the court administration to the digital case management file.

## RULE 25.—THE ARTIFICIAL INTELLIGENCE PRINCIPLE

**(1) The development and use of artificial intelligence (AI) must be**
  **(a) subject too and limited by the need to secure judicial independence;**
  **(b) consistent with the purposive principle;**
  **(c) consistent with procedural equality; and**
  **(d) transparent, intelligible, and accountable.**

**(2) To give effect to judicial independence, the development of AI further to this Code shall be subject to judicial oversight. Its adoption shall be subject to approval by both the Civil Dispute Resolution Council and the Lord or Lady Chief Justice.**

**(3) AI may be used to assist parties to prevent disputes arising or to resolve disputes consensually. It may also be used by the court (including court administration) to assist parties both pre-action and post-issue of proceedings to manage disputes and facilitate consensual settlement. It may also be used to assist the court in adjudicative decision-making.**

**(4) Where parties are assisted by AI in respect of adjudicative procedures they must inform the court and other parties of that fact and of how they have been assisted. Where the court uses AI to assist decision-making it must inform the parties of that fact and how it is has been assisted.**

**(5) AI may not be used to determine proceedings on their substantive merits, except where the parties consent to its use for that purpose. Such consent must be express and fully-informed. Where artificial intelligence is used in this way any decision made has the status of an arbitral decision, albeit one that may be enforced as if it is a judgment of the court.**

[283] R Koulu cited in J Sorabji, 'Compliance Problems and Digitising Case Management in England and Wales', in A Higgins and R Assy (2020) at 175.

*Sources: Council of Europe Rec R (84) 5, principle 9; Council of Europe, Recommendation CM/Rec (2020)1 of the Committee of Ministers to member States on the human rights impacts of algorithmic systems; European Commission for the Efficiency of Justice (CEPEJ), European Ethical Charter on the use of Artificial Intelligence in Judicial Systems and their Environment (2018); Consultative Council of European Judges, Opinion No 14, Justice and information technologies (IT) (2014); European Commission, Independent High Level Expert Group on Artificial Intelligence, Ethics Guidelines for Trustworthy AI (2019); Consultative Council of European Judges, Opinion 26: Moving forward: the use of assistive technology in the judiciary (2023).*

## COMMENTARY

1. Artificial intelligence (AI) can be defined broadly as the use of a machine or computer programme to replicate human cognition and decision-making through the purposive analysis of information.[284] Its use is now endemic within society as it underpins the operation of the Internet. Its increasing application in the justice system is, given its ubiquity, inevitable and, potentially, beneficial.[285] Its use does not, however, come without risk or limitation, neither of which should be overlooked.[286]
2. This rule seeks to facilitate the incorporation of AI into civil dispute resolution. It does so by articulating specific principles to guide its use and development, all of which are subject to judicial oversight. Its use should also be subject to approval both by the Civil Dispute Resolution Council, which is independent of Government, and the Lord or Lady Chief Justice. These safeguards are intended to ensure that the use of AI is consistent with the rule of law, and does not render prevention or resolution of disputes unfair. It is particularly intended to ensure that the development and use of AI does not undermine judicial independence or erode separation of powers, either through its design or through its application undermining the civil court's ability to hold the Government to account where judicial review is concerned.[287]
3. Its adoption is also subject to the application of four design principles. The primary one is that AI's development and use must be made subject to and limited by the principle of judicial independence.[288] AI must neither have an adverse impact on institutional independence nor may it have an adverse impact on individual independence. This is reflected specifically in rules 25(3), (4) and (5). This also requires limits to be placed upon any analysis carried out via AI, further to rules 24(3) and 27, to assess the operation of the civil justice system. AI cannot, for instance, properly be

[284] European Commission, Independent High Level Expert Group on Artificial Intelligence, *Ethics Guidelines for Trustworthy AI* (European Commission, 2019) at 36.

[285] A Lodder and J Zeleznikov, 'Artificial Intelligence and Online Dispute Resolution', in M Wahab, *Online Dispute Resolution: Theory and Practice* (Eleven, 2011) at 61; Susskind (2019); T Sourdin (2021).

[286] A Higgins, I Levy, and T Lienart, 'The Bright but Modest Potential of Algorithms in the Courtroom', in R Assy and A Higgins (2020).

[287] A Michaels, 'Artificial Intelligence, Legal Change, and Separation of Powers' (2020) 88(4) Cincinnati Law Review 1083 at 1085; T Sourdin (2021) at 192–197.

[288] CEPEJ, *European Ethical Charter on the use of Artificial Intelligence in Judicial Systems and their Environment* (2018), Principle 1. And see, the Consultative Council of European Judges, *Opinion 26: Moving forward: the use of assistive technology in the judiciary* (Council of Europe, 2023)] at [94], which sets out fourteen principles governing use of AI by the judiciary. Also see: Lady Carr LCJ et al, *Artificial Intelligence (AI)—Guidance for Judicial Office Holders* (Judicial Office, 2023); Courts of New Zealand, *Guidelines for Use of Generative Artificial Intelligence in Courts and Tribunals* (Courts of New Zealand, 2023); and, L. Bennett Moses, M Legg, J Silove, M Zalnieriute, and S Mahmood, *AI Decision-making in Courts and Tribunals* (The Australasian Institute of Judicial Administration, 2024).

used to identify specific judges and analyse the way in which they carry out their judicial functions. Such analysis could tend to undermine individual independence. It might, for instance, identify judges who work more slowly than others or who rule more often in favour of claimants or defendants, or whose decisions are appealed more often than others. This could lead to improper pressure being placed on them to change the ways they work. It could lead to public criticism or targeting of judges or attempts by parties to challenge allocation of their dispute to a specific judge. Such possibilities may undermine the proper administration of justice. This is not to say that analysis should not be carried out. Rule 24 provides for analysis to be carried out at a systems level to provide the basis for judicial training.

4. Individual independence may also be challenged through the use of AI to assist judicial decision-making. Judicial decision-making is a complex skill that requires constant honing over time. There is a danger that AI assistance of judges may, overtime, reduce judicial skills, which in turn would increase reliance on AI. A vicious circle could be then created, the end product of which would be a judiciary that was dependent upon AI to make decisions. Thus steps, whether it be by effective and regular training or by requiring judges to spend a minimum amount of time making decisions unaided per year, must be taken to ensure that individual independence is not adversely affected through the use of AI.[289]

6. The second design principle is that the development and use of AI shall be consistent with the purposive principle. As a necessary corollary, AI must also be consistent with all of the principles articulated within this Part of the Code. In this way, its design and use must be consistent with the various aspects of the right to fair trial guaranteed by the common law right to fair trial and article 6 of the European Convention on Human Rights, which are given expression in the principles set out in this Part. Compliance with this design principle is intended to ensure that the use of AI will not undermine the provision of a fair process for parties.[290] As a consequence the development and use of AI must be ethical.[291] One way that this should be secured is by limiting AI's use to assisting human decision-making.[292]

7. The third design principle is intended to ensure that problems that have become well-known about the use of AI are not replicated in the assistance it provides. AI bias and discrimination is all too well-known and has posed significant problems where used in criminal justice systems.[293] The problem is that, quite simply, AI draws upon the data it is provided with, which has an unfortunate tendency to be biased against individuals and groups within society.[294] Biased data produces biased analyses and results.[295] Such a consequence and the discriminatory effects it produces stand intrinsically in opposition to the need for the design and use of AI to be both ethical and for it to be consistent with procedural equality. Given the harm that can

289 H Fry, *Hello World—How to be Human in the Age of the Machine* (Penguin, 2019) at 131.

290 CEPEJ, *European Ethical Charter on the use of Artificial Intelligence in Judicial Systems and their Environment* (2018), principle 4.

291 CEPEJ (2018) principle 1.

292 T Sourdin (2021) at 236–271.

293 *Proposal for a Regulation of the European Parliament and of the Council Laying Down Harmonised Rules on Artificial Intelligence (Artificial Intelligence Act) and Amending Certain Union Legislative Acts*, Annex III, para 8(a).

294 M Raub (2018).

295 Not only may this have adverse effects on individuals and groups within society, but it may also have an adverse impact on the development of the law through bias and stereotyping: S Menon cited in T Sourdin (2021) at 27.

be caused to individuals and groups in society, the proper administration of justice, confidence in the justice system, and ultimately the rule of law, while procedural equality is inherent in the second design principle, it is specifically identified as an AI design principle in its own right. AI in the justice system must as a consequence be developed and used in ways that eradicate the prospect of bias in the system.[296] Additionally, this design principle places a positive obligation on AI development and design. It requires AI to be designed to enhance procedural equality, ie through helping to ensure that like cases are treated alike and different cases are treated differently, as considered further below.

8. The fourth design principle requires AI design and use to be transparent, intelligible, and accountable.[297] The Code, if it is to be consistent with the publicity principle, must be transparent and intelligible as must any assistance provided by it: it must thus be accessible. Where decisions are made by AI, where that is permissible under rule 25(5), they too must be transparent and intelligible to the parties, ie the parties must be able to understand the basis of the AI decision through an adequate explanation.

9. To secure intelligibility and accountability, the same design approach should be adopted to the development of AI as adopted in respect of the development of the digital procedure.[298] Accountability specifically comes through the requirement that the design of AI is subject to judicial oversight and that it is to be approved by the Civil Dispute Resolution Council and Lord or Lady Chief Justice. Further design accountability comes from the AI code itself being made available publicly. In this way it can be subject to both informed analysis and scrutiny and public, democratic accountability.

10. Rules 25(3), (4) and (5) identify the scope and limits of the use of AI. Where parties are concerned, it should also be developed to assist them in identifying the steps they can take to defuse or resolve their dispute prior to commencing litigation, as well as helping to explain the litigation process to them. Where dispute management is concerned, its use shall, primarily, be to assist the parties, courts, and the court's administration to manage disputes. The rule thus adopts an approach to the use of AI that is commonly known as one that provides a judicial '*decision support system*'.[299] This covers a range of tasks. AI could be used within the digital procedure to promote effective timetabling of disputes by suggesting optimal dispute management directions.[300] It could analyse use of the court's resources to optimise hearing schedules, ensuring that court buildings, for instance, were utilised effectively. It could also be used to analyse judicial workload, thus assisting court administration and judicial decision-making on the allocation of work to individual judges. The provision of AI analysis, as the data it used could be taken from the civil justice system as a whole, could also help promote greater consistency in judicial decision-making by bringing to the attention of judges and the parties how previous decisions in similar matters had been determined.[301] That base line could then, through party submissions and

[296] CEPEJ (2018) principle 2.

[297] CEPEJ (2018) principle 4.

[298] CEPEJ (2018) principle 3.

[299] A Lodder and J Zeleznikov (2011) at 62 and following; T Sourdin (2021) at 190.

[300] Dispute management could also be facilitated through AI being used: for automated document generation; to assist with the identification of proceedings that raise common issues so as to facilitate the making of group proceedings orders or representative proceedings orders; and, so on. Z Loebl, *Designing Online Courts—The Future of Justice for All* (Wolters Kluwer, 2019).

[301] E Katsh and O Rabinovich-Einy, *Digital Justice* (OUP, 2017) at 48.

judicial analysis, be adapted to fit the individual circumstances of the case, which the AI programme would not have been able to take into account.[302] AI could also be used to manage the monitoring of compliance with procedural obligations, providing automated alerts (or nudges) to parties of upcoming deadlines, as well as providing similar alerts to judges so they may monitor compliance effectively.[303] Consistently with the due notice and adversarial principles, where such assistance relates to judicial decision-making, any assistance provided to the judge must also be made available to parties. In the same vein where parties use AI to assist them during proceedings, particularly to formulate their cases, legal arguments, and submissions they must inform other parties and the court.[304] Notice is the basis of effective scrutiny of such assistance.

11. While there have been some suggestions that AI may be used to create 'Robot Judges' that replace human judges, this Code adopts a nuanced approach.[305] It accepts, as a possibility, that AI could replace human decision-making in dispute resolution. It also accepts that for some individuals a quicker, cheaper form of resolution that could be provided by AI might be acceptable and perhaps even preferable, particularly where a dispute is of a low value.[306] Were AI decision-making to be applied to make dispute management decisions and to determine disputes on their substantive merits, it is also likely, due to the cost and time saving, to promote systemic proportionality through its reduction in the use of court resources. It may also be more consistent in its determination of such matters, as its decisions would be the product of the application of mathematical logic. It would also not be susceptible to human foibles and biases.[307]

12. AI decision-making would not, however, as a consequence of applying mathematical analyses to data, be able to take account of factors that human decision-makers are able to consider. It is trite to say that human judges do not simply, if ever, apply mathematical analysis. When considering the burden of proof, for instance, they are not applying mathematical probability. When taking decisions generally, they are considering not simply the bare facts as applied to the law, they are looking at its application in its broader social context. They bring their own experience, and shared humanity to the task. For this reason, this Code adopts the position that human decision-making, whatever else it may be in comparison to AI decision-making, is incommensurate to it and must therefore remain the means by which disputes are managed and determined on their substantive merits.

13. Maintaining judicial decision-making does not, however, wholly exclude AI decision-making. Consistently with party autonomy, rule 25(5) facilitates the use of AI where parties expressly and in a fully informed manner opt to use it for the management and/or resolution of their dispute. In this way, they can opt to use

[302] A Higgins, I Levy, and T Lienart in A Higgins and R Assy (2020) at 122–124.

[303] J Sorabji, 'Compliance Problems and Digitising Case Management in England and Wales', in A Higgins and R Assy (2020).

[304] *Practice Direction Re: Use of Artificial Intelligence in Court Submissions* (Court of King's Bench of Manitoba, 23 June 2023); *Practice Direction: Use of Artificial Intelligence Tools* (Supreme Court of Yukon, 26 June 2023).

[305] T Sourdin (2021) at xi; R E Volokh, 'Chief Justice Robots' (2019) 68 Duke LJ 1135; A Michaels (2020).

[306] *Pyrrho Investments v MWB Property* [2016] EWHC 256 (Ch); M Grossman and G Cormack, 'Technology-Assisted Review in E-Discovery Can Be More Effective and More Efficient Than Exhaustive Manual Review' (2011) 17(3) Richmond Journal of Law & Technology 1.

[307] D Nugent, 'Judicial Bias' (1994) 42(1) Clev St L Rev 1; E Peer and E Gamliel, 'Heuristics and Biases in Judicial Decision-Making' (2013) 49 Court Review 114.

AI to secure a more economical and efficient approach to the management and resolution of their dispute. They must do so, however, in the full awareness that any decisions reached will lack the humanity of judicial decision-making, but will rather be the product of the application of mathematical analysis. Where parties opt for such an approach, any decision reached has the status of an arbitral decision: AI decision-making rests on party consent not the exercise of the judicial power of the State. To facilitate effective enforcement, however, such decisions may be enforced as if they were judgments. As party use of this approach promotes the public interest in the administration of justice through promoting systemic proportionality, obstacles to party consent should be minimised. Permitting AI decisions to be enforced as judgments is intended to assist in minimising such obstacles.

## RULE 26.—THE DIGITAL ACCESS PRINCIPLE

**(1) The digital procedure shall be reasonably intelligible and accessible to all users via the digital portal.**

**(2) For users who do not readily have access to the Internet or who need reasonable assistance to access it effectively, digital access shall be available for public use in all court buildings. Where a town or city has no court building, digital access shall be provided in town halls, other public buildings, and other venues authorised by the Civil Dispute Resolution Council.**

**(3) The court administration shall help court users to facilitate effective digital access. Assistance shall be delivered via a medium appropriate to the needs of the users.**

*Sources: Council of Europe Rec R (84) 5, principle 9.*

## COMMENTARY

1. If the introduction of a digital procedure is to secure not only increased access to justice in its widest sense[308] it will need to be intelligible and accessible. Consistently with procedural equality, this means that it will need to be both intelligible and accessible to all users. This may pose a significant challenge to those designing the digital process. Digital systems are, unfortunately, all too often designed in ways that fail to maximise accessibility. This can arise through poor design, which makes the system difficult to use. It can also arise through designers' implicit or unconscious bias, which may and can produce digital systems that discriminate against certain users. Discriminatory design may adversely affect individuals on the basis of race, gender, impaired vision, deafness or impaired hearing, vulnerability, or their ability to access or use the Internet due to cognitive impairment, neuro-diversity, or learning disabilities.[309]

2. To secure digital access, the Rule Committee, which will itself need to be diverse in its membership, will need to both ensure the digital design team responsible for the

[308] M Galanter, 'Justice in Many Rooms', in M Capelletti (ed), *Access to Justice and the Welfare State* (Alphen aan den Rijn: Sijthoff; 1981); T Sourdin (2021) esp chap 6; B Rose Hough, 'Let's Not Make it Worse: Issues to Consider in Adopting New Technology', in J Cabral et al, 'Using Technology to Enhance Access to Justice' (2012) 26(1) Harvard Journal of Law & Technology 243.

[309] M Broussard, *More than a Glitch—Confronting Race, Gender and Ability Bias in Tech* (MIT, 2023).

digital procedure and digital portal is itself diverse. It will also need to ensure the procedure and portal does not discriminate against its users while also complying with any statutory accessibility requirements.[310] Effective design on its own will not, however, be sufficient to secure effective access. Steps will also need to be taken to secure effective access to the Internet for those who need to access the digital portal and procedure.

3. Access to the digital portal should be provided through public access sites for those who have poor Internet connectivity or who need help in navigating the portal and digital procedure. Such sites should, primarily, be in court buildings. Where a town or city does not have a court building, they should be provided in other public buildings whether they are town halls, civic centres, or Citizens Advice centres. Where they are not available, the Civil Dispute Resolution Council should authorise the use of other premises, eg supermarkets, chemists, doctor's surgeries, or hospitals.
4. Access to the portal should additionally be supplemented by assistance that helps individuals use it and the digital procedure. Such assistance could be provided by an effective chatbot incorporated into the digital portal, in-person support from members of the court administration, or freely-accessible telephone assistance.[311]

## RULE 27.—THE DIGITAL INTEGRATION PRINCIPLE

**(1) The digital procedure shall be integrated holistically and coherently via the digital portal with other means for preventing and resolving civil disputes including: Citizens Advice, Ombudsman schemes and other conflict and dispute resolution service providers approved by the Civil Dispute Resolution Council.**
**(2) Integration shall be carried out to promote the prevention and resolution of conflicts and disputes.**

*Sources: Council of Europe Rec R (84) 5, principle 9.*

## COMMENTARY

1. This rule gives effect to the shift that the Code marks in the approach to dispute resolution. It directs the Rule Committee and those responsible for the digital procedure to ensure that it is fully integrated with a range of mechanisms for preventing civil disputes arising, resolving individual conflicts before they transform into disputes, and resolving disputes consensually and adjudicatively via the courts. It is thus intended to facilitate the development of a coherent, holistic system to deal justly with disputes. It is not, as noted above, intended do so by privileging the civil courts and their processes. As such it does not require preventive and conflict resolution measures to be built out from the court, but rather that the digital procedure integrates a range of measures independent of the court into a one-stop-shop digital portal and procedure, which secures access to the court as well as those other measures.

[310] Diversity will need to go far beyond the diversity of membership required for the Civil Procedure Rule Committee and the Online Procedure Rule Committee: Civil Procedure Act 1997, s 2; Judicial Review and Courts Act 2022, s 22; Public Sector Bodies (Websites and Mobile Applications) (No 2) Accessibility Regulations 2018 (SI 2018/952).

[311] B Leveson, *Justice for the 21st Century* (Judicial Office, 2015) at [45]–[46]; M Briggs (2016) at 40, 118; A Findley et al, *Preventing Digital Exclusion from Online Justice* (JUSTICE, 2018).

Rather than creating an 'extended court' or online multi-door courthouse,[312] digital integration is intended to integrate the civil courts into a wider, coherent whole.

2. The integration required by this rule is based on the premise that the digital portal provides the means by which anyone may access a range of dispute prevention and resolution resources. Those measures may be provided by the civil courts. They may be provided by public sector bodies such as Citizens Advice, Ombudsman, regulators, and complaints bodies. And they may be provided by a range of private sector Ombudsman, complaints bodies, and dispute resolution providers. The last would include the currently developing sector of pre-action dispute resolution portals.[313] Integration should thus be compendious. The key design issue is for the Civil Dispute Resolution Council to provide a guiding hand for the development and coherent integration of these various bodies and processes into the digital portal and procedure. That this guidance is not to be provided by the Civil Courts Rule Committee will ensure that this integration and coherence is not court centric.

[312] J Sorabji, 'The Online Solutions Court—a Multi-Door Courthouse for the 21st Century' (2017) 36(1) CJQ 86 at 100; S Menon, *Technology and the Changing Face of Justice* (Negotiation and Conflict Management Group (NCMG) ADR Conference, 2019).

[313] G Vos, *Online Courts: Perspectives from the Bench and the Bar* (Harvard, 2020); CPR PD27B; The Official Injury Claim Portal (https://www.officialinjuryclaim.org.uk).

# PART 2

# CIVIL COURT ADMINISTRATION

## SECTION 1: GENERAL

1. This Part details the civil court's structure and the status and role of its administration. While it generally maintains the current approach taken in England and Wales, it differs in one significant way: it proposes the creation of a unified civil court operated through a judicial model of court administration. The unification of the civil courts ought properly to have taken place when a single set of civil procedure rules was introduced in 1999. Their continued existence where process becomes increasingly digital in its delivery, will become ever more difficult to justify; not least to the public. Integration will also ensure that digital delivery will not be hampered by the differential distribution of resources across the two courts: a single civil court will eradicate the possibility that one court will be under-resourced in comparison with the other. A single civil court will also facilitate effective court reform, which will only need to be applied in one way to one court. It is also consistent with a simplified enforcement process.
2. This Part also proposes the introduction of a judicial model of court administration. This is intended to better support institutional judicial independence than the current ersatz-partnership model.

### RULE 1.—SCOPE AND PURPOSE

**(1) This Part concerns the structure and administration of the civil courts and the powers of judges and court officers.**
**(2) The civil court structure and administration ought to be designed and operated to particularly promote access to justice and the implementation of the economy, efficiency, and proportionality principles.**

*Source: CPR Pt 2.*

### COMMENTARY

1. This Part of the Code is intended to ensure that civil court structure and administration is more fully consistent with the economy, efficiency, and proportionality principles than is currently the case. It should also be read consistently with the digital procedure and accountability principle. They require the Code to be implemented in a way that facilitates ongoing improvement. This will require, as was intended with

*A Model Civil Procedure Code for England and Wales*. John Sorabji, Oxford University Press. © John Sorabji 2024.
DOI: 10.1093/oso/9780192848680.003.0003

the introduction of the power to alter the High Court's Divisions in the Judicature Act 1873,[1] that the civil court structure be revised and reformed to meet changing demands upon the courts. There is thus no presumption that the civil court structure, or its administration, provided for at the time the Code is introduced should remain unchanged or unchanging. Continuous, incremental improvement, where necessary, is to be inherent in the structure as much as it is to be in the Code and any digital procedure made under it.

## SECTION 2: CIVIL COURT STRUCTURE AND EXERCISE OF JURISDICTION

### RULE 2.—CIVIL COURTS

**(1) The civil courts of England and Wales are the High Court and the Court of Appeal (Civil Division).**
**(2) The High Court shall be divided into two tiers: the First-tier and Upper Tier. The Upper Tier shall be divided into such Divisions and contain such specialist courts as designated by the Head of Civil Justice.**
**(3) The First-tier of the High Court shall have jurisdiction to resolve all civil disputes to a value of £100,000. A dispute with a value greater than £100,000 may be transferred to the First-tier where it is in the interests of the administration of justice to do so.**
**(4) The High Court and Court of Appeal (Civil Division) may deal with proceedings anywhere they consider appropriate.**

*Sources: Senior Courts Act 1981, ss 1, 2, 4, 15(3), 57(1), 62; County Courts Act 1984, ss A1, 33; CPR r 2.7.*

### COMMENTARY

1. There are currently three courts in England and Wales that primarily deal with civil disputes: the County Court, High Court, and Court of Appeal (Civil Division).[2] The division of responsibility between the courts reflects an early commitment to structural proportionality: the County Court, historically, having its own simplified procedural code and a focus on lower value, less complex disputes, while the High Court with a more sophisticated procedural code, focused on higher value, more complex disputes.
2. The structural division between the County and High Courts has been the focus of criticism since the 19th century, not least as its dual structure is said to promote unnecessary complexity, cost, and delay. Their merger was first proposed in 1873.[3]

[1] Order in Council, of 16 December 1880. A Wilson, *Wilson's Supreme Court of Judicature Acts* (Stevens and Sons, 1882) 42–46. The First Report of the Royal Commission to inquire into the Operation and Constitution of the High Court of Chancery, Courts of Common Law, Central Criminal Court, High Court of Admiralty, and other Courts in England, and into the Operation and Effect of the Present Separation and Division of urisdiction between the Courts (No 4130; 1868–1869) at 10. Senior Courts Act 1981, s 7.

[2] Certain civil disputes also fall within the ambit of, eg the Employment Tribunal, Competition Appeal Tribunal, First-tier Tribunal, and Upper Tribunal. Effective reform would see them merge with the civil courts.

[3] The Second Report of the Royal Commission to inquire into the Operation and Constitution of the High Court of Chancery, Courts of Common Law, Central Criminal Court, High Court of Admiralty, and other Courts in England, and into the Operation and Effect of the Present Separation and Division of Jurisdiction between the Courts (C 631; 1872) at 13 and 15.

That did not occur.[4] It was revisited by the Beeching Commission in 1969.[5] It was again considered in 1987,[6] 1988,[7] 2007, and 2008.[8] Each time its merger was either not taken forward or rejected in favour of lesser reforms. Those decisions were taken primarily because merger's benefits were thought to be overstated, that it would pose problems for judicial specialisation,[9] and that systemic improvements could be achieved by reforms short of merger.[10]

3. Increasing digitisation will, however, make the County and High Court's continued dual existence increasingly anachronistic. Interaction with the courts will primarily be through a single digital website or portal. The distinction between two courts lying behind such a website or portal will be lost on all except those working within the courts. More substantively, their merger ought to facilitate ease of deployment of judges, more effective allocation of work, maintaining specialisation where necessary, and furthering the development of judicial skills and experience more generally than is currently the case. It ought to also ensure that resources, and particularly the provision, maintenance, and development of digital technology is properly provided to both courts, so that the County Court is not less-well-resourced in that respect than the High Court; a problem that became readily apparent during the Covid-19 pandemic.[11]
4. The County Court's merger with the High Court is not, however, intended to eliminate the distinction between them entirely. Adopting the model used for the creation of the unified Tribunals in 2007, this rule proposes the creation of a two-tier structure within the new High Court: a First-tier and an Upper Tier, which will, initially at least, correspond to the jurisdictional boundaries between the County Court and High Court. Alteration of those boundaries, in future, will be more straightforward than at present, as it will not be a matter of legislation.[12] This will maintain structural proportionality.
5. Rule 2(2) maintains the High Court Divisions and specialist courts within its new Upper Tier. Consistently with an intention that the High Court's structure should be more reflective of the business needs of the court and capable of revision to meet them, designation of the Divisions and specialist courts should be carried out by the Head of Civil Justice rather than, as at present, Order in Council.[13]
6. Finally, this rule confirms that the High Court and Court of Appeal may deal with proceedings anywhere in England and Wales, eg from a court building or elsewhere.

[4] T Snow, 'The Consolidation of the High Court and the County Courts' (1906) 22 LQR 127.

[5] The Report of the Royal Commission on Assizes and Quarter Sessions (Cmd 4153, 1969) at [250].

[6] J Jacob, *The Fabric of English Civil Justice* (Stevens & Sons, 1987) at 259–260.

[7] Civil Justice Review Body, Civil Justice Review 1988 (Cmd 394, 1988).

[8] H Brooke, *Should the Civil Courts be Unified?* (Judicial Office, 2008).

[9] Civil Justice Review Report (1988) at [104]–[105].

[10] H Brooke (2008) at 2.

[11] N Byrom, S Beardon, and A Kendrick, *The Impact of Covid-19 Measures on the Civil Justice System* (Civil Justice Council, 2020)

[12] The High Court and County Courts Jurisdiction Order 1991 (SI 1991/724); County Courts Act 1984, ss 15–24.

[13] Senior Courts Act 1982, s 7.

## RULE 3.—EXERCISING THE CIVIL COURTS' JURISDICTION

**(1) The jurisdiction of the Court of Appeal (Civil Division) may be exercised by any judge of the Court of Appeal and other persons authorised to exercise its jurisdiction judicially. Appeal hearings shall be heard by a minimum of two judges.**

**(2) The jurisdiction of the High Court may be exercised by any judge of the High Court, any judge of the Court of Appeal, any judge who may sit in the High Court, and any other persons authorised to exercise its jurisdiction judicially. Hearings in the Upper Tier of the High Court may be heard by two judges.**

**(3) Judges who may sit in the High Court may only sit in its Upper Tier if specifically authorised to do so. Authorisations may be made, as relevant, by the president of the Court, High Court Division, or specialist court.**

**(4) Where an individual exercises the jurisdiction of a civil court when**

**(a) they reasonably believed they were authorised to do so, but**

**(b) they were not properly authorised to do so**

**they are deemed to have been so authorised until the time they became aware of the fact that they were not properly authorised.**

*Sources: Senior Courts Act 1981, ss 2(1), 4(1), 9, 19, 54, 89, 91, 100, 102; County Courts Act 1984, s 5; Constitutional Reform Act 2005, ss 7(3), 94AA; Court and Tribunals (Judiciary and Functions of Staff) Act 2018, s 3; CPR rr 2.6, 3.1(3A).*

## COMMENTARY

1. A wide variety of judicial office holders can exercise the civil courts' jurisdiction. These range from the ex officio and ordinary judges of the Court of Appeal and High Court to judicial office holders who are authorised to act as judges of those courts and deputy judges.[14] This rule is intended to be consistent with the current judicial structure. It particularly maintains the ability for Divisional (two-judge) courts[15] to sit in the High Court and the minimum sitting requirement of two-judge courts hearing appeals in the Court of Appeal.[16]

2. There is, however, scope for simplifying the structure of judicial offices. One such approach is a creation of a four-tier judicial structure. This would retain, as at present, both ex officio judges (the Lord Chief Justice, Master of the Rolls, and Heads of Division) and ordinary judges of the Court of Appeal and the High Court. They would form the first and second tier of the judiciary. Tier three would be constituted of a new judicial office, resulting from the merger of all other full-time and part-time salaried judicial offices, including that of Circuit Judge. Tier four would be constituted of all part-time, fee-paid, judicial offices.

3. Judges in tiers one and two would be judges of the Court of Appeal and High Court. Judges in tier three would be judges who could sit in the High Court under rule 3(3). Judges in tier four could be authorised to sit in the Court of Appeal or High Court, according to criteria, such as that presently set out in section 9(1) of the Senior Courts Act 1981. This structure is intended to simplify judicial administration, particularly

[14] Senior Courts Act 1981, ss 2(1), 4(1), 9.

[15] Senior Courts Act 1981, s 54.

[16] Senior Courts Act 1981, s 19(3); CPR r 3.1(3A).

where authorisation to sit in specific courts was concerned. It would also help promote judicial continuity, as provided for in Part 11.

4. Rule 3(4) codifies the common law doctrine of de facto judicial authority.[17] This provides that where an individual exercises judicial authority without the requisite authorisation to do so, but does so in ignorance of that fact, they are deemed to have acted with the proper authority. This protects the administration of justice in situations where, through inadvertence, judicial authorisation has not been properly obtained for technical and similar reasons before an individual sits as a judge. It upholds any decisions made in such circumstances so that they are not nullities, which would otherwise require both the court and parties to expend additional time and expense in rehearing such matters. It does not, however, have any application where an individual either deliberately or knowingly purports to act as a judge when they were not authorised to do so.

## RULE 4.—CIVIL COURT PRECEDENCE

**(1) Judgments and orders of the Court of Appeal bind all civil courts other than the UK Supreme Court.**

**(2) The Court of Appeal is not bound by one of its previous decisions when**

**(a) its previous decision is inconsistent with a latter House of Lords or United Kingdom Supreme Court decision;**

**(b) there are two such conflicting decisions; or**

**(c) it was made in ignorance of a binding decision or it involved demonstrably wrong reasoning.**

**(3) Judgments of the Upper Tier of the High Court bind the First-tier of the High Court and should generally be followed by the Upper Tier. The Upper Tier need not follow one of its own previous decisions when, after full consideration, it concludes the previous decision was wrong.**

## COMMENTARY

1. This rule codifies precedent as it applies to the civil courts of England and Wales.[18] It makes clear that precedence operates between and within courts as courts, and not between different judicial office holders exercising a court's jurisdiction.[19] It also codifies the circumstances when the Court of Appeal and High Court may depart from their previous decisions. Where the Court of Appeal is concerned, it may only do so in three circumstances,[20] each of which is justified by the need to ensure that by departing from a past judgment it can give clarity and certainty to the law. Where the High Court's Upper Tier is concerned, clarity and certainty are secured, consistent with judicial comity within that court, by it generally following its previous decisions. Unlike the Court of Appeal, it is not however bound by its past decisions. It

[17] *Fawdry & Co v Murfitt* [2002] EWCA Civ 643; [2002] 3 WLR 1354; *Coppard v Customs and Excise Commissioners* [2003] EWCA Civ 511; [2003] QB 1428; *Baldock v Webster* [2004] EWCA Civ 1869; [2006] QB 315; *Sumukan Ltd v Commonwealth Secretariat* [2007] EWCA Civ 1148; [2008] 2 All ER (Comm) 175.

[18] R Cross and J Harris, *Precedent in English Law* (Clarendon Press, 1991).

[19] *Coral Reef Ltd v Silverbond* [2016] EWHC 3844 (Ch); [2018] 4 WLR 104 at [55]–[68].

[20] *Young v Bristol Aeroplane Co Ltd* [1944] KB 718; *R (King) v Secretary of State for Justice* [2012] EWCA Civ 376; [2012] 1 WLR 3602.

may depart from one when it concludes that it was wrongly decided. In this way, the High Court is able to correct past judicial error simply, straightforwardly, and proportionately, without the need for the matter to be dealt with on appeal to the Court of Appeal. It thus also helps to conserve the Court of Appeal's resources.

# SECTION 3: ADMINISTRATION

## RULE 5.—COURT ADMINISTRATION

**(1) Court administrative staff are employees of the Court of Appeal and High Court.**
**(2) Court employees may exercise the administrative functions of, and carry out any formal act of, the Court of Appeal (Civil Division) and High Court. Where authorised they may exercise its jurisdiction judicially.**

*Sources: Mount Scopus International Standards of Judicial Independence (2013); Courts Act 2003, ss 1, 3; HMCTS Framework Document (2014); Court and Tribunals (Judiciary and Functions of Staff) Act 2018, s 3.*

## COMMENTARY

1. The civil courts are administered by His Majesty's Courts and Tribunals Service (HMCTS), an arms-length body of the Ministry of Justice. Its staff are civil servants.[21] Since 2014, it has operated as a partnership between the Government and the Judiciary under the HMCTS Framework Agreement. It is a partnership granted by the Government and may be rescinded by it. It is not established, or protected, by statute or any other form of institutional guarantee as to its form or existence.
2. Rather than adopt the current partnership model, this rule adopts a judicial model of court administration.[22] It places responsibility for the management and administration of the courts in the hands of the judiciary. It does so because it more clearly reflects separation of powers and the need to promote institutional judicial independence. It also avoids any lack of clarity over to whom or to what court administrative staff and HMCTS's senior management are ultimately answerable. At present, HMCTS staff owe a statutory duty of loyalty to the Government rather than the courts or judiciary.[23] This would be overcome if they were to be employees of the court, which in turn was administered by the judiciary. A judicial model adopted also avoids the potential for explicit or implicit Government control or influence over the development and implementation of administrative policy concerning the court's operation, thus promoting judicial independence and impartiality.[24]
3. This rule also codifies the current position that court staff are able to exercise the court's administrative functions and, where authorised to do so, its judicial

[21] Courts Act 2003, ss 1, 3.

[22] Mount Scopus International Standards of Judicial Independence (2013) at 2.13.

[23] Constitutional Reform and Governance Act 2010, s 7; The Civil Service Code.

[24] T Bunjevac, *Judicial Self-Governance in the New Millennium* (Springer, 2020); Canadian Justice Council, Alternative Models of Court Administration (2006); Canadian Justice Council, *Comparative Analysis of Key Characteristics of Court Administration Systems* (2011).

functions.[25] The latter has become, and is becoming increasingly important. Since the CPR's introduction legally qualified members of the Court of Appeal's administration have been authorised to carry out certain case management functions.[26] That role has since been extended to legally qualified members of the High Court's administrative court staff.[27] With the increasing move towards procedural digitisation, a broader set of judicial functions can now be carried out by authorised members of the court administration, eg they may also make straightforward case management decisions.[28] This rule gives effect to that development and makes it of general application.

## RULE 6.—COURT SEAL

**(1) All official documents of the court must be sealed by the court.**
**(2) The court seal may be affixed digitally, by facsimile, or by hand.**
**(3) Any document purportedly affixed, either digitally or physically, with the court seal may be produced in evidence without further proof.**

*Sources: Senior Courts Act 1981, s 132; CPR rr 2.6, 40.3(2).*

## COMMENTARY

1. All courts have an official seal, which is affixed to official documents that they issue. Affixing the seal is evidence of the authenticity of the document.[29] It is also evidence of the date and time when the document was issued by the court. This is of importance when determining matters such as: whether proceedings were issued within an applicable limitation period or the applicable time period within which case statements have to be served on parties. Affixing the court seal to documents is also necessary to serve a particulars of claim and to perfect a judgment or order.
2. Traditionally, the seal was affixed physically. Digitisation means that the court seal may now be affixed in a variety of ways, not least digitally.

## RULE 7.—COURT LISTINGS

**(1) Scheduling hearings is a judicial function, which may be undertaken on behalf of the judiciary by the court administration.**
**(2) The civil courts must publish daily lists of scheduled hearings, which must contain the names of the parties, the name of the judge dealing with the hearing, the court, where the dispute is being dealt with, and how the public may attend the hearing.**
**(3) The court may as part of dispute management require the lists to be subject to such restrictions or limitations as required by exceptions to the publicity principle.**

*Sources: Department of Constitutional Affairs, Constitutional Reform—The Lord Chancellor's judiciary-related functions: Proposals (January 2004) (The Concordat), para 36; Constitutional Reform Act 2005, s 7(1); CPR Practice Direction 51Y; Courts Act 2003, s 85A.*

[25] CPR r 2.5; Lord Chief Justice's Authorisation of court staff to exercise judicial functions and Delegation of Authorisation of Function Orders Nos 1, 2, and 3 (2020).
[26] CPR r 52.24.
[27] CPR r 54.1A.
[28] CPR r 2.4A.
[29] Senior Courts Act 1981, s 132.

## COMMENTARY

1. The ability to control when and how proceedings are scheduled for hearing directly relates to the ability of parties to gain access to the court. It can therefore only properly be exercised by, or on behalf, of the court acting judicially. If it were, for instance, an executive function, it would place control of the judicial process in the hands of the Government contrary to the principle of judicial independence. This rule codifies the current approach to listing. It thus specifies that it is a judicial function. Additional to the power set out here, the Lord Chief Justice as President of the civil courts retains an inherent jurisdiction over the listing of civil proceedings.[30]
2. To ensure that parties and witnesses are aware when hearings are taking place and that the public and media are able to scrutinise them effectively, hearing lists must contain a minimum amount of information to enable the proceedings, and parties, to be identifiable. They must also be issued on a daily basis. In this way listing furthers the due notice and publicity principles. Identifiability and publicity are also a means by which potential witnesses or potential additional parties may become aware of, and potentially take part in, proceedings.[31] Hence, list publication also support the accuracy and finality principles.
3. To enable members of the public and media to attend hearings, where hearings are non-physical, published lists must also contain sufficient information to enable attendance through whichever non-physical medium is being used. The ability to attend physical and non-physical hearings must be comparable.

## RULE 8.—COURT RECORDS

**(1) All court records shall be kept by the court administration on behalf of the court for a period of six years after the conclusion of proceedings (the retention period). At the end of the retention period, the record, unless the court directs otherwise, shall either be transferred to the National Archives or destroyed.**

**(2) The court record includes: all documents and information, including evidence and exhibits, provided to the court by the parties; all documents and information, including judgments and orders, relating to proceedings generated by the court and its administration; any recording or transcript of proceedings; and, any other document directed by the court to form part of the record.**

**(3) Documents and information provided to the court solely for the purposes of settlement do not form part of the court record.**

**(4) The court record does not include administrative management information. Administrative Management information may include party and witness personal information.**

**(5) The civil court administration shall make available to the Civil Dispute Resolution Council, in anonymised form, administrative management information and information derived from court records to enable it to monitor and secure civil court accessibility and to give effect to the digital procedure principle. Such information shall also be published annually.**

[30] *R (McKenzie) v Leeds Crown Court* [2020] EWHC 1867 (Admin).

[31] *R v Socialist Worker, ex p Attorney-General* [1975] QB 637 at 652.

**(6) Access to the court record shall be provided by the court to a party or non-party on request. Access may be provided in court buildings or by any other appropriate method, including digital access or the provision of a paper copy of the record requested. Access to a non-party may be subject to payment of a fee.**

**(7) Where a request concerns access to an audio or video-recording of a hearing, the court may also direct that recordings be made available online for a specified period. Access may also be provided via a written transcript of the recording.**

**(8) Where access is provided in one form, a request for further access in an alternative form may only be granted in exceptional circumstances.**

**(9) Access to the court record or any part of it may be limited or made subject to such conditions, including derogation from the publicity principle, necessary to promote the proportionality principle and to protect**

**(a) confidential or privileged communications between parties and their lawyers; or**

**(b) the proper administration of justice or other legitimate interests.**

**(10) Conditions on access may include anonymisation, redaction, or the restriction of access to lawyers.**

*Sources: ALI/UNIDROIT Principles, principle 20.1; ALI/UNIDROIT Reporters' Study, r 23.1; ELI-UNIDROIT Model Rules, r 17; Freedom of Information Act 2000, s 32; CPR Pt 5, r 39.9; Practice Guidance (Court Proceedings: Live Text-Based Communications) (No 2) [2012] 1 WLR 12; Practice Direction (Audio Recordings: Access) [2014] 1 WLR 632; Law Commission of New Zealand, Access to Court Records (2006).*

## COMMENTARY

1. Access to court records is required by the publicity principle. The power to secure it arises under the inherent jurisdiction.[32] It is the means by which the public and media may gain a proper understanding of what goes on in the courts, what disputes are litigated, by whom they are brought and defended, and how they are determined. It is one of the means through which judicial accountability is secured. Access to such records is also the means by which parties to potential litigation may obtain information that could be relevant to their own claims.

2. To ensure that records, which will in future be predominately digital in nature, are preserved for a reasonable period of time, they shall be kept by the court administration for six years after the conclusion of proceedings. This ought to provide sufficient time for them to be accessed for reasons of public scrutiny. It should also provide sufficient time for parties to proceedings, and non-parties, to obtain access to the court record for reasons related to the initial proceedings. Such a time period should be sufficient, for instance, for parties to obtain information to enable them to apply to reopen the proceedings. It should equally be long enough to enable a non-party to obtain documents or information from the record that are relevant to proceedings or potential proceedings in which they have an interest. At the expiry of the retention period, unless the court directs otherwise, the record shall either be transferred to The National Archives[33] or destroyed.

[32] *Cape v Dring* [2019] UKSC 38; [2019] 3 WLR 429 at [41].

[33] Public Records Act 1958, s 8.

3. The court record is neither defined definitively in the CPR, at common law or in statute.[34] Rule 8(2) is intended, in the interest of simplicity and accessibility, to provide a compendious, definitive explanation of what is meant by the court record. It covers all documents and information relevant to specific proceedings whether submitted by the parties to the court or created by the court. It thus covers the following documents and information: formal documents for commencing proceedings, including appeal proceedings, documents in response, all other case statements, and application notices, including any relevant number allocated to identify the proceedings by the digital dispute management systems; exhibits to case statements and any documentary evidence, including witness evidence and experts' reports, provided to the court; parties' skeleton arguments and written submissions; judgments and court orders. Additionally, any further document or information may also form part of the court record if directed by the court on a case-by-case basis.
4. The various documents and information referred to in rule 8(2) come within the definition of court record because it is both necessary and desirable to retain them further to the publicity principle. Their retention is also necessary, to promote adjudicative accuracy, eg they promote the private interest in corrective justice where they are available for appeals, applications to reopen proceedings, or where non-parties require access to them because they are relevant to other proceedings or potential proceedings.
5. The court record does not, however, encompass two significant types of information. It does not include information concerning settlement processes. They are inherently private and do not fall under the publicity principle. It also does not include administrative management information. This is information created by the civil court administration or the civil courts for internal management purposes. This could include: judges' and court administrators' personal details, including remuneration, pension arrangements, health data, and travel arrangements to and from court for judges and court employees; and, operational information concerning the civil courts, including the digital management system. This information does not form part of the court record as public access to it does not concern individual proceedings. Public availability is not therefore necessary for the purposes of the publicity principle or the administration of justice in individual cases.
6. This is not to say that publication of administrative management information is neither important nor desirable in the public interest. Whether or not the court administration is efficient and capable of securing the timely and effective delivery of justice to all litigants is of significant public importance. Rule 8(5) facilitates the scrutiny of such information, in anonymised form, by the Civil Dispute Resolution Council. It also provides for it to be published annually again in anonymised form in so far as necessary, thus enabling civil society and the Government to scrutinise court administration.[35] In this way it can be assessed to ascertain if the courts are operating

[34] *Cape v Dring* [2019] UKSC 38; [2019] 3 WLR 429 at [19]; *R v Northumberland Compensation Appeal Tribunal ex p Shaw* [1952] KB 338, 351–352; *A-G v Leveller Magazine Ltd* [1979] AC 440 at 450; CPR r 39.9; *Practice Direction (Audio Recordings: Access)* [2014] 1 WLR 632; Freedom of Information Act 2000, s 32; *Mitchell v Information Commissioner* (IT, 10 October 2005) at [21]; *Peninsular Business Services Ltd v Information Commissioner & Ministry of Justice* [2014] UKUT 0284 (AAC) at [46]–[32]; *Edem v Information Commissioner & Ministry of Justice* [2015] UKUT 0210 (AAC) at [21]; *Brown v Information Commissioner & Ministry of Justice* [2016] UKUT 0255 (ACC) at [25] and [37].

[35] N Byrom, *Digital Justice: HMCTS data strategy and delivering access to justice—Report and recommendations* (Legal Education Foundation, 2019).

effectively or, if not, what reform is needed. Access to anonymised information shall also be made available to give effect to the three digital procedure principles.

7. As case statements, application notices etc, evidence, judgments, and orders form part of the court record, party, witness, and lawyers' information (name, address, profession) will also form part of the public record. Given the risk of misuse of this information where it is made available in a digital form, the court must consider whether any restriction on access should be imposed consistently with the publicity principle. This is not to suggest, in any way, that party, witness, or lawyers' names should be anonymised routinely. They should not: exercise of the judicial power of the State for and over legal and natural persons is and must generally be a matter of publicly available record. Public access to such information is a fundamental aspect of the delivery of open justice in England and Wales.

8. Rules 8(6) to (9) govern party and public access to the court record and, particularly, to audio and video-recordings of hearings. Rule 8(6) provides a wider right of access to recordings of hearings than is provided for under the CPR. The CPR provides a general right of access to written transcripts of proceedings (subject to a non-party paying a fee to reflect the cost of transcription),[36] but rejects a right to receive a copy of an audio or video recording.[37] Rule 8(6) provides a right of access for parties and non-parties to recordings in any format, on request. This is subject to a formal limitation, set out in rule 8(7): that the right of access is, generally, exhausted through the provision of one form of access. Access via multiple various mediums is not required by the publicity principle, which is satisfied by access in a single format. Multiple access is also generally disproportionate given the time and expense the court administration would be put to in dealing with such requests.

9. The right of access provided by rule 8(6) is primarily intended to enhance public scrutiny of hearings, and hence democratic accountability of the civil justice system. It also reflects the fact that a hearing is a public event and that—unless a derogation from the publicity principle applies—what occurs at a hearing is within the '*public domain*'.[38] As such there is no principled reason why access to a record of such public events ought not to be accessible by a participant in the event or the public generally. Again, a fee may properly be required from a member of the public to reflect the cost of providing such accessibility.

10. Any potential harm arising from access to a recording can properly be mitigated through the application of rule 8(9). This requires the court to consider, when dealing with an access request, whether it should either be refused or subject to conditions or limitations that either protect confidentiality, legal professional privilege, or the proper administration of justice.[39] The former two criteria are particularly concerned to ensure that any conversations between parties and their lawyers that have been inadvertently recorded by the court before, during, or after a hearing are not made available further to an access request. Breach of any such confidences or privilege would undermine confidence in the courts. The last criterion is linked to the publicity principle. It requires the court to consider the various legitimate interests that justify the imposition of a derogation from the publicity principle, eg national

[36] *Cape v Dring* [2019] UKSC 38; [2019] 3 WLR 429 at [47]; CPR r 5.4D.

[37] CPR r 39.9(2); *Practice Direction (Audio Recordings: Access)* [2014] 1 WLR 632 at 2.

[38] *Home Office v Harman* [1983] 1 AC 280 at 312.

[39] *Practice Direction (Audio Recordings: Access)* [2014] 1 WLR 632.

security, the interests of children, commercial confidentiality, as well as the effect access may have on the proper administration of justice.[40]

11. Access must also be proportionate so as not to impose too great a burden on the court administration. Where digital records on their own are concerned it will be difficult for access to be limited or denied on proportionality grounds.

[40] *Cape v Dring* [2019] UKSC 38; [2019] 3 WLR 429 at [45]–[47].

# PART 3
# COSTS

## SECTION 1: GENERAL

1. This Part concerns the cost of dispute resolution, specifically the approach taken to enable successful parties to recover the costs they incurred in proceedings.[1]
2. It is no understatement to describe the approach to costs under the CPR as disastrous; they are its '*biggest failure*'.[2] The current level of complexity in costs law is such that a leading authority suggests that it cannot '*be assumed that even diligent advocates will always be able to unearth all the relevant authorities*' or that district judges, who are generally responsible for carrying out costs assessments, will '*have the time to keep abreast of all developments*'.[3] This situation undermines the legitimacy of the courts.[4] Moreover, procedural complexity and particularly the use of adverse costs awards as a means to promote rule compliance[5] have also, perversely, led to increasing levels of costs, not least as both have resulted in unpredictability and large-scale satellite litigation about costs.
3. Further problems, and with them further increases in cost levels, have since the CPR's introduction also been caused by disputes over litigation funding arrangements as well as the introduction of costs budgeting and management.[6] The position reached is that, unlike any other jurisdiction, civil costs in England and Wales, as Zuckerman has very rightly put it, generates a level and amount of litigation cost that is without parallel.[7] It also unquestionably embeds disproportionate delay and inefficiency into the civil justice system as its resources are expended not on substantive disputes but rather on such disputes over litigation cost. That position is unsustainable. It is an insult to genuine access to justice and to a fair process.
4. It has been suggested that these problems are endemic; that devising a simple and fair approach to costs recovery is not possible, notwithstanding the fact that very many other countries do so.[8] The rules in this Part are intended to provide a fairer, simpler approach to costs recovery; one that controls costs so that they do not operate as a fetter

[1] M Friston (ed), *Friston on Costs* (OUP, 2023); S Middleton and J Rowley, *Cook on Costs* (LexisNexis Butterworths, 2023).

[2] N Andrews, *Andrews on Civil Processes* (Intersentia, 2019) at 523; M Friston (ed) (2023) chap 1.

[3] As rightly noted in M Friston, *Friston on Costs* (OUP, 2018) at viii.

[4] L Fuller, *The Morality of Law* (Yale, 1969) at 63; T Bingham, *The Rule of Law* (Penguin, 2010) at 37.

[5] A Zuckerman, *Zuckerman on Civil Procedure—Principles of Practice* (Sweet & Maxwell, 2021) at 1416.

[6] R Jackson, *Review of Civil Litigation Costs: Preliminary Report* (May 2009) Vol I, chap 3; S Clark and R Jackson, *The Reform of Civil Justice* (Sweet & Maxwell, 2018) at 8–9.

[7] A Zuckerman (2021) at 1413.

[8] *Lawrence v Fen Tigers Ltd (No 3)* [2015] UKSC 50; [2015] 1 WLR 3485 at [72]; compare with H Woolf, *Access to Justice: Interim Report to the Lord Chancellor on the Civil Justice System in England and Wales* (HMSO) (1995) at 11.

*A Model Civil Procedure Code for England and Wales*. John Sorabji, Oxford University Press. 
DOI: 10.1093/oso/9780192848680.003.0004

on effective access.[9] They do so by drawing on the approach taken in Germany, eg the application of set tariff costs. While this approach was considered and rejected by the Woolf Reforms,[10] it is not unknown historically to English and Welsh procedure.[11] It is also one that is akin to recent developments concerning fixed recoverable costs.[12] It can therefore be said to build upon that approach.[13] Through the general application of fixed tariff cost recovery, the adoption of a test for cost proportionality for disputes that fall outside the tariff scheme, and a more straightforward use of cost orders as a means to promote rule compliance, the rules in this Part seek to provide greater certainty concerning litigation costs while removing the scope for litigation about and concerning costs. Taken together with the rules on litigation funding in Part 4, they are intended to produce a scheme that secures effective access to justice for all litigants without producing disproportionate, time-consuming, and expensive satellite litigation.

5. This Part and that on funding are deliberately placed at the beginning of this Code. This is for one fundamental reason: access to funding lies at the heart of effective access to justice, no matter which dispute resolution method is to be used. Underpinning effective funding mechanisms lies an effective and predictable costs regime.[14] Hence cost and funding must be set out together and should, given their importance, be at the forefront of any Code governing dispute resolution. Their place here in and in Part 4 is intended to emphasise this and their centrality to the achievement of both the purposive and general access principles.

## RULE 1.—SCOPE AND PURPOSE

**(1) This Part concerns the allocation and recovery of costs incurred during pre-action and post-issue proceedings.**

**(2) The common law indemnity principle is abolished. Recoverable costs include**

**(a) court fees;**

**(b) costs provided for in this Part;**

**(c) expenses, charges, or disbursements incurred by or on behalf of a party, which includes the remuneration of lawyers; and**

**(d) any increase on costs permitted under this Code.**

**(3) The purpose of costs recovery is the promotion of access to justice through reimbursing such costs incurred by parties who bring or defend claims successfully as permitted under this Part. Costs recovery is also intended to promote compliance with procedural obligations and procedural equality; the latter through ensuring that the incidence of costs does not act as a fetter on access to justice.**

*Sources: ALI/UNIDROIT Principles, principle 25; ELI-UNIDROIT Model Rules, r 5, Part XII, esp r 241; Solicitors Act 1974, s 87(1); Senior Courts Act 1981, s 51(2); CPR r 44.1.*

[9] B Garth and M Cappelletti, 'Access to Justice: The Newest Wave in the Worldwide Movement to Make Rights Effective' (1978) 27 Buff L Rev at 186–188

[10] H Woolf, *Access to Justice: Final Report to the Lord Chancellor on the Civil Justice System in England and Wales* (HMSO) (1996) at 81–82.

[11] Rule 8.

[12] Civil Procedure (Amendment No 2) Rules 2023 (SI 2023/572).

[13] R Jackson, *Review of Civil Litigation Costs: Final Report* (December 2009) at 172; R Jackson, *Review of Civil Litigation Costs: Supplemental Report Fixed Recoverable Costs* (Judicial Office, July 2017); Ministry of Justice, *Extending Fixed Recoverable Costs in Civil Cases—The Government's Response* (September 2021).

[14] W van Boom, 'Litigation Costs and third-party funding' in W van Boom, *Litigation, Costs, Funding and Behaviour* (Routledge, 2017) at 7–9.

## COMMENTARY

1. This rule specifies that this Part applies to the recovery of costs between parties, whether they are incurred before or after proceedings are issued.[15] It does not apply to costs or expenses incurred between a lawyer and their client.[16]
2. By providing for cost recovery, the rule maintains what is variously known as the 'loser pays principle', 'the English rule', or 'European rule',[17] in contrast to the American no-cost-shifting rule. It thus maintains the principle that the successful party in proceedings can recover from the losing party, or a non-party, a sum of money to compensate them for the money they have expended in pursuing their claim or defence successfully. This approach is more apt to promote several procedural principles than a no-cost-shifting rule.
3. Primarily, it helps incentivise meritorious disputes to be litigated, while deterring the unmeritorious. It thus promotes the general access principle.[18] It also helps promote settlement as parties may, having assessed the merits of their respective cases, consider settlement in the light of their potential cost liability if their claim or defence were to fail.[19] Both of these issues help to promote economy, efficiency, and proportionality by reducing the number of disputes that are issued and/or proceed to judgment.[20] It thus promotes effective rationing and allocation of the resources provided by the state for dispute resolution to those who need to call upon them.[21]
4. Cost-shifting also promotes the purposive principle as it helps promote costs discipline on parties.[22] It does this through cost recovery being subject to defined limits, eg the recovery of tariff and proportionate costs. These limits are intended to focus parties' minds on the real issues in dispute, on what evidence etc is necessary to resolve them, and on those steps that promote effective dispute management and compliance with procedural obligations. They do so because parties know from the outset of litigation what their likely cost recovery will be. Hence, they are provided a clear incentive to conduct proceedings effectively and proportionately. By guiding party behaviour in this way, it ought to also reduce the amount of the court's time and resources each dispute utilises: incentivising effective dispute management and party proportionality ought to promote the wider public interest in systemic proportionality.[23]
5. Cost recovery is also intended to give effect to a fundamental principle of fairness, ie the principle of compensation. Parties to disputes ought not to be unreasonably out-of-pocket for advancing or defending their rights successfully. That, however, must itself be balanced by a need to ensure that a losing party is not also unreasonably out-of-pocket for reasonably advancing their claim or defence. Hence this Part seeks to strike a balance between these two aspects of procedural fairness. It

[15] Rule 5.
[16] Solicitors Act 1974, Part III; M Friston (ed) (2023) chap 35.
[17] ELI-UNIDROIT Model Rules, r 241.
[18] H Woolf (1995) at 9; B Garth and M Cappelletti (1978) at 186–188.
[19] *R v Lord Chancellor, ex p Child Poverty Action Group* [1998] 2 All ER 755 at 764.
[20] Part 1, rr 5, 11, 12, 16.
[21] F Wilmot-Smith, 'Just Costs', in R Assay and A Higgins, *Principles, Procedure, and Justice: Essays in Honour of Adrian Zuckerman* (OUP, 2020) at 229ff; A Zuckerman (2021) at 1432–1433.
[22] ELI-UNIDROIT Model Rules, r 5 commentary.
[23] R. Jackson (December 2009) at 35–36.

does so through, as Jackson put it in a related context, by seeking to strike a balance between compensation for the winning party, on the one hand, with proportionality on the other hand; the latter being the means to afford a losing party a degree of fairness.[24]

6. While it gives effect to cost recovery, this rule marks a significant departure from the common law position in England and Wales. It does so by abolishing the indemnity principle, as permitted by section 51(2) of the Senior Courts Act 1981. That principle had two elements: that the losing party in litigation had to reimburse the successful party for the costs they had incurred in conducting the litigation in respect of which they had a legal liability to pay; and, following from that, that costs recovery was neither punitive nor intended to permit the successful party to secure a profit.[25] The principle has been successively reduced in its application since the introduction of various forms of contingency fee agreements,[26] fixed fee recoverability in the CPR,[27] and the statutory power to award pro bono costs.[28] Its complete abrogation has, however, been resisted notwithstanding objections to its continued existence. The most important of those objections is that by maintaining it the development of contingency fee agreements has been retarded. It has also, just as problematically, formed the basis of a wealth of satellite litigation over the enforceability of conditional fee agreements in attempts to avoid cost recovery.[29] In both cases the principle promotes unnecessary complexity and technicality in procedure that is itself a further source of additional satellite costs litigation. As Sime and French put it, '... *it is inevitable that as the indemnity principle remains part of costs law, satellite litigation over costs will remain*'.[30] It may not be the only cause of such satellite litigation, but it is an important element underpinning it.
7. Rule 1(2) abolishes the indemnity rule for several related reasons. The centrepiece of this Part is the introduction of a general tariff costs regime. As this is a form of fixed cost recoverability scheme, it builds on and generalises the existing exception to the indemnity rule provided in CPR Pt 45. By generalising fixed costs, tariff costs render the indemnity principle otiose.
8. Where tariff costs do not apply, cost recovery is required to be proportionate. In assessing such costs, rule 1(2)(c) provides a definition of recoverable items of cost.[31]

[24] *R v Lord Chancellor, ex p Child Poverty Action Group* [1998] 2 All ER 755 at 764; R. Jackson (December 2009) at 35–36.

[25] *Harold v Smith* [1860] 5 H & N 381; *General of Berne Insurance Co v Jardine Reinsurance Ltd* [1998] 1 WLR 1231 at 1234.

[26] Courts and Legal Services Act 1990, ss 58, 58A; S Sime and D French, *Blackstone's Guide to the Civil Justice Reform 2013* (OUP, 2013) at 137–141.

[27] CPR r 45; *Nizami v Butt* [2006] EWHC 159 (QB); [2006] 1 WLR 3307; *Kilby v Gawith* [2008] EWCA Civ 812; [2009] 1 WLR 853.

[28] Legal Services Act 2007, s 197.

[29] R Jackson (December 2009) at 53–58; Civil Justice Council, *The Damages-based Agreements Reform Project—Drafting and Policy Issues* (August 2015) at 85–92; *Malone v Birmingham Community NHS Trust* [2018] EWCA Civ 376; [2018] 3 Costs LR 627; *The Winros Partnership v Global Energy Horizons Corporation* [2021] EWHC 3410 (Ch); *Zuberi v Lexlaw Ltd* [2021] EWCA Civ 16; [2021] 1 WLR 2729; *PACCAR Inc v Road Haulage Association Ltd* [2021] EWCA Civ 299; [2021] WLR 3648, and *R (PACCAR Inc) v Competition Appeal Tribunal* [2023] UKSC 28; [2023] 1 WLR 2594.

[30] S Sime and D French (2013) at 140.

[31] Solicitors Act 1974, s 87(1); CPR r 44.1; Litigants in Person (Costs and Expenses) Act 1975; CPR r 46.5. 'Lawyerless party' is chosen here to make clear the party is not in receipt of legal advice or representation from a lawyer. Other, established, terms lack clarity and can lead to confusion: *Practice Note: Terminology for Litigants- in- Person* (11 March 2013).

It thus provides the legal basis for their recoverability, notwithstanding the abolition of the indemnity principle. And it does so on a sure footing. It is thus intended to promote greater certainty and predictability in costs recoverability, while also eliminating a potential source of litigation about costs. Greater certainty and predictability are particularly important in respect of both tariff and proportionate cost recovery, as it essential for the development of effective litigation funding mechanisms, not least legal expenses insurance, as that is developed in Part 4.

9. Finally, by clarifying that costs may be used to promote compliance with procedural obligations, and deter non-compliance, rule 1(2)(d) clarifies that costs may be used punitively rather than simply as a means to compensate a party for the expense they have been put to for seeking to vindicate their rights.

## RULE 2.—THE COSTS AND FUNDING COUNCIL

**(1) The Costs and Funding Council shall be responsible for keeping the costs of dispute resolution under review, setting tariff costs, issuing guidance on the reasonable range of proportionate costs, and setting the financial thresholds for adjudication track classification. It shall also be responsible for reviewing the operation of funding arrangements and making recommendations to reform their nature, regulation, and availability.**

**(2) In carrying out its functions, the Council shall have regard to economic data, including data on the costs of disputes that settle and those which are determined by judgment. Data on settlement shall be made available through the digital procedure.**

*Sources: Woolf—Final Report, chap 4; Jackson Costs Review—Final Report, chap 6.*

## COMMENTARY

1. The creation of a Costs Council was first recommended in the Final Woolf Report. It was to evaluate the CPR's operation continuously, review annually the level at which fixed recoverable costs were set,[32] and review the whole costs regime triennially.[33] It was to carry out its evaluation through the collection of data from costs recovered on the CPR's fast track. The creation of such a Council was again recommended by the Civil Justice Council in 2005[34] and by the Jackson Costs Review.[35] The recommendations were never implemented.

2. In 2014, a Costs Subcommittee of the Civil Justice Council was, however, established. Its focus was not fixed recoverable costs. It provided advice on the level at which the Guideline Hourly Rates for the Summary Assessment of Costs (GHRs) should be set. Having reported, it fell into abeyance before it was re-established in 2021 to carry out the same task.[36]

[32] Fixed recoverable costs are those costs recoverable by a successful party in litigation from the losing party, where the level of recoverability is set in advance by statutory instrument or within the rules of court.

[33] Civil Justice Council, *Costs Review—Final Report* (May 2023) at 19.

[34] Civil Justice Council, *Improved Access to Justice—Funding Options and Proportionate Costs* (2005) at 63–64.

[35] R Jackson (December 2009) chap 6.

[36] Civil Justice Council, *Guideline Hourly Rates Working Group Report for Consultation* (January 2021) at 2–14.

3. This rule gives effect to those various recommendations and builds on the creation of the Civil Justice Council's costs subcommittee. It does so for the same reasons that those recommendations were made, ie to provide an effective, structured means to implement and maintain effective control of dispute resolution costs consistent with the purposes that underpin costs recovery.[37] Its establishment is particularly necessary to ensure that the approach taken to costs is kept under continuous, expert scrutiny and review; that the tariff costs regime introduced in rule 8 of this Part is effective and kept up to date; that guidance on proportionate costs (the successor in this Code to the GHRs) is maintained effectively; and that the level at which the financial thresholds for adjudication track classification (the successor in this Code to the CPR's procedural case tracks) is appropriate. Where necessary such scrutiny and review should result in reform to ensure both costs and funding secure their aims.
4. The Council is not, however, simply a Costs Council. Given the symbiotic relationship that exists between costs and funding it should also be responsible for the oversight of dispute resolution funding; hence it is a Costs and Funding Council. This dual role is particularly important as it ensures that the review of both costs and funding is carried out in an integrated and consistent manner; its twin focus is one aspect of the necessary, effective, co-ordination of the civil justice system's governance. To ensure the Council is properly integrated into that overall governance structure, it should be a subcommittee of the Civil Dispute Resolution Council.
5. So that the Costs and Funding Council is able to carry out its responsibilities effectively, it will need to draw on a range of expertise. Its membership will need, for instance, to include economists, insurers, members of the legal profession, consumer representatives, and members of the judiciary and government. To carry out its functions effectively it will also need to draw upon a range of evidence, not least evidence drawn from the digital procedure consistently with the digital procedure and accountability and digital integration principles. Drawing evidence from the digital procedure will enable the Council particularly to review the cost of pre-action settlement as well as post-issue settlement, adjudication, and enforcement. Further evidence could be drawn from external sources.[38] Such a breadth of evidence will enable the Council to take an overarching view of the operation of the costs regime and enable it to recommend necessary and properly evidence-based reforms.

## SECTION 2: CONTROL AND RECOVERY OF COSTS

### RULE 3.—DUTY TO PROMOTE PROPORTIONATE COST

**(1) Parties must co-operate with each other and the court to ensure, in so far as practicable, that their pre-action and post-issue expenditure is proportionate to the nature, complexity, amount in dispute, importance of the dispute, and any wider private or public interests.**

**(2) The court must actively manage proceedings to promote proportionate expenditure by parties.**

*Sources: ELI-UNIDROIT Model Rules, rr 5, 6 and 8; CPR rr 1.1(2)(b) and (c), 1.2–1.4, Pt 3, sections II and III, Pt 46, section VI.*

[37] R Jackson (December 2019) chap 6; Civil Justice Council (2005) at 63.

[38] Civil Justice Council, *Guideline Hourly Rates—Final Report* (April 2021).

## COMMENTARY

1. This rule is a specific application of the dispute management and co-operation principles. It is also a means to promote compliance with the proportionality principle. It specifies that the primary responsibility for ensuring disputes are resolved at proportionate cost lies with the parties. It does so by reference to the key criteria for determining proportionality. These criteria go beyond the value of the claim for relief: a narrow focus on value would improperly restrict access to justice for individuals with low value claims by rendering them economically unviable if recovery were strictly limited to a cost-benefit analysis focused on claim value.[39] The criteria include the requirement that parties consider wider private or public interests in approaching proportionality. Such wider interests may be that the specific dispute could led to the resolution of further disputes in which parties are involved. They also include consideration of systemic proportionality.
2. The court's role under rule 3(2) is facilitative. Through active dispute management it should provide parties with guidance on steps to be taken to ensure costs remain proportionate. This could include requiring parties to formulate a dispute management plan in cases where, due to the nature and complexity of the dispute, one would assist its effective management. Active management does not, however, include costs budgeting as is the case under CPR Pt 3. Its benefits, eg cost predictability, greater party understanding of their and their opponent's costs, and control over them,[40] can be better achieved through tariff costs, guidelines on proportionate costs, focused dispute management in specific proceedings, and the effective application of the test for the assessment of proportionate costs.[41] The particular use of tariff costs and recovery of proportionate costs ought generally to provide an effective means to guide parties to take steps to control their own costs, while understanding their potential exposure to adverse cost awards. They provide the key, with active court management, to effective prospective cost control rendering generic costs budgeting otiose. Moreover, by not adopting cost budgeting, this Part also removes unnecessary complexity, an avenue for satellite litigation over costs, and one element of the frontloading of litigation costs.
3. Active court management may also include the imposition of cost capping, ie an order that the recovery of costs be subject to a specified upper limit in those cases where tariff costs are not applicable. While such orders would generally be expected to be unnecessary given effective party co-operation, court management, and the application of proportionate costs, their availability and use may be required, and justified, in judicial review proceedings.[42]

[39] ELI-UNIDROIT Model Rules, r 8.

[40] S Clark and R Jackson (2018) at 155–161; M Friston (ed) (2023) at 384–388.

[41] To the contrary see, Civil Justice Council (2023) at 2–16.

[42] Criminal Justice and Courts Act 2015, ss 88–90.

## RULE 4.—PARTIES' POWER TO AGREE OR SEEK COSTS

**(1) Parties may agree the allocation, amount, and recovery of costs. They may do so in respect of the whole or part of the proceedings. They may do so where they reach a consensual settlement of the dispute and where it is concluded by a court judgment.**
**(2) Where, and in so far as the parties reach agreement on costs, the court will generally give effect to that agreement.**
**(3) Where parties do not agree the allocation, amount, or recovery of costs, they may apply to the court to recover costs.**

*Sources: ELI-UNIDROIT Model Rules, r 239.*

## COMMENTARY

1. Rule 4 is a specific application of the party autonomy principle.[43] As a matter of principle and authority costs agreements form part of English and Welsh civil procedure,[44] as it understands litigation to be a matter of the private interest of the parties, albeit one subject to the wider public interest of ensuring access to justice.[45] Settlement of costs, as a private interest of the parties, is as much a matter for them as is the ability to settle the substantive dispute.
2. The rule is drafted to emphasise that the primary responsibility for determining cost recoverability between the parties to proceedings lies with them. They are expected, consistently with the co-operation principle, to work together collaboratively to seek agreement on cost recovery and should be guided in their approach by the economy, efficiency, and proportionality principles.
3. While the parties may have primary responsibility, the rule acknowledges that any agreement they reach is subject to the court's overriding statutory discretion to determine costs.[46] Where parties have, however, reached an agreement on costs, the court would and should ordinarily give effect to such an agreement, not least because doing so furthers the proportionality principle.[47]

## RULE 5.—THE COURT'S POWER TO DETERMINE COSTS

**(1) The court has a general power to determine and award the costs of or incidental to pre-action and post-issue proceedings. Costs may be awarded prospectively or retrospectively. They may be awarded in favour of or against any party or non-party.**
**(2) The general power is subject to any restriction or exemption set out in this Part or in legislation.**
**(3) Costs of pre-action proceedings are those costs incurred by a party following the commencement of Pre-Action Dispute Resolution and Post-Issue Dispute Management in Part 5.**

[43] ELI-UNIDROIT Model Rules, r 329.
[44] *Mansfield v Robinson* [1928] 2 KB 353 at 359; *Gomba Holdings (UK) Ltd v Minories Finance Ltd (No 2)* [1993] Ch 171 at 193.
[45] J Jacob, *The Fabric of English Civil Justice* (Stevens & Sons, 1987) at 8; M Damaska, *The Faces of Justice and State Authority* (Yale, 1986) at 104.
[46] Senior Courts Act 1981, s 51.
[47] *Gomba Holdings (UK) Ltd v Minories Finance Ltd (No 2)* [1993] Ch 171 at 194 citing *Seavision Investment SA v Evennett* [1992] 2 Lloyd's Rep 26; *BCCI SA v Ali (Assessment of Costs)* [2000] 2 Costs LR 243.

**(4) Whether costs are incidental to pre-action and post-issue proceedings is a question of fact to be determined by the court.**

*Sources: Senior Courts Act 1981, s 51(1)–(3).*

## COMMENTARY

1. The civil courts have had a single, consolidated basis for the power to award costs since 1990, when section 51 of the Senior Courts Act 1981 was amended by section 4(1) of the Courts and Legal Services Act 1990.[48] There is no principled basis to depart from that approach. It is a power that overrides the parties' ability to agree costs.
2. The power to make costs awards includes the power to make protective costs orders, which includes the power to make cost capping orders. While the CPR draws a distinction between them,[49] the former making provision for costs in advance of their being incurred, the latter prescribing the maximum amount of recoverable costs, there is no real basis on which to treat the two differently. As both involve the court determining costs prospectively no distinction is drawn between them in this rule. Given the more general application of tariff costs in this Code than available under the CPR, it is unlikely that the use of either prospective costs orders or cost capping orders will be necessary other than exceptionally. The power also includes the jurisdiction to make wasted costs orders under Part 11.
3. While the statutory power is unfettered and enables costs awards to be made for or against any party or non-party,[50] it may be subject to restrictions set out in rules of court and, more generally, legislation.[51] That approach is restated in rule 5(2). There is, as the Supreme Court affirmed in *Competition and Markets Authority v Flynn Pharma Ltd* (2022), no general presumption that costs orders should not be made against public authorities.[52] Such a general rule would undermine the disciplinary effect on party behaviour that the potential of adverse costs award would otherwise have.
4. Rule 5 departs, however, from the current statutory position in two significant ways. First, the power to award costs under the Senior Courts Act 1981 depends on the commencement of proceedings, ie a claim having been issued.[53] Under this Code, the power to award costs arises where a party commences use of the Pre-Action Dispute Resolution and Post-Issue Dispute Management phases of pre-action dispute management in Part 5 of this Code. Secondly, this change requires a further broadening out of the current position that provides the power to award costs of or incidental to litigation.[54] Thus this rule provides the power to award the costs of and incidental to dispute resolution under that part of this Code.

[48] Civil Justice Review Body, Civil Justice Review 1988 (Cmd 394, 1988) at [287]–[293], recommendation 30.

[49] *McDonald v Horn* [1995] ICR 85; *R v Lord Chancellor, ex Parte Child Poverty Action Group* [1998] 2 All ER 755 at 766; *R (Corner House) Research v Secretary of State for Trade* [2005] EWCA Civ 192; [2005] 1 WLR 2600; Criminal Justice and Courts Act 2015, ss 88–90; *AB v Leeds Teaching Hospitals NHS Trust* [2003] EWHC 1034 (QB); CPR r 3.19.

[50] *Russian Commercial and Industrial Bank v Comptoir d'Escompte de Mulhouse* [1923] 2 KB 630; *Aiden Shipping Co Ltd v Interbulk Ltd* [1986] AC 965.

[51] Senior Courts Act 1981, s 51(1); Representation of the People Act 1983, s 156.

[52] *Competition and Markets Authority v Flynn Pharma Ltd* [2022] UKSC 14; [2022] 1 WLR 2972 at [97].

[53] M Friston (ed) (2023) at 139–140.

[54] *In re Gibson's Settlement Trusts* [1981] Ch 179 at 187.

5. These two changes are consistent with the Code's overall aim of integrating settlement and adjudicatory procedures into a single, coherent process. They are thus consistent with the consensual settlement and digital integration principles. Additionally, they are necessary to enable the court to fully manage costs. They will enable it to award costs where parties settle their substantive dispute before proceedings commence, but are unable to agree the costs of pre-issue settlement. In this they remove party inability to agree such costs as a fetter on their ability to settle pre-issue. They also clarify that where proceedings are issued, pre-action costs incurred in attempts to settle the dispute are recoverable. It will be a question of fact if pre-issue settlement costs incurred outside of the pre-action process provided for in Part 5 are recoverable as costs incidental to pre-action or post-issue proceedings.[55]

## RULE 6.—DETERMINING COSTS

**(1) Costs shall generally be awarded on a global basis in favour of the successful party. The court may, however, make any other costs order, including a percentage or issue-based order where there are substantial and reasonable grounds to do so.**

**(2) The successful party is the one who has in substance and reality achieved their objective in the proceedings or on a specific issue.**

**(3) In determining whether it is reasonable to make a costs order other than one in favour of the successful party, the court shall take account of the parties' pre-action and post-issue conduct, including the extent to which they have complied with the purposive principle, the extent to which they have been successful in respect of their claims or defences, and any steps taken to resolve the dispute consensually.**

*Source: ALI/UNIDROIT Principles, principle 25; ELI-UNIDROIT Model Rules, rr 239, 241; CPR r 44.2(2).*

## COMMENTARY

1. In exercising its discretion over costs, a court must determine two issues: whether to award recovery of costs and if so in whose favour; and, where costs are awarded, the quantum of costs. This rule is concerned with the former question. It restates the position under the CPR.
2. The basic rule is that costs should be awarded in favour of the successful party.[56] This presumption is intended to promote certainty and predictability, and hence reduce the scope for satellite costs litigation. As such it ought not unreasonably be displaced.[57] Success should generally be determined globally by reference to who achieved their objective in the proceedings. In money claims this was historically determined by reference to whether the defendant had to pay damages.[58] In non-money claims, the successful party was determined by reference to who, as a matter

[55] *McGlinn v Waltham Contractors* [2005] EWHC 1419 (TCC); [2005] 3 All ER 1126 at [6]–[9].

[56] M Friston (ed) (2023) at 151.

[57] *Fox v Foundation Piling Ltd* [2011] EWCA Civ 790; [2011] CP Rep 41; *Johnsey Estates (1990) v Secretary of State for the Environment* [2001] EWCA Civ 535 at [21]; *Multiplex Construction (UK) Ltd v Cleveland Bridge UK Ltd* [2008] EWHC 2280 (TCC) at [72].

[58] *Day v Day* [2006] EWCA Civ 415; [2006] CP Rep 35 at [16]–[17].

of substance and reality, achieved their objective in the proceedings.[59] In reality, the court is asking the same question in both cases; in money claims it is simply answering that question by the simple expedient of looking to the question of damages.

3. The rule does, however, enable in-roads to be made into the certainty and predictability provided by the basic rule. That it does so means that, as under the CPR, it provides some scope for the development of costs litigation.[60] First, it does so by permitting percentage-based and issue-based awards, eg awards of a proportion only of costs otherwise recoverable.[61] This enables the court to make a costs award based on which party succeeded on specific issues in the proceedings. Costs recovery does not therefore need to be a 'zero-sum' game.[62] Secondly, it does so by adopting the long-established approach that the court may make awards other than one in favour of the successful party. Thus, the court may make no award of costs, may order costs in favour of the unsuccessful party, or costs relating to specific phases of proceedings, or steps taken in the proceedings.
4. There are several rationales that justify the creation of a discretion to depart from the basic rule and the attendant risk of satellite litigation that that generates. From the perspective of doing justice in individual cases, the discretion enables courts to make costs awards that properly reflect differential success in proceedings. It enables the court to award the majority of costs in favour of the party that was successful overall, while making an award in favour of the other party in respect of issues where they were successful. Awards may therefore more properly reflect overall success or failure, particularly in complex proceedings where a large number of matters where in issue.[63]
5. From a systemic perspective, a discretion supports the achievement of the purposive and general access principles; a point reflected by the criteria the court is directed to consider when assessing the question whether to depart from the basic rule.[64] It enables costs awards to be used, for instance, to promote the proper use of settlement processes through adverse costs awards where such processes are either not used or not used effectively.[65] It also enables costs awards to be used to show the court's disapproval of non-compliance with procedural obligations or of meretricious conduct in proceedings.[66] As such they can, as noted in rule 1, act to promote procedural compliance and deter non-compliance.[67] They can also in this way be a means to promote effective co-operation between the parties, which can itself promote effective dispute management consistent with the purposive principle, and particularly proportionality. Care must, however, be taken when the court considers departing from the basic rule. It must consider the effect that doing so would have on the achievement of these various objectives: the discretion must not therefore be used as a means to subvert

[59] *Roache v Newsgroup Newspapers Ltd* [1998] EMLR 161 at 168–169; *Procter & Gamble Co v Svenska Cellulosa Aktiebolaget SCA* [2012] EWHC 2839 (Ch); [2013] 1 WLR 1464 at [8]–[10].

[60] A Zuckerman (2021) at 1429 and 1439.

[61] *Wilmott v Barber* [1880] 15 ChD 96 at 105; M Friston (ed) (2023) at 147–149.

[62] *Kastor Navigation Co Ltd v AGF MAT* [2004] EWCA Civ 277; [2005] 2 All ER (Comm) 720.

[63] *Phonographic Performance AEI Rediffusion Music Ltd* [1999] 1 WLR 1507 at 1523; *Budgen v Andrew Gardner* [2002] EWCA Civ 1125; [2003] CP Rep 8 at [25].

[64] CPR r 44.2(5).

[65] *Halsey v Milton Keynes General NHS Trust* [2004] EWCA Civ 576; [2004] 1 WLR 3002.

[66] *Peakman v Linbrooke Services Ltd* [2008] EWCA Civ 1239; [2009] CP Rep 14; *Sulaman v Axa Insurance Plc* [2009] EWCA Civ 1331; [2010] CP Rep 19; *Widlake v BAA Ltd* [2009] EWCA Civ 1256; [2010] CP Rep 1.

[67] *Straker v Tudor Rose* [2007] EWCA Civ 368; [2007] CPR Rep 32.

the various procedural principles that the discretion is intended to support. As noted above, the basic rule should not unreasonably be displaced.[68]

6. By limiting departures from the basic rule to where there are substantial and reasonable grounds,[69] the scope for satellite litigation is to be minimised; a point reinforced by the greater control over the quantum of costs available under the tariff and proportionate cost regime set out in this Part than arose under either the RSC or CPR.

## RULE 7.—TIME WHEN COSTS ARE DETERMINED AND NATURE OF ASSESSMENT

**(1) Cost orders shall be made at the conclusion of a hearing, except where the court orders otherwise.**
**(2) Where the court directs that a costs order be made otherwise than at the conclusion of a hearing, it may direct that costs shall be subject to a detailed assessment.**
**(3) A detailed assessment shall take place at the conclusion of proceedings, unless the court orders otherwise.**

*Sources: CPR rr 44.6, 44.10, PD44 paras 9.1–9.2, Pt 47; Guide to the Summary Assessment of Costs (2021).*

## COMMENTARY

1. This rule deals with two separate issues: when a costs order should be made and, if one is made, the process by which costs should be assessed.
2. The approach under the CPR that the question of costs should be dealt with at the conclusion of a hearing, and hence set out within the order made at that hearing, is maintained in this rule. The virtue of this is that it ensures that the parties and the court actively consider costs throughout the lifespan of proceedings. It facilitates a continuing understanding by the parties of the extent to which they are incurring costs, including irrecoverable costs. It thus helps promote effective dispute management.
3. The court may depart from the general rule and, for instance, adjourn or reserve the question until a later point in the proceedings. It may do so, for instance, where the question arises whether it should depart from tariff costs due to a party's unreasonable conduct or where it is necessary to carry out a detailed assessment of proportionate costs. One specific area where the court is likely to adjourn the question of costs to the conclusion of proceedings is where an interim injunction is granted. This is right in principle as the question of the costs of the application ought properly to be considered when the substantive right, which the injunction protects, is finally determined.[70]

[68] The discretion must not be exercised in ways that promote a general use of an issue-based approach, which provides a basis for the unjustifiable multiplication of costs: Bramwell LJ, Letter to Solicitors' Journal 341 (5 March 1881), cited in S Rosenbaum, *The Rule-making Authority in the English Supreme Court* (Boston, 1917) at 69.

[69] *Hall v Stone* [2007] EWCA Civ 1354; [2008] CP Rep 14.

[70] *Desquenne et Giral Ltd v Richardson* [2001] FSR 1; *Picnic at Ascot Inc v Derigs* [2001] FSR 2.

4. Where an order for costs is made, the question then arises how the amount of costs payable is to be determined. The established approach, which is adopted here, is for costs either to be assessed on a summary or detailed basis.
5. Summary costs assessment does not involve the court in a rigorous examination of the costs claimed to be recoverable. It ought to be the default approach where tariff costs apply as well as for hearings that deal with interim matters generally, whether or not tariff or proportionate costs apply. Where tariff costs apply summary assessment is justified as the nature and extent of those costs is provided for by the tariff issued by the Costs and Funding Council. Thus, detailed consideration is unwarranted. Proportionate costs may also be dealt with by summary assessment where it is reasonable, by reference to economy, efficiency, and proportionality, to do so in the circumstances.
6. A detailed assessment of costs requires a more rigorous, forensic examination of the costs said to be recoverable. It may be justified where the costs order provides for proportionate costs and there is a significant number of items of costs claimed. It will also be justified where reasonable costs recovery is being considered or has been ordered.
7. To promote efficient dispute management, detailed assessments ought generally to take place at the conclusion of proceedings, ie at a hearing after final judgment. This is due to the nature of such an assessment, which due to the time and resources needed to carry it out effectively, is likely to require time to prepare. A departure from the general rule may be permissible in respect of costs arising from a trial of a preliminary issue.[71]

## SECTION 3: TARIFF, PROPORTIONATE, AND REASONABLE COST RECOVERY

### RULE 8.—TARIFF COSTS

**(1) The level of tariff costs shall be set and reviewed by the Costs and Funding Council on a triennial basis.**
**(2) The Costs and Funding Council shall ensure that tariff levels are proportionate by reference to the following factors**
**(a) the value, amount, and importance of the relief claimed;**
**(b) the complexity of the proceedings;**
**(c) the cost to the parties of pursuing and defending the proceedings.**
**(3) Tariff costs shall include provision for costs of all stages of proceedings, including pre-action dispute resolution, post-issue proceedings, and enforcement. They shall also include provision for lawyerless parties and costs awards against intervenors. Different tariff rates shall be set for different categories of dispute.**
**(4) The court may only award costs tariff costs where**
**(a) pre-action costs are awarded;**
**(b) post-issue costs are awarded in claims where the relief claimed is £100,000 or less;**
**(c) post-issue costs are awarded in claims for non-monetary relief not classified as high value claims;**

[71] *Greencore (UK) Holdings Plc v Elementis Plc* [2005] EWHC 2139 (Comm).

**(d) the successful party is funded through legal expenses insurance; or**

**(e) the costs of enforcement are awarded in proceedings to which sub-rules (a)–(d) apply.**

**(5) The tariff amount will be reduced by 50 per cent where the successful party engaged in unreasonable conduct, unreasonably refused to engage in settlement efforts, or failed to achieve a judgment at least as advantageous to them as an offer to settle made by the paying party.**

**(6) The tariff amount will be increased by 50 per cent where the paying party has engaged in unreasonable conduct, unreasonably refused to engage in settlement efforts, or failed to achieve a judgment at least as advantageous to them as an offer to settle made by the successful party.**

*Sources: CPR r 1(2)(c), Pt 45.*

## COMMENTARY

1. English and Welsh civil procedure has a long history of fixed (scale or tariff) costs. Appendix N to the RSC 1883, Appendix 3 to RSC 1962, and Appendix 2 (as originally enacted) to RSC 1965 all provided for a fixed (scale) cost regime for a wide variety of litigation costs.[72] They remained in place until 1986, when they were '*swept away in the culmination of the Law Society's campaign for an all-discretionary bill of costs*'.[73] The Woolf Reports, however, recommended what would have been their re-introduction via a generic fixed costs regime in the CPR's fast track, albeit only a partial scheme was introduced in 1999.[74]
2. Following the CPR's introduction there were repeated calls to extend its fixed costs regime; the most significant of which was made in the Jackson Costs Review and its Supplemental Report.[75] In 2021, the Government announced that there would be a general extension of fixed costs; properly fixed recoverable costs. This regime was finally introduced in October 2023. This rule builds on and goes beyond that expansion of fixed recoverability. It does so through the introduction of a tariff costs regime applicable to: all costs incurred under pre-action dispute management; all claims that are not high value claims;[76] and any other claim funded by legal expenses insurance. As a consequence, the majority of civil disputes will fall under the fixed tariff regime. Where the tariff costs regime does not apply proportionate costs recovery, under rule 9, applies, but that too is guided by the principles applicable to tariff costs. On enforcement costs also see Part 16, rule 9.
3. The tariff rates are intended to give effect to the proportionality principle. They are to be proportionate by reference to well-established factors.[77] It is not, however, expected that the same tariffs will be set for all types of claim. They will need to be devised by applying the assessment factors to evidence relevant to each different category of dispute.[78]

[72] M Friston (ed) (2023) at 29–30.

[73] M Cook, *Cook on Costs* (LexisNexis, 2012) at 98.

[74] H Woolf (1995) chaps 7 and 8; CPR Pts 45 and 46 (as at April 1999).

[75] R Jackson (2017); Ministry of Justice (2021).

[76] R Jackson (2017) at 99–100; Part 11, r 11.

[77] CPR r 44.3(5); A Zuckerman, *Zuckerman on Civil Procedure—Principles of Practice* (Thomson Reuters, 2006) at 1032; A Zuckerman (2021) at 1456; R Jackson (December 2009) chap 3.

[78] CPR Pt 45 fixed costs.

4. The rationale for introducing a general tariff costs regime applicable to the majority of proceedings is threefold. It is an essential means through which greater simplicity, certainty, and predictability is to be introduced into costs recovery. Thus, it is intended to reduce the scope of litigation over costs, which is itself a major factor in the excessive cost of dispute resolution. It is also the basis on which a mandatory legal expenses insurance scheme for dispute resolution can be developed. The certainty and predictability of a fixed recoverable costs regime is well-understood to be an essential pre-requisite of the development of such schemes.[79] This is one reason why costs and funding must be viewed as two parts of a symbiotic whole. Finally, it is a means by which the proper balance is struck between compensating a successful party, promoting effective access to dispute resolution, and incentivising parties to conduct litigation in a speedy, economical, and proportionate fashion. Limiting recoverability provides parties with, as Jackson put it, an incentive to resolve their dispute economically.[80] Taken together the three factors ought to lead to the effective control of litigation cost.[81] From the perspective of each party, it ought also to control and limit their potential exposure to their opponent's costs; costs over which they would otherwise have no control.
5. The first two factors further support an approach that sees the tariff rates both set by the Costs and Funding Council and uprated or downrated triennially, as previously recommended by both the Woolf Review and Jackson Costs Review.[82] In this way, an appropriate balance would be struck between maintaining certainty and predictability and ensuring that the tariff rates remain reflective of both inflationary effects and broader changes in the cost of dispute resolution, eg cost reductions arising from technological developments.[83]
6. The tariff also includes provision for increasing or decreasing recoverable costs by a fixed percentage. This discretion allows the tariff to be modified in individual cases to promote procedural compliance and deter non-compliance, to promote effective settlement endeavours and to reflect a failure to achieve a result in proceedings that is better than an offer to settle. It thus maintains the court's discretion to use cost recoverability as a means to promote effective, and sanction ineffective, dispute management. It also replaces for disputes to which tariff costs apply the complex web of provisions in CPR Pt 36,[84] which concern offers to settle and the cost consequences that flow from them. It thus provides a simple, more certain approach, and one less likely to result in satellite litigation than CPR Pt 36. The court's discretion to modify the tariff is, however, limited to the fixed percentage set out in the rule. The reason for a fixed percentage is, again, to promote certainty and predictability and to reduce the potential for litigation over the appropriate level at which the increase or reduction should be set.[85]

[79] J Peysner, 'Costs in Personal Injury Cases: Searching for Predictable Costs' (2002) 2(2) Journal of Personal Injury Law 166; J Peysner, *Access to Justice: A Critical Analysis of Recoverable Conditional Fees and No Win No Fee Funding* (Palgrave) (2014) at 13; B Hess and R Hubner, 'Germany—National Report', in C Hodges, S Vogenauer, and M Tulibacka, *The Costs and Funding of Civil Litigation—A Comparative Perspective* (CH Beck, 2010) at 348–349; and, R Lewis, 'Litigation Costs and Before-the-event Insurance: The Key to Access to Justice?' (2011) 74 MLR 272 at 278.

[80] R Jackson (May 2017) at 213.

[81] A Zuckerman, 'Lord Justice Jackson's Review of Civil Litigation Costs—Preliminary Report' (2009) 28 CJQ 435.

[82] H Woolf (1996) chap 4, recommendation 11; R Jackson (2017) at 81.

[83] R Jackson (2017) at 81.

[84] Part 11, r 17.

[85] R Jackson (2017) at 80.

## RULE 9.—PROPORTIONATE AND REASONABLE COST RECOVERY

**(1) Where tariff costs do not apply, the court may only award costs that are proportionate unless reasonable cost recovery is ordered. Where proportionate cost recovery is ordered, costs that are other than proportionate are irrecoverable and must not be awarded.**

**(2) The party in whose favour a costs award is made must satisfy the court on the balance of probabilities that costs to be awarded are proportionate. Doubts as to whether costs are proportionate must be resolved in favour of the party against whom they are to be awarded.**

*Sources: ELI-UNIDROIT Model Rules, rr 8, 240; CPR rr 1.1(2)(c), 44.3(5).*

## COMMENTARY

1. Tariff costs do not, generally, apply to high value disputes ie ones with a value of over £100,000. To ensure that non-tariff costs strike an appropriate balance between compensating the successful party and promoting effective access to dispute resolution, recoverability is limited by reference to the proportionality principle, except where reasonable cost recovery is ordered. Costs that are not proportionate, irrespective of whether they were necessarily incurred, reasonably incurred, or are reasonable in amount, are irrecoverable.[86]
2. While the nature of proportionality in respect of costs is dealt with in rule 10, this rule makes clear that proportionality is the sole test for recoverability. By adopting this approach to high value and equivalent proceedings a degree of flexibility is permitted, which enables the parties and court to ensure that recoverable costs are tailored to reflect the value, nature, complexity, and importance of such claims on an individual basis. The fact that recoverability is limited by reference to proportionality nevertheless promotes effective dispute management and requires parties to co-operate effectively with each other and the court in managing proceedings and their attendant costs. Party co-operation is particularly required to ensure that disproportionate costs are not incurred, and hence that the disproportionate conduct of proceedings does not occur. While such costs could be borne by the parties without recoverability, their incidence would be likely to have a negative impact on the court's ability to ensure that the immediate dispute was managed proportionately, while adding to the cost, time, and disproportionality of work that would need to be done by opposing parties. It would thus not only undermine both aspects of proportionality, but more broadly it would be contrary to the purposive principle.
3. Placing the burden of proof to establish that costs are proportionate on the party in whose favour a costs award is made is consistent with the general principle that the party asserting is required to prove. It is also consistent with the approach taken under the CPR.[87]

[86] CPR r 44.3(2)(a); R Jackson (December 2009) at 37–38; *Malmsten v Bohinc* [2019] EWHC 1386 (Ch); [2019] 4 WLR 87 at [54]; *West v Stockport NHS Foundation Trust* [2019] EWCA Civ 1220; [2019] 1 WLR 6157 at [88]–[93].

[87] *Excelsior Commercial & Industrial Holdings Ltd v Salisbury Hamer Aspden & Johnson (Costs)* [2002] EWCA Civ 879 at [15]; *Callery & Gray (Nos 1–2)* [2002] UKHL 28; [2002] 1 WLR 2000 at [126].

## RULE 10.—THE ASSESSMENT OF PROPORTIONATE COSTS

**(1) Proportionate costs shall be assessed on a global basis. This requires the court to**
**(a) First, determine whether each specific item of costs claimed was incurred reasonably. Costs incurred unreasonably are irrecoverable and must not be taken into account;**
**(b) secondly, determine the total amount of reasonably incurred costs;**
**(c) thirdly, determine whether the total amount of reasonably incurred costs is proportionate.**

**(2) Where a party is a lawyerless party, proportionate costs include provision for the reimbursement of costs incurred in carrying out activities that would otherwise be carried out by a lawyer. The party must prove the nature and extent of any such costs claimed.**

**(3) In determining whether reasonably incurred costs are proportionate, the court shall take account of Costs and Funding Council guidance on the reasonable range of proportionate costs awardable and any information derived from the digital dispute management system indicative of proportionate costs for the immediate proceedings. It shall also consider the extent to which the reasonably incurred costs, in all the circumstances, have a reasonable relationship to**
**(a) the nature, amount, and importance to the parties of relief claimed;**
**(b) the complexity of the proceedings;**
**(c) work caused by the unreasonable conduct of the party or non-party against whom costs are awarded;**
**(d) wider private or public interests than those that arise in the proceedings. The court shall not take account of value-added tax.**

**(4) In determining its guidance on the reasonable range of proportionate costs, the Costs and Funding Council shall consider the factors applicable for determining tariff costs.**

*Sources: CPR rr 1.1(2)(c), 44.3(5), 46.5.*

## COMMENTARY

1. This rule, which is to be read with rule 10, sets out the approach that civil courts are to take to assess proportionate costs.[88] It is the means by which the proportionality principle is given effect in non-tariff costs.
2. The application of proportionality to costs has a long history in English and Welsh civil justice.[89] The particular approach adopted here is that lit upon following the Jackson Costs Review, which undid the damage caused by the previous, ineffectual,[90]

[88] The approach thus differs from the three stage approach to assessing proportionate costs set out by Etherton MR in *West v Stockport NHS Foundation Trust* [2019] EWCA Civ 1220; [2019] WLR 6157 at [87]–[93]. M Friston (ed) (2023) at 790–793. The *West* approach is rejected as it reintroduces the possibility of assessing proportionality during the assessment of each item's reasonableness and, while it notes the conceptual distinction of reasonableness and proportionality, provides a basis on which they could be elided. The better approach is to maintain that clear distinction between the reasonableness assessment of each item and the global assessment of proportionality.

[89] M Friston (ed) (2023) at 3-56.

[90] R Jackson (December 2009) at 37–38; D Neuberger, *Proportionate Costs* (15th Lecture in the Jackson Implementation Programme, 2012) at [4]–[9]; Compare M Friston (2018) at 759–763 with M Friston (ed) (2023) at 797–798 concerning the continuing lack of clarity on how proportionate costs are to be measured under the CPR.

approach that was encapsulated in *Lownds v Home Office* (2002).[91] That case wrongly assessed proportionality by reference to questions of necessity and reasonableness. Costs that were necessary and reasonable often were, when taken together, disproportionate.[92] To avoid that problem, this rule adopts and restates the approach currently taken by the CPR following the Jackson Costs Review, which properly excludes questions of necessity from the assessment of recoverability so as to give proper effect to party and systemic proportionality. It does so through adopting a three-stage process for the assessment of proportionate costs. The first two stages should determine, by reference to each item of costs, whether they were incurred reasonably, and if so, the reasonable amount that should, in principle, be recoverable for each of them. The court should then assess whether the total global amount of those reasonable costs, and only those costs, is proportionate. This ensures that costs are limited by proportionality, as that is the last matter to be assessed.[93] VAT is excluded from the assessment as it is a tax on the services provided to a party rather than a cost of those services in so far as they relate to the conduct of proceedings.[94]

3. The assessment of proportionality itself is to be carried out by reference to several criteria, which are intended to strike a balance between guiding the court's discretion and enabling it to determine proportionality by reference to the circumstances of the proceedings. General guidance, which is absent under the CPR notwithstanding the guidance given in *West v Stockport NHS Trust* (2019),[95] is needed to provide the courts[96] and parties with an idea of how to take account of both party and systemic proportionality in assessing costs. Guidance on systemic proportionality is particularly needed for both courts and parties to ensure their focus is not exclusively or predominately on the immediate proceedings. Such general guidance would thus have a prospective effect, helping to promote the effective management of proceedings and costs by providing a means to guide party conduct by reference to potential recoverability. It would also have a retrospective effect, helping to ensure that costs assessments of incurred costs are no more than proportionate. As with tariff costs, developing the general guidance is a task for the Costs and Funding Council.
4. In assessing proportionality, the court can also properly draw upon its digital procedure, and particularly information derived from its digital management system. Information could be drawn, via that system, from other proceedings and the proportionate costs they incurred. That data could be analysed via AI to provide guidance on the anticipated proportionate costs for the immediate proceedings. This could be made available to both parties and the court to help them determine prospectively the likely proportionate costs for their proceedings, taking account of the specific features of their dispute that differentiate it from the indicative assessment. It could also, in this way, guide the retrospective assessment of costs.

[91] *Lownds v Home Office* [2002] EWCA Civ 365; [2002] 1 WLR 2450.

[92] A May, speech to Cardiff Costs Conference (19 June 2009).

[93] *Malmsten v Bohinc* [2019] EWHC 1386 (Ch); [2019] 4 WLR 87 at [54]; *West v Stockport NHS Foundation Trust* [2019] EWCA Civ 1220; [2019] 1 WLR 6157 at [88]–[93].

[94] *Giambrone v JMC Holidays Ltd (formerly t/a Sunworld Holidays Ltd) (Costs)* [2002] EWHC 2932 (QB); [2003] 1 All ER 982 at [43].

[95] *West v Stockport NHS Foundation Trust* [2019] EWCA Civ 1220; [2019] WLR 6157 at [87]–[93].

[96] M Friston (2018) at 763. The point is not repeated in M Friston (ed) (2023) at 797–798 given *West v Stockport NHS Foundation Trust* [2019] EWCA Civ 1220; [2019] WLR 6157. However, *West* does not consider systemic proportionality.

5. In addition to the general guidance, the court should also take account of factors that relate to the specific proceedings. The factors identified in rule 10(3)(a)–(d) are drawn from CPR r 44.3(5). They highlight that the value of the dispute, either financial or otherwise, is not the sole or determinative factor for assessing proportionality. It is one factor only. Significant costs could then properly be justified in a low value case, even where the general guidance specifies that the reasonable range of proportionate costs is sharply below the level of actual costs incurred in such proceedings. Such costs could, for instance, be justified as being proportionate due to the complexity of the proceedings or due to their importance as a means to either develop precedent or bring to light a matter of public concern. And the converse is also the case. A high value case may only warrant a low level of costs where it raises a straightforward, single, issue or involves no wider public interest.
6. The rule also makes provision for recovery of proportionate costs by lawyerless parties. This may include recovery of costs incurred by the party for work they had carried out, which would otherwise have been carried out on their behalf by a lawyer. This gives effect to procedural equality, in that a lawyerless party should be able to recover their expenses on the same basis as a party who engages a lawyer.

## RULE 11.—REASONABLE COST RECOVERY

**(1) In place of proportionate costs, the court may award reasonable costs where the paying party's conduct or the circumstances were such as to be outside the ordinary and reasonable conduct of proceedings.**

**(2) Conduct of the party includes the conduct of persons acting for or on their behalf, including any person providing dispute funding.**

**(3) An award of reasonable costs is an award of all costs that were reasonably incurred by the successful party.**

**(4) The party against whom reasonable costs are awarded may contest whether items of cost were incurred reasonably. To do so they must satisfy the court on the balance of probabilities that any such costs to be awarded are unreasonable. Doubts as to whether costs are reasonable must be resolved in favour of the party to whom they are to be awarded.**

*Sources: CPR r 44.3.*

## COMMENTARY

1. This rule sets out the exception to the general approach to costs recovery. It provides for an award of costs on what is sometimes said to be a punitive basis.[97] The punitive element is, however, limited as the award cannot be for more than the successful party's reasonable costs. It is therefore an award of costs assessed by reference to rule 10(1)(a) and (b) and without reference to rule 10(1)(c). Under the CPR this approach is referred to as costs awarded on an indemnity basis. Under those rules, such an award does not amount to a full indemnity, as costs unreasonably incurred

[97] *Victor Kiam v MCN Ltd* [2002] EWCA Civ 66 at [12]. Compare with *Petrotrade Inc v Texaco* [2002] 1 WLR 497 at [63].

or unreasonable in amount are not recoverable.[98] It was under the CPR, as it is here, an approximation of full cost recovery.[99] The term 'reasonable costs' is preferred here to indemnity costs as, unlike the latter term, it captures the actual effect of the order.

2. As an exception to the application of the proportionality principle to recoverable costs, reasonable costs awards should only be made where the circumstances justify departure from it. This can be justified by reference to other procedural principles, such as the dispute management, co-operation, or general access principle. It could be based on a breach of the former two principles through a party bringing or defending the proceedings abusively.[100] The last could be breached through a party bringing a dishonest claim before the courts. In these and other such circumstances, it is appropriate for the court to 'mark its disapproval' through imposing an award of reasonable costs recovery.[101] Equally, that this form of award can be made ought to promote systemic proportionality by deterring parties from acting in ways that waste the court's resources improperly.
3. The general idea underpinning the examples given above is captured by the test for awarding this form of costs recovery: that the paying party's conduct, including that of, for instance, lawyers acting on their behalf,[102] or the circumstances of the proceedings, was outside the norm. Outside the norm does not mean there must be exceptional circumstances. It means that they are unreasonable, in all the circumstances,[103] due to their being outside the ordinary and reasonable conduct of proceedings.[104]
4. Where reasonable costs are to be awarded, it is for the paying party to persuade the court that specific costs claimed are unreasonable, and hence outside the scope of this form of recoverability. Any doubts are, however, to be resolved in favour of the party in whose favour the award is to be made.[105]

## SECTION 4: COSTS RELATING TO SETTLEMENT

### RULE 12.—COSTS RELATING TO SETTLEMENT ENDEAVOURS

**(1) Where parties resolve their dispute by consensual settlement, they should seek to agree both the allocation and amount of costs and include them within their settlement. Where they agree allocation but not the amount of costs, the amount**

[98] CPR r 44.3(1)(b); *Fourie v Le Roux* [2007] UKHL 1; [2007] Bus LR 925 at [39]; M Friston (ed) (2023) at 555 and following.

[99] *Petrotrade Inc v Texaco* [2002] 1 WLR 497 at [63].

[100] Such as bringing or pursuing a hopeless claim for commercial reasons or as to harass the other party, *Arcadia Group Brands Ltd v Visa Inc* [2015] EWCA Civ 883; [2015] Bus LR 1362.

[101] *Esure Services Ltd v Quarcoo* [2009] EWCA Civ 595 at [23]–[25]; *Excelsior Commercial and Industrial Holdings Ltd* [2002] EWCA Civ 879; [2002] CP Rep 67; *Whaleys (Bradford) Ltd v Bennett* [2017] EWCA Civ 2143; [2017] 6 Costs LR 1241 at 22.

[102] *Excalibur Ventures LLC v Texas Keystone Inc* [2016] EWCA Civ 1144; [2017] 1 WLR 221 at [24].

[103] *Reid Minty (a firm) v Taylor* [2001] EWCA Civ 1723 at [27].

[104] *Excelsior Commercial and Industrial Holdings Ltd* [2002] EWCA Civ 879; [2002] CP Rep 67; *Three Rivers DC v Bank of England* [2006] EWHC 816 (Com); [2006] 5 Costs LR 714 at [25]. Moral culpability is not a requirement for conduct to be held to be unreasonable.

[105] *Excelsior Commercial and Industrial Holdings Ltd* [2002] EWCA Civ 879; [2002] CP Rep 67 at [15]; CPR r 44.3(3).

**will be determined, according to the rules in this Part, for the period up to the date of settlement.**

**(2) Where a successful party has unreasonably refused to engage in pre-action and/or post-issue settlement endeavours and proportionate costs are awarded, the court may disallow all or some of the costs that would otherwise have been awarded. The burden of proof lies on the paying party to demonstrate that the refusal was unreasonable.**

**(3) Where a paying party has unreasonably refused to engage in pre-action and/or post-issue settlement endeavours, the court may order reasonable cost recovery on all or some of the costs. The burden of proof lies on the successful party to demonstrate that the refusal was unreasonable.**

**(4) In considering whether the refusal to engage in settlement endeavours was unreasonable the court shall take account of the following factors**

**(a) party conduct during phase 2 of the pre-action dispute management process;**

**(b) the nature and level of compliance with directions concerning settlement, including with any order mandating use of a consensual settlement process;**

**(c) the effect the refusal had on proportionate and effective dispute management.**

*Sources: CPR r 44.5(a).*

## COMMENTARY

1. Rule 12 seeks to promote the application of the settlement principle through providing adverse consequences where parties unreasonably refuse to engage in settlement endeavours. It thereby seeks to promote party autonomy and, inherent in that, party responsibility for settling their own disputes both for the benefits that may give them through cost-savings, efficiency, and in some cases, through more creative, interest-based forms of resolution. Inherent in party autonomy is also the responsibility that each party to a dispute has to draw on the justice system's resources as little as possible so as to promote systemic proportionality, and thus ensure that others, who need to, can draw upon those resources effectively.[106]

2. The starting point adopted here for determining recoverable costs where parties settle their dispute is that costs should form part of the settlement. Where parties cannot, however, agree costs, that ought not to form a barrier to resolving their substantive dispute. Hence this rule provides that, absent settlement of costs, recoverability is to be determined according to the rules in this Part. By setting a default rule for recoverability, it provides a clear guide to parties to the consequences of any failure to agree costs as part of the settlement, the aim of which is to help them settle by removing costs as a potential point of contention between them.

3. To promote party co-operation in the use of settlement endeavours rule 12 adopts the approach developed in the *Halsey* line of authorities.[107] While it accepts that there will, inevitably, be circumstances where a party can properly, ie reasonably, refuse to engage with a settlement process, it aims to deter unreasonable refusals

[106] *Rosalba Alassini v Telecom Italia* (Joined Cases C-317/08, C-318/08, C-319/08, and C-320/08) [2010] I-ECR 02213.

[107] *Dyson v Leeds City Council* [2000] CP Rep 42; *Cowl v Plymouth City Council* [2001] EWCA Civ 1935; [2002] WLR 803; *Dunnett v Railtrack* [2002] EWCA Civ 303; [2002] 1 WLR 2434; *Burchell v Bullard* [2005] EWCA Civ 358; *Halsey v Milton Keynes General NHS Trust* [2004] EWCA Civ 573; [2004] 1 WLR 2434; *PGF v OFMS* [2013] EWCA Civ 1288; [2014] 1 WLR 1386.

to engage. This is to be done, as under the CPR, through the imposition of adverse consequences. It should be noted that this approach is not adopted to enable adverse costs orders to be an implied means to introduce mandatory mediation.[108] The Code explicitly provides for mandatory ADR, as since 2023 has been the case under the CPR.[109] Non-compliance with any such mandatory order will be a significant factor to be considered under rule 12(4)(b) and (c) as the courts will need to ensure that compliance with such orders does not become, in effect, a matter of party discretion. Non-compliance would, inevitably, pose a problem for the court's ability to give effect to the proportionality principle and effective dispute management.

4. In considering how to assess whether there was unreasonable conduct, rule 12(2) and (3) adopt the principled approach that where a party asserts there has been such conduct it is for them to establish that fact.[110] The question is then what factors are relevant to assess whether a refusal was unreasonable.[111]

5. The Court of Appeal in *Halsey v Milton Keynes* (2004) set out a range of factors to be considered when determining if a refusal to engage in settlement endeavours is unreasonable.[112] They are: the nature of the dispute; the merits of the case, where the court finds that a (successful) party who reasonably believed they have a watertight case might well be justified in refusing to mediate; the extent to which other settlement attempts have been made, remembering that mediation often settled cases where negotiation had previously failed; whether the cost of ADR would have been disproportionately high; and, whether delay in setting up ADR would have been prejudicial to a trial date.[113]

6. The *Halsey* factors have, however, not been without criticism. The Civil Justice Council, for example, concluded that only two of the *Halsey* factors were valid reasons to be considered when approaching the question whether a refusal to engage in ADR was unreasonable: the nature, but not complexity or seriousness, of a dispute; and whether delay caused by ADR would prejudice the trial date.[114] There is a good degree of force in these criticisms. Underpinning each of the factors is, moreover, a further criticism. They focus entirely on whether the refusal was reasonable or unreasonable by reference to the immediate case. Only one of the factors takes proper account of the wider role that settlement's promotion plays in the proper management of the civil justice system. They do not consider the adverse impact that a refusal to mediate, and the court's approach to assessing such refusals might have, on systemic proportionality. The one factor that is relevant to that wider question is the potential impact ADR might have on the potential trial date, as moving a trial date may have an impact on management of the court's resources generally.

7. Given these considerations, rule 12 does not generally adopt the *Halsey* factors. It rather requires the court to focus its assessment more clearly on issues that concern

[108] M Ahmed, *Implied Compulsory Mediation* (2012) 32 CJQ 151.

[109] See Part 11, r 19(1)(a); *Churchill v Merthyr Tydfil County Borough Council* [2023] EWCA Civ 1416, which clarified that *Halsey v Milton Keynes General NHS Trust* [2004] EWCA Civ 573; [2004] 1 WLR 2434 was not to be followed in so far as its remarks concerning mandatory ADR were concerned. It specifically held that *Halsey* was wrong in law to hold that mandatory court-ordered mediation was contrary to the right to fair trial.

[110] *Halsey v Milton Keynes General NHS Trust* [2004] EWCA Civ 573; [2004] 1 WLR 2434 at [13]; M Friston (ed) (2023) at 174–176.

[111] The adverse consequences of unreasonable conduct where tariff costs are applicable is dealt with in r 9.

[112] *Halsey v Milton Keynes General NHS Trust* [2004] EWCA Civ 573; [2004] 1 WLR 2434.

[113] M Friston (ed) (2023) at 174 and following.

[114] Civil Justice Council, *ADR and Civil Justice—Final Report* (November 2018) at 8.29.

effective dispute management. Rule 12(4)(a) and (b) therefore focus the assessment of reasonableness on rule compliance. In that way they enable the court to consider the impact a refusal to engage in settlement had on the management of the immediate proceedings, which may include an assessment of pre-action attempts to settle. Rule 12(4)(c) focuses the assessment on broader principles of dispute management, particularly those that concern the effect that a refusal to engage with settlement processes may have had upon the court's ability to give effect to the purposive principle; particularly the effect on proportionate dispute management. This enables the court to consider both the effect a refusal may have had on the immediate proceedings, but also its potential effect on the operation of the justice system as a whole.

8. The two *Halsey* factors identified as valid by the Civil Justice Council are particularly relevant in respect of rule 12(4(c). Both those factors have the potential to adversely affect systemic proportionality. If, for instance, a dispute gave rise to a serious issue of principle, could clarify, or develop the law, or could have an effect wider than its effect on the parties, that could render a refusal to engage in settlement endeavours reasonable. Adjudication in such a case would, for instance, promote systemic proportionality through the effect it would have on preventive justice as well as consensual justice. Equally, an adverse impact on a potential trial date may result in changes being made to the court's ability to schedule and determine other applications and hearings. It thus may affect the proper use of its resource allocation in other proceedings. Again, refusal in such circumstances may be reasonable. In each case, the court will need to consider all the circumstances as they relate to the three issues set out in rule 12.

## RULE 13.—COSTS RELATING TO OFFERS TO SETTLE WHERE TARIFF COSTS DO NOT APPLY

**(1) Where a claimant makes an offer to settle in proceedings to which tariff costs do not apply, which is not accepted, and the claimant secures a judgment at least as advantageous as their offer, the claimant will be entitled to recover reasonable costs.**

**(2) Where a defendant makes an offer to settle in proceedings to which tariff costs do not apply, which is not accepted and secures a judgment at least as advantageous as that offer**

**(a) the defendant will be entitled to recover reasonable costs for their costs from the last date on which the offer could have been accepted; and,**

**(b) the claimant shall be entitled to such cost recovery as the court would ordinarily award them in respect of their costs up to that date.**

**(3) Where it would be unjust to make an order under sub-rule (1) or (2), the court may make another order as to costs. In considering whether, and the extent to which, it is unjust, the court shall take account of the following factors**

**(a) the terms of the offer to settle;**

**(b) when the offer was made;**

**(c) the conduct of the parties concerning the offer;**

**(d) the parties' ability to assess the offer at the time it was made;**

**(e) whether the offer was made in good faith.**

**(4) The burden of establishing that it would be unjust to make the normal award under this rule lies on the party asserting that it would be unjust.**

*Sources: CPR Pt 36.*

## COMMENTARY

1. Offers to settle can be made under Part 11, rule 17. The CPR's approach is not adopted in that rule. Rather than the degree of complexity provided for in that part of the CPR (CPR Pt 36), a simplified approach is taken.[115] Simplification is also at the heart of the approach taken in this rule to costs recovery where settlement offers have been made. This is, again, intended to rationalise the process and render it more certain, thus reducing the time and cost associated with it. It is also intended to contribute to the overall reduction in litigation over costs generally, which this Part aims to achieve. The rule only applies where proportionate costs apply.[116]
2. As under the CPR, rule 13 aims to place pressure on parties to accept reasonable offers to settle. This is done by providing clear and predictable incentives favouring acceptance. Claimants are incentivised to make offers that properly reflect likely recoverability were a judgment to be given by the court, and defendants are incentivised to accept them. This is done by providing for reasonable rather than proportionate cost recovery costs where such an offer is made but not accepted by a defendant and the claimant ultimately recovers the same or more than the offer. The rationale for applying reasonable cost recovery is that the defendant's conduct by refusing the offer in such circumstances was by its very nature unreasonable given the result. Defendants are also incentivised to make such offers, and thus place pressure on claimants to settle. This is done by providing them with reasonable cost recovery for the period up to the point on which their offer could have been accepted, with the claimant being entitled to an award of costs from that date where the judgment is at least as good as that set out in the defendant's offer. Again, this reflects the unreasonable nature of the claimant's refusal to accept the offer.
3. Rule 13(3) provides the court with a guided discretion to disapply or vary the general approach set out in rules 13(1) and (2).[117] It adopts the approach taken in the CPR to the question whether it would be unjust to apply the normal costs consequences of its rules concerning offers to settle.[118] It does so to give effect to the purposive principle, ie to ensure that the application of this rule is fair and just, and hence in the specific circumstances the refusal to accept the offer was not unreasonable. It is for the party asserting that the generally applicable order would be unjust to establish that that is the case.[119] Given the importance of the general approach, there ought to be a high threshold for satisfying the court that it would be unjust to apply it.[120]
4. There are many examples of when it would be unjust to apply the general rule. It may, for instance, be unjust to make an award where an offer was so unclear that it could not be assessed properly by the party to whom it was made. Equally, it may be unjust to make an award where the offer was made very late in proceedings, after a change of circumstances outside the control of the parties, or the party to whom it was made did not have sufficient information or evidence to assess it effectively. Importantly, the parties' conduct in respect of the offer may be important here, eg if it was a tactical offer, rather than genuine offer, if the party making the offer refused to provide material to the other party to enable them to assess it properly, or if it was

[115] M Friston (ed) (2023) at 612 and following.
[116] Rule 9.
[117] *Thinc Group Ltd v Kingdom* [2013] EWCA Civ 1306 at [22].
[118] CPR r 36.17(5).
[119] *Tinta Plc v Rawlinson & Hunter (A firm)* [2016] EWHC 3480 (QB) at [14].
[120] *Briggs v CEF Holdings Ltd* [2017] EWCA Civ 2363 at [20].

made in bad faith.[121] Such behaviour would all point away from the application of the general rule.

## SECTION 5: FUNDING COSTS

### RULE 14.—CONTINGENCY FUNDING AGREEMENT COSTS

**(1) Where costs are awarded in favour of a party funded through a contingency funding agreement, only costs in respect of the party's lawyer's base fee may be awarded as costs.**

**(2) The base fee refers to the fees that the lawyers would charge on a non-contingency basis.**

*Sources: ELI-UNIDROIT Model Rules, r 245(3); Courts and Legal Services Act 1990, ss 58, 58A, 58AA.*

### COMMENTARY

1. Contingency funding agreements, in the form of conditional fee agreements (CFAs) and latterly also damages-based agreements (DBAs) have formed a part of English civil procedure since 1995.[122] They are provided for in Part 4 of this Code.
2. Rule 14 adopts the position generally reached in England and Wales by the Jackson Costs Review.[123] It thus only permits a party to recover their lawyer's normal, base costs under a contingency funding agreement. To promote simplicity and reduce the scope for satellite litigation it does not, however, permit of exceptions to the general rule, as is allowed for specific types of claim under the CPR.[124] Any additional element of cost, however calculated, that is contingent upon success is irrecoverable. As only costs in respect of the base fee are recoverable, where a party takes out after-the event (ATE) insurance as part of or further to their contingency fee agreement, such insurance and any related insurance premiums are also irrecoverable as costs.
3. This approach is adopted for the cogent reasons advanced against success-fee recoverability, elaborated in the Jackson Costs Review: increasing a losing party's costs burden to cross-subsidise work done by lawyers on work for other CFA-funded clients whose claims are unsuccessful not only leads to an unjustified increase in costs but it is unjust, not least because it imposes a form of implicit taxation on losing parties.[125] From a principled perspective, any increase in costs to losing parties through requiring success fee recoverability undermines access to justice, as the risk of increased adverse costs is liable to deter meritorious claims being brought or defended.[126] For the same reason, it is also contrary to procedural equality. Moreover, as the Jackson Costs Review properly concluded, because other funding mechanisms exist, where parties choose to litigate on a contingency fee basis, they should do so at

[121] M Friston (ed) (2023) at 627–638.

[122] J Peysner (2014).

[123] Legal Aid, Sentencing and Punishment of Offenders Act 2012, ss 44 and 46.

[124] Mesothelioma, certain insolvency, publication, and privacy proceedings; Legal Aid and Punishment of Offenders Act 2012 (Commencement No 5 and Saving Provision) Order 2013.

[125] R Jackson (December 2009) chaps 9 and 10; S Clark and R Jackson (2018) chap 7.

[126] S Clark and R Jackson (2018) at 73.

their own expense and not that of the other party.[127] As the current Code promotes legal expenses insurance as the primary means of litigation funding, that latter reason from the Review is all the more pertinent a justification for maintaining success fee irrecoverability.

4. This rule does not make provision for qualified-one-way costs shifting (QOCS), which was introduced primarily as a means to protect personal injury claimants from adverse costs awards when funded by a post-Jackson CFA.[128] Absent such protection, it was anticipated that claimants would be denied access to justice. QOCS are not adopted here for two reasons. First, they introduce an unnecessary additional layer of complexity into costs, adding to the time and cost of determining such matters while also creating scope for satellite litigation over their application. They thus can undermine the provision of an economical, efficient, and proportionate process. Secondly, their introduction is unnecessary. Unlike under the CPR, CFAs are not a primary means to secure litigation funding. That role is taken by legal expenses insurance. By removing the basis on which they were introduced, ie the need to render post-Jackson CFAs fairer to claimants, the justification for their retention is set aside.

## RULE 15.—DISPUTE FUNDING COSTS

**(1) Where costs are awarded in favour of a party funded through a dispute funding arrangement, no costs over and above those that could have been awarded in the absence of a funding arrangement may be awarded as costs.**

**(2) Where a party has entered into a dispute funding arrangement, the court may direct that a funder pay all or part of any costs awarded against the funded party where it is just to do so.**

**(3) In determining whether it is just to direct that a funder is liable for an amount of costs, the court shall consider all the circumstances, and particularly shall consider**

**(a) the amount of funding provided; and**

**(b) the funder's conduct in respect of the proceedings, including the level of control, if any, they exercised over the proceedings.**

**(4) As a general rule where dispute funding, either under an agreement or otherwise, is provided altruistically, a funder shall not be held liable for any costs awarded against the funded party. The court may depart from this for good reason. Where it does so the funder shall be liable for costs as if they were a regulated funder.**

*Sources: ELI-UNIDROIT Model Rules, r 245; Courts and Legal Services Act 1990, s 58B.*

## COMMENTARY

1. Recovery of costs from a funder may arise in two circumstances; where the funding is provided by a commercial, ie regulated, funder on a for-profit basis via a dispute funding arrangement; or, where it is provided by a non-party, known as a pure funder, on an altruistic basis. This rule permits recovery of costs in both situations.

[127] R Jackson (December 2009) at 105.

[128] R Jackson (December 2009) chap 19; A Zuckerman (2021) at 1482ff; M Friston (ed) (2023) chap 8.

2. Where funding is provided by a dispute funding arrangement, cost recovery is limited to the amount of normal recoverable costs. The same approach is therefore taken to recovery here as is the case for contingency fee funding costs. As with such costs, recoverability is based on the principle that funding arrangements ought not to increase the amount of costs at risk for the opposing party to proceedings as that acts as a fetter on access to justice and runs contrary to procedural equality.[129]
3. This rule maintains the position under the CPR that a commercial funder under such an agreement ought to be at risk of contributing to any adverse cost award. The current, heavily criticised approach to assessing the nature of such liability is that set out in *Arkin v Borchard Lines Ltd* (2005) and *Chapelgate Credit Opportunity Master Fund Ltd v Money* (2020).[130] The *Arkin cap* as it is called provides that a commercial funder ought, normally, to be liable for no greater an amount of adverse costs than that of the level of funding they provided, including any funding provided to satisfy an order for security for costs.[131]
4. This rule does not adopt the *Arkin cap*. It follows the approach advanced in the Jackson Costs Review, which recommended it be abolished and that commercial funders be fully liable for any adverse costs, subject to a discretion to reduce the level of liability.[132] It did so on two bases. First, that there was no evidence that such a step would inhibit the development of commercial funding. The evidence from Australia, where full liability for costs was available, was in fact to the contrary. Secondly, the *Arkin cap* was wrong as a matter of principle. A funder who stood to gain from providing funding had to take the attendant burden in the event of failure. This was justified as otherwise access to justice and procedural equality would be undermined from the perspective of the non-funded party who would otherwise be unable to recover their costs. And, as the Review also concluded, without such liability, the funded party would be left with a costs liability that they might not be able to satisfy, which—implicitly—the funder had been responsible for creating.[133] These criticisms are cogent and well-founded.[134]
5. This rule therefore approaches the question of liability on the basis that the court has full power to hold a commercial funder wholly, or in a suitable case partially, liable for any adverse costs awards. In assessing what is just, the rule requires the court to take account of all the circumstances. Specifically, it must consider the amount of funding provided and the funder's conduct during the proceedings, including its control over them. These factors are the key means to determine whether, and the extent to which, a commercial funder has provided the funding in order to benefit from it, rather than simply increase access to justice for the funded party, and hence should take on the attendant burden of adverse costs.
6. By way of contrast, as a general principle, a pure, ie unregulated, funder will not be made liable for any costs awarded.[135] This is because such funding, provided

[129] *Essar Oilfield Services Ltd v Norscot Rig Management PvT Ltd* [2016] EWHC 2361; [2017] Bus LR 227; *Merricks v Mastercard* [2017] CAT 16; [2018] Comp AR 1.

[130] *Arkin v Borchard Lines Ltd* [2005] EWCA Civ 655; [2005 1 WLR 3055 at [38]–[45]; *Chapelgate Credit Opportunity Master Fund Ltd v Money* [2020] EWCA Civ 246; [2020] 1 WLR 1751.

[131] *Excalibur Ventures LLC v Texas Keystone Inc* [2016] EWCA Civ 1144; [2017] 1 WLR 221.

[132] R Jackson (December 2009) chap 11.

[133] R Jackson (December 2009) at 123.

[134] *Chapelgate Credit Opportunity Master Fund Ltd v Money* [2020] EWCA Civ 246; [2020] 1 WLR 1751 at [31]–[39]; *Lazer Trust v CFL Finance Ltd* [2021] EWHC 1404 (Ch).

[135] *Hamilton v Al Fayed* [2002] EWCA Civ 665; [2003] QB 1175 at [47], [63].

altruistically, promotes access to justice and procedural equality by helping to put the funded party into a financial position analogous to that of the other party.[136] Unlike a commercial funder, a pure funder does not seek to benefit personally from the proceedings. There is therefore no principled basis on which to impose an attendant burden on them.[137] Where such funding promotes the prosecution or defence of an unmeritorious claim steps can, of course, be taken to bring the proceedings to an early conclusion through strike out or summary judgment applications (see Part 11).

7. In certain circumstances the general rule for pure funders can be set aside. Where they have exercised control over the funded proceedings, they will have done more than simply further the public interest in facilitating access to justice. As the Privy Council put it in *Dymocks Franchise Systems (NSW) v Todd (Costs)* (2004),[138] by taking control of proceedings they are '*gaining access to justice for [their] own purposes*'. They should thus become liable for costs. Moreover, they may be liable for costs if they provide funding in bad faith or in such a way as to undermine the effective administration of justice.[139] As such they should again be liable for adverse costs on the same basis as a commercial funder.
8. Where reasonable costs recovery is ordered, it may be ordered to apply to any costs for which a commercial funder is liable.[140] There is no basis on which to take a different approach where a pure funder has been held to be liable for adverse costs.

# SECTION 6: SPECIAL CASES

## RULE 16.—MULTI-PARTY ACTION COSTS

**(1) Where proceedings are conducted as group litigation, the group parties are severally liable for an equal proportion of any common issue costs awarded against them. They remain individually liable for any individual costs awarded against them.**
**(2) Where proceedings are conducted as representative proceedings any costs liability shall only be borne by the representative party.**
**(3) Where it is necessary in the interests of justice the court may vary group or representative parties' liability for costs. This includes the power to order a group party or represented party to contribute to any costs liability incurred on their behalf.**

*Source: ELI-UNIDROIT Model Rules, r 238; CPR rr 19.8(4), 46.6, and PD19B para 16.1.*

## COMMENTARY

1. This rule concerns the approach to costs where a group proceedings or representative proceedings order is made under Part 11. It is based on CPR r 19.8(4) in respect of the latter, and r 46.6, in respect of the former.

[136] *Hamilton v Al Fayed* [2002] EWCA Civ 665; [2003] QB 1175 at [70].
[137] *Hamilton v Al Fayed* [2002] EWCA Civ 665; [2003] QB 1175 at [40].
[138] *Dymocks Franchise Systems (NSW) v Todd (Costs)* [2004] UKPC 39; [2004] 1 WLR 2807 at 2815.
[139] *Gulf Azov Shipping Co Ltd v Idisi (Costs)* [2004] EWCA Civ 292.
[140] *Excalibur Ventures LLC v Texas Keystone Inc* [2016] EWCA Civ 1144; [2017] 1 WLR 221.

2. The general rule in group litigation is that there should be a common costs sharing order: group parties, each of whom benefit from the determination of common issues in the litigation, should bear the burden of any adverse costs awards order.[141] Rule 16(1) adopts the general rule contained in CPR r 46.6(3) to make provision for this.[142] There may, however, be circumstances where it would be unjust to adopt the general rule. A fair process therefore requires the court to maintain a discretion to depart from it. Departure may, for instance, be justified, where the conduct of one or more group parties increased the overall costs. This may arise where a number of group parties' claims go forward as test cases, and it cannot properly be said that the entire group benefited from those issues. The court may also depart from the general rule where one or more group parties are held to have acted improperly. In such cases it would not be just to visit the cost of their misconduct upon the other group parties.[143] Finally, it may also arise where group parties did not intend any adverse costs to be shared equally amongst them in respect of those test cases[144] or where they entered into a cost sharing agreement. While the court ought to generally respect such an expression of party autonomy, it need not do so: party agreements as to costs remain subject to the court's overarching costs discretion.[145] Group parties will always remain responsible for adverse costs incurred in respect of issues unique to their own claims.
3. Where a group party exited the group prior to determination of the common issues, the court should ordinarily apply the general rule. This protects the interests of other group members and defendants who may have incurred work and costs relating to issues raised by that party.[146] The determination of costs in such circumstances should be made when the common issues are themselves determined finally. It will only be at that time that the court will be in a position to consider properly if there is good reason to deviate from the general rule.[147]
4. The approach to costs differs in representative proceedings, where only a representative party is a proper party to proceedings. Consequently, only they are liable for any adverse costs award.[148] As the Supreme Court explained in *Lloyd v Google LLC* (2021), it is difficult to envisage a situation when liability for costs could be imposed on a represented party who had had no say in the nature and conduct of the proceedings. A power to do so, however, is provided for here as a specific application of the court's general power to make an award of costs against a non-party. Costs may therefore be awarded against a represented party on the same basis as awarded against a non-party generally. Should a represented party, for instance, provide funding for the representative action, that would provide a basis to vary the representative party's liability and impose costs liability on the represented party. Such liability would, at the least, amount to the level of funding provided.[149]

[141] *Re Interest Rate Swap Litigation*, The Times, 19 December 1991.

[142] *Greenwood v Goodwin* [2014] EWHC 227 (Ch).

[143] *BCCI SA v Ali (Assessment of Costs)* [2000] 2 Costs LR 243.

[144] *Ochwat v Watson Burton* [2000] CP Rep 45.

[145] *BCCI SA v Ali (Assessment of Costs)* [2000] 2 Costs LR 243.

[146] *Sayers v Merck SmithKline Beecham Plc* [2001] EWCA Civ 2017; [2002] 1 WLR 2274.

[147] *Afrika v Cape Plc* [2001] EWCA Civ 2017; [2002] 1 WLR 2274.

[148] *Handforth v Storie* (1825) 2 Sim & St 196 at 198; *Moon v Atherton* [1972] 2 QB 435 at 441.

[149] *Lloyd v Google LLC* [2021] UKSC 50; [2021] 3 WLR 1268 at [79]; *Davey v Money* [2020] EWCA Civ 246; [2020] 1 WLR 1751.

## RULE 17.—SECURITY FOR COSTS

**(1) The court, on the application of a party, may order the provision of security for the costs of proceedings. An order may only be made against a claimant or a person from whom the claimant has obtained the assignment of the cause of action that forms the subject matter of the proceedings.**

**(2) An order for security for costs may be made by the court where it is just to do so. In considering this the court shall take account of the following factors**

**(a) whether the subject of the order resides out of the jurisdiction;**

**(b) whether an award of costs could be enforced against the claimant under a relevant international treaty;**

**(c) whether security for costs is permitted by a relevant international treaty;**

**(d) whether the subject of the order is a legal person;**

**(e) the pre-action and post-issue conduct of the subject of the order up to the date when the application for security was made;**

**(f) the purposive principle.**

**(3) Where an order for security for costs is made, proceedings shall be stayed until the order is satisfied or the court orders otherwise.**

**(4) Where a party is funded by a dispute funding arrangement and a non-funded party applies for security for costs, or the court considers making such an order of its own initiative, it is for the funded party to satisfy the court that such an order is not necessary.**

*Source: ALI/UNIDROIT Principles, principle 3; ELI-UNIDROIT Model Rules, r 243; CPR r 1.1(2)(a), Pt 25, Section II.*

## COMMENTARY

1. English and Welsh civil procedure does not generally provide parties with the ability to obtain security for judgment.[150] It does, however, provide the court with discretionary powers to stop a party from evading judgment and the payment of costs.[151] The former is considered in Part 13. The latter is the power to award security for costs, the aim of which is protect a defendant against the risk that a claimant may not be able to satisfy any costs liability that may arise.[152] This power is unusual as it can validly fetter access to justice.[153] This is because once made, proceedings are stayed until the order is satisfied, varied, or set aside.[154]

2. In assessing whether it would be just to exercise its discretion to order security for costs, and thus whether an order would be a proportionate means to protect the defendant's general access right, the court should consider the factors set out in rule 17(2). They require the court to consider whether there is a specific factor that justifies the imposition of a fetter on a claimant's right of access. It may be, for instance, that the claimant is outside the jurisdiction and in a jurisdiction where it would not be possible for costs to be enforced, that their conduct may indicate that

[150] Part 16, r 17.

[151] *Bestfort Developments LLP v Ras Al Khaimah Investment Authority* [2016] EWCA Civ 1099; [2017] CP Rep 9 at [82]; M Friston (ed) (2023) chap 15.

[152] N Andrews (2019) at 555.

[153] A Zuckerman (2021) at 557.

[154] *Abraham v Thompson* [1997] CLC 1370 at 1386.

they are seeking to avoid costs, or that the claimant is a nominal claimant.[155] It may also do so where a company without assets was specifically established as a means to take the litigation forward on such a basis or where a claimant has, objectively, taken steps to frustrate the enforcement of an award of costs against them.[156] In each case, the claimant might properly be viewed as being immunised from the risk of paying costs, which would expose the defendant to litigating in the knowledge that any costs order made would be of little practical utility. A fair process would, in such circumstances, require positive steps to be taken to protect the defendant's access right.

3. Another factor that must be considered where the court is considering whether it is just to make an order is whether there is any international treaty that prohibits the enforcement of security for costs. If there is, an order ought not to be made as it would be futile.[157] The general access and procedural equality principles must also be considered when the court considers the purposive principle. This is to ensure it takes proper account of the claimant's as well as the defendant's rights. Particularly important here is for the court to assess whether an order would stifle an impecunious claimant's access to the court, thus treating them less favourably or fairly than the defendant who seeks an order. Just as security for costs is intended to protect the defendant's rights, it must not improperly fetter a claimant's rights.
4. Finally, the rule creates a presumption in favour of awarding security for costs against a party who is funded via a dispute funding arrangement. The rule is applied here to protect the non-funded party against the risk that the funded party's commercial funder might become insolvent.[158]

[155] *White v Butt* [1909] 1 KB 50 at 55; *Envis v Thakkar* [1997] BPIR 189.

[156] *Ackerman v Ackerman* [2011] EWHC (Ch) at [16].

[157] Carriage of Goods by Rail (Berne) Convention 1952, art 55(4); Hague Access to Justice Convention (1980), art 14).

[158] *Australian Law Reform Commission, Integrity, Fairness and Efficiency—An Inquiry into Class Action Proceedings and Third-Party Litigation Funders* (2018) at 6.48.

# PART 4
# FUNDING

## SECTION 1: GENERAL

1. This Part concerns funding dispute resolution. There is no analogue to it in the CPR, nor was there in its predecessors. Litigation funding has, historically, either been a matter dealt with at common law or via statute. Champerty and maintenance, for instance, restricted the use and development of contingency fee and third-party litigation funding until the start of the 21st century.[1] More positively, the Legal Aid and Advice Act 1949 established the civil legal aid funding scheme, which remains in place today, albeit in a significantly etiolated form following the Legal Aid, Sentencing and Punishment of Offenders Act 2012.[2] The need to consider and deal with questions of funding as part of civil procedural codes has, however, recently been recognised both generally and specifically. The ELI-UNIDROIT Model Rules, for instance, incorporate generic legal aid, contingency fee, and third-party funding rules within their treatment of litigation costs.[3] They also make provision for specific funding rules in respect of multi-party proceedings for collective redress.[4]
2. This Part adopts the approach adopted by ELI-UNIDROIT. In doing so it rejects the current two-pronged approach to litigation funding adopted in England and Wales. It thus also rejects the longstanding policy of shifting responsibility for litigation from the public sector—legal aid[5]—to the private sector primarily through the promotion of forms of contingency fee and third-party funding.[6] It also rejects the implicit underpinning of the HMCTS reform programme and its approach to digitisation of the civil court process. That approach is that the civil process should be digitised in a way that means individuals can litigate disputes without legal assistance or representation.[7] The implicit underpinning is that funding for legal representation, whether through civil legal aid or contingency and third-party funding mechanisms will not generally be available for a significant proportion of civil disputes. Hence digitisation makes a virtue out of an absence of funding by seeking to create a civil

[1] *Wallersteiner v Moir (No 2)* [1975] 1 All ER 849 at 860.

[2] T Goriely, 'Gratuitous Assistance to the "Ill-dressed": Debating Civil Legal Aid in England and Wales from 1914 to 1939' (2006) 13(1) International Journal of the Legal Profession 41; A Flynn and J Hodgson, *Access to Justice and Legal Aid* (Routledge, 2017) chap 1.

[3] ELI-UNIDROIT Model Rules, rr 244 and 245.

[4] ELI-UNIDROIT Model Rules, r 237.

[5] W van Boom, 'Litigation Costs and Third-Party Funding', in W Van Boom (ed), *Litigation, Costs, Funding and Behaviour: Implications for the Law* (Routledge, 2017) at 5.

[6] Courts and Legal Services Act 1990, s 58 (as originally enacted); Access to Justice Act 1999, ss 27 and 28; J Peysner, *Access to Justice: A Critical Analysis of Recoverable Conditional Fees and No Win No Fee Funding* (Palgrave, 2014) chap 5; R Mulheron and P Cashman, 'Third Party Funding: A Changing Landscape' (2008) 27 CJQ 312.

[7] M Briggs, *Civil Courts Structure Review—Interim Report* (December 2015) at 7–8 and 122.

*A Model Civil Procedure Code for England and Wales*. John Sorabji, Oxford University Press. 
DOI: 10.1093/oso/9780192848680.003.0005

justice system where legal advice and representation is, for those who cannot afford it, unnecessary. It ought to go without saying that that approach embeds procedural inequality, as those who can afford legal advice and representation will undoubtedly continue to avail themselves of such.

3. Litigation funding is incorporated into the Code for three specific reasons. Primarily, doing so properly reflects the importance of funding as the means by which access to dispute resolution is achieved. Effective funding transforms the theoretical right of access to justice, whether that is achieved through court judgment or settlement, into a practical and effective one: incorporation thus gives concrete effect to the funding right that forms part of the general access principle.[8] Incorporation thus transforms any Code of Procedure, from one that is capable of securing formal, theoretical access and particularly procedural equality, into one that secures practical and substantive access.

4. Incorporation particularly improves access in two specific ways. Funding's availability and an awareness of its availability play an important part in the emergence of disputes. Lack of funding or awareness of its availability, linked with an awareness of the potential cost of dispute resolution, can play an important role in leading individuals whose rights have arguably been infringed to take no steps to assert or vindicate them.[9] Incorporation is intended to help overcome any such culture of constraint; the sense of powerlessness which leads to individuals on low incomes to limit their resort to effective dispute resolution mechanisms.[10] Funding's incorporation, and the manner of it, thus has an impact on the emergence of disputes and steps to resolve them.[11] Secondly, where a dispute does emerge, questions of funding have an important role in determining choice of dispute resolution method as well as party behaviour during dispute resolution. Limited funding may, for instance, push a party towards the use of low-cost dispute resolution, eg, negotiation or mediation, and away from litigation. Objectively, that may not be problematic, but in some instances, it may be, eg, where the dispute is more properly suited to resolution through litigation. Questions of funding may also have an impact on the extent to which parties can participate effectively in any resolution process. An imbalance of funding between parties may, for instance, influence settlement of a dispute at an undervalue because the party with more limited funding cannot afford to continue to prosecute or defend their position.[12] Incorporation is thus also intended to reduce

[8] M Cappelletti and B Garth, 'Access to Justice and the Welfare State: An Introduction', in M Cappelletti (ed), *Access to Justice* (Sijthoff & Noordhoff, 1979) at 1; B Garth and M Cappelletti, 'Access to Justice: The Newest Wave in the Worldwide Movement to Make Rights Effective' (1978) 27 Buff L Rev 181 at 196–198; and see, in respect of legal aid provision, *Airey v Ireland* (1979) 2 EHRR 305; *Tolstoy Miloslavsky v UK* (1995) 20 EHRR 442; *R (Gudanaviciene) v The Director of Legal Aid Casework and The Lord Chancellor* [2014] EWCA Civ 1622 at [72].

[9] A point most clearly made in the US literature: I Weinstein, 'Access to Justice in America: What do we Know', in S Estreicher and J Radice (eds), *Beyond Elite Law: Access to Civil Justice in America* (CUP, 2016) at 6–8; P Pleasance and N Balmer, *How People Resolve 'Legal' Problems* (PPSR/Legal Services Board, 2014) at 4.

[10] R Sandefur, 'The Importance of Doing Nothing: Everyday Problems and Responses of Inaction', in P Pleasance, A Buck, and N Balmer (eds), in *Transforming Lives: Law and Social Process* (Stationary Office Books, 2006) at 115–117.

[11] W Felstiner, R Abel, and A Sarat, 'The Emergence and Transformation of Disputes: Naming, Blaming, Claiming' (1980) 15 Law and Society Review 631 at 637.

[12] O Fiss, 'Against Settlement' (1984) 93 Yale LJ 1073 at 1076–1078; R Jackson, *Review of Civil Litigation Costs: Final Report* (December 2009) at 41.

the negative impact that funding questions might have on the nature of dispute resolution.

5. Incorporating funding into the Code also helps overcome the likelihood that parties, due to funding concerns, are led to use resolution methods that are not well-suited to their dispute. It does so through the second main reason for incorporation: conduct guidance, which refers to the ability to use funding methods to promote the use of different pathways to dispute resolution. The Code adopts mandatory multi-tier legal expenses insurance as the default funding mechanism. This can promote a staged approach to dispute resolution for funded disputes, eg initial funding is provided for negotiation or Ombudsman schemes, second stage funding for mediation or early neutral evaluation (ENE), third stage funding for arbitration or litigation. In that way, the nature and level of funding available can be tailored to early, lower-cost, simpler, and speedy forms of resolution moving up to higher-cost, more complex, and slower forms of resolution. Thus, it can also promote procedural proportionality, as it ensures that parties properly utilise the various aspects of the dispute resolution system in a structured way. Through that it also helps to ensure that the system as a whole operates effectively, with disputes being considered through appropriate processes, so that its resources are targeted and distributed effectively across disputes. It is thus a means to help match disputes to appropriate dispute resolution processes.

6. For the first and second reasons for incorporation to be implemented effectively there needs to be coherence between funding and cost. That is most apparent where legal expenses insurance is concerned. Predictability and certainty where costs are concerned is a premise on which such insurance is based. Equally, coherence is needed to ensure that funding does not undermine the operation of the system. Where the two are treated separately from each other it is easier for funding reforms to be considered and made without consideration of their impact on the dispute resolution system's operation. Since the 1990s, there have been two significant instances where funding reform had a detrimental impact on the operation of the civil courts. The Woolf reforms were introduced in 1999 via the CPR at the same time as significant changes to the operation of contingency fee funding were effected by the Access to Justice Act 1999. The funding changes played a significant part in undermining the success of the Woolf reforms due to their adverse effect on the cost of litigation.[13] The Jackson Cost Review, which subsequently identified and sought to remedy the problems caused by the 1999 Act, was itself then undermined by the rejection of one of its recommendations concerning legal aid. Its reform proposals were predicated on no change being made to legal aid provision.[14] Separately from its recommendations, legal aid was reduced starkly, which not only led to a reduction in access to justice but also had a negative impact on the operation of the justice system through increasing the numbers of litigants-in-person. In both cases, the lack of coherence and appreciation of the likely consequences of the funding developments had an adverse impact on effective dispute resolution.[15]

7. In essence then, by incorporating funding provision in the Code, and linking it closely with the Part on costs, the intrinsic link between the two, and their importance,

[13] R Jackson (December 2009) at 43, also see chaps 9 and 10.

[14] R Jackson (December 2009) at 70.

[15] Civil Justice Council, *Access to Justice for Litigants-in-Person (or self-represented litigants* (November 2011); The Low Commission, *Report of the Low Commission on the Future of Advice and Legal Support, Tackling the Advice Deficit—A Strategy for Access to Advice and Legal Support on Social Welfare Law in England and Wales* (January 2014).

is highlighted. Incorporation is also to ensure that funding is considered as an integral part of the system, thus promoting systemic coherence. In a system that is not inquisitorial, but which rather depends upon party autonomy to raise, pursue, and to a significant extent resolve disputes by consent, access to effective funding is fundamentally important. Incorporation reflects that fact.

## RULE 1.—SCOPE AND PURPOSE

**(1) This Part concerns public and private funding mechanisms, the primary purpose of which is to secure effective and practical access to dispute resolution.**

**(2) Funding also enables parties to obtain effective advice and representation so as to best effect their procedural autonomy. It also promotes the economy, efficiency, and proportionality principles.**

**(3) A party's right to receive public and private funding is subject to any restriction or exemption set out in this Part or in legislation.**

*Sources: ELI-UNIDROIT Model Rules, rr 244, 245.*

## COMMENTARY

1. Article 6 of the European Convention on Human Rights requires the provision of practical and effective access to justice. This includes effective economic access. It leaves the choice of means by which effective access is secured to the State. Securing it does not necessarily require the provision of civil legal aid.[16]
2. This Part gives effect to the requirement to secure effective economic access, as part of the general access principle. It does not do so, as had been the case since the creation of the Welfare State, via the provision of civil legal aid as a, or the, key element of funding. Nor does it posit private funding via contingency fee or third-party funding as the primary funding source. On the contrary, it promotes a combined approach to funding, which incorporates both public and private funding mechanisms, the principal one of which is before-the-event (BTE) legal expenses insurance. Funding is also intended to encompass both access to funding for consensual settlement processes and for adjudicative processes. To ensure the approach to funding operates coherently the right to receive public and private funding may be subject to restriction or exemption, albeit they must not be such as to reduce funding below the minimum necessary to secure practical and effective access.[17]
3. In addition to promoting effective access to dispute resolution, funding is also intended to promote several other procedural principles. Funding enables parties to obtain legal advice and assistance. This can help them to properly identify and assess their dispute, identify any appropriate dispute resolution methods, and participate in them effectively. It is thus also a means to promote effective party autonomy in dispute resolution. Through this, funding also promotes economy, efficiency, and proportionality. Effective advice and representation can promote the use of the most speedy and economic dispute resolution method. Effective participation, facilitated

[16] *Golder v UK* (1975) 1 EHRR 524 at [24]–[26]; A A Matić, *Just Words—The Effectiveness of Civil Justice in European Human Rights Jurisprudence* (CUP, 2020) at 182–195.

[17] *Airey v Ireland* (1979) 2 EHRR 305 at [26].

through funded assistance, can promote greater understanding of the resolution process used and satisfaction in it; an issue of particular importance to vulnerable parties who need specific assistance, over-and-above that which can be provided by a digital procedure, to access means of dispute resolution effectively. In turn, funding can help to promote procedural equality, early resolution, and the prospect that the parties will abide by any resolution reached, the last of which stems from the additional understanding and confidence in the resolution process and its fairness driven by more effective participation.[18] Proportionality's promotion follows on from the fact that funding promotes speedier and more economic resolution. It should also be noted that the presence of lawyers within the system to advise and represent parties is one of the means by which the publicity principle, and the accountability it instils in the system, is given effect.[19] Effective funding thus variously promotes a range of procedural principles that underpin an effective dispute resolution system and is, accordingly, a matter that promotes the public interest.

## RULE 2.—PRESUMPTION IN FAVOUR OF PRIVATE FUNDING

**(1) Parties are primarily responsible for securing funding for civil dispute resolution. This is to be carried out principally through self-funding or, where that is not available or sufficient, through a means of private funding specified in this Code.**
**(2) Where parties are unable to self-fund or secure private funding, subject to any restrictions in this Code or in legislation, they may apply for public funding.**

## COMMENTARY

1. This rule establishes a hierarchy in funding provision. Parties are primarily responsible for funding the resolution of their disputes. Where self-funding is not available, the secondary funding basis is private funding. This also places responsibility for funding on the parties, albeit it is a responsibility that is promoted by the State mandating individuals to take out BTE legal expenses insurance. Only where self-funding and private funding are unavailable is the safety net of civil legal aid available.
2. This approach, which gives precedence to party-based funding, is adopted for a number of reasons. It is intended to promote individual responsibility. Whether and how to resolve a dispute is a serious question that ought to be taken seriously. Placing responsibility on individuals to fund dispute resolution promotes that. It also, through the promotion of BTE legal expenses insurance, promotes individual responsibility by increasing awareness of dispute resolution processes and the ability to access them. Requiring individuals to take out insurance can also play a key role in promoting public legal education. An educated population is one that is properly

[18] C Menkel-Meadow, 'Toward Another View of Legal Negotiation: The Structure of Problem-solving' (1984) 31 University of California Los Angeles Law Review 754; T Tyler and J Sevier, 'How Do the Courts Create Popular Legitimacy?: The Role of Establishing the Truth, Punishing Justly, and/or Acting Through Just Procedures' (2013/2014) 77(3) Albany Law Review 1095; S Diacoff, 'Collaborative Law: A New Tool For the Lawyer's Toolkit' (2009) 20 University of Florida Journal of Law & Public Policy 131.

[19] J Sorabji, 'Justice without Lawyers', in X Kramer, A Biard, J Hoevenaars, and E Themeli (eds), *New Pathways to Civil Justice in Europe* (Springer, 2021).

able to exercise individual responsibility, and thus preventive justice is made more effective.

3. Giving precedence to party-based funding is also intended to meet a further objective, that of helping individuals exercise self-restraint in terms of use of the State's resources. Responsible individuals should draw on the State as little as possible and only where absolutely necessary. By doing so, they help the State to more effectively distribute scarce resources across the community and particularly to those who truly need to call upon them. Individual responsibility here thus promotes distributive justice, which underpins the purposive and proportionality principles.
4. Finally, and again in order to promote the proportionality principle, where an individual is directly responsible for funding dispute resolution, either through self or private funding methods, they have a direct interest in the effective management of dispute resolution. One of the problems that arose in respect of CFA funding from 2000 to 2013 was that parties had no financial interest in managing the cost of litigation, and hence no interest in managing the nature and extent of it. This was part of the reason why litigation costs expanded post-2000 rather than being reduced by the Woolf reforms.[20] This rule and the precedence it creates is intended to ensure that such a situation cannot arise again in future.

## RULE 3.—COMBINATION OF FUNDING SOURCES

**Parties may utilise any combination of private funding sources, including self-funding. Where available, public funding may supplement private funding.**

## COMMENTARY

1. This rule makes clear that mixed funding, whether of private funding methods or private and public funding methods, is permissible. It thus eliminates any possibility that satellite litigation could arise seeking to challenge the validity of such approaches. The mixing of private and public funding can, however, only properly be used where public funding supplements private funding. As such, questions concerning whether it is appropriate for private funding to provide an additional or top-up source of funding over and above public funding are minimised if not avoided entirely,[21] as are questions such as those relating to the use and validity of hybrid DBAs, ie ones that involve the use of DBAs and other forms of lawyer's retainer.[22] Thus this approach avoids a rich source of satellite litigation over such matters that has bedevilled the CPR.
2. In addition to eliminating the potential scope for challenges to the use of mixed funding, this rule serves a positive purpose. By specifying that mixed funding is permissible, it seeks to promote access to dispute resolution consistently with the general approach to funding based on individual responsibility.[23] By expressly permitting

[20] R Jackson (December 2009) at 43.

[21] *Merrick v Law Society* [2007] EWHC 2997 (Admin); *Hyde v Milton Keynes NHS Foundation Trust* [2017] EWCA Civ 399; [2018] 1 WLR 597. The prohibition on top-up funding is not repeated here due to the primacy given to the use of private funding and public funding's supplementary role.

[22] Civil Justice Council, *The Damages-based Agreements Reform Project—Drafting and Policy Issues* (2015) at 26–32; *Zuberi v Lexlaw Ltd* [2021] EWCA Civ 16; [2021] 1 WLR 2729.

[23] S Clark and R Jackson, *The Reform of Civil Justice* (Sweet & Maxwell, 2018) at 73.

the use of mixed funding, it creates the basis on which individuals can consider how best to finance their approach to resolution; it is thus intended to promote greater consideration by individuals, and advice from lawyers in that regard, of how best to utilise the various funding sources available to them. It is also intended to promote innovation and competition in private funding methods, as different funding providers are incentivised to devise and market different funding products (eg basic BTE legal expenses insurance products, mixed insurance, and contingency funding products), differing forms of contingency funding product, and so on. Innovation and competition serve to promote greater access to funding that matches different parties' funding needs.

## SECTION 2: PRIVATE FUNDING MECHANISMS

### RULE 4.—LEGAL EXPENSES INSURANCE

**(1) The principal source of private civil dispute resolution funding shall be before-the-event legal expenses insurance. After-the event legal expenses insurance may also be obtained.**

**(2) Before-the-event legal expenses insurance shall cover pre-action and post-issue legal advice and representation. All such insurance must contain provisions requiring the use of pre-action dispute management provided for under Part 5 of this Code.**

**(3) All adults and minors resident in England and Wales must obtain a minimum level of before-the-event legal expenses insurance each year. Such insurance shall apply to all civil disputes. Greater levels of insurance may be obtained.**

**(4) Insurance for minors under the age of 18 shall be included within the minimum level of before-the-event legal expenses insurance obtained by an adult who has parental responsibility for them.**

**(5) During any period when an adult is in receipt of State benefits, the State may either pay the premium applicable to the minimum level of before-the-event legal expenses insurance, provide such individuals with access to a State-run before-the-event expenses insurance scheme providing such cover, or provide them with access to civil legal aid that provides an equivalent level of insurance cover.**

**(6) Use of any available before-the-event or after-the event legal expenses insurance is not mandatory. However, where legal expenses insurance is in place a party may not apply for public funding except, where necessary and available, as a means to supplement it.**

**(7) Legal persons may obtain either before-the-event or after-the event legal expenses insurance.**

### COMMENTARY

1. Before-the-event legal expenses insurance is well-established in England and Wales,[24] although it is generally under-utilised as a form of litigation

[24] 'Before-the-event' because it is insurance that is taken out before a cause of action has accrued. 'After-the-event' insurance is taken out after a cause of action has accrued.

funding.[25] It is typically found in mandatory car insurance or home contents insurance policies, albeit many individuals with such policies are unaware of that fact.[26] Such insurance generally covers legal expenses relating to road traffic accident, home insurance, and employment disputes.[27] After-the-event legal expenses insurance is equally well-established and is typically used in conjunction with CFA funding. The funding scheme set out in this Part builds on the current market. It seeks to make BTE legal expenses funding the primary form of litigation funding; an approach which is already to a significant degree established in several European jurisdictions.[28] It does so by making it mandatory for individuals to take out such insurance. Such a step is predicated on the introduction of greater predictability and certainty concerning the costs of dispute resolution, as provided for in Part 3 of this Code.[29] Companies and other legal persons may also take out such insurance.

2. From a principled perspective this approach promotes individual responsibility rather than reliance upon the State to provide litigation funding.[30] It also enables the State to focus resources drawn from general taxation on other areas, such as the proper provision of criminal legal aid, financial support for individuals who are unable to pay the cost of their legal expenses insurance premiums, or the provision of civil legal aid (in so far as it needs to be made available). It thus helps the State, from a general perspective, avoid or at least minimise in one area what Calabresi and Bobbitt described as the tragic choice to be made where the State has multiple competing and urgent demands on its resources and the allocation to one means the lack of allocation to another.[31]
3. From a practical perspective, on any realistic assessment it is also unlikely that publicly funded civil legal aid will be reinvigorated and returned to its pre-LASPO provision, never mind the level of assistance it provided at its height. In any event, a return to legal aid as the primary mechanism for securing litigation funding is sub-optimal. Even at its height, legal aid did not provide universal provision for meritorious cases. To expect a shift to universal provision of legal aid is worse than unrealistic. Mandatory BTE legal expenses insurance can, however, provide universal cover both in terms of scope, ie, the causes of action it applies to, and in terms of population. Rather than providing a minimum level of legal assistance sufficient for compliance with article 6 of the European Convention on Human Rights, it could fully realise practical and effective access to a fair trial, and more broadly, to dispute resolution. Its promotion could thus provide a more comprehensive and effective form of funding than has previously been put in place in England and Wales.

[25] S Clark and R Jackson (2018) at 75; Civil Justice Council, *The Law and Practicalities of Before-The-Event (BTE) Insurance—An Information Study* (2017) at xiii and Section G; C Hodges, *Delivering Dispute Resolution* (Hart, 2019) at 140.

[26] Civil Justice Council (2017) at 134.

[27] Civil Justice Council (2017) at 90.

[28] G Hadfield and J Heine, 'Life in the Law-Thick World: Legal Resources for Ordinary Americans', in S Estreicher and J Radice (2016) at 47; J Peysner (2014) at 13; L Follett, 'Access to Justice—Rights or Rations? Comparing European Legal Aid Systems in the Context of a Shrinking Budgetary Environment' (2008) 1 Plymouth Law Review 1 at 6, 18. S Choudhry, M Trebilcock, and J Wilson, 'Growing Legal Aid in Ontario into the Middle Class: A Proposal for Public Legal Expenses Insurance', in M Trebilcock, A Duggan, and L Sossin, *Middle Income Access to Justice* (University of Toronto Press, 2012).

[29] J Peysner (2014).

[30] S Butler, *Assuring Affordable Healthcare for All Americans*, The Heritage Lectures 218 (Heritage Foundation) at 6.

[31] G Calabresi and P Bobbitt, *Tragic Choices* (Norton, 1978).

4. Mandatory coverage would have other advantages. By mandating coverage, it would ensure that everyone had such cover. Permissive uptake would not produce such a result. Individuals generally do not believe they will be involved in legal disputes. As a result, many would choose not to take out insurance, which would either leave them unable to cover dispute resolution costs where disputes arise or would lead them to either not pursuing a dispute or under-settling it, which in turn would hamper the promotion of preventive justice. A mandatory approach, achieved through auto-enrolment for those in employment and through state welfare provision for those who are not, would obviate the lack-of-cover problem.[32] It would also help ensure that insurance premiums were as low as possible, as it would secure the broadest spectrum of risk within the insured population, which by definition would be a very large pool. Rule 4 does, however, provide the State with three options where provision of assistance to individuals who are in receipt of State benefits are concerned. It could either fund their minimum level of insurance cover as a State benefit. If, however, that option is too costly,[33] it could provide an equivalent level of cover via a publicly run and funded legal expenses insurance scheme solely applicable to those in receipt of state benefits. Or it may fund an equivalent level of cover to that provided by the minimum level of cover provided by private BTE legal expenses insurance cover through civil legal aid, which is provided for under rule 8.
5. More broadly, a mandatory approach would also promote dispute formation as it could be used to promote awareness of the possibility of access to justice. For individuals who are financially or socially vulnerable or marginalised within society and thus less likely to perceive that they have suffered an actionable harm or, if they perceive they have done so are less likely to take steps to resolve it because they view the justice system as out-of-reach, knowledge that they have insurance can help overcome those issues.[34] It can help them secure advice as to their rights and the means to seek redress for harm. It can thus help overcome what would otherwise be a structural barrier to access by redressing financial or social marginalisation and could thus promote procedural equality.[35]
6. While mandatory insurance could promote dispute formation, this would not, however, produce an increasingly litigious society.[36] In the first instance, ready access to dispute resolution mechanisms would be expected to promote behaviour that was less likely to result in disputes arising. Access to legal advice can help individuals order and carry out their affairs consistently with their legal obligations, ie, access to advice can help promote preventive justice thus reducing the prospect that disputes

[32] In Germany the question of mandatory insurance was considered, but rejected; P Gottwald, 'Funding Civil Litigation Through Legal Expenses Insurance in Germany', in R Assy and A Higgins (eds), *Principles, Procedure, and Justice: Essays in Honour of Adrian Zuckerman* (OUP, 2021) at 200.

[33] S Choudhry, M Trebilcock, and J Wilson, in M Trebilcock, A Duggan, and L Sossin (2012) at 395; J Sorabji, 'Legal Expenses Insurance and the Future of Effective Litigation Funding' (2022) 4 Erasmus Law Review 189.

[34] OECD, *Building a Business Case for Access to Justice*, <https://www.oecd.org/gov/building-a-business-case-for-access-to-justice.pdf>; P Pleasance and N Balmer, 'Caught in the Middle: Justiciable Problems and the Use of Lawyers', in M Trebilcock, A Duggan, and L Sossin (2012); C Hodges (2019) at 140.

[35] It would thus overcome the problem identified by G Hadfield and J Heine (2014) that specific groups within society view the justice system as 'not for them'.

[36] E Blankenburg, 'Access to Justice and Alternatives to Courts: European Procedural Justice Compared' (1995) 14 (Jul) CJQ 176 at 183.

will form.[37] Practical access to conflict and dispute resolution would also help promote behaviour consistent with such obligations obviating resort to litigation, ie it would help to promote conflict defusion and early resolution. Ready access to the courts would, equally, help promote rule-compliance, thus reducing the prospect of resort of dispute resolution. Additionally, because mandatory insurance must be integrated with the systemic approach to dispute resolution within the Code funded parties would be directed to the most appropriate dispute resolution pathway prior to resort to litigation. In that way, early resolution is likely to be promoted more effectively. Mandatory insurance would, in this way, also help embed the integrated approach to dispute resolution set out within the Code. Particularly, it could help mandate use of consensual forms of resolution prior to the commencement of proceedings through insurance requiring a tiered approach to dispute resolution funding.

## RULE 5.—CONTINGENCY FUNDING AGREEMENTS

**(1) Parties may enter into a contingency fee agreement with their lawyers. Such agreements may be entered into irrespective of the nature of the dispute.**

**(2) A contingency fee agreement is one**

**(a) where the lawyer agrees to provide the party with legal advice and/or representation on the basis that the party is under no obligation to pay them in the event their dispute is not resolved in their favour; and**

**(b) the party agrees to pay their lawyer in the event the dispute is resolved in their favour.**

**(3) A dispute is resolved in a party's favour when it either concludes by way of consensual settlement or judgment in their favour.**

**(4) Payment under a contingency fee agreement may be made on a fee-plus-uplift-basis or a damages-basis, or any combination of the two.**

**(5) Payment on a fee-plus-uplift basis is calculated by reference to the lawyer's base fee, which is a fee for the total work done for their client, and an additional fee. The base fee may be calculated on an hourly rate or as a fixed fee. The additional fee is to be calculated as a percentage of the base fee.**

**(6) Payment on a damages-basis is calculated as a percentage of the damages or settlement amount recovered by the party.**

*Sources: ELI-UNIDROIT Model Rules, rr 245; Courts and Legal Services Act 1990, ss 58, 58A, 58AA.*

## COMMENTARY

1. England and Wales have permitted the use of contingency fee funding since 1995.[38] Since then contingency fee funding, in the form of CFAs and latterly DBAs, has been promoted as the primary form of litigation funding. CFAs were particularly

[37] Increasing the efficacy of the shadow of the law through making access to dispute resolution more readily available and by making access to the law itself more readily available would be expected to achieve this end; R Mnookin and L Kornhauser, 'Bargaining in the Shadow of the Law' (1978–1979) 88 Yale LJ 950.

[38] The Courts and Legal Services Act 1990 (Commencement No 9) Order 1993 (SI 1993/2132); Conditional Fee Agreements Order 1995 (SI 1995/1674): Conditional Fee Agreements Regulations 1995 (SI 1995/1675).

expanded in 1999 on the basis that they would replace legal aid.[39] Prior to these developments such funding was prohibited, primarily on the basis that it was unethical as it gave lawyers an interest in litigation. Such an interest it was believed would tend to corrupt the administration of justice by leading to witness coaching, the manufacture of evidence, improper examination of witnesses, and the proliferation of meretricious legal arguments, all of which were aimed at helping a lawyer secure success at the expense of justice in order to benefit themselves.[40] These concerns were rejected in the late 1990s on the basis that contingency funding could promote access to justice, while also facilitating a retrenchment of the state through the withdrawal of legal aid.[41] Experience has shown that the fears around its introduction have not been realised.[42]

2. This rule maintains the general availability of CFA and DBA funding. It does so by adopting a simplified approach, which is aimed at maximising its utility as a secondary form of private funding. It does not, as a consequence, maintain the technical distinction between CFAs and DBAs. It does, however, provide that contingency funding can be provided, without limit in terms of the type of dispute, on either of those two bases. Rule 5(4) promotes maximum flexibility by expressly permitting a contingency agreement to incorporate a combination of the two (CFA and DBA) approaches to the calculation of payment; an instance of the approach outlined in rule 3, that any combination of funding method may be used. It also does so by adopting a simplified regulatory approach to CFAs, which differs from the cautious approach of the 1990 Act.
3. Where lawyers' fees are concerned, rules 5(5) and (6) adopt the approaches taken to both CFAs and DBAs. Rule 5(5) clarifies that which is, at the least, implicit in the approach taken to CFAs under the Courts and Legal Services Act 1990 that a lawyer's base fee may be calculated by reference to a fixed fee rather than by way of an hourly rate. While the use of fixed fees in this way is out of the ordinary under the 1990 Act,[43] within the scheme set out in the Code and its promotion of tariff fees, the use of fixed fees as a means of setting the contingency fee base rate could develop as lawyers' business models adapt to fixed fee recoverability. Fixing the base rate by reference to the tariff fees may further promote proportionate dispute management by aligning lawyer-client fees with the level of recoverability. It may also, if the success fee were calculated by reference to a fixed base fee improve access to the full range of dispute resolution methods via this funding method by increasing a party's certainty in terms of their total potential fee liability where their own lawyer is concerned in the event of success.
4. Neither rule 5(5) or (6) provide any cap on the level of uplift or percentage of damages to be paid under a contingency fee agreement. This is justified on two grounds.

[39] The Conditional Fee Agreements Order (1998) (SI 1998/1860); M Zander, 'Will the Revolution in the Funding of Civil Litigation in England Eventually Lead to Contingency Fees?' (2002) 52 DePaul Law Review 259 at 269; *Callery v Gray* [2001] EWCA Civ 1117; [2001] 1 WLR 2112.

[40] Royal Commission on Legal Services, *Final Report* (Cmnd Paper, 7648 of 1979) at 176 (The Benson Commission).

[41] P Middleton, *Report to the Lord Chancellor* (September 1997) at 5.47; J Peysner (2014) chap 6; Access to Justice Act 1999, ss 27 and 28.

[42] ELI-UNIDROIT Model Rules, r 245 commentary.

[43] P Hurst, S Middleton, R Mallalieu KC, J Ayling KC, N Creaney KC, and S Kapoor, *Costs and Funding Following the Civil Justice Reforms: Questions and Answers* (Thomson Reuters, 2023) at 59.

The amount an individual is willing to pay their lawyer is and ought to be a matter for them; it is a question of party autonomy. Secondly, as the scheme under this Code understands this form of funding to be secondary to BTE legal expenses insurance, any argument that the State needs to protect litigants by regulating fee levels is met by the fact that the primary means of funding does not provide for uplift payments. Thus, the use of contingency fee agreements does not stand in need of regulation in the same way as it would were they to continue to be the primary source of private funding.

## RULE 6.—DISPUTE FUNDING

**(1) Parties may enter into dispute funding arrangements.**

**(2) A dispute funding arrangement is one where a non-party provides funding to a party to a dispute to enable them to pay their costs and does so to promote access to dispute resolution.**

**(3) A dispute funding arrangement is valid if provided in total or partial consideration of a percentage of any damages awarded or settlement due to the funded party or some other sum.**

**(4) Dispute funding may also be provided altruistically.**

*Sources: ELI-UNIDROIT Model Rules, rr 237, 245; Courts and Services Act 1990, s 58B.*

## COMMENTARY

1. Dispute funding is the term adopted in this Code for what is known as litigation or third-party funding. The change in name reflects the general approach taken in the Code that focuses on dispute resolution rather than litigation. Such funding can be provided altruistically (pure funding).[44] It can also, and increasingly is, provided for financial gain through commercial or 'third party' funding.[45] It can also be provided to fund strategic, ideological litigation, via the Internet: crowd-funding.[46] On the different approaches to costs awards to different forms of dispute funding see, Part 3, rule 15. This rule and rule 5 draw a clear distinction between dispute funding arrangements and contingency funding agreements. They thus avoid the possibility of confusion arising as to whether dispute funding arrangements are, or can be, contingency funding agreements and thus subject to the same regulation as the latter.[47]

[44] *Hamilton v Al Fayed* [2002] EWCA Civ 665; [2003] QB 1175.

[45] *Arkin v Borchard Lines Ltd* [2005] EWCA Civ 655; [2005] 1 WLR 3055; Civil Justice Council, *Improved Access to Justice—Funding Options & Proportionate Costs—The Future Funding of Litigation—Alternative Funding Structures* (2007); R Mulheron and P Cashman, 'Third Party Funding: A Changing Landscape' (2008) 28 CJQ 312; R Jackson, *Review of Civil Litigation Costs: Preliminary Report* (Judicial Office, May 2009) Vol I, chap 15.

[46] J. Tomlinson, 'Crowdfunding Public Interest Judicial Reviews' (2019) Public Law; J Ren, V Raghupathi, and W Raghupathi, 'Exploring the Factors that Determine the Success of Litigation Crowdfunding: Implications for Social Justice' (2021) 169 Technological Forecasting & Social Change 120813.

[47] It thus avoids the problem that arose from *R (PACCAR Inc) v Competition Appeal Tribunal* [2023] UKSC 28; [2023] 1 WLR 2594, where the Supreme Court, surprisingly, held that some forms of third party funding agreements were DBAs.

2. Dispute funding promotes access to dispute resolution whether provided altruistically, for commercial or for ideological reasons.[48] It enables claims to be prosecuted or defended where other funding sources are unavailable or are available on less favourable terms. This is particularly the case where commercial funding is available for higher value cases that may not come within the scope of legal expenses insurance. It is also likely to be the case where, as in the European Union or Australia, multi-party claims are pursued by way of representative proceedings.[49] Commercial funding is unlikely, however, to provide an effective means to promote access to justice for low or intermediate value claims given the limited likelihood of a sufficient financial reward in return for providing the funding,[50] albeit the growth of portfolio funding is increasing the broader availability of this form of funding to such claims.[51] Altruistic and ideological funding, where available, is however able to promote access to justice more generally across dispute type and value.[52]
3. This rule defines the nature of dispute funding. Generally, it does so without drawing a difference between the three types of funding arrangement. In doing so it emphasises that giving effect to the general access principle is the rationale for permitting parties to enter into such funding arrangements.[53] It specifically defines the broad scope of commercial funding arrangements, which are those generally provided on a no-win, no fee basis, with the fee, in the event of success, being a percentage share of the damages or settlement award.[54] The rule acknowledges that the fee may, however, be a defined lump sum or other financial arrangement.

## RULE 7.—CONTROL OF CONTINGENCY FEE AGREEMENTS AND DISPUTE FUNDING ARRANGEMENTS

**(1) Contingency fee agreements and dispute funding arrangements must comply with the requirements set out in this rule.**
**(2) Champerty and maintenance do not apply to contingency funding agreements or dispute funding arrangements. Such agreements may, however, be held to be unenforceable where they are not consistent with the general access principle.**
**(3) Except where funding is provided altruistically by way of a gift, both contingency fee agreements and dispute funding arrangements must comply with the law of contract.**
**(4) Funders providing dispute funding other than altruistically must be licenced. Legislation shall provide for an appropriate licensing scheme operated by the Financial Conduct Authority. Lawyers may not provide dispute funding to their clients.**

48 *Gulf Azov Shipping Co Ltd v Idisi (Costs)* [2004] EWCA Civ 92 at [54].
49 Directive (EU) 2020/1828 of the European Parliament and of the Council of 25 November 2020 on representative actions for the protection of the collective interests of consumers and repealing Directive 2009/22/EC, art 10; *Campbells Cash and Carry Pty Ltd v Fostif Pty Ltd* (2006) 229 ALR 58, (2006) 80 ALJR 1441; Australian Law Reform Commission, *Integrity, Fairness and Efficiency—An Inquiry into Class Action Proceedings and Third-Party Litigation Funders—Final Report* (2018).
50 J Peysner, 'Playing the Man Not the Ball', in W van Boom (2017) at 69.
51 Portfolio funding arises where a funder packages together a number of different disputes, with differing risk profiles from the same client, and secures funding for the package.
52 ELI-UNIDROIT Model Rules, r 245, comments.
53 D Neuberger, *From Barretry, Maintenance and Champerty to Litigation Funding* (8 May 2013).
54 R Jackson (May 2009) Vol 1 at viii.

**(5) Where a party has entered into either a contingency fee agreement or dispute funding arrangement, they must disclose the fact of such matters to all other parties and to the court. The identity of any dispute funder must be disclosed. Disclosure must be made within a reasonable time of the agreement or of the arrangement commencing. Where necessary, for a legitimate purpose, the court may require disclosure of the details of a contingency fee agreement or dispute funding arrangement. Disclosure may be ordered subject to necessary redactions to protect the disclosing party from undergoing a disadvantage arising from the disclosure.**

**(6) Contingency fee agreements and dispute funding arrangements must not undermine a funded party's ability to exercise effective control over the conduct of proceedings. Nor may they provide for the effective assignment of a claim to a lawyer or funder.**

*Sources: ELI-UNIDROIT Model Rules, rr 237, 245; Courts and Services Act 1990, ss 58, 58A, 58AA, and 58B; Federal Court of Australia Practice Note CM17.*

## COMMENTARY

1. This rule concerns the regulation of contingency fee agreements and dispute funding arrangements. The former are currently regulated by sections 58, 58A, and 58AA of the Court and Legal Services Act 1990. The latter are not subject to statutory regulation, despite the basis for such regulation having been enacted through the Access to Justice Act 1999, which inserted section 58B into the 1990 Act.[55] That section has never, however, been brought into force. Such regulation as there is of dispute funding arises at common law.[56] Commercial funders have, since 2011, also been subject to self-regulation through the Code of Conduct of the, voluntary, Association of Litigation Funders of England and Wales.[57]

2. The Code does not seek to replicate the approach taken to regulation under the 1990 Act or the common law. Regulation of both CFAs and DBAs under the 1990 Act is complex. It has led to considerable satellite costs litigation, and where DBAs are concerned, their underutilisation.[58] Regulation of dispute funding (third-party funding) has broadly arisen against the backdrop of the continued half-life of the doctrines of champerty and maintenance.[59] This rule's starting point is that both types of funding are now accepted to be permissible due to the role they play in enhancing access to justice (the general access principle) and that that policy objective outweighs historic concerns about the possibility that their use could undermine the proper administration of justice. Hence there is no need to maintain the application of champerty and maintenance.[60] The control mechanism that replaces them is based on the rationale for rendering such forms of funding permissible: that it must be provided consistently with the general access principle. Funding cannot thus be provided for other, ulterior, motives, such as to harass a defendant or where it would tend to corrupt public justice because it is provided to increase damages,

[55] Access to Justice Act 1999, s 28.

[56] Competition Appeal Tribunal Rules, r 113. M Friston (ed), *Friston on Costs* (OUP, 2023) at 1118–1124.

[57] Code of Conduct of Litigation Funders (2018); R Jackson, *Third Party Funding or Litigation Funding* (6th Lecture in the Implementation Programme, 2011); M Friston (ed) (2023) at 1116–1117.

[58] R Mulheron and N Bacon, *An Independent Review of the DBA Regulations 2013* (The Damages-Based Agreements Regulations Reform Project 2019, 2019).

[59] M Friston (ed) (2023) chaps 29 and 33.

[60] A Zuckerman, *Zuckerman on Civil Procedure—Principles of Practice* (Sweet & Maxwell, 2021) at 1427.

suppress evidence, or suborn witnesses.[61] Rule 7 thus more clearly reflects the fact that public policy has changed to promote the use of funding mechanisms generally.[62] It also accepts that promotion of both forms of funding increases competition between funders, and against the backdrop of mandatory BTE legal expenses insurance, should increase the range, variety, and cost-effectiveness of funding methods. A multiplicity of competing funding methods ought also to ensure that the widest range of disputes, particularly those involving small and medium-sized businesses that might not otherwise utilise legal expenses insurance, can be pursued.[63]

3. The basic mechanism provided by rule 7 to control both forms of funding arrangement is the requirement that they must comply with the law of contract and that, in respect of dispute funding, commercial funders must be licenced. The latter point is an explicit rejection of the self-regulatory framework currently in place for third party litigation funding, which was introduced in 2011 and endorsed by the Jackson Costs Review.[64] Such an approach may have been appropriate while such funding was in its nascent phase; heavy-handed regulation may have stifled its development.[65] The market is now more fully developed. That risk does not therefore remain a valid reason to avoid formal regulation. Moreover, inherent in such funding is a risk that the funder may not have adequate capital to cover any potential cost liability. Statutory licensing, as was accepted in Australia,[66] provides an effective means of minimising that risk. It would ensure that an appropriate body, such as the Financial Conduct Authority, could assess the financial viability of a funder before they are permitted to enter or remain in the market thus protecting their clients and their opponents against the risk that they might not be able to meet their funding obligations.
4. Rule 7(4) maintains minimum limits on what lawyers can provide by way of funding. Were a lawyer to seek to provide dispute funding, they would need to be licensed. The rule prohibits licences to be given to permit lawyer to provide this form of funding to their own client. Thus, the rule maintains the prohibition on lawyers funding their own client's litigation, outside of contingency fee funding or the assignment to them of the cause of action. On one level this might appear unprincipled. All funding gives rise to conflicts of interest between lawyer and client and provides incentives to the former to act in unethical ways. Having accepted the validity of lawyers providing one form of funding it might appear incoherent to prohibit them from providing the other. However, as has been recognised in other common law jurisdictions, the nature of the conflict of interest arising from commercial funding, were lawyers to provide it to their own clients, is particularly acute. Where contingency fee arrangements are entered into, the lawyer remains a representative of the party for whom they act. Where there is an assignment of the cause of action, the lawyer is acting for themselves. Where dispute funding is provided, the nature of the relationship is

[61] M Friston (ed) (2023) at 1057–1058; *R (Factortame) v Secretary of State for the Environment, Transport and the Regions (No 8)* [2002] EWCA Civ 932; [2003] QB 38 at [36]; *London & Regional (St George's Court) v Ministry of Defence* [2008] EWHC 526 (TCC) at [103].

[62] *Kellar v Williams* [2004] UKPC 30; [2005] 1 LRC 582 at [21].

[63] Victorian Law Commission (Australia), *Access to Justice—Litigation Funding and Group Proceedings: Report* (2018).

[64] R Jackson (December 2009) chap 11.

[65] R Jackson (December 2009) at 119.

[66] *Australian Law Reform Commission, Integrity, Fairness and Efficiency—An Inquiry into Class Action Proceedings and Third-Party Litigation Funders* (2018) For the current position, see S. Friel, *The Law and Business of Litigation Finance* (Bloombsury, 2024).

different: they take on more of the quality of the client while remaining their client's legal adviser. In such a case there is an increased risk that they would be able to exercise a greater degree of control, either consciously or subconsciously, over the client for their own ends. Given this risk, and the availability of a wide range of other funding sources and means by which lawyers could finance claims, it is reasonable to place this restriction on lawyers' ability to provide dispute funding to their own clients.[67]

5. Rule 7 also contains transparency provisions requiring funding arrangements to be disclosed[68] and funders to be identified.[69] These are intended to put the parties and court on notice of the existence of such arrangements. Thus, for instance, they enable parties, or the court to consider of its own initiative, whether to seek or make an order for security for costs where a dispute funding arrangement is in place. Disclosure of the details of such arrangements should generally not be required. It may, however, be required where, for instance, it is necessary for an application for costs against a non-party or in respect of an application for security for costs.[70] It may also be required to enable the court and the other party to proceedings to consider whether the provision of funding and the nature of the agreement or arrangements are such as to undermine the proper administration of justice, and is thus contrary to the general access principle.[71] Disclosure is thus intended to secure a fair process. Further to that last point, disclosure should not be such as to put the funded party at a procedural disadvantage. Before it is ordered the court should consider what steps may need to be taken to redact the terms of any agreement necessary to protect against that possibility.
6. In addition to protection for the non-funded party, the rule also protects funded parties by prohibiting lawyers or funders from exercising control over the conduct of a dispute. Funding is provided to enhance access, ie, the party's ability to resolve their dispute, not primarily to promote the financial interests of the lawyer or commercial funder. The latter may be a by-product of the former and may properly incentivise provision of such funding arrangements, but it must not be viewed or treated as their primary purpose.

## SECTION 3: PUBLIC FUNDING MECHANISMS

### RULE 8.—PUBLIC FUNDING

**(1) The State shall provide parties with public funding where no other form of funding is available.**

**(2) Public funding shall cover both legal advice and representation before and after proceedings commence. It shall be no more than necessary and reasonable to secure a fair procedure to resolve the parties' dispute.**

*Sources: ELI-UNIDROIT Model Rules, r 244; Rushcliffe Committee Report on Legal Aid and Legal Advice in England and Wales (Cmd 664).*

[67] Victorian Law Commission (Australia), *Access to Justice—Litigation Funding and Group Proceedings: Report* (2018) at 3.45.

[68] *Wall v The Royal Bank of Scotland PLC* [2016] EWHC 2460 (Comm); [2017] 4 WLR 2.

[69] *Reeves v Sprecher* [2007] EWHC 3226 (Ch); [2009] 1 Costs LR 1.

[70] *Re RBS Rights Litigation* [2017] EWHC 463 (Ch); [2017] 1 WLR 3539.

[71] *Campbells Cash & Carry Pty Ltd v Fostif Pty Ltd* (2006) 229, 386; M Legg, *Case Management and Complex Civil Litigation* (Federation Press, 2011) at 233.

## COMMENTARY

1. Public assistance for individuals who are unable to finance dispute resolution is long-established. Before the court's power to award costs was introduced in the 13th century, judges could, for instance, remit legal fees for impecunious litigants. This power was formalised in 1494 and 1531 with the development of the *in forma pauperis* procedure, which enabled impecunious litigants to issue claims for no fee and be provided with counsel who also acted for no fee. It also provided some protection from adverse cost awards.[72] A formal civil legal aid scheme was not, however, introduced until 1949.[73] Currently, its scope is such that it has forcefully been said to provide no more than the bare minimum provision needed to comply with the requirements of article 6 of the European Convention on Human Rights.[74]
2. This rule makes continuing provision for civil legal aid funding. It does not set out a detailed scheme, which ought to be set out in legislation and integrated and consistent with this Code. Integration is necessary to ensure that it is developed as a necessary supplement only to the general approach to costs and funding.[75] Integration is also intended to ensure that public funding is separated out from criminal legal aid provision. This would help ensure that the two sets of funding are not conflated, and resource pressure on one does not adversely affect the other.
3. This rule does not, as might be expected, limit public funding to access to the court and to a fair trial.[76] It encompasses funding other forms of dispute resolution, including pre-action dispute resolution. It is also, unlike the current legal aid scheme, not limited in terms of scope. It is a universal scheme. This is to maintain consistency with the general approach to funding, and particularly to ensure that it promotes the same tiered approach to prevention, consensual resolution, and adjudication that is to be provided for by BTE legal expenses insurance.
4. Finally, rule 8 does not make provision for the introduction of either a contingent legal aid fund (a CLAF) or a supplementary legal aid scheme (a SLAS). While the introduction of such schemes has been suggested in England and Wales, they are mechanisms to supplement provision of publicly funded legal aid.[77] As this Code provides public funding as a safety net, secondary to private funding and particularly BTE legal expenses insurance, there is no need to introduce either a CLAF or SLAS as a means to make up for any shortfall in public legal aid funding.

[72] R Egerton, *Legal Aid* (Routledge, 1945) chaps 1 to 4.

[73] Legal Aid and Advice Act 1949. And see, Legal Aid Acts 1974, 1979, and 1988; Access to Justice Act 1999; Legal Aid, Sentencing and Punishment of Offenders Act 2012.

[74] R Smith, 'After the Act: What Future for Legal Aid?' JUSTICE Tom Sargant memorial annual lecture 2012 (16 October 2012) at 2.

[75] ELI-UNIDROIT Model Rules, r 244 commentary; *Steel & Morris v UK* (2005) 41 EHRR 22.

[76] *Airey v Ireland* (1979) 2 EHRR 305.

[77] JUSTICE, *CLAF—Proposals for a Contingency Legal Aid Fund* (1978); Civil Justice Council, *Improved Access to Justice—Funding Options and Proportionate Costs* (2007) at 30–31; R Jackson (May 2009) chap 18; R Jackson (December 2009) chap 13.

# PART 5
# PRE-ACTION DISPUTE MANAGEMENT

## SECTION 1: GENERAL

1. Rules of court have historically not concerned themselves with what happens regarding a dispute before litigation commences. They have historically been focused on one thing: guiding litigants to trial and judgment, notwithstanding the fact that the vast majority of disputes end in settlement.[1] The CPR changed that to a degree with the introduction of Pre-Action Protocols (PAPs), the aim of which is to promote pre-action settlement and, where that is not achieved, more effective post-issue dispute management.[2] The PAPs, despite forming part of the 'architecture' of litigation,[3] formally sit outside the CPR. They are best practice guides to pre-action conduct and do not have the force of rules of court.[4] They mark a limited but important step towards achieving what was said to be the aim of the CPR: to render litigation a last resort.[5] The proposals in this Part go beyond the PAP approach. Their introduction would require primary legislation.
2. Pre-Action Dispute Management incorporates and goes beyond the CPR's approach. First, it seeks to reduce the prospect that disputes will arise in the first place. It does so by giving effect to the preventive justice principle. It introduces a process that at a general level seeks to reduce the prospect that disputes will arise, while also helping individuals understand their rights and obligations more effectively so as to also reduce the prospect that individual disputes will arise. It draws on the preventive law movement for this approach.[6] Secondly, where this fails it adopts a digital triage model, which has in various different ways been promoted by Susskind's extended court model, Hodges' holistic approach to dispute resolution, and the different

[1] H Woolf, *Access to Justice: Interim Report to the Lord Chancellor on the Civil Justice System in England and Wales* (HMSO) (1995) at 194; A Sarat, 'Exploring the Hidden Domains of Civil Justice: "Naming, Blaming, and Claiming" in Popular Culture' (2000) 50 DePaul L Rev 425 at 426–427; AKC Koo, 'The Role of the English Courts in Alternative Dispute Resolution' (2018) 38 Legal Studies 666, at 677 notes that no more than 4 per cent of claims commenced result in judgment. Such figures fail to note the reserve army of disputes that never progress to being issued as proceedings: M Galanter, 'Reading the Landscape of Disputes: What We Know and Don't Know (and Think We Know) About Our Allegedly Contentious and Litigious Society' (1983) 31 UCLA L Rev 4.

[2] CPR PD—Pre-Action Conduct and Protocols, para 3; Civil Justice Council, *Review of Pre-Action Protocols Interim Report* (CJC, 2021), Appendix 3—A Brief History of Pre-Action Protocols.

[3] *Jet 2 Holidays Ltd v Hughes* [2019] EWCA Civ 1858; [2020] 1 WLR 844, at [36]–[43].

[4] N Andrews, *Andrews on Civil Processes* (Intersentia, 2019) at 53.

[5] H Woolf (1995) at 5; H Woolf, *Access to Justice: Final Report to the Lord Chancellor on the Civil Justice System in England and Wales* (HMSO) (1996) at 4.

[6] L Brown, *Preventive Law* (Praeger, 1970).

*A Model Civil Procedure Code for England and Wales*. John Sorabji, Oxford University Press. © John Sorabji 2024.
DOI: 10.1093/oso/9780192848680.003.0006

iterations of the HMCTS digitisation process.[7] This sees early advice and guidance being provided to parties once a conflict arises to try to defuse it before it becomes a full-blown dispute. Should that fail, it moves to pre-action dispute resolution. This Part can, through this approach, be seen as one way in which a combination of Susskind's and Hodges' proposals can be given effect.

3. Taken together the various pre-action mechanisms in this Part form part of a single, coherent, and integrated process that spans conflict and dispute formation to the means to resolve disputes consensually and then, if necessary, adjudication by a court.[8] It might be said that this approach, as it is said of settlement promotion in general, will be injurious to the public interest as it will reduce the number of disputes that come to public attention. This it could be argued would diminish the public good achieved through adjudicative justice, as it could, for instance, reduce public scrutiny of tortious behaviour, inhibit public discussion of court judgments and the norms they articulate, as well as inhibit the development of the law, and so on.
4. The approach taken in this Part, and particularly its use of the digital procedure is, however, intended to overcome those potential problems. As it provides for anonymised information concerning conflicts and disputes to be collected and provided to Ombudsman, regulators, government, and through publication on the digital portal, to the media and public, it brings to light those very issues, the ones that consensual settlement has traditionally been said to hide from public scrutiny. It is, in the same way, also intended to facilitate law reform and development. In this way and in tandem with its promotion of public legal education, this Part is intended to ensure that its processes do not harm but rather enhance public understanding and scrutiny of the nature of conflict and disputes that arise in society.

## RULE 1.—SCOPE AND PURPOSE

**(1) This Part concerns the management of conflict and dispute resolution before proceedings have commenced (pre-action dispute management).**
**(2) Pre-action dispute management has three objectives. These are: to promote the public interest by reducing conflict and dispute formation through educative and evaluative processes; to promote consensual settlement once a dispute has arisen; and to promote effective post-issue dispute management.**
**(3) In giving effect to its aims, this Part implements the flexible process, settlement, preventive justice, digital integration, digital access, and artificial intelligence principles.**
**(4) Steps taken further to this Part are without prejudice to any jurisdictional challenge that a party may wish to make when proceedings are commenced.**

*Sources: ALI/UNIDROIT Principles, principle 24.3; ELI-UNIDROIT Model Rules, r 9.*

[7] R Susskind, *Online Courts and the Future of Justice* (OUP, 2019) at 61 and following; C Hodges (2019); M Briggs, *Civil Courts Structure Review—Interim Report* (2015); M Briggs, *Civil Courts Structure Review—Final Report* (2016); T Etherton (2017) at [20] and following; G Vos and J Sorabji, 'Digital Technology and the Development of Integrated Dispute Resolution', in X Kramer, S Voet, L Ködderitzsch, M Tulibacka, and B Hess, *Delivering Justice—A Holistic and Multidisciplinary Approach* (Hart, 2022); Civil Justice Council, *Online Dispute Resolution for Low Value Claims* (2015). The 2023–2024 iteration of the HMCTS digitisation programme, articulated by Sir Geoffrey Vos MR and Birss LJ, does not go as far as the model proposed in this Part as it rests on a shift towards private sector provision of all pre-action means of dispute resolution. In that way it is a very different model from that proposed by Susskind and that set out in M Briggs (2015) and (2016): see C Birss, *Is a focus on data the way to improve access to justice in a multifaceted world?* (Judicial Office, 2023).

[8] C Hodges, *Delivering Dispute Resolution* (Hart, 2019) at 550–551.

## COMMENTARY

1. This Part marks a significant departure from the approach taken by English and Welsh civil procedure. It formally integrates into an expanded civil justice system processes to prevent conflicts arising, defuse those that do arise, and, where conflicts are transformed into disputes, processes to resolve them without proceedings having to be commenced. It therefore plays a central role in the fundamental reshaping of the State's role in dispute resolution intended by this Code (see Part i).
2. It has three main objectives that are intended to both give effect to the preventive and consensual justice principles and enable adjudicative justice to be achieved proportionately. It is initially intended to achieve these objectives through promoting public legal education. A more legally literate society is one that should be better able to order their affairs on a sound legal footing, and do so in ways that minimise the prospect that conflict and disputes will arise. It is also intended to facilitate law reform, such that the causes of conflict and disputes are remedied at a societal level, thus helping to prevent future disputes arising. Where conflicts do arise, this Part is then intended to promote their early resolution or defusion so that they are not transformed into full blown disputes. Where disputes do, however, arise, consensual settlement through various, flexible processes should then be made available to help parties resolve them without recourse to litigation. Finally, where litigation is unavoidable, the measures taken to resolve disputes under this Part are intended to promote effective and proportionate post-issue dispute management to both settlement and adjudication.
3. This approach is adapted from one developed by Ury, Brett, and Goldberg.[9] They argued that the optimum approach to the design of dispute resolution systems is one that enables parties to a dispute to move from low-cost, quick, interest-based forms of resolution, eg negotiation, via increasingly time-consuming and costly interest-based methods, to formal rights-based resolution via a binding adjudication. The benefit of this tiered approach is that it promotes proportionate, economical, and efficient resolution for parties to conflict and then disputes. For the system itself, it also promotes proportionality as it helps ensure that the most resource intensive forms of resolution, eg mediation and court adjudication, are reserved for only those disputes that truly require them. This Part, while it incorporates this approach, goes beyond it through its incorporation into its tiered approach of steps to help prevent disputes arising.
4. It is important that the incorporation of the measures in this Part does not adversely affect a party's right to challenge the court's jurisdiction over them. It might be argued that by extending the court's role so that it applied to the pre-action stage of dispute resolution might do so. If that were the case, jurisdiction challenges would need to be made at this stage. To ensure that they do not, and that parties can properly focus on defusing or resolving their conflicts and disputes prior to issuing proceedings, this rule makes clear that any steps taken under this Part are made without prejudice to any jurisdictional issues.

[9] W Ury, J Brett, and S Goldberg, *Getting Disputes Resolved* (PON, 1993) chap 3.

## RULE 2.—PARTY DUTIES DURING PRE-ACTION DISPUTE MANAGEMENT

**(1) At all stages during pre-action dispute management parties shall co-operate with each other effectively in seeking to**
**(a) defuse conflict between them;**
**(b) resolve their dispute consensually; and**
**(c) at all times promote the purposive principle.**
**(2) Parties may seek to resolve their dispute before issuing proceedings through means outside those provided by this Code.**

*Sources: ELI-UNIDROIT Model Rules, r 9.*

## COMMENTARY

1. Rule 2 gives effect to the co-operation principle. It requires parties to work together to try to defuse conflict that arises between them. Where that fails they are required to take steps to resolve their dispute. They are to do so to promote the purposive principle. This aspect of the duty to co-operate is, as the ELI-UNIDROIT Model Rules make clear, one that has '*developed into a common European standard over the last two decades*'.[10] In England and Wales it lives within the PAPs and the shift in procedural philosophy underpinning the CPR that requires parties to settle their disputes prior to litigation where that is reasonably possible.[11]
2. As with the PAPs, the secondary aim of pre-action dispute management is to ensure that should proceedings commence steps parties have taken pre-action enable them and the court to manage proceedings fairly both to the parties and other litigants.[12] Party co-operation pre-action must therefore, at the very least, be carried out so as to ensure that any subsequent proceedings can be managed efficiently, effectively, and proportionately.
3. Provision is not made in this rule for parties to co-operate in good faith. That is despite the fact that good faith requirements in consensual dispute resolution processes are not uncommon, not least in other common law jurisdictions,[13] and have been recommended by the Civil Justice Council for incorporation into the PAPs.[14] There are two reasons for this. The first is that an express good faith requirement is otiose. Parties are already subject to a requirement to co-operate with each other to promote the purposive principle both before and after proceedings commence. That requirement is explicit in rule 2(1)(c). Parties acting in bad faith during the pre-action phase could not properly be said to promote the purposive principle. Secondly, as has been seen in Australia, the introduction of an explicit good faith requirement would tend to lead to disputes over the meaning of good faith in pre-action dispute resolution and whether parties had complied with the obligation. It is likely that such an obligation would be a fertile source of

[10] ELI-UNIDROIT Model Rules, r 9, comment 1 and r 51, comment 2.
[11] H Woolf (1995) at 19; A Clarke, *The Future of Civil Mediation* (2008) Arbitration (74.4) 419.
[12] Pre-Action Protocol for Personal Injury Claims, para 2.1.
[13] Administrative Appeals Tribunal Act 1975 (Cth), s 34A(3); Civil Dispute Resolution Act 2011 (Cth), ss 4, 15, 16; Civil Justice Council (2021) at 108.
[14] Civil Justice Council (2021) at 12–13, 98.

costly, time consuming and disproportionate satellite litigation.[15] It would thus appear to pose a potential risk to the promotion of effective and proportionate pre-action resolution with little real benefit over and above that already provided for through requiring parties to promote the purposive principle, which carries with it the clearer objectives of reducing the cost, complexity and disproportionality of dispute resolution.

4. Rule 2(2) makes clear that parties may use any form of pre-action dispute resolution process that falls outside this Code. This Part does not create a monopoly, nor should it.

## RULE 3.—COURT JURISDICTION DURING PRE-ACTION DISPUTE MANAGEMENT

**(1) The court's pre-action dispute management jurisdiction over an identified claimant begins when they first use settlement facilitation.**

**(2) A court's pre-action dispute management jurisdiction over identifiable defendants begins when a claimant first communicates commencement of settlement facilitation to them.**

*Sources: ELI-UNIDROIT Model Rules, r 10; Jackson Costs Review—Final Report, recommendation 85.*

## COMMENTARY

1. Neither the CPR nor the ELI-UNIDROIT Model Rules make provision for court involvement in the pre-action process.[16] Under the CPR the reason for this is that the court's jurisdiction over parties arises once proceedings have commenced.[17] Exceptionally, where statute makes provision for it, it can arise on application by a party.[18] Rule 3, consistently with the general approach taken by this Code[19] goes beyond this and provides the court with jurisdiction over parties before proceedings have commenced. Primary legislation is required to create this power.

2. The rationale for this extension of the court's role and jurisdiction is to enable it, consistently with its duty to further the purposive principle, to promote pre-issue settlement. The specific role the court has is, however, limited to phase 2 of the pre-action dispute management process. It is simply neither feasible nor appropriate for the court to engage in pre-action processes that are provided in phase 1 of the process as they go wider than the court's experience or proper role: they require the expertise of organisations separate from the court. They also go significantly beyond the court's constitutional role.

[15] T Sourdin, 'Good Faith, Bad Faith? Making an Effort in Dispute Resolution' (2013) 2(1) Victoria University Law and Justice Journal 19.

[16] ELI-UNIDROIT Model Rules, r 10.

[17] H Woolf (1996) at 104; Civil Justice Council (2021) at 77.

[18] Senior Courts Act 1981, s 33; CPR r 31.16. Part 12, r 13.

[19] R Jackson, *Review of Civil Litigation Costs: Final Report* (December 2009) recommendation 85.

3. The specific approach taken to establishing the court's jurisdiction in this rule is analogous to that taken where proceedings are concerned under Part 7, rule 2.

## SECTION 2: PHASE 1: PREVENTION AND DEFUSION

### RULE 4.—PROSPECTIVE PREVENTION

**(1) Prospective prevention shall increase public awareness of legal rights and obligations to reduce the prospect that conflicts and disputes will arise. It will be facilitated through the digital portal, which shall provide**
**(a) online public legal education;**
**(b) access to approved public and private legal education bodies; and**
**(c) where appropriate, individualised analysis and advice.**
**(2) The approval referred to in this rule shall be given by the Preventive Justice Council.**

### COMMENTARY

1. This rule provides the primary means by which the Code supports the implementation of preventive justice. It rests on the fact that substantive law is not self-effectuating.[20] Individuals and companies may not fully appreciate, or in some cases appreciate at all, their legal rights and obligations nor how they should be effected properly, ie in ways that minimise the risk that conflicts and disputes will arise. This is particularly the case now as society has become '*law-thick*'.[21] Law pervades and underpins all human activity and not in a simple way. It is all too easy given its ubiquity and complexity that conflict can arise through misunderstanding or misapplication of the law.
2. This rule seeks to give effect to the idea that prevention is better than cure; that individuals should be given access to information about the law and its application both generally and in specific circumstances, so as to help them avoid conflict and disputes arising. In the context of digitisation of court processes this has been referred to as legal health promotion.[22] It is simply an extrapolation of the idea developed by the preventive law movement that sees lawyers helping their clients to understand what caused a dispute to arise so as to help them avoid it reoccurring. It is also a specific application of the idea that individuals should have effective public legal education made available to them.[23] Taken together these two features, as they are promoted by this rule, are not simply a means to prevent disputes arising, they are

[20] G Postema, 'The Principle of Utility and the Law of Procedure: Bentham's Theory of Adjudication' (1976–1977) 11 Georgia Law Review 1393 at 1402.

[21] G Hadfield and J Heine, 'Life in a Law-Thick World: Legal Resources for Ordinary Americans', in S Estreicher and J Radice (2016) at 21.

[22] R Susskind (2019) at 69–70; J Bentham, 'Principles of Judicial Procedure, with the outlines of a Procedure Code', in *The Works of Jeremy Bentham* (ed Bowring) (William Tait, 1843) Vol 2 at 6–20; F Sander, 'Varieties of Dispute Processing' (1976) 70 FRD 79 at 111–112; M Briggs (2016) at 58.

[23] G Hadfield and J Heine in S Estreicher and J Radice (2016) at 21.

also a means to promote the empowerment of individuals within civil society so that they benefit fully from living in a rule-of-law-based society.

3. The development of a digital portal provides a means to facilitate this aim as it can make public legal education and, where necessary, individualised preventive advice more accessible. This can take several forms. At a basic level, the portal could provide access to information and to bodies that provide public legal education. It could also provide access to tailored information and advice from, for instance, Citizens Advice and other legal advice centres. The digital portal could quite properly incorporate Citizens Advice within it. Additionally, the portal could provide access to a trained, human adviser either online or via the telephone. Such access ought to increase accessibility as individuals would not need to travel to advice centres. It could also provide, via the use of Generative AI, an analysis of prospective legal relations between parties to enable them to identify where conflict might arise with tailored recommendations as to the steps that could be taken to avoid or mitigate such possibilities.

4. To ensure the widest and most effective provision of information and advice under this rule, the digital portal should provide a plurality of sources for information and advice. It should provide its own information and advice resources. It should also act as a conduit for access to other, external independent providers.[24] All of this could be provided via the use of AI. Its provision via the portal should be a public-private partnership in the best sense of the term. To maintain quality control of the information and advice providers, and particularly to ensure they take account of users' needs and are non-discriminatory only those approved by the Preventive Justice Council should be incorporated into the digital portal. Approval will also ensure that any Generative AI used is operated consistently with the AI principle. It should provide a basis for users to have confidence in the information sources and any advice given. It should also help promote a form of simplified, coherent means of securing any such information and advice.[25] Gaps in coverage as well as unnecessary duplication should be avoided.

5. That rule 4 can not only provide information and advice but can also direct users to appropriate information, advice or external providers ought also to help reduce what has been identified, by Pleasance and Balmer, as advice fatigue.[26] This is the idea that individuals when searching for advice or information often go down blind alleys, ie the first or second advice source turns out to be the wrong one and, consequently, individuals do not then go on to find the right source of information and advice and are left with an unresolved legal issue. While their work has highlighted the problem at the stage when disputes have arisen,[27] it is equally problematic earlier than that. At the preventive stage, advice fatigue can form the basis for future conflict and disputes as it reduces the possibility that individuals will gain an understanding of their rights and obligations and order their affairs and act accordingly. The digital portal will therefore need to be designed and operated as a one-stop-shop so to reduce advice fatigue and its adverse consequences and thus promote a more legally literate populous.

[24] V Flango and T Clarke, *Reimagining Courts—A Design for the Twenty-First Century* (Temple, 2017) at 158.

[25] C Hodges (2019) at 205–206.

[26] P Pleasance and N Balmer, *How People Resolve 'Legal' Problems—A Report to The Legal Services Board* (Legal Services Board, 2014).

[27] P Pleasance and N Balmer (2014) at 4.

## RULE 5.—SYSTEMIC PREVENTION

**(1) Systemic prevention shall improve the law and its implementation to reduce the possibility of disputes arising.**
**(2) The digital portal shall facilitate this by providing Ombudsman, regulators, and the government with anonymised information concerning identified systemic legal problems. This information shall be obtained from the digital portal and digital dispute management files. It must also be published on the digital portal.**

## COMMENTARY

1. This rule provides the secondary means through which preventive justice is implemented. Its focus is promoting systemic reform, the aim of which is to reduce the prospect that conflict and disputes will arise. It does so by incorporating one of the functions of Ombudsman schemes into the Code. It is well-established that such schemes can play three broad roles: they can help resolve individual disputes; they can help to prevent individual future disputes arising; and, they can help promote general systemic reform and improvement.[28] This rule facilitates the last of the three.
2. To work effectively, this rule requires Ombudsman schemes, regulators, and government to be properly integrated with the digital portal and, through that, the wider civil justice system. As with rule 4, this does not engage the courts. Thus, it maintains the traditional position that they are not involved in dispute prevention, except and in so far as that arises through the shadow of the law. The intention underpinning this rule is that the digital portal will be designed to enable the collation and transmission to Ombudsman etc anonymised data derived from a wide variety of sources. This will encompass data drawn from information and advice searches on the portal, from conflicts and disputes that are identified through use of the portal, and which are either unresolved or resolved consensually. Once this information has been provided to the various recipients, they will then be able to analyse it to ascertain whether there are any systemic or general legal problems in specific areas.[29] This approach could, for instance, bring to light widespread problems that would otherwise go unnoticed due to their not transforming into disputes that are resolved by the courts.[30] It could also enable problems that might otherwise be hidden from public scrutiny, such as those covered by non-disclosure agreements that form part of settlement agreements, being brought to light.
3. With this information, the various recipients could then bring to public view these issues and/or make recommendations for regulatory or law reform. Implementation of those recommendations could then help reduce the prospect that future conflict or disputes in the areas subject to reform will arise.

[28] C Gill, 'The Evolving Role of the Ombudsman: A Conceptual and Constitutional Analysis of the "Scottish Solution" to Administrative Justice' (2014) Public Law 662.

[29] A Arden et al, *Solving Housing Disputes* (Justice, 2020) at 23–24.

[30] Such an approach could bring to light areas where the law is not clear, and hence compliance is a general problem, or where the law is in need of reform as it no longer meets the needs of modern society. In all such cases, systemic review could result in measures intended to reduce the prospects of future conflict and disputes through, for instance, guidance being issued or law reform. G Vos and J Sorabji in X Kramer, S Voet, L Ködderitzsch, M Tulibacka, and B Hess (2022) at 259.

## RULE 6.—CONFLICT DEFUSION

**(1) When a conflict arises, parties should seek to defuse it at the earliest opportunity so that it does not develop into a full-blown dispute.**

**(2) Access to conflict defusion measures shall be provided by the digital portal and non-digital procedure by providing parties with information and access to approved public and private complaints mechanisms, conciliation and advisory services, Citizens Advice, regulatory bodies, and Ombudsman schemes the aim of which are to de-escalate conflicts through early intervention.**

**(3) The approval referred to in this rule shall be given by the Preventive Justice Council. Approval of Ombudsman schemes shall be given by the Consensual Dispute Resolution Council.**

## COMMENTARY

1. The English and Welsh courts have traditionally taken a broad view to what constitutes a dispute. *Hayter v Nelson* (1990)[31] and *Halki Shipping Corp v Sopex Oils Ltd* (1998),[32] for instance, adopted the approach that a dispute encompasses a disagreement or difference between parties. This is necessarily a very wide definition, which would encompass anything from social and political disputes, disputes over where to go on holiday or which school a child should attend, to disputes between a shop and a consumer over the standard of service received by the latter or disputes between multi-national corporations over financial transactions. This Code rejects this broad approach and draws a distinction between conflicts and disputes.
2. The term conflict is used here to refer to a disagreement or difference between parties over something.[33] The reason for this is that a difference or disagreement between parties may remain nothing more than that. A shop's customer may have and express a different view to the shop owner over the standard of service they have received, but do nothing more than that. The disagreement or difference need not lead to any particular steps being taken by either party to it. It is only when steps are taken by one party that a conflict should be understood to have been transformed into a dispute. Were a shop customer to ask for their money back or refuse to pay for a service received then a conflict might be transformed into a dispute, and only then if the shop owner refused to give the money back or took steps to require payment.
3. A dispute then, for present purposes, is a conflict that leads to a demand from one party that is then refused by that other party. A dispute is thus a subset of conflict.[34] Consensual settlement and adjudication via litigation are the primary means to resolve disputes, particularly those concerning legal rights. Neither are apt to resolve conflict, a point which is latent in Hodges' work, the CJC's Online Court proposals,[35] and proposals such as *JUSTICE's* recommendation to develop a Housing Dispute Service.[36] Hodges, for instance, focuses on the need to integrate different resolution

[31] *Hayter v Nelson* [1990] 2 Lloyd's Rep 265.

[32] *Halki Shipping Corp v Sopex Oils Ltd* [1998] 1 WLR 726.

[33] J Brett, 'Negotiation' (2000) 35(2) International Journal of Psychology 97.

[34] S Shipman, B Waters, and W Brown QC, *Brown & Marriot's ADR Principles and Practice* (Sweet & Maxwell, 2019), at 6.

[35] Civil Justice Council (2015).

[36] A Arden et al (2020).

pathways to resolve disputes, such as regulatory or problem-solving pathways that change behaviour, or reduce or resolve conflict before it is transformed into a legal dispute.[37] Similarly the Civil Justice Council's approach to court reform,[38] adopted and endorsed by the Briggs' Civil Court Structure Review,[39] proposed a three tier approach to dispute resolution. Its first tier, described as dispute avoidance through online evaluation, focused on the need to provide parties with the means to understand and evaluate their grievance (not their dispute) and their rights. It was to enable them to avoid moving to dispute resolution through giving them the tools to resolve the cause of their grievance, or to gain an understanding that it is not justiciable.[40] By using the language of 'grievance' the CJC implicitly draws the same distinction as that drawn here between conflict and dispute.[41] This rule makes explicit what these various proposals acknowledge implicitly: that there is a distinction between a conflict and a dispute, and resolving or defusing the former requires a different approach to that taken to resolving disputes.

4. This rule is intended to provide the basis on which parties can be given assistance to analyse and evaluate their conflict, the reasons why and how it arose, while also providing access to procedures that help to reconcile the parties, ie to defuse the conflict. It should also provide the means to effect referrals to Ombudsman schemes, regulators and their regulatory redress mechanisms or conciliation services, both public and private sector, the aim of which is to help parties set aside their conflict. This rule thus provides a form of individualised preventive justice: prevention here focusing on preventing a conflict from escalating and becoming a dispute. This assistance is to be delivered by the digital portal and, where necessary, the non-digital procedure. This rule thus differs from rules 4 and 5, which are intended to help prevent conflict and disputes arising by minimising the prospect that that will happen. Here the focus is on dealing with conflict after it has arisen.
5. To ensure that the digital portal integrates the various means through which conflicts can be defused effectively, including their integration with the civil courts, the Preventive Justice Council and the Consensual Dispute Resolution Council are required to approve the organisations that are to provide conflict resolution mechanisms via the portal. This recognises that access must be subject to a degree of co-ordination and quality control.[42] Co-ordination is needed to ensure that parties are provided with access to the right source of information and advice and are not passed from one source to another or directed to an inappropriate source. It is also needed to ensure that there are no gaps in information and advice sources.
6. This rule also highlights a key feature of this Code. It rejects the idea that the civil courts and their procedural rules should be extended to incorporate other forms of dispute resolution. It thus partially rejects Susskind's idea that future development of

[37] C Hodges (2019).

[38] Civil Justice Council (2015) at 19.

[39] M Briggs, (2015) and (2016), which see as the first stage of dispute resolution the provision of education, information and evaluation to enable parties to take steps to resolve their 'dispute' without the need to resort to consensual settlement or litigation.

[40] R Susskind, (2021) at 135.

[41] A Arden et al (2020) at 32–34.

[42] This is in contrast to the approach currently being adopted that sees approval falling within the remit of the court rule committees: G Vos and J Sorabji in X Kramer, S Voet, L Ködderitzsch, M Tulibacka, and B Hess (2022) at 249.

courts should see them become 'extended courts' carrying out a range of functions not previously carried out by courts, such as those referred to in this rule as well as consensual settlement.[43] The focus here is on recognising that the civil courts form one part of a wider conflict and dispute resolution landscape. It is a focus that promotes the integration via a single digital portal and procedure of the non-court related aspects of the landscape (dispute prevention and conflict defusion) and the court related aspects (pre-action dispute resolution and post-issue dispute management).

7. Finally, the approach taken here is one that views early intervention as a means to defuse conflicts as an essential part of a wider civil justice process: early intervention both reducing the time and cost to parties and the State. It is thus a further means to promote the purposive principle, and particularly the economic, efficient, and proportionate resolution of, in this case, conflict.

## RULE 7.—AVAILABILITY OF DISPUTE PREVENTION AND CONFLICT DEFUSION

**Dispute prevention and conflict defusion measures shall be available through the digital portal without charge.**

## COMMENTARY

1. The provision of dispute prevention and conflict defusion is intended to benefit those involved in potential or actual disputes and the public interest generally. Cost barriers should not be placed in the way of access to them.[44] Such a model is not in itself innovative. It is the approach routinely taken to Ombudsman schemes.[45]
2. While there will be a significant cost to the State for the provision of measures through the digital portal, that cost ought to be offset by the benefit derived from their provision. As the National Audit Office has noted, where individuals cannot access the means to enable them to resolve disputes via litigation there are likely to be wider adverse costs to the State, eg through an increase in welfare payments and through increased health care costs.[46] Intervention reduces the prospect of adverse outcomes arising from conflict and disputes.[47] Early intervention and, particularly prevention, are likely to do so to a greater extent. The social and economic benefit derived from the measures provided by the digital portal may come at a price, but that is a price worth paying for a healthier, more prosperous society; it is also a price that, to the extent the various measures work, ought to provide benefits that outweigh the cost.

[43] R Susskind (2019) at 60–62.

[44] While legal expenses insurance is the default funding mechanism (Part 3), it would typically apply from the consensual settlement phase of pre-action dispute management (r 8).

[45] P Verkuil, 'The Ombudsman and the Limits of the Adversary System' (1975) 75 Columbia L Rev 845; C Gill and C Hirst, *Defining Consumer Ombudsman—A Report* (Queen Margaret University, Edinburgh, 2016).

[46] National Audit Office, *Implementing reforms to civil legal aid* (HC 784 Session 2014–15, 20 November 2014) at 19.

[47] On the adverse consequences to individual's lives, and the costs that are incurred to them, the broader economy and the State: J Organ and J Sigafoos, *The impact of LASPO on routes to justice* (Equality and Human Rights Commission, 2018) at 43–51.

# SECTION 3: PHASE 2: PRE-ACTION DISPUTE RESOLUTION AND POST-ISSUE DISPUTE MANAGEMENT

## RULE 8.—SETTLEMENT AND POST-ISSUE DISPUTE MANAGEMENT

**(1) If dispute prevention and conflict defusion measures are not successful, parties shall co-operate in attempts to resolve their dispute consensually and, if necessary, promote post-issue dispute management.**

**(2) Effective pre-action co-operation requires parties to**
  - **(a) provide each other with concise details of the dispute and any response;**
  - **(b) identify, and where possible narrow, the legal and factual issues in dispute;**
  - **(c) identify relevant evidence;**
  - **(d) provide each other with copies of relevant documentary evidence and a concise outline of any witness evidence;**
  - **(e) take stock of the progress of steps taken to resolve their dispute; and**
  - **(f) where possible, provide each other with an estimate of their likely costs of pursuing or defending the claim.**

*Sources: ELI-UNIDROIT Model Rules, r 51; Practice Direction—Pre-Action Conduct.*

## COMMENTARY

1. Where a conflict cannot be defused and a dispute arises, parties may move to the pre-action settlement phase of the pre-action process. This has much in common with the approach taken under the CPR and its PAPs and is modelled on them.[48] Specifically, it is modelled on their approach to pre-action party co-operation, bolstered here by the co-operation principle. It is supported by requiring parties to engage in the early exchange of information between them as a means to promote early resolution and to co-operatively take stock of the steps taken to resolve the dispute.[49]

2. Where parties have taken steps under phase 1 of this Part, a large degree of information to be exchanged under this rule will already have been uploaded to the digital dispute management file and may have already been exchanged. Where it is has not, this rule provides the basis for uploading and exchanging it. The rationale for early exchange of information is straightforward. It is the basis on which parties can more effectively assess the merits of their respective claims and defences and the likely cost of pursuing the dispute if proceedings are issued. Such information exchange and assessment lies at the heart of any successful negotiation between the parties or, if necessary, any mediation. There is no reason why, as part of the promotion of settlement, the digital portal may not provide access to the means by which Generative or predictive AI could provide the parties with its assessment of the merits of their dispute as part of settlement.

[48] It is also analogous to stage 2 of the Briggs' Online Solutions Court and Tier 2 of the Civil Justice Council's proposed online court: M Briggs (2015) at 76; M Briggs (2016) at 36ff; Civil Justice Council (2015) at 18–20.

[49] H Woolf (1996) at 107–111; Civil Justice Council (2021) at 8–9; CPR Practice Direction—Pre-Action Conduct, para 12.

3. The secondary aim of this phase of pre-action dispute management, as it is under the PAPs, is to facilitate the effective management of disputes if proceedings commence: see rule 10.

## RULE 9.—SETTLEMENT FACILITATION

**(1) The court shall initially facilitate consensual pre-action settlement by**
  **(a) ensuring parties have considered accessing a relevant Ombudsman or similar public or private scheme, an aim of which is to promote consensual settlement; and**
  **(b) providing access to its pre-action settlement scheme, which should be approved by the Consensual Dispute Resolution Council.**

**(2) The court shall provide parties with an assessment of the relative suitability of dispute resolution methods to the dispute. The assessment will be carried out by means of automated decision-making based on information uploaded by the parties to the digital dispute management file through the process set out in Part 11, rule 15(3).**

**(3) Except as permitted by the court on application, parties may not issue proceedings until they have engaged in the pre-action settlement scheme.**

*Sources: ELI-UNIDROIT Model Rules, r 51; Practice Direction—Pre-Action Conduct.*

## COMMENTARY

1. Settlement facilitation is the first point at which the civil courts become involved in dispute resolution. Their role is to promote the use of various measures aimed at promoting consensual settlement further to the court's duty to promote settlement.[50] This takes two forms.
2. First, it is to be carried out by ensuring that the parties have properly considered use of any available consensual settlement scheme provided by an Ombudsman. This is particularly important where parties have not engaged with Ombudsman schemes as part of conflict defusion. It is also important where they have engaged with Ombudsman, but not with any settlement process they provide, such as negotiation, mediation, or ENE.
3. Secondly, it requires the court to provide access to its own consensual settlement scheme. It thus requires the incorporation of what for the Civil Justice Council and Briggs was stage 2 of their proposed reformed court processes: the introduction of a negotiation, mediation and ENE process integrated into the court procedure.[51] The rule does not itself specify the nature of such a process. Different models are available. One model is a scheme that requires parties to first go through negotiation and then mediation or ENE.[52] The drawback of this type of approach lies both in its sequential nature and its assumption that at best there are two or three forms of negotiated process available: mediation and ENE are simply forms of facilitated negotiation. The former assumes that moving in a sequence is always the most suitable approach.

[50] Practice Direction 31, para 1 (Hong Kong).
[51] Civil Justice Council (2015) at 18–20; M Briggs (2015) at 76; M Briggs (2016) at 36ff.
[52] G Vos and J Sorabji in X Kramer, S Voet, L Ködderitzsch, M Tulibacka, and B Hess (2022) at 249.

The latter assumes that the sequence proposed is the optimum one for each specific disputes.

4. The approach adopted here provides for more flexibility than a sequential approach. The pre-action settlement scheme provided by the court should be designed so as to provide parties with a range of dispute resolution processes that start with the simplest, quickest, and least expensive, ie facilitated negotiation.[53] From there a range of other processes should be available, which the parties may access. They need not do so in any prescribed sequence. Rather, through the assessment provided under rule 9(2), they should be provided with a range of recommended options. Recommendations should detail the suitability of the method to their dispute and its likely time and cost to the parties. Parties may thus be provided with an analysis of the utility, and applicability to their dispute, of facilitative mediation, evaluative mediation, ENE, collaborative law, med-arb, arb-med, or binding arbitration. The digital portal should then, as part of the pre-action scheme, provide access to such measures. For low value claims, for instance, the most suitable form of process might be a facilitative mediation or binding arbitration. For higher value claims, evaluative mediation or ENE may be more appropriate. For complex commercial claims, it may be the case that a formal arbitration procedure or Executive Tribunal process might be most suitable. The key is for the scheme to provide a range of measures and provide the parties with an assessment of the options.
5. Delivery of the settlement scheme, consistently with the digital procedure and AI principles, ought to be facilitated by and delivered via the digital procedure. This would mean that negotiation, mediation, and ENE processes should be delivered primarily online. Telephone-based and in-person options ought, however, to be made available where necessary and proportionate. A low-value binding arbitration scheme could also be delivered online or in-person. Any collaborative law scheme, as it would involve the parties and their lawyers rather than the court would simply be facilitated by the court, eg it would provide a venue, whether online or physical, for the collaborative process to take place.
6. This rule thus acknowledges the utility of pre-action settlement processes and mandates engagement with the court in respect of it. Parties should engage constructively with them (rule 2). The Code thus creates an environment of robust and consistent promotion of such measures. Rule 9(3) does, however, provide the court with a discretion to permit parties to issue proceedings even though they have not engaged in its pre-action settlement scheme. Parties can thus, effectively opt-out of mandatory pre-action settlement processes. The rationale for this is to enable parties that have undertaken a number of such steps prior to engaging with the court's pre-action process, including during conflict defusion, to move directly to issuing proceedings. Where parties have engaged in negotiation or mediation outside the courts or have engaged with Ombudsman schemes to the same purpose as part of conflict defusion they ought not be put to the disproportionate time and expense of engaging in further pre-action processes. In assessing whether to exercise its discretion under this rule, the court should, however, take account of the rule 9(2) suitability assessment. It might, for instance, be the case that while parties have already engaged in a number of settlement processes, it identifies one as being more suitable for their dispute. In such a situation, the court, having considered the views of the parties, will need to consider whether requiring use

[53] W Ury, J Brett, and S Goldberg (1993) chap 3.

of the identified scheme would serve the purposive principle. Where it would, the discretion should not be exercised.

## RULE 10.—PROMOTION OF POST-ISSUE DISPUTE MANAGEMENT

**To promote effective post-issue dispute resolution, parties shall co-operate with each other to try to narrow the issues in dispute. They shall review their positions before proceedings commence and seek to agree a proposed dispute management timetable, including whether there is the need for early applications concerning jurisdiction, limitation, provisional or protective measures. The review and timetable should be consistent with the purposive principle and made available to the court when proceedings commence.**

*Sources: ELI-UNIDROIT Model Rules, r 51; Practice Direction—Pre-Action Conduct, paras 3, 12; Pre-Action Protocol for Personal Injury Claims, paras 2.1(a)–(d), 9.1.3, 11.*

## COMMENTARY

1. This rule is influenced by both the approach taken in the ELI-UNIDROIT Model Rules, especially its rule 51, and the CPR's PAPs. Both emphasise the secondary aim of pre-action dispute management: the promotion of economical, effective, and proportionate dispute management if proceedings commence. This is to be achieved in two fundamental ways.
2. Throughout the course of their pre-action engagement, parties to a dispute should actively consider whether there are issues that they can either resolve or set to one side because they are tangential to the real issue or issues in dispute. They should seek to narrow the issues in dispute. Where they can do so they will not only be promoting a more proportionate use of court resources, when proceedings commence, but they will also be reducing the cost and time they will need to expend on proceedings.
3. Once it is apparent that the claimant will commence proceedings, the parties should take steps to ensure that the benefits of engaging in pre-action dispute management are transferred effectively, as the CJC has argued, to the post-issue phase of the dispute.[54] This is to be achieved through effective forward planning, akin to that which underpins the CPR's introduction of costs budgeting and Disclosure Review.[55] In this regard, the requirement that parties seek to agree a proposed timetable is intended to ensure they take seriously the obligation to co-operate with each other to narrow the issues in dispute. It is intended to focus their minds on what the real issues in dispute are, whether there are any preliminary issues that need to be dealt with at an early stage (and which by being dealt with at such a stage may promote the proportionate management and resolution of the dispute). It is thus intended to provide an effective spur to the review of the position reached by the parties once pre-action measures have come to an end without them having to engage in detailed planning; too detailed an approach here could lead to too great a frontloading of costs.[56]

[54] CJC (2021) at 24.
[55] CPR Pt 3, Section II, CPR PD57AD para 10.
[56] CJC (2021) at 13.

# SECTION 4: PROCEDURE

## RULE 11.—DIGITAL PROCEDURE

**The digital procedure shall provide**

**(a) the means to increase public knowledge and understanding of the law and its application;**
**(b) a digital process through which parties can gain an understanding of the nature of their conflict or dispute, an early evaluation of it and of the merits of any legal action, access to means to defuse any conflict or to resolve their dispute; and**
**(c) the means through which pre-action communication and exchange of documents and information between parties can be carried out, and by which they can be uploaded to the digital dispute management file.**

## COMMENTARY

1. The three features of the digital procedure relevant to the pre-action phase of a dispute are: educative, which concerns dispute prevention; conflict defusion; and, the means to promote consensual settlement. This rule specifies that the digital procedure must make provision for these three features of the system. It does so to provide clear guidance to those responsible for its design and approval of the nature and parameters of the digital procedure. It also provides the means by which the public, and civil society generally, can scrutinise and hold accountable the digital procedure.
2. The rule is to be implemented consistently with the digital procedure and accountability and digital access principles.[57]

## RULE 12.—DIGITAL DISPUTE MANAGEMENT ACCOUNT AND FILE

**(1) Access to the digital portal is unrestricted prior to the commencement of conflict defusion. To access conflict defusion and later phases of pre-action and, if necessary, post-issue procedure, parties to a conflict must create a digital dispute management account.**
**(2) Lawyers that engage in conflict and dispute resolution must have, at all times, a registered digital dispute management account.**
**(3) A single digital dispute management file shall be created for each conflict and dispute. If it is not created at the conflict defusion phase of pre-action dispute management, it must be created at the earliest other opportunity.**
**(4) The digital management file shall contain all information and documents relevant to a specific conflict and/or dispute. Where the non-digital procedure is used, all non-digital documents and information shall be uploaded to a digital dispute management file through digital assistance provided by the digital dispute resolution service.**
**(5) Access to and the use of content contained in each digital dispute management file will be provided to third parties consistently with the digital integration principle.**
**(6) Access to the digital dispute management file by the public shall be secured consistently with the publicity principle.**

[57] Part 1, rr 24 and 25.

## COMMENTARY

1. English and Welsh procedure does not accept the position that natural or legal persons must generally register with the court. The Court of Appeal in *Estate Acquisition & Development Ltd v Wiltshire* (2006), for instance, deprecated the suggestion that individuals might be required to register with the court simply on the basis that they had entered into a legal relationship with each other.[58] A general requirement that individuals and legal persons register with the court would be a significant step beyond that which was rejected. This Code maintains the general position. By doing so it maintains a proper balance in the relationship between the State and citizen. State-based dispute resolution is something that the State provides in the public interest. It is not something that the State mandates. To do so would impinge unnecessarily on party autonomy and individual liberty. It is for parties to determine how they wish to resolve their disputes and, importantly, engage with the State.
2. Consistently with this approach, and with the digital integration principle, this rule does, however, make provision for the creation of digital dispute management accounts and digital dispute management files. Maintaining the accepted position on mandatory registration for natural and legal persons, it only requires them to create a dispute management account when they wish to access the provision of conflict defusion measures provided via the digital dispute resolution portal. They are not required to create an account generally. The position is, however, different for lawyers. They are required to generally register with the portal and thus create their own account when they provide conflict and dispute resolution services. This reflects both the reality that lawyers are repeat players in dispute resolution and will have an ongoing relationship with the court and other dispute resolution services. It also is an aspect of the co-operation principle as it applies to the legal profession.
3. Creation of a dispute management account for parties will, in many cases, run in tandem with their creation of the digital dispute management file for their conflict and, if necessary, their dispute. That is, it should be created at the point in time when parties first intend to use conflict defusion measures. That is the starting point for engagement with conflict and dispute resolution where parties will be required to provide case specific information and, in all likelihood, evidence. Creation of the file is the means by which each dispute can be managed effectively by both the parties, their lawyers, dispute resolution services, and the court. For each conflict a unique file is created.
4. A signal advantage of requiring the creation of a unique digital file for each conflict and, if necessary, dispute that follows on from it, is that it enables parties to upload information once only. As the file is intended for use at all stages of conflict and dispute resolution it means that parties will not have to incur the time and expense of uploading the same information and, where appropriate, evidence on multiple occasions to different organisations. This will streamline the conflict and dispute management process, rendering it more economical and proportionate.
5. While the digital management file is intended to contain all relevant information and, where necessary, documentary evidence, the possibility remains that parties may engage with the process through a physical, non-digital procedure. This is required, as it is under any Online Procedure Rules authorised under the Judicial Review

[58] *Estate Acquisition & Development Ltd v Wiltshire* [2006] EWCA Civ 533 at [18]–[24].

and Courts Act 2022,[59] to enable individuals who may have difficulty accessing the digital procedure to be guaranteed practical and effective access to justice. Under this Code use of non-digital procedure ought to be rare given the provision of litigation funding to enable parties to be legally represented. However, given the right to self-representation, parties who choose to exercise that right ought to be afforded the means of accessing dispute resolution services in a non-digital manner.

6. Access to the contents of dispute management files are made available under rules 12(5) and (6). This is to ensure, consistently with the digital integration principle, that anonymised information can be extracted from them so that dispute prevention can be carried out effectively under rules 4 to 6. This should also ensure, through providing public access to information concerning the nature and types of conflicts, the characteristics of parties engaged in conflicts and disputes, and resolution rates, that effective democratic scrutiny of the nature of conflict and disputing can be carried out.

[59] Judicial Review and Courts Act 2022, s 19(7).

# PART 6
# PARTIES

## SECTION 1: GENERAL

1. This Part concerns the participants in a dispute resolution process, primarily the parties to proceedings. Its focus is on ensuring that proceedings are properly constituted. It thus provides rules concerning the joinder of parties to proceedings, see Part 9 on the removal, addition, or substitution of parties. It also makes provision for parties who lack the capacity to conduct proceedings to do so through a third party as well as for specified non-parties to take an active part in proceedings.

### RULE 1.—SCOPE AND PURPOSE

**(1) This Part concerns who may bring or defend proceedings and the capacity in which they may do so. It also concerns the role that specified non-parties may have in proceedings.**
**(2) Rules concerning parties and non-parties primarily give effect to the autonomy, accuracy, and settlement principles. They also give effect to the general access, due notice, and participatory principles. Such rules also enhance the court's ability to carry out its public function of developing, correcting, and refining the law.**

*Sources: ELI-UNIDROIT Model Rules, Part II.*

### COMMENTARY

1. The purpose of proceedings, whether pre-action or post-issue, is to resolve disputes between parties, whoever they may be. Exceptionally, proceedings may also provide a definitive ruling on legal issues where there is no live dispute.[1] In both situations there need to be adverse parties, eg claimants and defendants. Certain non-parties may also participate in proceedings. This rule identifies this Part's application to both parties and specified non-parties. In respect of the former it identifies their role as bringing or defending proceedings; it thus adverts to rule 2 and the manner in which it defines parties to proceedings, as well as the limitations it imposes on that definition. In respect of the latter it adverts to rules 4 and 5, which make provision for intervenors and advocates to the court.
2. This Part's importance cannot be understated. Effective identification and joinder of parties is an essential prerequisite for several aspects of the litigation process. At its most basic level it forms the basis of, and thus also limits, the court's jurisdiction. On the one hand, that jurisdiction is invoked by one party, the claimant, when they

[1] *Financial Conduct Authority v Arch Insurance (UK) Ltd* [2021] UKSC 1; [2021] AC 649.

*A Model Civil Procedure Code for England and Wales*. John Sorabji, Oxford University Press. © John Sorabji 2024.
DOI: 10.1093/oso/9780192848680.003.0007

issue proceedings. On the other hand, it applies to the party against whom the court's jurisdiction is invoked, the defendant. Proper joinder of parties is also the basis on which the scope of proceedings is defined effectively. It is for the parties to do that through their case statements. Effective identification and joinder of parties thus not only forms the basis of the court's jurisdiction, but also provides the basis on which that jurisdiction is defined and limited. Implicit in these points is the principle of party autonomy; that it is for parties to pursue, defend, withdraw, or settle proceedings in respect of their dispute; a point inherent in rule 2.

3. Through delineating the basis on which natural or legal persons may seek to resolve their disputes through legal proceedings, the rules in this Part are also the starting point for securing compliance with several procedural principles. Party autonomy in bringing or defending proceedings to establish or vindicate rights or obligations, is a means by which access to the court, the general access principle, is given effect. That can only be achieved where parties are properly identified. That parties are properly identified is then a prerequisite for the effective implementation of the due notice principle. That cannot be given effect if parties do not know who is bringing or defending proceedings. Equally evidence cannot be obtained and tested without such notice. Effective participation, and confidence in the dispute resolution process,[2] is also secured by proper identification and joinder of parties. Clarity over who the parties are and their joinder also promotes adjudicative accuracy and settlement by ensuring that the right parties are contesting the issues in dispute. It also does so, in combination with the publicity principle, as parties' proper identification can facilitate witnesses coming forward who might otherwise not know about the dispute and whose evidence could prove important to determine proceedings on the substantive merits or promote consensual settlement.[3]
4. In so far as non-parties are concerned, this Part focuses on those who can properly play a role in promoting the accuracy and settlement principles as well as supporting the civil court's ability to fulfil its constitutional role of stating, refining, correcting, and developing the law.

## RULE 2.—PARTIES

**(1) A party is a natural or legal person that brings or defends proceedings to resolve a dispute by establishing or vindicating legal or equitable rights or obligations, including those that have not yet been recognised as such by a court. That proceedings are brought to establish or vindicate such rights or obligations does not preclude the possibility that the dispute may be resolved consensually.**

**(2) A person may also be a party to proceedings where**

**(a) a rule of law permits them to bring or defend proceedings in the public interest;**

**(b) a statutory provision permits them to bring or defend claims;**

**(c) they are an interested party in judicial review proceedings; or**

**(d) the court authorises them to bring or defend proceedings in a representative capacity.**

[2] T Tyler, 'Procedural Justice, Legitimacy, and the Effective Rule of Law' (2003) 30 Crime & Justice 283; R Hollander-Blumoff and T Tyler, 'Procedural Justice and the Rule of Law: Fostering Legitimacy in Alternative Dispute Resolution' (2011) 1 Journal of Dispute Resolution 3.

[3] *R v Legal Aid Board, ex parte Kaim Todner (a firm)* [1999] QB 966 at 977.

**(3) Multiple persons may be party to a single proceeding. A single person cannot, however, both bring and defend the same cause of action in proceedings.**

*Sources: ELI-UNIDROIT Model Rules, rr 29, 36; Interpretation Act 1978, schedule 1; Senior Courts Act 1981, s 151; CPR rr 2.3(1), 19.1; PD 7A.*

## COMMENTARY

1. Disputes exist between parties. They may be individuals. They may be corporate entities, partnerships, trade unions, charities, unincorporated associations, or the Government. Rule 2 captures this longstanding position, well-established across civil procedure systems. It does so by defining parties by reference to them being either natural or legal persons. A legal person is a '*body of persons corporate or unincorporated*'.[4] On the need to identify parties see Part 7, r 2.
2. Some jurisdictions have begun to extend the scope of parties to include, for instance, natural parks, rivers, or mountains.[5] Additionally, in the future, the definition of legal persons could be extended, in principle at least, to forms of artificial intelligence. At the present time, the expansion of 'parties' to include aspects of the natural world appears unlikely in England and Wales, not least given the approach of the High Court in *Moosun v HSBC Bank Plc* (2015),[6] which held that a claim could not be brought by an animal (a dog). The most obvious reason cited for that, apart from the fact that it was noted that a dog was not a person (albeit that leaves open the broader question of whether in the future animals could be recognised as legal persons) was that an animal could not give instructions. The same could be said for trees and rivers, and so on. This rule does not exclude the possibility that future statutory developments could provide for animals, trees, plants, rivers, etc, as well as artificial intelligence to be recognised as legal persons. Such developments would, however, fall outside the scope of procedural law. Were they to occur, this rule in tandem with rule 4 would provide for any new forms of party to litigate via a litigation friend acting on their behalf, which would undoubtedly be necessary in all cases bar that, potentially, of artificial intelligence.
3. The basic criterion to be a party to proceedings is that a person brings or defends proceedings to resolve a dispute that involves legal or equitable rights, including rights not yet recognised but which the proceedings seek to have recognised.[7] Disputes involving rights includes 'stakeholder claims', eg those where a party seeks to establish which of a number of competing claims to an item of, for instance, property is valid even though the claimant themselves has no legal or equitable interest in the matter.[8] While pre-action dispute resolution may involve the resolution of conflicts that do not (yet) involve legal or equitable rights, legal proceedings require there to be a dispute over rights.

[4] Interpretation Act 1978, schedule 1.

[5] Te Urewera Act 2014 (New Zealand: mountain region as a legal person); Te Awa Tupua (Whanganui River Claims Settlement) Act 2017 (New Zealand: river as a legal person); Te Anga Pūtakerongo—Record of Understanding 2017 (New Zealand: Mount Taranki as a legal person).

[6] *Moosun v HSBC Bank Plc (t/a First Direct)* [2015] EWHC 3308 (Ch) at [10].

[7] *X v Bedfordshire CC* [1995] 2 AC 633 at 741; *Barrett v Enfield London Borough Council* [2001] 2 AC 550 at 557–558.

[8] CPR Pt 86.

4. Rule 2(2) provides for individuals who do not themselves have a legal or equitable interest that forms the basis of a dispute to be party to proceedings. First, it permits persons authorised by a rule of law to bring or defend proceedings in the public interest, eg the Attorney-General when bringing proceedings for contempt of court,[9] when acting in proceedings that give rise to human rights issues[10], or when bringing applications under section 42 of the Senior Courts Act 1981. Secondly, it acknowledges that legislation may permit a person to bring or defend proceedings when they would not otherwise be able to do so. Examples of such legislation are statutes that authorise non-parties to bring collective proceedings[11] or derivative claims.[12] Thirdly, it acknowledges the role of interested parties in judicial review proceedings (Part 7, rule 4). And, finally, it recognises that the court may authorise a person to bring representative proceedings even though they have no legal or equitable interest in the dispute.[13]

5. Rule 2(3) restates the longstanding position that multiple parties may be joined to a single set of proceedings. This can be traced to the approach taken in proceedings in the Court of Chancery and is intended to promote the principle of finality by ensuring that all relevant parties to a dispute are before the court and will, therefore, be subject to any judgment given or, now also, any settlement.[14] This also serves to promote the effective administration of justice through promoting procedural economy, efficiency and proportionality, again through avoiding multiplicity of proceedings and the repetitious costs and temporal demands that they may create, while also maximising the effect of any resolution of the dispute.[15] There is no limit to the number of parties who may be joined as parties.[16] Multiple claimants must, however, develop their cases consistently with each other. The court does, however, as part of its general dispute management power, maintain the discretion to permit multiple claimants to set out differing cases via separate legal representation.[17]

6. Rule 2(3) also specifies a point that ought to be obvious: a single person may not bring or defend proceedings against themselves in respect of the same cause of action. This is due to the nature of a cause of action, which is the basis of proceedings.[18] A cause of action requires there to be a factual situation '*the existence of which entitles one person to obtain from the court a remedy against another person*'.[19] Courts thus exist to resolve disputes between people; they provide remedies to resolve their disputes. Equally, they provide a process to enforce judgments on behalf of one person against another. They do not provide the means for enforcement action to be brought by a person against themselves, which could then give effect to a judgment brought by that person to bind themselves. Individuals cannot, as a matter of logic, enforce rights against themselves. That is not to say, however,

[9] *Solicitor-General v Jones* [2013] EWHC 2579 (Fam); [2014] 1 FLR 852 at [14]; *R v Yaxley-Lennon* [2018] EWCA Crim 1856; [2018] 1 WLR 5400 at [26].

[10] Human Rights Act 1998, s 5.

[11] Competition Act 1998, s 47(B)(8).

[12] Companies Act 2006, Part 11, chap 1.

[13] *Google LLC v Lloyd* [2021] UKSC 50; [2021] 3 WLR 1268.

[14] R W Millar, *Civil Procedure of the Trial Court in Historical Perspective* (New York University, 1952) at 98–99.

[15] *CE Heath Plc v Ceram Holding Co* [1988] 1 WLR 1219 at 1229.

[16] CPR r 19.1; *Morris v Williams & Co Solicitors (A Firm)* [2024] EWCA Civ 376.

[17] *Lewis v Daily Telegraph (No 2)* [1964] 2 QB 601.

[18] Part 7, r 5.

[19] *Letang v Cooper* [1965] 1 QB 232 at 243.

that in specific circumstances an individual may be a claimant and defendant in the same proceedings but in different capacities, eg in a personal capacity and in a representative capacity. Examples of this are probate proceedings, where an individual may be a party in their personal capacity and as a personal representative of another person.[20]

## RULE 3.—PARTY CAPACITY

**(1) A protected party is either a natural person under the age of eighteen or a natural person who otherwise lacks legal capacity to conduct proceedings.**
**(2) A natural person under the age of eighteen must, unless permitted by the court, conduct proceedings through a litigation friend.**
**(3) A natural person who lacks capacity to conduct proceedings must conduct proceedings through a litigation friend.**
**(4) A litigation friend is a person who is able, and consents, to conduct proceedings fairly and effectively for a protected party or, where no such person can be appointed, the Official Solicitor.**
**(5) A legal person must conduct proceedings through a named director, employee or equivalent natural person.**
**(6) References in this Code to party includes reference to a litigation friend where a party acts through a litigation friend, the Official Solicitor, or an individual who may conduct proceedings on behalf of a legal person.**

*Sources: ELI-UNIDROIT Model Rules, r 30; Senior Courts Act 1981, s 99; CPR Pt 21, r 39.6.*

## COMMENTARY

1. The rule on capacity to bring or defend legal proceedings tracks that of legal capacity to exercise rights generally.[21] Where a person lacks legal capacity because they are either under the age of eighteen or are under a form of incapacity as defined by the Mental Capacity Act 2005 (a protected party) proceedings must be conducted by a litigation friend, ie a third party responsible for the conduct of proceedings for the protected party.[22] Where a person is under the age of eighteen, the court however retains a discretion to permit them to conduct proceedings on their own behalf. This discretion reflects the possibility that the court may conclude that the individual concerned is fully able to understand the nature of the proceedings, to give instructions to lawyers, and make fully-informed decisions about the conduct and resolution of the proceedings.[23] The requirement to act via a litigation friend is one of the means through which the general access and participation principles are given effect for the protected party. Because of this, a court should take care to consider the issue of legal capacity where there is a real suspicion that a party lacks it.[24] In some cases, it may have to do so over the objections of the party concerned or other parties in the

[20] Inheritance (Provision for Family and Dependants) Act 1975.
[21] *Re Whittall* [1973] 1 WLR 1027 at 1030; *Masterman-Lister v Brutton & Co* [2002] EWCA Civ 1889; [2003] 1 WLR 1511 at 1539.
[22] *Bailey v Warren* [2006] EWCA Civ 51; Mental Health Act 2005, s 1; *Saulle v Nouvet* [2007] EWHC 2902 (QB).
[23] *Dunhill v Burgin* [2014] UKSC 18; [2014] 1 WLR 933; CPR 21.2; Mental Capacity Act 2005, s 5.
[24] *Masterman-Lister v Brutton & Co* [2002] EWCA Civ 1889; [2003] 1 WLR 1511.

proceedings.[25] Ordinarily, however, it will be obvious if a party stands in need of a litigation friend as the court will be informed of that fact by the person who seeks to be appointed as one.

2. There are two main categories of litigation friend. First, they are individuals who can manage the proceedings, including the pursuit of settlement where appropriate, in the best interests of the protected party. This requires them to be both willing and able to fairly and effectively conduct proceedings, which includes furthering the purposive principle,[26] for the protected party.[27] Given this a litigation friend ought not to be appointed where they have a conflict of interest with the protected party. In some cases a litigation friend will be a family member.[28] Where an individual seeks appointment as a litigation friend, they must provide evidence of the necessity of an appointment. The court must also be satisfied that there is nothing to suggest that the appointment is being sought for any improper reason.[29] Where a litigation friend can no longer satisfy the basis on which they were appointed the court should terminate their appointment.[30]
3. Secondly, where no one is capable of appointment on the first basis, the Official Solicitor may consent to being appointed as a litigation friend.[31] The Official Solicitor has indicated that it will only do so in the last resort, where no one else is capable or willing to do so and where there is evidence that there is security for the costs of legal representation.[32] Where costs cease to be available, the Official Solicitor may withdraw from acting, in which case the court will need to carefully consider what steps it can take to manage the dispute, not least to ascertain if a further party can be appointed as a litigation friend, or to direct that the other parties to proceedings defray the Official Solicitor's costs as costs of the proceedings.[33]
4. Where costs are concerned, the litigation friend of a claimant protected party would typically be expected to be liable for the costs of the party on whose behalf they conduct litigation and to give an undertaking to that effect.[34] A defendant protected party's litigation friend may also be held liable for costs, not least where they fail to discharge their duty to carry out the conduct of litigation fairly and effectively.[35]
5. Rule 4 also provides for legal persons to act through natural persons. This reflects the general position that, for instance, companies act through their directors or employees.[36] To promote certainty the legal person should notify the court and other parties who it is acting through. Such a person should be of sufficient authority within

[25] *Saulle v Nouvet* [2007] EWHC 2902 (QB); *Greetham v Greetham* [2021] EWHC 998 (QB).

[26] *Bushby v Galazi* [2022] EWHC 136 (Ch) at [59].

[27] CPR r 21.4(3)(a) and (b); *R (Raqeeb) v Barts NHS Trust* [2019] EWHC 2976 (Admin); *Hinduja v Hinduja* [2020] EWHC 1533 (Ch); [2020] 1 WLR 93.

[28] Mental Capacity Act 2005, ss 16 and 18.1(k).

[29] *Folks v Faizey* [2006] EWCA Civ 381; [2006] CP Rep 30 at [19].

[30] Consent to act as a litigation friend is essential. Only exceptionally should a court refuse to permit a person to cease acting as a litigation friend: *Major v Kirishana* [2023] EWHC 1593 (KB) at [111]–[118].

[31] Senior Courts Act 1981, s 99.

[32] Paufley J, 'Guidance in cases involving protected parties in which the Official Solicitor is being invited to act as guardian ad litem or litigation friend' (December 2010) at [3] in P Coulson (ed), *Civil Procedure 2024* (Sweet & Maxwell, 2024) Vol 2 at 6B-26+.

[33] *Bradbury v Paterson* [2014] EWHC 3992 (QB); [2015] COPLR 425; *Major v Kirishana* [2023] EWHC 1593 (KB).

[34] *Glover v Barker* [2020] EWCA Civ 1112; [2021] 1 WLR 231 at [64].

[35] *Bushby v Galazi* [2022] EWHC 136 (Ch) at [84]–[94].

[36] CPR r 39.6.

the company etc to be able to take decisions necessary to properly conduct the proceedings.

## SECTION 2: NON-PARTIES

### RULE 4.—INTERVENORS

**(1) The court may permit any person to intervene, either in writing or at a hearing, in proceedings where it is in the interests of justice. Where intervention is permitted by a rule of law, permission is not required.**

**(2) An application to intervene should be made through the digital procedure and will be determined without a hearing, unless the court orders otherwise. An order on an application to intervene may not be subject to appeal.**

**(3) In considering whether it is in the interests of justice, the court must take account of all the circumstances, including whether the intervention**

**(a) would assist the court in ways that the parties could not;**

**(b) would promote adjudicative accuracy; and**

**(c) the extent to which it would further the purposive principle.**

**(4) Intervenors shall bear their costs of intervention. Generally, they shall not be subject to an adverse award of costs. Adverse costs may be awarded where an intervenor conducts their intervention in a way that is contrary to the interests of justice.**

*Sources: ALI/UNIDROIT Principles, principles 12.2, 13; ELI-UNIDROIT Model Rules, rr 39–43; CPR rr 52.25, 54.17; UK Supreme Court Rules, rr 15, 26; Practice Direction 8A, paras 8.8.1, 8.8.2*

### COMMENTARY

1. Intervention in proceedings by non-parties is a generally recognised feature of civil procedural codes.[37] Neither the CPR nor its predecessors, however, contain general provision for intervention. The CPR limits its provision for intervention to judicial review proceedings, statutory appeals, and where it is otherwise authorised by statute.[38] Outside such provision intervention is generally governed by the court's inherent jurisdiction.[39] The CPR's approach can be compared with that of the UK Supreme Court Rules, which contain a rule on intervention of general application.[40]

2. This rule codifies the UK Supreme Court's approach. It does so as intervention, if controlled carefully by the court, has several benefits that further the purposive principle. It can, for instance, help bring to light matters that assist the court in making relevant findings of fact.[41] Correspondingly, such findings may assist parties to reach a consensual settlement by shedding new light on their assessment of their respected cases.

[37] ALI/UNIDROIT Principles, *Transnational Rules of Civil Procedure (Reporters' Study)* (*ALI/UNIDROIT Reporters' Study*) r 6; ELI/UNIDROIT Model Rules, r 43.

[38] CPR r 52.25, r 54.17, and r 57.31 (intervention under Guardianship (Missing Persons) Act 2017, s 21(1)).

[39] *Roe v Sheffield City Council* [2003] EWCA Civ 1; [2004] QB 653 at [84]–[85]; *Halsey v Milton Keynes General NHS Trust* [2004] EWCA Civ 576; [2004] 1 WLR 3002; *Bowman v Fels* [2005] EWCA Civ 226; [2005] 4 All ER 609.

[40] *E v The Chief Constable of the Royal Ulster Constabulary (Northern Ireland Human Rights Commission intervening)* [2008] UKHL 66; [2009] 1 AC 536 at [2]–[3].

[41] *R v Lord Chancellor, ex parte Witham* [1998] QB 575.

Intervention can also enable the specialist, expert, perspective of the intervenor on legal issues to be put before the court. In that way, the court would have the benefit of it and of any submissions by the parties in response it. Thus, its judgment would be better informed as the intervention would provide the court with a '*more rounded picture than it would otherwise obtain*'.[42] Where judgment is given in the light of intervenors' submissions, that could also further promote the broader public interest by helping to develop or clarify the law more effectively than might otherwise have been the case. Such points are as relevant to private law disputes as they are to public law disputes.[43]

3. Accepting that intervention has particular benefits for the court and parties does not, of itself, justify the introduction of a rule of general application. Two further rationale support that. At a basic level, effective access to dispute resolution calls for the court's powers to be accessible. Codification of the general power to appoint intervenors in a single rule promotes such accessibility. Linked to that, the introduction of a general rule, promotes procedural equality, and through that the provision of a fair procedure. That it does so was illustrated by Sir Henry Brooke. He noted how, in the absence of a rule on intervention, the Court of Appeal had adopted three different approaches to dealing with applications to intervene. They ranged from the court giving informal directions following requests to intervene to it requiring either informal or formal applications to intervene. Differing approaches tend to result in differential treatment, which can result in different parties in different proceedings being treated unequally. A single, express rule obviates this problem; a point recognised by Sir Henry but not acted upon by the Civil Procedure Rule Committee.[44]
4. This rule establishes the general procedure to be followed. It applies to all proceedings. To promote procedural efficiency and proportionality, and also limit the potential costs that might be incurred by applications to intervene, they ought to be made by the digital procedure and determined without a hearing. This limitation is justified, in general, as intervention is not necessary to determine proceedings, but is a means to enhance the quality of judicial decision-making and settlement endeavours. The rule does, however, provide a discretion to determine the application at a hearing. That may be justifiable where it is not apparent that the benefits of intervention outweigh the disadvantages. It may also be justified where there are a number of intervenors who wish to make submissions on the same issue, and a hearing will enable the court to determine which of them ought to be permitted to intervene either orally or via written submissions.
5. Intervention should only be permitted where it is in the interests of justice.[45] In determining that question, the court ought to take account of the extent to which intervention will enable it to better perform its adjudicative role. It also ought to take account of the extent to which it will more broadly promote the purposive principle. This ought to require the court to consider the extent to which intervention would help to promote settlement. In considering the interests of justice, however, the court should also bear in mind its wider constitutional role. This requires it to consider the extent to which intervention may enable it to develop, correct, or clarify the law (and in that way also promote preventive justice).

[42] *E v The Chief Constable of the Royal Ulster Constabulary (Northern Ireland Human Rights Commission intervening)* [2008] UKHL 66; [2009] 1 AC 536 at [2].

[43] *Roe v Sheffield City Council* [2003] EWCA Civ 1; [2004] QB 653 at [85].

[44] H Brooke, 'Interventions in the Court of Appeal' (2007) 3 Public Law 401 at 406 and 408.

[45] *R (British American Tobacco UK Ltd) v Secretary of State for Health* [2014] EWHC 3515 (Admin); [2015] 1 CMLR 35.

6. Taking into account the extent to which intervention promotes the purposive principle also requires the court to consider the extent to which it would cause '*inconvenience, delay and expense*' to the parties,[46] and importantly to the court. Thus it must consider the extent to which intervention is consistent with both aspects of the proportionality principle. With this in mind, it should generally only be permitted where it is targeted to specific points on which the intervenor can assist the court in ways that go beyond that which the parties themselves can do. As a necessary corollary, it ought not to be permitted where the intervenor simply wishes to act as an advocate for a specific position, to repeat points made by the parties or other intervenors,[47] or raise or advance issues not directly in issue in proceedings.[48] Where intervention is permitted, the court should use its general dispute management powers to make provision for how the intervention is to be conducted, eg whether it should be by written or oral submissions and, if the latter, whether they should be subject to time limits.
7. Where intervention is authorised or required by any rule of law, such as intervention by the Crown in proceedings that raise human rights issues under section 5 of the Human Rights Act 1998, permission to intervene is not required.
8. As a general rule, an intervenor should bear their own costs of intervention as they are voluntarily choosing to assist the proper administration of justice. Similarly, they ought ordinarily not to be subject to an adverse costs award.[49] However, where an intervenor makes unnecessary or repetitive oral submissions, tries to expand the scope of the proceedings to accommodate points that are no more than indirectly related to the proceedings, or otherwise conduct themselves unreasonably, an adverse costs award may be justified. The same approach should thus apply to intervenors as it does to litigation friends who fail to carry out their duty of conducting proceedings on behalf of a protected party fairly and effectively. In both cases, the jurisdiction to award costs against the non-party arises under section 51 of the Senior Courts Act 1981.[50]

## RULE 5.—ADVOCATE TO THE COURT

**(1) The court may request, on its own initiative or on application of a party, the appointment of an Advocate to the Court by the Attorney-General.**
**(2) The Attorney-General may make an appointment where it is in the public interest because there is a real risk that the court will not be provided with submissions from the parties on an important point of law, the application of which to facts in dispute will be difficult to decide. Exceptionally, an Advocate to the Court may be authorised to examine witnesses.**
**(3) An Advocate to the Court does not represent, nor shall they take instructions from, any party to proceedings.**

*Sources: ELI-UNIDROIT Model Rules r 43; CPR PD3F.*

[46] *R (Northern Ireland Human Rights Commission) v Greater Belfast Coroner* [2002] UKHL 25; [2002] HRLR 35 at [32].
[47] *E v The Chief Constable of the Royal Ulster Constabulary (Northern Ireland Human Rights Commission intervening)* [2008] UKHL 66; [2009] 1 AC 536 at [3].
[48] *R (Burke) v The General Medical Council* [2005] EWCA Civ 1003; [2006] QB 273 at [82].
[49] *R (British American Tobacco UK Ltd) v Secretary of State for Health* [2014] EWHC 3515 (Admin); [2015] 1 CMLR 35.
[50] Applying the approach taken to litigation friends; *Bushby v Galazi* [2022] EWHC 136 (Ch) at [84]–[94].

## COMMENTARY

1. This rule integrates the CPR's approach to advocates to the court (formerly amicus curiae) into the Code. Until 2019, the CPR did not formally deal with the question of their role or appointment. Previously to that, the approach to be taken was governed by a protocol agreed in 2001 by the Lord Chief Justice and Attorney-General.[51] The substance of that protocol was incorporated into the CPR as its Practice Direction 3F.[52]
2. Advocates to the court assist the court through making submissions on particularly important and difficult legal issues and their application to the facts of proceedings. Their primary function then is to facilitate accuracy in judicial decision-making and they are generally appointed where one or more of the parties is without legal representation. Their appointment is also an indirect means to promote procedural equality where one party is unrepresented and without the advocate to the court's assistance the court may not have legal issues fully elaborated or tested. This role thus differs from that known as an amicus curiae brief in the United States of America, albeit the two roles have a common origin in English procedural law. They both developed from a common root, which permitted non-parties to assist the court by making submissions to it.[53] The US amicus brief, by way of contrast, is more akin to that of an intervenor.[54]
3. This rule maintains the position that an advocate to the court is appointed by the Attorney-General. In doing so it differs from the best practice approach taken by the ELI-UNIDROIT Model Rules, as that rule combines the role of the advocate to the court with that of the US amicus brief.[55] This Part maintains the distinction between advocates to the court and intervenors. It does so on the basis that advocates to the court are and should only be appointed when it is in the public interest to do so because there is a real risk that the court will not be able to decide an issue in proceedings that involves an important of law and its application.

[51] Memorandum of Understanding agreed by the Attorney General and the Lord Chief Justice, dated 19 December 2001, on the appointment of an Advocate to the Court (amicus curiae).

[52] CPR Update 104 (February 2019).

[53] S Krislov, 'The Amicus Curiae Brief: From Friendship to Advocacy' (1963) 72 Yale LJ 694.

[54] *ALI/UNIDROIT Reporters' Study*, r 6.

[55] ELI-UNIDROIT Model Rules, r 43.

# PART 7

# JURISDICTION, SCOPE, AND TERMINATION

## SECTION 1: GENERAL

1. This Part concerns the civil court's jurisdiction over parties and non-parties once legal proceedings have commenced. Its focus is the establishment and limits of the court's jurisdiction. In the latter regard it also sets out the rules concerning the scope of proceedings and parties' ability to terminate proceedings. Jurisdiction in respect of pre-action dispute resolution is dealt with in Part 5.

### RULE 1.—SCOPE AND PURPOSE

**(1) This Part concerns the basis on which the civil court exercises its adjudicative jurisdiction over natural and legal persons and their disputes.**
**(2) Rules concerning jurisdiction, scope and termination give effect to party autonomy by defining the court's jurisdiction over disputes and to due notice by requiring parties to be informed that the court's jurisdiction has been invoked and over that which it has been invoked. It also provides the framework within which courts reach accurate decisions and promote settlement through an adversarial process.**

*Sources: ALI/UNIDROIT Principles, principle 2; ALI/UNIDROIT Reporters' Study, r 4.*

### COMMENTARY

1. The civil courts in England and Wales operate according to an adversarial model of procedure.[1] They are not inquisitorial or investigative.[2] This is due to the centrality of both the party autonomy and adversariality principles, to which this Part gives effect. One particular consequence of the former principle is that proceedings cannot commence, and hence a court's jurisdiction to resolve a dispute by way of accurate judgment or consensual resolution cannot arise, unless and until its jurisdiction has been invoked by a natural or legal person.
2. The court's jurisdiction is not only limited, however, by reference to whether or not proceedings are commenced by a party to a dispute. There are two further significant limitations to it. The first concerns the scope of proceedings. An inquisitorial process

[1] Part 1, rr 6.1 and 18.1.
[2] Judicial Working Group on Litigants-in-Person, *Report* (Judicial Office, 2013) at 8, 24–25; Lord Thomas CJ, *Reshaping Justice* (Justice Lecture) (3 March 2014) at [25]–[32].

*A Model Civil Procedure Code for England and Wales*. John Sorabji, Oxford University Press. © John Sorabji 2024.
DOI: 10.1093/oso/9780192848680.003.0008

would enable a court, of its own initiative, to range widely over all matters relating to a dispute. If, for instance, it determined that the parties had not raised certain issues, whether factual or legal, which it considered relevant to their dispute, an inquisitorial court could investigate and determine the dispute by reference to them. This Code limits the civil court's ability to investigate matters on its own initiative. It thus maintains this longstanding further effect of party autonomy by limiting the court's jurisdiction to the dispute as defined by the parties. It further gives effect to party autonomy by making provision for either the claimant or defendant to terminate the proceedings without them being resolved adjudicatively or by consensual resolution process.

3. Party autonomy is not, however, the only procedural principle with which this Part is concerned. An equally well-established procedural principle, both at common law and under article 6(1) of the European Convention on Human Rights, is that of due notice. In this Part, this is particularly focused on the right of a defendant to be made aware of the fact that proceedings have commenced against them. In doing so due notice plays a central role in establishing the civil court's jurisdiction over them, thus also providing the foundation for defendants to exercise their own autonomy by way of determining their response to the proceedings.

## RULE 2.—JURISDICTION

**(1) The court's adjudicatory and settlement jurisdiction over an identified claimant begins when they commence proceedings, including issuing an application for pre-commencement measures.**
**(2) The court's adjudicatory and settlement jurisdiction over an identifiable, even if unknown or unidentified, defendant begins when a defendant is served or is deemed to be served with proceedings.**
**(3) Jurisdiction over non-parties, including intervenors and witnesses, arises when they commence acting in proceedings, are served with or are deemed to be served with proceedings, or as provided for at common law or in legislation.**
**(4) A party may challenge the court's jurisdiction.**
**(5) Adjudicatory jurisdiction is the power to determine a dispute through the application of right law to right fact. Settlement jurisdiction is the power to facilitate consensual settlement of a dispute after proceedings have commenced.**

*Sources: ALI/UNIDROIT Principles, principle 2; ALI/UNIDROIT Reporters' Study, r 4.*

## COMMENTARY

1. The civil court's jurisdiction over claimants commences when they seek its aid by commencing proceedings[3] or invoking its powers in respect of pre-action process. This is a consequence of the autonomy principle: individuals are responsible for resolving their own disputes, but may choose, where necessary, to call upon the court and its powers to determine them by way of judgment or help promote consensual resolution within proceedings.

[3] First Report of the Common Law Commissioners into the Practice and Proceedings of the Superior Courts of Common Law (House of Commons) (1829) at 80.

2. Matters are different with defendants where commencing proceedings is concerned. Defendants cannot choose to submit to the court's jurisdiction. If they were able to do so they would be able to frustrate the civil process. Moreover, if jurisdiction was based on the defendant's election it would result in them being able, as Zuckerman notes, to deny claimants their right of access to justice: it would frustrate the general access principle.[4] To give effect to a claimant's ability to secure such access, party autonomy over the court's jurisdiction does not therefore apply to defendants. Commencement of proceedings is a unilateral act. This is not to say that a defendant may not, for valid reasons, challenge the court's jurisdiction. Nor is it to say that it is simply commencement that creates jurisdiction over defendants. For that, there must not only be commencement, but the fact and nature of proceedings must be or be deemed to have been brought to the defendant's attention. Thus jurisdiction over defendants begins with service or deemed service of proceedings, which is also a unilateral act either effected by the court or by the parties, and thus not capable of frustration by a defendant.
3. Proceedings must also be commenced against a, generally, identified defendant.[5] In some cases a claimant may not know the defendant's identity. A claimant may be threatened or harassed over the Internet by persons unknown. Unknown squatters may have moved into a claimant's property. Unknown protestors may block access to property or disrupt trade or business activities. In such circumstances, to require a claimant to identify the defendant by, for instance, name and address as would ordinarily be the case, would deny them access to the court. To give effect to the general access principle, therefore a claimant need only take steps to ensure that the defendant is, at a minimum, identifiable by description. The description given must enable the court to conclude that reasonable steps were taken to bring the fact of the proceedings to the defendant's notice, ie to effect service of the particulars of claim upon them, and thus satisfy the due notice principle.[6] This is because it is as the Supreme Court has explained '*a fundamental principle of justice that a person cannot be made subject to the jurisdiction of the court without having such notice of the proceedings as will enable [them] to be heard*'.[7]
4. In addition to the parties to proceedings, the court has jurisdiction over a range of non-parties. It retains, for instance, jurisdiction over solicitors as officers of the court.[8] While not officers of the court, it also has jurisdiction over barristers, for instance, in respect of non-party costs orders.[9] Jurisdiction over intervenors arises from the point at which they are granted permission to intervene, and over witnesses, whether lay or expert, when they too become involved in proceedings.
5. Finally, rule 2(1) and (5) make clear that the court has, in addition to its adjudicatory jurisdiction, which is its power to determine disputes through the application of right law to right fact, a settlement jurisdiction. It thus makes clear that the management of consensual settlement processes is an exercise of the judicial power of

[4] A Zuckerman, *Zuckerman on Civil Procedure—Principles of Practice* (Sweet & Maxwell, 2021) at 193.

[5] *Re Harris (Puisne mortgage)* [2021] EWHC 1771 (Ch); Part 6, r 2(3).

[6] *Cameron v Liverpool Victoria Insurance Co Ltd* [2019] UKSC 6; [2019] 1 WLR 1471 at [18]–[20].

[7] *Cameron v Liverpool Victoria Insurance Co Ltd* [2019] UKSC 6; [2019] 1 WLR 1471 at [17], also see [12]–[16], [25]; *R v London Quarter Sessions Appeal Committee, ex parte Rossi* [1956] 1 QB 682 at 691, 696. A. Zuckerman (2021) at 276–277.

[8] Solicitors Act 1974, s 50; *Stephens v Hill* (1842) 10 M & W 28; *Myers v Elman* [1940] AC 282 at 319; *Gupta v Comer* [1991] 21 QB 629; *Holden & Co v Crown Prosecution Service* [1990] 2 QB 261.

[9] Part 3, r 2(4); Part 11, r 33.

the State, and hence is within judicial immunity from suit. It also provides the basis on which the consensual settlement principle is given effect, not least as it forms the basis for the court's general dispute management powers concerning settlement developed in Part 11.

6. In commencing or defending proceedings, it is essential that a claimant or defendant must identify themselves to the court. As Warby J rightly noted, where commencement is concerned, '*A right to bring a claim on behalf of a person whose identity is known but kept secret from the Court has never yet been recognised.*'[10] The same is true for defendants. Parties cannot therefore be permitted to commence proceedings or defendants to defend them using a pseudonym or otherwise hide their identity from the court, and by extension from the other party and the public.[11] To recognise such a right would be to fatally undermine the proper administration of justice, and not least the publicity principle.[12]

7. That the courts have not recognised such a right arises through the operation of several principles. The publicity principle requires the court to ensure that justice is done in the open. It could not do so if it were ignorant of who the parties were. Nor could it properly assess whether an exception to the publicity principle applied absent such knowledge. Witnesses might also not be able to come forward, frustrating that particular rationale of the publicity principle. Courts would also not be able to be held properly accountable by either appellate courts or the public if the parties' identities were unknown. Public knowledge of who is litigating, as it is the means by which the public becomes aware over whom the State is exercising its authority is essential.[13] This is not to say that specific information concerning parties may not properly be anonymised[14] or that, for instance, a claimant's address may not properly be withheld from a defendant where, for instance, knowledge of it would put the claimant in danger.[15] Such matters may, where justified in the circumstances of a particular case, be appropriate derogations from the publicity principle. Anoymisation necessarily presupposes that the court is aware of party identity.

8. Further issues arise. Permitting a party to withhold their identity from the court would frustrate the objective that proceedings should be conducted fairly. It is an aspect of procedural fairness for a defendant to know who their accuser is, just as it is for the claimant to know that they are proceeding against the right defendant and not some third party purporting to be the right defendant. Where a party withholds their identity, the court would also not be in a position to ascertain if claimant or defendant could properly be a party to proceedings such that, if not, the proceedings were a nullity.[16] Moreover, it would not be able to take steps to secure procedural equality or to enforce compliance with procedural orders or final judgments. It would thus frustrate effective dispute management, enforcement, and finality.

[10] *SMO (A Child) v Tiktok Inc* [2020] EWHC 3589 (QB); [2021] 2 FLR 917 at [8].

[11] *R (C) v Secretary of State for Justice* [2016] UKSC 2 (at [1] and [18]; *Wright v The person or persons unknown responsible for the operation and publication of the website www.bitcoin.org* [2022] EWHC 2982 (SCCO), esp at [43]; *Persons Unknown v Wright* [2023] EWHC 2292 (Ch) at [42]–[44].

[12] *R (C) v Secretary of State for Justice* [2016] UKSC 2; [2016] 1 WLR 444 at [1]; *Persons Unknown v Wright* [2023] EWHC 2292 (Ch) at [32].

[13] *Astrovlanis Compania Naviera SA v Linard* [1972] 2 QB 611.

[14] D. Neuberger et al, *Report of the Committee on Super-Injunctions: Super-Injunctions, Anonymised Injunctions and Open Justice* (Judicial Office, 2011).

[15] *Axnoller Events Limited v Brake* [2022] EWHC 1162 (Ch) at [16] and following.

[16] *Lazard Brothers & Co v Midland Bank Ltd* [1933] AC 289 at 296; *Fielding v Rigby* [1993] 1 WLR 1355 at 1359; *Persons Unknown v Wright* [2023] EWHC 2292 (Ch) at [42]–[44].

9. Were a claimant to hide their identity from the court, and hence the defendant, due notice would also not be satisfied. While a defendant might suspect who had started proceedings they would not know. Their suspicion might be wrong. For all they might suspect, there is no basis on which they could be sure that proceedings, which alleged a genuine cause of action against them, was not being brought by a third party to, for instance, harass them. In such a situation neither the court nor the defendant would, furthermore, be in a position to properly assess whether the claim was being brought abusively, for a criminal purpose, contrary to the principle of finality, or simply to harass the defendant.

## SECTION 2: COMMENCEMENT

### RULE 3.—COMMENCEMENT AND NOTICE OF PROCEEDINGS—GENERALLY

**(1) Where a dispute is not resolved during pre-action dispute management, a claimant may provide the court with particulars of claim. For the purposes of any applicable limitation period, proceedings are brought when they are provided to the court.**

**(2) Proceedings commence when the court issued particulars of claims that have been provided to it by a claimant. In exceptional circumstances, the court acting judicially and without generally holding a hearing may refuse to issue proceedings. It may do so, for instance, to protect its processes from abuse.**

**(3) Unless the court orders otherwise, the date of issue is the date on which the court seals, either digitally or physically, the particulars of claim.**

*Sources: ALI/UNIDROIT Principles, principle 10.1; ALI/UNIDROIT Reporters' Study, r 11; ELI-UNIDROIT Model Rules, r 52; CPR Pt 7.*

### COMMENTARY

1. The primary function of this rule is to provide for the formal commencement of proceedings. It stresses that prior to commencement parties ought to have engaged in pre-action dispute resolution. Thus, it reinforces the integration of court processes into a holistic approach to dispute resolution. It also makes clear that the decision whether to commence proceedings lies in the hands of the claimant. It thus emphasises both the consensual settlement principle, as it recognises that disputes may settle pre-issue, and party autonomy over the choice to commence proceedings. It also emphasises the unilateral nature of commencement, which ensures effective access to the court for claimants.

2. The process for commencing claims is twofold.[17] The first part is unilateral and is intended to give effect to the general access principle. It requires the claimant to file their particulars of claim with the court, eg to deliver it to the court. Historically, this would have been done through the delivery of a physical writ and, then from 1999,

[17] *Salford City Council v Garner* [2004] EWCA Civ 364; *Barnes v St Helens Metropolitan Borough Council* [2006] EWCA Civ 1372; [2007] 3 All ER 525 at [30]; *Page v Hewetts Solicitors* [2012] EWCA Civ 805.

a physical claim form.[18] Present and future better practice will see filing generally carried out electronically through the digital procedure.[19]

3. Providing that this aspect of the commencement process is unilateral and is based on provision of particulars of claim to the court is essential for a further reason. It is the means by which a claimant can be sure that they have brought proceedings within any applicable limitation period.[20] If, for instance, for limitation purposes a claim was not brought until issued by a court, the claimant could never guarantee that their claim was brought within a limitation period. They could not as they could never be certain when the court would carry out its role and issue the proceedings. Or, if a question over whether the claimant had paid the correct filing fee applicable to the claim for relief could affect the determination of whether, and if, a claim had been filed for limitation purposes, neither parties nor the court would be able to ascertain simply and with certainty limitation questions.[21] Lack of certainty here would open up an avenue for satellite litigation that could otherwise properly be avoided through the application of a bright line rule based purely on the unilateral act of a claimant. As a consequence, maintenance of this longstanding approach to filing and limitation is consistent, not only with facilitating access to justice for claimants, but also with the aim of securing an efficient, economical and proportionate process through minimising the risk of such litigation.
4. The second part of the commencement process is transactional and formal. It relies upon the court to issue the particulars of claim once they have been deposited with it. Courts do this by sealing and dating the particulars of claim as a single process.[22] Generally, this is an administrative process, which provides a definite date on which proceedings commence. This provides a sure means to determine the procedural timetable for the dispute's proper management. It sets, for instance, the starting point for the procedural time limit within which the particulars of claim must be served on a defendant. It also clearly defines the time from which the court's jurisdiction over the dispute arises, and hence it defines when the court's obligations concerning the dispute, not least its obligation to manage the dispute consistently with the purposive principle, arises.
5. Exceptionally, civil courts may refuse to issue proceedings. The basis of this jurisdiction to refuse to issue proceedings is the court's inherent jurisdiction to protect the administration of justice from abuse. Only a senior judge, eg at least a judge of the High Court's Upper Tier, may exercise this jurisdiction,[23] and will do so without holding a hearing. Where necessary the court may, however, do so at a hearing.

[18] RSC Ord 6; CPR Pt 7.

[19] CPR PD7E para 5.1; CPR PD51O—The Electronic Working Pilot Scheme, para 2.2; CPR PD51R—Online Civil Money Claims Pilot Scheme, para 4; CEPEJ, *Guidelines on electronic court filing (e-filing) and digitalisation of courts* (Council of Europe, 2021).

[20] A. Zuckerman (2021) at 193–194.

[21] *Dixon v Radley House (A firm)* [2016] EWHC 2511 (TCC); *Wells v Wood* [2016] WLUK 226; *Atha & Co Solicitors v Liddle* [2018] EWHC 1751 (QB); [2018] 1 WLR 4953.

[22] *Walton v Pickerings Solicitors* [2023] EWCA Civ 602.

[23] *Re Benmusa (No 3)* [2017] EWHC 966 (Fam) at [3].

## RULE 4.—COMMENCEMENT AND NOTICE OF PROCEEDINGS—JUDICIAL REVIEW

**(1) In addition to the requirements of Part 7, rule 3,**
   **(a) judicial review proceedings may only be commenced by a person with sufficient interest in bringing such proceedings with the court's permission;**
   **(b) permission may only be granted where an application for permission, which accompanies the claimant's particulars of claim, discloses an arguable ground or grounds of review, which has or have a real prospect of success, and where there are no other available remedies; and**
   **(c) permission must, unless the court directs to the contrary or a statute provides otherwise, be sought promptly and, in any event, no later than three months after the basis on which the judicial review proceedings are founded arose.**

**(2) Notice of the application for permission to bring judicial review proceedings must be served on any interested party. Interested parties are those persons directly affected by the proceedings.**

**(3) The application for permission will be decided without a hearing, unless the court orders otherwise.**

**(4) Where the permission application is determined without a hearing, the claimant may apply for it to be reconsidered at a hearing.**

*Sources: CPR Pt 54; Senior Courts Act 1981, s 29, s 31.*

## COMMENTARY

1. The civil courts have full jurisdiction to determine both private and public law disputes.[24] This Code, like the CPR, thus applies to both private and public law disputes. The CPR makes, however, specific provision for public law—judicial review—claims within its Pt 54. This Code does not have an equivalent to Pt 54. Rather this rule makes provision for additional requirements applicable to commencing judicial review proceedings. Other Parts of the Code either make specific provision for judicial review or they are generally applicable to public law claims.

2. This rule sets out five essential features of the approach to commencing judicial review proceedings. It defines the nature of such claims.[25] It specifies, consistently with the long-established approach to judicial review, that permission is required by a person with sufficient standing for such proceedings to commence.[26] It articulates the applicable test for the grant of permission,[27] the time limit for seeking permission,[28] and it requires interested parties to be given notice of such proceedings.[29] That interested parties must be given notice, ie served with the application for permission, arises from the fact that they will be, or are likely to be affected, by the outcome of the

[24] *R (Good Law Project) v Secretary of State for Health and Social Care* [2022] EWCA Civ 355.

[25] Senior Courts Act 1981, s 31; CPR rr 54.1(1)(a) and see rr 54.2 and (3); *R v East Berkshire Health Authority, ex p Walsh* [1985] QB 152 at 162; *R v Panel on Takeover and Mergers, ex p Datafin* [1987] QB 815 at 838.

[26] CPR r 54.4; Senior Courts Act 1981, s 31.

[27] *R v Legal Aid Board, ex p Hughes* [1992] 5 Admin LR 623; *Sharma v Brown-Antoine* [2007] 1 WLR 780 at [14]; *Simone v Chancellor of the Exchequer* [2019] EWHC 2609 (Admin) at [112].

[28] CPR r 54.5.

[29] CPR r 54.1(2)(f).

proceedings.[30] As they are in a comparable position to a party to proceedings they must therefore be afforded due notice of the claim being made.

## RULE 5.—COMMENCEMENT AND NOTICE OF PROCEEDINGS—PROCEEDINGS ON AGREED FACTS

**(1) In addition to the requirements of Part 7, rule 3, where there is a dispute between the parties but no substantial factual dispute between them, they may agree to bring proceedings on agreed facts. Agreed facts must not be hypothetical or academic.**

**(2) There may be no substantial factual dispute even if there are some factual issues on which the parties do not agree. In such a case proceedings on agreed facts may still be commenced.**

**(3) The court may also, alternatively, permit proceedings on agreed facts where:**

**(a) there is no present cause of action but if the court did not rule on an issue it is likely that a dispute would arise;**

**(b) the parties have opposed interests;**

**(c) the proceedings would raise an important point of law of general application on which declaratory relief could be granted; and**

**(d) dealing with the issue would further the purposive principle.**

**(4) Proceedings on agreed facts shall be commenced through a joint particulars of claim, as provided for under Part 8 rule 10, rather than through the claimant issuing their own particulars of claim that would then be responded to by a defence.**

**(5) The court, at any time on its own initiative or on application of a party, may direct that the proceedings cease to be proceedings on agreed facts. Where such an order is made, the court will give dispute management directions appropriate for the further management of the proceedings.**

**(6) Generally, all parties will bear their own costs when proceedings are brought on agreed facts. Where, however, contentious factual issues are resolved by the court, the general rule concerning costs applies to those issues.**

*Sources: ELI-UNIDROIT Model Rules, r 23; French Code of Civil Procedure, art 57; CPR Pt 8, PD63AA, para 6.*

## COMMENTARY

1. This rule makes provision for two circumstances where parties may wish to bring proceedings where there is little to no factual dispute between them. Both rules are intended to reduce the cost and time of proceedings.

2. This rule, first, adopts the approach taken to CPR Pt 8. It thus requires proceedings brought under it to involve no substantial disputes of fact.[31] To agree the use of such proceedings, parties will need to co-operate with each other prior to finalising their joint particulars of claim. As a bare minimum this requires compliance with the guidance set out in *Cathay Pacific Airlines Ltd v Lufthansa Technik AG* (2019).[32] That guidance requires a claimant to notify the defendant of the issue

[30] RSC Ord 53, r 5(3); *R v Liverpool City Council, ex p Muldoon* [1996] 1 WLR 1103.

[31] *ING Bank NV v Ros Roca SA* [2011] EWCA Civ 353; [2012] 1 WLR 472 at [77].

[32] *Cathay Pacific Airlines Ltd v Lufthansa Technik AG* [2019] EWCH 484 (Ch); [2019] 1 All ER (Comm) 265 at [42].

and surrounding facts, their proposed intention to use this procedure and why it is suitable. It further requires the proposed agreed facts to be identified. Under the CPR, proceedings under Pt 8 were capable of being issued without this guidance having been complied with in cases of urgency.[33] Given the centrality of party agreement under this rule, that is not possible. In cases of urgency, a claimant should issue their particulars of claim as normal and include with them an application for a stay of proceedings to permit time for the steps to be complied with, ie to ascertain if the defendant is prepared to agree to the facts. Where a defendant agrees, the court may then direct the proceedings to continue as proceedings on agreed facts. Where a defendant does not agree, the stay may be lifted and proceedings continue as normal. If a stay is not a viable option for a claimant, then they may simply use the normal procedure.

3. Notwithstanding there being no substantial factual dispute between the parties, there may be some factual issues on which they are unable to disagree. In such a case, this procedure may still be used.[34] It may, however, only be used if contentious factual issues do not predominate. In such a case, the contentious issues must clearly be identified and the parties' respective positions set out in the joint particulars of claim.
4. The court always retains a discretion to transfer proceedings on agreed facts to the normal procedure. It would ordinarily do so where it becomes apparent that there are, in fact, substantial factual issues in dispute between the parties. See further Part 8, rule 10 on the joint particulars of claim.
5. The second function of this rule, provided for specifically by rule 5(3), enables parties to bring proceedings where there is, as yet, no cause of action between the parties,[35] but there is a dispute over the correct interpretation of a legal issue. This situation is currently provided for, to a limited degree, by CPR PD63AA, para 6: the Financial Markets Test Case Procedure. That scheme is of limited application. It only applies to specialist claims that would fall within the Financial List, eg capital or financial markets disputes.[36] In turn this specialist procedure is based on previous case law developments, ie those summarised and applied in *Rolls-Royce plc v Unite the Union* (2009) that acknowledged that the court has jurisdiction to grant declaratory relief on matters that do not involve a dispute between the parties if: (i) the issue was likely to lead to a dispute between the parties if declaratory relief was not granted, ie it was not a purely academic issue;[37] (ii) the issue was of public importance; and (iii) court resolution would further the overriding objective, specifically through being a justifiable use of court resources.[38] Similar approaches to such matters are taken in other procedural schemes. French civil procedure, for instance, provides a simplified procedure through which parties may submit a joint pleading where they agree on factual issues, but want the court to determine specific legal and, limited, factual

[33] *Standing v Power* [2021] EWHC 1744 (Ch) at [19]–[21].

[34] *Vitpol Building Service v Samen* [2008] EWCA 2283 (TCC); [2009] Const LJ 25(4) 319 at [18].

[35] *Letang v Cooper* [1965] 1 QB 232 at 242; *Cooke v Gill* (1872–73) LR 8 CP 107 at 116; *Read v Brown* (1888) 22 QBD 128 at 131; *Central Electricity Board v Halifax Corp* [1963] AC 785 at 800.

[36] CPR Pt 63A.

[37] *Ainsbury v Millington* [1987] 1 WLR 379 at 381. See *Montlake Qiaif Platform Icav v Tiber Capital LLP* [2021] EWHC 202 (Comm) at 44 for a summary of the general principles governing the grant of declaratory relief.

[38] *Rolls-Royce plc v Unite the Union* [2009] EWCA Civ 387; [2010] 1 WLR 318 at [52]–[58]; CPR PD63AA para 9.2

matters in dispute. A similar approach is also adopted as best practice in the ELI/ UNIDROIT Model Rules.

6. Rule 5(3) codifies and generalises the approach taken by the *Rolls-Royce plc* jurisdiction and by the Financial Markets Test Case procedure. It does so because the position taken under the CPR is unprincipled as it is subject-specific rather than trans-substantive and was particularly designed to further the status of the Commercial Court in London as '*the global leader in efficient, specialist, and high quality financial dispute resolution*'.[39] While there is no reason why procedure should not be developed to promote the efficacy, and attractiveness, of specialist courts, the benefit of this procedure is one that is generally applicable, not least as judgments made under it would enrich the legal framework, and hence the shadow of the law it creates through judgments that give definitive guidance on legal issues of general importance. Such a position promotes not only dispute prevention, but also—as acknowledged in respect of the Financial Markets Test Case procedure– consensual resolution.[40] As such it should be of general and not just specialist application. As this rule may accordingly reduce the potential number of disputes through the guidance it can facilitate this rule is equally capable of promoting procedural proportionality, and particularly systemic proportionality.
7. Given the nature of the two approaches under this rule, there should generally be no order as to costs. Both parties should bear their own costs. Where, however, such proceedings include contentious issues of fact that need to be determined by the court, in so far as those matters are concerned, the normal rule concerning costs applies.
8. Use of pre-action dispute management may be of limited value in proceedings on agreed facts given the absence of a current dispute or cause of action.

# SECTION 3: SCOPE OF PROCEEDINGS

## RULE 6.—SCOPE OF PROCEEDINGS

**(1) The scope of proceedings is defined by the parties' case statements.**
**(2) The court may only determine proceedings within the limits set by the parties' case statements.**
**(3) Where a court considers that a case statement does not properly identify a relevant legal or factual issue, it should invite the relevant party to apply to amend the statement.**

*Sources: ALI/UNIDROIT Principles, principle 10.3; ELI-UNIDROIT Model Rules, r.23, r.61.4.*

## COMMENTARY

1. This rule concerns the nature of the court's jurisdiction. Within an adversarial system of procedure, the scope of proceedings falls within the ambit of party autonomy.[41]

[39] Civil Procedure Rule Committee Meeting Minutes (20 June 2020) cited in in P Coulson (ed), *Civil Procedure 2023* (Sweet & Maxwell, 2023) at 2FA-12.1.

[40] *Financial Conduct Authority v Arch Insurance (UK) Ltd* [2021] UKSC 1; [2021] AC 649 at [43].

[41] A Zuckerman (2021) at 329.

It is thus for the parties through their statements of case to determine the scope of the proceedings.[42] As Lord Woolf MR noted case statements (pleadings) '*mark out the parameters of the case that is being advanced by each party*'.[43] They do so for a number of reasons, the most important of which is jurisdictional. As Brooke LJ explained,

> *... It is fundamental to our adversarial system of justice that the parties should clearly identify the issues that arise in the litigation, so that each has the opportunity of responding to the points made by the other. The function of the judge is to adjudicate on those issues alone. The parties may have their own reasons for limiting the issues or presenting them in a certain way... One consequence of this may be that the judge is compelled to reject a claim on the basis on which it is advanced, although he or she is of the opinion that it would have succeeded if it had been advanced on a different basis. Such an outcome may be unattractive, but any other approach leads to uncertainty and potentially real unfairness.*[44]

Were a judge to go beyond the parameters of the dispute set by the case statements or pleadings, they would as Brooke LJ went on to explain have impermissibly departed from their proper role within an adversarial system. They would have acted as if they were operating within an inquisitorial system of justice.[45]

2. Party autonomy may provide the basis for defining the scope of the court's jurisdiction, but it is not the only procedural principle in play. Rule 6 recognises that there may be circumstances where a court reaches the view that the parties have not pleaded their case effectively, and that a key issue in the dispute—whether factual or legal—ought properly to have been pleaded. To rectify such a situation, case statements may be amended; an approach which promotes adjudicative accuracy. However, it is for the parties to determine if they wish to seek amendment, as much as it is for the court to determine, in the event of such an application, if it is proper to permit it. To take account of this, consistently with the need to promote effective dispute management, this rule codifies the approach endorsed by the Court of Appeal in *Loveridge and Loveridge v Healey* (2004). Thus where the court concludes that an issue is outside the scope of the proceedings due to the way a party has pleaded their case it should invite them to apply to amend their case statement if they want the court to rule upon it.[46] There is, however, no duty on the court to make such an inquiry and to raise such issues with the parties.[47] In the absence of amendment, the opposing party is perfectly entitled to require the court to confine itself and any judgment to the pleaded cases as defined by the case statements.[48] Moreover, where facts are established at trial that are unconnected with the pleaded case, the claim may properly fail.[49]

[42] A party is perfectly entitled to leave out of their pleaded claim, or defence, any matter that they could reasonably have pleaded: *Khiaban v Beard* [2003] EWCA Civ 358; [2003] 1 WLR 1626 at [13].

[43] *McPhilemy v Times Newspapers Ltd* [1999] 3 All ER 775 at 793.

[44] *Al-Medenni v Mars UK Ltd* [2005] EWCA Civ 1041 at [21]; *Loveridge v Healey* [2004] EWCA Civ 173; [2004] C P Rep 30 at [22].

[45] *Al-Medenni v Mars UK Ltd* [2005] EWCA Civ 1041 at [22]–[25]. In certain circumstances, where it is clear that all parties have come to court to argue an unpleaded point the court could go on to determine it: *Lombard North Central plc v Automobile World (UK) Ltd* [2010] EWCA Civ 20 at [79]. Rather than view the court's approach as acting inquisitorially or going outside the parameters set by the case statements, the court can be understood to be dispensing with case statements in so far as the unpleaded issue is concerned.

[46] *Loveridge v Healey* [2004] EWCA Civ 173; [2004] C P Rep 30 at [25].

[47] *Lombard North Central plc v Automobile World (UK) Ltd* [2010] EWCA Civ 20 at [78].

[48] *Loveridge v Healey* [2004] EWCA Civ 173; [2004] C P Rep 30 at [23]; *Al-Medenni v Mars UK Ltd* [2005] EWCA Civ 1041 at [21].

[49] *Waghorn v George Wimpey & Co Ltd* [1969] 1 WLR 1764 at 1771.

3. Limiting the court's jurisdiction by reference to the contents of the case statements serves further purposes. It stops parties being surprised by new issues that are raised without having been pleaded, and thus secures due notice.[50] It provides clarity for the parties concerning facts to be established, evidence to be obtained and challenged, and legal submissions to be made and met. As such it forms the basis on which the court, and parties co-operating with it, can conduct litigation economically, efficiently, and proportionately; confining, for instance, the evidence and legal submissions to issues in dispute and, as a corollary, managing and limiting court and party time and resources to such matters. It also forms the basis on which the court can effectively promote settlement. And, in the event, the dispute does not settle, it forms the basis on which the court may adjudicate effectively. It also, by providing a clear record of the dispute enables the public to properly understand and scrutinise the proceedings further to the publicity principle.

# SECTION 4: TERMINATION

## RULE 7.—TERMINATION OF PROCEEDINGS

**(1) A claimant may bring the dispute to an end, in whole or in part, at any time by discontinuing proceedings.**

**(2) If a defendant has not been served with any order obtained before proceedings commenced or with the particulars of claim, discontinuance may be effected without the court's consent. In all other circumstances, discontinuance may only be effected with the court's consent.**

**(3) Unless the court orders otherwise, a claimant who discontinues proceedings with the court's consent shall be liable for the defendant's costs up to the date of discontinuance. The court may not order otherwise unless the claimant demonstrates that there is good reason for it to do so.**

**(4) Where proceedings are discontinued without the court's consent there shall be no order as to costs.**

**(5) Where a claimant discontinues with the court's consent they may not commence fresh proceedings in respect of the same dispute without the court's consent. Consent may only be given if the claimant has good reason for seeking to do so.**

*Sources: ALI/UNIDROIT Principles, principle 10.5; ELI-UNIDROIT Model Rules, r 56; CPR Pt 38.*

## COMMENTARY

1. This rule concerns the ability of claimants to bring disputes to an end by terminating proceedings. Where a defendant wishes to terminate proceedings they may do so by admitting the claimant's claim. The ability to discontinue proceedings is an aspect of party autonomy.
2. A claimant may terminate proceedings as of right where it can properly be said that neither the court nor the defendant has a legitimate interest in them continuing. This is clearly the case where neither court nor defendant have been engaged by the

[50] *Davie v New Merton Board Mills Ltd* [1956] 1 WLR 233.

proceedings, e.g., because no hearings or orders, including pre-action orders, have been made. Where they have been, consent is required to discontinue.

3. The rationale for this approach was made clear in the ELI-UNIDROIT Model Rules.[51] Once a claimant has taken steps that have required the defendant and court to engage with the proceedings, they can be said to have progressed to a point when they both have a legitimate interest in the dispute being determined by the court, so as to give effect to both the proportionality and finality principles. On this basis, consent to terminate is unnecessary where a defendant has had no notice of proceedings or not been subject any orders made prior to or after commencement. In such circumstances, an interest in having the dispute resolved does not arise: the defendant has not been troubled by the claimant and may not even know there is a dispute. Equally, there will have been little use of the court's resources to properly engage the court's duty to promote proportionality or its interest in the dispute being disposed of finally.

4. Where, however, steps have been taken by a claimant that have engaged the defendant, they are likely to have incurred time and costs on preparing their defence. Additionally, the court will have expended some of its resources on the dispute and may have already started to carry out its dispute management role. In these circumstances, defendants and courts have an interest in scrutinising discontinuance. They have an interest in ensuring, for instance, any applicable interim injunctive relief is set aside, or undertakings are released before discontinuance takes effect. They have an interest in giving effect to finality and proportionality, not least as discontinuance may potentially be followed by the claimant at a future point in time seeking to recommence proceedings. Such factors will weigh increasingly heavily the further advanced proceedings have progressed, ie the further proceedings will have progressed the greater defendant and court time and costs will have been expended and the greater the defendant's need to see their rights put on a certain footing will be.[52]

5. Where discontinuance is granted with court consent, the default position is that the claimant will pay the defendant's costs incurred to the date on which discontinuance is effected. This is an aspect of procedural fairness. Having been troubled by proceedings, and incurred costs as a consequence of them, the claimant—not having pursued their claim to resolution—should compensate the defendant for causing them to take steps to defend their interests. For the court to depart from the general rule, the claimant must show that there is a good reason for it do so.[53] Departures from the general rule may, nevertheless, be made. This will usually require the claimant to show a change in circumstances has arisen independently of anything they have done, eg due to unreasonable conduct by the defendant. Neither changes in financial circumstances nor practical or pragmatic reasons on the claimant's part for discontinuing will amount to a good reason. That it is obvious that the claim would have failed is a reason to support the application of the general rule. Equally, the fact that the claim would or may have succeeded at trial is not a good reason to disapply the general rule.[54]

[51] ELI-UNIDROIT Model Rules, r 56 commentary.

[52] *Ernst & Young v Butte Mining Plc* [1996] 1 WLR 1605.

[53] *Brookes v HSBC Bank PLC* [2011] EWCA Civ 354 at [6]; *Nelson's Yard Management Co v Eziefula* [2013] EWCA Civ 235; [2013] CP Rep 29 at [14]; *Ashany v Eco-Bat Technologies Limited* [2018] EWCA Civ 1066; [2018] 3 Costs LO 387 at [16].

[54] *Brookes v HSBC Bank PLC* [2011] EWCA Civ 354 at [6] and [10].

6. In many cases, a defendant will not object to discontinuance. Where they do, they and the claimant ought to be heard on the issue before the court decides whether to exercise its discretion to consent to the discontinuance. Where, however, a defendant does not object, it ought—further to the co-operation principle—to inform the court and the claimant of that fact. In such circumstances, the court may give its consent without holding a hearing. If it considers that it may withhold its consent, a with-notice hearing should take place. Where discontinuance is granted with consent, the rule provides, consistently with the CPR, that the claimant may only commence new proceedings concerning the same dispute with the court's permission.[55] A claimant will need to satisfy the court that there is a good reason justifying the grant of consent, ie that there is good reason for it to seek to commence fresh proceedings in respect of the same dispute.[56] Good reason may arise where, for instance, new evidence has come to light since discontinuance.[57]

[55] CPR r 38.7.

[56] *Hague Plant Ltd v Hague* [2014] EWCA Civ 1609; [2015] CP Rep 14 at [61].

[57] P Coulson (ed), *Civil Procedure 2024* (Sweet & Maxwell, 2024) Vol 1 at 38.7.1.

# PART 8

# CASE STATEMENTS

## SECTION 1: GENERAL

1. Case statements or pleadings have been a central feature of English civil procedure since its earliest stage of development.[1] The process has always been one where the claimant (historically the plaintiff) pleaded first with the defendant responding, with the parties thereafter taking it in turns to set out further pleadings in response. Prior to 1873 the claimant's initial pleading, at common law, was known as a '*declaration*', the defence was a '*plea*' and a response to that was a '*replication*'. From 1873 the claimant's initial pleading became a statement of claim and then from 1999 a particulars of claim. The plea became a defence and the replication became a reply.[2] Here pleadings are referred to, functionally, as case statements. The names used may have changed, but case statements' essential function has remained the same: to define the nature and ambit of the dispute between the parties, to determine the extent of the court's jurisdiction, and provide the basis on which it can adjudicate.
2. Historically different approaches have been taken to the pleading process. Prior to 1873, the common law adopted a highly technical approach to pleading via the forms of action (Form of Action Pleading).[3] This required pleadings to comply with the strict requirements of the form of action relevant to the substantive cause of action; what needed to be pleaded and how it was to be pleaded was governed by each individual form of action. It also led to the situation where legal conclusions were pleaded. Each of which could be borne out by different factual scenarios. This, in addition to formal technicality, led to surprise at trial where a defendant would be informed, for the first time, of the actual case advanced against them that was said to bear out the legal conclusion that was pleaded. Neither consequence was conducive of economy, efficiency, or the proper delivery of justice on the substantive merits of the dispute.[4]
3. Since 1873, English civil procedure has adopted what is sometimes referred to as Fact Pleading.[5] Parties are simply required to set out the facts that are alleged to give rise to a specific cause of action. It is unnecessary to plead law as the court

[1] W Blake Odgers, *The Principles of Pleading and Practice in Civil Actions in the High Court of Justice* (Stevens & Sons, 1912) at 74.

[2] W Blake Odgers (1912) at 74–76.

[3] W Maitland, *The Forms of Action at Common Law* (CUP, 1965).

[4] W Blake Odgers (1912) at 84.

[5] In the United States, fact pleading is commonly known as Code Pleading: C Clark, 'The Code Cause of Action' (1923) 33 Yale LJ 817 at 821; C Clark, 'The Complaint in Code Pleading' (1926) 35 Yale LJ 259; C Hepburn, *The Historical Development of Code Pleading in America and England* (Classic Reprint) (Forgotten Books reprint, 2019; Anderson, 1897) at 11–16. The US generally adopts what is known as Notice Pleading, where parties only need to be given notice of the cause of action; A Miller, 'From Conley to Twombly to Iqbal: A Double Play on the Federal Rules of Civil Procedure' (2010) 60 Duke LJ 1.

*A Model Civil Procedure Code for England and Wales*. John Sorabji, Oxford University Press. 
DOI: 10.1093/oso/9780192848680.003.0009

is understood to draw appropriate conclusions concerning the law from the facts and the evidence.[6] It is unnecessary to plead evidence as including it in pleadings is generally liable to render the civil process unnecessarily complex due to the conflation of the means to define the dispute with the means to establish the parties' rival contentions.

## RULE 1.—SCOPE AND PURPOSE

**(1) This Part concerns the manner in which parties define their disputes and provide each other and the court with information necessary to promote both settlement and, where necessary, accurate adjudication.**

**(2) This Part also gives effect to the autonomy, due notice, adversariality, and participatory principles. It also promotes the concentration, dispute management and finality principles.**

*Sources: ALI/UNIDROIT Principles, principle 5.1; ALI/UNIDROIT Reporters' Study, r 11, r 12; ELI-UNIDROIT Model Rules, r 52; CPR Pt 16.*

## COMMENTARY

1. The pleading process has, as Odgers noted, four key aims. It enables the parties to understand the exact nature of the dispute.[7] Hence parties must plead their cases with precision.[8] It also enables them, within an adversarial system, to understand what needs to be proved, and hence the evidence needed[9] and, perhaps more importantly, what is not needed and would if obtained and tested simply lead to disproportionate cost and delay.[10] It also enables both the parties and the court to manage the dispute effectively. It, for instance, provides the basis for determining what, if any, provisional or protective measures may be needed to secure the proper administration of justice, how to classify proceedings and what dispute management track to allocate them to, and whether a party could apply to strike out the proceedings or seek summary judgment.[11] It can also provide the basis on which the mode of trial can be determined. And, finally, it provides a clear record, for the parties and the public, of the issues in dispute.[12]
2. Underpinning each of these aims are various procedural principles. That what is pleaded in the parties' case statements is a matter for them is a fundamental aspect of party autonomy. They frame the terms of the dispute. That the case statements define the issues and thus define the scope of enquiry as to which evidence will be required is a prerequisite to settlement. Parties need to understand the nature of their dispute and the issues involved before settlement can properly be considered. Framing the

[6] *Hanmer v Flight* 24 W & R 346, 35 LT 1127; W Blake Odgers (1912) at 190–191.

[7] *Duke v Wisden* (1897) 77 LT 67 at 68; *Al Rawi v Security Service* [2011] UKSC 34; [2012] 1 AC 531 at [18].

[8] *Lombard North Central plc v Automobile World (UK) Ltd* [2010] EWCA Civ 20 at [75]. Implicit in this aim is a further function of the pleading process, that it protects parties '*from inadvertently making a false admission*': N Andrews, *Andrews on Civil Processes* (Intersentia, 2019) at 84.

[9] *Thorp v Holdsworth* (1876) 3 ChD 637 at 639.

[10] *Prudential Assurance Company Ltd v HM Revenue and Customs* [2016] EWCA Civ 376; [2017] 1 WLR 4031 at [20].

[11] N Andrews (2019) at 84 identifying track allocation and strike out as two specific functions of the pleading process.

[12] W Blake Odgers (1912) at 73–74 and 79.

dispute in this way also provides the basis on which evidentiary disclosure can take place, which can additionally then assist settlement by helping the parties assess the merits of their respective claims effectively.

3. Going beyond settlement, accuracy in adjudication also cannot properly come about without the exact scope of the dispute, and with it the court's jurisdiction, being defined. Moreover, by defining the nature of the dispute, case statements provide the courts with a baseline for understanding what steps need to be taken to actively manage the dispute, eg what needs to be done to determine the order in which issues may need to be resolved, whether the proceedings are better allocated to the settlement or adjudication track, what evidence needs to be obtained etc. Effective pleadings thus also promote the accuracy and dispute management principles.
4. By defining the issues and providing a basis to understand what evidence may be necessary,[13] case statements are also instrumental in securing due notice of each parties' case.[14] Case statements enable parties to know what needs to be tested and what needs to be supported by evidence and legal argument. They thus enable the parties to understand what they need to prove at trial and what they need to do to make out their case.[15] They also therefore underpin the adversarial process. Inherent in these points is the fact that case statements also promote effective participation in proceedings, not least through guarding against surprise at trial.[16]
5. Effective case statements equally enable parties to understand the matters on which they need to obtain legal advice. They thereby enable them to make informed choices on legal advice as to how they wish to conduct the dispute, or what steps may need to be taken to promote its settlement or secure a judgment on the substantive merits.
6. Underpinning all of these points is that case statements are one of the primary means by which a fair trial is secured,[17] that the proceedings are kept within properly defined limits,[18] and that litigation cost[19] and delay are minimised. It ought to be understood that flowing from these points, it is evident that properly defined case statements further the achievement of an economical, efficient, and proportionate process.
7. Finally, the four aims of the pleading process also promote the concentration and finality principles. By providing a clear definition of the nature of the dispute, they enable the parties and the court to understand if all relevant issues or parties are before the court. It may be, for instance, that case statements reveal the need to join a third party to the proceedings as a co-claimant, co-defendant, or by way of a claim for contribution by the defendant. They may also, due to publicity regarding the proceedings, bring forward further claims and or claimants that can properly be joined to the proceedings so that '*the parties and their successors may not fight the same battle over again*' in further proceedings.[20]

[13] Not least by setting the scope and limits of disclosure: *Yorkshire Provident Life Assurance Co v Gilbert* [1895] 2 QB 148 at 152, and ensuring that disclosure is not and cannot be used to ascertain if a party has a defence to a claim: *Zierenberg v Labouchere* [1893] 2 QB 183 at 188; *HRH Duchess of Sussex v Associated Newspapers Ltd* [2020] EWHC 1058 (Ch); [2020] EMLR 21 at [59].

[14] *Lombard North Central plc v Automobile World (UK) Ltd* [2010] EWCA Civ 20 at [75]–[76].

[15] *Conticorp SA v Central Bank of Ecuador* [2007] UKPC 40 at [38].

[16] *Spedding v Fitzpatrick* (1888) 38 ChD 410 at 413.

[17] *British Airways Pension Trustees Ltd v Sir Robert McAlpine & Sons Ltd* [1994] Con LR 1 at 5.

[18] *Milbank v Milbank* [1900] 1 Ch 376 at 385.

[19] *Astrovlanis Compania Naviera SA v Linard* [1972] 2 QB 611 at 620.

[20] W Blake Odgers (1912) at 74.

8. The pleading process also promotes finality in another way. By providing a basis on which other individuals and the public generally can understand the nature of the dispute, where it is resolved by adjudication, it can provide the basis on which they may order their own affairs. The pleading process thus also has a key role to play in the promotion of preventive justice through its link to developing the shadow of the law.

## RULE 2.—CASE STATEMENTS

**(1) Case statements include: a claimant's particulars of claim; a defendant's response to the particulars of claim; a claimant's reply to the response; additional case statements; and, an admission statement.**
**(2) Case statements must contain sufficient information to identify the nature of the dispute between the parties, define its scope, and enable parties to know the claim made against them or the defence to the claim that is made. They must, particularly, contain all the factual issues arising from the dispute so as to enable the court to finally determine them all, in so far as possible, within a single proceeding.**
**(3) A court may, on application by a party or its own initiative, dispense with case statements other than the particulars of claim where that would not adversely prejudice the proper administration of justice.**
**(4) Case statements must be verified by a statement of truth signed by the party or their lawyer. They must also be sealed by the court and stamped with the date on which they are issued.**
**(5) A case statement not verified by a statement of truth otherwise remains valid. The court may require an unverified case statement to be verified or may strike out an unverified case statement.**
**(6) Case statements are not evidence to be relied on at any trial in the proceedings. They may, however, otherwise be relied upon as evidence in proceedings if verified by a statement of truth.**

*Sources: ALI/UNIDROIT Principles, principle 5; ALI/UNIDROIT Reporters' Study, rr 11, 12 and 13; ELI-UNIDROIT Model Rules, s 2; CPR Pts 7, 8.5(7), 14, 15, 16, 32.6(2), and PD32 para 26.1; RSC Ord 18, r 21(2).*

## COMMENTARY

1. This rule identifies the four main types of case statement or, as they were historically known, pleadings. It also includes an admission statement, under the CPR an admission under its Pt 14, as a case statement. They all, as Clark put it, '*serve the primary purpose of acquainting the court and the parties with the facts in dispute*'.[21] They do so whether they identify the nature and scope of the dispute or, as in the case of admissions, the absence of a dispute.
2. Rule 2(2) sets out the general rule concerning the content of case statements. They should contain all the material facts concerning the dispute and, which therefore, underpin the claimant's cause of action and defendant's response to it. All such facts should be pleaded, consistently with the concentration principle, to enable the court to determine all disputes arising from them within a single proceeding. This

[21] C Clark, 'History, Systems and Functions of Pleading' (1925) 11 Virginia Law Review 517 at 518.

approach also ensures that both parties and the court know the case they are to meet and the likely evidence they will need to secure for trial. In that way it promotes a fair, open, and well-managed process; one consistent with a '*cards on the table*' approach to litigation.[22] As the Court of Appeal has said, '*Proper pleading of the material facts is essential for the orderly progress of the case and for its sound determination . . .*'[23]

3. To ensure that case statements are concise and to the point only those material facts necessary to make out a cause of action, and which will need to be established at trial, should be pleaded.[24] As case statements define the scope of the proceedings and the court's jurisdiction, a party cannot adduce evidence to prove a material fact not pleaded[25] except where the court grants permission to amend the pleading to add that material fact to a case statement. Parties must therefore take care to ensure that their case statements are not too concise that necessary elements are missed.
4. The court may dispense with case statements, other than a particular of claim as that initiates proceedings.[26] It may do so where they are unnecessary and where doing so would not undermine the administration of justice.[27] This latter limitation is intended to ensure that dispensing with case statements does not undermine the court's ability to determine cases accurately or would not prejudice other procedural principles by, for instance, frustrating a defendant's right to due notice or the public's right to know what is taking place in proceedings.
5. Dispensing with case statements is not unknown. It may arise where liability has been admitted and questions of quantum are set out by the parties in an exchange of correspondence. It may also occur where the court has directed or permitted parties to set out their respective contentions in a short statement of points to be determined.[28]
6. Under the digital procedure formal case statements could equally be replaced by parties completing digital court forms or by following a digital process that enabled them to identify from a database of causes of action their dispute through inputting material facts or selecting text from digital precedents; the use of generative AI may thereafter transform the information provided into a concise statement of the issues in dispute. Each of these various situations may avoid the need for formal case statements, but they would each amount to 'pleadings' in a broader sense of the term. They do so because they would identify the nature and scope of the dispute and, thereby, set the scope of the court's jurisdiction. They would thus be functionally equivalent to case statements, howsoever they were set out.
7. Case statements must be verified by a statement of truth. As under the CPR this requirement serves several aims. It is intended to ensure that parties only bring and defend claims where they have a reasonable belief in the contentions.[29] It thus serves

[22] *Astrovlanis Compania Naviera SA v Linard* [1972] 2 QB 611 at 620.

[23] *Boake Allen Ltd v Revenue and Customs Rev 1* [2006] EWCA Civ 25; [2006] STC 606 at [131].

[24] *Philipps v Philipps* (1878) 4 QBD 127, necessity turns on the circumstances; *In re Wrightson* [1908] 1 Ch 789 at 799, '*The plaintiff is not entitled to relief except in regard to that which is alleged in the pleadings and proved at trial.*'

[25] *West Rand Gold Mining Co Ltd v Rex* [1905] 2 KB 391 at 399–401.

[26] The court may, however, dispense with the need for the particulars of claim to contain all the details required by r 3 as long as the defendant is given sufficient notice of the nature of what is being claimed and why.

[27] RSC (1893) Ord 18; W Blake Odgers (1912) at 61.

[28] *Hill v Scott* [1895] 2 QB 371.

[29] *Clarke v Marlborough Fine Art (London) Ltd* [2002] 1 WLR 1731 at [20] and following.

to deter the bringing of unmeritorious claims or defences, which would unjustifiably consume the parties' and the court's time and resources. It also promotes settlement. It does so by enabling parties to have confidence in the fact that they are facing genuine claims and defences.[30]

8. Sealing case statements with the court seal, and dating them on the date of sealing, provides a definitive date of issue for the purpose of calculating procedural time limits, not least those relating to service.[31]
9. Finally, case statements are not, generally, evidence at trial. They should not therefore ordinarily contain evidence, nor should they be viewed as evidence. That is not to say that a party may not, in their evidence at trial, adopt, in whole or in part, what is said in their case statements as evidence.[32] Parties may, equally, adopt their case statements as written evidence in proceedings that are determined solely on the papers or in proceedings on agreed facts. Case statements may be relied upon as evidence in application hearings where evidence is given in writing.

## SECTION 2: TYPES OF CASE STATEMENT

### RULE 3.—PARTICULARS OF CLAIM

**(1) A claimant's particulars of claim must set out their claim. It must, at a minimum, identify**
- **(a) the court in which proceedings are to be pursued;**
- **(b) the parties. This includes all persons with whom the claimant is jointly entitled to a remedy claimed in the proceedings;**
- **(c) the cause of action, set out in a concise statement of material facts, pursued by the claimant;**
- **(d) the remedy sought by the claimant, including interest on any monetary amount claimed and costs;**
- **(e) a statement of pre-issue steps taken to resolve the dispute, including a copy of any proposed initial dispute management timetable and directions;**
- **(f) the steps, and time limits for taking them, a defendant may make in response to the claim and the consequences of taking or not taking those steps.**

**(2) Particulars of claim must contain all matters relating to the cause of action that forms the basis of the claimant's claim for relief. Any such matters, which could and should have been set out within the proceedings, may not be the subject of any subsequent proceedings.**

*Sources: ALI/UNIDROIT Principles, principle 5.1; ALI/UNIDROIT Reporters' Study, rr 11.1, 12; ELI-UNIDROIT Model Rules, r 52; CPR r 7.4, Pt 16, Pt 19.*

### COMMENTARY

1. Under the CPR proceedings were commenced via a claim form within which a claimant could set out their claim. They could, however, and in the vast majority

[30] *Zurich Insurance Co Plc v Hayward* [2011] EWCA Civ 641; [2011] CP Rep 39 at [33].
[31] Senior Courts Act 1981, s 132.
[32] *Kimathi v The Foreign and Commonwealth Office* [2018] EWHC 2066 (QB) at [35].

of cases did so, set out their claim in a separate document: a particulars of claim. Particulars of claim could either be attached to the claim form or filed with the court and served separately and at a later date. This Part does not replicate this approach. It does not separate out the claim form, the means for initiating proceedings, from the particulars of claim. In this it adopts the better practice approach endorsed by the ELI-UNIDROIT Model Rules, which provide for a single document to both commence proceedings and set out the claimant's claim. Due notice of both the fact and the nature of proceedings is thus given at the same time. This approach is adopted for two reasons.

2. First, the bifurcation of the means of commencing proceeding and articulating the claim is unnecessary. This is particularly the case given the integration of pre-action dispute resolution into the dispute resolution process. Given that, both parties ought to be fully aware of their claim in good time before any relevant limitation period may apply. There is thus no good reason why a claimant would need to issue a claim form, as a protective measure, to preserve their claim prior to finalising their particulars of claim as can be the case under the CPR. That this option does not exist under this Part is also a means to promote the use, as standard, of pre-action dispute resolution so as to ensure that claimants are not in the position where their claim needs to be commenced at short notice prior to expiry of a relevant limitation period. Where proceedings do, in what should be rare circumstances, need to be issued at short notice, that can be done by uploading relevant information via the digital procedure. In so far as, the particulars need to be further elaborated later that may be done via amendment.

3. Secondly, it is unnecessary as Part 7 and this Part, unlike the CPR, do not provide for two different ways in which proceedings can be commenced. Rule 3 achieves what has been a long-term aim of civil procedure reform: the elimination of multiple ways to commence proceedings. In this it seeks to finally achieve procedural simplicity in this aspect of the civil process.[33] Taking this step now is also consistent with the development of digital procedures. A significant amount of information should have been uploaded to the court's digital dispute management file by both claimants and defendants during the pre-action dispute resolution process. That information will be susceptible to extraction by claimants to populate a digital particulars of claim. A separate claim form, within such a process, would serve no function. Commencement will occur once the claimant has completed the process of setting out the information required by this rule via the digital procedure, has paid the relevant issue fee and taken the necessary step required by the system to digitally file the particulars of claim. Again, there is no role for a separate claim form.

4. Rule 3 prescribes the information that a claimant must set out in their particulars of claim. This information is necessary to enable the defendant to know the claim made against them and to enable the court to deal with the proceedings effectively. Rule 3(1)(a) and (b) require the claimant to identify the court in which proceedings are to be brought.[34] They also require the claimant to identify the parties, including itself, any co-claimants and the defendants. Where co-claimants are concerned it is necessary to identify them either as such, or if they refuse consent to be joined as

[33] The First Report of the Royal Commission to inquire into the Operation and Constitution of the High Court of Chancery, Courts of Common Law, Central Criminal Court, High Court of Admiralty, and other Courts in England, and into the Operation and Effect of the Present Separation and Division of Jurisdiction between the Courts (No 4130; 1868–1869) at 11.

[34] This is done in order to differentiate civil proceedings from those commenced in, for instance, the Family Court.

co-claimants then they must be identified as defendants.[35] This is consistent with the concentration and finality principles.

5. Rule 3(1)(e) requires the claimant to identify what pre-action steps have been taken and to set out indicative dispute management directions. This is intended to better enable the court to determine from the outset how best to manage the dispute. Requiring such matters to be set out in the particulars of claim is also intended to promote compliance with the requirement that parties consider dispute management during the pre-action process.[36] Rule 3(1)(f) requires the provision of information to defendants of any relevant procedural time limit; the most pressing of which will be the time limit to file and serve their defence or, if appropriate, an admission. By requiring a claimant to set out the consequences of not taking any necessary steps this rule also ensures that defendants are fully aware of, amongst other things, that default judgment may be entered against them.[37] It thus puts them on notice of the need to take steps to respond where they wish to do so or, of the fact that if they wish to concede the claim they need do nothing. This is particularly intended to assist lawyerless and/or vulnerable parties understand the process and steps that they need to take. These requirements, and those in rules 3(1)(a) and (b) could properly be said to be administrative or formal in nature.
6. In addition to the administratively focused rules, rules 3(1)(c) and (d) set out substantive requirements. They prescribe the minimum level of information a claimant must give to a defendant and the court for them to have effective notice of the nature of the claim that lies at the heart of the dispute. Thus, they require the claimant to set out their cause of action by reference to the material facts and the claim for relief. Such matters must be to the point and concise.[38] Discursive, vague or unclear pleading is to be avoided; as has long been accepted to be the case: '*[b]revity ... is the soul of good pleading.*'[39] The focus should thus be on ensuring that the issues in dispute are clearly identified so that a defendant is able to fully and easily understand the claim they are being required to meet. It is also necessary as a means to enable the court to clearly understand the scope of its jurisdiction over the parties.
7. One important limitation, which is maintained in this rule and in respect of which the approach taken in the ELI-UNIDROIT Model Rules is not adopted,[40] is not to include within the particulars of claim the claimants' response to what they might understand to be the defence. The ELI-UNIDROIT Model Rules suggests that such a response may reasonably be set out where the claimant has a reasonable belief as to what the defendant's defence is likely to be. English and Welsh civil procedure has experience of this type of approach. It was a common feature of pre-1873 equity proceedings and was one of the reasons why equity pleadings in the Court of Chancery were unduly complex, and led to unnecessary cost and delay. It particularly led to the pleading of imaginary defences.[41] Even assuming that a claimant could reasonably anticipate what a defence may be from prior discussion with the defendant during the pre-action phase that would not justify anticipatory pleading. First, it may be

[35] Part 8, r 2(4); Part 9, r 2(1)(d).

[36] ELI-UNIDROIT Model Rules, r 53(2(e).

[37] Derived from ELI-UNIDROIT Model Rules, r 69.

[38] *Hague Plant v Hague* [2014] EWCA Civ 1609 at [76]; H Woolf, *Access to Justice: Interim Report to the Lord Chancellor on the Civil Justice System in England and Wales* (HMSO) (1995) at 162–163.

[39] C. Hepburn (1897) at 209.

[40] ELI-UNIDROIT Model Rules, r 53(6).

[41] *Hall v Eve* (1876–7) 4 ChD 341 at 345.

unnecessary as a defendant may ultimately not plead the anticipated defence. Secondly, if the defence is pleaded, it may not be set out in exactly the way in which the claimant anticipated. In the first case, the anticipatory pleading is redundant. In the second case, it will again be redundant, at least in part. In both cases, it will have done nothing but add unnecessary complexity, time and expense to the proceedings. Moreover, such an approach confuses the purposes of particulars of claim, which is to set out the claimant's claim for relief in a concise manner so as to put the defendant on notice of the nature of the claim. It also conflates the particulars of claim with the reply to the defence. There is, on analysis, no good reason for adopting the ELI-UNIDROIT approach to anticipatory pleading, whereas there are good reasons not to do so. English and Welsh civil procedure's prohibition on anticipated defences is thus maintained.

8. Finally, the rule gives effect to the public policy that underpins the rule in *Henderson v Henderson* (1843);[42] that it is an abuse of process to either raise again in a single set of proceedings an issue that has been finally determined in them or to bring in later proceedings that which ought to have properly been brought before the court in earlier proceedings. This is primarily aimed at giving effect to the concentration principle; that all related claims and defences ought to be brought in a single proceeding.[43] It also gives effect to the finality principle by ensuring that parties are not troubled by matters arising out of or related to the same dispute more than once. It enables parties therefore to be confident that their rights have been finally determined, and thus there is post-judgment a certain and effective basis for them to order their affairs. It is also a means to promote economy and efficiency, and implicitly also proportionality, through ensuring that all issues are resolved through one set of proceedings.[44] This becomes a particularly important factor in the light of the emphasis given in this Code to securing systemic proportionality.

## RULE 4.—RESPONSE TO PARTICULARS OF CLAIM, INCLUDING CHALLENGE TO JURISDICTION

**(1) A defendant does not have to respond to a particulars of claim. Where they do not do so the claimant may apply for judgment in default of a defence (default judgment).**

**(2) A defendant may respond to a particulars of claim by**

**(a) admitting the claim or part of it;**

**(b) raising a procedural defence challenging either the court's jurisdiction to try the claim or the court's ability to exercise jurisdiction to try the claim on its merits;**

**(c) setting out a substantive defence to the claim.**

**(3) Where a defendant wishes to challenge the court's jurisdiction they must set out the basis of that procedural defence to the claim in their defence. Failure to do so acts as a waiver of the right to challenge the jurisdiction.**

[42] *Henderson v Henderson* (1843) 3 Hare 100; *Orji v Nagra* [2023] EWCA Civ 1289 at [46]–[47].

[43] In *Barrow v Bankside Members Agency Limited* [1996] 1 All ER 981.

[44] *Vervaeke (formerly Messina) v Smith* [1983] 1 AC 145 at 157; *Divine-Bortey v Brent LBC* [1998] ICR 886 at 898; *Atlantic Airways Ltd v Zodiac Seats UK Ltd (formerly known as Contour Aerospace Ltd)* [2013] UKSC 46; [2014] AC 160 at [17]–[26].

**(4) Where a defendant challenges the court's jurisdiction they are not deemed to have submitted to it. Nor do they do so by appealing from a decision to dismiss such a challenge.**

**(5) Where a defendant challenges the court's jurisdiction, the court must determine that matter before any further step is taken in the proceedings.**

**(6) Where a defendant challenges the court's jurisdiction they may also set out their substantive defence to the claim in their defence. If they do so, they are not to be taken to have waived the right to assert the procedural defence. Where the court concludes that it has jurisdiction, if they have not already done so the defendant may then respond to the particulars of claim with a substantive defence.**

**(7) A substantive defence to the claim must set out the defendant's response to the allegations contained in the particulars of claim. It must specify, in respect of each allegation, whether it is admitted, denied or can be neither admitted nor denied. The response must set out a concise statement of all relevant material facts on which reliance is made to support the defence. It must specifically do so where an allegation is denied and the defendant intends to set out an alternative account to that advanced in the particulars of claim.**

**(8) Where an allegation is denied or neither admitted nor denied, concise reasons must be given in the defence why that it is case.**

**(9) Where a substantive defence fails to respond either specifically or generally to an allegation, it is deemed to have been admitted.**

**(10) Where a defendant does not pursue a matter that they could and should have set out in either their procedural or substantive defence within the proceedings, they may not do so in any subsequent proceedings.**

*Sources: ALI/UNIDROIT Principles, principles 5.1, 10.5; ALI/UNIDROIT Reporters' Study, r 13; ELI-UNIDROIT Model Rules, r 54; CPR r 3.4, PD3A, Pts 11, 14, and 15.*

## COMMENTARY

1. This rule identifies the range of responses to a particulars of claim that a defendant may make. It also makes clear that responding to a claim is optional. A defendant may perfectly properly choose to do nothing when served with particulars of claim; that is an aspect of their procedural autonomy. They should, however, understand that no response may result in the claimant seeking a default judgment. Where the defendant does not wish to contest the claim a non-response may be the most proportionate response as it involves no expense on their part and enables the claimant to quickly and economically move to obtaining an enforceable judgment.
2. If a defendant chooses to respond to particulars of claim they have several options. They may formally admit the claim or part of it. In the latter case, they further the purposive principle by narrowing the issues and thus saving time and expense. Where partial admissions are made they can properly be made in any substantive defence to the claim. Before making a substantive defence, a defendant may, however, wish to challenge the court's jurisdiction. There may do so in in either of two ways that are '*logically and juridically separate and distinct*.'[45]

[45] *IMS SA v Capital Oil & Gas Industries Ltd* [2016] EWHC 1956 (Comm); [2016] 4 WLR 163 at [28]; *Hoddinott v Persimmon Homes (Wessex) Ltd* [2007] EWCA Civ 1203; [2008] 1 WLR 806 at [28].

3. First, a procedural challenge may be made to the court's ability to exercise jurisdiction over the parties.[46] A defendant may, for instance, want to argue that the English and Welsh courts are not the best forum to resolve the dispute, that there is a valid jurisdiction agreement in place between the parties that provides for another country's courts to have jurisdiction,[47] or that there is a valid multi-tier dispute resolution clause in place that precludes, at that time, resort to the courts. Secondly, a procedural challenge may be made to the court's ability to try a claim on its merits. Such a challenge may, for instance, be made on the grounds that proceedings were not properly served on the defendant, ie that the court's jurisdiction over the defendant had not properly been established consistently with the fundamental requirement of due notice.[48] Such challenges also encompass applications by a defendant to strike out or seek summary judgment on the claimant's claim. Taking such steps at the outset of proceedings, particularly where they are sought on the basis that the particulars of claim do not disclose reasonable grounds for bringing proceedings or that, taking it at its highest, the claim does not disclose that it has a real prospect of success, is one way in which proceedings can be managed with a view to minimising systemic proportionality.[49]
4. Where a defendant wishes to raise a procedural defence they may do so in two ways mindful of their obligation to assist the court in managing proceedings consistently with the purposive principle. They may either submit a procedural defence without providing any details of their substantive defence or they may combine the two in a single composite defence. They should choose the option that in the circumstances of the case is the most economical, efficient, and proportionate. Where they choose to adopt the composite approach, the rule again makes clear that by setting out their substantive defence they are not to be taken to have submitted to the jurisdiction.[50] An appeal from a decision rejecting a challenge to jurisdiction also, and logically, does not amount to a submission to the jurisdiction.
5. Where the defendant raises a procedural defence that matter must be determined before further steps are taken in the proceedings. If, for instance, they have only filed a procedural defence, they are not required, nor may they go on, to file a separate substantive defence until the procedural issue is determined.[51] Where they have filed a composite defence no steps, by either party, may be taken on substantive matters until the procedural issue is determined.
6. Where a defendant submits a substantive defence, which may include a counterclaim and a claim for set-off,[52] they must set out, in concise terms, the nature of their response to the claimant's factual allegations. They must do so through pleading all relevant material facts.[53] They may either admit or deny the claimant's allegations. They may also, where they are not in a position to either admit or deny the

[46] Such a challenge may be made notwithstanding the parties having engaged in pre-action dispute resolution under Part 5.

[47] L Collins and J Harris, *Dicey, Morris & Collins on the Conflict of Laws* (Sweet & Maxwell, 2022).

[48] *Hoddinott v Persimmon Homes (Wessex) Ltd* [2007] EWCA Civ 1203; [2008] 1 WLR 806; *Caine v Advertiser and Times Ltd* [2019] EWHC 39 (QB).

[49] *Okpabi v Royal Dutch Shell Plc* [2021] UKSC 3; [2021] WLR 1294 at [20].

[50] *Deutsche Bank AG London Branch v Petromena ASA* [2015] EWCA Civ 226; [2015] 1 WLR 4225.

[51] *Multimedia International Ltd v ARA Media Services* [2006] EWHC 3612 (Ch); [2007] 1 All ER (Comm) 1160.

[52] A Zuckerman, *Zuckerman on Civil Procedure—Principles of Practice* (Sweet & Maxwell, 2021) at 210–212.

[53] W Blake Odgers (1912) at 214.

allegations, put the claimant to proof. Where they deny an allegation, to give the claimant effective notice of the defendant's case on the issue they must set out their positive case for the denial in concise terms. By adopting this approach, the parties and court are able to gain an effective understanding of the nature of the dispute. Rule 4(9) is the equivalent to rule 3(2), ie it gives effect to the public policy that underpins the rule in *Henderson v Henderson* (1843).[54]

7. Under the CPR, a defendant also has the option of filing an acknowledgement of service prior to filing a defence.[55] This enables them to obtain a short, extension to the period to file their defence. It also provides certainty that the defendant has received the defence. Given the general application under the CPR, and this Code, of deemed service provisions the utility of an acknowledgement of service in terms of certainty is minimal, at best. Where a defendant needs additional time to serve their defence, rules 13(5) and (6) provide the functional equivalent to the CPR's acknowledgement of service.

## RULE 5.—REPLY TO A DEFENCE

**(1) A claimant may respond to a defence through a reply to the defence. They may do so to respond to any new facts set out in the defence.**
**(2) Where a claimant either does not provide a reply to a defence or does not deal with a matter contained in a defence in their reply to it, the defendant is put to proof.**
**(3) A claimant may not raise a new claim in a reply. New claims may only be brought by an amendment to the particulars of claim.**

*Sources: ALI/UNIDROIT Principles, principle 5.2; ALI/UNIDROIT Reporters' Study, r 13.3; ELI-UNIDROIT Model Rules, r 54(6); CPR Pt 14, PD 14 para 7.2.*

## COMMENTARY

1. A reply to a defence is an optional case statement. Defendants join issue, or not, with the claimant in the defence. Ordinarily, therefore, there is no basis on which a claimant need take any further step in the pleading process. However, it may be beneficial to do so, especially if the defendant raises new issues or facts in their defence. A defendant may, for instance, set up a positive defence, such as one of self-defence to a claim alleging trespass to the person. Where a defendant pleads a limitation defence, for instance, it may also be necessary for the claimant to set out in its reply material facts that it alleges show such a defence is not available.[56] Alternatively, the claimant may wish to confess and avoid the points raised by the defendant.[57] They may also want to admit the matters raised in the defence, thereby helping to narrow the issues in dispute. In setting out such various matters in the reply the aim is to ensure that the parties and the court clearly identify the issues in dispute, have proper notice of them and, in the court's case, be in a position to take them into account when considering how best to manage the proceedings.

[54] *Henderson v Henderson* (1843) 3 Hare 100.
[55] CPR Pt 10.
[56] *Kronstein v Korda* [1937] WN 67.
[57] *Hall v Eve* (1876) 4 ChD 341 at 345.

2. Because, a reply is optional, a default rule is needed for circumstances where a claimant does not provide one. Rule 5(2) provides that by placing on the defendant the onus of proving the matters raised in the defence. The absence of a reply does not therefore amount to an admission by the claimant of any matters set out in the defence.
3. Rule 5(3) codifies an important and longstanding qualification on the use of a reply.[58] A reply to a defence cannot be used as a means by which a claimant may raise a new claim, ie one not raised in the particulars of claim, against the defendant.[59] Its sole purpose is to join issue with matters raised by the defendant in its defence to the claimant's original claim. Any new claims must be brought by way of an amendment to the particulars of claim. In that way, the court can consider whether the new claim can properly be added by way of amendment.[60]

## RULE 6.—ADDITIONAL CASE STATEMENTS

**Exceptionally where doing so would further the purposive principle, a court may permit additional case statements subsequent to a reply to a defence.**

*Sources: CPR r 15.9; RSC Ord 18 r 4.*

## COMMENTARY

1. Generally, there ought to be no need for any further case statements beyond a reply to a defence. The CPR and before it the RSC acknowledged that exceptionally there may be circumstances where their provision may be justified. Prior to the introduction of the RSC such further case statements were referred to as follows: a response to a reply to a defence was a 'rejoinder'. A response to a rejoinder was a 'surrejoinder'. A reply to a surrejoinder was a 'rebutter'. A response to a rebutter was a 'surrebutter.'[61] While neither the RSC nor the CPR formally adopted these names to describe such additional case statements, they were maintained in practice in so far as it was necessary for such case statements to be used.
2. Under the RSC all but a rejoinder were noted to be all but extinct. They were, however, noted to be used in proceedings for defamation where it became necessary to respond by pleading express malice as a response to a plea of qualified privilege raised for the first time in a claimant's reply and defence.[62]
3. Rule 6 maintains the historic approach that additional case statements are exceptional and subject to the court's discretion. The discretion, as is generally the case, must be considered by reference to the purposive principle. Where, therefore, additional case statements would better enable the court to resolve a dispute justly without giving rise to disproportionate expense or delay they ought to be permitted. It may be, for instance, that an additional case statement would enable a counterclaim to

[58] *Williamson v L & N W Railway* (1879) 12 ChD 787; *D&G Cars Ltd v Essex Police Authority* [2013] EWCA Civ 514 at [70].

[59] Historically known as a 'departure'; C Hepburn (1897) at 233.

[60] It may, for instance, refuse to grant permission where the claim is time-barred or where it does not have sufficient connection with the original claim.

[61] R Scott, *Supreme Court Practice 1999* (Sweet & Maxwell, 1999) Vol 1 at 18/4/1.

[62] R Scott (1999) Vol 1 at 18/4/1.

be brought, which if not joined to the present proceedings would form the basis of additional and separate proceedings. If such a claim was brought independently of the present proceedings, it would, when issued, in all likelihood be joined with the present proceedings at additional and unnecessary cost and delay.

## RULE 7.—FURTHER INFORMATION

**(1) Subject to any rule of law to the contrary, the court may, on application or its own initiative, require a party to clarify or expand on matters in dispute that are set out in a case statement.**

**(2) Sanctions may be imposed where a party does not comply with an order for further information. Non-compliance arises where a response to such an order is plainly incomplete or could not reasonably be thought to be complete and sufficient.**

*Sources: CPR Pt 18.*

## COMMENTARY

1. Rule 7 restates the court's power to order a party to clarify or expand on any matter detailed within a case statement. It enables parties, upon application, to seek further information from their opponent to assist their understanding of the claim or defence where matters set out in it are unclear, imprecise or otherwise lacking in sufficient detail to enable an effective response to be made to them. It is not a means by which a party can seek the court's assistance to investigate matters that are not raised within a case statement.[63] The further information sought must therefore relate to matters that are in dispute and said to be so within an extant case statement.[64]
2. The power to direct the provision of further information is generally unfettered, albeit it must be applied consistently with the purposive principle. There is, however, one significant express limitation upon it. Further information cannot be ordered contrary to any rule of law to the contrary. The provision of further information contrary to, for instance, the application of legal professional privilege cannot be ordered.[65]
3. Generally, this power is exercisable on application by a party. The court may, however, exercise it of its own initiative. It may, for instance, do so where a lawyerless party's case statements lack clarity or sufficient specificity and further information is necessary to enable other parties to proceedings and the court to understand that party's claim or defence.
4. Rule 7(2) restates the test for determining non-compliance with a request for further information.[66]

[63] *Hennessy v Wright (No 2)* (1888) 24 QBD 445; *Lovell v Lovell* [1970] 1 WLR 1451.

[64] *Trader Publishing Ltd v Autotrader.com Inc* [2010] EWHC 142 (Ch) at [16].

[65] CPR r 18.1(2).

[66] *Owners of the Gravity Highway v Owners of the Maritime Maisie* [2020] EWHC 1697 (Comm); [2021] 2 All ER (Comm) 340; *QPS Consultants Ltd v Kruger Tissue (Manufacturing) Ltd* [1999] BLR 366.

# SECTION 3: SPECIFIC FORMS OF CASE STATEMENT

## RULE 8.—COUNTERCLAIMS AND ADDITIONAL CLAIMS

**(1) A defendant may raise in their defence a claim against the claimant. Such a claim is a counterclaim.**

**(2) A defendant, including a third party defendant, may also commence an additional claim. An additional claim is either a claim against another party or a third party, including a claim for a contribution or indemnity in respect of the claimant's claim.**

**(3) A counterclaim may only be made with the court's permission, except where it is filed by the defendant with their defence. An additional claim may only be made with the court's permission.**

**(4) Permission to bring a counterclaim or additional claim should be sought at the earliest possible opportunity. Permission may be granted where**

**(a) there is a reasonable degree of connection between the original claim and the counterclaim or additional claim;**

**(b) the counterclaim or additional claim concerns or is reasonably connected with the factual and/or legal issues raised in the original claim.**

**(5) Any counterclaim or additional claim must, so far as necessary, comply with the requirements applicable to particulars of claim.**

*Sources: ALI/UNIDROIT Principles, principle 5.1; ALI/UNIDROIT Reporters' Study, r 13.1; ELI-UNIDROIT Model Rules, r 54; CPR Pt 20; RSC Ord 15, Ord 16.*

### COMMENTARY

1. Rule 8 states the defendant's ability to issue a claim against the claimant where the defendant's claim arises from the same facts as the claimant's claim: a counterclaim.[67] Thus where a claimant's claim is for breach of contract, a defendant, in addition to defending that claim, can bring their own claim against the claimant concerning the same facts that give rise to the claimant's claim. Such a counterclaim may equally be for breach of contract. It may, however, concern a separate cause of action, eg the counterclaim may be in tort.[68] As a counterclaim is independent of the original claim it is not affected by procedural decisions that affected the viability of the original claim. If, for instance, the original claim is struck out for abuse of process or is subject to summary judgment, that does not affect the viability of the counterclaim.[69]

2. The rule also provides for the ability to join other claims to the proceedings initiated by the claimant: additional claims.[70] Additional claims can take a variety of forms. These include: claims brought by a defendant against a co-defendant or third party seeking a contribution or indemnity in respect of any liability the defendant may

[67] Judicature Act 1873, s 24; Senior Courts Act 1981, s 49(2)(a); *Padwick v Scott* (1876) 2 ChD 736; RSC Ord 15.

[68] *Stooke v Taylor* 5 QBD 576; *Re Richardson, Richardson v Nicholson* [1933] WN 90; *Beddall v Maitland* (1881) 17 ChD 181.

[69] *Amon v Bobbett* 22 QBD 548.

[70] RSC Ord 16.

be found to have against the claimant;[71] claims brought by a defendant against a third party; and, claims brought by third parties, against whom additional claims are brought, against further third parties. Additional claims may also be independent of the original claim and, like a counterclaim, may not therefore be adversely affected by procedural decisions concerning the original claim.

3. The aim of this rule, as was the case under the CPR and the RSC before it, is to enable proceedings to be '*managed in the most convenient and effective manner*'.[72] It does this by promoting the concentration and finality principles through enabling all matters relevant or connected to the immediate dispute between claimant and defendant to be resolved in a single set of proceedings. Where, for instance, a building contractor is sued by their client, it is preferable for any separate claim that the contractor may have against their sub-contractors to be resolved together with the original claim rather than in separate proceedings. Such concentration of claims promote procedural economy, efficiency and proportionality as it means that the same factual and legal issues do not have to be litigated more than once in respect of different parties and claims. It also promotes the proper administration of justice by ensuring that inconsistent judgments concerning the same factual and legal issues are not reached by different courts in different proceedings arising from a common dispute. Inconsistent judgments would not only promote appeals unnecessarily, which would itself undermine the efficient and proportionate use of the court's resources and through that the proper administration of justice, but would also undermine confidence in the administration of justice. Through that it would undermine the legitimacy of the courts.
4. The test for permission ensures that defendants or third parties do not seek to bring within the original proceedings disputes that are unconnected with the original claim. Such claims should properly be brought by separate proceedings. Were defendants or third parties able to bring unconnected claims within the original proceedings, it would tend to undermine effective dispute management as it would complicate and prolong both it and, in all likelihood, the trial process.[73]
5. Effective dispute management calls for counterclaims and additional claims to be brought at an early a stage of a dispute as possible. Hence, this rule encourages defendants to commence counterclaims at the same time as they file their defence.[74] It further encourages defendants to bring additional claims at an early a stage as possible for the same reason.

## RULE 9.—CASE STATEMENTS IN JUDICIAL REVIEW PROCEEDINGS

**(1) In addition to the general requirements concerning the content of particulars of claim, particulars of claim in judicial review proceedings must include**

**(a) the name and contact details of any interested party;**

**(b) that permission to bring such proceedings is sought;**

**(c) clear and concise details of the basis or bases, and all relevant material facts, whether supportive or adverse to them, on which judicial review sought;**

71 Civil Liability (Contribution) Act 1978; Law of Property Act 1925, s 76(1)(d).

72 CPR r 20.1; The First Judicature Report at 11–12. The introduction of the ability to bring counterclaims was, for instance, viewed as a means to prevent '*unnecessary litigation, expense and delay*'.

73 *Chatsworth Investments v Amoco (UK) Ltd* [1969] Ch 665.

74 A Zuckerman (2021) at 208–209.

**(d) the remedy sought and any alternative remedy or mechanism available to the claimant;**

**(e) details of any statutory provision relevant to the court's jurisdiction to grant the remedy sought; and**

**(f) any further information required by law.**

**(2) A defendant and any interested party taking an active part in the proceedings must also provide the court with all material facts relevant to the proceedings and where known the reasoning behind them. They must do so whether they are supportive or adverse to their case.**

**(3) Non-compliance with the requirement to set out all relevant material facts may result in permission to apply for judicial review being refused. It may also justify a refusal by the court to grant the remedy sought in the proceedings and/or an award of costs against a non-compliant party.**

*Sources: CPR r 54.6, PD54A para 4.2; Senior Courts Act 1981, s 29, s 31.*

## COMMENTARY

1. This rule supplements Part 7, rule 4. It restates the approach taken in CPR r 54.6, which makes provision for additional information to be included by claimants bringing judicial review proceedings in their claim forms. It also requires, consistently with CPR PD54A para 4.2(1), information concerning the basis or bases (the grounds) on which judicial review is sought. Information concerning interested parties is required to enable them to be given notice of the proceedings. Clear and succinct details concerning the judicial review issues are required to enable the defendant and any interested parties to understand the nature of the claim, consistently with the requirements of due notice.[75] Their provision also enables the court to assess whether it can determine the question of permission to bring the proceedings without a hearing.

2. The requirement to provide all material facts relevant to the basis on which the claim is brought is the claimant's 'duty of candour'. This is a duty to make full and frank disclosure of all relevant facts known or which would have been known to the claimant had they made reasonable enquiries.[76] Thus it imposes a duty on judicial review claimants to make reasonable enquiries before commencing proceedings to ascertain matters supportive or not of their claim.

3. Similarly, a claimant should set out any statutory provision that may be relevant to the question of whether the court has jurisdiction to grant the remedy sought. If the claimant has an alternative route to an effective remedy that too is reason to refuse permission to apply for judicial review, which is a remedy of last resort. As such a claimant should identify any relevant alternative remedies and, if there are any, they will need to explain why they have not been or could not be pursued.[77]

4. Compliance with the duty to make full and frank disclosure and to provide the further details identified above, is important for two reasons. It enables the court to

[75] *R (Dolan) v Secretary of State for Health & Social Care* [2020] EWCA Civ 1605; [2021] 1 All ER 780 at [119]–[120].

[76] *R v Lloyd's of London, ex p Briggs* [1993] 1 Lloyd's Rep 176; *R (Khan) v Secretary of State for the Home* Department [2016] EWCA Civ 416.

[77] CPR PD 54A para 4.1(2).

fully consider the question whether to grant permission to apply for judicial review. It provides it with as complete a view, both positive and negative, of the proposed claim.[78] It also enables the defendant and any interested parties to fully understand the proposed claim. They can therefore then take an informed view of the proposed claim and, particularly in the case of interested parties, of whether and how to respond to it.

5. To facilitate the effective adjudication of the claim and procedural equality, both defendants and any interested party actively engaged in the proceedings also come under a 'duty of candour'.[79] They too must disclose to the claimant and court any relevant material that is either supportive or adverse to their position in the proceedings. Again, this is to enable the court to have '*full and accurate explanations of all the facts relevant to the issue the court must decide*'.[80] It also requires, where known, the provision of the reasoning that gave rise to those facts.[81] The defendant and any interested party must therefore be as candid in their approach as the claimant.[82] This approach, developed through case law, can also be seen as a specific application of the co-operation principle to public law claims.[83]
6. Given the importance of the duty of candour as a means, primarily, to enable the court to fully consider whether to grant permission and adjudicate on the claim, and due to it being a continuing obligation throughout proceedings, non-compliance with it by a claimant may result in the court refusing to grant the remedy sought.[84] It may equally result in adverse costs being awarded. Non-compliance by a defendant or interested party may equally result in adverse costs being awarded.

## RULE 10.—CASE STATEMENTS ON AGREED FACTS

**(1) Where proceedings are commenced on agreed facts, the parties shall agree a single, joint case statement setting out those facts and affirming that the dispute is neither hypothetical nor academic. Where proceedings are brought where there is no cause of action between the parties, the single, joint case statement must also satisfy the requirements of Part 7, rule 5(3).**
**(2) Where there are any contentious factual issues between the parties, they shall separately set out their respective positions in the single, joint case statement.**
**(3) No further case statements shall be submitted, although a court may direct the provision of further information.**

*Sources: ELI-UNIDROIT Model Rules, r 23; French Code of Civil Procedure, art 57; CPR Pt 8, PD63AA, para 6.*

[78] *R v Humberside CC, ex p Bodgal* (1992) 5 Admin LR 405.
[79] *Belize Alliance of Conservation Non-Governmental Organisations v Department of the Environment* [2004] UKPC 6; [2004] Env LR 38 at [87].
[80] *R (Quark) v Secretary of State for Foreign and Commonwealth Affairs (No.1)* [2002] EWCA Civ 1409 at [50].
[81] *R v Lancashire CC, ex p Huddleston* [1986] 2 All ER 941.
[82] *Tweed v Parades Commission for Northern Ireland* [2006] UKHL 53; [2007] 1 AC 650 at [31].
[83] *Belize Alliance of Conservation Non-Governmental Organisations v Department of the Environment* [2004] UKPC 6; [2004] Env LR 38 at [86].
[84] *Peerless Limited v Gambling Regulatory Authority (Mauritius)* [2015] UKPC 29; [2015] LLR 539 at [23] citing *R v Wirral Metropolitan Borough Council, ex p Bell* (1994) 27 HLR 234 at 242.

## COMMENTARY

1. This rule supplements Part 7, rule 5. It diverges from the general approach to case statements by requiring the parties to agree a single, joint case statement, which sets out the agreed facts, the nature of the dispute between them and that there are no substantial factual issues in dispute. In the interests of economy, efficiency and proportionality, where there are some factual issues in dispute rather than providing for additional and separate particulars of claim and defences, the parties are, in a separate part of the single, joint case statement, to set out their respective cases on them.
2. Where the parties bring proceedings on an agreed basis where there is no present cause of action, the single, joint case statement must also satisfy the requirements of Part 7, rule 5(3).

## RULE 11.—ADDITIONAL INFORMATION IN CASE STATEMENTS

**(1) Case statements may include points of law and may identify witnesses and evidence where doing so would further the purposive principle.**
**(2) Documentary evidence that a party intends to rely upon in support of their pleaded allegations and which is available to that party at the time the case statement is to be filed and served must be annexed to the case statement as provided for in Part 12, rule 14(2).**

*Sources: ALI/UNIDROIT Principles, principle 5.4; ALI/UNIDROIT Reporters' Study, r 12.2; ELI-UNIDROIT Model Rules, r 53(2)(c); CPR r 16.4(1)(a), PD 16 para 13.3; RSC Ord 18, rr 7 and 11.*

## COMMENTARY

1. Parties have not been required to plead law or evidence since 1873 due to the shift towards Fact Pleading.[85] While not permitted to plead evidence under the RSC they could, however, plead law.[86] The CPR adopted a more relaxed approach.[87] It continued the permissive rule that law could be pleaded. It also, however, permitted evidence and the identification of witnesses to be pleaded.[88] This rule generally maintains the approach taken by the CPR.
2. Pleading law and/or evidence may be permitted under this rule but it should be kept under strict control. Pleadings should not become a confusion of fact, law and evidence as that would frustrate its aims, and would particularly undermine effective and proportionate dispute management.[89] The test then for when law or witness identification may be pleaded is whether it would promote the purposive principle. Would it effect, for instance, due notice or better enable the parties to consider the

[85] RSC Ord 19, r 4.

[86] H Woolf (1995) at 161; *N W Salt Co Ltd v Electrolytic Alkali Co Ltd* [1913] 3 KB 422 at 425; R Scott (1999) Vol 1 at 314ff.

[87] CPR r 16.4(1) and PD16 para 13.3.

[88] H Woolf (1995) at 162–163.

[89] A Zuckerman, *Zuckerman on Civil Procedure* (Sweet & Maxwell, 2013) at 296; *Willers v Joyce (Re Gubay (Deceased)* [2017] EWHC 1225 (Ch) at [32]; *Hague Plant v Hague* [2014] EWCA Civ 1609 at [76].

merits of their respective claims? Would it, as Woolf intended, lead parties to plead allegations that were '*likely to be substantiated*'?[90]

3. Pleading law may properly be done where there is, for instance, no dispute as to the facts and the sole issue in dispute is one of law. It ought to be done when it would dispose of the claim or a substantial issue in dispute.[91] It may be done where the defendant admits the facts but wishes to assert a defence in law. An example of the latter might, for instance, be where a defendant to a data protection claim alleges unlawful processing of personal data by pleading that the defendant disclosed the claimant's data by talking about them to a third party. The defendant may not contest the facts, but assert that as a matter of law an oral disclosure does not amount to processing personal data.
4. Pleading evidence within this rule goes further than that permitted by the CPR in one respect. It generalises the effect of the Initial Disclosure process under CPR PD57AD: see Part 12, rule 14(2).[92] It requires the provision by parties, as an annex to their case statement, of a list of documents and copies of key documents that support their claim or defence. The rationale for this, as under the CPR PD, is to enable parties to better understand the claim or defence they are required to meet from an early stage of proceedings. Through that it is intended to promote early settlement as parties are better able to assess the strengths of their respective claims. It is also intended to promote efficiency, economy and proportionality through focusing the parties on the main issues in the dispute from the outset of proceedings, eg by helping them to narrow the issues by conceding those that are weak, settling others or by identifying the key areas where further evidence is required. Thus, early provision of evidence is intended to narrow the later scope, time and cost of disclosure.[93]
5. Not pleading a point of law does not, however, mean that a party is precluded from raising the issue at trial.[94] As pleading a point of law is discretionary, not pleading it does not give rise to such an adverse consequence. Similarly, not identifying relevant evidence or witnesses in a case statement does not preclude a party from adducing such matters at a later stage in the dispute management process.

## RULE 12.—ADMISSIONS

**(1) A defendant may admit the claim or part of a claim made against them in an admission statement. Where the claim is admitted in whole or in part, the defendant may also apply for time to provide the claimant with the relief sought in the claim.**
**(2) An admission, including one made before proceedings were commenced where the court has commenced pre-action dispute management, may only be withdrawn with the court's permission.**
**(3) In exercising its discretion to permit a defendant to withdraw an admission the court will consider all the circumstances of the case, including**
**(a) whether the defendant has a good reason for seeking to withdraw the admission;**

[90] H Woolf (1995) at 161.
[91] *Independent Automatic Sales Ltd v Knowles & Foster* [1962] 1 WLR 974 at 976.
[92] P Coulson (ed), *Civil Procedure 2024* (Sweet & Maxwell, 2024) Vol 2 at 2AA-60.
[93] A Zuckerman (2021) at 330, fn 13.
[94] *Independent Automatic Sales Ltd v Knowles & Foster* [1962] 1 WLR 974 at 981; *Loveridge v Healey* [2004] EWCA Civ 173; [2004] C P Rep 30 at [29].

- **(b) whether the defendant has a real prospect of success in respect of the claim or part of it that is subject to the application;**
- **(c) the conduct of the parties;**
- **(d) any prejudice to a party if the application is allowed or if it is refused;**
- **(e) whether allowing the application will further the purposive principle.**

**(4) The court may grant permission to withdraw an admission subject to conditions.**

*Sources: ALI/UNIDROIT Principles, principles 5.2, 10.5; ALI/UNIDROIT Reporters' Study, r 13.2; ELI-UNIDROIT Model Rules, r 56(2); CPR Pt 14, PD 14 para 7.2.*

## COMMENTARY

1. This rule, like rule 4(8), is an example of party autonomy; a defendant's ability to either expressly or implicitly choose not to contest the claim or issues within it. Unlike rule 4(8), which concerns admissions in defences, this rule enables a defendant to make an admission at any time during proceedings. The same rationale underpins this rule as that which applies to rule 4(8), eg it promotes settlement and efficiency, economy and proportionality.[95]
2. Admissions may be withdrawn, including those made before proceedings commence. This includes admissions made in any case statement. Admissions can, however, only be withdraw with the court's permission, except where they were made prior to the court's involvement in managing pre-action dispute management. Rule 12(3) sets out the basis on which permission may be granted. In doing so it substantively reproduces the approach taken under the CPR.[96] The approach taken is intended to ensure that admissions are not withdrawn lightly given the need to protect the claimant's interest in relying upon them and the court's interest in effective dispute management. Both claimant and the court will, ordinarily, proceed to manage the proceedings on the basis of an admission. The former may, for instance, tailor their approach to evidence-gathering based on an admission. They may also tailor their legal advice and trial strategy based on any partial admission. Withdrawal of an admission may cause them prejudice as evidence that would have been available but for the admission may no longer be available. Withdrawal may also cause unnecessary delay in determination of the proceedings. Equally, it may give rise to additional costs that may not be capable of being remedied by an award of costs against the defendant. More generally, withdrawal may adversely affect the court's ability to manage the proceedings proportionately both in terms of the immediate proceedings and in respect of other proceedings.
3. To place proper limits on a defendant's ability to withdraw an admission, the court must take account of a number of factors in considering whether to grant permission. The most important factor is whether the defendant has a good reason for seeking to withdraw the admission.[97] Withdrawal for tactical reasons or to put pressure on a claimant by introducing the delay and expense of revising their approach to proceedings in the light of it would, obviously, not amount to a good reason. Withdrawal

[95] Rule 4(8). Part 15, r 2(7).
[96] *Kojima v HSMC Bank Plc* [2011] EWHC 611 (Ch); [2011] 3 All ER 359 at [19]; CPR PD para 7.2.
[97] *Woodford v Stopford* [2011] EWCA Civ 266; [2011] Med LR 237 at [26].

due to fresh evidence coming to light would, on the contrary, likely amount to a good reason, as could the fact that it was made on the basis of a genuine mistake by the defendant.[98]

4. Where the defendant can demonstrate a good reason, they must also demonstrate that the defence or issue with which the withdrawal is concerned has a real prospect of success if permission is to be granted. It would serve no proper purpose to grant permission in respect of a matter that was without such a base level of merit. The other factors in rule 12(3) require the court to consider the extent to which prejudice would be caused to the claimant, by permitting withdrawal, or to the defendant by refusing permission. In considering all the circumstances, the court may also, for example and as relevant, have regard to the promptness with which the defendant made the application to withdraw, the value of the issue subject to the application, whether the defendant was acting in good faith in seeking to withdraw the admission, and whether it would enable the court to determine the claim on the correct legal basis.[99]
5. Where the claimant is concerned, rule 12(3)(d) requires consideration of the extent to which they have relied upon the admission to their detriment and the extent to which that detriment can be rectified by steps taken by defendant, such as an award of costs on a reasonable costs basis. It equally calls for consideration of the extent to which the parties are blameworthy in respect of the admission having been made. A defendant who admitted an issue but then wished to withdraw because evidence came to light after the admission, but which could have been obtained prior to it being made, can properly be viewed as the author of their own misfortune. Such would point away from granting permission to withdraw. If, however, they had been led to believe by another party or third party that such evidence did not exist that might point the other way.
6. Finally, although the criteria are non-exhaustive, the purposive principle must be considered. Significantly here, the court must consider the effect that permitting withdrawal may have on its ability to secure a proportionate process. Permitting a late withdrawal may, for instance, cause such disruption to the economical and efficient management of proceedings that it has an adverse impact on both the proportionate management of those proceedings, but also on that of other proceedings. In such circumstances, permission could properly be refused to promote proportionately, not least systemic proportionality. An admission cannot be withdrawn, however, after judgment given the importance of giving effect to the principle of finality.[100]
7. Permission may be made subject to conditions, which may include requiring a defendant to compensate the claimant for the costs arising from the withdrawal. To promote or protect systemic proportionality conditions might also impose strict limits on evidence to be adduced in respect of the issue or strict limits on trial time relating to it. A condition may also, for instance, provide that the issue only be dealt with by way of written submissions.

[98] *Moore v Worcestershire Acute Hospitals NHS Trust* [2015] EWHC 1209 (QB) at [28]–[32].

[99] *Tchenguiz v Director of the Serious Fraud Office* [2014] EWCA Civ 472; [2014] CP Rep 35.

[100] *Kojima v HSMC Bank Plc* [2011] EWHC 611 (Ch); [2011] 3 All ER 359.

# SECTION 4: TIME LIMITS AND CLOSURE OF CASE STATEMENTS

## RULE 13.—TIME LIMITS

**(1) Particulars of claim must be served within four months of the commencement of proceedings where they are to be served within the jurisdiction or within six months of commencement where they are to be served outside the jurisdiction. Failure to do so invalidates the particulars of claim. Proceedings may be recommenced if the particulars of claim are reissued by the court.**

**(2) Where a claimant has commenced proceedings and the court has authorised service of the particulars of claim to be effected on its behalf and service has not been effected within fourteen days of the court's order, or any other time limit specified within that order, the defendant may apply to the court for an order that the court serve the particulars of claim.**

**(3) Unless the time limit for response to a particulars of claim is set out in statute or an international instrument, a response to a particulars of claim must be filed with the court and served on the claimant within fourteen days of deemed service of the particulars of claim where they were served within the jurisdiction, otherwise any response must be served within twenty-one days of deemed service. Where no response is made within the time limit for filing and serving a response, the claimant may apply for default judgment. Further case statements must be served within fourteen days, if within the jurisdiction, or twenty-one days, if outside the jurisdiction, of the deemed service date of the case statement to which they respond.**

**(4) Where no steps have been taken in the proceedings six months from service of the particulars of claim, the proceedings shall be stayed for twelve months. During that twelve month period any party may apply to the court to lift the stay and take a step in the proceedings. At the expiry of the stay the proceedings shall stand dismissed. An application to lift the stay may be granted where the applicant can show a good reason for delay. An application to set aside a dismissal is an application for relief from sanction.**

**(5) Time limits to serve case statements may be extended by consent of the parties for up to fourteen days after the dates specified in rules 13(2) and (3). Any further extensions and any retrospective applications for extensions of time may only be granted by the court under Part 11, rule 9.**

**(6) A defendant may give notice to the court and claimant that they require an extension of time to serve their defence. Where such notice is given by the defendant, the time limit for service shall automatically be extended by fourteen days if service is to be effected within the jurisdiction or twenty-one days if it is to be effected outside the jurisdiction.**

*Sources: State Immunity Act 1978; CPR rr 7.5, 7.6, 7.7, 10.3, 15.4, 15.11, and PD6B.*

## COMMENTARY

1. This rule provides the time limits for the validity of the particulars of claim following the commencement of proceedings. It adopts the approach taken under the CPR, ie that service must be effected within four months of the date of issue.[101] The rule needs

[101] CPR r 7.5.

to be read consistently with the rules on service, especially regarding the approach to deemed service.

2. The adoption of time limits for the validity of particulars of claim, as well as providing the defendant with the power to compel service of the particulars if they are aware that proceedings have commenced, is intended to promote finality in litigation. It, as Zuckerman notes, serves a similar purpose to the imposition of limitation periods for bringing actions. These time limits, as well as limitation periods, ensure that potential claims do not have an indefinite existence. If they did individuals would be in an indefinite state of uncertainty as to their rights and obligations, which would not be conducive to social or economic activity. Both rules 13(1) and (2) thus act as '*extensions of the limitation period*'.[102] They do so as they can extend the lifespan of a claim by four or six months, not least where proceedings are brought at the end of any applicable limitation period. Where the validity period expires before the end of the limitation period, there is no reason why a claimant should not reissue their particulars and recommence proceedings. Permitting them to do so is not inconsistent with the promotion of finality in litigation due to the fact that the statutory limitation period has not expired.
3. Rule 13(3) provides the time limits for responding to particulars of claim by any of the methods set out in rule 4. It further provides the time limits for responding to any defence or further case statements. It acknowledges that time limits for responding to particulars of claim may be set out in statute, eg the State Immunity Act 1978. Other than when statutory time limits apply, it adopts the standard approach to time limits: fourteen days where service is to be effected within the jurisdiction and twenty-one days where it is to be effected outside the jurisdiction. This approach is maintained notwithstanding the move to digital procedure. The ease of filing and serving case statements may increase due to digitisation, but there is a continuing need nevertheless to provide defendants (and claimants) with a reasonable period of time within which to consider their response, draft and file it. Affording parties such a reasonable period of time is an inherent aspect of a fair procedure and, particularly, of the general access principle.
4. Proper management of proceedings requires parties to actively pursue the resolution of their dispute. Proceedings cannot therefore be commenced with no steps taken thereafter. It is, as has been made clear by the High Court, an abuse of process to commence proceedings with no intention to pursue them.[103] Rule 13(4) aims to promote the effective management of proceedings by the parties and to promote their co-operation with the court in so doing.[104] It does so by policing inaction by claimants following the service of particulars of claim. It places the onus on them to take active steps in the face of inaction by a defendant, eg to seek judgment in default of a defence, to withdraw the proceedings or, where the parties wish to pause the progress of the proceedings, to seek a stay of the proceedings.[105] There is, of course, no onus on a defendant to take any steps following service of the particulars of claim. Any failure to take steps on their part could, as they will know, lead to judgment in default.

[102] A Zuckerman (2021) at 221.

[103] *Grovit v Doctor* [1997] 1 WLR 640; *Arbuthnot Latham Bank Ltd v Trafalgar Holdings Ltd* [1998] 1 WLR 1426; *Kazakhstan Kagazy Plc v Zhunus* [2016] EWHC 1048 (Comm); [2016] 4 WLR 86 at [40]; *Kazakhstan Kagazy Plc v Zhunus* [2016] EWCA Civ 1036; [2017] 1 WLR 1360 at [20]); Part 8, r 13.

[104] *Bank of America Europe DAC v CITTA Metropolitana Di Milano* [2022] EWHC 1544 (Comm) at [22].

[105] *Asturion Foundation v Alibrahim* [2020] EWCA Civ 32 at [62]; Part 11, r 3(2)(b).

5. In the absence of the claimant taking any active step to pursue their claim for relief, proceedings are subject to an automatic stay. During that period any party may seek to lift the stay. A claimant may do so in order to seek judgment in default or to proceed to trial in the absence of a response by the defendant.[106] A defendant may apply to lift the stay in order to seek permission to strike out the particulars of claim or file their defence or an admission. Absent any such steps, to give effect to the principle of finality, the claim will then stand dismissed after twelve months. This relatively low threshold test is justified given the short length of time the stay is in place.[107] A more draconian test would place too great a fetter on the general access principle. The test for setting aside a dismissal is, however, the higher relief from sanction test. This is justified not only to promote finality in litigation, but also due to neither party having complied with the duty to co-operate with the court in managing proceedings consistently with the purposive principle. The application of the relief from sanction threshold is thus also justified as a means to promote party compliance with their duties to the court.
6. Rule 13(5) makes explicit provision for the service time limits for case statements to be extended either by consent of the parties for a limited period or otherwise by court order. That parties may need additional time to prepare and serve their case statements is a commonplace of litigation. Parties ought, consistently with the co-operation principle, to agree reasonable requests for extensions of time. Such agreement not only promotes economy and proportionality between the parties, as it avoids the necessity of an application being made to the court, but for the same reason it promotes systemic proportionality as it does not unjustifiably consume court resources.
7. Parties may, however, only agree extensions up to fourteen days beyond the general time limit. This is to ensure they do not unnecessarily prolong proceedings by repeatedly agreeing extensions of time. By thereafter requiring an application to the court, which does not necessarily have to be a contested one, the rule ensures that it can scrutinise the application effectively further to its duty to manage the dispute effectively. Applications for extensions are governed by the general power in Part 11.
8. Finally, rule 13(6) is functionally equivalent to the extension of time to serve a defence that is provided under the CPR by filing an acknowledgment of service. Under this Code, the necessity of filing such a notice ought to be less than is the case under the CPR. Due to the co-operation principle, parties will be expected to agree a fourteen-day extension of time for service of a defence, ie rule 13(5) ought to be the default rule concerning such extensions. The intention underpinning this approach is to replace the acknowledgment of service process and the cost and time attendant upon it, with a less costly and time-consuming process.

[106] *Berliner Bank AG v Karageorgis* [1996] 1 Lloyd's Rep 426; *Habib Bank Ltd v Central Bank of Sudan* [2006] EWHC 1767 (Comm); *Eurasia Sports Ltd v Tsai* [2020] EWHC 81 (QB).

[107] *Football Association Premier League Ltd v O'Donovan* [2017] EWHC 152 (Ch); [2017] FSR 31; *Bank of Beirut (UK) Ltd v Sbayti* [2020] EWHC 557 (Comm). The lower threshold approach is preferred here to that taken in *New Zealand Cricket v Neo Sports* [2016] EWHC 3615 (Comm) at [8] and *Bank of America Europe DAC v CITTA Metropolitana Di Milano* [2022] EWHC 1544 (Comm).

## RULE 14.—CLOSURE OF CASE STATEMENTS

**(1) Case statements are deemed to be closed fourteen days, if the parties are within the jurisdiction, or twenty-one days, if a party is outside the jurisdiction, after deemed service of, whichever is later**
**(a) the defence;**
**(b) the reply to the defence or further case statement;**
**(c) the defence to any counterclaim or additional claim;**
**(d) the reply to a defence to any counterclaim or additional claim or further case statement; or**
**(e) a date as directed by the court on its own initiative or on application of the parties.**

**(2) Closure of case statements marks the commencement of the dispute management phase of proceedings.**

*Sources: ELI-UNIDROIT Model Rules, r 63; RSC Ord 18, r 20.*

## COMMENTARY

1. This rule reintroduces the formal close of case statements, which was contained in RSC Ord. 18, r 20 but not adopted by the CPR. It serves two purposes. First, it marks the formal joinder of issues between the parties.[108] Secondly, it marks the formal point, for the court and parties, from which the formal dispute management process begins. This is not to say, however, that the court will not be responsible for the active management of the proceedings prior to close of case statements. It may, for instance, be involved in managing the process by which the parties are filing and serving their case statements. It may also be involved in the management of interim applications. Close of case statements, however, is intended to identify clearly the point from which proceedings shift to, for instance, allocation to procedural management track. Given the shift to a digital procedure, this process can easily be automated, with the date on which case statements close operating as the key date from which later dates in the dispute management timetable can be calculated and provided to both parties and the judge assigned to manage the proceedings. The time limits set out here, as with time limits generally, may be extended.
2. Close of case statements does not preclude the later amendment of case statements or, where necessary, the provision of additional case statements. Nor is it a barrier to the defendant filing and serving an admission. All these steps may properly take place at any time after close of case statements with, as necessary, the court's permission. This rule does not mark a barrier to such steps due to its formal nature.

[108] R Scott (1999) Vol 1 at 18/20/1.

# PART 9

# AMENDMENT

## SECTION 1: GENERAL

1. This Part supplements Part 8. It concerns amendments to case statements and other procedural documents. It draws together various rules that are set out disparately within the CPR. The aim here is, once again to promote procedural simplicity; to draw together those rules that have the same function, albeit they are applied differently.
2. A general power to amend case statements has been a feature of English and Welsh civil procedure since the 1850s when reforms effected by the Common Law Procedure Act 1852 provided the common law courts with a general power to amend pleadings that was analogous to the, then, long extant power to do so in the equity courts.[1] The power was endorsed by the Judicature Commissioners in 1868[2] and adopted, and applied liberally, by the RSC[3] and, less liberally, under the CPR.[4]
3. Specific powers to amend other procedural documents are also well-established and flow from the court's common law inherent jurisdiction. Thus, the CPR implicitly restated both the general power to amend documents other than case statements[5] and the 'slip rule', the power to amend documents administratively to correct, for instance, typographical errors.[6]

### RULE 1.—SCOPE AND PURPOSE

**(1) This Part concerns the manner in which amendments may be made to procedural documents.**

**(2) This Part primarily gives effect to the autonomy, accuracy and settlement principles. Its parameters are also set by the economy, efficiency and, particularly, proportionality principles.**

*Sources: ALI/UNIDROIT Principles, principle 5; ALI/UNIDROIT Reporters' Study, r 14; ELI-UNIDROIT Model Rules, rr 55, 59; CPR Pt 17.*

[1] Common Law Procedure Act 1852, s 222 and its preamble; E Daniell, *Treatise on the Practice of the High Court of Chancery, with Some Practical Observations on the Pleadings in That Court* (1845), chap 5.

[2] The First Report of the Royal Commission to inquire into the Operation and Constitution of the High Court of Chancery, Courts of Common Law, Central Criminal Court, High Court of Admiralty, and other Courts in England, and into the Operation and Effect of the Present Separation and Division of Jurisdiction between the Courts (No 4130; 1868–1869) at 11.

[3] RSC (1875) Ord 27 r 1; RSC (1962) Ord 20 r 8.1; RSC (1965) Ord 20 r 8.

[4] CPR Pt 17.

[5] RSC Ord 20 r 8; CPR r 3.1(2)(m).

[6] RSC Ord 20 r 11; CPR r 40.12.

*A Model Civil Procedure Code for England and Wales*. John Sorabji, Oxford University Press. 
DOI: 10.1093/oso/9780192848680.003.0010

## COMMENTARY

1. From the middle of the 19th century, English and Welsh civil procedure adopted a liberal approach to the amendment of procedural documents and, particularly, case statements. Amendment was permitted to cure procedural error, drafting error or to enable new or additional matters to be brought within the scope of the proceedings. This approach flowed from what has been described as the '*dominant policy*', '*positive objective*', or '*general idea*'[7] of procedure during this time; it being that procedure should operate to enable disputes to be resolved substantively on their merits. As Hepburn put it, the power to permit amendments, which flowed from procedural reforms in the 1850s and 1870s, was exercised consistently with the view that it was more '*a duty rather than the mere privilege of a court to allow amendments at all stages of the case in furtherance of justice*'.[8] This was given effect in a line of authority that firmly established a strong presumption that amendment of case statements be permitted where it would better enable the courts to determine the case on its substantive merits and where any prejudice caused to the opposing party by the amendment was compensated by costs.[9]
2. The underpinning of this liberal approach was that amendment was primarily a manifestation of a commitment to the accuracy principle, which at the time was unfettered by concerns relating to economy and efficiency, never mind proportionality. Bowen LJ in *Cropper v Smith* (1884) emphasised the centrality of this aim in his statement of principle concerning the basis on which the amendment power should be exercised,

> . . . *the object of the Courts is to decide the rights of parties, and not to punish them for mistakes they make in the conduct of their cases by deciding otherwise than in accordance with their rights . . . I know of no kind of error or mistake which, if not fraudulent or intended to overreach, the Court ought not to correct, if it can be done without injustice to the other party. Courts do not exist for the sake of discipline, but for the sake of deciding matters in controversy, . . . It seems to me that as soon as it appears that the way in which a party had framed his case will not lead to a decision of the real matter in controversy, it is as much a matter of right on his part to have it corrected, if it can be done without injustice . . .*[10]

3. This Part maintains the commitment to the idea that amendment is, primarily, a means by which the accuracy principle can be given effect. It also, for the first time, makes explicit that amendment is also a means to promote consensual settlement. Consistently with developments under the CPR, it does not however adopt as liberal an approach to amendment as was the case from the 1850s until the end of the 20th century. Under the CPR greater importance was placed on amendment

[7] J Jolowicz, '"General Ideas" and the Reform of Civil Procedure' (1983) 3 Legal Studies 295 at 297; First Report of Her Majesty's Commissioners into the Process, Practice and System of Pleading in the Court of Chancery (HMSO) (1852) (The 1852 Report) at 34 and following; Common Law Procedure Act 2852, s 222.

[8] C Hepburn, *The Historical Development of Code Pleading in America and England* (Classic Reprint) (Forgotten Books reprint, 2019; Anderson, 1897) at 267; A Zuckerman, *Zuckerman on Civil Procedure—Principles of Practice* (Sweet & Maxwell, 2021) at 8–12.

[9] *Tildesley v Harper* (1878) 10 ChD 393; *Collins v The Vestry of Paddington* (1879–1880) LR 5 QBD 368 at 379; *Clarapede & Co v Commercial Union Association* (1883) 32 WR 262 at 263.

[10] *Cropper v Smith* (1884) 26 ChD 700 at 710; J Sorabji, *English Civil Justice after Woolf and Jackson* (CUP, 2014) at 56 and following.

being permitted consistently with principles other than that of accuracy, not least economy and efficiency.[11] The approach under the CPR to amendment thus moved away from that established under the RSC, and now does not reflect the position under *Cropper v Smith* (1884),[12] a point particularly stressed by the Supreme Court in *Prince Abdulaziz v Apex Global Management Ltd (Rev 2)* (2014).[13] Amendment must now be carried out consistently with the purposive principle, and must particularly take account of systemic proportionality.[14] The rules in this Part are intended to maintain and give further effect to this step change in approach effected under the CPR.

## RULE 2.—AMENDMENT OF A CASE STATEMENT

**(1) Amendments to case statements may**
  **(a) revise the contents of the case statement;**
  **(b) add or substitute a new cause of action;**
  **(c) remove a cause of action;**
  **(d) add, substitute, or remove a party; or**
  **(e) alter the capacity of a party.**

**(2) A case statement may be amended by a party at any time before it is served on another party or by consent of the parties at any time. Such amendments may be disallowed by the court. Otherwise, case statements may either be amended on application with the court's permission or, exceptionally, by the court on its own initiative.**

**(3) An application to amend a case statement to add or substitute a new party may be made by an existing party or by a person seeking to be added or substituted as a party.**

**(4) A case statement may not be amended to add or substitute a person as a claimant without their consent.**

**(5) Any amendment to the content of a case statement must be verified by a statement of truth signed by the party or their lawyer. Where an amendment is not verified by a statement of truth it cannot be relied on as evidence, but otherwise remains valid. The court may require an unverified amendment to be verified or may strike it out.**

*Sources: ALI/UNIDROIT Principles, principle 5.1; ALI/UNIDROIT Reporters' Study, r 14; ELI-UNIDROIT Model Rules, r 55; CPR Pt 17; rr 19.2, 19.4, 19.5, PD19.2, para 2.*

[11] *Charlesworth v Relay Roads Ltd* [2000] 1 WLR 231 at 238; *Savings and Investment Bank Ltd (In Liquidation) v Fincken* [2003] EWCA Civ 1630; [2004] 1 WLR 667; *Swain-Mason v Mills and Reeve LLP* [2011] EWCA Civ 14; [2011] 1 WLR 2735; *Prince Abdulaziz v Apex Global Management Ltd (Rev 2)* [2014] UKSC 64; [2014] WLR 4495; *CIP Properties (AIPT) Ltd v Galliford Try Infrastructure Ltd* [2015] EWHC 1345 (TCC); 160 Con LR 73 at [15]; *Quah v Goldman Sachs International* [2015] EWHC 759 (Comm) at [38]; *Prudential Assurance Company Ltd v HM Revenue and Customs* [2016] EWCA Civ 37; [2017] 1 WLR 4031; *Nesbit Law Group LLP v Acasta European Insurance Co Ltd* [2018] EWCA Civ 268 at [41]–[44].

[12] *Quah v Goldman Sachs International* [2015] EWHC 759 (Comm) at [38]; *Georgiev v Kings College Hospital NHS Foundation Trust Appeal* [2016] EWHC 104 (QB) at [8]; *Henderson v Dorset Healthcare University Foundation NHS Trust* [2016] EWHC 3032 (QB); ELI-UNIDROIT Model Rules, r 55, comments 2 and 5.

[13] *Prince Abdulaziz v Apex Global Management Ltd (Rev 2)* [2014] UKSC 64; [2014] WLR 4495 at [27].

[14] *Mitchell v News Group Newspapers Ltd* [2013] EWCA Civ 1537; [2014] 1 WLR 795; *Denton v TH White Ltd* [2014] EWCA Civ 906; [2014] 1 WLR 3926; J Dyson, 'The Application of the Amendments to the Civil Procedure Rules' (2014) 33 CJQ 124.

## COMMENTARY

1. This rule provides the basis on which case statements may be amended both in respect of causes of action and parties.[15] The CPR deals with this power in its Pts 17 and 19. A consolidated approach to amendment is adopted in this Part for reasons of procedural simplicity: its substantive function is amendment and that need not be split across different Parts of the Code.
2. The focus of this rule is amendment of case statements.[16] This power is a broad one;[17] a point emphasised by the test for the grant of permission to amend. Specifically, the rule covers three situations: amendment of causes of action; amendment to join or remove a party; and, amendment to alter the capacity of a party. It does not deal with the situation where amendment is sought after the expiry of a relevant limitation period. That is dealt with in rule 7 for reasons of clarity.
3. Rule 2(2) maintains a distinction between two approaches to amendment: those where the court's permission is not required and those where it is required. Where a case statement has not been served on another party it may be amended without the need to obtain either the consent of all the parties or the permission of the court. An unserved case statement is one to which other parties have not been given notice. They have not therefore, potentially, been put to any trouble or expense in formulating their response to it.[18] Nor will it, generally, have engaged the court in active dispute management. Thus, the amendment will neither prejudice other parties nor the court's ability to secure systemic proportionality. The broader power, also maintained in this rule, to amend case statements without the court's permission if there is all-party consent has existed since RSC Ord 20 r 12 was introduced in 1982. It may see an amendment effected where there is agreement at any time during proceedings.[19] Both these forms of amendment give full effect to the principle of party autonomy. They are, however, both subject to the court's power to disallow the amendment. There are two reasons for this.
4. First, a power to disallow is consistent with the dispute management principle. An amendment effected through either of these two methods might, for instance, have an adverse impact on the court's ability to effectively and proportionately manage the dispute. It may also have an adverse impact on other litigants and their right of access to an effective and proportionate process. The power to disallow thus ensures that the court can effectively control the proceedings, which as the ELI-UNIDROIT Model Rules note is an '*essential aspect of the court's case management role*'.[20] Noting that, this rule does not go as far as those Model Rules, which provide that no amendment may be made without the court's permission. Such a prescriptive rule is itself contrary to effective and proportionate management because it unnecessarily involves the court in considering formal applications in all cases, thus wastefully utilising its resources where the amendment would itself have no adverse impact on the proper management of proceedings. The present rule, which maintains the approach under

[15] *Re Pablo Star Ltd* [2017] EWCA Civ 1768; [2018] 1 WLR 738 at [47]; *Molavi v Hibbert* [2020] EWHC 121 (Ch); [2020] 4 WLR 46 at [48]; E Daniell (1845) chap 5.

[16] *R (Johnson) v Secretary of State for Health* [2006] EWHC 288 (Admin); *Hounslow LBC v Cumar* [2012] EWCA Civ 1426; [2013] HLR 17 at [14].

[17] *Hounslow LBC v Cumar* [2012] EWCA Civ 1426; [2013] HLR 17 at [11]–[13].

[18] A Zuckerman (2021) at 344.

[19] SI 1982/1786; R Scott, *Supreme Court Practice 1999* (Sweet & Maxwell, 1999) Vol 1 at 20/12/2.

[20] ELI-UNIDROIT Model Rules, r 55, comment 2.

both the RSC and CPR, strikes the more effective balance between party autonomy and effective dispute management.

5. Secondly, the power to disallow enables the court either on application of a party (exceptionally including one that had previously consented to the amendment),[21] or its own initiative to disallow amendments that ought not properly have been made. It would, for instance, enable the court to disallow an amendment that is challenged on the basis that it seeks to: add a new cause of action after a relevant limitation period has expired;[22] add a claimant without their consent; add unnecessary material to the contents of a case statement or a cause of action that is not properly connected with the claims already pleaded. Again, this gives expression to the dispute management principle. That the court has the power to amend a case statement of its own initiative may appear unusual given the autonomy and the adversariality principles. It suggests an inquisitorial power on the part of the court. It is a power, however, that, exceptionally, enables the court to ensure that proceedings are properly constituted, eg by adding or substituting a party as a defendant where that is necessary to enable the dispute to be properly dealt with by the court.[23] It is thus justified by reference to both the dispute management and finality principles. That a party may challenge such an amendment once made by the court ensures that party autonomy is properly respected.[24]

6. Other than the two circumstances noted, an amendment can only be effected with the court's permission. Where this is required, a formal application must made. This ensures that all other parties have proper notice of the proposed change and are able, if they wish, to oppose it before the court rules on it. It also ensures that a proper record, for dispute management purposes is maintained. This minimises the prospect of procedural confusion in respect of the amendment, and enables proper judicial consideration of the matter.[25] It also helps to promote effective public understanding and scrutiny of the proceedings. From a practical perspective, it ensures that an appropriate court fee is paid. By properly contributing to court funding it better enables the court to secure systemic proportionality. The court may, however, waive the need for a formal written application where, for instance, an amendment seeks to correct minor errors in case statements, which do not effect substantive changes.

7. Amendments to case statements may broadly take two forms: ones that relate to their substantive contents; and, ones that concern the parties to the proceedings. The former includes revisions to the contents of a case statement. For instance, a party may need, or be required by order, to amend their case statement to clarify or expand on factual allegations where they were initially unclear or too concise.[26] Equally, where amendments are made by one party, the opposing party may need to amend

[21] *Cape Distribution Ltd v Cape Intermediate Holdings Plc* [2016] EWHC 1786 (QB); [2017] Lloyd's Rep IR 1 at [171]–[173]. The basis of such an exceptional application would be if the party alleged they had been misled into consenting to the amendment.

[22] *Cape Distribution Ltd v Cape Intermediate Holdings Plc* [2016] EWHC 1786 (QB); [2017] Lloyd's Rep IR 1; *Qatar Airways Group QSCS v Middle East News FZ LLC* [2020] EWHC 2975 (QB).

[23] *Nottage v Jackson* (1883) 11 QBD 627 at 638; *TSB Private Bank International SA v Chabra* [1992] 1 WLR 231; RSC Ord 20 r 8; J Jolowicz, 'The parties and the judge', in J Jolowicz, *On Civil Procedure* (CUP, 2000) at 201.

[24] *Cropper v Smith* (1884) 26 ChD 700 at 715.

[25] *Magdeev v Tsvetkov* [2019] EWCA Civ 1802 at [26]–[27].

[26] *Maradive & Oil Services (SAE) v CAN Insurance Company (Europe) Ltd* [2002] EWCA Civ 369; [2002] 1 All ER (Comm) 653.

their own case statement to deal with changes effected by the initial amendments to their opponent's case statement. A party may also seek to amend their case statement to add a new cause of action,[27] substitute one or remove one. This may be necessary where, for instance, a new cause of action has arisen between the parties after the case statement was served.[28]

8. Case statements may also be amended to add or substitute a person as a new party on the application of either an existing party or the person who is to be joined as a new party.[29] Consistently with the party autonomy, concentration and finality principles, such an application ought to be capable of being made in both of these situations. Permitting existing and potentially new parties to make the application better enables the court to consider who ought to be a party to proceedings and whose joinder, therefore, will better enable it to manage and resolve the proceedings effectively.

9. A person can, however, only be added to proceedings as a claimant with their consent. This requirement exists for an obvious reason.[30] The principle of autonomy means it is for a putative party to determine if they want to *bring* proceedings, and thus commit to the potential obligation to pay their own and other parties' costs. This applies at whatever stage proceedings have reached. It thus applies if proceedings have been issued but not served, issued and served, or at any stage of the proceedings thereafter.[31] Where a person does not consent to be added or substituted as a claimant it may be necessary to add them as a defendant to the proceedings. A person does not, by contrast, need to consent to be sued. They may be joined as a defendant therefore against their will in an analogous manner to which a defendant generally becomes party to proceedings upon their commencement.

10. Case statements may also be amended to remove a party from proceedings. This may be necessary, for instance, where their joinder is not necessary to finally determine the issues, where it renders proceedings unnecessarily complex, or they were simply joined in error. Party capacity can also be amended. This may be necessary where, for instance, a claimant acting in a representative capacity seeks to act in a personal capacity eg after a representative proceedings order is set aside or they are bringing proceedings as an executor or administrator of an estate.[32]

11. An amendment to the content of a case statement, including ones that add, substitute or remove a cause of action, must be verified with a statement of truth. The rationale for this is the same as applies to case statements.[33]

12. Case statements do not include notices of appeal or responses to notices of appeal. Part 17, rule 15, however, applies the rules concerning amendment of case statements to them, subject to the requirement set out in that rule that any such amendments can only be made with the appellate court's consent.

[27] A new cause of action will be one that is not implied by the material facts already pleaded: *Savings v Investment Bank (In Liquidation) v Fincken* [2001] EWCA Civ 1639; (2001) 98(48) LSG 29 at [30]–[31].

[28] *British Credit Trust Holdings v UK Insurance Ltd* [2003] EWHC 2404 (Com); [2004] 1 All ER (Comm) 444.

[29] CPR r 19.4(2).

[30] CPR r 19.4(4).

[31] *Various Claimants v G4S Plc* [2021] EWHC 524 (Ch) is to be preferred to that in *Rawet v Daimler AG* [2022] EWHC 235 (QB).

[32] *Haq v Singh* [2001] 1 WLR 1594.

[33] *Clarke v Marlborough Fine Art (London) Ltd* [2002] 1 WLR 1731 at [20]–[30].

### RULE 3.—AMENDMENT OF DOCUMENTS OTHER THAN CASE STATEMENTS

**Documents other than case statements and notices of appeal and responses may be amended. They may only be amended with the court's permission.**
*Sources: CPR r 3.1(2)(m); RSC Ord 20 r 8.*

### COMMENTARY

1. This rule provides for the amendment of documents other than case statements or notices of appeal and responses. Amendment of the former is dealt with in rule 2. Amendment of the latter is provided for in Part 17, rule 15.
2. An equivalent power to this one was contained in RSC Ord 20 r 8, but not replicated in the CPR. It was, however, held under the CPR that, at least in so far as application notices were concerned, a power to amend was implicit in the general case management power contained in CPR r 3.1(2)(m).[34] This rule makes explicit the power and, in doing so, makes clear that it applies to all procedural documents other than those specifically excluded from it. It thus applies to application notices, documents that stand in place of case statements where the court has dispensed with them, or administrative documents such as court lists. It would also apply to documents used in specialist proceedings to which this Code is applied under Part 1, rule 1(2).
3. On the court's power to correct its own judgments and orders, see Part 14, rule 9.

## SECTION 2: PERMISSION TO AMEND

### RULE 4.—PERMISSION TO AMEND A CASE STATEMENT OR OTHER DOCUMENT—GENERALLY

**(1) Permission to amend a case statement or other document may be granted where**
  **(a) there is a good reason to make the amendment; and,**
  **(b) the amendment would, consistently with the purposive principle, assist the court and parties to resolve the real dispute in the proceedings.**
**(2) In considering whether granting permission to amend is consistent with the purposive principle, a court must particularly seek to balance the injustice to the party seeking the amendment of refusing permission with the injustice to other parties in the proceedings and to the wider public interest in enabling other litigants to obtain justice efficiently and proportionately should permission be granted.**
**(3) Prejudice to other parties in the proceedings may be mitigated by the payment of costs to those parties. The payment of such costs is not to be taken into account when considering the wider public interest.**
**(4) Where a proposed amendment is to a case statement, the party seeking to amend must also establish that the amended case statement has a real prospect of supporting the underlying claim or defence or, if the opposed amendment seeks to introduce a new claim or defence, that that new claim or defence has a real prospect of success.**
**(5) Permission to amend may be granted subject to any condition that the court considers just.**

*Sources: ALI/UNIDROIT Principles, principle 5.1; ALI/UNIDROIT Reporters' Study, r 14; ELI-UNIDROIT Model Rules, r 55; CPR Pt 17.*

[34] *Agents Mutual Ltd v Moginnie James Ltd* [2016] EWHC 3384 (Ch) at [8]–[10].

## COMMENTARY

1. The liberal approach to proceedings that prevailed from the 1850s, as noted earlier, placed significant weight on the need to ensure that disputes were resolved on their substantive merits. Mistakes by parties in respect of their pleadings were not to stand in the way of this being achieved. Amendment was generally to be permitted to ensure justice on the merits was achieved. Similarly, other amendments were to be permitted on the same basis. This approach was subject to two caveats. First, where mistakes were concerned, they must not be attributable to some form of misfeasance, eg they must not have been the product of fraud. Secondly, any prejudice caused to the other party by way of the amendment had to be capable of being compensated, which it generally but not necessarily was, by an award of costs.[35] This approach, however, took no account of its effect on the effective management of proceedings. It led to a lax approach to rule compliance, which in turn engendered an increase in contested applications and satellite litigation over whether amendment should be allowed. This in turn increased procedural cost and delay for parties to such proceedings. More broadly, it took no account of the impact this had on the court's resources and on other litigants' ability to secure a resolution of their disputes in reasonable time and at reasonable cost. The liberal approach led to disproportionate litigation time and cost, which acted as a significant barrier to access to justice.[36]
2. It is now generally recognised that factors other than the need to secure adjudicative accuracy (justice on the merits) must be taken into account when managing proceedings. Economy, efficiency and, most particularly, proportionality must be taken into account. As the ALI/UNIDROIT Reporters' Study rightly puts it, a court approaching amendment needs to ensure that it does not '*unreasonably delay or otherwise cause injustice*'.[37] The same approach is adopted as best practice in European procedure in the ELI/UNIDROIT Model Rules.[38] It is equally evident under the CPR generally under its overriding objective as interpreted following the Court of Appeal's decision in *Mitchell v News Group Newspapers Ltd* (2013), and particularly in terms of the application of its emphasis on the importance of procedural proportionality.
3. As a consequence of these developments, the idea that was central to the pre-CPR's approach to amendment, that any harm caused to a party as a result of their opponent amending their pleadings could be cured by way of compensation in costs, is no longer sufficient. The approach under the CPR, which is maintained here, is that in considering whether to grant an amendment the court must first consider if there is a good reason to permit the amendment. Secondly, consideration must be given to whether the amendment will further the purposive principle. This requires consideration of whether it is likely to promote the prospect of the court securing adjudicative accuracy or the parties reaching a properly informed settlement. It requires consideration of the harm, and possibility of compensation for it, to other parties of allowing the amendment; it thus maintains the pre-CPR approach established by *Cropper v Smith* (1884) to that extent. More importantly

[35] *Tildesley v Harper* (1876) 3 Ch D 277; *Cropper v Smith* (1884) 26 ChD 700 at 710; *Clarapede & Co v Commercial Union Association* (1883) 32 WR 262 at 263.

[36] A Zuckerman, Civil Procedure (Butterworths, 2003) at 31; J Sorabji (2014) at 67–74.

[37] *ALI/UNIDROIT Reporters' Study*, r 14.1.

[38] ELI-UNIDROIT Model Rules, r 55, and comment 5.

though, it requires consideration of the effect that the amendment has on proportionality, and particularly systemic proportionality, ie its impact on the court's resources and other litigants' ability to secure access to a proportionate process. It is a test that is therefore aimed at balancing the interests of justice in the immediate case with the wider public interest in managing the civil justice system as a whole in a way that secures proportionate access for all litigants. That balance may, in some cases, require an amendment to be refused where allowing it would harm the wider public interest, notwithstanding the fact that that might hamper the court's ability to give effect to the accuracy principle in the immediate proceedings.[39]

4. Additionally, where a proposed amendment is to a case statement, the party seeking the amendment must show that the amended case statement has a real prospect of success or, if the amendment seeks to introduce a new claim or defence, that that has a real prospect of success.[40] This is intended to ensure that only viable amendments are made. In the absence of a real prospect of success, the court would be asked to unnecessarily expend its time and resources to the detriment of other litigants on the expanded claim before it. It would also result in the other party to the proceedings being put to disproportionate time and expense.

## RULE 5.—PERMISSION TO AMEND A CASE STATEMENT AFTER THE CLOSE OF PROCEEDINGS

**(1) There is no presumption that a late amendment to a case statement should be allowed.**

**(2) A case statement may be amended after the close of case statements if the general requirements for permission to amend are satisfied and**

**(a) there is good reason for the lateness of the amendment. The later the amendment is sought the stronger such reasons must be;**

**(b) justice to the party seeking the amendment and other parties in the litigation requires the amendment to be made; and**

**(c) permitting the amendment does not prejudice either the wider public interest in enabling other litigants to obtain justice efficiently and proportionately or affect finality in litigation disproportionately.**

**(3) Where a late amendment is very late such that it would put at risk a set trial date, it is sought at trial, after the conclusion of a trial, or on appeal, particularly strong reasons for the lateness of the amendment are required and the court must consider the strength the case.**

*Sources: ALI/UNIDROIT Principles, principle 5; ALI/UNIDROIT Reporters' Study, r 14; ELI-UNIDROIT Model Rules, rr 55, 59; CPR Pt 17.*

[39] *AON v Australian National University* [2009] HCA 27; (2009) 239 CLR 175 at [93]–[103]; *Kowalski v MMAL Staff Superannuation Fund Pty Ltd* (2009) 178 FCR 401, 414.

[40] *Elite Property Holdings Ltd v Barclays Bank Plc* [2019] EWCA Civ 20 at [41]; *Kawasaki Kisen Kaisha Ltd v James Kemball Ltd* [2021] EWCA Civ 33; [2021] 3 All ER 978 at [18]. In assessing whether an amendment has a real prospect of success the court must consider the law as it is at the time of the amendment: *Mandrake Holdings Ltd v Countrywide Assured Group Plc* [2005] EWHC 311 (Ch).

## COMMENTARY

1. This rule applies to applications to amend case statements after the close of proceedings. It applies therefore to what under the CPR and its predecessors were generally known as *'late or very late amendments'*, although that term was not used formally in the procedural rules. The CPR marked a shift in approach to such amendments. Prior to, and for some time after, its introduction, late amendments (consistently with the approach to amendments in general) were considered by reference to the approach set out in *Clarapede v Commercial Union* (1883)[41] and *Cropper v Smith* (1884).[42] Reflecting the significant shift towards rule compliance[43] and the need for disputes to be managed proportionality, late and very late amendments latterly under the CPR were subject to the approach articulated in *Swain-Mason v Mills and Reeve LLP* (2011)[44] and *Quah v Goldman Sachs International* (2015)[45] as summarised in *CNM Estates (Tolworth Tower) Ltd v Carvill-Biggs* (2023).[46] This rule codifies that approach.
2. Under the CPR, 'lateness' was properly noted as a relative concept;[47] any amendment could be construed as being late. This rule adopts a clear temporal approach to lateness. An amendment is late if it is made after the close of case statements. By definition such amendments occur at a point where both the parties and the court have utilised more of their resources than they would have done prior to that point. Amendment at this stage will therefore have an increasingly greater impact on the court's ability to effectively manage other proceedings. The later the amendment the greater such an impact, and particularly the greater the prospect that the immediate proceedings, if the amendment is granted, will draw on a disproportionate share of the court's resources to the detriment of other litigants. Hence the later the amendment the stricter the test for granting permission must be to take proper account of the need to secure systemic proportionality.[48] Under the CPR that required consideration of its overriding objective, which by analogy here requires consideration of the purposive and proportionality principles.[49] It should also be noted that the approach adopted under the CPR also gave effect to the finality and enforcement principles. The later an amendment the greater the adverse effect on achieving finality[50] and effective enforcement in good time. The same approach is taken here.
3. In the light of the above, this rule takes as its starting point that there is no presumption that a late amendment should be granted. Each amendment must be

[41] *Clarapede & Co v Commercial Union Association* (1883) 32 WR 262 at 263.

[42] *Cropper v Smith* (1884) 26 ChD 700 at 710.

[43] *Mitchell v News Group Newspapers Ltd* [2013] EWCA Civ 1537; [2014] 1 WLR 795; *Denton v TH White Ltd* [2014] EWCA Civ 906; [2014] 1 WLR 3926; J Dyson (2014).

[44] *Swain-Mason v Mills and Reeve LLP* [2011] EWCA Civ 14; [2011] 1 WLR 2735.

[45] *Quah v Goldman Sachs International* [2015] EWHC 759 (Comm).

[46] *CNM Estates (Tolworth Tower) Ltd v Carvill-Biggs* [2023] EWCA Civ 480.

[47] *Quah v Goldman Sachs International* [2015] EWHC 759 (Comm) at [38]; *CIP Properties (AIPT) Ltd v Galliford Try Infrastructure Ltd* [2015] EWHC 1345 (TCC); 160 Con LR 73 at [19].

[48] *Prudential Assurance Company Ltd v HM Revenue and Customs* [2016] EWCA Civ 37; [2017] 1 WLR 4031 at [21].

[49] H Woolf, *Access to Justice: Final Report to the Lord Chancellor on the Civil Justice System in England and Wales* (HMSO) (1996) at 24.

[50] *Nesbit Law Group LLP v Acasta European Insurance Co Ltd* [2018] EWCA Civ 268 at [44].

considered by reference to general criteria set out in rule 4 and the specific criteria set out in this rule. They must be considered consistently with the purposive principle. It will not therefore be the case, as it is with amendments in general, that permission will be granted solely on the basis that the amendment will enable the court to determine the real issues in dispute, where any prejudice caused to the opposing party by allowing the amendment can be compensated in costs. Where permission is sought for a late amendment, strong reasons justifying the grant of permission are required. This places a heavy burden on the applicant to discharge. The later the amendment is sought, the heavier the burden, ie the stronger the reasons for granting permission. In setting out those reasons, as Carr J put it, the applicant must show '*why justice to him, his opponent and other court users requires him to be able to pursue it*'.[51] Of necessity then, the justification goes beyond consideration of the impact of amendment on the immediate parties: systemic proportionality is built into the test.

4. Where an amendment comes so late it would adversely affect a trial date, amongst other things, it is viewed as coming 'very late'. Particularly strong reasons are required to justify the grant of such an amendment. Furthermore, in these cases, the stronger the prospects of success must be. Thus, the court must also, in those cases but not in cases of late amendment, consider the strengths of the case.[52] This is because, further to both the proportionality and finality principles, parties have a legitimate interest in trial dates being kept. Other litigants also have a legitimate interest in parties keeping to their trial dates: a set trial date marks the end point of proceeding's proportionate resource allocation. Rescheduling a trial date to accommodate additional work, and court time, to deal with the consequences of an amendment means those proceedings will utilise more than their proportionate share of the court's resources, and will negatively affect other litigants and their right to access an economical, efficient, and proportionate process. Similar considerations apply where an amendment is sought at trial or after judgment.[53] The reason for granting the amendment must outweigh the countervailing interests of the opposing party and other litigants. It must do so against a backdrop where, in the interests of maintaining a proportionate procedure, it undermines the court's ability to fully give effect to the accuracy principle in the proceedings where amendment is refused.[54]
5. Amendments may also be made on an appeal. An amendment raising a point of law is more likely to be permitted than one raising a new factual issue. That being said, due to the public interest in proceedings being conducted proportionately, and particularly the need to take account of the scarcity of the Court of Appeal's resources, the grant of permission in either case would require particularly cogent and strong reasons to outweigh the public interest in proportionality and finality.[55]
6. Taking a graduated approach to late and very late amendments ensures that a proportionate approach is taken to the tests for permission. It enables the court to

[51] *Quah v Goldman Sachs International* [2015] EWHC 759 (Comm) at [38(b)].

[52] *CNM Estates (Tolworth Tower) Ltd v Carvill-Biggs* [2023] EWCA Civ 480 at [76]–[77].

[53] *Chiron Corporation v Organon Teknika Ltd (No 4)* [1994] FSR 252.

[54] *Beachley Property Limited v Edgar* (CA 26 November 1996, unreported) at 30; *Flaxman-Binns v Lincolnshire County Council (Practice Note)* [2004] EWCA Civ 424; [2004] 1 WLR 2232 at [41]; *Sutradhar v Natural Environment Research Council* [2006] 4 All ER 490 at [42].

[55] *Prudential Assurance Company Ltd v HM Revenue and Customs* [2016] EWCA Civ 37; [2017] 1 WLR 4031 at [24]–[25]; *Nesbit Law Group LLP v Acasta European Insurance Co Ltd* [2018] EWCA Civ 268 at [40]–[41].

match the tests to the nature of the adverse effect on the administration of justice. This approach is to be compared with the regime for amendment set out in rules 2 and 3, which provide a more liberal regime for amendment. The difference between the two regimes is to promote early amendment, wherever possible, consistently with the economy, efficiency, and proportionality principles as well as effective dispute management.

## RULE 6.—PERMISSION TO AMEND A CASE STATEMENT TO ADD, SUBSTITUTE, OR REMOVE A PARTY

**(1) The addition or substitution of a party to proceedings may be permitted at any time, including after judgment or where a relevant limitation period has been disapplied, where**

**(a) it would enable the court to further the purposive principle by resolving one or more of the issues in dispute in the proceedings or resolve issues connected to the dispute and is desirable to do so; or**

**(b) an existing party's liability or interest in the proceedings has passed to a new party, including by succession.**

**(2) A party may be removed as a party to proceedings where their joinder will not further the purposive principle.**

**(3) Permission to add, substitute or remove a party may only be granted with-notice to existing parties to the proceedings.**

*Sources: CPR Pt 17; r 19.2; Limitation Act 1980, ss 33 and 35.*

## COMMENTARY

1. This rule complements rule 3. It is concerned with ensuring that all persons who have an interest in the proceedings are joined to them. Its primary aim is thus to give effect to the concentration and finality and certainty principles. It is also intended to further the effective management of disputes, consistently with the economy, efficiency and proportionality principles. It does so through facilitating the resolution of all issues connected with the dispute that form the basis of the proceedings.
2. Addition or substitution, the latter of which implicitly includes the removal of an existing party, may be effected by the court in a number of situations.[56] A new party may be added where, for instance, their joinder is necessary to determine all the issues arising in the dispute or to ensure that they are bound by any judgment. It may be effected so the court can resolve an issue between the current parties by determining an issue between one or more of them and the new party. Moreover, a party may be substituted if they have, for instance, succeeded to the interest, or to a liability, of an existing party to the proceedings through, for instance, inheritance. Addition may be effected where the outcome of the immediate proceedings would affect an interest of the new party. In such circumstances, not joining the new party would lead to further, separate proceedings between them and the successful party

[56] *Cameron v Hussain* [2017] EWCA Civ 366; [2018] 1 WLR 657.

in the original proceedings. Joinder through addition or substitution would thus promote the purposive principle.[57]

3. This latter issue highlights the importance of the principles of concentration, finality and certainty to questions of party joinder. All support provision of a power to secure the joinder of the right parties to proceedings so that the court can resolve all relevant issues in a single set of proceedings. It further highlights, as Zuckerman has stressed, that the ultimate test to be applied to addition or substitution is one of '*convenience*':[58] will joinder enable the court to resolve all the issues in dispute. If it will, it is likely to be in the interests of justice to permit addition or order substitution, even where addition or substitution is to be effected post-judgment.[59] A further aspect of this can be seen as addition or substitution is in the interests of justice where it promotes effective dispute management. In such situations, it is not simply convenient in the interests of justice to effect the addition or substitution from the parties' perspective: it is necessary in the interests of justice as it promotes systemic proportionality. This is particularly the case where addition is concerned, as joinder of parties through addition may enable multiple disputes to be more economically, efficiently and proportionately resolved through one set of proceedings where several individual claimants might otherwise bring separate claims against the same defendant arising from the same cause of action.[60]
4. Addition or substitution can be effected after the expiry of a limitation period, such as those imposed under the Landlord and Tenant Act 1954, Limitation Act 1980, or Foreign Limitation Periods Act 1984. This can occur either under this rule or in limited circumstances under rule 7.[61] It is to be effected under this rule where a relevant limitation period has been disapplied. This may occur, for instance, in personal injury claims.[62] In such circumstances, the general rule, in rule 6(1)(a) and (c), concerning addition or substitution should apply, ie it may be effected where it furthers the purposive principle and is desirable.[63] This is a logical approach as the question whether the limitation period applies will have been determined by reference to the substantive law. If it has been disapplied, limitation is not in issue and there is no basis to take the situation outside the general rule.
5. Rule 6(1) sets out the test for granting permission to amend case statements to add or substitute a party. It applies the general requirement that permission be granted where, consistently with the purposive principle, it facilitates the resolution of the issues in dispute and the grant of permission is desirable.[64] This particularly enables those persons whose rights are likely to be affected by the proceedings, and more specifically any judgment, to have effective notice of the proceedings and issues, and to be heard on them.[65]

[57] *Nottinghamshire CC v Bottomley* [2010] EWCA Civ 756; [2010] Med LR 407 at [20], making clear that the power to add or substitute a party should be construed broadly.

[58] Zuckerman (2021) at 720.

[59] *River Thames Society v First Secretary of State* [2006] EWHC 2829 (Admin); [2007] JPL 782; *Dunwoody Sports Marketing v Prescott* [2007] EWCA Civ 461; [2007] 1 WLR 2343 at [23].

[60] *Hounslow LBC v Cumar* [2012] EWCA Civ 1426; [2013] HLR 17 at [11].

[61] *River Thames Society v First Secretary of State* [2006] EWHC 2829 (Admin); [2007] JPL 782 at [3]–[6].

[62] Limitation Act 1980, s 33.

[63] Under the CPR this remained an open question; *Pawley v Whitecross Dental Care Ltd* [2021] EWCA Civ 1827 at [48].

[64] *Re Pablo Star Ltd* [2017] EWCA Civ 1768; [2018] 1 WLR 738 at [48].

[65] *Re Pablo Star Ltd* [2017] EWCA Civ 1768; [2018] 1 WLR 738 at [60].

6. Rule 6(2), again consistently with the purposive provision, enables a party that was joined to proceedings to be removed as such where their joinder will not or no longer assist the resolution of issues in dispute.[66]
7. Various factors ought to be taken into account when considering whether to grant permission under this rule.[67] Relevant considerations where permission is sought to add or substitute a party include whether joinder will better enable the court to resolve the issue(s) or the dispute. In *Molavi v Hibbert* (2020),[68] for instance, the party to be joined could give evidence as a witness and hence their joinder would not improve the court's ability to resolve the dispute and was not permitted. On the other hand, it may be desirable to join a principal to proceedings brought or defended by their agent as that could better enable matters in dispute to be resolved. Where permission is sought to resolve connected issues, relevant considerations include whether there is an issue connected to the dispute, which need not be a cause of action,[69] between an existing party and the party to be joined. The connection could, for instance, be evidential.[70] It could be that the outcome of the proceedings would affect the party to be joined, such that it would be beneficial for them to be bound, as a party, to any judgment given. As was stressed in *Molavi*, whether there is a connection justifying joinder is a matter of fact to be determined on a case-by-case basis.
8. In assessing whether it is desirable to grant permission a variety of further factors could potentially be relevant, eg to what extent would joinder increase the cost or complexity of the proceedings and the time taken to resolve them? Would such an increase outweigh the benefit to be gained from the joinder? To what extent would it prejudice existing parties to the proceedings if it was permitted? To what extent would it benefit or adversely affect the court's ability to properly manage the dispute consistently with the proportionality and finality principles by, for instance, extending the scope of the proceedings and issues in dispute? In other words, what affect would joinder have on systemic proportionality?
9. Similar considerations apply to the question of whether to remove a party. Is the existing party's continued joinder necessary to enable the court to determine an issue or issues in the dispute? Does its continued joinder render the proceedings unnecessarily complex or unnecessarily add to the costs and time of resolution? Where there is a negative answer to such questions their continued joinder would be unnecessary and they ought to be removed from the proceedings.
10. Finally, it should be noted that joinder of parties is an aspect of party autonomy. It is again necessary therefore to inform both existing parties and any new party of any proposed order under this rule.[71] Notice is particularly necessary where a new claimant is to be joined, as they cannot be joined without their consent. Notice is also important for all existing parties where a new defendant is to be added or a

[66] CPR r 19.2(3).

[67] *Gaia River SA v Behike Ltd* [2020] EWHC 2981 (Comm); *Molavi v Hibbert* [2020] EWHC 121 (Ch); [2020] 4 WLR 46.

[68] *Molavi v Hibbert* [2020] EWHC 121 (Ch); [2020] 4 WLR 46.

[69] *XYZ v Various (Including Transform Medical Group (Cs) Ltd & Spire Healthcare Ltd)* [2014] EWHC 4056 (QB) at [22].

[70] *Dunlop Haywords (DHL) Ltd v Erinaceous Insurance Services Ltd* [2009] EWCA Civ 354; [2009] Lloyd's Rep IR 464.

[71] *Molavi v Hibbert* [2020] EWHC 121 (Ch); [2020] 4 WLR 46 at [43] citing RSC Ord 15, r 6; *Tildesley v Harper* (1876) 3 Ch D 277; *In re Colbeck* (1888) 36 WR 259.

defendant is to be removed or substituted. This is because it is, as a general rule, for the claimant as a matter of party autonomy to determine against whom they pursue proceedings.[72] They should thus be given notice to enable them to make representations on the question of addition, substitution or removal. It is equally important, from a defendant's perspective, as a matter of due notice, for them to know if they are to be added to or removed from proceedings. Where an application is not contested the court may determine it without a hearing. A contested application for permission should, however, be determined at a dispute management hearing.

## RULE 7.—PERMISSION TO AMEND A CASE STATEMENT AFTER THE EXPIRY OF A RELEVANT LIMITATION PERIOD

**(1) A case statement may be amended to add a new, or substitute a, cause of action after the expiry of a relevant limitation period. Amendment may be made if that cause of action arises from the same or substantially the same facts as an existing cause of action in the proceedings.**

**(2) A case statement may be amended to correct the name of an existing party after the expiry of a relevant limitation period. Permission may not be granted unless the party initially named was named by mistake and that mistake has not reasonably mislead other parties to the proceedings as to the misnamed party's identity.**

**(3) A case statement may be amended to add or substitute a new party after the expiry of a relevant limitation period where**

**(a) the original party was wrongly named in the proceedings albeit they were properly identified by description and the error has not reasonably misled other parties to the proceedings as to the wrongly named party's identity;**

**(b) the addition or substitution of a new party is necessary in the interests of justice to enable the court to resolve the proceedings; or**

**(c) the substitution is required by succession.**

*Sources: CPR Pt 17; rr 19.2, 19.4, 19.5, PD19.2, para 2; Limitation Act 1980, ss 33 and 35.*

## COMMENTARY

1. After the expiry of a relevant limitation period, the public interest in finality in litigation generally takes precedence over other public interests. In limited circumstances, it is, however, well-established that case statements can be amended after the expiry of a relevant limitation period. Amendment is justifiable in those circumstances not because there is a derogation from the finality principle, but rather because, given the nature of the amendment, that principle is not properly engaged.
2. A new cause of action may be added or substituted for an existing one after the expiry of a limitation period if it arises from the same facts as an existing cause of action pleaded in the proceedings. In such a case the new cause of action can be understood to have been inherent in the proceedings when they were issued within the limitation period. The amendment simply makes patent what was latent. This is a consequence of the adoption of Fact Pleading, which is inherently not cause of action specific. The same material facts could and do often give rise to multiple different causes of action.

[72] *Dolfus-Mieg et Compagnie SA v Bank of England (No 2)* [1951] Ch 33 at 38.

Material facts that give rise to a claim in contract can, for instance, equally give rise to claims in tort and/or in unjust enrichment. By seeking to amend a case statement to add a claim for unjust enrichment in the alternative or additional to a claim for breach of contract, a claimant would simply be extrapolating from that which the defendant already had notice of prior to the expiry of any limitation period.

3. Where parties are concerned the approach is subject to greater restrictions. Clarification or correction of a party's name may not be permitted if it would effectively bring a new party into the proceedings, thus taking from them the benefit of an expired limitation period. Hence clarification can only take place if it is to correct a mistake as to a party's name and the mistake did not reasonably mislead anyone as to their identity. Correction in such a situation does not change who is a party. As such there is no question of an accrued limitation right being impinged upon.
4. In a similar vein, addition or substitution so as to add a new party or replace an existing party, can only properly be effected where there was a mistake as to the name of the party to be joined to the proceedings, ie the claimant always intended to bring proceedings against the person to be added or substituted but failed to do so effectively by mis-naming them and thus commencing proceedings against the wrong person.[73] To effect substitution in reliance on this provision, it must be clear from the proceedings that the person to be added or substituted was originally intended to be joined to the proceedings.[74] In this way post-limitation joinder is only available against new parties who would reasonably have expected to be the subject to proceedings before the expiry of the limitation period. Thus rule 7(3)(a) protects the accrued limitation rights of those who would not reasonably have expected to be the subject of proceedings. This approach both furthers the finality principle where such individuals are concerned, but does so by striking a proper balance between it and the general access principle as it applies to the party seeking to effect the addition or substitution of an individual who ought reasonably to have expected to be joined as a party and because, for instance, they otherwise had due notice of the potential proceedings that were commenced against someone else in error.[75]
5. The other two bases on which post-limitation addition or substitution is permissible are also of limited scope. First, they apply where a claim could not be carried on effectively without substitution because an existing claimant did not have standing to bring proceedings, eg where a liquidator or administrator of a company was to be substituted by the company itself,[76] or where a new party has succeeded to the interest or liability of an existing party through, for instance, inheritance or bankruptcy.[77] In both situations proceedings were properly brought against a defendant within limitation. In the first type of case, the substitute claimant was, through its liquidator or administrator, before the court, and hence it can be said to be in the interests of justice to permit the substitution. In the second type of case, the party to be substituted has, as a matter of law, taken over the existing party's interest in the proceedings and ought therefore to be joined to them.

[73] *Gregson v Channel Four Television Corp* [2000] CP Rep 60 at [18]–[29].

[74] *The Sardinia Sulcis* [1991] 1 Lloyds Rep 201; *Kesslar v Moore & Tibbits (A firm)* [2004] EWCA Civ 1551; *Adelson v Associated Newspapers Ltd* [2007] EWCA Civ 701; [2008] 1 WLR 585 at [55].

[75] *Parsons v George* [2004] EWCA Civ 912; [2004] 1 WLR 3264 at [8]–[9].

[76] CPR r 19.5(3)(b); *Irwin v Lynch* [2010] EWCA Civ 1153; [2011] 1 WLR 1364; *Roberts v Gill & Co* [2010] UKSC 22; [2011] 1 AC 240.

[77] CPR r 19.5(3)(c).

## RULE 8.—PERMISSION TO AMEND A CASE STATEMENT TO CHANGE PARTY CAPACITY

**(1) Permission to amend a case statement to change the capacity of an existing party to proceedings may be granted where the party had that capacity at the time proceedings commenced or later acquired it and amendment would further the purposive principle.**

**(2) Where a party commences proceedings in a capacity that they do not have but later acquire, permission to amend may be granted where it would further the purposive principle. That the party did not have capacity to commence proceedings prior to the amendment is a procedural irregularity that is cured by the amendment.**

*Sources:* RSC Ord 20, r 5; *CPR r 17.4.4; Limitation Act 1980, s 35.*

## COMMENTARY

1. This rule restates the power to amend a case statement to change an existing party's capacity that was set out in both RSC Ord 20, r 5 and CPR r 17.4. Such an amendment can change the party's capacity to one that it had at the time proceedings were commenced. It also provides for a party to change the capacity in which it is a party to one that it has gained consequent to proceedings having commenced. Either a claimant or defendant may make an application under this rule.
2. Under the CPR there was uncertainty whether this power could be used to amend party capacity where a claimant commenced proceedings in a capacity that they did not have at that time. This arose typically in circumstances were an individual commenced proceedings as a personal representative of a deceased before the grant of administration.[78] In such cases, it was held that the proceedings were a nullity that could not be cured. Therefore, there was no basis on which to permit a later change of capacity. Under this rule, the commencement of proceedings in such a situation is not treated as a nullity. Consistently with the purposive principle, and specifically the need to properly manage the court's resources proportionately, rule 8(2) deems such a situation to be a procedural irregularity. The error can thus be cured by an amendment. By taking effect as from the date when the proceedings were issued, the change in capacity to the after-acquired one, deems the party to have had the capacity at the date on which proceedings commenced (rule 9(1)).
3. Maintaining the CPR's nullity approach would require, assuming limitation was not in issue, the proceedings having to be recommenced, which would achieve little more than to add unnecessary delay and increase litigation cost.[79] It would be to maintain an unnecessary technicality, which is not justified by reference to the need to ensure that proceedings were commenced by an '*appropriate claimant*'.[80] If the court is in a position to properly amend the party's capacity, the claim will have been brought by an appropriate claimant. Where limitation is in issue, it would remain open to a defendant to contest the grant of permission to amend on that basis.

[78] *Ingall v Moran* [1944] KB 160; *Millburn-Snell v Evans* [2011] EWCA Civ 577; [2012] 1 WLR 41; *Haq v Singh* [2001] 1 WLR 1594; *Roberts v Gill & Co* [2010] UKSC 22; [2011] 1 AC 240.

[79] It is also an approach consistent with the spirit of RSC Ord 2, r 1; R Scott (1999) Vol 1 at 2/0/2, 2/1/2.

[80] *Millburn-Snell v Evans* [2011] EWCA Civ 577; [2012] 1 WLR 41 at [41].

## SECTION 3: EFFECT OF AMENDMENT

### RULE 9.—TIME WHEN AMENDMENT TAKES EFFECT

**(1) Unless the court orders otherwise so as to give effect to the purposive principle and except as provided by legislation, amendments take effect from the date of the case statement or document not from the date on which the amendment is made.**
**(2) Amendments to add a new claimant to proceedings take effect from the date on which they consent to be joined to proceedings.**
**(3) Amendments to add a new defendant to proceedings take effect from the date on which the defendant is given notice of those proceedings.**

*Sources: CPR Pts 17 and 19, PD19A, paras 2 and 3; Limitation Act 1980, s 35.*

### COMMENTARY

1. Amendments generally take effect not from the date on which they are made, but from the date of the document that they amend. An amendment to a particulars of claim, for instance, takes effect not from the date of the amendment, but from the date when the particulars of claim was issued. The date of the amendment '*relates back*' to the date of the original document. This rule sets out three provisions; one of general application, subject to exceptions; one related to new claimants; and one related to new defendants.[81]
2. The general rule gives effect to the doctrine of relation-back for the principled reason that the amendment stands in the place of the original. An amendment to a case statement does not result in a new case statement being issued or new proceedings being commenced. It alters the content of the existing case statement or proceedings.[82] However, exceptions to this general rule are permissible and in some cases are necessary.
3. One such exception arises where an amendment adds a new cause of action that has arisen between the parties after service of the relevant case statement. Obviously, the date of the case statement cannot stand as the date of the new cause of action: the former will predate the cause of action having arisen. At one time in such a circumstance a new claim could not be joined by way of amendment.[83] Separate proceedings had to be issued. Rule 9(1) takes a more purposive approach. If permission would be granted to amend the particulars of claim to add the new cause of action, the court can under its discretion in rule 9(1), provide that the doctrine of relation-back does not apply. The date of the amendment stands as the date on which it takes effect. In this way, effect can be given to the economy and proportionality principles, as well as the concentration principle.
4. The second main exception to the general rule arises under the Limitation Act 1980. Its section 35 makes specific provision for certain new claims to be deemed to be '*separate actions*' when raised in the course of existing proceedings. It specifically provides that the general rule applies except in respect of a '*new claim*' that is '*made*

[81] P Coulson (ed), *Civil Procedure 2024* (Sweet & Maxwell, 2024) Vol 1 at 17.3.3.
[82] *Sneade v Wotherton Barytes and Lead Mining Company Limited* [1904] 1 KB 295 at 297.
[83] *Halliard Property Co Ltd v Jack Segal Ltd* [1978] 1 WLR 377.

*in or by way of third party proceedings*'.[84] In such a case the effective date is the date on which those third party proceedings were commenced. Section 35(2) defines a new claim as any claim of set-off, any counterclaim, and any claim that involves the addition or substitution of a new cause of action or new party. Third party proceedings are defined as '*any proceedings brought in the course of any action by any party to the action against a person not previously a party to the action, other than proceedings brought by joining any such person as defendant to any claim already made in the original action by the party bringing the proceedings.*'

5. Turning to the second and third provisions in the rule, first, an amendment joining a new claimant takes effect from the date on which they consent to be joined to the proceedings. This reflects the voluntary nature of participation by claimants in proceedings. Claims commence only when the claimant issues them. By consenting to join proceedings a claimant is, in effect, 'issuing' proceedings in so far as they are concerned. Secondly, and consistently with Part 7, rule 2(2), where a defendant is joined to proceedings, they do so as from their being given notice, ie the amended case statement is served on them. This reflects the need for defendants to be given effective notice of proceedings before they come under the court's jurisdiction.

[84] Limitation Act 1980, s 35(1)(b).

# PART 10
# SERVICE

## SECTION 1: GENERAL

1. This Part concerns service of procedural documents. The development of the approach to service can be divided into five phases, with the rules in this Part forming the suggested fifth phase.[1]
2. Initially, service of process required, at common law, the defendant to be produced in court via a writ of capias. This initial phase, which guaranteed notice and participation in an adversarial process, gave way in the 19th century to a second phase, which also sought to guarantee due notice of proceedings. It required defendants to be served with process personally via a writ of summons.[2] The third phase properly began in 1979 where postal service was generally permitted. It had previously been permitted, in limited circumstances, in the County Courts where the plaintiff could certify that they had reason to believe that service by post would bring the summons (the initiating process) to the defendant's attention.[3] It had also been permitted in the High Court in limited circumstances as a form of substituted (alternative) service.[4] As Zuckerman notes, permitting postal service generally had first been proposed in the 19th century by Bentham.[5]
3. The fourth phase was introduced by CPR Pt 6. It broadly adopted the approach to service taken in the County Courts. It also simplified it by consolidating all service rules into a single Part of the CPR. It also contained provisions permitting service to be effected in a variety of different ways, eg service by fax, by DX, and, where there was prior agreement, by email.[6] It also moved away from the concept that for service to be effective documents had to come to the actual attention of the recipient. To introduce certainty into the service rules irrebuttable deemed service provisions were included in the CPR. This was, however, problematic as it meant that defendants could not demonstrate that they had not, in fact, received notice of proceedings and, as required by the due notice principle, have any default judgment against them set aside as of right. Consequently, CPR Pt 6 was a source of a significant amount of satellite litigation in the CPR's first decade.[7] New and far more complex service rules

[1] This short summary is drawn from A Zuckerman, *Civil Procedure* (Butterworths, 2003) at 142–146.
[2] Uniformity of Process Act 1832, s 1.
[3] CCR (1936) Ord 8, r 8(2).
[4] RSC (1875) Ord IX, r 15 and Ord X; RSC (1965) Ord 65, r 4; Companies Act 1948, s 437(1).
[5] A Zuckerman (2003) at 143.
[6] CPR rr 6.3, 6.20.
[7] Eg *Vinos v Marks & Spencer* [2001] 3 All ER 784; *Infantino v MacLean* [2001] 3 All ER 802; *Godwin v Swindon BC* [2001] EWCA Civ 1478; [2002] 1 WLR 997; *Anderton v Clwyd CC* [2002] EWCA Civ 933; [2002] 1 WLR 3174; *Cranfield v Bridgegrove Ltd* [2003] EWCA Civ 656; [2003] 1 WLR 2441; *Akram v Adam* [2004] EWCA Civ 1601; [2005] 1 WLR 2762; *Collier v Williams* [2006] EWCA Civ 20; [2006] WLR 1945; *Kuenyehia v International Hospitals* [2006] EWCA Civ 21; [2006] CP Rep 34; *Hoddinott v Persimmon Homes (Wessex) Ltd* [2007] EWCA Civ 1203; [2008] 1 WLR 806.

*A Model Civil Procedure Code for England and Wales.* John Sorabji, Oxford University Press. © John Sorabji 2024.
DOI: 10.1093/oso/9780192848680.003.0011

were introduced in 2008 to ameliorate that issue. They continue to generate satellite litigation.[8]

4. The rules in this Part are designed to move beyond the fourth phase of service and make electronic or digital service the default means to effect service of both case statements and other procedural documents. As noted in the United States as long ago as 1980 and where greater consideration of the use of electronic and now digital service has been given,

   *Courts ... cannot be blind to changes and advances in technology. No longer do we live in a world where communications are conducted solely by mail carried by fast sailing clipper or steam ships. ... No longer must process be mailed to a defendant's door when he can receive complete notice at an electronic terminal inside his very office, even when the door is steel and bolted shut.*[9]

   So far, the English and Welsh civil justice system while not being blind to changes and advances in technology has almost been as reticent to embrace it as it was to embrace postal service.

5. These rules embrace digital technology as a means to effect service. They do so by making service by the court via its digital dispute management system the default service method. This is to be possible because of the introduction of digital dispute management accounts, which will provide the means by which the court will effect document service on the parties in a way that can reasonably guarantee they will come to their notice. Even where service via this method is not used, digital technology will remain the primary vehicle for service, with it being effected by, for instance, email, social media platforms (Facebook, WhatsApp, Twitter, etc),[10] blockchain etc.[11] Only where digital service methods are unavailable will traditional service methods, whether postal service or personal service etc, be used.

6. Adopting an approach where service via the digital dispute management system is the default carries with it several advantages. Where both claimant and defendant have a digital dispute management account it guarantees actual service[12] as well as facilitating a clear deemed service date. It is thus an effective means to satisfy all service's functions, as defined in rule 1. It also ensures that parties can be sure that the documents received are not spam or some form of malicious communication. Where other forms of digital service method are used, steps will, however, need to be taken to ensure that the recipient can be confident that the documents served are genuine and the sender is either the court or an individual properly authorised to serve procedural documents. Steps will also need to be taken to ensure that such alternative digital methods are reasonably capable of providing actual notice, ie by

[8] *Barton v Wright Hassal LLP* [2018] UKSC 12; [2018] 1 WLR 1119; *Kennedy v National Trust for Scotland* [2019] EWCA Civ 648; [2020] QB 663; *Axnoller Events Limited v Brake* [2022] EWHC 1162 (Ch); *Ideal Shopping Direct Ltd v Mastercard Inc* [2022] EWCA Civ 14.

[9] *New Eng Merch Nat'l Bank v Iran Power Generation & Transmission Co*, 495 F Supp 73, 81 (SDNY 1980) cited in K Knapp, *#serviceofprocess @socialmedia:* 'Accepting Social Media for Service of Process in the 21st Century' (2014) 74 La L Rev 547 at 555.

[10] *Gray v Hurley* [2019] EWHC 1636 (QB) (service by WhatsApp).

[11] Service by Twitter was first effected in 2009. Service by Facebook was first permitted in 2012. Service by Blockchain via an NFT (non-fungible token) was first permitted in 2022: *D'Aloia v Binance Holdings* [2022] EWHC 1723 (Ch). On the first two see, K Rushton, *Legal claims can now be served via Facebook in Britain, after a landmark ruling in the English High Court* (Daily Telegraph, 21 February 2012).

[12] K Knapp, *#serviceofprocess @socialmedia:* 'Accepting Social Media for Service of Process in the 21st Century' (2014) 74 La L Rev 547 at 563 and following.

the claimant providing evidence that it was the recipient's social media account and that the recipient uses it regularly.[13] Such evidence may become increasingly available through the use of machine learning tools, which would enable parties to search the internet effectively to identify the intended recipient and effective means by which they could be served.[14]

7. In addition to the shift to a more technological approach, the other main difference between this Part and the CPR is that it contains nine rules in contrast to CPR Pt 6's 52 rules and two Practice Directions. There are two main reasons for this. The rules here, like the initial 1999 version of CPR Pt 6, do not provide two essentially discrete codes of procedure: one for service of claim forms and the other for service of other documents. They do not therefore have numerous rules across the two sets of provision that are essentially identical. There is little justification for such procedural repetition. Any necessary differences between approaches taken to service of the two categories of document can be dealt with via discrete rules. More significantly, the rules and practice directions within the CPR set out a substantial amount of technical detail. CPR PD 6B, for instance, sets out the types of claim where service out of the jurisdiction may be effected, the documents that need to be served where claims are served out of the jurisdiction, and lists the time limits for responding to claim forms and application notices. In respect of the latter, specific time limits are set out for over 100 jurisdictions. All of this type of detail could, with ease, be set out within the court's digital procedure, with parties directed to the appropriate requirements depending on the cause of action and where and upon whom service is to be effected, and the appropriate time limit etc applied as a digital default. Digitisation of process thus provides the means to not only simplify the rules and how service is effected, at an overarching Code-level, but it also means that the mechanics of service that currently are set out in great detail within the CPR can be instantiated in the digital procedure. In both cases, the process for service can, it is intended, be put into effect in the simple and straightforward manner that the CPR had itself intended consistently with the aim of achieving a properly intelligible and accessible procedure.[15]

## RULE 1.—SCOPE AND PURPOSE

**This Part concerns the provision of procedural documents to parties, non-parties and the court. It primarily gives effect to the due notice, adversariality and participatory principles. It further gives effect to the digital procedure and accountability principle. It also requires the court administration to give effect to the digital access principle.**

*Sources: ALI/UNIDROIT Principles, principle 5; ALI/UNIDROIT Reporters' Study, r 7; ELI-UNIDROIT Model Rules, Part VI; CPR Pt 6.*

## COMMENTARY

1. The rules in this Part govern the procedure through which procedural documents are provided to the court and served on parties and non-parties to proceedings.

[13] K Rushton (2012).

[14] Z Niesel, 'Machine Learning and the New Civil Procedure' (2020) 73 SMU L Rev 493 at 533.

[15] R Scott, *Supreme Court Practice 1999* (Sweet & Maxwell, 1999) at 41; *Collier v Williams* [2006] EWCA Civ 20; [2006] WLR 1945 at [1].

They are of fundamental importance to any procedural code. They, first, provide the basis on which the court's jurisdiction over parties and non-parties is established. While jurisdiction over claimants begins when they commence proceedings[16] it is established over defendants, subject to any jurisdictional challenge, when particulars of claim are formally provided to them via the service process. Secondly, they are the primary means by which any civil procedural code gives effect to the due notice principle. For that reason, service has rightly been described as going '*to the root of our conceptions of the proper procedure in litigation*'.[17]

2. Without due notice, via service of case statements, parties would be unaware of the fact of proceedings, the nature of the claim pursued, of any defence and the nature of that defence. Service of case statements and procedural documents generally, whether they be application notices, evidence, court orders, or judgments, are equally the means by which the adversariality and participation principles are given effect. Without service of such documents, parties would not have reasonable time within which to consider their position and the arguments advanced by other parties. Nor would they have time to consider what evidence to obtain, which witnesses, including expert witnesses, may need to be secured and what evidence needed to be disclosed. Only with timely service of the various procedural documents are parties able to put themselves in the position to conduct and participate in an adversarial process effectively. Looked at more broadly, service by giving effect to these procedural principles is also the means by which parties can put themselves in the position to best secure the accurate adjudication of their dispute or, if possible, a settlement based on a full and proper appraisal of the issues, arguments and evidence relevant to their dispute. It is for these reasons that service can and has been properly described as '*a fundamental requirement of justice*'.[18] It is the pivot around which implementation of all the procedural principles that underpin a fair process turn. Moving to a digital approach to service ought to ensure this pivot operates more effectively and certainly in future.

3. Service also serves further purposes. It promotes finality in litigation. This is achieved by the service rules, and specifically the rules concerning deemed dates of service, which provide a certain date when service is formally, rather than actually effected. By providing such certainty the rules enable parties to know, without a doubt, whether particulars of claim were served within the time limit for service. Failure to serve them within the time limit would bring the proceedings to an end, subject to the possibility of a fresh claim being issued if any relevant statutory limitation period had not expired. Thus, the deemed service rules are a means by which procedural limitation periods are given effect and statutory ones can also be given effect.

4. Certainty provided by the deemed service dates plays a further role. It is the basis on which effective dispute management can be implemented.[19] It does this by providing definitive dates when procedural obligations have been carried out and others need to be carried out. The application of deemed service dates for service of

[16] Traditionally known as filing: CPR r 2.3(1).

[17] *Craig v Kanseen* [1943] KB 256 at 262; *Cameron v Liverpool Victoria Insurance Co Ltd* [2019] UKSC 6; [2019] 1 WLR 1471 at [17].

[18] A Zuckerman, *Zuckerman on Civil Procedure—Principles of Practice* (Sweet & Maxwell, 2021) at 221 citing *White v Weston* [1968] 2 QB 647.

[19] *Anderton v Clwyd CC* [2002] EWCA Civ 933; [2002] 1 WLR 3174 at [36]. A Zuckerman (2021) at 222–223.

the particulars of claim, for instance, gives certainty for obtaining default judgment. It, and equivalent deemed service dates for other procedural documents, provide a certain basis to determine if and when procedural obligations have fallen due, such as the time by which a defence needs to be filed and served. They are also then the means by which the court can determine when automatic reminders should be sent to parties concerning compliance with upcoming procedural deadlines. Finally, they are thus also a means by which party co-operation with effective dispute management can be promoted.

## RULE 2.—GENERAL

**(1) Procedural documents shall be provided to the court and served on parties and, where relevant, non-parties in accordance with the rules in this Part.**

**(2) Procedural documents include, case statements, documents amending case statements, evidence, and evidentiary statements, application notices, notices of appeal and responses to notices of appeal, and any other document relevant to the proceedings.**

*Sources: ELI-UNIDROIT Model Rules, rr 68, 80; CPR Pt 6, Section II and Section III.*

## COMMENTARY

1. This rule states the general rule that procedural documents shall be provided to the court and served on parties and relevant non-parties. It also provides a non-exhaustive list of procedural documents, the most important of which are case statements, application notices and notices of appeal and responses to them. Service of such documents is the means by which the Code gives effect to the due notice principle. It also gives effect to the right to be represented, as that too depends on being given effective notice of the fact, nature and content of proceedings and any applications made within them.[20] Evidentiary statements refer to witness statements, witness summaries and expert reports.
2. The rule does not draw a distinction between service of case statements and other documents. This is intended to ensure that the rules on service are as simple as possible and simpler in approach than either the CPR or its predecessors. Simplification can particularly be achieved through the development and use of digital technology, such that digital court-based service should become the default approach. By using a court-based dispute management system to serve documents, the three aims of service (actual notice, deemed notice, effective procedural timetabling) can more straightforwardly be achieved. Digital service can, particularly, give greater certainty in terms of actual and deemed notice. Digital date and time stamps can show when documents were sent. They can show delivery and receipt. And, they are able to form the basis of effective timetabling as such data can be used automatically by the dispute management system to calculate deemed service dates and, via that, plan the procedural timetable, not least through the use of digital scheduling tools.[21]

[20] *R v London Quarter Sessions Appeal Committee, ex parte Rossi* [1956] 1 QB 682 at 691 and 696.

[21] ELI-UNIDROIT Model Rules, r 74 commentary.

# SECTION 2: PROVIDING PROCEDURAL DOCUMENTS TO THE COURT AND PARTIES

## RULE 3.—RESPONSIBILITY FOR PROVIDING THE COURT WITH PROCEDURAL DOCUMENTS

**(1) Parties, including non-parties, are responsible for filing with the court all relevant procedural documents.**

**(2) Where parties have created a digital dispute management account during the pre-action phase of dispute management documents will be filed through it. Otherwise all procedural documents will be filed with the court via a digital dispute management account, which must be created**

**(a) by a claimant at the time they initiate proceedings;**

**(b) by any other party or non-party to proceedings at the time they provide the court with their response to either the first procedural document or other communication concerning the proceedings they receive.**

**(3) Exceptionally, parties may, with the court's permission, file procedural documents through the non-digital procedure.**

**(4) Where a procedural document must be provided to the court on a date when the court is closed, that date is deemed to be the first subsequent date when the court is open.**

*Sources: ALI/UNIDROIT Principles, principle 5; ALI/UNIDROIT Reporters' Study, r 7; ELI-UNIDROIT Model Rules, r 71; CPR rr 2.8(5), 6.21.*

## COMMENTARY

1. This rule is a product of logic, party autonomy, effective dispute management, and efficiency. It states the general rule that it is the responsibility of a party, or non-party, who is in possession or control of a procedural document to ensure that it is provided to the court. That person will be in the best position to do so, and in many cases will be the only person able to do so.

2. This rule adopts as the default position that the English and Welsh courts ought to have in place fully-operational digital management systems that enable all documents to be uploaded electronically via digital dispute management accounts. It can then ensure that those documents are accessible to the court, relevant parties, and non-parties and, in so far as they are accessible to the public under the publicity principle, to the public. A digital by default approach in this way is an extrapolation of the introduction of CE-File,[22] the Online Civil Money Claims,[23] and County Court Online pilots.[24] A fully digitised dispute management system based on individual party and non-party dispute management accounts is a reasonable, and to be expected if not inevitable, extension of these developments.[25] A non-digital procedure may, however, be used with the court's permission by parties who are unable to use the digital procedure effectively.

[22] CPR PD51O—The Electronic Working Pilot Scheme and https://www.gov.uk/guidance/ce-file-system-information-and-support-advice.

[23] CPR PD51R—Online Civil Money Claims Pilot Scheme.

[24] CPR PD51S—The County Court Online Pilot Scheme. CPR PD510, and CPR PD51R, and PD 51V.

[25] Z Loebl, *Designing Online Courts—The Future of Justice is Open to All* (Walters Kluwer, 2019) at 39 to 54.

3. The rule is predicated on the assumption that both claimant and defendant will have engaged in the pre-action dispute resolution process and will, as a consequence, already have set up digital dispute management accounts. Where they have not done so this rule sets the requirement for parties, and also non-parties engaged in proceedings to create their own accounts. This rule therefore serves a wider purpose than effective document management. It ensures that effect is given to the digital procedure and digital access principles.
4. Finally, the rule codifies the rule in *Kaur v S Russell & Sons Ltd* (1973),[26] concerning the provision of documents to the court on a date when the court is closed. When a limitation period or procedural time limit expires on such a day, it would be unjust for a party to lose their entitlement to provide the court with documents on it. Consequently, where the last date for providing the court with a document falls on a day when the court is closed (a Saturday, Sunday, public or bank holiday), it can be provided to the court on the first date thereafter when it is open.

## RULE 4.—COURT OR PARTY SERVICE

**(1) Except where parties agree on a method of service, the court is responsible for serving procedural documents on parties in England and Wales, Scotland and Northern Ireland. The court may authorise service to be effected on its behalf.**
**(2) Service may also be effected by any method authorised by statute. Personal service may not be effected by or against the Crown.**
**(3) Service by the court shall be effected through the digital dispute management system, except where alternative provision is made in another rule.**
**(4) Where a document cannot be served through the digital dispute management system or where the court authorises service to be effected by a party, non-party, or third party, service may be effected by any method that is reasonably likely to bring the procedural document to the intended recipient's attention. The method authorised must be cost-effective and proportionate.**
**(5) Where parties agree a service method or where service is effected by a person authorised to do so by the court, the parties or the authorised person must provide the court with a certificate, verified by a statement of truth, stating when and how service was effected and the deemed date of service.**
**(6) Only a sealed copy of a case statement may be served validly. Non-compliance may be cured as a procedural error.**

*Sources: ELI-UNIDROIT Model Rules, rr 74, 78; CPR rr 6.11, 6.15, 6.27, 6.40(2).*

## COMMENTARY

1. The aim of service is to bring a procedural document to the intended recipient's intention. Service must therefore be carried out by a method that is reasonably likely to achieve that end to give effect to the due notice principle and, where a particulars of claim is concerned, thus found the court's jurisdiction. This rule adopts a dual approach to this analogous to that adopted under the CPR.[27]

[26] *Ex parte Saffery* (1877) 5 ChD 365; *Kaur v S Russell & Sons Ltd* [1973] QB 336; *Matthews v Sedman* [2019] EWCA Civ 475; [2020] Ch 85; CPR r 2.8(5).
[27] CPR r 6.40(2).

2. Primary responsibility for service lies with the court through the digital dispute management system. This ought to be effected most efficiently through the development of a digital court website or digital application (app).[28] The general rule may, however, be displaced where an alternative approach is required by specific provision, eg where an order for committal to prison for contempt of court is to be served. The court may also authorise service to be carried out on its behalf. It may, therefore, authorise a party or non-party,[29] including a process server or other professional, to effect service on its behalf. Where the court authorises service to be carried out on its behalf the method chosen must be cost-effective and proportionate.
3. The rule also maintains the position that parties may agree a method of service between themselves.[30] Party agreement may thus form part of a procedural agreement between contract parties through which they agree a streamlined approach to dispute management. Such agreement may also, consistently with effective dispute management and the co-operation principle, be a means by which parties can both guarantee actual notice through the service method chosen, reduce the cost of service to the court through not involving it in the process, and reduce the prospect of disputes over service. Consequently, it may reduce the cost and time taken up with serving documents.
4. Rule 4 also reflects the fact that there may be circumstances were statute requires service to be effected in a specific way or, as in the case of service on the Crown, prohibits the use of certain service methods.[31] More significantly, it permits the court to authorise service by methods other than by party consent or by it through the digital dispute management file for the proceedings. Rule 4(4) therefore enables the court to authorise the use of any method that was previously permissible under the CPR eg personal service, service at a last known address, service by email, service by DX, and alternative service.[32] The rule does not, however, require that service by email be effected only where there is prior consent to use that method.[33] Given the ubiquitous availability and use of email maintaining that requirement is in no way justifiable now.[34] However, before a court can properly authorise service by email as an alternative service method, it would need to be satisfied that it is a method that is likely to bring the documents to the attention of the intended recipient. The party seeking to use email service would need to be able to satisfy the court that the email address was one the intended recipient used and was likely to check regularly. If it was a business e-mail address, they would have to show that it was one that was likely to bring the documents to the attention of an individual who was likely to appreciate the nature of the documentation.[35]

[28] All parties and their lawyers must have such an account: Part 4, r 11(2). A model for the app could be Singapore's Singpass app: https://app.singpass.gov.sg.

[29] Part 8, r 9.

[30] *Kenneth Allison Ltd v A E Limehouse & Co* [1992] 2 AC 105; RSC Ord 10, r 3; CPR r 6.11. *Cranfield v Bridgegrove* [2003] EWCA Civ 656; [2003] 1 WLR 2441 at [85].

[31] Crown Proceedings Act 1947, s 18; CPR r 6.10; Companies Act 2006; Limited Liability Partnerships Act 2000; State Immunity Act 1978.

[32] CPR r 6.3.

[33] CPR r 6.3(1)(d), PD6A para 4.1(1); *R (Tax Returned Ltd) v Commissioners for His Majesty's Revenue and Customs* [2022] EWHC 2515 (Admin). Compare with *Entertainment One UK Limited v Công Ty TNHH Đầu Tư Công Nghệ Và Dịch Vụ Sconnect Việtnam also known as Sconnect Co Ltd* [2022] EWHC 3295 (Ch).

[34] *Axnoller Events Limited v Brake* [2022] EWHC 1162 (Ch) at [16] to [19]; CPR Update 153 (February 2023), amendment to PD6A, para 4.1.

[35] ELI-UNIDROIT Model Rules, r 74, comment 6 to 8.

5. The key test for authorising the use of alternative service methods is, except where consensual service applies, that court service via the digital management system cannot be used. That may well be the case where a defendant is unknown, they do not have a digital dispute management account,[36] or they are using the non-digital procedure. Where this test is met the court should authorise the most proportionate and cost-effective method likely to bring the procedural document to the intended recipient's attention.[37] What the most effective service method may be will inevitably be context dependent.
6. Where service is carried out by the parties or by a person authorised by the court, they must provide the court with evidence that they have effected service.[38] This is particularly important from the perspective of dispute management. The court and parties need to be in a position to know that service of a document has been effected so that there can be certainty about the procedural timetable, effective monitoring of it and of compliance with court orders. Non-compliance with the requirement to file a certificate confirming service of particulars of claim would, necessarily, have an impact on a claimant's ability to obtain default judgment. While it would not mean that they could not seek default judgment, they would need to evidence in another way the fact that service had been effected properly and that the time period for responding to the particulars of claim had expired.[39]
7. Finally, the rule codifies the approach taken under the CPR that where service of a case statement is concerned only a sealed copy may be served validly.[40] This is to ensure, especially where particulars of claim are concerned, that the case statement has been issued properly prior to service. This protects the principle of finality as given effect by statutory limitation periods. Were parties able to serve unissued particulars of claim, questions may arise whether or not a claim was issued within the limitation period or whether a defendant, by responding to proceedings served prior to issue, had waived limitation. Where, however this rule is not complied with by the serving party, the court may dispense with formal service under rule 9 where there is evidence of actual notice of the unsealed case statement. The non-compliance may be cured as a procedural error.

## RULE 5.—ALTERNATIVE METHODS OF SERVICE

**(1) Where service is not to be effected through the digital dispute management system, the court shall give precedence to electronic methods that can reasonably guarantee delivery to the intended recipient when authorising alternative service methods.**

**(2) Where electronic service methods cannot reasonably be used, the following methods, in order of precedence, may be used**

**(a) non-electronic methods that reasonably guarantee delivery;**

**(b) any other method that is reasonably likely to bring the procedural document to the intended recipient's attention.**

*Sources: ELI-UNIDROIT Model Rules, rr 78, 80; CPR rr 6.15, 6.27.*

[36] Which may arise innocently or because a defendant is seeking to avoid service.

[37] *Cameron v Liverpool Victoria Insurance Co Ltd* [2019] UKSC 6; [2019] 1 WLR 1471 at [21].

[38] The document will, or ought, already to have been provided to the court under r 3.

[39] *Henriksen v Pires* [2011] EWCA Civ 1720.

[40] *Ideal Shopping Direct Ltd v Mastercard Inc* [2022] EWCA Civ 14; [2022] 1 WLR 1541.

## COMMENTARY

1. This rule supplements rule 4. It maintains the precedence given in that rule, and under the digital procedure and digital access principles, to the use of electronic procedure. Alternative methods of service that are electronic are thus given precedence over non-electronic methods. Service via email, digital platforms, blockchain, etc are thus to be given precedence to service via the post, courier services, or process servers.
2. Any approved non-electronic method must be one that either reasonably guarantees delivery, eg postal service, or is reasonably likely to bring the procedural document to the intended recipient's attention, eg a notice in a newspaper or delivery to their last known address. The former are to be preferred given the greater likelihood that actual delivery will be effected and, through that, that the document will come to the attention of the recipient than if the latter forms of service method were used.

# SECTION 3: SERVICE OUTSIDE ENGLAND AND WALES

## RULE 6.—SERVICE OUT OF THE JURISDICTION

**(1) Procedural documents may be served on a defendant outside the court's jurisdiction.**
**(2) Where documents are to be served outside the jurisdiction they must be accompanied by a translation of the document into an official language of the jurisdiction to be served.**
**(3) A case statement may only be served out of the court's jurisdiction without the court's permission where such service is**
**(a) authorised or otherwise permitted by statute;**
**(b) authorised or otherwise permitted under an international instrument;**
**(c) the court has jurisdiction under a contractual term to that effect.**
**(4) Where permission to serve procedural documents, including case statements, out of the court's jurisdiction is required, permission may be granted where**
**(a) the proceedings disclose a substantial and not merely casual or adventitious link between the cause of action and England and Wales;**
**(b) there is a serious issue to be tried on the substantive merits of the claim;**
**(c) England and Wales, in all the circumstances, is clearly or distinctly the appropriate forum to try the claim.**
**(5) Permission to serve outside the jurisdiction may be granted retrospectively under Part 8, rule 13.**
**(6) Procedural documents other than case statements may only be served out of the court's jurisdiction without the court's permission where such service is**
**(a) to be effected in Scotland or Northern Ireland;**
**(b) permission has previously been granted to serve a case statement or procedural document out of the jurisdiction.**
**(7) Where a procedural document is served out of the jurisdiction it must specify, if applicable, the date by which a response to the document is required.**

*Sources: ELI-UNIDROIT Model Rules, rr 82, 85; CPR rr 2.3(1), 6.32, 6.33, 6.37, 6.38, 6.45, PD6B.*

## COMMENTARY

1. This rule specifies the procedure to be followed where a party seeks to invoke the court's jurisdiction where a defendant is outside the jurisdiction. It does not confer any substantive jurisdiction over them; that is a matter of the general law and particularly private international law.[41]
2. Service may be effected without the court's permission where that is authorised by statute. The relevant statute here is the Civil Jurisdiction and Judgments Act 1982. Its main focus is service in Scotland and Northern Ireland.[42] Service may also be effected further to the Service Convention, where that applies to proceedings.[43] Finally, it may also be effected where the parties to proceedings have entered into a contractual agreement conferring jurisdiction on the English and Welsh courts. This approach mirrors the position set out in CPR rr 6.32 and 6.33. In each case service can be effected without permission because jurisdiction is conferred on the English and Welsh courts under the general law.
3. Service may also be effected outside the jurisdiction with the court's permission in several circumstances. Here the rule restates the approach taken under the CPR, the aim of which is to ensure that permission to serve outside the jurisdiction may only be granted, and thus the court's jurisdiction established, where the proceedings can properly be pursued in England and Wales. To ensure this is the case permission will only be granted where the cause of action underpinning the proceedings has a substantial link to England and Wales, a serious substantive issue needs to be tried, and England and Wales is the most suitable forum for determining the claim. Permission to serve outside the jurisdiction may also be granted retrospectively.[44]
4. Procedural documents, other than case statements, may be served out of the jurisdiction where case statements or other procedural documents have already been properly served outside the jurisdiction.[45] This approach was adopted by the CPR in 2022,[46] albeit only where case statements had previously and properly been served out of the jurisdiction. The rationale behind the CPR amendment and the broader approach taken here is to ensure that unnecessary and disproportionate cost and delay is not created through multiple applications being made where the question of the primary right to serve has already been determined.
5. To enable the recipient of any document served outside the jurisdiction to understand what has been sent, it must be accompanied with a translation in an official language of the jurisdiction where service is to be effected.[47] Without a translation, service will not be guaranteed to give the recipient due notice of the proceedings or their content. Moreover, any documentation served outside the jurisdiction must also

[41] A. Zuckerman (2021) at 289; L Collins and J Harris, *Dicey, Morris & Collins on the Conflict of Laws* (Sweet & Maxwell, 2022).

[42] *Spiliada Maritime Corp v Cansulex Ltd* [1987] AC 640; *Vedanta Resources Ltd v Lungowe* [2019] UKSC 20; [2020] AC 1045.

[43] The Convention on the Service Abroad of Judicial and Extrajudicial Documents in Civil or Commercial Matters 1965 (the Hague Service Convention).

[44] *Neshein v Kosa* [2006] EWHC 2710 (Ch); [2007] WTLR 149.

[45] An order made under Part 16, r 5 is not a procedural document under this rule: *Vitol AS v Capro Marine Ltd* [2008 EWHC 378 (Comm); [2009] Bus LR 27; *Masri v Consolidated Contractors International Co SAL (No 4)* [2009] UKHL 43; [2009] 3 WLR 385.

[46] Civil Procedure (Amendment No 2) Rules 2022 (SI 2022/783), reg 7.

[47] CPR r 6.45.

specify within it the time limit for taking any procedural steps consequent upon service.[48] This is an aspect that could be described as procedural due notice. It gives the recipient, who (with their lawyers) may not be familiar with the operation of the English and Welsh civil justice system effective notice of what they need to do and by when. Through giving recipients explicit notice of procedural time limits, this rule also promotes effective dispute management not least because it puts them in a position where they can co-operate effectively with the court and other parties with the management of the proceedings.

## RULE 7.—METHODS OF SERVICE FOR SERVICE OUTSIDE THE UNITED KINGDOM

**(1) Where service is to be effected outside the United Kingdom, it may be effected**
- **(a) according to the rules in this Part for service within the jurisdiction unless they are excluded by any international instrument;**
- **(b) by any method specified in legislation or an international instrument; or**
- **(c) by any method permitted by the jurisdiction in which service is to be effected.**

**(2) Precedence shall be given to service by the rules in this Part where they are applicable.**

**(3) The cost of and any expenses arising from effecting service outside the jurisdiction shall be borne by the claimant. Expenses may be incurred by the UK government, courts, or foreign authorities in giving effect to service outside the jurisdiction.**

*Sources: CPR rr 6.40, 6.42, 6.43, 6.44.*

## COMMENTARY

1. This rule supplements rule 6. It specifies the methods that may be used to serve procedural documents outside the jurisdiction. The primary service methods are those applicable generally in this Part, unless they are excluded by an international instrument. To give effect to the general preference for court-based digital service, these methods are given preference in so far as possible. The rule also acknowledges that international instruments may make specific provision for applicable service methods.[49] Finally, it provides for service methods applicable within the jurisdiction where service is to be effected to apply.
2. Where costs and other expenses are incurred by any official channel for effecting service out of the jurisdiction, the party seeking service by that method must reimburse such costs. This rule restates CPR r 6.46. Such costs may be incurred, for instance, by the Foreign, Commonwealth, and Development Office when documents are served further to the State Immunity Act 1978.
3. Within the CPR this rule is supplemented by a detailed Practice Direction, CPR PD6B, which provides details, amongst other things, of the process to be adopted for different types of claim, for documents that need to be filed with the court, and applicable time limits for responding to claim forms. Such practical details can properly be set out and applied within the digital procedure.

[48] CPR PD6B para 6.6.

[49] For instance, The State Immunity Act 1978; The Hague Service Convention.

# SECTION 4: PROCESS FOR DEEMING AND DISPENSING WITH SERVICE

## RULE 8.—DEEMED SERVICE DATE

**(1) Procedural documents served via the digital dispute management system, an electronic service method that reasonably guarantees delivery, or via personal service are deemed to have been served:**

**(a) on the date of transmission, sending or personal service, if transmitted, sent or actually served on the intended recipient before 16.30 on that day;**

**(b) otherwise, on the first day after the date of transmission, sending or, where personal service is effected, actual service.**

**(2) Where non-electronic service methods that reasonably guarantee delivery are used to effect service, service is deemed to take place on the second day after use of the service method was commenced.**

**(3) Where the court authorises service by another method, it shall stipulate in the order authorising service the deemed service date.**

**(4) Where service is effected by a statutory service method, the deemed date of service shall be that specified in the statute where there is one.**

**(5) Where service is effected out of the jurisdiction via the digital dispute management system or, where served in Scotland or Northern Ireland by that or any other service method, the deemed date of service is that applicable to service by that method within the jurisdiction. Where it is effected outside the United Kingdom by any other service method, the deemed date of service is either the date specified in any relevant international instrument, by the law of the jurisdiction or, otherwise as provided for in the digital procedure or as directed by the court in the order granting permission to serve out of the jurisdiction.**

*Sources: CPR rr 7.17, 6.26.*

## COMMENTARY

1. Deemed service dates are intended to create procedural certainty, which is fundamental to enabling the procedural timetable to run and dispute management to be carried out effectively. Deemed service is not relevant to certainty of notice nor is it intended to create an irrebuttable factual presumption of service.[50]
2. To promote certainty, this rule adopts a simpler approach to deemed service than that taken under the CPR, which provides a range of different deemed service dates depending on the service method adopted. This rule adopts a binary approach. Where service is effected by digital service methods or personal service, the deemed service date is either the date on which the documents were transmitted, sent or actually given to the recipient, or if those actions were carried out after 16.30, the following day. Where any other service method is used, the second day after use of the service method was commenced is the deemed service date. To ensure the parties have clarity over the deemed service date, any order that requires a procedural step to be carried out must specify the applicable deemed service date relevant to the service method to be used. Limited exceptions to these provisions are acknowledged in the rule where deemed service dates are set out in legislation or in any international instrument relevant to service outside the jurisdiction.

[50] A Zuckerman (2003) at 169–174.

3. The deemed service date cannot be rebutted by proof of actual service.[51] This enables parties and the court to have the necessary degree of certainty to manage the procedural timetable. It, particularly, enables claimants to calculate the date by which they may apply for default judgment. This is not to say that a defendant is prohibited from demonstrating that they did not receive actual notice or that actual notice was effected on a date other than the deemed service date. That they can do so is necessary to give effect to the general access principle, particularly where applications to set aside default judgment are concerned.[52]

## RULE 9.—POWER TO DISPENSE WITH SERVICE

**(1) The court on its own initiative or on application of a party may dispense with service of a procedural document. Service may be dispensed with either prospectively for good reason or retrospectively. An order dispensing with service may also cure any procedural non-compliance.**
**(2) Service of a particulars of claim or defence may only be dispensed with in exceptional circumstances.**
**(3) Any retrospective application to dispense with service is an application for relief from sanction.**
**(4) Service may not be dispensed with where it is required by legislation or any international instrument.**
**(5) Service may be dispensed with subject to conditions.**

*Sources: ELI-UNIDROIT Model Rules, r 81; CPR rr 3.10, 6.16, 6.28.*

## COMMENTARY

1. Rule 9 provides a single rule that enables the court to dispense with service of a procedural document. It codifies the approach in the CPR set out in its r 6.16 (power to dispense with service of a claim form) and r 6.28 (power to dispense with service of other documents). Procedural simplicity and intelligibility strongly point to both powers being set out in a single, compendious rule.[53]
2. The rule does, however, draw a distinction in approach to particulars of claim and defences and other procedural documents. Particulars of claim are the means by which jurisdiction over a defendant is established. With a defendant's defence, it is the primary means by which the court's jurisdiction is defined. Taken together these documents provide parties with due notice of proceedings and of their respective claims and defences. The need for there to be formal service of these documents is more important therefore than it is where other procedural documents are concerned. For this reason, formal service of these documents may only be dispensed with exceptionally.[54] This rule thus adopts the approach taken under the CPR to the power to dispense with service of a claim form.[55]

[51] *Godwin v Swindon BC* [2001] EWCA Civ 1478; [2002] 1 WLR 997.

[52] A Zuckerman (2021) at 251–253; Part 15, r 8.

[53] The CPR originally had one rule dealing with both situations, CPR r 6.9 (prior to 2008); *Anderton v Clwyd CC (No 2)* [2002] EWCA Civ 933; [2002] 1 WLR 3174.

[54] *Lonestar Communications Corp LLC v Kaye* [2019] EWHC 3008 (Comm) is thus rejected. For other criticism of the decision, P Coulson (ed), *Civil Procedure 2024* (Sweet & Maxwell, 2024) Vol. 1 at 6.28.1.

[55] P Coulson (ed) (2024) Vol 1 at 6.16.1, noting that unlike here procedural equality was the basis of the CPR's approach.

3. Rule 9(1) permits prospective and retrospective applications. Consistently with the promotion of party co-operation and through that effective and proportionate dispute management, the approach to such applications is one that is stricter where retrospective applications are concerned. Good reason, such as a document had been brought to a party's attention other than by an applicable service method before expiry of any applicable service time limit, is required to justify service to be dispensed with prospectively. Requiring formal service in such circumstances would involve additional time and cost for no good reason.
4. An order dispensing with service retrospectively raises considerations beyond economy and efficiency. Where particulars of claim or a defence are concerned, dispensing with service retrospectively may effectively enable a party to side-step the service time limits. It may have an impact on a claimant's ability to seek default judgment. Retrospective applications also involve non-compliance with procedural rules, contrary to the compliance principle. Retrospective applications must therefore be subject to the same test as that which applies to retrospective applications to extend time limits to serve case statements, ie they are applications for relief from sanction.[56]
5. A common reason why a retrospective application may be granted is where the document in question has been brought to the actual attention of the intended recipient within an applicable time limit but not via a formal means of service. In such a situation the due notice requirement has been satisfied, albeit without meeting the formal, technical requirements of service. To give effect to the compliance principle, and through it effective and proportionate dispute management, an order curing the non-compliance, which may relate to either service within or outside the jurisdiction, is still needed.[57] Such an order, if granted, would justify an order dispensing with service.
6. This Code, as a statutory instrument, is subject to any primary legislation. It should also be subject to any international obligation on the UK, particularly those concerning service outside the jurisdiction. Where legislation or an international obligation requires formal service to be effected, the court cannot dispense with service.
7. Where the court dispenses with service it may do so subject to conditions. Any such conditions should be consistent with the purposive principle. A relatively standard condition would be, where it had not already been done, to require the document subject to the order to be provided to the court via the party's digital dispute management account.

[56] *Godwin v Swindon BC* [2001] EWCA Civ 1478; [2002] 1 WLR 997; *Anderton v Clwyd CC (No 2)* [2002] EWCA Civ 933; [2002] 1 WLR 3174; *Kuenyehia v International Hospitals Group Ltd* [2006] EWCA Civ 21; [2006] CP Rep 34; *Olafsson v Gissurarson (No 2)* [2008] EWCA Civ 152; [2008] 1 WLR 2016.

[57] *Abela v Baadarani* [2013] UKSC 44; [2013] 1 WLR 2043.

# PART 11

# DISPUTE MANAGEMENT

## SECTION 1: GENERAL

1. Within the CPR management powers are dispersed across a variety of Parts and rules. CPR Pt 3 contains general case management rules as well as those concerning civil restraint orders. CPR Pt 19 provides rules governing multi-party litigation, while Pt 23 contains rules governing applications. Its Pt 26 sets out the rules concerning allocation to procedural case management track, while its Pt 36 promotes early settlement. Additionally, its Pt 81 contains rules concerning contempt of court. Consistently with the accessibility principle (Part 1, rule 2(1) of this Code), this Part draws all those rules together to provide a single point of reference for the effective management of disputes.
2. This Part also effects some significant changes to case management. It introduces judicial continuity as standard. It revises the approach to representative actions to bring them into greater conformity with the approach taken in the Competition Appeal Tribunal. Most significantly, it gives greater effect than the CPR to the settlement principle through bifurcating case management through the introduction of a dedicated settlement management track.

### RULE 1.—SCOPE AND PURPOSE

**(1) This Part concerns dispute management, which is the active management of proceedings by the civil courts from their commencement to, where necessary, enforcement.**

**(2) Its purpose is to secure the just, economical, efficient, and proportionate resolution of disputes either through consensual resolution or adjudication. Effective dispute management shall be given effect consistently with the purposive, co-operation and compliance principles. Its implementation shall be supported by the digital procedure and accountability and artificial intelligence principles.**

*Sources: ALI/UNIDROIT Principles, principle 14; ALI/UNIDROIT Reporters' Study, rr 18, 32.5; ELI-UNIDROIT Model Rules, rr 4, 5, 47–50; CPR r 1.4, Pt 3.*

### COMMENTARY

1. This Part complements Part 5. Whereas that earlier Part concerned pre-action dispute management, this one is solely concerned with the management of disputes from the point at which formal proceedings are initiated to, if necessary, enforcement.[1]

[1] D Steelman, J Goerdt, and J McMillan, *Caseflow Management. The Heart of Court Management in the New Millennium* (National Center for State Courts, 2000).

*A Model Civil Procedure Code for England and Wales*. John Sorabji, Oxford University Press. © John Sorabji 2024.
DOI: 10.1093/oso/9780192848680.003.0012

2. Dispute management under rule 1(2) has a wider explicit purpose than under the CPR. Under CPR r 1.4, the court is under a duty to actively manage cases to further its overriding objective. Implicitly this requires the court to manage cases to a just resolution, ie to either a just consensual resolution as much as to a just adjudication.[2] This rule makes explicit that dual function.
3. Rule 1(2) also highlights the importance that other procedural principles play in the proper management of disputes. Effective management rests on party co-operation with other parties and the court. This was recognised to a certain extent under the CPR, as parties were required to assist the court in managing cases so as to further the overriding objective.[3] They were not, however, placed under a duty to give effect to it.[4] Here parties are under an express duty to co-operate with each other and the court to achieve the purposive principle. As a consequence, while under the CPR parties were not under an obligation to point out their opponent's procedural errors to them, they are required to do so here. This change represents an inroad into party autonomy. It is, however, justified due to the need to ensure that proceedings are determined accurately, ie that decisions are not the product or consequence of inadvertent procedural error. It is also based on the need to ensure that unnecessary party and court cost and time are not incurred through applications that would need to be made to rectify errors that are not pointed out at the earliest opportunity. It is thus justified by reference to the purposive principle, generally, and more specifically, the accuracy, economy, efficiency, and proportionality principles.
4. One of the central problems that undermined effective case management under the CPR was the approach taken to rule-compliance. Lax, negligent, or deliberate non-compliance with case management directions and orders was one of the main reasons why the CPR, until the restatement of the approach to rule compliance following the Jackson reforms, failed to give effect to the overriding objective effectively. Rule 1(2) also therefore acknowledges the importance of the compliance principle to dispute management. Section 7 makes specific provision for the approach to compliance and non-compliance.
5. To enable the parties to give proper effect to their obligations regarding dispute management, it is to operate consistently with the digital procedure and accountability and artificial intelligence principles. Dispute management must, as a consequence, primarily be carried out via the digital procedure, as made available via the digital portal. It must also, where appropriate, be assisted by the use of appropriate artificial intelligence programmes that are to form part of the digital procedure. Also, consistently with the digital integration principle, information concerning disputes, derived from the dispute management process, is to be made available to Ombudsman, regulators, government, etc, consistently with the approach to dispute information derived from the pre-action dispute management process being made available to them. Again, the intention here is to facilitate effective scrutiny, and, where necessary, reform of the Code and its operation where it is deficient as well as to enhance dispute prevention and conflict defusion.

[2] M Briggs, *Chancery Modernisation Review—Final Report* (Judicial Office, December 2013) at 67–68; A Zuckerman, *Zuckerman on Civil Procedure—Principles of Practice* (Sweet & Maxwell, 2021) chap 11.

[3] CPR r 1.3.

[4] *Hallam Estates Ltd v Baker* [2014] EWCA Civ 661; [2014] CP Rep 38; *Barton v Hassall LLP* [2018] UKSC 12; [2018] 1 WLR 1119; *Woodward v Phoenix Healthcare Distributions Ltd* [2019] EWCA Civ 985.

## RULE 2.—PRESUMPTION IN FAVOUR OF DIGITAL PROCEDURE

**Dispute management shall be effected through the digital procedure, except where the court orders the use of the non-digital procedure.**

*Sources: Judicial Review and Courts Act 2022, s 19(7).*

## COMMENTARY

1. This rule gives effect to the general principle that proceedings should be carried out through the digital procedure, subject to a discretion to order the use of the non-digital procedure. The presumption in favour of digital dispute management is important for two fundamental reasons. Both promote economy, efficiency, and proportionality. The second reason is also intended to promote greater procedural fairness by helping ensure that like cases are treated alike, and different cases are treated differently.
2. First, it is intended to integrate the pre-issue and post-action process effectively. It will do so by facilitating the use of a single, continuous dispute resolution process for parties, rather than one that requires them to set out their respective cases and provide evidence etc to multiple different pre-action and post-issue dispute resolution systems. Information provided by the parties would, for instance, only need to be provided once rather than multiple times to different systems and processes.
3. Secondly, it ought to help overcome one of the well-documented and commented upon problems associated with the CPR and its predecessors: party non-compliance with procedural obligations, time limits, and case management orders. Non-compliance lay at the heart of problems such as satellite litigation over procedural issues, and the associated unnecessary, disproportionate cost and delay that they generated for both parties and the court; effects that undermined the civil court's ability to secure access to a proportionate process for all litigants.[5] Eliminating or, at the very least reducing non-compliance, is one important way in which to promote the purposive principle.
4. Increasing rule-compliance is only, however, a partial solution as it depends upon securing compliance with orders that themselves promote the purposive principle. It is generally assumed that dispute management orders are consistent with that principle. However, the assumption may not necessarily be borne out in practice. Different judges quite naturally take different approaches to such matters. Moreover, there is evidence to suggest that individual judges may take different approaches to the same factual and legal matrix presented at different times when making decisions.[6] The possibility thus arises that some decisions may be consistent with the purposive

[5] C Crifo, 'Enforcement of Process Requirements: A Search for Solid Grounds' (2014) 34(2) Oxford Journal of Legal Studies 325.

[6] W Austin and T Williams III, 'A Survey of Judges' Responses to Simulated Legal Cases: Research Note On Sentencing Disparity' (1977) 68(2) Journal of Criminal Law and Criminology 366; M Dhami and P Ayton, 'Bailing and Jailing the Fast and Frugal Way' (2001) 14 Journal of Behavioral Decision-making 141; J Sorabji, 'Compliance Problems and Digitising Case Management in England and Wales', in A Higgins and R Assy, *Principles, Procedure, and Justice: Essays in Honour of Adrian Zuckerman* (OUP, 2020).

principle, others may not. Such inconsistency could tend to undermine judicial legitimacy just as it could procedural equality.

5. More generally, judges under the CPR take case management decisions based on the individual case before them, without necessarily having any detailed knowledge of its impact on the court's overall resources; a point underscored by the fact noted in *Mitchell v News Group Newspapers Ltd* (2014) that non-compliance in one case may adversely affect the court's ability to secure the fair distribution of its resources across other disputes, which was done by reference to other cases that the Master had listed before her but not by reference to other disputes in the system or any detailed administrative data.[7] This may mean that, even where decisions are taken consistently across cases, due to a lack of systems knowledge an order may not give effect to the purposive principle and, particularly, the aim of achieving systemic proportionality.
6. The default use of the digital procedure for dispute management is intended to help overcome these deficiencies, whether actual or potential. Consistently with the artificial intelligence and digital integration principles, it is intended to facilitate the extraction and analysis of information on how individual judges approach dispute management issues. This material can be used in two ways. It can help shape judicial training. It may, for instance, be used to provide training to judges on issues to consider, and the relative weight to be given to them, when they consider not just the individual factors in any particular management question but, importantly, when they consider questions of systemic proportionality. It can also, in specific proceedings, provide information to individual judges and parties on comparable approaches to the same or similar issues from across the civil courts to those in the instant matter. The aim here is to promote greater judicial consistency across different proceedings, and hence a fairer process for all litigants.
7. Additionally, use of this information is intended to facilitate the achievement of the purposive principle. Data from all proceedings that are being managed, if made available to the court and parties, could facilitate a greater understanding of the impact of judicial decisions, and non-compliance with those decisions, on the effective management of the civil court's resources. It could thus be used by judges to tailor their directions more consistently with the constraints placed by resource supply and litigant demand. Application of an effective machine learning AI programme could, for instance, provide tailored, recommended directions and orders for judicial and party consideration based on an assessment of factors such as procedural economy, efficiency, and systemic proportionality. It could be based on evidence derived from past decisions and present and predicted future demands on the court's resources.[8] The aim here is not to take decision-making out of the hands of individual judges, but to assist them. It is to provide them with more and better information on factors necessary for consistent, effective, and proportionate dispute management than would otherwise have been available.

[7] *Mitchell v News Group Newspapers Ltd* [2013] EWHC 2355 (QB) at [28] and [59].

[8] E Troulinos, *The Prospects of Artificial Intelligence in a Court Information System* (3 September 2020, Athens, Greece) <https://ceur-ws.org/Vol-2844/ethics3.pdf>.

## RULE 3.—ROLE OF THE COURT

**(1) The court is responsible for the effective management of proceedings consistently with the purposive principle. It shall have such powers, under this rule or its inherent jurisdiction, as are sufficient to make or vary any order necessary to give effect to this responsibility.**

**(2) Effective management requires the court to actively manage proceedings. Active management includes, at any time,**

**(a) making any order for the proper timetabling and/or management of proceedings, including settlement and adjudication procedures (a dispute management order) either on its own initiative or on application of the parties;**

**(b) scheduling, when necessary, hearings to plan and make orders concerning the effective management of proceedings (dispute management hearings);**

**(c) making provision for the submission of skeleton arguments;**

**(d) adjourning any hearing;**

**(e) staying proceedings;**

**(f) ensuring technology is used appropriately throughout the proceedings;**

**(g) encouraging or mandating the use of any non-binding settlement procedure;**

**(h) monitoring and securing party compliance with court orders concerning the proper management of proceedings.**

**(3) Active management also requires the court to take account of any characteristics of parties, witnesses, or non-parties that either require, or otherwise for good reason justify, the modification of any procedural step, direction, court order, or process. In doing so the court must not compromise its independence and impartiality.**

**(4) The court may use artificial intelligence to assist in the proper management of proceedings. Assistance may include**

**(a) providing the court with an assessment of the most appropriate procedure for managing the proceedings;**

**(b) determining the suitability of specific settlement procedures;**

**(c) compliance monitoring.**

**(5) Where the court relies on the assistance of artificial intelligence it must make such assistance available to the parties and consider any submissions they have in respect of it either before making or reconsidering any order.**

**(6) Anonymised information concerning disputes shall be provided to Ombudsman, regulators, and the government through the same process applicable to pre-action dispute prevention.**

*Sources: Council of Europe Rec R (84) 5, principle 3; ALI/UNIDROIT Principles, principles 9.3, 14; ALI/UNIDROIT Reporters' Study, r 18; ELI-UNIDROIT Model Rules, rr 48, 49, 50; CPR rr 1.4, 3.1(8), Pt 3.*

## COMMENTARY

1. Rule 3 gives effect to the dispute management principle. The power to make or vary orders to manage proceedings effectively is wide-ranging. It arises both under this rule and under the civil court's inherent jurisdiction, which is acknowledged in rule 3(1).[9]

2. Rule 3(2) signals the most important aspects of effective dispute management. Of those the most important is effective timetabling. An effective timetable is the central

[9] *Hinkley and South Leicestershire PBS v Freeman* [1941] Ch 32; *Agents Mutual Ltd v Moginnie James Ltd* [2016] EWCH 3384 (Ch); *Cocker v Tempest* (1841) 7 M & W 502 at 503–504; *Bremer Vulcan v South India Shipping* [1981] AC 909 at 977.

means by which the court can distribute its resources across all potential proceedings consistently with the purposive principle. As the ALI/UNIDROIT Principles rightly note, an '*orderly schedule facilitates expeditious conduct of... litigation*'.[10] The same is true of economy and proportionality. It is thus an essential means by which systemic proportionality is achieved. It is also the means through which the court, with party co-operation, can match procedure to the needs of the dispute.

3. Effective timetabling is not, however, a sufficient condition to meet such ends. For that, there also has to be effective compliance with procedural obligations and deadlines. For that reason, rule 3(2)(h) goes beyond the CPR and requires the court to take active steps to monitor and secure party compliance.[11] The introduction of a digital procedure could help to achieve this effectively. It could, for instance, issue automatic prompts, or e-alerts, to the court and parties reminding them of time limits and compliance deadlines.[12] Given judicial continuity, provided by rule 14, those prompts would go to a single, designated judge responsible for managing the proceedings. That judge would be both familiar with them and have at their fingertips the e-dispute management file that would enable them to take any appropriate step to promote compliance, such as sending further reminders to the parties,[13] scheduling short telephone or non-physical hearings to discuss with the parties progress towards compliance, or proactively considering any necessary, prospective extensions of time, stays, or adjournments. Adjournments may particularly be necessary to afford parties a fair process or procedural equality if, for instance, a party is unable to attend a hearing for reasons outside their control. They may also be necessary to provide parties with a proportionate opportunity to consider fresh evidence or a novel point that arises in proceedings or to deal with an amendment granted during a hearing.[14] In considering whether to grant an adjournment, a court must take particular account of the need to maintain procedural equality, while ensuring proceedings are managed economically, efficiently, and proportionately (in all its senses).[15]
4. Where scheduling hearings is concerned, this should be carried out not only to ensure effective management on the adjudication and settlement management tracks, but also to ensure that a proactive stance is taken by the court and parties generally to settlement and use of settlement processes.[16] More broadly, as active dispute management is focused on managing disputes to resolution and not adjudication,[17] rules 3(2)(a), (b), and (f) make explicit provision for settlement processes. The last of the provisions adopts and generalises the approach set out in CPR r 3.1(2)(m), which acknowledges the court's power to mandate ENE.[18] It makes explicit that which the CPR failed

[10] ALI/UNIDROIT Principles, comment P-9B to principle 9.

[11] CPR r 3.1(8).

[12] R Jackson, *Review of Civil Litigation Costs: Final Report* (December 2009) at 398; J Cabral and T Clarke, 'Access to Justice Integration with Emerging Court Technologies' (2012) 26(1) Harvard Journal of Law & Technology 278 at 289; J Sorabji in A Higgins and R Assy (2020) at 168; CEPEJ, *Revised Saturn Guidelines for Judicial Time Management* (2021) at 6.

[13] Steps taken to prompt party compliance as a result of monitoring ought generally to be carried out via the digital procedure to ensure that there is a record of the prompt. Digital communication also ensures that the same message is given to all parties: *Constantinou v Wilmot-Josife* [2010] EWCA Civ 747; [2010] 2 FLR 1449.

[14] *Boyd & Hutchinson (A Firm) v Foenander* [2003] EWCA Civ 1516 at [9]; *R v Kingston-upon-Thames Justices, ex parte Martin* [1994] Imm AR 172.

[15] *Robinson v Mentmore Towers* [2009] EWHC 3070 (TCC); [2010] CP Rep 15.

[16] Rules 16 and 19.

[17] Rule 1.

[18] *Lomax v Lomax* [2019] EWCA Civ 1467; [2019] 1 WLR 6527.

to do originally, that the court has the power to mandate the use of any non-binding settlement procedure.[19] This power may be exercised irrespective of whether proceedings have been allocated to the adjudication or settlement management tracks.

5. Rule 3(2)(c) makes provision for directions to be given concerning skeleton arguments. These should generally be provided to the court and other parties prior to hearings. They should only be used where they are likely to promote economy and efficiency. Where used they should, as a general rule, set out a clear concise summary of the matter at hand and any factual and legal submissions to be developed at a hearing, with relevant citation of authority.
6. Active dispute management also requires the court to take such steps as are necessary to utilise appropriate technology. Most obviously, this requires the court to ensure the digital procedure is used to manage proceedings. It also requires it to ensure that appropriate use of technology, whether telephonic, digital, or otherwise, is used to manage and hear proceedings. This would include appropriate use of digital technology in evidence-gathering and exchange.
7. Rule 3(3) gives effect to the purposive and procedural equality principles. It is intended to ensure, amongst other things, that appropriate consideration is given to the specific needs of vulnerable parties or witnesses.[20] It may, for instance, require a party's or a witness's contact details to be withheld from other parties. It may require the provision of breaks in hearings at regular intervals, consideration of taking evidence via a non-physical hearing, or of the need for a party to be provided with reasonable assistance in court. However this rule is applied, it must not be applied so as to compromise judicial independence or impartiality.
8. Rule 3(4)(a) and (b) provide the basis for the use of artificial intelligence as an aid to decision-making, whether that is in the classification of proceedings, track allocation, and the determination of a suitable settlement process for proceedings allocated either to the adjudication or settlement management tracks. Consistently with the due notice principle, where the court does use AI in such circumstances parties must be given an opportunity to make submissions in respect of it prior to any decision being made.
9. Rule 3(6) mirrors the comparable rule in Part 5, rule 5(2) and serves the same purpose. Also see rule 6(3), below.

## RULE 4.—ROLE OF THE PARTIES

**(1) Parties shall co-operate with each other and the court in the effective management of disputes. This includes, but is not limited to, taking steps, in so far as reasonable, to**
**(a) settle disputes consensually;**
**(b) agree the proper and proportionate management of proceedings;**

[19] The power to mandate use of a binding settlement procedure would amount to a denial of the right to fair trial: *Deweer v Belgium* (1980) 2 EHRR 439. On proposals to amend the CPR to provide a mechanism to mandate the use of settlement processes following *Churchill v Merthyr Tydfil County Borough Council* [2023] EWCA Civ 1416 see, Civil Procedure Rule Committee, Alternative Dispute Resolution consultation (Ministry of Justice, 2024).

[20] CPR r 1.6, PD1A; Civil Justice Council, *Vulnerable Witnesses and Parties with Civil Proceedings* (February 2020); *AXX v Zajac* [2022] EWHC 2463 (KB) at [23]–[35].

**(c) minimise non-contentious and contentious procedural applications; and**
**(d) minimise the cost of, and time to, the resolution of proceedings.**

**(2) Where required by this Code, a Practice Direction, or court order, parties shall verify the truth of procedural documents by a statement of truth. Verifying a statement falsely may amount to a contempt of court.**

**(3) Non-compliance with this rule may result in the imposition of sanctions.**

*Sources: ALI/UNIDROIT Principles, principles 11.1, 11.2; ELI-UNIDROIT Model Rules, r 6; CPR r 1.3, Pt 22.*

## COMMENTARY

1. Rule 4 is intended to complement the parties' pre-action duty to co-operate with each other (Part 5, rule 2). As such it gives concrete effect to the co-operation principle during the post-issue phase of a dispute.
2. As with the approach to pre-action dispute management, this rule is intended to mark a shift away from an adversarial approach to dispute management to one that is more co-operative and collaborative. It does not, however, assume that it is possible to secure a wholly consensual and collaborative approach to the conduct of proceedings.[21] A realistic approach is taken here, as it is to the co-operation principle generally and the equivalent of this rule in Part 5. This is given expression by rule 4(1) only requiring parties to take reasonable steps to settle their dispute (thus supporting settlement management under Section 4), to agree a proportionate management timetable for their dispute,[22] and to minimise contentious applications. The latter requirement should, however, be read as requiring parties to take steps to point out to each other in good time procedural mistakes so that they may be rectified without the need to resort to non-contentious or contentious applications: see rule 1(2).
3. More generally, effective co-operation requires parties to take such steps as are reasonable to minimise the cost and time of proceedings. Rule 4, and particularly rule 4(2)(d) should be read consistently with the proportionality principle. Accordingly, they should be read as requiring parties to co-operate not only to promote their own private interest in resolving their dispute as efficiently and economically as possible, but also through that to promote the public interest by ensuring that they draw on no more than a proportionate share of the court's resources. Rule 4 must specifically therefore be applied to give effect to systemic as well as individual proportionality.
4. Rule 4(3) sets out the general rule that, where required, parties shall confirm the truth of documents submitted in proceedings through signing a statement of truth. It is intended to ensure that anyone submitting a document that must be signed by such a statement takes seriously the fact that they are submitting material that will have an impact on the exercise of State power by the court. Signing a statement of truth is not something that ought to be taken lightly. It is a matter of substance, not form.[23] Swearing a false statement, as it undermines the proper administration of justice, may result in proceedings for contempt of court (rule 41(8)).
5. In seeking to minimise adversarial conduct, and hence promote co-operation, non-compliance with this rule can result in the imposition of sanctions (rule 33).

[21] W Brazil, 'The Adversary Character of Civil Discovery' (1978) 31 Vand LR 1295 at 1299 to 1302.
[22] This should build on the duty imposed under Part 5, r 10.
[23] *Clarkson v Future Resources FZE* [2022] EWCA Civ 230 at [47].

## RULE 5.—PROHIBITED COMMUNICATIONS BETWEEN THE COURT AND PARTIES OR NON-PARTIES CONCERNING PROCEEDINGS

**(1) Private communication between the court, a party, or a non-party once proceedings have commenced is prohibited except in respect of formal administrative matters, matters concerning without-notice applications and hearings, and settlement processes. Breach of this prohibition may result in proceedings for contempt of court.**

**(2) Formal administrative matters are those that do not concern the management or determination of proceedings by a judge.**

**(3) The court will take steps to ensure that any prohibited private communication it receives is provided to all other parties in proceedings. It must also take no account of the communication.**

*Sources: ALI/UNIDROIT Principles, principle 1.4; ALI/UNIDROIT Reporters' Study, r 10.4; ELI-UNIDROIT Model Rules, r 13; CPR r 39.8.*

## COMMENTARY

1. This rule prohibits parties and non-parties communicating privately with the court. This is to protect the integrity of the administration of justice.[24] It is required by various procedural principles. The due notice and adversariality and accuracy principles require judicial decisions to be taken following and in the light of representations by all parties.[25] Adjudication, if carried out properly, is based on the testing of both parties' positions, evidence, and legal submissions. The general access and procedural equality principles require all parties to have equivalent access to the court prior to decisions that affect them being taken. Private communications between one party and the court if generally permitted would run counter to those principles. They would place one party in a privileged position in the proceedings inimical to the provision of a fair process.

2. Enabling one party, or a non-party, to secure a privileged position within proceedings such that the court but not all parties had access to their views or evidence also poses a significant problem vis a vis judicial impartiality and independence.[26] Were one party or a non-party to communicate with the court regarding proceedings, there is a risk that the court could act on them. Its decision-making could be tainted by their influence. Even if the communications did not relate to any specific issue in the proceedings, depending on their content, they would run the risk of prejudicing the court's view of either or both parties. Such communications could then either affect or be seen to affect judicial impartiality. Were the communications to come from, for instance, a Member of Parliament, a civil servant, a member of the Government, or a more senior judge, they might also run the risk of undermining judicial independence[27] and ultimately the rule of law. For this reason, civil servants

[24] *R (Binyam Mohamed) v Secretary of State for Foreign and Commonwealth Affairs* [2010] EWCA Civ 158; [2011] QB 218 at [6].

[25] *Pamplin v Express Newspapers Ltd* [1985] 1 WLR 689 at 691 stressing the rationale against private communications lies in the due notice and adversariality principles.

[26] ELI-UNIDROIT Model Rules, r 13, comment 1.

[27] *ALI/UNIDROIT Reporters' Study*, comment R-10D to r 10.4.

and members of the Government are under statutory, constitutional duties not to interfere with ongoing proceedings.[28]

3. To both deter parties and non-parties from attempting to communicate privately with the court, rule 5(3) requires the court to inform all parties of any such communications and their content. Thus, were a party or non-party to seek to influence a court improperly through such a communication, its attempt would be exposed to all parties who could then take such steps as they saw fit to counter the attempt. Such steps could, of course, include exposing the attempt to public scrutiny. Deterrence is further promoted as the court is specifically prohibited by this rule from taking account of any such communication. Finally, as such communications are inimical to the proper administration of justice any party or non-party who breaches the prohibition may be subject to proceedings for contempt of court.
4. Exceptions to this general rule only arise in limited circumstances. Private communications are permissible where they are made further to a without-notice application. This is because the court is not finally determining such a matter (Part 14, rule 6; Part 13). Further, limited exceptions arise where formal administrative matters are concerned, such as enquiries concerning court fees applicable to proceedings or applications or enquiries concerning when hearings may be or have been listed. Such communications fall outside the general prohibition as they do not play any role in either the management of proceedings or adjudication of issues in dispute by a judge.
5. A further exception arises in respect of settlement processes. Where the court, either through a court officer or judge, takes part in a mediation process and quite properly receives private communications as part of that process this rule has no application. Such communications, as part of private caucusing, are typical of mediation and often play an essential role in its success. Were this rule to apply in such circumstances it would undermine the efficacy of the court's promotion of settlement contrary to the settlement principle. Where settlement is not, however, achieved through such a process, to ensure that any private communications do not thereafter taint the integrity of the administration of justice, the court officer or judge who took part in the settlement process must, generally, play no further role in the proceedings (see rule 15(10)).

## RULE 6.—NOTIFICATION OF SETTLEMENT

**(1) Parties shall inform the court promptly if they settle their dispute.**
**(2) Upon confirmation of settlement, the court may schedule any necessary hearings or make any necessary consequential orders.**
**(3) Where a dispute settles, anonymised information shall be provided to Ombudsman, regulators, and the government through the same process applicable to pre-action dispute prevention.**

*Sources: CPR r 39.10, PD52A, para 6.3.*

[28] Constitutional Reform Act 2005, s 3(1).

## COMMENTARY

1. Effective management of the court's resources requires parties to notify it promptly of settlement. This enables the court to ensure that it can manage its resources effectively, not least for the benefit of litigants in other proceedings. Prompt notification, for instance, enables the court to vacate hearing dates related to the settled proceedings and thus schedule hearings in other proceedings. It also saves what would otherwise be wasted judicial and administrative time preparing for any hearings that need to be vacated in the event of settlement.
2. When notified of settlement, the court may need to make further orders in the proceedings. Costs order may, for instance, need to be made (Part 3, rule 12). Judgment by consent may need to be entered and, where settlement applies to a party represented by a litigation friend, a hearing approving the settlement may need to be held (Part 15, rule 16). Rule 6(2) is accordingly a facultative provision, which applies the general dispute management power to such post-settlement situations.
3. The public interest in settlement goes beyond the effective management of the court's resources. Information obtained from settlement should play an important role in the promotion of systemic dispute prevention. This rule thus applies the approach provided for in the pre-action phase of a dispute, which requires Ombudsman, regulators, and the government to be provided with anonymised information concerning the dispute and its settlement (Part 5, rule 5(2)).

# SECTION 2: APPLICATIONS

## RULE 7.—APPLICATIONS—GENERAL

**(1) A party or non-party may apply for a court order. Applications may be made at any time. Generally, they should be made through the digital procedure. They may also be made orally at a hearing.**
**(2) Applications should only be made where necessary. They should be made as soon as necessary and desirable. They may be supported by evidence.**
**(3) Applications should, generally, be held with-notice consistently with Part 14, rule 6.**
**(4) Written applications must be verified by a statement of truth signed by the party or their lawyer where the party making the application wishes to rely on evidence contained within it.**
**(5) The court may dispense with the need to make an application.**
**(6) Renewed or successive applications for the same relief, which seek to vary or set aside the order made on the original application, may be made in accordance with Part 15, rule 12.**

*Sources: ELI-UNIDROIT Model Rules, r 50; CPR Pt 23, PD23A.*

## COMMENTARY

1. Effective dispute management requires parties, as well as the court, to be pro-active in their conduct of proceedings. Applying for court orders is the main way in which parties can do so. Applications can be made in respect of all aspects of procedure.

They can be made before proceedings commence. They can be made to seek permission to amend case statements, to obtain provisional or protective measures, to seek permission to appeal, for enforcement, or for a myriad of other reasons.

2. Parties should consider carefully whether an application is necessary. Examples where it is necessary to apply to the court for an order are: where a provisional or protective order, such as an interim injunction, is required; where an extension of time to comply with a procedural time limited is sought; or where relief from sanction is required. An application will also be necessary to vary or set aside court orders or directions. To promote effective and proportionate dispute management applications should be made as soon as it becomes apparent to the party making it that it is necessary and desirable.[29]
3. Parties should also co-operate with each other, as much as reasonably possible, to avoid the necessity of making applications. They should, for instance, seek wherever possible to agree directions, thus obviating the need for applications and hearings concerning them to be made. Equally, they should seek to agree directions such that where a court order is required an application could be determined via a written procedure or without a hearing.[30] In this way compliance with the co-operation principle will help promote economy, efficiency, and proportionality.
4. Applications can be made both in written form and orally. The digital procedure ought to provide the means to do this, ie making an application should be digital by default. They should also, generally, be made with-notice to other parties. They may also be made orally in court, ie without a prior written application having been made. Whether or not an application is supported by evidence will depend on the nature of the application made, eg an application for an interim injunction will require evidence to make out the case for it being granted or refused.[31]
5. A party may make renewed or successive applications for the same relief. The procedure governing such applications is set out in Part 15, rule 12. Additionally, where an application is heard without-notice it may be reheard with-notice consistently with Part 14, rule 6(10).
6. As with case statements, written applications must be accompanied by a statement of truth.[32]

## RULE 8.—APPLICATIONS—DETERMINATION AT A WRITTEN HEARING OR WITHOUT A HEARING

**(1) The court may determine an application without holding an oral hearing where permissible under Part 14, rule 4(7).**

**(2) The court may also determine an application without holding any form of hearing. It may do so where the parties consent to the judgment or an order under Part 15, rule 16.**

*Sources: CPR r 23.8.*

[29] CPR PD23A, para 2.7.

[30] Parties should seek to agree extensions of time for compliance.

[31] CPR PD 23A, para 9.

[32] Part 8, r 2.

## COMMENTARY

1. Applications will, generally be determined at a hearing, which includes a written hearing. Additionally, they may also be determined without any form of hearing taking place at all. This latter situation may arise where the parties consent to judgment or to an order.

## RULE 9.—APPLICATIONS FOR EXTENSIONS OF TIME TO COMPLY WITH PROCEDURAL TIME LIMITS

**(1) A party may apply to extend the time for compliance with any procedural time limit. The court may also vary time for compliance of its own initiative.**

**(2) An application to extend time to comply may be made prospectively or retrospectively. Parties may agree a prospective extension. No agreed extension may be for longer than twenty-eight days after the expiry of the original time limit. Where parties agree an extension they must inform the court.**

**(3) A prospective application may be granted by the court for good reason where the applicant has taken all reasonable steps to comply with the time limit and where the extension would not undermine effective dispute management.**

**(4) A retrospective application is an application for relief from sanctions for non-compliance.**

*Sources: CPR rr 3.1(2)(a), 3.8(4), 7.6(2).*

## COMMENTARY

1. Parties should generally expect to be held to time limits that require them to comply with procedural obligations. General compliance is a necessary feature of the effective management of individual proceedings, but also of the court's overarching duty to secure systemic proportionality. Notwithstanding the need to secure general compliance with procedural obligations, there will inevitably be a need in many—if not all—proceedings for procedural time limits to be extended. Parties may, for instance, need additional time than provided to serve their case statements. They may need further time to comply with their disclosure obligations. Examples can be multiplied.
2. This rule provides the basis under which parties can apply to extend any procedural time limit.[33] It is intended to simplify the approach set out under the CPR by providing a single rule setting out the test for such applications.[34] It is thus consistent with procedural accessibility. Parties may apply to extend time both prospectively and retrospectively. As under the CPR, parties ought properly to approach extensions prospectively. Doing so is an aspect of party co-operation and effective dispute management. It demonstrates that parties are paying proper attention to the need to ensure that proceedings are managed efficiently and economically.

[33] *Mucelli v Government of Albania* [2009] UKHL 2; [2009] 1 WLR 276.

[34] Under the CPR, the general power to extend time limits was displaced by other specific rules; *Vinos v Marks & Spencer Plc* [2000] EWCA Civ B526; [2001] 3 All ER 784 and *Titmus v General Motors UK Ltd* [2016] EWHC 2021 (QB).

3. A prospective application may, however, only be granted where the applicant has taken all reasonable steps to comply with the time limit before it expires. Time limits are to be complied with and the presence of this discretionary power should not be taken as licence for parties to adopt a laissez-faire approach to compliance. It may also only be granted for good reason.[35] The courts have consistently stressed that a party's lawyer's incompetence, oversight, or a failure to properly manage their practice is unlikely to amount to a good reason.[36] Finally, such an extension may only be granted where the extension itself would not disrupt the effective management of proceedings. The court will thus also have to consider the effect that granting an extension may have on the management of the immediate and other proceedings.[37] Where, for instance, an extension might require a future hearing and particularly a trial date to be set aside and rescheduled that might have a negative impact on the efficient, economical, and proportionate management of the immediate proceedings. It may also, due to the need to reschedule a hearing, adversely affect the court's ability to list for hearing other proceedings. That may negatively affect other parties' ability to secure effective and timely access to justice through delaying the effective management and resolution of their dispute.
4. As under the CPR, rule 9(2) permits parties to agree prospective extensions of time for compliance with procedural requirements. Again, this is intended to promote effective management. There is no good reason why parties should not, as part of their duty to co-operate with the court in carrying out the effective management of disputes, take an active role in seeking to agree extensions of time to comply. Effective court management, however, requires it to retain oversight of such extensions. Parties must inform the court of any such extensions. This ensures that the court can police agreed extensions, varying them where necessary for the proper management of the dispute. It also ensures that the dispute management timetable is updated effectively, which again enables the court to carry out its management function and monitor compliance effectively. Oversight is also retained by party agreed extensions being limited to a maximum of twenty-eight days. Any extension beyond that time can only be obtained on application. Where parties cannot agree extensions, a party may apply to extend a time limit.
5. The test for the grant of a retrospective application is stricter than that for the grant of prospective applications.[38] That a retrospective application is made, by definition, means that the party making it has failed to comply with a procedural obligation. They will have thus failed to adhere to the compliance principle. They will also have failed to co-operate effectively with the court in the effective management of the dispute. Necessarily, this will also mean that the non-compliant party will have failed to act in a way that promotes a fair process for their opponent (by unreasonably delaying it) and for other litigants in general (by failing to promote systemic proportionality). For these reasons, a party that seeks a retrospective application must satisfy the test for the grant of relief from sanction for non-compliance (rule 34). That this stricter test applies is also intended to encourage a pro-active approach to making applications and, conversely, deter the making of retrospective applications.

[35] *Collier v Williams* [2006] EWCA Civ 20; [2006] WLR 1945 at [87].
[36] *Hashtroodi v Hancock* [2004] EWCA Civ 652; [2004] 1 WLR 3206 at [131].
[37] *Jalla v International Trading & Shipping Co Ltd* [2021] EWCA Civ 1559 at [29]–[30].
[38] *Collier v Williams* [2006] EWCA Civ 20; [2006] WLR 1945.

# SECTION 3: DETERMINATION OF PROCEDURAL MANAGEMENT TRACK

## RULE 10.—CLASSIFICATION OF PROCEEDINGS AND ALLOCATION TO A PROCEDURAL MANAGEMENT TRACK

**(1) The court shall classify all proceedings and allocate them to an appropriate procedural management track.**

**(2) Classification and allocation is a single, automated decision-making process carried out via the digital procedure, except where the court directs otherwise on application of the parties. It is carried out on the basis of information provided to the court by the parties.**

**(3) Classification and allocation shall take place after service of a substantive defence in the proceedings.**

**(4) Where a procedural defence is served, classification and allocation will not take place until it is finally determined.**

*Sources: ELI-UNIDROIT Model Rules, r 49; CPR Pt 26.*

## COMMENTARY

1. Classification and allocation of proceedings serve two distinct purposes. The former is concerned with the maintenance of the CPR's incorporation of formal, structural proportionality into civil procedure via its procedural case tracks (CPR Pts 27, 28, and 29).[39] The latter forms part of this Code's approach to integrating settlement processes into dispute management.
2. Classification and allocation is the initial stage of the post-issue dispute management process. It is generally intended to be carried out through an automated process, based on information provided by the parties via the digital procedure. Information provided should be sufficient to satisfy the requirements of rules 11 and 12. This will ensure that the majority of disputes, ie those that are low and moderate value disputes will be classified and allocated in the most timely and cost-efficient way (rule 11(2)(a) and (b)). Disputes that are likely to be intermediate or high value (rule 11(2)(c) and (d)) or those that are likely to involve complex issues of fact or law are likely to fall within the exception provided by rule 10(2). In these latter cases, classification and allocation is likely to require detailed consideration by the court in the light of party submissions and should, therefore, take place at a non-physical hearing.
3. To ensure that parties are not unnecessarily put to the time and expense of providing the court with sufficient information for effective classification or allocation, this process shall only take place after any procedural defence advanced has been finally determined and a substantive defence has been served.

[39] J Sorabji, *English Civil Justice after Woolf and Jackson* (CUP, 2014) at 188.

## RULE 11.—CLASSIFICATION OF PROCEEDINGS

**(1) Unless there is good reason not to do so, the court will classify proceedings that include a claim for relief for a specified sum of money as follows**
**(a) all proceedings where the claim for relief is below the value of £10,000 are low value proceedings;**
**(b) all proceedings where the claim for relief is valued at £10,000 to £25,000 are moderate value proceedings;**
**(c) all proceedings where the claim for relief is valued above £25,000 to £100,000 are intermediate value proceedings;**
**(d) all proceedings where the claim for relief is above the value of £100,000 are high value proceedings.**
**(2) Where proceedings do not include a claim for relief for a specified sum of money the court shall take account of the following in determining their classification as low, moderate, intermediate, or high value proceedings**
**(a) the number of parties involved;**
**(b) the nature and complexity of the dispute, and the issues involved;**
**(c) the importance of the dispute to the parties and the public.**
**(3) High value proceedings will be managed and tried in the Upper Tier of the High Court. All other proceedings will be managed and tried in the First-tier of the High Court. The court may, on its own initiative or on application of a party, transfer the management of an intermediate value claim to the Upper Tier of the High Court where there is good reason to do so.**

*Sources: ELI-UNIDROIT Model Rules, r 49; CPR r 26.8.*

## COMMENTARY

1. The use of procedural case tracks based on dispute value was introduced into the CPR by the Woolf reforms.[40] Their introduction was specifically intended to promote both individual and systemic proportionality by matching procedure to the nature of the dispute.[41] This particularly ensured that within a trans-substantive procedure, a differential approach could properly be taken to ensure that like cases could be treated similarly and different cases could be treated differently: the basis of differentiation being dispute value, the nature and complexity of the dispute, the issues it involved and their importance both to the parties and the public.[42]
2. Rule 11 maintains the CPR's approach. It does so in common with approaches in several other jurisdictions.[43] In this the Code differs from the ELI-UNIDROIT

[40] H Woolf, *Access to Justice: Interim Report to the Lord Chancellor on the Civil Justice System in England and Wales* (HMSO) (1995) at 21; J Sorabji (2014) at 188–196. S Clark and R Jackson, *The Reform of Civil Justice* (Sweet & Maxwell, 2018) at 214.

[41] H Woolf, *Access to Justice: Final Report to the Lord Chancellor on the Civil Justice System in England and Wales* (HMSO) (1996) at 24.

[42] S Subrin, 'The Limitations of Transsubstantive Procedure: An Essay on Adjusting the "One Size Fits All" Assumption' (2010) 87(2) Denver University Law Review 377; S Subrin, 'Uniformity in Procedural Rules and the Attributes of a Sound Procedural System: The Case for Presumptive Limits' (1997) 49(1) Alabama Law Review 795; C Crifo, 'Does Procedural mean trans-substantive? A historical and normative analysis of English Civil Procedure Rules', in R Assy and A Higgins, *Principles, Procedure, Justice—Essays in Honour of Adrian Zuckerman* (OUP, 2020)

[43] E Jeuland, *Introduction to French Business Litigation* (Joly) (2016) at 128–131; S Nieuwendijk et al, 'The Paradox of Access to Justice—Empirical Research Into The Attitude Of The Cantonal Judge Towards

Model Rules,[44] which do not adopt procedural case tracks, preferring to give courts a greater discretion to match procedure to disputes on a case-by-case basis. That approach is rejected here on grounds of proportionality. Requiring the court to consider the exact nature and amount of process to be afforded to each dispute on a case-by-case basis would involve a disproportionate use of both court and party time and resources. Providing a mechanism that classifies disputes according to standardised criteria and which matches them to broad procedural categories that then have standard dispute management directions provides a more efficient basis on which to manage them proportionately. The ELI-UNDROIT approach further provides a basis for inconsistent approaches to be applied to similar cases, which runs contrary to the aim of providing procedural equality—like cases being treated alike—and a fair process overall.

3. Rule 11(1) establishes four procedural case tracks. It thus adopts the approach recommended by the Jackson Fixed Costs Review, which was not introduced into the CPR until October 2023.[45] It does so for the reason succinctly stated by Clark and Jackson, that a single track—the CPR's multi-track—being available for relatively low value claims to significantly complex claims valued in the billions of pounds '*sits uneasily with the basic intention of the track system*'. A single track for disputes above the value of £25,000 is not a proportionate approach. Rule 11(1) provides that more proportionate approach, which can tailor procedure to the needs of disputes that are valued between £25,000 and £100,000.[46] Each track should be supplemented by standardised directions provided for in the digital procedure.
4. Not all disputes involve a claim for damages. To classify them, rule 11(2) restates the approach taken under CPR rr 26.7 and 26.8(1). It thus takes account of the number of parties, the nature and complexity of the issues, and their importance in determining classification. The greater the number of parties and the greater the number, complexity, and importance of the issues in dispute, the greater the likelihood that a dispute ought to be classified as intermediate or high value proceedings.
5. Rule 11(3) ensures that the right level of judge deals with the right type of dispute. Only those disputes classified as high value ought to be dealt with in the Upper Tier of the High Court. This reserves such disputes for what is, at present, the High Court. All other disputes ought to be dealt with in the First-tier of the High Court, which is equivalent to the County Court. This ensures that a clear general distinction is maintained between the High Court's Upper and First-tier in terms of their workload, with the most complex, high value, and important disputes being the province of the Upper Tier. Where, however, there is good reason to do so an intermediate value dispute may be transferred to that tier. Good reason could arise where the dispute raised a particularly complex issue or one of general public importance or where the First-tier was bound by an Upper Tier precedent and one issue in the dispute concerned the validity of that precedent.

Unrepresented Parties In Dutch Civil Procedure', in A Uzelac and CH van Rhee, *Revisiting Procedural Human Rights* (Intersentia) (2017).

[44] ELI-UNIDROIT Model Rules, r 49.

[45] R Jackson, *Review of Civil Litigation Costs: Supplemental Report Fixed Recoverable Costs* (Judicial Office, July 2017); S Clark and R Jackson (2018) at 214–215. Civil Procedure (Amendment No 2) Rules 2023 (SI 2023/105).

[46] Civil Procedure Rule Committee, October 2022 Minutes at [27].

## RULE 12.—ALLOCATION OF PROCEEDINGS

**(1) Following classification, the court will allocate proceedings to either the settlement or adjudication management track.**
**(2) Where proceedings are low or moderate value they will be allocated to the settlement track. They may be allocated to the adjudication track where that is in the public interest or the parties have substantially engaged in pre-action dispute management.**
**(3) Other proceedings will be allocated to the adjudication track. With party consent they may be allocated to the settlement track where that furthers the purposive principle.**

*Sources: ALI/UNIDROIT Principles, principle 24; ALI/UNIDROIT Reporters' Study, r 18.5; Briggs, Chancery Modernisation Review, 5.9–5.16.*

## COMMENTARY

1. It has long been known that not all disputes are best suited to adversarial, rights-based adjudication.[47] Rule 12 recognises that, and with rules 15 and 18 gives effect to the idea that the civil courts should provide a holistic approach to dispute resolution through integrating consensual settlement processes into civil procedure.[48]
2. Allocation takes place through the same process as classification (rule 11). To promote proportionality, it presumptively allocates low and moderate value proceedings to the settlement track.[49] This is not to say they cannot be allocated to the adjudication track, eg where they raise issues of fraud or novel issues of law. Where novel issues are concerned the possibility of differential allocation provides a safety valve that protects the court's ability to carry out its constitutional function concerning the law and its development. Where the parties have engaged substantively in settlement processes during pre-action dispute resolution that too may militate against allocation to the settlement track. Much will depend upon the extent and nature of such engagement.
3. Other proceedings will generally be allocated to the adjudication track. This presumption may be set aside where the parties consent to allocation to the settlement track.

## RULE 13.—RECLASSIFICATION AND REALLOCATION OF PROCEEDINGS

**(1) A party may apply to vary the classification and/or initial allocation of proceedings. The application shall be considered at a hearing.**
**(2) Where proceedings are reclassified any fixed or proportionate costs applicable to the initial classification apply to the date of reclassification and thereafter any fixed or proportionate costs applicable to the subsequent classification apply.**

*Sources: ELI-UNIDROIT Model Rules, r 50(3); CPR rr 26.10, 27.15.*

[47] L Fuller, 'The Forms and Limits of Adjudication' (1978) 92 Harvard Law Review 353; V Flango and T Clarke, *Reimagining Courts—A Design for the Twenty-First Century* (Temple, 2017) chap 7.

[48] F Sander (1976) at 131.

[49] Civil Justice Council, *Online Dispute Resolution for Low Value Civil Claims* (2015) at 19–20; M Briggs, *Civil Courts Structure Review—Final Report* (July 2016) at 59.

## COMMENTARY

1. The rule builds on the power provided within CPR r 26.10, for reallocation of proceedings after initial allocation to the CPR's procedural case tracks. It is necessarily wider than that rule due to the provision here of both classification according to value etc, and allocation to either the settlement or the adjudication tracks. It also incorporates provision, analogous to that in CPR r 27.15, which governs the application of costs where proceedings under the CPR are reallocated from its small claims track to either its fast track or multi-track.
2. Consistently, with the AI principle, decisions concerning reclassification or reallocation may be assisted by an assessment of the proceedings carried out by any applicable AI programme that forms part of the digital procedure. Use of such information is, as in general, intended to increase the quality of judicial decision-making by rendering it more consistent with decisions made in like cases. It is also intended to improve decision-making by providing judges with an assessment of the suitability of the proceedings for reallocation or reclassification. This may include an assessment of the suitability of any particular form of settlement process to assist judicial consideration of whether proceedings should be reclassified out of or into the settlement track. All such information must be made available to the parties prior to any decision being made to enable them to make submissions in respect of it (see rule 3(5).

## RULE 14.—JUDICIAL CONTINUITY

**(1) Upon allocation to a management track the court will assign responsibility for the management and, where necessary, determination of proceedings to a designated judge.**

**(2) Where during the course of proceedings and for good reason the designated judge can no longer manage or determine the proceedings, they may recuse themselves either temporarily or permanently.**

**(3) Where a designated judge recuses themselves, another judge will be assigned responsibility, either temporarily or permanently as the case may be, for the management and determination of the proceedings.**

**(4) During the course of proceedings a designated judge may be replaced on the application of a party. Replacement may only be effected where it is necessary in the interests of the proper administration of justice.**

**(5) The designated judge may authorise a member of the court administration to assist them in managing the proceedings. A member of the court administration authorised to exercise judicial functions may exercise those functions whilst assisting the designated judge.**

**(6) A designated judge may not authorise a member of the court administration to assist them in any part of the process where the court is exercising adjudicatory functions.**

*Sources: Woolf—Interim Report, chap 11; Jackson Costs Review—Preliminary Report, chaps 43, 58, and 60.*

## COMMENTARY

1. Rule 14 marks a departure for English and Welsh civil procedure. It introduces a novel rule that makes provision for judicial continuity or, as it is otherwise known, docketing. It requires individual judges to be assigned responsibility for managing and where necessary determining proceedings once they are allocated to a management track. Thus, a single judge will be responsible for proceedings from allocation until they are resolved via settlement or judgment. That judge, if proceedings are allocated to the settlement track, may also be responsible for facilitating settlement. Consistently with the judicial independence principle, determination of which judge is assigned responsibility for which proceedings is a judicial decision. It is thus to be determined by the judiciary, or by members of the court administration who are authorised to exercise judicial functions, as an aspect of judicial deployment.[50]
2. Allocation is not necessarily definitive. A designated judge may recuse themselves at any point during the management of proceedings for good reason. They may do so, for instance, temporarily, if they are unable to deal with proceedings due to ill-health and their absence would have a negative impact on the court's ability to secure the purposive principle, ie it would cause unnecessary delay in the management of proceedings. They may do so permanently where their management results in them being unable to manage, resolve, or adjudicate fairly, ie where bias arises from their management or due to their conduct being such as to prejudice the parties' ability to obtain a fair procedure.
3. Rule 14(4) also provides a power to replace a designated judge with another where that is in the interests of the administration of justice. This ensures that the decision whether a judge is replaced is not left solely in the hands of the designated judge. One instance where this power is likely to be exercised is where a designated judge is not available to hear a trial in proceedings.[51] This is likely to arise where they are still dealing with another matter, most likely to be the trial in other proceedings that has over-run its timetable. In such circumstances, giving effect to the purposive principle would require the trial to go ahead with a different judge. It also enables parties to seek the removal of a designated judge where bias etc arises.
4. Judicial continuity was to be introduced into the CPR following the Jackson Costs Review. It concluded that its implementation would '*promote effective case management and help to reduce costs*',[52] as it did in other jurisdictions, such as the United States of America and Australia,[53] and as it did in England and Wales in the Technology and Construction Court.[54] That conclusion was not, however, made a reality. A more targeted approach was to be adopted. Only those cases, primarily those on the multi-track,

[50] Lord Chancellor's Department, *The Lord Chancellor's Judiciary-Related Functions: Proposals (The 'Concordat')* at [36] (January 2004).

[51] M Briggs (2013) at 56–58.

[52] R Jackson, *Review of Civil Litigation Costs: Preliminary Report* (May 2009) Vol II at 433–434, 586–587.

[53] R Jackson (May 2009) Vol II, chaps 58 and 60; R Fox, *Justice in the Twenty-First Century* (Cavendish, 2000) at 30 and following; H Woolf (1995) at 63–72; K Takeshita, 'Overcoming Judicial Reluctance to Secure Effective Case Management' (2014) 33 CJQ 281.

[54] R Jackson (May 2009) Vol II at 434.

were to be allocated to designated judges.[55] Assignment was then effected either on application of the parties or on the court's own initiative, but was generally confined to claims proceeding in specialist jurisdictions such as the Commercial Court.[56]

5. This rule thus departs from the approach adopted by the CPR not only by introducing a specific rule governing judicial continuity, but also by entrenching it as of general application. It does not, for instance, accept the view taken by Lord Woolf and then Lord Neuberger MR that judicial continuity should only be applied to multi-track cases.[57] The benefit of judicial continuity, as evident from other jurisdictions, which the Jackson Review and Lord Neuberger MR relied upon to support its introduction, stems from its universal application in those jurisdictions. Evidence particularly from the United States, for instance, demonstrates that its general application is a key means by which efficiency is increased through a reduction in unnecessary delay.[58] It has also been shown to increase individual judicial motivation to ensure that management is carried out effectively, not least through promoting a sense of individual accountability for the assigned proceedings, which would not otherwise exist.[59] Assignment to individual judges also ensures, as Lord Neuberger MR noted, that judges would not come to case management hearings ignorant of what has happened prior to their involvement. A single judge managing proceedings thus does not have to familiarise themselves with the proceedings, what hearings had previously taken place, or which directions had previously been made, as would be the case where a new judge dealt with the proceedings at different hearings. Court and party time and cost would thus be reduced as a result.[60] These general benefits apply irrespective of the nature or value of a dispute. Added value through judicial continuity is likely, however, to particularly arise where claims are high value or complex,[61] but that is additional to the general improvement in effective management that the evidence suggests accrues where judicial continuity is applied generally to all proceedings.

6. Allocation to designated judges would also enable judges to maintain, and where necessary, develop specialist skills and experience. Increased experience will, as noted consistently over the last twenty years, also promote more efficient and cost-effective management,[62] further to the purposive principle.

7. The main reason why judicial continuity was not introduced generally under the CPR was due to its perceived incompatibility with the way in which the English and Welsh judiciary is organised. The assignment of judges to circuits, particularly High Court judges who only spend part of the year on Circuit, and the requirement for judges to work across civil, family, and criminal justice systems are said to militate against its general introduction.[63] There is, however, no good reason why either of

[55] R Jackson (December 2009) chap 39; D Neuberger, *Docketing: Completing Case Management's Unfinished Revolution* (Ninth Lecture in Implementation Programme) (Solicitors' Costs Conference 2012) at [30].

[56] S Clark and R Jackson (2018) at 119–121; Admiralty and Commercial Court Guide 2022, D1.4-D1.8. Financial List claims under CPR PD63AA are automatically assigned to designated judges.

[57] H Woolf (1995) at 63; D Neuberger (2012) at [30]–[31].

[58] T Church, *Justice Delayed—The Pace of Civil Litigation in Urban Trial Courts* (1978) Williamsburg, Virginia: National Center for State Courts at 55; D Neuberger (2012) at [20]–[22]; M Solomon, *Caseflow Management in the Trial Court* (American Bar Association, 1973) at 21; N Taylor and B Fitzpatrick, 'Docketing Lite: An Analysis of a Process of Assigning Multi-Track Cases to Individual Judges' (2012) 31 CJQ 430.

[59] K Takeshita (2014) at 285.

[60] D Neuberger (2012) at [22]–[23].

[61] D Neuberger (2012) at [30]–[31].

[62] H Woolf (1995) at 64; D Neuberger (2012) at [32].

[63] H Woolf (1995) at 63; D Neuberger (2012) at [29].

these reasons should stand in the way of its introduction. Digital procedure, and particularly digital case management systems, ought to enable a judge sitting in any part of England and Wales to manage and hear proceedings effectively irrespective of which Circuit's geographic area it falls within. That judges are required to sit across different jurisdictions, whether family, civil, criminal, or increasingly that of the tribunals, ought to make no difference for the same reason. Effective use of digital procedure across those jurisdictions ought to enable judges to manage their workload, as allocated to them across the whole of the jurisdictions, effectively. To suggest otherwise is to accept that the justice system as a whole cannot be managed effectively. That cannot be right, and in so far as it might be that calls for further reform of the Circuits and judicial allocation.

8. The success of judicial continuity does not simply depend upon assignment of proceedings to individual judges. It also calls for close co-operation between judges and the court administration.[64] This is provided for by rules 14(5) and (6). Co-operation can take two forms.
9. First, where they are authorised to exercise judicial functions, court staff may assist a designated judge in managing proceedings judicially. They may, for instance, work with the designated judge by dealing with routine or uncontested applications, eg for extensions of time or to amend case statements. Such routine applications would not impinge upon the benefits derived from judicial continuity as they would not tend to undermine the designated judge's familiarity with the proceedings or the manner in which they had progressed.
10. Secondly, they may also be authorised by a designated judge to facilitate a settlement process. The benefit here would be to ensure that the designated judge would not then have to potentially recuse themselves from any further dealing with the proceedings should the settlement process not result in resolution, as might be necessitated by rule 15(8) if they conducted the settlement process.
11. These forms of assistance are in addition to the fact that court staff authorised to exercise judicial functions could themselves be assigned to manage proceedings classified as low value proceedings (rule 11(2)(a)). Court staff may also, as normal, assist by carrying out necessary administrative functions for the management of proceedings.

## SECTION 4: SETTLEMENT MANAGEMENT

### RULE 15.—SETTLEMENT MANAGEMENT PROCESSES

**(1) Where proceedings are allocated to the settlement track, the court will**
- **(a) assign low and moderate value proceedings to the court's mediation process, which may either be low-cost and timely telephone-facilitated mediation or e-mediation. The parties may opt-out of mediation if they enter into a binding arbitration process to resolve their dispute;**
- **(b) provide other proceedings with a settlement management assessment.**

**(2) The assessment will consider the following**
- **(a) the time and cost of settlement processes;**
- **(b) the extent to which the parties have differing views on the law and the facts;**

64 H Woolf (1995) at 68; D Neuberger (2012) at [33].

**(c) the extent to which evidence of fact is necessary and disclosure will be required;**
**(d) the importance of privacy to the parties;**
**(e) the importance of maintaining a future relationship between the parties;**
**(f) the importance of an independent evaluation of the dispute;**
**(g) the extent to which communication between the parties may need to be facilitated;**
**(h) the nature of the relief sought; and**
**(i) whether the parties consent to an adjudicative form of settlement process.**

**(3) The assessment will determine the proceedings relative suitability to different settlement methods. Those methods, include**
**(a) negotiation;**
**(b) mediation;**
**(c) early neutral evaluation;**
**(d) mini trial (or executive tribunal);**
**(e) collaborative law; and**
**(f) arbitration, either binding or non-binding.**

**(4) The assessment will be carried out by means of automated decision-making based on information uploaded by the parties to the digital dispute management file. Parties shall be given a reasonable opportunity to supplement any information that is on the file before the court carries out its assessment.**

**(5) Once the assessment is made, the parties may make submissions to the court to assist its consideration before any order is made.**

**(6) Where negotiation, mediation, or early neutral evaluation are suitable, parties may utilise e-negotiation, e-mediation, or early e-neutral evaluation provided by the court. Alternatively, they may utilise telephone-facilitated negotiation or mediation, or early neutral evaluation provided by the court or by a third party of their choice.**

**(7) Where arbitration is suitable, and the parties consent to its use, the court may**
**(a) provide access to a court-based e-arbitration scheme; or**
**(b) refer the parties to an arbitration scheme approved by the Consensual Dispute Resolution Council.**

**(8) Where the court provides telephone-based negotiation, or telephone-based mediation for low or moderate value proceedings, it shall be facilitated by a court officer with negotiation or mediation training, respectively.**

**(9) Where the court provides e-mediation, in-person mediation, e-early neutral evaluation, or in-person early neutral evaluation, for intermediate and high value proceedings a court officer may not act as the mediator or evaluator.**

**(10) Where an evaluative form of process does not result in settlement, the mediator or evaluator where they are a judge must have no further involvement in the proceedings. This prohibition may be waived by consent of the parties under Part 1, rule 13.**

*Sources: ALI/UNIDROIT Principles, principle 24; ALI/UNIDROIT Reporters' Study, r 18.5; ELI-UNIDROIT Model Rules, r 10; Civil Justice Council, Online Dispute Resolution for Low Value Claims (2015); Briggs, Civil Courts Structure Review—Interim Report (December 2015); Briggs, Civil Courts Structure Review—Final Report (July 2016).*

## COMMENTARY

1. Rule 15 reflects a fundamental reality that has been historically glossed over and under-emphasised within English and Welsh civil procedure: that the civil justice system is '*not a system of trials but a system of alternative means of resolution*'.[65] That

[65] A Hinshaw, A Kupfer Schneider, and S Rudolph Cole, *Discussions in Dispute Resolution* (OUP, 2021) at ix.

truth, recently stated but long recognised, is underpinned by the reality that if all disputes were to require adjudication civil courts would need far more resources, administrative staff, and judges than they currently have, have ever been provided, or which the State could reasonably provide.

2. The starting point for settlement track management is to provide parties with a proportionate process. Rule 15(1)(a) gives effect to this by requiring parties to engage in a form of low-cost, speedy mediation where a claim is classified as low or moderate value. Parties may, however, opt-out of mediation if they agree to enter into binding arbitration, which may be provided by either a low-cost court-based e-arbitration scheme or through a suitable scheme[66] approved by the Consensual Dispute Resolution Council.
3. For other proceedings the form of settlement process is determined by the court in the light of an automated settlement management assessment. This should recommend the most suitable form of resolution process for the proceedings. The incorporation of this multi-factorial assessment as a basis for matching dispute to settlement process may be novel in England and Wales but is well-established in the United States where it has formed part of the *Guide to Judicial Management of Cases in ADR* since 2001.[67] Such assessments will become increasingly commonplace given the decision in *Churchill v Merthyr Tydfil* (2023) that ADR can be mandated by the courts.[68] The key is to consider the features of the dispute and party characteristics so that the optimum form of process is identified. By way of example, a dispute that involves discrete questions of law may be more suited to an evaluative process carried out by a lawyer or judge as a third party. Hence an evaluative mediation or early neutral evaluation may be suitable. A commercial dispute between businesses might equally be suited to a mini-trial process if, for instance, it would otherwise require a long, expensive adjudicative process and senior decision-makers from the businesses could take part and thus be persuaded to progress the settlement process as a business negotiation. Where parties are involved in, and will continue to maintain a long-term relationship after resolution, more interest-based processes such as a lawyer-led negotiation, a collaborative law process, or facilitative mediation may be more appropriate. Much will depend on the individual circumstances.
4. Parties should have a choice of provider for each form of settlement process. The court should provide, as a default, electronic resolution schemes, which may be used by the parties. It should also provide telephone-facilitated negotiation or mediation, in-person mediation, or early neutral evaluation (rule 15(6)). A similar approach is taken to arbitration (rule 15(7)). The intention underpinning this

[66] CIArb's Business Arbitration Scheme provides a low-cost arbitration process for low value business disputes. There is no reason why other such schemes could not be established for other types of dispute.

[67] R Niemic, D Stienstra, and R Ravitz, *Guide to Judicial Management of Cases in ADR* (Federal Judicial Center, 2001) at 39–47; F Sander and S Goldberg, 'Fitting the Forum to the Fuss: A User-Friendly Guide to Selecting an ADR Procedure' (1994) 10 Negot J 49; F Sander and L Rozdeiczer, 'Matching Cases and Dispute Resolution Procedures: Detailed Analysis Leading to a Mediation-Centered Approach' (2006) 11(1) Harv Neg Law Rev 1.

[68] *Churchill v Merthyr Tydfil County Borough Council* [2023] EWCA Civ 1416 at [60]–[63], where Vos MR set out guidelines for the courts to consider in assessing whether to mandate the use of an ADR process. Those guidelines require consideration of the form of ADR proposed to be mandated. The courts will thus have to become much more familiar than in the past with the many and different forms of ADR and their utility for different disputes.

is to balance party autonomy in the choice of provider, with the need to ensure that effective processes are available in the circumstances that parties are unable or unwilling to utilise a privately-run settlement scheme. It is also intended to promote competition amongst private sector providers, which it is anticipated will lead to the development of specialisation, expertise, and competitive pricing for the provision of such services. It further reflects an understanding that the court is unlikely to be able to provide access to its own schemes for all proceedings allocated to the settlement track. Thus, the provision of settlement processes should operate as a complementary partnership between the civil courts and the private sector facilitated through the digital portal. The promotion and maintenance of standards amongst private sector providers, as well as court-based schemes, ought to be secured through their endorsement by the Consensual Dispute Resolution Council.

5. Rule 15(10) makes clear that where an evaluative form of resolution process, whether mediation, early neutral evaluation, mini-trial, or non-binding arbitration, is carried out by a judge and it does not result in settlement that judge must, generally, have no further involvement with proceedings.[69] Effective management thus requires that a judge-evaluator in such schemes ought not to be the judge responsible for managing the proceedings under rule 14. The reason for this prohibition on further engagement is to avoid problems arising from any perception of judicial bias following on from the evaluation. This prohibition as it concerns the protection of impartiality may, however, be waived.

## RULE 16.—SETTLEMENT MANAGEMENT DIRECTIONS

**(1) The court may give any directions necessary to manage the settlement process. It may apply and/or vary any standard directions applicable to specific types of claim for relief or classification of proceedings. It may particularly give directions concerning**
**(a) the timing for completion of any settlement process;**
**(b) steps parties are to take to complete a settlement process;**
**(c) steps necessary to enable parties to take stock of the settlement process;**
**(d) the sanctions applicable for non-compliance with settlement management directions.**

**(2) Where a settlement process does not result in settlement, the court will give directions either reallocating the proceedings**
**(a) to a further settlement process or processes; or**
**(b) to the adjudication track.**

**(3) In considering reallocating the proceedings, the court shall consider**
**(a) the views of the parties;**
**(b) the settlement management assessment;**
**(c) whether any further settlement process would be proportionate;**
**(d) the effect any further settlement process would have on the parties' ability to secure a timely and cost-effective judgment.**

[69] D Foskett, *Foskett on Compromise* (Sweet & Maxwell, 2024) at 585, Appendix 6.

## COMMENTARY

1. Rule 16 is a specific instance of the general dispute management power. It does not limit it. On the contrary, it is intended to highlight particular matters that must be taken into consideration by the court when managing proceedings allocated to the settlement track.
2. Standard directions ought to be provided via the digital procedure as part of dispute management generally. They should be tailored to specific types of dispute, eg there ought to be specific standard directions for personal injury, clinical negligence, breach of contract, commercial disputes, etc. They should also be tailored to the particular classification, eg standard directions for low value disputes ought not to be as detailed as those for high value disputes. Standard directions are, however, only the starting point. They may require modification depending on the individual circumstances of the dispute. Thus, the court can, consistently with the purposive principle, modify or vary any standard direction as necessary.
3. Rule 16(1) highlights particular directions that should be given to further effective management of the settlement process. Proportionality is key here. Directions must therefore ensure that the settlement process does not infringe the general access principle through the cost and time taken to conduct that process. To promote compliance with settlement management directions, and hence a more effective settlement process, any directions should also set out the consequences of non-compliance. Those consequences should underscore the importance of compliance and that the parties ought to take the settlement process seriously.
4. Inevitably, and quite properly, not all disputes will be resolved via the settlement process. Where this occurs the court and parties should consider two options: whether to embark upon a further settlement process; or whether to move to adjudication. In some instances, use of a further settlement process may be proportionate and economical and may not act as an unreasonable fetter on the general access principle. Where, for instance, the initial settlement process was a low cost, relatively simple one such as negotiation, it may be appropriate to direct the use of mediation or ENE. Just as in the use of contractual multi-tiered dispute resolution clauses, it may also be economical and proportionate to move from negotiation to mediation to a third form of settlement process such as an advisory adjudication or, where the parties agree, a binding arbitration. In other cases it will not be economical or proportionate to engage in further settlement processes and the court should direct reallocation to the adjudication track.
5. Rule 16(3) articulates the factors to be considered when determining the question of what steps to take where a settlement process does not resolve a dispute. The parties' views will be an important factor to be considered. They should not, however, be determinative. The factors are intended to ensure that the court's decision is properly informed both by the anticipated efficacy and appropriateness of any further, and specific, settlement process and by the need to ensure that the use of settlement processes remains consistent with procedural principle.

## RULE 17.—OFFERS TO SETTLE

**(1) Any party may make a genuine offer to settle the dispute to one or more parties in proceedings.**
**(2) An offer must be in writing and clearly specify the terms on which it is made and that it is made under this rule. It must, particularly, make clear whether it is an offer to settle the whole dispute or part of it and, if the latter, which part. It must also specify if the offer is inclusive of interest and/or costs.**
**(3) An offer must be open for acceptance for a specified period, which must not be less than twenty-one days. Where, however, an offer is made less than twenty-one days before trial or the final scheduled event of a continuous digital process it shall remain open for acceptance until they have concluded.**
**(4) An offer remains open unless rejected, replaced by a subsequent offer, or withdrawn in writing.**
**(5) A party to whom an offer is made may make their own offer to settle (a counter-offer). A counter-offer when made is a rejection of the other party's offer to settle.**
**(6) An offer to settle is without prejudice save as to costs. A judge dealing with an adjudicative hearing must not be informed of the fact and nature of such an offer. Where the adjudicative hearing deals with some but not all matters in dispute, the judge may be informed of an offer to settle in respect of matters already determined and of the existence but not terms of other offers to settle. Where a judge is informed of any prohibited matters before judgment, they may continue to deal with the proceedings unless such knowledge would give rise to an appearance of bias.**
**(7) Parties may make offers to settle proceedings outside this rule. Where they do so the costs consequences applicable to this rule shall not apply.**
**(8) Except as varied by any provision in this rule, offers to settle are governed by the law of contract.**
**(9) Part 3 governs the costs consequent on settlement when reached under this rule.**

*Sources: ALI/UNIDROIT Principles, principles 24.3, 25.2; ALI/UNIDROIT Reporters' Study, rr 16, 32.5; ELI-UNIDROIT Model Rules, rr 9, 241; CPR Pt 36.*

## COMMENTARY

1. Since 1999, the CPR has provided through its Pt 36 a comprehensive mechanism to promote settlement through parties making offers to settle their dispute.[70] It provides a self-contained code governing such offers. It is not a complete code; such offers are also governed by other aspects of the CPR and the substantive law of contract.[71] CPR Pt 36's history is not, however, altogether satisfactory. It has been subject to significant substantive revision four times and was replaced in its entirety in 2015.[72] It is a detailed, complex, and technical part of the CPR, contrary to the explicit intention of the Woolf reforms and the Civil Procedure Act 1997.[73]
2. Notwithstanding CPR Pt 36's problematic drafting and complexity, it is accepted to have been a successful innovation of the CPR.[74] It was also accepted in the ALI/

[70] RSC Ord 22 and CCR Ord 11.
[71] D Foskett (2024) at 195–198.
[72] D Foskett (2024) chaps 14 to 20; A Zuckerman (2021) chap 27.
[73] H Woolf (1995) at 218; H Woolf (1996) at 4; Civil Procedure Act 1997, ss 1(3) and 2(8).
[74] R Jackson (May 2009) Vol II at 476; R Jackson (December 2009) at 420.

UNIDROIT Principles as an inspiration for its principles 24.3 and 25.2, which make provision for formal settlement offers to be made and to carry cost consequences where they are not accepted. More significantly, it formed the basis of the simply expressed and straightforward model rule 16 in the ALI/UNIDROIT Reporters' Study. That rule was based on both CPR Pt 36 and a comparable rule in Ontario's civil procedure rules.[75] Rule 16 of the ALI/UNIDROIT Reporters' Study more closely follows the drafting approach of the Ontario rules than that of CPR Pt 36. It is simple and simply expressed. Rule 17 adopts the ALI/UNIDROIT Reporter's Study approach.

3. To promote certainty and predictability in the offer to settle regime, offers must be set out in writing and must state their terms clearly.[76] They must also state that they are an offer made under this rule. To facilitate compliance with that last point, a standard form offer to settle should be made available through the digital procedure. The form should make provision for the offeror to set out all the information required by rule 17(2). It should also make provision for variation, withdrawal, or acceptance of an offer, as well as for the making of subsequent offers or counter-offers.
4. Certainty and predictability are further provided by the requirement in rule 17(3) that offers remain open for a specified period of time, after which they lapse. Once an offer lapses, there is no reason why a further offer cannot be made. A specified period of time need not be calculated by reference to the passing of time. It could also be calculated by reference to a specified event, eg an offer could be specified as remaining open until the commencement of the trial or the conclusion of the trial in the proceedings.
5. Procedural equality is promoted through the ability for parties to make counter-offers to settle.[77] A counter-offer to settle must also comply with the requirements of rule 17. Such an offer operates to reject the other party's original offer. Again, this is intended to promote certainty and predictability.
6. Offers to settle under this rule are without prejudice save as to costs.[78] This replicates the position under the CPR. It thus requires an offer to settle not to be disclosed to any judge dealing with an adjudicative hearing,[79] whether at first instance or on an appeal. Where an offer is disclosed inadvertently, as under the CPR, the judge may continue to deal with the proceedings except where the disclosure would give rise to an appearance of bias.[80] Where the adjudicative hearing deals with some but not all matters in dispute, eg a split trial is taking place, and the court is considering issues of quantum having already determined issues of liability, the judge may not be informed of any offer to settle made in respect of quantum although they may be informed of the existence of such an offer.[81]

[75] Rules of Civil Procedure (Ontario) (RRO 1990, Reg 194) r 49.

[76] *Gibbon v Manchester City Council* [2010] EWCA Civ 726; [2010] 1 WLR 2081 at 6; A Zuckerman (2021) at 1380–1381.

[77] *ALI/UNIDROIT Reporters' Study*, commentary to rule 16.

[78] Part 3, r 13; Part 12, r 33.

[79] *Williams v Boag* [1941] 1 KB 1.

[80] CPR rr 361.16, 52.22; *Garrett v Saxby* [2004] EWCA Civ 341; [2004] 1 WLR 2152.

[81] CPR r 36.16(3)(d) and (4).

## SECTION 5: ADJUDICATION MANAGEMENT

### RULE 18.—ADJUDICATION MANAGEMENT PROCESSES

**Where proceedings are allocated to the adjudication track, the court will primarily manage proceedings to judgment. It will also actively encourage parties to take steps to settle their dispute consensually. Both the court and the parties will also keep under continuing review whether the proceedings should be reallocated to the settlement track.**

*Sources: Briggs, Chancery Modernisation Review, 5.9–5.16.*

### COMMENTARY

1. Adjudication management's primary aim is to ensure proceedings are managed effectively to trial, judgment, and—where necessary—enforcement. In doing so the court must act consistently with the purposive principle. It must particularly seek to give effect to the economy, efficiency, and proportionality principles. Parties must co-operate with the court in pursuit of these aims.
2. Notwithstanding its primary aim, adjudication management must still give effect to the settlement principle. The court is still required to consider the suitability of settlement processes to proceedings, and to promote their use by the parties. Parties are still required to consider the use of such processes. If appropriate, proceedings may be stayed to enable settlement processes to take place, whether they are mandated by court order or carried out voluntarily. Offers to settle may still be made (rule 17). That there is a discrete adjudication management process is not to be taken as providing a limit on the integration of settlement processes in this Code, and particularly its integration into adjudication management.
3. This rule also makes provision for the court to continuously monitor whether proceedings should be reallocated to the settlement track (rule 18). It thereby provides an example of what Ury, Brett, and Goldberg argue is an essential feature of an effectively structured dispute resolution system: a loopback rule, ie a rule which enables the dispute resolution process to move back to a simpler, more efficient, and cost-effective form of resolution process than the one it has currently reached.[82] Such rules help promote not only proportionate cost and time effective resolution for parties, but also help to promote systemic proportionality through directing disputes away from the more expensive, complex, rights-based form of resolution provided by adjudication to less expensive, simpler forms of interest-based resolution or rights-based resolution (rule 15(3)).

### RULE 19.—ADJUDICATION MANAGEMENT DIRECTIONS

**(1) The court may give directions necessary to manage the adjudication process. It may apply and/or vary any standard directions applicable to specific types of claim for relief or classification of proceedings. It may particularly give directions concerning**
**(a) the promotion of settlement, including mandating parties to use non-binding forms of settlement process;**

[82] W Ury, J Brett, and S Goldberg, *Getting Disputes Resolved* (PON, 1993) at 52–56.

**(b) the timetable for the pre-trial phase of proceedings or the preparatory phase of a continuous digital process;**
**(c) procedural steps to be taken by the parties and/or the court during the pre-trial or preparatory phase of proceedings including, where appropriate, steps to set aside the closure of case statements;**
**(d) the nature of the trial process;**
**(e) the date by which a trial shall be heard;**
**(f) the timetable for commencing and completing the adjudicative phase of a continuous digital process;**
**(g) evidence-gathering and exchange;**
**(h) the identification of witnesses and exchange of witness evidence;**
**(i) the appointment of expert witnesses, including court-appointed experts and assessors;**
**(j) scheduling dispute management hearings;**
**(k) automated compliance review dates;**
**(l) the sanctions applicable for non-compliance with adjudication management directions;**
**(m) the date by which judgment shall be given;**
**(n) procedural steps consequent upon judgment.**

**(2) The court may also, either on its own initiative or on application of a party, direct the proceedings be managed as multi-party proceedings or, at any time, reallocate them to the settlement track.**

**(3) In considering reallocating the proceedings, the court shall consider**
**(a) the views of the parties, albeit they are not conclusive;**
**(b) the suitability of any settlement process, particularly taking account of the criteria for allocation to the settlement track;**
**(c) the extent to which the pursuit of settlement without formal reallocation to the settlement track is proportionate;**
**(d) the effect reallocation to the settlement track would have on the parties' ability to secure a timely and cost-effective judgment.**

## COMMENTARY

1. Rule 19 supplements the general dispute management power. It makes specific provision for a range of directions that ought properly to be made when a dispute is allocated to the adjudication track. It further makes provision for the court to direct that proceedings be managed as multi-party proceedings.
2. The rule also makes provision concerning settlement. First, it highlights the power to make directions to promote settlement. Secondly, it includes specific provision for reallocation of proceedings to the settlement track. Both measures ensure the full incorporation of settlement processes even though a dispute has been allocated to the adjudication track. The former includes court encouragement of the use of settlement processes by parties. It also includes the power to mandate parties to engage in non-binding forms of settlement process, including those available to parties allocated to the settlement track.[83] The latter enables the court to go further and reallocate proceedings to the settlement track.

[83] *Churchill v Merthyr Tydfil County Borough Council* [2023] EWCA Civ 1416 at [50].

3. Standard directions should be made available via the digital procedure. Where appropriate, the court may use AI to assist a judge in deciding appropriate directions, subject to prior notice being given to the parties concerning the nature of the assistance so that they may make submissions in respect of it.

## RULE 20.—MANAGEMENT OF CONTINUOUS DIGITAL PROCESS

**During a continuous digital process, the court will actively manage the order and manner in which parties communicate with each other and the court, including how and when they submit and challenge evidence and legal argument. The court may also seek clarification from the parties of any matters raised in the proceedings.**

## COMMENTARY

1. The court may direct that adjudicative proceedings take place as a continuous digital process where at least one party is unrepresented.[84] Where it does so it will need to consider and manage the manner in which parties communicate with each other and the court. The court will have to ensure that the parties are given reasonable time to communicate with both. This will need careful management due to the process being asynchronous. Without such management parties may either not be given sufficient time to respond or, as problematically, they may not respond within a reasonable time. Careful management is thus required to secure a fair process for all parties.
2. Effective management by the court will also need to go beyond the strictly procedural. To a limited degree it will need to involve some substantive dispute management. Where parties are unrepresented, they may need the court to help them clarify points they are making in their submissions via the digital procedure. It may therefore be of particular importance for the court to seek clarification of matters raised by the parties so that both it and they fully understand any points being made. Also see Part 12, rules 1, 8, and 9 on evidence management generally.

## RULE 21.—ADJUDICATIVE HEARING MANAGEMENT

**(1) The court shall determine the order in which issues are to be determined at adjudicative hearings. It shall determine the manner and order in which the parties shall present and test evidence and submit their legal arguments. In determining these matters the court shall consider submissions and any agreement made by the parties.**
**(2) Adjudicative hearings may include: parties' opening speeches; the submission and testing of evidence; submissions on the law; closing arguments.**
**(3) Parties shall be afforded a reasonable opportunity to present their evidence and legal arguments and respond to evidence and legal arguments presented by other parties.**
**(4) An adjudicative hearing shall close once the parties have completed the presentation of their evidence, legal arguments, and any closing arguments.**

[84] Part 14, r 5.

**(5) The court may reopen an adjudicative hearing on its own initiative or on application of a party at any time before judgment is given but not perfected where there is a compelling reason for doing so.**

*Sources: ALI/UNIDROIT Reporters' Study, r 29; ELI-UNIDROIT Model Rules, r 64; RSC Ord 35, r 7; CPR rr 1.4(2)(l), 28.6, 29.8, 39.4, PD28, para 8; PD29, para 10.*

## COMMENTARY

1. Active dispute management applies to a trial and its equivalent during a continuous digital process as much as it does to all other stages of the dispute resolution process. Trials and other adjudicative hearings typically involve four stages: opening submissions, evidence presentation and testing, legal submissions, and closing arguments. There is no necessity for all four stages to be included. Opening submissions may, for instance, be dispensed with to promote economy, efficiency, or proportionality. Where there are opening submissions, the party on whom the burden of proof lies ought generally to commence first.[85] A party may decide not to give a closing submission. The court may also not call on a party to give a closing submission where it does not need to hear further from that party on any issues raised by their opponent.
2. Primary responsibility for effective planning and management remains with the court, although it must necessarily be carried out in close co-operation with the parties. It should also take place at as early a stage as possible in the dispute management process so that both the court and the parties may plan effectively for it, and thus ensure in so far as possible that the cost and time taken at any trial or other adjudicative hearing are proportionate.
3. Early consideration of the trial process also helps both the court and parties to consider if they wish to truncate the trial process by, for instance, concentrating on specific issues or taking various issues in a particular order. It may make sense, for instance, for parties to focus the trial on liability or on damages. To promote party engagement in this process, rule 21(1) provides explicitly for party agreement on the nature of the trial or adjudicative phase process. While such agreements do not bind the court, which must manage proceedings in the public interest, they should be given particularly strong weight when management decisions are made. This provision is intended to give general effect in the Code to the approach that underpins the Shorter and Flexible Trial Schemes, contained in CPR PD57AB, which apply to proceedings in the Business and Property Courts. Rule 21(1) is thus intended to generalise and render trans-substantive that approach so that its ability to promote a more proportionate trial and adjudicative process is available to all proceedings and not just business or commercial ones. Rule 21(3) makes explicit a limit on the court's power to determine how evidence should be given at a trial or adjudicative process. It should be read consistently with both the evidential and adversarial principles and the rule concerning party submission of evidence at Part 12, rule 6. The trial timetable must at a bare minimum provide the parties with reasonable opportunity to submit and challenge relevant evidence.
4. Rule 21(3) is a formal rule. It specifies that trial or adjudicative proceedings come to an end following the submission of evidence, legal argument and closing submissions. Closing arguments may be dispensed with by the parties or by the court. Once proceedings have closed, the court will either give judgment orally or will take time to

[85] *Seldon v Davidson* [1968] 1 WLR 1083.

prepare and then issue a written judgment. Proceedings may, however, be reopened at any time after the close of proceedings and before judgment is given. Reopening may either be on application of a party or on the court's own initiative. The court retains jurisdiction to do so as it retains jurisdiction of the dispute until its decision is perfected.[86] A compelling reason must be given to justify reopening proceedings, eg new evidence or a new matter has come to light that would not reasonably have been available prior to the conclusion of proceedings. Consideration of the purposive principle will be particularly important in such circumstances, as reopening will inevitably have an impact on the court's ability to secure systemic proportionality. It will also require consideration of that factor in relation to the interests of the immediate parties to have the court consider and adjudicate upon the fresh issue. Where any new matter requires the amendment of a case statement, the court will also need to consider the test applicable to late amendments. To reopen it must be satisfied that a late amendment would be granted, ie reopening would be conditional on the amendment being allowed. A compelling reason would still be needed to justify reopening even where the amendment itself would be allowed.

## RULE 22.—SUBMISSION OF NO CASE TO ANSWER

**(1) At the conclusion of a claimant's case at an adjudicative hearing, a defendant may elect not to submit any evidence and seek judgment in their favour on the basis that the claimant has failed to establish that they have a case to answer.**

**(2) Exceptionally where it is obvious that the claimant has submitted no evidence to support their case, the court may permit a defendant to seek judgment on the basis that there is no case to answer without electing to submit no evidence.**

*Sources: RSC Ord 35, r 7.*

## COMMENTARY

1. Neither the CPR nor its predecessors made provision for a defendant choosing to make a submission of no case to answer.[87] Such a process was, however, well established having been approved by the Court of Appeal prior to and after the CPR's introduction.[88] Rule 22 codifies the established approach. A defendant may make a submission of no case to answer in two ways at the conclusion of a claimant's case at trial, ie at an adjudicative hearing.
2. First, it may do so while electing not to submit any evidence of its own. In this situation, the court is determining whether, on the balance of probabilities, the claimant has made out their case based solely on their own evidence. Putting a defendant to their election helps minimise the risk of judicial bias. Were a court to express a view on the merits of a claimant's case before, assuming the submission is rejected, having to then go on to determine it in the light of the defendant's evidence such a risk might arise.

[86] Part 15, rr 5 and 7.

[87] R Scott, *Supreme Court Practice 1999* (Sweet & Maxwell, 1999) Vol 1 at 35.7.3.

[88] *Alexander v Rayson* [1936] 1 KB 169; *Parry v Aluminium Corp* [1940] WN 44 at 46; *Laurie v Raglan Building Co* [1942]1 KB 152 at 155; *Graham v Chorley Borough Council* [2006] EWCA Civ 92; [2006] CP Rep 24.

3. Secondly, and very exceptionally, the court may allow a defendant to make a submission of no case to answer without having to elect not to submit evidence of their own. This should only be permitted where it is obvious that the claimant has failed to adduce any evidence to support their case.[89]
4. Submissions of no case to answer under this rule, as a general rule, are very rare. Hence the second basis on which they can be brought should be rarer still. There are principled reasons why this is the case. As Zuckerman explains they run the risk of ultimately wasting the courts and parties' time and financial resources.[90] Were a submission to succeed and later be overturned on appeal, it would require a new trial to be held. Thus, it would unnecessarily generate wasted costs of an appeal and of the original trial that was brought to an end after the claimant's case concluded. They should only therefore be made and granted where they promote the purposive and economy, efficiency, and proportionality principles. This is only likely to be the case where it is apparent that the claimant has either failed to satisfy the burden of proof or, in terms of the second basis on which the submission can be made, the claimant's case has '*suffered a serious collapse*'.[91] The latter may occur, for instance, where the claimant's key witness gave evidence that fundamentally controverted their case.
5. This rule can thus be seen to be a residual jurisdiction. The general approach to dealing with weak cases ought properly to be via an application for summary judgment, which may be made at any time including at trial.[92]

## SECTION 6: MULTI-PARTY PROCEEDINGS MANAGEMENT

### RULE 23.—MULTI-PARTY DISPUTE MANAGEMENT

**(1) The court may, where it is just and reasonable, take any of the following steps to manage multi-party disputes**
- **(a) direct that one or more proceedings continue as test proceedings;**
- **(b) consolidate separate proceedings into a single proceeding;**
- **(c) join parties to proceedings.**

**(2) The court may also direct proceedings continue as**
- **(a) group proceedings under rule 24; or**
- **(b) representative proceedings under rule 27.**

**(3) Multi-party proceedings are:**
- **(a) individual proceedings that involve more than one claimant or more than one defendant; and/or**
- **(b) individual proceedings that raise the same, similar, or related (common) legal and/or factual issues that are raised in other individual proceedings.**

*Sources: ELI-UNIDROIT Model Rules, r 49(6); CPR rr 3.1(g), (h), 19.8, 19.22.*

[89] *Benham Ltd v Kythira Investments Ltd* [2003] EWCA Civ 1749; [2004] CP Rep 17 at [39]; *Graham v Chorley Borough Council* [2006] EWCA Civ 92 at [29]–[30].
[90] A Zuckerman (2021) at 1114.
[91] A Zuckerman (2021) at 1116.
[92] Part 11, r 36; Part 15, r 11.

## COMMENTARY

1. The paradigm form of proceedings are individual, unitary proceedings between a single claimant and defendant. Closely linked are proceedings with one or more claimants or defendants. Social and legal relations are such, however, that in many instances multiple parties, either as claimant or defendant, may have an interest in the same legal proceedings. Many claimants may have the same cause of action against the same defendant or against multiple defendants arising from the same or similar facts. Were such situations to be dealt with by multiple, individual proceedings several problems would arise. Most obviously, the prosecution of 100s, 1000s, or 100s of 1000s of individual disputes as individual claims would overwhelm the court's resources. There is simply no reasonable way in which the civil courts could manage such claims, as well as other claims, effectively, economically, and in a reasonable period of time if they were all to proceed individually. It is equally inefficient from an individual and societal perspective for individual party resources to be expended in multiple proceedings prosecuting and defending the same dispute. For defendants this is particularly problematic as they would need to expend their resources multiple times to defend the same cause of action against multiple claimants.[93] That is an unreasonable allocation of resources. Such an approach could also, due to it raising a risk that each claim might result in a different result, undermine confidence in and the legitimacy of the courts. As significantly, multiple conflicting judgments undermines the shadow of law, making it more difficult for individuals and businesses to gain a reasonable understanding of what the law requires. It would thus undermine both preventive justice and consensual settlement.
2. So that such problems do not arise, civil procedure has evolved several mechanisms for the effective management of multi-party proceedings. Within the CPR those mechanisms are provided for under both the general case management power in CPR r 3.1(h) and (g) and r 19.1 (joinder and consolidation), the court's inherent jurisdiction (test cases), CPR r 19.8 (representative actions), and CPR r 19.21 (Group Litigation Orders).[94] Rule 23 consolidates those various rules. The most basic approach is to identify one set of proceedings to go forward to trial as a test case, while the other proceedings are stayed until that case has been determined. This enables the court to determine the test case, following which the other proceedings can be reassessed by the parties to them in the light of the judgment in that case. Those proceedings ought, generally, to settle based on the judgment or, where issues other than that which they have in common with the test case exist, they can be managed more effectively as the issues in dispute will have been narrowed.[95]
3. Slightly more involved than test cases, further mechanisms can see multiple claims that raise the same, similar, or related issues of fact or law consolidated into a single proceeding to which all the parties from the original, individual proceedings become parties.[96] Similarly, proceedings can remain individual and thus separate from each other but are joined together. In this way they are capable of being managed together, with a single judge responsible for their management and trial. Both these approaches enable a more economic and efficient approach to be taken to the management

93 A Zuckerman (2021) at 724.
94 Part 6, r 3(2).
95 *The Office of Fair Trading v Abbey National Plc & Others* [2008] EWHC 875 (Comm).
96 *Lubbe v Cape* [2000] 1 WLR 1545.

of proceedings. A single law firm may, for instance, take on the carriage of the proceedings for multiple claimant(s) or defendant(s). The dispute may be managed singularly without resort to multiple hearings before multiple judges. Orders may be made that bind all the parties, where there is consolidation, or can be drafted so as to apply to all the separate but individual proceedings where there is joinder. In such ways, resolution can be reached in reasonable time and at reasonable cost consistently with the purposive principle.

4. Orders directing proceedings continue as test cases or that they are subject to consolidation or joinder may be made where they further the purposive principle. Particularly, consideration will need to be given to the public interest in securing systematic proportionality given the amount of the court's resources that multiple proceedings may utilise where they would require the court to resolve the same or similar issues repeatedly. Consideration will also need to be given to which order is most appropriate given the dispute at the heart of the multiple claims, the parties' resources, and legal representation. A test case may, for instance, be the more effective mechanism where multiple proceedings involve low or moderate value claims for damages. Consolidation or joinder may be more effective where there is a large number of parties raising higher value claims or multiple related issues that would otherwise require several test cases to be selected. Equally, finality of litigation may point towards consolidation or joinder from a defendant's perspective.
5. Rule 23(2) further provides that the court may order that multi-party disputes may be managed as either group proceedings or as representative proceedings.

## RULE 24.—GROUP PROCEEDINGS

**(1) The court may make a group proceedings order, on its own initiative or on application, at any time after proceedings have commenced where**
**(a) more than one proceeding involves the same, similar, or related issues of law or fact; and**
**(b) it is just and reasonable to do so.**

**(2) In determining whether it is just and reasonable to make a group proceedings order, the court must take account of all the circumstances, including whether, given the number of proceedings, the nature and complexity of the common issues, the value of the claims, and any funding arrangements, the proceedings can be managed as separate proceedings or through another form of multi-party dispute management process in an efficient, economical, and proportionate way.**

*Sources: Woolf—Final Report, chap 17, para 8-41; CPR rr 19.21, 19.22.*

## COMMENTARY

1. Group proceedings were first introduced in the Final Woolf Report as part of its proposed multi-party action. The other aspect of such an action was a reformed representative action. While the latter reform was not effected when the CPR was introduced, group proceedings were introduced in 2000 as Group Litigation Orders or GLOs.[97]

[97] Civil Procedure (Amendment) Rules 2000 (SI 2000/221).

2. Reforms to multi-party actions were recommended in the Final Woolf Report to achieve three objectives: to improve access to justice for situations where large numbers of individuals had suffered alleged harm, but their claims were not economically viable to litigate as individual claims; to provide an expeditious, economical, and proportionate means of resolving multi-party claims; and, to secure a balance between claimant and defendant rights.[98] The reformed representative action would have achieved all three objectives.
3. GLOs were, however, less able to achieve the first of the three objectives.[99] On the contrary, their practical focus was to secure the second and third objectives. Hence, their proper focus was and is to secure an expeditious, economical, and proportionate means of resolving multi-party disputes that are individually economically viable. As both Andrews and Zuckerman have rightly highlighted, the GLO was in reality no more than a sophisticated management mechanism for high value claims.[100]
4. Rule 24 restates the approach to GLOs contained in CPR r 19.22.[101] It does so, however, in the context of the introduction in rule 27 of a reformed representative action. It thus provides, with rule 27, what the Woolf Final Report intended to be a holistic approach to the effective management of multi-party disputes that could secure all three of the objectives it identified.
5. The decision to make a GLO is one the court may take on its own initiative or on application. The former may, for instance, arise where the digital case management system alerts a judge or judges who are managing individual disputes that they potentially raise the same, similar, or related issues of law and fact to those raised in other proceedings. The management system thus should be calibrated to identify such issues across proceedings and suggest how they can be grouped together. The discretion to make such an order, however, rests with a judge. It will depend on their assessment that the proceedings raise the same, similar, or related issues of law or fact (the commonality test). There would be no proper basis for making such an order if proceedings did not involve common issues as that would mean that a judgment would not bind all the group members on the common issue. The question is thus intimately linked with the promotion of finality of litigation: would making the order promote finality in litigation through adjudication that would bind all the group members in respect of the common issue.
6. Where the commonality test is satisfied, the court must also be satisfied that it is just to make the order. It must consider each of the factors identified in rule 24(2). It must thus consider whether such an order provides a fair means of managing multi-party disputes from both the perspective of claimants and defendants and from that of the court's ability to secure systemic proportionality.[102] The question of cost-savings through the making of such an order is an important issue to consider here,[103] as is whether it provides a more effective way to secure individual and

[98] H Woolf (1996) at 223.

[99] R Mulheron, 'Some Difficulties with Group Litigation Orders—and Why a Class Action is Superior' (2005) 24 Civil Justice Quarterly 40; S Gibbons, 'Group Litigation, Class Actions and Lord Woolf's Three Objectives—A Critical Analysis' (2008) 27 Civil Justice Quarterly 208; R Mulheron, *Reform of Collective Redress in England and Wales: A Perspective of Need* (Civil Justice Council, 2008).

[100] N Andrews, *English Civil Procedure: Fundamentals of the New Civil Justice System* (OUP, 2003) at 974–976; A Zuckerman (2021) at 738–739.

[101] Ministry of Justice, GLO Register.

[102] *Schmitt v Depuy International Ltd* [2016] EWHC 638 (QB).

[103] *Boake Allen Ltd v Revenue & Customs Commissioners* [2007] 1 WLR 1386 at 1394.

systemic proportionality. It is also important to assess whether the common issue or issues predominate over other issues in the various proceedings, such that it is thus more appropriate a management method than proceeding by way of a test case or via consolidation or joinder.

7. Making a GLO must not only be just it must also be reasonable. While rule 24(1)(a) only requires there to be more than one proceeding, the court must ask itself the question whether, given the number of proceedings, it is reasonable to make the order and thus apply the panoply of procedure required by rule 24 for the management of the group. It may not, for instance, be reasonable to create a group register, identify lead parties and lawyers and give detailed directions for the management of the proceedings where there are only a small number of proceedings. Two proceedings will, for instance, generally be more reasonably managed via joinder or consolidation. The court should also consider the viability of individual disputes where, for instance, a small number had commenced prior to consideration of group proceedings but large numbers of potential disputes had not but were likely to do so once an order was made. In such a circumstance making an order might be reasonable. Alternatively, it may be the case that there is little likelihood of further disputes commencing and thus being able to join the group proceedings as funding is not likely to be available. In such circumstances, it may not be reasonable for a GLO to be made unless or until a critical mass of proceedings had in fact been issued.[104]
8. Unlike GLOs under the CPR, this rule does not require approval of a group proceedings order to be given by a senior judge before it takes effect.[105] While that can be seen to provide oversight of the use of group proceedings orders, it is difficult to justify. The making of such an order is, as is the making of other multi-party orders, a dispute management order. Those other orders, and particularly representative proceedings, do not require the grant of consent of a senior judge. It is difficult to see why group proceedings orders should be treated differently. All such decisions require consideration of the nature of the proceedings and whether an order is justified by reference to the circumstances and the purposive principle. Those are judicial decisions that are properly taken by the judge who is seized of the application. That a senior judge should be placed in a position to, administratively, review that decision is inconsistent with the approach taken to other such applications. It is also inconsistent with judicial independence. The proper approach to policing the use of group proceedings orders ought to be, as it is here, by way of appeal.

## RULE 25.—MANAGEMENT OF GROUP PROCEEDINGS

**(1) Where a group proceedings order is made, the court shall**

**(a) specify the common issues in order to identify those proceedings that come within the scope of the order;**

**(b) establish a digital register (the group register) to manage the proceedings;**

[104] *Austin v Miller Argent (South Wales) Ltd* [2011] EWCA Civ 928; [2011] Env LR 32.

[105] CPR PD19B para 3.

**(c) direct all proceedings within the scope of the order at the time the order is made to be placed on the group register;**

**(d) give directions for the group proceedings order to be publicised and take steps to identify proceedings already issued that may be within the scope of the order;**

**(e) specify a date by which proceedings issued after the group proceedings order was made should be registered on the group register;**

**(f) stay all proceedings within the scope of the group proceedings order that are not registered by the specified date;**

**(g) allocate or re-allocate proceedings entered on the group register to the settlement or adjudication track, and make directions for the management of proceedings post-allocation or re-allocation.**

**(2) Parties to any proceedings that are not registered by the specified date may apply for permission to join the register after that date by making an application for relief from sanction.**

**(3) Any party may, at any time after their entry on the group register, apply for their removal from it.**

**(4) The court may also**

**(a) specify one or more claimants and/or defendants as lead parties;**

**(b) specify that the lawyers for one or more of the claimants and/or defendants be designated as lead representatives;**

**(c) direct that one or more proceedings on the group register proceed as test proceedings.**

*Sources: CPR rr 19.22.*

## COMMENTARY

1. Rule 25 restates CPR r 19.22. It makes provision for specific dispute management orders that are required for the effective management of group proceedings. It is thus a specific application of the general dispute management power.

2. The most important issues that need to be identified are the common issues. This is necessary to enable the identification of proceedings that are to come within the ambit of the group proceedings, and thus placed on the group register. It is also important to enable steps to be taken to publicise the fact that a group proceedings order is made. This should include requirements for the identification of a lead party and their lawyers to take steps to bring the proceedings to public attention.

3. Steps should also be taken to bring the fact of the order to the attention to parties that have already commenced other proceedings and who may not know about the order. The court should use the digital procedure to identify such proceedings. Parties to such proceedings should thereafter be notified of the order, again via the digital procedure. Other means should also be used to advertise the fact that such an order has been made. The intention here is to ensure that as many parties as possible are able to join the group register, and thus promote effective management and finality of litigation. In this way the possibility that individual, parallel proceedings are commenced or continued will also be minimised. Contrary to the position under the CPR, any costs of publicising the fact of the order should be costs in the proceedings. Such costs are not, as held under the CPR, advertising costs incurred by lawyers in the pursuit of business. They are necessary costs incurred by the parties further to a court order, the aim of which is to promote both

the effective and efficient management of court and party resources and finality of litigation.[106]

4. It is also important to set a date by which no new proceedings may be entered on the group register.[107] This is to ensure that the group proceedings can be planned and managed by the parties and the court properly. This does not, however, preclude individual proceedings being issued beyond that date. Such proceedings can be issued, but if issued they should be subject to a stay. That is required to ensure that the benefits of group proceedings are not undermined by individual proceedings continuing in parallel. Parties may apply to join the register after the cut-off date has passed. Rule 25(2) codifies the approach under the CPR that such an application is an application for relief from sanction for non-compliance.[108] Consistently with the principle of party autonomy, a party may also apply to be removed from the register. They may do so to, for instance, proceed as an individual proceeding outside the group. In such a case removal from the register will lead to those proceedings being subject to the stay under rule 25(1)(e). Removal may also foreshadow an application to discontinue proceedings under Part 7.
5. To promote the effective management of group proceedings, the court should also consider whether there is a need to allocate or re-allocate the group proceedings to the settlement of adjudication management tracks (rule 25(1)(f)).
6. The court will ordinarily appoint one of the parties as the lead party. They, and their lawyers, will be responsible for managing and prosecuting the dispute on their and the other group parties' behalves. The court may also direct that one or more group proceedings be identified as test cases. Those proceedings, which should typify the common issues, should then go forward to judgment. This approach marries together the benefit of the test case procedure with the binding effect of group proceedings across all group members. It is intended to further promote the efficient, economical, and proportionate management and resolution of group proceedings. Where a lead party or test case within group proceedings settles before judgment, the court should consider substituting them for another party from the group. The court should particularly consider with the other group parties the question of settlement of their claims or of the common issue or issues in the light of such a settlement.

## RULE 26.—EFFECT OF A GROUP PROCEEDINGS ORDER

**Where a group proceedings order is made**

**(a) any judgment or order on a common issue shall bind all the parties entered on the group register at the time the judgment or order is given or issued. Any party subsequently entered on the register shall also be so bound, except where the court directs otherwise either on its own initiative or on application of a party;**

**(b) a party that joins the group register after a judgment or order is issued or made may not appeal from or otherwise challenge that judgment or order;**

**(c) any evidentiary disclosure by a party on the group register is disclosure to all parties on the group register;**

**(d) any costs incurred in respect of the common issues shall be shared equally between the parties liable for costs, unless the court directs otherwise.**

*Sources: CPR rr 19.23.*

[106] *Motto v Trafigura* [2011] EWCA Civ 1150; [2012] 1 WLR 657.

[107] *Pearce v Secretary of State for Energy & Climate Change* [2015] EWHC 3775 (QB); *Weaver v British Airways Plc* [2021] EWHC 217 (QB).

[108] *Holloway v Transport Medical Group (CS) Ltd* [2014] EWHC 1641 (QB).

## COMMENTARY

1. Rule 26 specifies the most important consequences of the making of a group proceedings order. The most important of these is that any judgment or order on common issues binds all the parties entered on the group register. This secures finality of litigation for those parties and for defendants to the group proceedings. That it also provides that such judgments and orders bind parties that join the group register after the judgment or order is given further extends the utility of group proceedings. Late joining parties are thus spared the need to otherwise prosecute individual proceedings, saving them and the court time and expense. This approach also reduces the possibility of multiple inconsistent decisions, which might arise if late joining parties were not bound by the past judgments or orders in the group proceedings. The court does, however, retain a discretion to disapply the binding nature of such judgments and orders to late joining parties where that is necessary in the circumstances of the case.
2. Linked to the foregoing provision, a late joining party may not appeal or otherwise challenge past judgments or orders. This is to ensure finality of litigation for the parties who were group members at the time such judgments or orders were given and had either chosen not to challenge them or had done so and the challenge had been unsuccessful. That late joiners cannot challenge such judgments and orders does not place them at a procedural or substantive disadvantage. They may apply under rule 26(a) for an order disapplying the judgment or order's application to them.
3. Rule 26(c) provides that disclosure by one party is disclosure to all parties on the group register. This is intended to promote effective dispute management as it eliminates any argument about the extent to which disclosure has been made. Consequently, it obviates the prospect that multiple applications for disclosure would need to be made. It is also intended to ensure that all group parties are able to obtain evidence in a timely manner and thus consider what, if any, issues may arise and need to be tested. It thus promotes the evidential access and adversarial principles, consistently with the economy, efficiency, and proportionality principles.
4. Group parties may reach an agreement on the apportionment of costs under a cost sharing agreement. They should be encouraged to do so to save cost and time. The most likely situation where they may do so is where one or more proceedings within the group are identified and managed as lead or test cases. Group parties may not, however, restrict access to the group register by requiring parties that wish to join the group proceedings to enter into a cost sharing agreement as a pre-condition to entry.[109] Such a requirement is an improper fetter on the court's jurisdiction and the exercise of its dispute management powers. Where parties do enter into such an agreement it cannot, however, displace the court's power to award costs.[110]

[109] *Crossley v Volkswagen* [2018] EWHC 723 (QB).

[110] *Bank of Credit and Commerce International SA v Ali (No 5)* [2000] Costs LR 243 at 259. Part 3, r 5.

## RULE 27.—REPRESENTATIVE PROCEEDINGS

**(1) The court, on the application of a party, may make a representative proceedings order.**

**(2) A representative proceedings order is one that designates a specified claimant or defendant as a representative party.**

**(3) A representative party is a party that continues proceedings, including enforcement proceedings on behalf of a represented class of persons (the represented class). The represented class may include the representative party.**

**(4) The court may make a representative proceedings order where**

**(a) one or more parties' claims for relief or defences to claims for relief in proceedings or potential proceedings involve the same, similar, or related (common) issues of law or fact;**

**(b) it is possible to determine either by name or by description membership of the representative class at the time the representative proceedings order is made;**

**(c) management of the proceedings or potential proceedings through representative proceedings is superior, by reference to the purposive principle, to management as separate proceedings or through any other form of multi-party proceeding. In considering this issue the court will have regard to the number of proceedings or potential proceedings, and their nature, complexity, and value; and**

**(d) it is just and reasonable to permit the applicant to bring or defend proceedings in a representative capacity.**

**(5) Where a represented proceedings order is made, the represented class are not parties to the proceedings.**

**(6) The court may, on its own initiative or on application of a party, vary or set aside the representative proceedings order if at any time during the course of the representative proceedings the conditions for making the order are no longer met. Where such an order is made the court shall give consequential directions for the future management of any individual proceedings.**

*Sources: ELI-UNIDROIT Model Rules, rr 207, 212, 213; Civil Justice Council (2008),*[111] *Recommendations 1, 2, 3, 4, Draft Civil Procedure Rules rr 19.17; 19.19; Competition Act 1998, s 47B; CAT Rules, rr 78, 79, 80, 85.*

## COMMENTARY

1. English and Welsh civil procedure has contained a representative or class action since the Middle Ages.[112] It is currently contained in CPR r 19.8.[113] Since 2002, there has also been a representative action within the Competition Appeal Tribunal (CAT).[114] Rule 27 and subsequent rules on representative proceedings maintain the commitment to such a form of proceeding, albeit the approach taken here differs

[111] Civil Justice Council, *Improving Access to Justice through Collective Actions—Developing a More Efficient and Effective Procedure for Collective Actions—Final Report* (CJC, 2008).

[112] S Yeazell, 'Group Litigation and Social Context: Toward a History of the Class Action' (1977) 77 Colum L Rev 866; S Yeazell, 'From Group Litigation to Class Action—Part I: The Industrialization of Group Litigation' (1980) 27 UCLA L Rev 514; S Yeazell, 'From Group Litigation to Class Action—Part II: Interest, Class, and Representation' (1980) 27 UCLA L Rev 1067; S. Yeazell, *From Mediaeval Group Litigation to the Modern Class Action* (Yale, 1990); T Snow (ed), *The Annual Practice* (Sweet & Maxwell, 1904) Vol 1 at 162.

[113] RSC Ord 15, r 12 and CCR Ord 5, r 5. It was until 2022 set out in CPR r 19.6.

[114] Competition Act 1998 s 47B, as originally introduced via the Enterprise Act 2002, s 19.

substantively from that taken under the CPR.[115] The approach taken is closer to that set out in the CAT Rules.[116]

2. A representative action is one that enables a large number of persons to bring proceedings against a common defendant (or vice versa) in a single proceeding.[117] Several rationales underpin the existence of this form of multi-party proceeding.[118] It promotes the efficient and proportionate management of the proceedings. A single set of proceedings, with one party representing 100s or 1000s is a more effective means of achieving such management than if each dispute were dealt with individually. It ensures that the court's resources are not overwhelmed by having to deal with very large numbers of similarly situated claims on an individual basis. It thus promotes systemic proportionality, as well as procedural efficiency. That one proceeding deals with many disputes also promotes procedural economy, both for the court and the various parties as, for instance, the same issues do not have to be evidenced and argued over multiple times.

3. Perhaps most significantly, this form of proceeding can help promote effective access to justice for claims that would not be economically viable to pursue as individual claims. It does this through the preceding benefits, but also through ensuring that—particularly where proceedings are brought on an opt-out basis under rule 30—that disputes that would not rationally be brought by claimants due to their low economic value can be pursued or defended. It is thus more advantageous for this purpose than a group proceeding, which depends on the individual group claims being economically viable in their own right.

4. Representative proceedings also help secure confidence in the law through ensuring that a single judgment is given across all the disputes. It thus, like a group proceedings order, obviates the possibility that each individual dispute could result in differing judgments if, as would be the case, they were heard by different judges.[119] Finally, it also ensures that there is an effective shadow of the law. It thus promotes preventive justice and consensual settlement, as well as the rule of law. It does this by ensuring that the law is able to effectively shape social and economic behaviour, to promote compliance with obligations imposed by the substantive law, eg those imposed by the law of tort, as well as those voluntarily undertaken, eg those imposed under contracts, particularly where individual represented claims are not economically viable as individual proceedings. Given their lack of individual viability, the likelihood would be that if not pursued via a representative proceeding, the disputes would not be pursued and the substantive law at the heart of the dispute would go unenforced. Were that to occur, the rule of law would be compromised.

5. Rule 27(1) provides the basis for the court to make a representative proceedings order. It may only do so on the application of the putative representative party. The court cannot make such an order of its own initiative as it would impose a significant obligation, particularly a financial one, on a party to act as a representative. Equally, absent an application by a party the court would not have sufficient information to make an order, such as that required by rules 27(5)(c), 28, 29, and 30.

[115] D Grave, M McIntosh, and G Rowan, *Class Actions in England and Wales* (Sweet & Maxwell, 2022).

[116] CAT Rules, Part 5.

[117] R Mulheron, *The Class Action in Common Law Legal Systems* (Hart, 2004) at 3.

[118] A Zuckerman (2021) at 730; H Woolf (1996) at 223.

[119] *Mastercard Incorporated v Walter Hugh Merricks CBE* [2020] UKSC 51; [2021] 3 All ER 285 at [37]; *Hollick v Toronto (City)* 2001 SCC 68; [2001] 3 SCR 158.

6. Rule 27(4) provides the basis on which a representative proceedings order may be made.[120] It is a discretionary power. It is essentially a certification or authorisation rule. Such rules are commonplace in representative or class actions and are intended to police their use, ie ensure they are not used abusively.[121] Authorisation thus helps avoid the prospect that representative claims are brought vexatiously or by way of so-called blackmail suits.[122] A blackmail suit is one where a representative claim is brought solely with the purpose of extracting a settlement from the defendant due to the likely costs of the proceedings in circumstances where the represented claims are without any real merit.[123]
7. Rule 27(4)(a) establishes the primary criteria for making an order: that there is a class of claims that are capable of being represented (the numerosity criterion) and that they involve the same, similar, or related issues of law or fact (the commonality criterion). The former does not specify a minimum number of claims or defences necessary for the making of a representative proceedings order. This is intended to provide the court with the flexibility to determine what is an appropriate number in the circumstances of each individual case. It follows the approach adopted under CPR r 19.8.[124] Generally, there will need to be a large number of similarly situated claims or defences to satisfy this criterion. The larger the number the more likely that the use of such a proceeding will be a proportionate use of the court's resources and will promote the effective administration of justice.[125]
8. The commonality criterion is based on that currently applicable for GLOs and, specifically, that set out for collective proceedings brought in the CAT.[126] It is broader than that set out for representative actions under the CPR. Its stricter approach has tended to limit the applicability and utility of the representative action.[127] It requires the represented class members to each have a common interest in the action. That requires a common interest, common grievance and a claim for relief that was common to all class members.[128]
9. Notwithstanding the UK Supreme Court's more flexible and purposive reinterpretation of the CPR's approach in *Lloyd v Google* (2021), which may in time widen out the application of the CPR r 19.8,[129] rule 27 explicitly expands the scope of certification wider than the CPR so that it is akin to the approach taken in GLOs. Adopting the same approach to the similarity criterion for the two forms of proceeding ensures that they can genuinely complement each other. It also ensures that for low value claims representative proceedings are a valid option.

[120] *Mastercard Incorporated v Walter Hugh Merricks CBE* [2020] UKSC 51; [2021] 3 All ER 285 at [64].

[121] *Mastercard Incorporated v Walter Hugh Merricks CBE* [2020] UKSC 51; [2021] 3 All ER 285 at [98]–[99].

[122] Federal Rules of Civil Procedure, r 23(a) (US); CAT Rules, r 79; R Mulheron, 'Justice Enhanced: Framing an Opt-Out Class Action for England' (2007) Modern Law Review 550 at 569.

[123] B Hay and D Rosenberg, 'Sweetheart and Blackmail Settlements in Class Actions: Reality and Remedy' (2000) 75 Notre Dame L Rev 1377; C Silver, 'We're Scared to Death: Class Certification and Blackmail' (2003) 78 New York University Law Review 1357.

[124] *Lloyd v Google* [2021] UKSC 50; [2022] AC 1217 at [69].

[125] *Mark McLaren Class Representative Ltd v MOL (Europe Africa) Ltd* [2022] CAT 10 at [144].

[126] Competition Act 1998, s 47B(6).

[127] *Markt & Co Ltd v Knight Steamship Co Ltd* [1910] 2 KB 1021; J Sorabji, 'The Hidden Class Action in English Civil Procedure' (2009) 28 CJQ 498; R Mulheron, 'Emerald Supplies Ltd v British Airways plc: A Century Later, the Ghost of Markt Lives On' (2009) 8 Competition Law Journal 159.

[128] *Markt & Co Ltd v Knight Steamship Co Ltd* [1910] 2 KB 1021 at 1040.

[129] *Lloyd v Google* [2021] UKSC 50; [2022] AC 1217 at [71].

10. The approach to the commonality criterion under the CAT Rules was considered in *Gutmann v First MTR South Western Trains Ltd* (2021).[130] It stressed that where there were the same, similar, and related issues as well as other issues, it was not necessary for the former to predominate over the latter. The issue was whether a representative proceeding was the most superior means of resolving the common issues. The more and the more significant the former, the more likely the commonality criterion will be satisfied. The CAT also, rightly, considered that in interpreting the commonality criterion the court was to take a purposive approach. It thus has to be considered by reference to the rationales underpinning representative proceedings.
11. In assessing commonality, all class members do not necessarily have to satisfy the criterion on the same basis. Sub-classes of represented class members may, for instance, have different claims for relief or defences from those of other sub-classes. Equally, in an undifferentiated represented class it is not necessary for there to be no difference in claims for relief or defences amongst the class members. The issue is whether there is a commonality across the represented class members of claims and defences. It does not mean that their claims and defences must be identical.
12. Rule 24(4)(b) maintains the requirement, currently under CPR r 19.8, that the represented class must be capable of identification prior to the proceedings being determined. This does not mean that each class member must be identified. It simply requires them to be capable of identification. This approach follows that endorsed in *Emerald Supplies Ltd v British Airways plc* (2011),[131] which held that the represented class had to be capable of determination prior to judgment being given. An approach that permitted the class to be determined on judgment, would—if the proceedings failed—leave it unclear as to whom the judgment bound. It is simply unjust to a successful defendant for them to be left in the position that they do know who is bound by a judgment issued in their favour.[132]
13. Rule 24(4)(c) introduces a superiority criterion. This requires the court to conclude that the use of a representative proceeding is superior to other forms of proceeding. This is aimed at ensuring an order is only made where it is the most effective and proportionate process for securing the administration of justice. Particular consideration must be given to the nature, complexity, and value of claims as well as the number of them. Unlike the Civil Justice Council, which recommended that any superiority criterion also considered if a representative action was superior to the use of an Ombudsman, regulatory or other form of ADR process,[133] this rule does not incorporate such a requirement. Such a requirement is otiose. In assessing the effective management of multi-party disputes the court will necessarily need to consider whether an adjudicative or settlement process is preferable. This includes under rule 31(1)(d), consideration whether a representative proceeding be allocated to the settlement management track.
14. The court will also have to consider under 24(4(c) whether certification is justified by reference to the purposive principle. This requires it to conduct a cost-benefit analysis in a manner analogous to that required by CAT Rules, r 79(2)(a) and (b). The former requires consideration whether such a form of proceeding would secure a fair process for the representative, the represented class members, and the defendant. It further requires consideration of the effect of such a proceeding on systemic proportionality

130 *Gutmann v First MTR South Western Trains Ltd* [2021] CAT 31 at [107].
131 *Emerald Supplies Ltd v British Airways plc* [2010] EWCA Civ 1284; [2011] Ch 345.
132 *Lloyd v Google* [2021] UKSC 50; [2022] AC 1217 at [56].
133 Civil Justice Council (2008) at 152; CAT Rules, r 79(2)(g).

and, thus, on the court's ability to effectively manage its overall resources across all proceedings. Both issues will particularly call for consideration of the comparative merits of representative proceedings versus other forms of proceeding to determine the optimum approach. The latter requires the court to consider the cost, both financial and non-financial, of representative proceedings against the likely benefit to be achieved. This could include consideration of the financial cost likely to be incurred by the parties versus the way in which such proceedings could promote compliance with the law in future, the level of expected damages,[134] and the benefit to the defendant (of, for instance, finality of litigation across the class).

15. Rule 24(4(d) requires the court to conclude that it is just and reasonable to permit a person to pursue or defend proceedings as a representative. The requirements necessary to determine this question are specified in rule 28. It makes explicit what is implicit, through the operation of the Interpretation Act 1978, in CAT collective proceedings that more than one person may be appointed as a representative party in proceedings.[135]

16. Rule 27(5) confirms that where a representative proceedings order is made, as under the CPR and the CAT Rules,[136] the represented class are not parties to the proceedings. They remain, however, bound by any judgment or order made in the proceedings.[137] One consequence of this is that where evidence is sought from represented class members by a defendant it must be sought on the basis that they are non-parties.

17. Rule 27(6) provides the power to vary or set aside a representative proceedings order. The court may do so of its own initiative or on application of a party.[138] This reflects the concept under the CAT Rules that certification is an ongoing process and must be kept under active review by the court and the parties. The rule specifies that this power may be exercised where it becomes apparent that the conditions specified in rule 27(4) no longer apply to the proceedings. The broadest criterion of note for the purpose of this rule is rule 27(4)(c), ie where it becomes apparent that representative proceedings are no longer superior to other forms of proceedings. Variation or setting aside may be ordered where the representative party is unable to obtain sufficient evidence to make out an aggregate damages claim as that would mean such a proceeding was no longer superior to group or individual proceedings.[139] It may also be justified where it becomes apparent that the represented class is smaller than originally understood and, as a consequence, joinder or consolidation of individual proceedings is a superior form of proceeding.[140] Variation may also be ordered to replace the representative party, to alter the definition of the class,[141] to create sub-classes or to alter the proceedings from opt-in to opt-out or vice versa. Variation or set aside decisions ought to be taken at an appropriate time in proceedings. As the CAT has noted, decisions to set aside due to problems securing evidence to bear out an aggregate damages claim ought to wait until after case statements, disclosure and expert evidence had been obtained.[142]

[134] *Gutmann v First MTR South Western Trains Ltd* [2021] CAT 31 at [165]–[178].

[135] *Boyle v Govia Thameslink Railway Ltd* [2022] CAT 35 at [10]–[13].

[136] CPR r 19.8(4); CAT Rules, r 91.

[137] *Meux v Maltby* (1818) 2 Swans 277 at 281.

[138] CAT Rules, r 85.

[139] *Merricks v Mastercard Inc* [2019] EWCA Civ 674; [2019] Bus LR 3025 at [53].

[140] *Mark McLaren Class Representative Ltd v MOL (Europe Africa) Ltd* [2022] CAT 10 at [62].

[141] *UK Trucks Claim Ltd v Stellantis NV* [2022] CAT 25 at [255].

[142] *Merricks v Mastercard Inc* [2019] EWCA Civ 674; [2019] Bus LR 3025 at [53].

18. This rule does not include a merits criterion. Consistently with the approach under the CAT Rules the merits of the proposed representative proceedings are not to be taken into account in determining certification.[143] Incorporation of such a criterion would inevitably transform the certification process into a mini-trial, and a particularly disproportionate one at that. Such a process would also lead to considerable front-loading of litigation cost: parties would seek to adduce and compel the disclosure of evidence prior to certification, which if certification was not granted could well be wasted costs.

## RULE 28.—AUTHORISATION OF A REPRESENTATIVE

**(1) In determining whether it is just and reasonable to permit a person to bring or defend proceedings in a representative capacity, the court must consider whether that person**

**(a) has any material conflict of interest with those persons whom they seek to represent;**

**(b) is able to fairly and adequately act in the best interests of those persons whom they seek to represent; and**

**(c) has sufficient resources to conduct the proceedings properly and to satisfy any undertakings to the court or as to damages or any costs liability.**

**(2) In determining whether a person is able to fairly and adequately act in the interests of those persons whom they seek to represent, the court must consider all the circumstances, including whether they**

**(a) share a common interest with those persons whom they seek to represent;**

**(b) are authorised by any rule of law to act as a representative party either generally or in respect of the subject matter of the proceedings;**

**(c) the reasons why they wish to act as a representative party if they do not share a common interest with the persons to be represented or are not authorised by law to act as a representative party; and**

**(d) the extent to which they have prepared, and the adequacy of, a representative proceedings management plan.**

**(3) Where the court has authorised a person to act as a representative party, it may either on its own initiative or on the application of a party, vary or set aside the authorisation where the person no longer satisfies the criteria for authorisation.**

**(4) Where the court varies or sets aside a representative party's authorisation to act as such, it may substitute another person as the representative party where they satisfy the authorisation criteria. If no other person satisfies the criteria, the court shall set aside the representative proceedings order and make any necessary directions.**

*Sources: ELI-UNIDROIT Model Rules, rr.208, 209, 214; Civil Justice Council (2008), Recommendation 2, Draft Civil Procedure Rules r 19.20; CAT Rules, r 78.*

## COMMENTARY

1. Two different approaches have been taken in England and Wales to the question of who may bring or defend representative proceedings in a representative capacity. Under the CPR, and its predecessors, only a person who falls within the represented class can act in a representative capacity.[144] Under the CAT process, non-class

[143] *Mastercard Incorporated v Walter Hugh Merricks CBE* [2020] UKSC 51; [2021] 3 All ER 285 at [59].

[144] CPR r 19.8(1).

members may be authorised. These can either be organisations that have been authorised by the State to act as representative parties[145] or persons authorised on a case-by-case basis by the CAT to act as representative parties.[146] In both these situations the authorised representative does not have to be a class member.

2. The CPR approach limits the potential scope for representative proceedings to be pursued, particularly where class claims are of low or moderate value and the potential cost to the representative party would significantly outweigh any damages award. The two approaches that operate within the CAT raise other potential problems. Extending the ability to act as a representative party to State-authorised bodies requires those bodies to initiate proceedings to secure effective access to dispute resolution for the represented class. Their ability to do so will be limited by their resources and by the number of potential proceedings they may need to consider commencing, as well as by any other commitments they have. When this approach was the sole one in place in the CAT only one organisation was authorised. It only commenced one collective proceeding.[147] Under its current approach, which also permits case-by-case authorisation, there is far broader scope for organisations and individuals to act as representatives. It thus provides the more effective basis for proceedings to be pursued.
3. Rule 27(4)(d) and 28 adopt the broader approach currently in place in the CAT.[148] It is an approach that is also consistent with, albeit wider than, the best practice approach endorsed by the ELI-UNIDROIT Model Rules.[149] The basic premise is that any organisation or individual can, in principle, be authorised as a representative party. The question for the court in considering authorisation is whether it is appropriate—just and reasonable—for them to do so. This is the same test as applicable in the CAT.[150] In determining that question rule 28 requires the court, irrespective of the opposing party's stance,[151] to consider a number of factors to determine whether authorisation is appropriate. Those factors are intended to ensure problems that might otherwise arise from enabling a wide range of organisations and individuals to be representative parties are mitigated and that the representative is able to properly carry out its role, which as the CAT Guidance rightly notes imposes '*significant and serious obligations [upon representative parties, which are not] to be taken on lightly*'.[152]
4. Broadening the scope of authorisation does, however, raise questions of conflicts of interest between the representative and represented class. Thus, the court must consider what, if any, material conflicts of interest exist or might arise. Their existence would point away from authorisation. This makes it particularly unlikely that a law firm or any organisation or individual that provides funding to enable proceedings to be conducted will be authorised.[153]

[145] As was the case when the CAT collective proceeding was opt-in only: Competition Act 1998, s 47B as inserted by Enterprise Act 2002, s 19.

[146] CAT Rules, r 78(1)(b).

[147] Civil Justice Council (2008) at 88–89.

[148] CAT, *Guide to Proceedings (2015)*, at 72–74.

[149] ELI-UNIDROIT Model Rules, r 208.

[150] CAT Rules, r 78(1)(b).

[151] *Gutmann v First MTR South Western Trains Ltd* [2021] CAT 31 at [49].

[152] CAT, *Guide to Proceedings (2015)*, at 72.

[153] CAT, *Guide to Proceedings (2015)*, at 72.

5. The court must also consider if the putative representative is able to fairly and adequately act in the class members' best interests. This requires, for instance, consideration of their ability to manage the proceedings effectively through being able to give effective instructions to their lawyers. It will also require them to have in place effective mechanisms to manage any relationship they may have with insurers or funding organisations.[154] To adequately and fairly represent the class means more than this. Rule 28(2) sets out a number of factors that the court must consider when determining this issue.[155]
6. Rule 28(2)(a) requires the court to consider if the representative is a class member, and hence due to having a common interest with the represented class is likely to pursue a representative claim or defence in a proper manner. Rule 28(2)(b) focuses on the question whether the putative representative is authorised by the State to act as a representative. Where they are, they are more likely to be properly situated to act in the class's best interests.
7. Rule 28(2)(c) focuses on the third class of potential representatives: those that have no connection with the dispute, ie they fall outside the class and are not a State-authorised organisation. Here the court must focus on the reasons why they seek to act as a representative. Such a putative representative may, for instance, wish to act in such a capacity because they are a campaigning organisation or a consumer representative organisation and are thus seeking authorisation to protect the interests of individuals harmed or to deter future harmful action by potential defendants within their field. They may also and to the contrary wish to bring such proceedings for abusive or mischievous reasons, eg to harass defendants or to seek to obtain settlement of unmeritorious or vexatious claims to enable them to make a profit from the litigation. Their reasons may therefore either be in the private interest of the class and the wider public interest or they may be contrary to the public interest.
8. An important factor which ought to be considered when assessing rule 28(3)(c) is whether the organisation was well-established prior to the cause of action arising or whether it was established after that date and/or specifically for the purpose of pursuing proceedings as a representative party. If, as noted above, the organisation is a well-established consumer representative or trade association that may point to their authorisation. If they are, by contrast, a special purpose vehicle created after the cause of action arose that may point away from their being authorised.[156] That may particularly be the case if it is apparent that its creation was primarily intended to be a vehicle to profit from the dispute rather than to pursue the private interests of class and the public interest that underpins the availability of representative proceedings.[157] It may be, however, that a special purpose vehicle is established and managed for the benefit of those interests and can, on the individual facts of the case, properly be authorised. Much will depend on the nature and management of the special purpose vehicle, and particularly who are behind it, their reasons for establishing it, and their ability to manage proceedings effectively.[158]

[154] *Michael O'Higgins FX Class Representative Ltd v Barclays Bank Plc* [2022] CAT 16 at [345]–[346].
[155] ELI-UNIDROIT Model Rules, r 209.
[156] *Michael O'Higgins FX Class Representative Ltd v Barclays Bank Plc* [2022] CAT 16 at [263]–[269].
[157] *Gibson v Pride Mobility Products Limited* [2017] CAT 9; [2017] 4 CMLR 33 at [138].
[158] *UK Trucks Claim Ltd v Stellantis NV* [2022] CAT 25 at [26].

9. Rule 28(2)(d) is specifically intended to enable the court to determine if the putative representative is able to adequately represent the class.[159] By providing the detail required by rule 29, the court will be put in the position to determine whether the putative representative understands the nature of the claim, the legal and factual issues it raises, the extent to which they have properly understood the management issues that are likely to arise and the basis on which they are able to deal with them, their ability to manage and secure any expected expert evidence, and their ability to fund the proceedings.[160] Particular consideration of this question will need to take place where the court is considering making an order under rule 30 that representative proceedings operate on an opt-out basis. In such a case, and in contrast to opt-in proceedings, the class members are unlikely to be known to the representative and are likely to be particularly numerous and, perhaps, only identified by description. There is thus a much greater need, as noted rightly in the CAT Guidance, to ensure that the putative representative is able to both adequately represent such a class.[161]

10. Authorisation is a continuing process. Once authorised a representative must ensure that it acts consistently with the basis of its authorisation. Where it does not or cannot do so, the court should consider varying or setting aside the authorisation. As the court may do this on its own initiative, it should monitor the representative's compliance with the basis of authorisation. Equally, a representative ought to apply to the court to set aside the authorisation where it becomes aware of the fact that it is no longer able to satisfy the basis of its authorisation because, for instance, a conflict of interest has arisen or it no longer has the resources to adequately act in the class's best interests. Where authorisation is set aside the court may appoint a new representative party. If that is not possible, it is required to give such directions as are necessary to enable the proceedings to continue as individual proceedings or, as may be necessary, to release the suspension of any limitation period applicable to the represented class members' claims.[162]

## RULE 29.—REPRESENTATIVE PROCEEDINGS MANAGEMENT PLAN

**(1) A person seeking authorisation as a representative party must prepare a representative proceedings management plan.**

**(2) The plan must, particularly, identify the steps that are proposed to be taken to manage the proceedings efficiently, economically, and proportionately, including how the costs of the proceedings will be managed. It must also provide information on any steps taken to settle the proceedings, what steps are proposed to be taken to promote settlement, the remedies sought and how any damages award is to be calculated and allocated amongst the represented class and how any unclaimed damages are to be managed.**

**(3) Where authorisation as a representative party is granted, the plan will be considered in determining appropriate dispute management directions under rule 31.**

*Sources: Civil Justice Council (2008), Part 10, Draft Civil Procedure Rules r 19.20(1)(b); CAT Rules, r 78(3)(c).*

[159] *Gibson v Pride Mobility Products Limited* [2017] CAT 9; [2017] 4 CMLR 33 at [134].

[160] CAT Rules, r 78(3)(a) and (c); r 29(2).

[161] CAT, *Guide to Proceedings (2015)*, at 72.

[162] CAT, *Guide to Proceedings (2015)*, at 74.

## COMMENTARY

1. This rule makes further provision for the representative proceedings management plan, which the court must consider when dealing with an application to authorise a party to act as a representative party under rule 28(2)(d). It is based on the recommendation made by the Civil Justice Council in the draft rules for representative actions set out in its 2008 Report, which was adopted by CAT Rules, r 78(3)(c).
2. The plan serves two purposes. Primarily, it provides the court with sufficient information to determine whether to grant an application for authorisation as a representative party. Its secondary purpose, if such an application is granted, is to provide the court with information necessary to determine appropriate dispute management directions. It must therefore be sufficiently detailed to deal with both circumstances. It should, as explained in respect of the CAT Rules, r 78(3)(c),

   '*... be sufficiently detailed and comprehensive to correspond to the nature of the particular case. It should explain how the proposed class representative and its lawyers intend to ensure that the collective proceedings will be effectively and efficiently pursued in the interests of the class, referring to the issues likely to arise in the particular case.*'[163]

   The plan should thus deal with those issues that are likely to arise in the proceedings and should be drafted accordingly. It should particularly ensure it provides detail concerning the representative party's ability to fund any potential costs.[164] As the plan is prepared at an early stage in proceedings the court will not expect it to go into specific detail regarding the various issues that are likely to arise. The approach to be taken is that adopted in Canada, as endorsed by the CAT, ie that

   *... At the certification stage, the standard [the] plan must meet is not one of perfection; ... the plan need only set out "a framework within which the case may proceed" and "demonstrate that the representative plaintiff and class counsel have a clear grasp of the complexities involved in the case.*[165]

3. Given the requirement under rule 32 that representative proceedings must be proportionate, the plan will also need to ensure that it sets out a proportionate procedure for managing the dispute. It will therefore need to consider and deal with the question of an appropriate classification for the proceeding, eg low, moderate, intermediate, or high value, and an appropriate management track allocation. The plan will need to be consistent with the proposed classification.
4. In so far as the plan must be detailed, that requirement is itself subject to the proportionality principle. A proceeding that is likely to be classified as low or moderate value will therefore require a less detailed plan than that of one likely to be classified as intermediate or high value.
5. A crucial feature of any management plan will concern remedies. It must identify clearly the remedies sought and, as will generally be the case, how damages are to be calculated and awarded. Under the CPR's representative rule, the availability of damages was limited. Generally a declaration as to damages was all that could be

163 CAT, *Guide to Proceedings (2015)*, at 72.

164 *Merricks v MasterCard Inc* [2021] CAT 28; [2021] 5 CMLR 17 at [19]–[20]; *UK Trucks Claim Ltd v Fiat Chrysler Automobiles NV* [2019] CAT 26 at [109].

165 *UK Trucks Claim Limited v Stellantis NV* [2022] CAT 25 at [32]; *Godfrey v Sony Corp* [2017] BCCA 302 at [255]; *Mastercard Inc v Merricks* [2021] UKSC 51; [2021] 3 All ER 285 at [42].

obtained.[166] Under the CAT procedure damages can, however, be sought on either an individual or aggregate basis; the latter being an award of damages reached without having to assess the damages incurred by each class member individually.[167] The former, traditional form of assessment is typical of unitary litigation, including group proceedings and opt-in representative proceedings. The latter, given the nature of opt-out classes and particularly the difficulty in identifying the individual class members and the numbers within the class, are typical of effective opt-out proceedings.[168]

6. Where aggregate damages are sought, and thus detailed in the management plan, sufficient information in terms of methodology for calculating the award[169] must be set out to enable the court to assess, on the facts of the case, whether there is '*a realistic prospect of establishing loss on a class-wide scale. . .*'.[170] While the information provided need not be such as to enable an assessment of the merits of such an award, there must be sufficient information to enable the court to conclude that information/evidence exists that will enable such an award to be calculated if this aspect of the management plan is to satisfy the court that approval of representative proceedings and, opt-out proceedings particularly, should be granted.[171]

## RULE 30.—DETERMINATION WHETHER REPRESENTATIVE PROCEEDINGS OPERATE ON AN OPT-IN OR OPT-OUT BASIS

**(1) Where a representative proceedings order is to be made, the court must determine whether the proceedings are to operate on an opt-in or opt-out basis.**

**(2) Opt-in proceedings require members of the represented class to explicitly consent to their being represented by the representative party in the proceedings. Opt-out proceedings require members of the represented class to explicitly decline to be represented by the represented party in the proceedings.**

**(3) Where the proceedings or potential proceedings within the scope of the order are individually low or moderate value claims, the proceedings will operate on an opt-out basis, unless the court directs otherwise.**

**(4) Represented class members domiciled outside the court's jurisdiction may only opt-into proceedings.**

**(5) In determining whether proceedings are opt-in or opt-out proceedings, the court shall consider all the circumstances, and particularly which basis best promotes access to justice, economy, efficiency, and proportionality.**

*Sources: ELI-UNIDROIT Model Rules, r 215; Civil Justice Council (2008), Recommendation 3, Part 10, Draft Civil Procedure Rules, rr 19.19(7), 19.21, 19.22, 19.23; Competition Act 1998, s 47B; CAT Rules, r 80(1)(h).*

166 *Lloyd v Google* [2021] UKSC 50; [2022] AC 1217.

167 Competition Act 1998, s 47C(1) and (2).

168 *Mastercard Incorporated v Walter Hugh Merricks CBE* [2020] UKSC 51; [2021] 3 All ER 285 at [76]–[77]: the introduction of aggregate damages was intended to obviate the problem of individual damages assessment in opt-out proceedings.

169 Statistical analysis is a typical approach to the calculation of aggregate damages awards.

170 *Pro-Sys Consultants Ltd v Microsoft Corp* [2013] SCC 57; *Mastercard Incorporated v Walter Hugh Merricks CBE* [2020] UKSC 51; [2021] 3 All ER 285 at [40]–[42]; *London & South Eastern Railway Ltd v Gutmann* [2022] EWCA Civ 1077; [2022] ECC 26 at [52]–[63].

171 *Mark McLaren Class Representative Ltd v MOL (Europe Africa) Ltd* [2022] CAT 10 at [74], [100]–[106].

## COMMENTARY

1. The question whether representative, or collective, proceedings should operate on an opt-in or opt-out basis is and remains controversial. Opt-in proceedings are commonly criticised as being an inadequate means to secure access to justice for multi-party low value disputes. The rationale for this is that individuals are, rationally, unlikely to pursue (opt-into) such claims. Consequently, the substantive law in such cases tends to go unenforced and potential defendants are not deterred from behaviour that would give rise to such harm. Opt-out proceedings are, on the other hand, said to give rise to vexatious and unmeritorious claims being pursued in the expectation that defendants will settle to avoid the potential costs of such litigation. This debate has played itself out both in England and Wales and the European Union[172] particularly since the turn of the 21st century, although the debate in the former properly commenced in 1987.[173]
2. The debate is now to a significant degree settled. Public policy in England and Wales has followed the approach advocated by both the Woolf Report and the Civil Justice Council and adopted within the CAT: an opt-in/opt-out form of collective or representative proceeding. That approach is now accepted to be the optimum one to balance the need to promote proportionate access to justice for multi-party claims, particularly low value ones.[174] The same approach has been endorsed in the European Union and in the ELI-UNDIROIT Model Rules.[175] Concerns about the drawbacks of opt-out proceedings are now largely understood to be overstated where there are effective means to control access to a representative procedure through robust certification or authorisation processes.[176] Equally, effective dispute management, court scrutiny and approval of any settlement, and an effective loser-pays costs rule ensure that opt-out proceedings are not capable of abuse. Each of these protective mechanisms are present in this Code.[177]
3. Rules 30(1) provide the basis for the court to direct that representative proceedings should proceed as either opt-in or opt-out proceedings. This decision is to be taken as part of the process to consider authorisation under rule 27. It should be considered after the court has determined that an order will be made.[178]
4. Rule 30(1) is, however, subject to the presumption contained in rule 30(3). It creates a presumption in favour of opt-out proceedings for low and moderate value

[172] Eg Commission Communication, *Towards a European Horizontal Framework for Collective Redress*, COM (2013) 401/2 (11 June 2013); Commission Recommendation, *On Common Principles for Collective Redress Mechanisms in the Member States for Injunctions against and Claims on Damages caused by violations of EU rights*, COM (2013) 3539 (11 June 2013).

[173] *Davies v Eli Lilly* [1987] 1 WLR 1136 at 1139; J Sorabji, 'Collective action reform in England and Wales: Are class actions really on the way?', in D Fairgrieve and E Lein, *Extraterritoriality & Collective Redress* (OUP, 2012).

[174] H Woolf (1996) at 236, 249; Civil Justice Council (2008), Recommendation 3; Consumer Rights Act 2015, s 81.

[175] Directive (EU) 2020/1828 of the European Parliament and of the Council of 25 November 2020 on representative actions for the protection of the collective interests of consumers and repealing Directive 2009/22/EC, recitals 43–46; ELI-UNIDROIT Model Rules, r 215.

[176] Civil Justice Council (2008) at 145–150; ELI-UNIDROIT Model Rules, r 215, comment 1 to 3.

[177] CAT Rules, rr 88, 94, 95, 98.

[178] CAT Rules, r 79(3); *Le Patourel v BT Group Plc* [2021] CAT 30 at [110]; *Gutmann v First MTR South Western Trains Ltd* [2021] CAT 31 at [182]; *Michael O'Higgins FX Class Representative Ltd v Barclays Bank Plc* [2022] CAT 16 at [80]–[89].

claims, and has two aims.[179] It is primarily intended to secure access to justice for them.[180] Such claims are typically not economical to pursue on an individual basis and individual claimants, where opt-in proceedings are available,[181] typically and rationally do not opt-in.[182] This leaves rights unvindicated or at the least it leaves the alleged infringement of rights untested judicially. An opt-in procedure thus, generally, fails to secure effective access to justice for such claims. It also creates a second problem, which the present approach is intended to rectify. Where small numbers of represented parties opt-in, the law is likely to go unenforced for the potentially large number who do not opt-in. There is thus a strong incentive or at least no proper disincentive for potential defendants to act within the law. This would tacitly encourage an environment where public confidence in the civil justice system is undermined as is the rule of law. A presumptive opt-out approach for low and moderate claims is intended to counter both problems. It is, however, only a presumption. There may be circumstances were the nature and complexity of the legal or factual issues involved in such claims merit the proceedings being classified as opt-in.

5. In determining whether representative proceedings should be classified as opt-in or opt-out, the court must also consider which classification would further the purposive principle.[183] This requires the court to take account of all the circumstances of the claims.[184]
6. Questions of economy, efficiency, and proportionality must also be taken account of by the court, both in terms of how those factors affect the parties, and represented class members, but also how they affect the court and its ability to allocate its resources to the proceedings and other proceedings. Important issues to consider in assessing these questions, and therefore whether opt-in or opt-out is more suitable are the size of the represented class,[185] the nature of the representative party's funding and the extent to which the represented claims will require individual damages assessments or whether aggregate damages are sought and are likely to be awarded. Aggregate damages are likely to reduce the complexity of proceedings and point towards classification as an opt-out form of proceeding, whereas the need for individual damages assessment may well point towards the need for an opt-in procedure.[186]

[179] In this it differs from the approach taken to CAT collective proceedings: *BT Group Plc v Le Patourel* [2022] EWCA Civ 593; [2022] Bus LR 660 at [61]–[67]; H Woolf (1996) at 236.

[180] *Mastercard Incorporated v Walter Hugh Merricks CBE* [2020] UKSC 51; [2021] 3 All ER 285 at [37], [45]; *BT Group Plc v Le Patourel* [2022] EWCA Civ 593; [2022] Bus LR 660 at [107].

[181] Opt-in proceedings typically yield low numbers opting in. Opt-out systems due to status quo bias yield low opt-out rates: R Mulheron, *Reform of Collective Redress in England and Wales: A Perspective of Need* (Civil Justice Council, 2008); W Samuelson and R Zeckhauser, 'Status Quo Bias in Decision Making' (1988) 1(1) Journal of Risk and Uncertainty 7.

[182] R Mulheron (2008); S Gibbons (2008).

[183] The comparable question in the CAT is which form of procedure is most practicable: CAT r 79(3); *BT Group Plc v Le Patourel* [2022] EWCA Civ 593; [2022] Bus LR 660 at [83].

[184] *BT Group Plc v Le Patourel* [2022] EWCA Civ 593; [2022] Bus LR 660 at [68] and [107]; *O'Higgins FX Class Representative Ltd v Barclays Bank Plc* [2022] CAT 16 at [122]–[123]: an opt-out process would not be practicable if it was clear that the represented class members or a large number of them had all previously indicated that they would opt-out. Conversely, if sufficient members of the class would not opt-in, then an opt-out process may be more practicable: *Le Patourel v BT Group Plc* [2021] CAT 30 at [30]; although see *Mark McLaren Class Representative Ltd v MOL (Europe Africa) Ltd* [2022] CAT 10 at [166]. Low value, particularly consumer, claims are the paradigm example of claims most suitable for opt-out proceedings.

[185] *Gutmann v First MTR South Western Trains Ltd* [2021] CAT 31 at [183].

[186] *BT Group Plc v Le Patourel* [2022] EWCA Civ 593; [2022] Bus LR 660 at [107].

7. Rule 30(4) is intended to ensure that representative proceedings do not incorporate an exorbitant jurisdiction. It incorporates into the Code the approach taken under the Competition Act 1998, which excludes individuals not domiciled in the UK from the opt-out regime and requires them to opt-into the CAT collective proceeding.[187]

## RULE 31.—MANAGEMENT OF REPRESENTATIVE PROCEEDINGS

**(1) Where a representative proceedings order is made, the court must give directions concerning**
- **(a) the reasonable steps to be taken by the representative party to publicise the proceedings;**
- **(b) the date by which represented class members may opt-into or opt-out of proceedings;**
- **(c) the establishment and management of a digital register for represented class members;**
- **(d) disclosure of any contingency fee or funding arrangements that the representative party has put in place;**
- **(e) the effective management of the proceedings, including classification and procedural track allocation.**

**(2) Directions may also be given at any time once a representative proceedings order is made to**
- **(a) divide the represented class into sub-classes and to appoint a representative party for each sub-class;**
- **(b) suspend the operation of any applicable limitation period;**
- **(c) determine the approach to the nature, calculation, and distribution of damages, including the distribution of damages unclaimed by class members albeit such distribution must not provide for their return to the defendant.**

**(3) The court may also stay any proceedings brought by represented class members who either did not opt-into opt-in proceedings or opted-out of opt-out proceedings. Where a stay is imposed, the party affected may apply to vary or set-aside the stay.**

*Sources: ELI-UNIDROIT Model Rules, rr 217, 218, 219; Civil Justice Council (2008), Recommendation 6; CAT Rules, rr 78(4), 88.*

## COMMENTARY

1. The effective management of representative proceedings involves a number of specific features that go beyond ordinary dispute management.[188] Rule 31 makes provision for them.
2. Rule 31(1) requires the court to give directions that serve the due notice, party autonomy and dispute management principles. It requires directions to be given to publicise the proceedings. The intention here is to give notice to class members of the proceedings to enable them to take such steps as they see fit concerning the vindication of their rights through the proceedings. In opt-in proceedings it serves

[187] Competition Act 1998, s 47B(11)(b).
[188] H Woolf (1996) at 230.

to enable class members to opt-in. In opt-out proceedings it enables them to opt-out. In both cases, it gives effect to the party autonomy principle enabling them to choose whether and how they wish to vindicate their rights. In opt-out proceedings it also provides a basis to justify what might otherwise be viewed as a general abrogation of party autonomy for class members. They are to be given effective and due notice of the proceedings and of the consequences of inactivity. If, having been given reasonable notice by the representative through appropriate channels, eg media adverts, text alerts, social media, etc, they choose not to opt-out, that decision is itself an act of party autonomy. Inevitably some class members will not receive actual notice. To require that would place too high a burden on the representative, which in turn would undermine the utility of representative proceedings. Hence reasonable steps need only be taken. Different notice periods will need to be set for class members outside the court's jurisdiction.

3. The court must also set a date by which class members must opt-in or opt-out. In opt-in proceedings, the date should provide sufficient time for class members to receive reasonable notice and decide whether they wish to opt-in. In opt-out proceedings, the converse applies. In both cases, the date helps provide the representative party with notice of the extent of the represented class so that it can plan its approach to the proceedings effectively. While the same is true of the defendant, the date also provides them with notice of the extent to which the proceedings will secure finality of litigation. A class member may be permitted to opt-in or opt-out after the cut-off date. To do so though they will have to satisfy the test applicable to relief from sanctions, as a failure to comply with the date is a breach of a court order (rule 34). Different dates should also be set for those class members outside the court's jurisdiction to give them sufficient time to receive notice and decide if they wish to opt-in.
4. Effective management of the proceedings also requires the establishment of a digital register of represented class members. This promotes effective communication between them and the representative party and the court. It also promotes effective management of the assessment and allocation of any damages.
5. Details of funding arrangements must be disclosed: Part 4, rule 7(5). Directions must be given as to when that is to take place.
6. Finally, rule 31(1) emphasises the need for effective management, including classification and allocated to procedural track. The emphasis on effective management here is intended to highlight its particular importance given the need to ensure that such proceedings are carried out proportionately. Classification is important given the differential approach taken in these rules to types of representative proceedings, eg different approaches to low and moderate value as against other value proceedings (rule 32). Allocation to track is also of importance as these rules do not make specific provision for collective or representative settlements, as is the case in the ELI-UNIDROIT Model Rules[189] and the CAT Rules.[190] The promotion of settlement is achieved via allocation of representative proceedings, where appropriate, to the settlement management track (rule 15).
7. Rule 31(2) provides for three distinct situations. Rule 31(2)(a) enables the represented class to be divided into sub-classes, each of which should have its own representative party. Representatives are authorised under rule 28. The creation of sub-classes

[189] ELI-UNIDROIT Model Rules, rr 221–226.

[190] Competition Act 1998, s 49A; CAT Rules, rr 94–97.

may arise for a number of reasons. There may be a spread of issues arising across the represented class, which justify sorting the class into distinct classes, eg some members may have suffered distinct forms of damage not suffered by others, eg direct or indirect loss. There may be a difference in relative merits of claims within the class. Some members may, for instance, have no issue concerning causation whereas others do, which would suggest that the former have stronger claims on the merits than others. There may be gradations of damage suffered across the class, such that some class members' claims are high value, whereas others are moderate or low value.[191] Or, there may be conflicts of interest between parts of the represented class, which can only be managed through its division into sub-classes.[192] More creative approaches to the creation of sub-classes could involve the creation of one to act as a lead or test case for the class as a whole; the sub-class in this case enabling more streamlined and cost-effective management than management of proceedings involving the whole, undifferentiated class.[193]

8. Rule 31(2)(b) concerns the suspension of limitation periods.[194] Where individual proceedings are issued, limitation periods cease to run once they are issued. Where a representative party falls within the represented class, for them too limitation will cease to run when proceedings commence. For represented class members, however, as they are not party to representative proceedings, limitation would ordinarily continue to run.[195] This is the case whether the proceedings are opt-in or opt-out because they are not parties to the proceedings. To protect their ability to vindicate their substantive rights, representative proceedings typically provide the means to suspend the running of limitation periods for class members. This serves several purposes. It ensures that they do not need to issue proceedings to protect their rights. It thus saves court and party time and cost on activity that would otherwise undermine one of the aims of introducing representative proceedings in the first place. It ensures that where a representative party has to be substituted during the course of proceedings, there remain class members who still have substantive rights that would enable them to issue proceedings and thus be substituted for the original representative party. The ability to suspend limitation periods also puts defendants on-notice of the nature of the class and that the rights of the represented class members remain viable and capable of prosecution pending the outcome of the representative proceedings.[196]

9. Rule 31(2)(c) is concerned with the calculation of damages. The representative party ought to have outlined its proposed approach to this issue within its management plan. As the representative proceedings develop and more information comes to light, that initial approach will inevitably need to be refined. Directions will need to be given concerning how damages are to be calculated, the evidence needed to bear out the calculation, and how damages are to be distributed. It may, for instance, be

[191] *Michael O'Higgins FX Class Representative Ltd v Barclays Bank Plc* [2022] CAT 16 at [275]–[278]; *Mark McLaren Class Representative Ltd v MOL (Europe Africa) Ltd* [2022] CAT 10 at [141], [188].

[192] R Mulheron, *The Class Action in Common Law Legal Systems: A Comparative Perspective* (Hart Publishing, 2004) at 184–188.

[193] R Mulheron (2004) at 186 citing *Eisen v Carlisle & Jackuelin*, 417 US 156 at 180.

[194] Competition Act 1998, s 47E; H Woolf (1996) at 228.

[195] *Moon v Atherton* [1972] 2 QB 435 at 442.

[196] R Mulheron (2004) at 373–381.

that expert evidence, particularly statistical evidence, will be needed on the question of calculation in opt-out proceedings. Equally, lump sum awards may be awarded, which in turn will require directions concerning their distribution to class members. In opt-in proceedings, individual calculations may, however, be necessary and proportionate.

10. In opt-out proceedings, there is generally a significant amount of unclaimed damages. Different approaches can be taken here.[197] Unclaimed damages could be: held in trust until claimed or a deadline for claiming expires; returned to the defendant; transferred to the State for distribution either generally or for specific purposes;[198] or, applied through a *cy pres* mechanism. The last, the approach taken in the United States, sees unclaimed damages applied for purposes closely related to the cause of action.[199] A famous example of this type of approach is that evidenced in the taxi overcharging case in Los Angeles. The class action in that case settled, but no compensation was able to be paid to class members as it was not possible to identify them: it was simply impossible to establish who had been overcharged. The settlement was consequently applied to secure a price rollback for future taxi users until the award was exhausted.[200] It is difficult to see how such an approach satisfies the compensatory principle where damages are concerned.
11. This rule does not specify the approach the court may take to unclaimed damages. In that it differs from the approach under the CAT Rules and as proposed by the Civil Justice Council in 2008. The former provides for distribution to a charity.[201] The latter provided three options. It suggested that unclaimed damages either be: applied against the costs of proceedings; forfeit to the Crown, ie transferred to the State; or returned to the defendant. The approach here is to leave the decision to the court on the facts of the individual proceedings, subject to one limitation. Unclaimed damages may not be returned to the defendant. To do so would undermine the rationale underpinning representative proceedings, as it would leave the defendant in practically no worse a position than if the proceedings had not been brought. Damages, unclaimed or otherwise, are the price of vindication of the law and the rights provided by it. To return damages to the defendant would undermine that vindication and the promotion of law-abiding behaviour.
12. Rule 31(3) is intended to ensure that parallel proceedings concerning the same cause of action as that subject to representative proceedings are not continued while it is live. It is thus intended to protect both the court from dealing with multiple proceedings concerning the same cause of action, contrary to the aim of representative proceedings, and also to protect the defendant to any such proceedings from having to defend in multiple proceedings. In this way, it also mitigates the risk of the court reaching multiple, potentially conflicting judgments.

[197] Civil Justice Council (2008), Part 10, r 19.42(4).

[198] This type of approach has been criticised for denuding the proceedings of any compensatory function, eg *State of California v Levi Strauss & Co* 715 P 2D 564, 575 (Cal 1986).

[199] S Shephard, 'Damages Distribution in Class Actions: The Cy Pres Remedy' (1972) 39 Univ Chi Law Rev 448, 498; R Mulheron, *The Modern Cy Pres Doctrine* (Routledge, 2016).

[200] *Daar v Yellow Cab Co* 67 Cal 2D 695; R Mulheron (2016) at 220.

[201] The Legal Services Act 2007, s 194(8).

## RULE 32.—PROPORTIONALITY OF REPRESENTATIVE PROCEEDINGS

**Representative proceedings, their classification and management, must be proportionate to the unaggregated value of the represented claims for relief and the nature and complexity of the dispute.**

*Sources: Civil Justice Council, Draft Rules for Collective Proceedings, rule 19.20(1).*

## COMMENTARY

1. Representative proceedings should provide a proportionate means to manage multi-party claims to either adjudication or settlement. It is important therefore that they do not themselves become disproportionate. This rule is intended to ensure that representative proceedings remain proportionate. It has no analogy in either the CPR's representative action or the CAT's collective proceeding, albeit the former ought to be managed consistently with the CPR's overriding objective and its commitment to proportionality.
2. To ensure that representative proceedings remain proportionate, rule 32 requires the court to classify and manage them based on two factors. First, it requires consideration of the nature and complexity of the claims. In this it modifies rule 11, as that ordinarily only applies nature and complexity as classification criteria, and hence as a guide to future management, where a claim has no financial value. Secondly, it requires consideration of the unaggregated value of the represented claims. Classification by reference to the aggregated value of represented claims would, almost always, ensure that the representative proceeding was classified as a high value claim due to the, ordinarily, large number of individual claims that would fall within the procedure. Focusing on the value of unaggregated claims enables the court to ensure that representative proceedings can be classified as low, moderate, intermediate, or high value.
3. Taken together, in so far as classification is concerned, these two factors are intended to ensure that, as can be the case, complex low value individual claims can be classified and then managed as moderate, intermediate, or high value and thus afforded a procedure that fits the claim and the issues it raises. It can also ensure that a straightforward low value claim, which goes forward as a representative proceeding, remains a low value claim and both the represented party and the defendant to that claim ought to be afforded an analogous process to that afforded to parties to low value claims that proceed as individual claims, ie one that is less complex and procedure heavy than that afforded to moderate, intermediate or high value representative proceedings. Standard directions should be incorporated into the digital procedure accordingly.
4. The rationale underpinning this approach is that a representative proceeding ought to not enable individual claims to be subject to a form of procedure more sophisticated than they would have had available to them otherwise. While the CPR does not make provision for the possibility of a small claim or fast track representative action under CPR Pts 19, 27 and 28, this rule ensures that such an approach can be taken to disputes that proceed as representative proceedings under rule 27.
5. Proportionate classification and management based on individual unaggregated claims ought not, however, to alter the approach to costs of representative proceedings. If a defendant to a representative proceeding were only able to recover the tariff costs,

in the event of success, as if the proceedings were for a single, individual claim, they would not be afforded a fair process. Tariff costs of such proceedings will therefore need to be calibrated to take account of the classification, nature and complexity of the proceeding, its management and, in so far as they effected the management of the proceedings, the number of represented claims. This approach underpins costs in multi-party proceedings in Part 3.

6. The approach adopted here was to a limited degree incorporated in the Civil Justice Council's 2010 draft rules for collective proceedings.[202] Its rule 19.20(1) made express reference to collective proceedings only being authorised where to do so would further the overriding objective. This required the proceedings to be capable of being carried out proportionately. Under the Civil Justice Council's approach, authorisation would therefore not be granted if collective proceedings could not be carried out proportionately. This rule gives effect to that idea, but does so not by reference to authorisation/certification but rather by reference to the nature of representative proceedings once certification has occurred. It thus provides that proportionality pervades the whole representative proceeding process and not just certification.

## SECTION 7: COMPLIANCE WITH PROCEDURAL REQUIREMENTS AND RELIEF FROM SANCTION

### RULE 33.—COMPLIANCE WITH PROCEDURAL REQUIREMENTS

**(1) Parties shall comply with procedural requirements in this Code, any Practice Direction, the digital or non-digital procedure and any court order. Court orders must specify the sanction for non-compliance with any procedural requirement unless the sanction is set out within this Code, any Practice Direction, or the digital or non-digital procedure.**

**(2) All court orders that require parties to take steps or refrain from taking steps in the proceedings must specify the time and date for compliance.**

**(3) Time for compliance with a procedural requirement or court order should be complied with unless extended under rule 9. Where time for compliance is extended, parties should comply with the extended period.**

**(4) Non-compliance with a procedural requirement may result in sanctions being imposed on the non-compliant party. A sanction is an adverse consequence imposed on the non-compliant party.**

**(5) Non-compliance by way of an error of procedure shall not invalidate any step permitted by this Code taken by a party before proceedings commence, to commence proceedings, or within proceedings. Such non-compliance may be regularised by court order.**

**(6) A sanction may be imposed where it is reasonable to do so and the sanction for non-compliance is itself proportionate. Reasonableness and proportionality shall be assessed, amongst other things, by reference to**

**(a) the nature of the proceedings;**

**(b) the nature and any history of non-compliance;**

**(c) the effect of non-compliance on the proceedings;**

[202] Civil Justice Council, *Draft Rules for Collective Proceedings* (February 2010) r 19.20(1).

**(d) the effect of the proposed sanction; and,**

**(e) the court's ability to further the purposive principle.**

**(7) Sanctions for non-compliance may include**

**(a) imposing a truncated time limit for future compliance;**

**(b) imposing conditions on future compliance;**

**(c) staying proceedings;**

**(d) striking out a claim, defence, or issue in the proceedings;**

**(e) prohibiting a party from taking a step or steps in the proceedings;**

**(f) limiting or excluding evidence;**

**(g) limiting or prohibiting cross-examination;**

**(h) requiring a party to give security for costs or make a payment into court as a condition precedent to permitting the non-compliant party to continue with their claim or defence;**

**(i) imposing adverse costs orders, including the payment of costs on a reasonable cost recovery basis.**

**(8) Contempt of court proceedings are not sanctions for non-compliance with procedural requirements.**

*Sources: ALI/UNIDROIT Principles, principle 17; ELI-UNIDROIT Model Rules, rr 7, 47; CPR rr 1.3, 2.11, 3.1(3), 3.8, 3.9, 3.10.*

## COMMENTARY

1. Rule 33 gives effect to the compliance principle and through that effective dispute management. Party compliance with procedural requirements, including the co-operation principle is necessary not only for the efficient, economical, and proportionate management of their dispute, but also for the proportionate management of the court's resources.[203] The rule does not, however mandate compliance. The language of the rule—parties *shall* comply—reflects the fact that compliance is also affected by party autonomy. Parties should comply but they may elect not to do so.[204] They should, for instance, but are not compelled to, comply with the requirement that service be effected by a specified time and via a specified method. Similarly, they shall but are not compelled to comply with the purposive and other procedural principles, with disclosure requirements, or the requirement to give full and frank disclosure of information at a hearing held without-notice.

2. Party compliance is thus the default but not mandated position. Compliance is required, but a party can elect not to do so and undergo the adverse consequences (the sanction[205]) of their election: non-compliance may thus result in the imposition of adverse consequences, as made clear by rule 33(4). Failure to comply with the service requirements may thus result in the non-compliant party not being able to rely on an unserved defence. Failure to comply with disclosure requirements may result in the non-compliant party not being able to rely on evidence, and so on. Serial non-compliance with procedural requirements may result in a claim being struck out.[206]

[203] *Mitchell v News Group Newspapers Ltd* [2013] EWCA Civ 1537; [2014] 1 WLR 795 at [38].

[204] A Zuckerman (2021) at 584–586.

[205] *Summit Navigation Ltd v Generali Romania Assigurare Reasigurare SA* [2014] EWHC 398 (Comm); [2014] 1 WLR 3472 at [27].

[206] *Flaxman-Binns v Lincolnshire County Court* [2004] EWCA Civ 424; [2004] 1 WLR 2232.

Deliberate non-compliance is thus party election to undergo an applicable adverse consequence.[207]

3. Non-compliance may also, however, be inadvertent. In such circumstances, it cannot properly be said that the defaulting party has elected to undergo the adverse consequence applicable. The imposition of adverse consequences in such a situation is nevertheless also justified. Their imposition and the existence of the likelihood of such consequences is both intended to deter inadvertent non-compliance by incentivising good practice and compliance and by punishing the non-compliant party for failing to give proper effect to the purposive principle.[208]
4. Given the importance of rule compliance, it is essential that parties understand the adverse consequences that may flow from non-compliance. If they are to elect effectively, they must know what they are choosing. Equally, if adverse consequences are to be an effective deterrent to, and thus help minimise, inadvertent non-compliance they must be known in advance. Unlike the CPR, which has adopted an approach that does not require the adverse consequences of non-compliance to be spelt out in advance and has, in some circumstances adopted an approach where it will imply sanctions for non-compliance where a rule provides no express sanction,[209] rule 33(1) requires sanctions to be set out expressly in any relevant court order. It thus makes mandatory what under the CPR was a permissive power under CPR r 3.1(3)[210] to specify the adverse consequences of non-compliance in court orders.
5. By requiring the date and time for compliance to be specified in court orders, rule 33(2) is also intended to further promote effective dispute management by providing, in all cases, clarity to the parties and the court. This not just enables parties and their legal representatives to manage their conduct of the dispute effectively, it also enables the court—through the digital procedure—to provide effective and timely prompts to the parties concerning compliance. Clear dates thus promote effective compliance monitoring.
6. Sanctions where they are imposed must be proportionate and serve a legitimate aim.[211] Were they not to be they would amount to a fetter on the general access principle.[212] The court is thus provided with the discretion to determine whether a sanction can be imposed and if so it must then ensure that it fits the particular circumstances. In assessing whether it is reasonable to impose a sanction consideration should be given to the individual history of non-compliance in the proceedings and also to the overall need to further the purposive principle. In the former respect, it is likely to be more reasonable to impose sanctions, and increasingly severe ones, on a party that has engaged in serial non-compliance. Equally, the imposition of standard sanctions for non-compliance, eg the imposition of adverse cost orders or orders requiring compliance within a short time period are more likely to be reasonable as measures to promote effective dispute management and systemic proportionality.

[207] *Prudential Assurance Co Ltd v Fountain Page Ltd* [1991] 1 WLR 756.

[208] *Mitchell v News Group Newspapers Ltd* [2013] EWCA Civ 1537; [2014] 1 WLR 795 at [48].

[209] *Sayers v Clarke Walker (a firm)* [2002] EWCA Civ 645; [2002] 1 WLR 3095 at [21]; *R (Hysaj) v Secretary of State for the Home Department* [2014] EWCA Civ 1633; [2015] WLR 2472; *Warren v Yesss (A) Electrical Ltd* [2024] EWCA Civ 14.

[210] *Marcan Shipping (London) Ltd v Kefalas* [2007] EWCA Civ 463; [2007] 1 WLR 1864.

[211] *Hennings v Germany* (1992) 16 EHRR 83; *Jones v T Mobile (UK) Ltd* [2003] EWCA Civ 1162; [2004] CP Rep 10.

[212] *CIBC Mellon Trust Co v Stolzenberg* [2004] EWCA Civ 827 at [161].

7. In determining the nature of any sanction, the key issue will be the aim it seeks to achieve. This will, at a general level, be the court's ability to further the purposive principle. Consideration of the other procedural principles, and particularly those of economy, efficiency, and proportionality, will also be required.
8. Care will also need to be taken to consider the effect of non-compliance and of the proposed sanction. These points will need to be considered in the context of the immediate proceedings. It may, for instance, be the case that a party has failed to comply with their obligation to disclose evidence by a specified date. The proposed sanction may be to debar them from relying on the evidence. If the party had had several opportunities to disclose the evidence and failed to do so, and if they had been subject to an 'unless order'[213], ie an order requiring them to disclose on pain of being debarred from relying on the evidence, the imposition of the sanction debarring them would, generally, be proportionate. If, however, there had been technical non-compliance, a sanction debarring the party from reliance would, generally, be disproportionate.
9. Non-compliance and a proposed sanction must also be considered in the context of other proceedings. Effective promotion of rule compliance through a consistent approach to sanctions for non-compliance is a key element of effective dispute management. Were the court to take an arbitrary or lax approach to both the imposition and nature of sanctions, as well as relief from sanctions, effective dispute management and, hence, the purposive principle would be frustrated.
10. Given the need to ensure that sanctions are proportionate, rule 33(7) provides a non-exhaustive list of possible sanctions. This mirrors the approach under the CPR, which provides and required the use by the court of a broad range of potential sanctions for non-compliance. Striking out a claim or defence, given its severity, should be reserved for the most egregious instances of non-compliance.[214]
11. Discussion of sanctions for non-compliance must be kept separate from proceedings for contempt of court. While both may be viewed at a general level as adverse consequences for non-compliance with court orders, they have different jurisprudential bases and serve different purposes. As Zuckerman has rightly pointed out, contempt of court proceedings arise for non-compliance with court orders that concern substantive rights or the proper administration of justice. Unlike sanctions for non-compliance under this rule their jurisprudential basis is not the promotion of compliance with, nor does it arise out of, procedural requirements.[215] Contempt proceedings arise where, for instance, there is non-compliance with the terms of an interim injunction or asset preservation order (freezing injunction), both of which protect substantive rights. Compliance with such orders is not a matter of election, ie a defendant cannot choose whether to comply with the terms of an interim injunction: compliance is not optional nor is it an aspect of party autonomy as is the case with compliance with procedural obligations. Parties are required to comply with orders that give effect to substantive rights and through them give effect to the proper administration of justice. Breach is therefore a different and more serious matter than that of breach of an electable procedural requirement.

[213] Such orders are generally only made where a party has already failed to comply with a procedural requirement: *British Gas Trading Ltd v Oak Cash & Carry Ltd* [2016] EWCA Civ 153; [2016] 1 WLR 4530 at [38]–[39].

[214] *Biguzzi v Rank Leisure Plc* [1999] 1 WLR 1926 at 1933.

[215] A Zuckerman (2021) at 692–693.

12. This rule, through rule 33(5) also gives effect to a long-standing principle that non-compliance by way of an error of procedure does not invalidate any step carried out by a party.[216] For instance, use of the wrong form to commence proceedings or to commence an appeal is an error of procedure, which would not invalidate commencement and could be regularised by a court order.[217] With the extension of this Code to pre-action dispute management this aspect of the compliance principle is extended to cover that phase of a dispute. While it restates the general power to regularise procedural mistakes, it cannot however override or be applied to specific provisions within the Code that set out the consequences of non-compliance and any attendant procedure for relief from the adverse consequences of such non-compliance.[218] In such cases, the specific provision applies.[219]

## RULE 34.—APPLICATION FOR RELIEF FROM SANCTIONS FOR PROCEDURAL NON-COMPLIANCE

**(1) Sanctions for procedural non-compliance takes effect automatically upon default by a party, unless the court orders otherwise.**
**(2) A party may apply for relief from sanctions for procedural non-compliance, including where the court declines to regularise an error of procedure and thus invalidates the step taken in error.**
**(3) The court may grant relief where**
**(a) the application was made promptly;**
**(b) the non-compliance was neither serious nor significant;**
**(c) the applicant had good reason for their non-compliance; and**
**(d) in all the circumstances, the grant of relief would further the purposive principle.**
**(4) Where relief from sanctions for non-compliance is sought in the form of an application for a retrospective extension of time to serve a case statement, notice of appeal or response to a notice of appeal, the applicant must also demonstrate that they had taken all reasonable steps to comply with the time limit before it expired.**
**(5) Where the court grants relief it may do so subject to such conditions as are just, including ordering the applicant to compensate any non-defaulting party for any costs incurred as a consequence of their non-compliance and the application for relief.**

*Sources: ALI/UNIDROIT Principles, principle 17; ELI-UNIDROIT Model Rules, rr 7, 47; CPR rr. 3.8, 3.9, 3.10, 7.6(3)(b).*

## COMMENTARY

1. How the court gives effect to sanctions and grants relief from them is of fundamental importance to the proper management of proceedings. Too lax an approach to the imposition of and relief from sanctions and compliance with procedural

[216] CPR r 3.10; previously RSC Ord 2.
[217] *Reddy v General Medical Council* [2012] EWCA Civ 310.
[218] *Vinos v Marks & Spencer Plc* [2000] EWCA Civ B526; [2001] 3 All ER 784; *Ideal Shopping Direct Ltd v Mastercard Inc* [2022] EWCA Civ 14; [2022] 1 WLR 1541 at [146].
[219] Eg Part 10, r 9(3); Part 11, r 9.

requirements will become at best arbitrary and at worst voluntary. Consequently, effective management will exist in name only. Too strict an approach and rule-compliance will come at the expense of parties' ability to secure a just resolution of their dispute. In both cases, such an approach will tend to create perverse incentives for parties to engage in meretricious satellite litigation to their cost and to the cost of the court and litigants in other proceedings. English and Welsh civil procedure has historically and unfortunately taken both approaches to the imposition of and relief from sanctions.[220] Under the CPR an attempt was initially made to introduce a more consistent and stricter approach, one that aimed to create a situation where relief from sanction was granted less readily. That approach was taken to promote rule compliance and ensure that the court's limited resources were used as efficiently and proportionately as possible.[221] It did not succeed.

2. Rule 34 enables parties to apply for relief from the adverse consequences of procedural non-compliance, including where the court has refused to exercise its discretion to regularise an error of procedure.[222] It adopts the second approach taken by the CPR, which followed the Jackson Cost Review. More pertinently rule 34(3) codifies the test developed in *Mitchell v Mitchell v News Group Newspapers Ltd* (2013)[223] and *Denton v White* (2014).[224] They gave effect to Lord Dyson MR's explanation of the role, purpose and approach to rule compliance and relief from sanctions in the 18th Jackson Implementation Lecture.[225] This test has generated a wealth of jurisprudence.[226] Its primary aim was to strike an effective balance between a too lax and a too strict approach to rule-compliance and in that way promote effective rule compliance.[227] It is adopted here as the optimum approach to securing a fair and effective approach to applications for relief from sanction. The four criteria for the grant of relief set out in rule 34(3) are intended to ensure that relief is not granted where it would undermine the purposive principle.

3. First, such sanctions for non-compliance take effect automatically on default unless the court orders otherwise, as is the case under CPR r 3.8. This ensures they take effect as cost-effectively and efficiently as possible without the need for the non-defaulting party to apply for them to take effect. Equally, it ensures that where non-compliance is a consequence of the defaulting party's election, no costly and time-consuming steps need to be taken to give effect to their election.

4. An application for relief must therefore be made promptly upon the sanction coming into effect. This is a consequence of the need for the defaulting party to act consistently with the efficiency and effective management principles. It is also a consequence of the procedural equality principle: defaulting parties ought not to be

[220] J Sorabji (2014), chaps 2 and 4–6.

[221] A Zuckerman (2021) at 634–650.

[222] This generalises the approach taken in *Walsham Chalet Park Ltd v Tallington Lakes Ltd* [2014] EWCA Civ 1607; [2015] CP Rep 15 at [44], where relief from an order striking out a statement of case for non-compliance was considered by reference to the approach to relief from sanction.

[223] *Mitchell v News Group Newspapers Ltd* [2013] EWCA Civ 1537; [2014] 1 WLR 795 at [38].

[224] *Denton v TH White Ltd* [2014] EWCA Civ 906; [2014] 1 WLR 3926.

[225] J Dyson, 'The Application of the Amendments to the Civil Procedure Rules' (2014) 33 CJQ 124; A Zuckerman (2021) at 647–657; J Sorabji (2014) chap 7. This was an approach that was foreshadowed by *Hoddinott v Persimmon Homes (Wessex) Ltd* [2007] EWCA Civ 1203; [2008] 1 WLR 806; D Neuberger (2012) at [19].

[226] P Coulson (ed), *Civil Procedure 2024* (Sweet & Maxwell, 2024) Vol 1 at 3.9.1–3.9.25.

[227] *Hashtroodi v Hancock* [2004] EWCA Civ 652; [2004] 1 WLR 3206; *Hoddinott v Persimmon Homes (Wessex) Ltd* [2007] EWCA Civ 1203; [2008] 1 WLR 806 at [59]; A Zuckerman (2021) at 652.

granted indulgence at the expense of the non-defaulting party who may incur time and expense in managing their conduct in reliance upon the sanction having been imposed.

5. The non-compliance must be neither serious nor significant for relief to be capable of being granted. The more serious and significant a breach the less appropriate it ought to be for relief to be granted. This is the case for two reasons. First, the grant of relief in such circumstances would undermine the compliance principle and, consequently, systemic proportionality. It would send out a message to parties that the court is likely to take a lax approach to non-compliance, which would undermine the efficacy of the sanctions regime and lead to satellite litigation over compliance and relief from non-compliance. Secondly, it is likely to lead to the individual parties in the immediate proceedings adopting a lax approach to dispute management. This criterion does, however, properly ensure that trivial, technical, or non-serious breaches are more likely to be subject to relief from sanction.[228]
6. The third criterion requires the defaulting party to have a good reason for their default.[229] This is, again, intended to ensure that their default was not deliberate, intended to harm or inconvenience their opponent, or due to incompetence or a lax approach to compliance.
7. Finally, the grant of relief must further the purposive principle. This requires a focus on both the immediate proceedings and, particularly, the court's ability to secure systemic proportionality and the compliance principle.
8. Rule 34(4) makes additional provision where relief from sanction is sought where there has been non-compliance with the time limits for serving case statements, notices of appeal or responses to notices of appeal. Where the application for an extension of time is made retrospectively, it is essential that the defaulting party demonstrates that they took all reasonable, active steps to comply with their procedural obligations in advance of the time limit expiring.[230] This is particularly important in these cases as the defendant or respondent will expect to be able to rely upon the fact that proceedings have not been commenced effectively against them. The defaulting party is thus seeking the court's permission to treat them in a way that impinges upon procedural equality, as the grant of relief would adversely affect the legitimate expectation of the defendant/respondent that their rights are not to be subject to challenge.
9. Rule 34(5) confirms that relief from sanction may be conditional. Typical conditions, aimed at promoting future compliance are requirements to comply within a specified time limit or that the defaulting party compensate the non-defaulting party in costs lost as a consequence of the default. Given the greater emphasis on the importance of systemic proportionality and the recognition that default may have an adverse impact on the ability of the court to properly manage its resources for the wider public benefit, the court may also impose as a condition that the defaulting party compensate the court for its costs in dealing with the non-compliance. The rationale here is to enable the court to use that compensation to improve its ability to manage

[228] The non-defaulting party, further to the dispute management and co-operative principles, ought not to adopt an opportunistic approach to trivial or technical non-compliance. They ought to therefore, where they can, properly seek to agree to any application for relief from sanctions in such circumstances, particularly where there is a good reason for the default: *Denton v TH White Ltd* [2014] EWCA Civ 906; [2014] 1 WLR 3926 at [39]–[43].

[229] *Mitchell v News Group Newspapers Ltd* [2013] EWCA Civ 1537; [2014] 1 WLR 795 at [41].

[230] See r 9 on extensions of time. CPR r 7.6(3)(b).

other proceedings consistently with the purposive principle by, for instance, funding additional part-time deputy judges to deal with proceedings. To secure consistency the court administration should prepare and publicise a set of standard fees applicable to such situations.

# SECTION 8: PROTECTING THE ADMINISTRATION OF JUSTICE

## RULE 35.—THE COURT'S POWER TO PROTECT AND PROMOTE THE ADMINISTRATION OF JUSTICE

**(1) The court may take such steps as necessary and as provided for by its inherent jurisdiction or a rule of law to protect its process from abuse and/or protect and promote the administration of justice.**

**(2) In particular, the court may at any time take any of the following steps to protect its process and/or protect and promote the administration of justice from abuse**

**(a) strike out a case statement or proceedings, including appellate proceedings;**

**(b) make a restriction order, civil restraint order or an order under section 42 of the Senior Courts Act 1981; or**

**(c) make a committal order, including for the sequestration of assets under Part 16 of this Code.**

**(3) Steps to protect the court's process and/or protect and promote the administration of justice may be taken by the court on its own initiative or on application of a party or non-party.**

**(4) The administration of justice is a continuing process. It is not limited by reference to any specific proceeding.**

*Sources: CPR r 3.4(2)(b).*

## COMMENTARY

1. Courts and their procedural rules are intended to enable disputes to be resolved fairly whether by adjudication or consensual settlement. Both the court and parties are required to co-operate with each other in managing proceedings to that end, consistently with the purposive principle. Inevitably, there will be and are instances where parties and some non-parties may act in ways that abuse or misuse the court's processes.[231] They may also act in ways that undermine the court's ability to secure the proper administration of justice.[232] Individuals may, for instance, issue applications or proceedings that are totally without merit. They may issue proceedings concerning a dispute that has already been resolved by a final judgment or which is subject to an extant binding settlement. They may issue proceedings or applications for purposes other than resolving a dispute, eg to harass or waste the resources of defendants, respondents, or the court.

[231] *Attorney-General v Barker* [2000] 1 FLR 759 at [19].

[232] Such as where a party's conduct demonstrates that they are intent upon frustrating the court's ability to secure a fair trial: *Arrow Nominees Inc v Blackledge* [2000] EWCA Civ 200; [2000] CP Rep 59 at [54].

2. Rule 35(1) gives effect to the court's inherent and unlimited jurisdiction to protect the proper administration of justice and its processes from abuse or misuse.[233] It does not codify it. By not doing so, it maintains that jurisdiction's flexibility so that it can adapt as necessary where novel forms of abuse or misuse arise. The rule also acknowledges that there may be statutory powers[234] and other rules of law[235] that may be relied upon to give effect to this jurisdiction.
3. Rule 35(2) refers to specific rules that may be used to protect the court's processes from abuse and to protect and promote the proper administration of justice. Additionally, the court may stay proceedings to achieve these ends.
4. When considering the administration of justice under this rule, and generally throughout this Code, it is to be understood as a concept that goes beyond any individual proceedings. It is continuing process.[236]

## RULE 36.—STRIKE OUT

**(1) The court, on its own initiative or application of a party, may strike out a case statement or proceedings where they disclose no reasonable grounds for bringing or defending the proceedings such that the claim or defence is bound to fail.**
**(2) The court may also strike out a case statement, proceedings, or document in proceedings where it is proportionate to do so where**
**(a) it is an abuse of the court's process;**
**(b) is likely to obstruct the court's ability to secure the purposive principle; or**
**(c) where a cause of action has been determined finally.**
**(3) A case statement, proceeding or document is likely to be an abuse of process where it is brought for a purpose significantly different from its ordinary and proper use.**
**(4) The court may make any necessary consequential order where a case statement, proceedings or document is struck out.**

*Sources: CPR r 3.4(2).*

## COMMENTARY

1. This rule restates CPR r 3.4(2).[237] It is one of the means through which the court may protect its processes, and hence the proper administration of justice, from abuse. It gives effect to a broad protective jurisdiction, which arises under the court's inherent common law jurisdiction.[238] The rule's focus is to ensure that neither the court's time and resources nor another party's time and resources are wasted. It is thus a key mechanism through which the court can give effect to the economy, efficiency, and

[233] *Cocker v Tempest* (1841) 7 M & W 502 at 503–504; *Hunter v Chief Constable of West Midlands* [1982] AC 529 at 536.
[234] Contempt of Court Act 1981; Senior Courts Act 1981, s 42.
[235] See Part 15, r 14 and the doctrine of merger and of res judicata: *Virgin Atlantic Airways Ltd v Zodiac Seats UK Ltd* [2013] UKSC 46; [2014] AC 160. Also see the torts of abuse of process (*Grainger v Hill* (1838) 4 Bing NC 212) and of malicious prosecution of civil proceedings *(Willers v Joyce (Re Gubay (Deceased) (No 1)* [2016] UKSC 43; [2016] 3 WLR 477.
[236] *Moevao v Department of Labour* [1980] 1 NZLR 464 at 481; Part 1, r 5.
[237] The jurisdiction is distinct from the substantive tort of abuse of process.
[238] J Jacob, 'The Inherent Jurisdiction of the Court' (1970) 23 CLP 23.

proportionality principles, and particularly systemic proportionality. It is thus to be considered along with provisions that provide for summary judgment, default judgment, civil restraint and civil proceedings orders, and contempt of court and rules concerning finality of litigation. It is a jurisdiction that promotes the purposive principle by controlling and effectively rationing access to court process.

2. Rule 36 achieves its aim in two ways. First, by giving effect to the jurisdiction through which case statements or proceedings may be struck out where they do not reasonably disclose a valid cause of action or defence.[239] A claim that does not reasonably disclose a cause of action known to the law is one that is bound to fail and ought not to be permitted to continue.[240] Equally, where facts alleged in a case statement are completely implausible or do not disclose a cause of action or defence to one, the claim or defence ought not to be permitted to continue.[241] In both cases, they may be struck out under rule 36(1).[242] This approach is not inconsistent with the general access principle: access only applies to the pursuit of genuine claims.[243] The rule is thus a filter that eliminates claims or defences that do not meet that standard.

3. The second way in which the rule secures its aim is through giving effect to three distinct circumstances where case statements etc may be struck out. First, it provides the basis to strike out where a case statement, proceedings or a document is an abuse of the court's process. This is a broad criterion: what is an abuse of process is not definitively specified to enable the court to develop the jurisdiction to meet circumstances as they arise. The essence of what amounts to an abuse of process is, however, codified by rule 36(3). It gives effect to the statement of principle from *Attorney-General v Barker* (2001)[244] that abuse of process occurs where the court's process is being used for a purpose significantly different from its ordinary and proper use. Circumstances that are likely to amount to an abuse of process are therefore, for instance, proceedings that are not pursued to vindicate rights, but rather to harass or put other parties to inconvenience and expense. Equally, where proceedings are brought without any genuine intention of pursuing them to resolution,[245] or where documents are served not to further the effective management of proceedings but to increase the costs and time incurred by the other party to proceedings, they are likely to amount to an abuse of process. In such situations the process is not being used for its ordinary or proper purpose.

4. The second distinct circumstance where a case statement etc could be struck out is where it is likely to obstruct the court's ability to secure the purposive principle. This is a specific form of abuse of process. It can arise where, for instance, a party has systematically failed to comply with procedural requirements or repeatedly made pointless applications[246] or applications for the same purpose where there has been no change in circumstance.[247] Such conduct is '*a challenge to the administration of*

[239] *X (Minors) v Bedfordshire County Council* [1995] AC 633 at 740–741.

[240] *Price Meats Ltd v Barclays Bank Plc* [2000] 2 All ER (Comm) 346; *Bridgeman v McAlpine-Brown* [2000] EWCA Civ 524.

[241] *Ministry of Defence v AB* [2012] UKSC 9; [2012] 2 WLR 643 at [149].

[242] Care should be taken, however, to provide a party an opportunity to amend their case statement where the failure to disclose a cause of action or defence is a matter of defective pleading.

[243] *Matthews v Ministry of Defence* [2003] UKHL 5; [2003] 1 All ER 689 at [3]; *Z v UK* (2001) BHRC 384 at [97].

[244] *Attorney-General v Barker* [2000] 1 FLR 759.

[245] *Johnson v Gore Wood & Co* [2002] 2 AC 1; *Arbuthnot Latham Bank Ltd v Trafalgar Holdings Ltd* [1998] 1 WLR 1426.

[246] *Tejendrasingh v Metsons* [1997] EMLR 597.

[247] *Otkritie International Investment Management Ltd v Urumov* [2017] EWCA Civ 134.

*justice*'.[248] It improperly consumes and wastes the scarce public resources provided to the courts. It harasses and causes other parties to suffer prolonged litigation at unnecessary expense. And it undermines the court's ability to secure a just resolution of proceedings.[249] Finally, rule 36(2)(c) provides for strike out where a cause of action has been finally determined.[250]

5. Where the court is considering a strike out it must ensure that that is a proportionate response. Strike out is a harsh and draconian step to take. It ought therefore only to be exercised where it is necessary.[251] Rule 36(4) enables the court to give appropriate directions upon striking out a case statement, proceeding or document. This is a specific exercise of the general dispute management power.

## RULE 37.—RESTRICTION ORDERS

**(1) In exceptional circumstances, where there is a substantial likelihood that unwarranted disruption of the proper administration of justice would occur through a person's misconduct a court may make a restriction order against that person.**

**(2) Unwarranted disruption is misconduct that takes the form of serious abuse that will significantly impede the proper administration of justice. It can take the form of, but is not limited to, abuse of or attacks on members of the court administration, wasting court administrative staff time, or misbehaviour in a court building or during a hearing.**

**(3) A restriction order may, for instance, restrict**

**(a) access to a court building;**

**(b) the manner in which a person may take part in, access or observe proceedings and/or hearings;**

**(c) the manner in which a person may communicate with the court, a judge, or the court administration.**

**(4) A restriction order must be proportionate. It may be made in respect of a specific hearing or proceedings or generally. It must not exceed three years, but may be renewed where it is appropriate to do so.**

## COMMENTARY

1. The proper administration of justice may be disrupted in more ways than those that can or should be dealt with through proceedings for contempt of court. Individuals may, unfortunately, treat members of the court administration abusively. They may verbally or physically attack them. They may send them abusive or offensive communications or make abusive or offensive telephone calls. Judges may be subject to similar conduct. The court's inherent jurisdiction has to a degree developed to respond to this type of disruptive behaviour.[252] It has done so by developing a

[248] *Raja v Van Hoogstraten* [2006] EWHC 1315 (Ch) at [32].

[249] *Logicrose Ltd v Southend United Football Club* [1988] 1 WLR 1256.

[250] Part 15.

[251] *Waltham Chalet Park Ltd v Tallington Lakes Ltd* [2014] EWCA Civ 1607.

[252] *Weston v Central Criminal Courts' Administrator* [1977] QB 32; *In re de Court, The Times*, 27 November 1997; *Agarwala v Agarwala* [2016] EWCA Civ 1252; [2017] 1 P&CR DG17.

jurisdiction, separate from contempt of court, that enables orders to be made that control a disruptive individual's future conduct.[253]

2. Rule 37(1) and (2) codifies the test that governs the exercise of this jurisdiction.[254] To ensure that the jurisdiction is not too readily resorted to, eg where conduct is rude rather than offensive or abusive, it must only be exercised exceptionally.[255] It ought not, therefore, be exercised in response to a singular act unless that is particularly warranted due to the nature of the behaviour, eg due to there being a physical assault on, or an egregious example of abusive language directed towards, a member of the court administration. Its exercise in defence of judges should be particularly rare as judges are expected to have particularly broad shoulders.[256] A judge's reliance on the jurisdiction should thus be more exceptional than that applicable to members of the court administration.
3. To justify making such an order there must be more than seriously abusive misconduct. There must also be a substantial likelihood that the proper administration of justice will be subject to or is being subjected to unwarranted disruption as a result of that misconduct.
4. Consistently with the approach taken to civil restraint orders, and for the same reason, restriction orders must be proportionate. They should be targeted to meet the particular harm that justifies the order being made. They may therefore be targeted towards specific hearings, proceedings or, where necessary, may be of general application. They must also be time-limited, although where necessary and proportionate their duration may be extended. The approach to questions of proportionality and temporal duration is that, mutatis mutandis, applicable to civil restraint orders.
5. Individuals subject to such orders may be prohibited from entering court buildings unless required to by court order. They may only be permitted to enter for limited and specified purposes.[257] They may also be required to apply in writing to a specified judge to seek access to a court building or attend a hearing. They may be prohibited from contacting court administrators or judges by telephone or via electronic forms of communication.[258] They may also be required to only communicate with a specific, named member of the court administration and then only by letter.[259]

## RULE 38.—TOTALLY WITHOUT MERIT ORDERS

**(1) A court may dismiss proceedings or an application as being totally without merit where it is truly bound to fail.**
**(2) Where proceedings or an application are dismissed as totally without merit**
**(a) the dismissal is final and may only be challenged by way of an appeal;**

[253] *Attorney-General v Ebert* [2001] EWHC 695 (Admin) at [35]–[41]; *Bhamjee v Forsdick (No 2)* [2003] EWCA Civ 1113; [2004] 1 WLR 88 at [14]–[15].

[254] The jurisdiction is distinct from statutory mechanisms such as those that arise under the Public Order Act 1986, ss 4, 4A, and 5, the Communications Act 2003, s 127(1), (2), the Malicious Communications Act 1998, s 1, or the Protection from Harassment Act 1997.

[255] *Attorney-General v Ebert* [2001] EWHC 695 (Admin) at [35]–[41]; *Bhamjee v Forsdick (No 2)* [2003] EWCA Civ 1113; [2004] 1 WLR 88 at [14]–[15].

[256] *Attorney-General v Ebert* [2001] EWHC 695 (Admin) at [28].

[257] *In re de Court, The Times*, 27 November 1997.

[258] *R v Ex Parte Winston Leachman* [1998] EWHC 22 (Admin).

[259] *Binder v Binder* (9 March 2000, CA unreported).

**(b) the court must consider whether to impose a civil restraint order.**

**(3) An order recording dismissal as being totally without merit, and the judgment to which it gives effect, cannot be subject to reconsideration.**

*Sources: CPR rr 23.12, 52.20.*

## COMMENTARY

1. The power to dismiss matters as being totally without merit was introduced into the CPR at the same time as the power to make civil restraint orders was codified.[260] Within the CPR the power is explicitly provided both generally under its Pt 23 and to the Court of Appeal under its Pt 52. Procedural simplicity necessitates its codification as a single rule.
2. Parties should pursue proceedings both reasonably and proportionately if they are to do so consistently with the purposive principle. The pursuit of applications that are bound to fail, marks a failure do so. It not only tends to waste court time and resources that should properly be utilised dealing with meritorious matters, it also wastes the time and resources of other parties to proceedings. It also breaches the co-operation and dispute management principles.[261] This rule is intended to deter the making of such applications.
3. To be totally without merit an application or proceedings is one that is bound to fail. Thus dealing with it amounts to an unreasonable and disproportionate use of the court's and other parties' resources. It need not be abusive or vexatious. Where a matter is recorded as being totally without merit, the court's jurisdiction to make a civil restraint order is triggered, although the court is not required to make such an order. However, it must consider whether one is justified.
4. To further protect the court's and parties' time and resources a finding that a matter was totally without merit cannot be subject to any application for reconsideration or variation. Where a party has applied for a totally without merit order to be made and it has been rejected that decision may be subject to an appeal.[262] Once a totally without merit order is made the question whether it was properly made cannot be revisited in any future proceedings.[263] Past findings that applications or proceedings were totally without merit can be considered by the court when considering whether to impose a civil restraint order or a civil proceedings order.

## RULE 39.—CIVIL RESTRAINT ORDERS

**(1) The court may make an order which restrains a person's ability to issue or continue proceedings or applications without first obtaining the court's permission to do so (a civil restraint order). Such permission may only be granted following an application submitted to a judge named in the civil restraint order.**

[260] Civil Procedure (Amendment No 2) Rules 2004 (SI 2004/2072); CPR rr 23.12, 52.20.

[261] *Wasif v The Secretary of State for the Home Department* [2016] EWCA Civ 82; [2016] 1 WLR 2793 at [9]–[12].

[262] *R (Grace) v Secretary of State for the Home Department* [2014] EWCA Civ 1191; [2014] 1 WLR 3432 at [13]–[15].

[263] *Re Glass Slipper Live Events—Events 1 Ltd* [2020] EWHC 942 (Ch).

**(2) A civil restraint order may also be made to restrain a person from providing reasonable assistance to a litigant.**

**(3) An application for permission must be made in writing and will be determined without a hearing. The same process applies to the exercise of a right of appeal from a refusal of permission.**

**(4) A civil restraint order may be of limited, extended, or general application.**

**(5) A limited civil restraint order of up to two years' duration may be made where a person makes at least two applications that are dismissed as being totally without merit. It prohibits making or continuing applications in specific proceedings.**

**(6) An extended civil restraint order of up to two years' duration may be made where a person issues at least three sets of proceedings or applications that are totally without merit. It prohibits the issue of new proceedings and the making or continuing of proceedings or applications that relate to specific proceedings.**

**(7) A general civil restraint order of up to three years' duration may be made where the conditions for the making of an extended civil restraint order are met but such an order would not be sufficient to protect the court's processes and/or the administration of justice from abuse. It prohibits the issue of new proceedings and the making or continuing of proceedings or applications generally.**

**(8) Limited and extended civil restraint orders may be made by a judge authorised to sit in the Upper Tier of the High Court, a judge of the High Court, or a judge of the Court of Appeal (Civil Division). A general civil restraint order may only be made by a judge of the High Court or Court of Appeal (Civil Division).**

**(9) The prohibition contained in an extended or general civil restraint order may apply to all courts if made by a judge of the Court of Appeal (Division), the High Court if made by a judge of the High Court, and the First-tier of the High Court if made otherwise.**

**(10) The duration of a civil restraint order may be extended where it is appropriate to do so. An extension may be granted both before or after the duration of the order has expired.**

**(11) Any proceedings or application issued or continued in breach of a civil restraint order is automatically struck out or dismissed without further order. Any procedural step taken in breach of a civil restraint order is a nullity. Where steps are repeatedly taken in breach of an order, contempt of court proceedings may be commenced.**

**(12) Any application to vary or set aside a civil restraint order must be made in writing and will be determined without a hearing, unless the court directs otherwise. The same process applies to the exercise of a right of appeal from a refusal to vary or set aside the order.**

**(13) Where a person subject to a civil restraint order makes repeated applications for permission to issue or continue proceedings or applications that are refused as being totally without merit, they may only seek permission to appeal from the judge who refused the application.**

*Sources: CPR r 3.11(2), PD3C.*

## COMMENTARY

1. The general access right does not include a right to abuse the court's process.[264] Access, and the provision of a fair and proportionate process for all litigants, requires

[264] *Bhamjee v Forsdick* (No 2) [2003] EWCA 1113; [2004] 1 WLR 88 at [3], [8]–[9].

the court to have the power to protect its processes from abuse by restraining parties from bringing proceedings or applications. That power was, until the start of the 21st century, exercised rarely under the High Court's inherent jurisdiction.[265] It was primarily used to restrict an individual's ability to issue applications within proceedings without the prior permission of the court. Where such permission was not sought and obtained, any such application was automatically dismissed without being heard.[266]

2. Following the CPR's introduction in 1999, a series of judgments developed this aspect of the inherent jurisdiction.[267] While it initially applied to the High Court, its application was extended to cover the County Court and Court of Appeal. It also developed so that it could restrain individuals from issuing new proceedings without prior permission. It was also applied to restrain individuals from providing reasonable assistance to litigants who did not otherwise have legal representation.[268] It was also applied to stop non-parties from, in effect, directing litigation on behalf of a named party to proceedings.[269] And, finally, the jurisdiction was extended to apply restrictions analogous to those that would otherwise be made under section 42 of the Senior Courts Act 1981,[270] albeit without having to demonstrate that the party's conduct was vexatious.[271]
3. This rule restates the CPR's three-tier codification of limited, extended, and general civil restraint orders as they were developed under the inherent jurisdiction. A limited civil restraint order may be made where a party or non-party has made a minimal number of applications held to be totally without merit. An extended civil restraint order requires a party or non-party to have persisted in making applications or issuing proceedings that are totally without merit.[272] And, a general civil restraint order may be made where the party or non-party's conduct in issuing applications and proceedings would not be managed effectively through the imposition of an extended civil restraint order.[273] This differential approach ensures that the restriction on the party or non-party's access is proportionate.
4. The justification for making such an order may continue after it has been made. Their duration may therefore be extended both before or after the order expires. Where the party subject to an order's conduct warrants it, it may also become necessary to replace an existing order with a more or less stringent one. Where, for instance, it becomes apparent that a party subject to a limited or extended order is continuing to abuse the court's process, an extended or general civil restraint order may be made, subject to the test for those orders being met. Where, however, it

[265] *Milissich v Lloyd's* (unrep, 18 December 1880); *Butson v Davies* (unrep, 5 June 1888); *Rawlins v Burton Yeates & Co* (unrep, 5 February 1889); *Torkington v Torkington* (unrep, 22 May 1889); *Milissich v Lloyd's* (unrep, 20 May 1892); *Marcuson v Postmaster General & Governor & Company of the Bank of England* (unrep, 29 October 1894).

[266] *Grepe v Loam* (1887) 37 ChD 168.

[267] *Ebert v Venvil* [2000] Ch 484; *Bhamjee v Forsdick (No 2)* [2003] EWCA 1113; [2004] 1 WLR 88; *Mahajan v Department of Constitutional Affairs* [2004] EWCA Civ 946; [2004] 101 EG 26.

[268] *Attorney-General v Purvis* [2003] EWHC 3190 (Admin).

[269] *CFC 26 Ltd v Brown Shipley & Co Ltd* [2017] EWHC 1594 (Ch); [2017] 1 WLR 4589; *Sartipy v Tigris Industries Inc* [2019] EWCA Civ 225; [2019] 1 WLR 5892.

[270] Rule 40.

[271] *R (Kumar) v Secretary of State for Constitutional Affairs* [2006] EWCA Civ 900; [2007] 1 WLR 536 at [69].

[272] *Sartipy v Tigris Industries Inc* [2019] EWCA Civ 225; [2019] 1 WLR 5892.

[273] *R (Kumar) v Secretary of State for Constitutional Affairs* [2006] EWCA Civ 900; [2007] 1 WLR 536 at [60]; *Chief Constable of Avon & Somerset* [2019] EWCA Civ 1675.

becomes evident that an order is too wide in its application or that an order is no longer necessary the court may vary or set aside a civil restraint order prior to the date of its expiry.[274]

5. Compliance with these orders, where necessary, may be supported by the power to bring proceedings for contempt of court.[275] Where there is persistent non-compliance with a civil restraint order, particularly an extended or general one, a civil proceedings order may be made.[276]

## RULE 40.—CIVIL PROCEEDINGS ORDER

**(1) A court on the application of the Attorney-General may make an order under section 42 of the Senior Courts Act 1981 to limit the ability of a person to carry out the following acts for either a specified or indefinite period of time**

**(a) engage in pre-action dispute resolution under Part 5, section 3 of this Code;**

**(b) issue or continue civil proceedings and applications; and/or**

**(c) initiate criminal proceedings.**

**(2) An order may only be made where a person habitually and persistently and without any reasonable ground institutes or continues vexatious proceedings or applications in the High Court, Family Court, or any inferior court, against the same or different persons, or institutes vexatious prosecutions. Vexatious applications may be commenced by or on behalf of the person against whom the section 42 order is sought.**

**(3) Vexatious proceedings, applications or prosecutions are those that**

**(a) have little or no discernible basis in law;**

**(b) subject the defendant to inconvenience, harassment and expense out of all proportion to any gain likely to accrue to the claimant; and**

**(c) involve an abuse of the court's process.**

**(4) A person subject to an order under section 42 may not carry out an act subject to the order without the prior permission of the High Court. Permission shall only be granted where the act to be carried out is not an abuse of the court's process and there are reasonable grounds for carrying out the act. Permission may only be sought in writing. A refusal of permission is not subject to a right of appeal. Any act done without prior permission is a nullity.**

**(5) The burden of proof to be discharged by the Attorney-General is the civil standard of proof.**

*Sources: Senior Courts Act 1981, s 42; CPR r 3.11(1).*

## COMMENTARY

1. The court's inherent jurisdiction codified in rule 39 to protect its processes from abuse is supplemented by a statutory power, which can be deployed to limit the activities of vexatious litigants, to issue a civil proceedings order. That power originated in the

[274] *Middlesbrough Football & Athletic Club Co (1986) Ltd v Earth Energy Investments LLP (In Liquidation)* [2019] EWHC 226 (Ch); [2019] 1 WLR 3709. Part 15, r 12(4)(b).

[275] *HM Solicitor-General v Ellis* [2020] EWHC 2727 (QB).

[276] *Attorney-General v Perrotti* [2006] EWHC 1002 (Admin).

Vexatious Actions Act 1896. It is now contained in section 42 of the Senior Courts Act 1981. It is intended to protect the court's processes, and particularly its resources, from being abused.[277] It also protects a wide range of defendants from the time and expense of having to deal with and respond to such litigation.[278] It thus supports the economy, efficiency, and proportionality principles, as well as implementation of the general access principle for other litigants.

2. The imposition of a civil proceedings order does not amount to a complete prohibition on pursuing proceedings. It simply controls the subject of the orders ability to commence or continue proceedings. It is thus a proportionate rather than absolute means to protect the court's processes from abuse. In so far as the nature of control is concerned, rule 40(1)(b)–(c) codifies the position as it is under section 42 of the 1981 Act. Rule 40(1)(a) does, however, expand the control provided under the 1981 Act so that it applies to pre-action dispute management. This is intended to ensure that that process is also not capable of being abused.
3. Only the Attorney-General may apply for a civil proceedings order.[279] They do so further to their role as guardian of the public interest. The test for determining whether an order should be made was articulated in *Attorney-General v Barker* (2000).[280] It is codified in rule 40(2) and (3).[281] Thus an individual must habitually and persistently and without reasonable grounds pursue vexatious claims, ie there must be repeated applications made over a period of time. Such applications must have no real basis in law. They must have the effect, irrespective of their intention or stated intention, of harassing defendants. And they must amount to an abuse of the court's process. The onus lies on the Attorney-General to satisfy the court to the civil standard of proof that the test has been met and an order should be made.[282]
4. Once an order has been made an individual subject to it must seek permission to bring or continue proceedings. Permission may only be sought in writing and will be determined without a hearing. This is to protect the court's processes from the adverse effect of abusive applications for permission. Where a person subject to a civil proceedings order takes any step subject to the order without seeking prior permission, that step is a nullity.[283] It cannot therefore be cured as a procedural error, through the grant of retrospective permission or through an application for relief from sanction. This is due to the fundamental nature of the protection given by the order to control the litigant's conduct. Any other approach would inevitably see individuals subject to such orders take such steps and then engage in satellite litigation over their validity.

[277] *Attorney-General v Jones* [1990] 1 WLR 859 at 865.

[278] M Taggart, 'Alexander Chaffers and the Genesis of the Vexatious Actions Act 1896' (2004) 63(3) Cambridge Law Journal 656.

[279] Senior Courts Act 1981, s 42(1).

[280] *Attorney-General v Barker* [2000] 1 FLR 759 at [22].

[281] *Attorney-General v Barker* [2000] 1 FLR 759 at [19]–[24].

[282] *Attorney-General v Hayward, The Times*, 20 November 1995.

[283] *Williamson v The Bishop of London* [2023] EWCA Civ 379.

## RULE 41.—COMMITTAL FOR CONTEMPT—GENERAL

**(1) The court may, on its own initiative or on application of a party or the Attorney-General acting as guardian of the public interest, commence proceedings for contempt of court (contempt proceedings).**

**(2) Where contempt of court arises from breach of a court order, the application should be made by a party to the proceedings. Only where a party does not commence proceedings may the Attorney-General make the application. The court may act on its own initiative only where neither the party nor the Attorney-General makes an application.**

**(3) Where contempt arises other than by breach of a court order, the application should be made by the Attorney-General. The court may also in such circumstances act on its own initiative. Where the court initiates proceedings, generally the judge who initiates them should not manage or determine the proceedings. A party may also initiate such proceedings.**

**(4) The court and any individual may refer any matter it considers may give rise to contempt of court to the Attorney-General.**

**(5) Where the court initiates contempt proceedings it must order the alleged contemnor to attend court for directions to be given for the management of the proceedings. It may also require any other party to proceedings in which the alleged contempt has been committed to afford the court such assistance as is proportionate in respect of the proceedings.**

**(6) Contempt of court is conduct that interferes with the proper administration of justice.**

**(7) Where contempt proceedings are commenced other than by the court, they must be issued in the High Court. Contempt proceedings initiated by the Court of Appeal will automatically be transferred to the High Court.**

**(8) Permission is required to issue contempt proceedings where the contempt concerns**

**(a) an alleged interference with the proper administration of justice in proceedings that have either not yet commenced or have concluded; or**

**(b) an allegation that a false statement of truth was knowingly made.**

**(9) Permission may be granted for each allegation of contempt where the applicant demonstrates that the public interest requires contempt proceedings to be issued and determined. In considering that question the court shall take into account whether**

**(a) there is a case on the face of it that there was an interference with the proper administration of justice where the application is brought by the Attorney-General or a strong case on the face of it otherwise;**

**(b) there is a strong case on the face of it that a false statement of truth was knowingly made;**

**(c) contempt proceedings are proportionate and would further the purposive principle.**

**(10) Except where this requirement is varied by the court, a defendant to committal proceedings must be provided with specific information identified in the digital procedure by the applicant bringing the proceedings or the court where it acts on its own initiative.**

**(11) An application for permission shall be determined by a judge of the Upper Tier of the High Court or a judge who is otherwise authorised to deal with contempt proceedings. The application must be heard with-notice.**

**(12) An order made on application for permission may be renewed, varied, or revoked.**

*Sources: County Courts Act 1984, ss 14, 38; CPR Pt 81.*

## COMMENTARY

1. The court has a general summary jurisdiction to protect the proper administration, both in terms of potential and ongoing proceedings.[284] The jurisdiction has two facets. The first is civil contempt: '*contempt by disobedience*'. The second is criminal contempt: '*contempt by interference*',[285] ie interference with the proper administration of justice.
2. Contempt by disobedience is intended to promote and secure compliance with court orders. Typically, this is focused on securing compliance either with orders that direct an individual to act or refrain from acting in a specified way or with undertakings. The rationale underpinning this aspect of the jurisdiction was summarised succinctly in *Mid-Bedfordshire DC v Brown (Thomas)* (2004).[286] In that case the jurisdiction was explained as ensuring that respect for court orders would not be diminished, the court's authority was not undermined, and the rule of law not subverted through disobedience with court orders. It thus promotes the public interest by ensuring that the court's orders are obeyed and the parties' private interest in securing the same.[287]
3. Contempt by interference is intended to protect the court's process from being subject to abuse. This could occur in many different ways. Threatening witnesses, parties or judges, evidence tampering, disrupting a court hearing, abusing members of the court administration, all could potentially fall within this aspect of the jurisdiction.[288] Again, similar public and private interest rationales apply to this as to contempt by disobedience.[289] Where proceedings are disrupted through hearings being interrupted by improper conduct in the court room or through witnesses being intimidated by non-parties (or parties), parties are unable to secure their right to a fair, efficient and economical procedure. They are unable to secure their rights and the rule of law is subverted.
4. The jurisdiction has two bases. For the High Court it arises under its inherent common law jurisdiction.[290] The County Court has a similar, albeit more limited statutory jurisdiction.[291] The unified civil court, provided for under Part 2, as the successor to the High Court and the County Court, is intended to have all the jurisdiction of the High Court. Rule 41(11), to an extent, echoes the current jurisdictional distinction. It generally limits exercise of the jurisdiction to judges of the High Court's Upper Tier. This ensures that the most serious cases are dealt with by those judges who would have exercised the High Court's unlimited jurisdiction under the CPR. It also provides for other judges to be authorised to exercise the jurisdiction. By doing so it enables, consistently with the need to secure the efficient and proportionate management of proceedings, a flexible approach so that it can be exercised by other members of the judiciary. This also ensures that less serious cases and those that arise

[284] P Londono, *Arlidge, Eady & Smith on Contempt* (Sweet & Maxwell, 2019) at 3–78 and following; *Balogh v Crown Court at St Albans* [1975] QB 73 at 93; *Attorney-General v Times Newspapers Ltd* [1974] AC 273 at 310–311; *National Farmers' Union v Tiernan* [2015] EWCA Civ 1419 at [51].

[285] A Zuckerman (2021) at 1187.

[286] *Mid-Bedfordshire DC v Brown (Thomas)* [2004] EWCA Civ 1709; [2005] 1 WLR 1460 at [27].

[287] *JSC BTA Bank v Solodchenko (No 2)* [2011] EWCA Civ 1241; [2012] 1 WLR 350 at [45].

[288] *Director of the Serious Fraud Office v O'Brien* [2014] UKSC 23; [2014] AC 1246 at [42].

[289] P Londono (2019) at 3-7 to 3-12.

[290] *Attorney General v Times Newspapers Ltd* [1992] 2 AC 191.

[291] County Courts Act 1984, ss 14 and 38.

in proceedings in the High Court's First-tier are dealt with by tier three and four judges.[292]

5. The contempt jurisdiction may be exercised by the court on its own initiative or on application.[293] Applications can be made by parties or the Attorney-General; the latter acting as a guardian of the public interest and of the proper administration of justice.[294] Rule 42(2) codifies the current approach to making these applications.[295] Hence where contempt by disobedience is concerned, it is primarily for the parties to take steps to commence contempt proceedings, ie to protect their private interest and through that the public interest. Only where they do not may the Attorney-General and, if necessary, the court take steps to protect the public interest. This hierarchy is reversed in rule 41(3), where alleged contempt primarily engages the public interest. In such cases, it is primarily for the Attorney-General to take steps. The court, however, retains a discretion to act on its own initiative, which may typically be exercised where the alleged contempt takes place during a court hearing.[296] Consistently with rule 41(1), a party to proceedings may also take steps to commence contempt proceedings in such a situation. In doing so, even if they are primarily concerned with their own private interest in the proceedings, the application serves the public interest. It remains possible under rule 41(4) for the court and any individual, whether a party to proceedings or not, to raise with the Attorney-General the question whether specific conduct gives rise to contempt of court.[297]
6. Where contempt proceedings are initiated by the court the judge who initiates them should not then go on to manage or determine the contempt proceedings (rule 42). This is intended to ensure that the judge is not then capable of being seen to be a judge in their own cause.[298] This is most pertinent where the alleged contempt occurred during a hearing. This requirement in rule 41(3) is thus intended to secure judicial independence and impartiality (Part 1, rule 13), and in that way the integrity of the administration of justice is not undermined by proceedings that are themselves intended to protect its integrity.
7. Where the court initiates contempt proceedings it must take steps to require attendance before the court of the alleged contemnor. It may also require any other party to proceedings, ie any party other than the one against whom the proceedings are taken, to assist it. In this way it limits the extent to which the court would otherwise have to act in an inquisitorial manner. Rule 41(5) in this way restates CPR r 81.6(2) and (3).
8. Rule 41(7) ensures that contempt proceedings are commenced in the High Court. Where an alleged contempt occurs in a court other than the High Court, eg the Employment Tribunal, the Upper Tribunal, or the Court of Appeal, and contempt

[292] Part 2.

[293] *Isbilen v Turk* [2021] EWHC 854 (Ch) at [22]–[46].

[294] The Attorney-General's role was established in 1954: *R v Hargreaves, Ex parte Dill*, The Times, 4 November 1953: *Attorney-General v Times Newspapers Ltd* [1974] AC 273 at 311; *Solicitor-General v Jones* [2013] EWHC 2579 (Fam); [2014] 1 FLR 852 at [14]; *Re Yaxley-Lennon* [2018] EWCA Crim 1856; [2018] 1 WLR 5400 at [26].

[295] *Bedfordshire Constabulary v RU* [2013] EWHC 2350 (Fam); [20014] Fam 69 at [32]–[35]; *Attorney-General v Times Newspapers Ltd* [1974] AC 273 at 311 and 326.

[296] Typically referred to as '*contempt in the face of the court*'; *Balogh v Crown Court at St Albans* [1975] QB 73.

[297] *Attorney-General v Times Newspapers Ltd* [1974] AC 273 at 326.

[298] *Re Yaxley-Lennon* [2018] EWCA Crim 1856; [2018] 1 WLR 5400 at [26]–[28].

proceedings are initiated by a party or the Attorney-General they must be commenced in the High Court. Where the Court of Appeal commences contempt proceedings on its own initiative, they are commenced in that court and automatically transferred to the High Court.

9. Where contempt proceedings are not initiated by the court, they may only be issued with the court's permission except where they concern ongoing proceedings. Hence where there is an alleged interference with administration of justice prior to proceedings commencing or after proceedings have concluded, permission is required. Permission is also required where there is an allegation that an individual has knowingly made a false statement of truth. In both situations, this is intended to protect the alleged contemnor from contempt proceedings being brought improperly.[299] It is particularly required to ensure that contempt proceedings are not brought abusively or without good cause, and thus are not used improperly to harass or otherwise threaten an individual. The permission requirement thus protects the process from abuse and requires careful thought to be applied before an application is made.[300] To further protect the rights of the alleged contemnor, a permission application must be heard with-notice.

10. Rule 41(9) provides the basis on which permission may be granted. The overall test is one that requires the court to be satisfied that it is in the public interest for contempt proceedings to be pursued.[301] Where the contempt concerns an interference with the proper administration of justice, the court must be satisfied that there is, on the face of it, a case against the alleged contemnor (a *prima facie* case) where the application is brought by the Attorney-General. In all other circumstances a strong case on the face of it must be shown.[302] In each case the aim is to filter out weak or trivial applications.

11. The lower permission threshold applies to those applications brought by the Attorney-General as they are required to act in the public interest and would thus be expected to be more circumspect in bringing applications than might otherwise be the case where a party to proceedings is concerned. In assessing whether it is in the public interest to grant permission the court must also consider such proceedings to be a proportionate response to the alleged interference or false statement.[303] Proceedings may not, for instance, be proportionate where they are pursued in response to a technical or minor interference with the administration of justice. Proceedings must also further the purposive principle. This latter criterion will be particularly relevant in determining whether it is in the public interest for permission to be granted to ensure proceedings are not brought for vexatious or abusive reasons. Equally, it will help ensure they are not used as a vehicle for meretricious satellite litigation.[304] Permission is required separately for each allegation of contempt.[305] It is for the applicant to satisfy the court that the threshold for the grant of permission has been met.

[299] *Attorney-General v Yaxley-Lennon* [2019] EWHC 1791 (Admin); [2020] 3 All ER 477 at [95(1)].

[300] *MBR Acres Ltd v McGivern* [2022] EWHC 2072 (QB).

[301] *KJM Superbikes Ltd v Hinton* [2008] EWCA Civ 1280; [2009] 1 WLR 2411, esp at [41].

[302] *Stobart Group Ltd v Elliott* [2014] EWCA Civ 564 at [44]; *Ocado Group Plc v McKeeve* [2021] EWCA Civ 145 at [65]–[69].

[303] *PJSC Vseukrainskyi Aktsionernyi Bank v Maksimov* [2014] EWHC 4370 (Comm).

[304] A Zuckerman (2021) at 1194.

[305] *Patel v Patel* [2017] EWHC 1588 (Ch).

12. To further protect the defendant's rights, they must be provided with specific information. This requirement is currently contained in CPR r 81.4(2). It is a means by which a defendant is afforded due notice, which is particularly important given the potential penal consequences of contempt proceedings. Information to be given includes, the nature of the alleged contempt, when it is said to have occurred, confirmation that any application has been served personally on the defendant, notice of the right to remain silent, the right to secure legal representation, the potential consequences of an adverse finding, notice that the proceedings will be in public, and that any judgment or order made will be made in public. The specific requirements should be set out in the digital procedure rather than in the Code.
13. Any order made on an application for permission may be renewed, varied, or revoked, as is generally the case for applications under rule 7(6).[306]

## RULE 42.—COMMITTAL FOR CONTEMPT—MANAGEMENT AND DETERMINATION

**(1) Contempt proceedings are commenced by application. They are neither classified nor allocated to a procedural management track. They will be assigned to a designated judge who shall give such directions as necessary for their proper management and determination. Standard directions will be given through the digital procedure.**

**(2) The court must ensure that the person against whom contempt proceedings are brought has been informed of their right to remain silent in any contempt hearing.**

**(3) The burden of proof lies on the claimant to establish contempt of court beyond a reasonable doubt. Where the court makes a finding of contempt it may impose any punishment permitted by a rule of law, including a sentence of imprisonment, a fine, or the confiscation of assets. It may also grant permission for the sequestration of assets.**

**(4) An order for committal to prison may be issued with a power of arrest. A sentence of imprisonment may be suspended. It may also be combined with any other form of punishment.**

**(5) Unless the court directs otherwise, an application for permission to bring contempt proceedings and any order for committal must be served personally on the defendant.**

**(6) In addition to service on the parties to contempt proceedings, any order for committal to prison must be served on the Official Solicitor. The Official Solicitor must review such orders and take such steps as appropriate in the circumstances to challenge the decision or encourage the contemnor to discharge their contempt.**

**(7) Any person who is held to be in contempt of court may apply to the court to discharge their contempt. Generally, the judge who made the committal order should hear the application to discharge. Where the court grants such an application it may vary or set aside any punishment imposed regarding the contempt.**

*Sources: Contempt of Court Act 1981, s 14; CPR rr 81.3, 81.4, 81.7, 81.8, 81.9, 81.10.*

[306] *Zurich Insurance Plc v Romaine* [2018] EWHC 3383 (QB).

## COMMENTARY

1. Contempt proceedings are incidental to substantive proceedings. They are therefore commenced by application and are not subject to classification or allocation to a procedural management track.
2. Once commenced, committal proceedings should be assigned to a specified, designated judge, who will be responsible for managing and determining the proceedings consistently with judicial continuity. Generally, this judge ought to be the same one who dealt with the substantive proceedings out of which the contempt proceedings arise. This approach is intended to promote the economical, efficient, and just management of contempt proceedings.[307] This is particularly the case as the designated judge assigned to the substantive proceedings will be familiar with the issues that gave rise to the alleged contempt. Time and expense will not therefore need to be expended by the court and the parties in familiarising a new judge with the background to the contempt proceedings. There is no objection to this on the grounds that it would result in a judge being judge in their own cause. Contempt proceedings are not brought, as made clear in *Wilkinson v Lord Chancellor's Department* (2003),[308] to protect any specific judge. They are intended to protect the administration of justice generally. Valid objection to the designated judge in the substantive proceedings dealing with the contempt proceedings may, however, be made where there is an appearance of judicial bias. Where, however, the proceedings are initiated by a judge under rule 41(3), they would be judge in their own cause and ought therefore not to manage or determine the proceedings.
3. Any person against whom contempt proceedings is brought has the right to remain silent.[309] The existence of the right, a specific application of the privilege against self-incrimination,[310] ought to be brought to the defendant's attention by the applicant. The court must also ensure that the defendant is aware of it.[311] This duty is an aspect of the purposive principle, ie it is required to secure a fair procedure. It is of particular importance where contempt proceedings are concerned given the defendant's liberty is at stake.[312]
4. Unlike in civil proceedings generally, the criminal standard of proof applies. This reflects the fact that both forms of contempt as they may result in imprisonment are deemed to be criminal proceedings for the purpose of proof.[313] Where an individual is held to be in contempt of court, the court may impose a range of sanctions, including the imposition of fines.[314] The object of sentencing is primarily to promote compliance with the court order. Its secondary objective is to punish the contemnor.[315]

[307] *Fairclough Homes Ltd v Summers* [2012] UKSC 26; [2012] 1 WLR 2004 at [59].

[308] *Wilkinson v Lord Chancellor's Department* [2003] EWCA Civ 95; [2003] WLR 1254 at [25].

[309] *Comet Products UK Ltd v Hawhex Plastics Ltd* [1971] 2 QB 67 at 73–77.

[310] *Cobra Golf Inc v Rata* [1998] Ch 109; P Londono (2019) at 3-202 and following. It falls under the specific immunity of an individual from being compelled to give evidence against themselves or answer questions when they are undergoing a trial that may result in their committal to prison, which would ordinarily be a criminal trial: *AT & T Istel Ltd v Tully* [1993] AC 45. This right is not affected in this context by the revision to the privilege against self-incrimination in Pt 12, r 32 as that rule applies to proceedings other than criminal proceedings.

[311] *Invideous Ltd v Thorogood* [2014] EWCA Civ 1511 at [41].

[312] *Yianni v Yianni* [1966] 1 WLR 120 at 124.

[313] *Re Bramblevale Ltd* [1970] Ch 12 at 137; *Newman (t/a Mantella Publishing) v Modern Bookbinders* [2000] 1 WLR 2559; P Londono (2019) at 3-78.

[314] Senior Courts Act 1981, s 40(1).

[315] *Crystal Mews Limited v Metterick* [2006] EWHC 3087 (Ch) at [8]–[13].

In the most serious cases, and as a measure of last resort, a sentence of imprisonment for up to two years may be imposed.[316] For less serious cases, a fine may be imposed, assets may be subject to confiscation or sequestration (Part 16, rule 4(4)(e)). A combination of sanctions may also be imposed.[317] In an appropriate case, a sentence of imprisonment may be suspended. The power to suspend arises at common law.[318] Rule 42(4) codifies that power.[319]

5. To ensure a defendant subject to an application for permission to bring contempt proceedings, to contempt proceedings, or to an order for committal for contempt, is made aware of them or any order made in them, they must be served personally.[320] This is an exception to the general approach to service where it is sufficient that a method of service only needs to reasonably guarantee delivery. A higher threshold of certainty is in the public interest where a defendant's liberty is at stake. This exception to the general approach to service may itself, however, be set aside. The court may permit service by an alternative method or dispense with service where, for instance, a defendant is taking steps to evade personal service and thereby frustrate the court's process.[321]
6. Contempt proceedings must be held in public. Orders and judgments must also, as is the general rule, be publicly available. Exceptions can be made where justified by an applicable exception to the publicity principle.[322] Where an individual is committed to prison for contempt, the fact of that must be made public. No exception to the publicity principle can justify the imprisonment of an individual in secret. Moreover, to ensure that an individual who is committed to prison is able, if necessary, to obtain legal assistance notice of their imprisonment must be provided to the Official Solicitor. The Official Solicitor may act in the public interest by taking such steps as are necessary to protect the liberty of the person. They should do this by scrutinising committal orders and providing advice and encouragement to the contemnor regarding any potential challenge to the order and/or discharging their contempt. They may also act as the contemnor's litigation friend. Through making provision for this rule 42(5) reintroduces a role carried out by the Official Solicitor, which was improperly abolished for financial reasons in 2012.[323] It is reintroduced as it plays an important role in ensuring that there is official scrutiny of all committals for contempt by an officer of the court who is not linked to the proceedings and who is acting in the public interest.
7. Consistently with the primary objective of sanctions imposed on contemnors, rule 42(7) specifies that a contemnor may apply to discharge (historically 'purge') their contempt. Generally, this requires them to apologise to the court for their actions that led to the finding of contempt. They will also ordinarily be required to assure

[316] Contempt of Court Act 1981, s 14(1); *McKendrick v Financial Conduct Authority* [2019] EWCA Civ 524; [2019] 4 WLR 65 at [40]–[41]; *Oliver v Shaikh* [2020] EWHC 2658 (QB) at [17]; *Liverpool Victoria Insurance Co Ltd v Zafar* [2019] EWCA Civ 392; [2019] 1 WLR 3833 at [64]–[69].

[317] *Phonographic Performance Ltd v Ellis* [2018] EWCA Civ 2812; [2019] Bus LR 542 at [51]–[57].

[318] *Liverpool Victoria Insurance Co Ltd v Zafar* [2019] EWCA Civ 392; [2019] 1 WLR 3833 at [69].

[319] *Lee v Walker* [1985] QB 1191 at 1199–1202.

[320] See, for instance, CPR r 81.5(1).

[321] *Isis Housing Co-Operative v Evelyn* [2019] EWCA Civ 1299 at [15]–[22].

[322] Unlike under the CPR no specific provision is made for committal hearings and orders to be made in public. The general rule concerning publicity applies.

[323] *Devon County Council v Kirk* [2016] EWCA Civ 1221; [2017] 4 WLR 36 at [45]–[49]. Also see Contempt of Court Act 1830 and subsequently the Court of Chancery Act 1860; Hansard, Commons, Volume 842, col 155: Wednesday, 2 August 1972.

the court of their future conduct, eg future compliance with ongoing or future orders or that they will not repeat such conduct as led to the finding of contempt.[324] To maintain judicial continuity and its advantages, the same judge who dealt with the contempt proceedings ought to hear any discharge application.[325] If an application is granted, the court may set aside the sentence in its entirety. It may also vary it, eg a committal may be varied so that any remaining period of committal to prison be suspended.[326]

[324] *Harris v Harris (Contempt of Court: Application to Purge)* [2001] Fam 502; The Criminal Justice Act 2003, s 258.

[325] *Swindon Borough Council v Webb* [2016] EWCA Civ 152; [2016] 1 WLR 3301 at [24].

[326] *Harris v Harris (Contempt of Court: Application to Purge)* [2001] Fam 502.

# PART 12

# ACCESS TO EVIDENCE AND PRIVILEGES

## SECTION 1: GENERAL

1. English and Welsh civil procedure provides a range of methods for evidence-gathering. This Part codifies them. It does so consistently with the established approach that places responsibility for evidence-gathering, and its submission, in the hands of the parties. Access to evidence is thus an instance of court-assisted party autonomy. This Part does, however, depart to a limited degree from that approach by providing the court with a limited power to assist parties with evidence-gathering. In doing so it does not place responsibility for the management of evidence-gathering in the hands of the court. It does not therefore introduce to any real extent a form of what might in some civil justice systems be known as substantive case management,[1] ie the management of the substance of the parties' cases.[2] This minor incursion into court-assisted party autonomy only arises where one or more parties are unrepresented and thus may not be in a position to determine effectively what evidence may be relevant and thus necessary to obtain.
2. This Part also makes provision for what are commonly known as evidentiary privileges, eg legal professional privilege. These various rules, which govern whether specific evidence is immune from compulsory disclosure or inadmissible as evidence, do not form part of civil procedure in England and Wales. Their introduction here is thus a novel development.
3. On access to physical evidence see Part 13.

### RULE 1.—SCOPE AND PURPOSE

**(1) This Part concerns the provision of documentary and witness evidence. It is concerned with how parties establish the factual contentions in their respective claims and defences. It is a specific application of the party autonomy principle, as parties may determine the extent to which they wish to rely upon evidence. It is also a means to further the general access, due notice, evidential access, and accuracy principles.**

**(2) The rules in this Part are also intended to put parties in the best position to assess the merits of their dispute. They therefore also promote consensual settlement. Evidential access also promotes the publicity principle.**

[1] *Materielle Prozessleitungspflicht* or substantive case management as it is known in Austria and Germany, for instance.

[2] German Code of Civil Procedure, Section 139—Direction in substance of the course of proceedings.

*A Model Civil Procedure Code for England and Wales*. John Sorabji, Oxford University Press. © John Sorabji 2024.
DOI: 10.1093/oso/9780192848680.003.0013

**(3) Evidence identification, gathering, exchange between the parties, and submission to the court is also subject to the economy, efficiency, and proportionality principles.**

*Sources: ALI/UNIDROIT Principles, principles, 16, 18; ALI/UNIDROIT Reporters' Study, rr 25, 26, 27; ELI-UNIDROIT Model Rules, Part VII; CPR Pts 31, 32, 34, 35, PD57AC.*

## COMMENTARY

1. No fair and effective dispute resolution system can operate without a process by which evidence is gathered and tested.[3] This Part is thus concerned with the means by which the two main forms of evidence can be adduced to support or undermine parties' factual contentions. It is thus concerned with documentary evidence, which includes electronically produced data, and witness evidence. Witness evidence encompasses both lay and expert witness evidence.
2. Rules concerning evidence-gathering engage a significant number of procedural principles. Their necessity is recognised by article 6 of the European Convention on Human Rights. It specifically identifies the need for there to be power to enable the court to assist the parties to secure evidence where necessary.[4] Hence effective, practical measures must be made available to parties to enable them to secure, and thereafter test, evidence.[5] The evidential access principle is in this way intrinsically linked with the general access principle.
3. Given the centrality of party autonomy to English and Welsh civil proceedings and, relatedly, the fact that proceedings are adversarial with the court having no inquisitorial powers, the rules in this Part are primarily facilitative. They enable parties to take steps to secure evidence from their opponents and, where necessary, non-parties. Whether they wish to rely upon such evidence is, however, ultimately a matter for them.
4. The facilitative nature of the rules also gives effect to procedural equality and due notice. If parties were unable to obtain evidence that was in the hands of their opponents, they would be at a procedural disadvantage. This would be acute where all or the majority of evidence was in their opponent's hands. Equal access is thus required for all parties to be able to put their best case forward and to test their opponent's case, thus enabling the court to determine the '*truth by the best evidence available*'.[6] Additionally, were a party able to withhold evidence that they were intending to rely upon until trial, as was the position in the common law courts prior to the middle of the 19th century, their opponent would not know the case they had to meet.[7] Due notice militates against a party being able to maintain evidential secrecy prior to trial. Moreover, it prevents surprise at trial.[8] Advance notice also

[3] ELI-UNIDROIT Model Rules, Part VII, Introduction; A Zuckerman, *Zuckerman on Civil Procedure—Principles of Practice* (Sweet & Maxwell, 2021) at 182 and following.

[4] *Feldbrugge v The Netherlands* (1986) 8 EHRR 425.

[5] *Airey v Ireland* (1979) 2 EHRR 305 at 24; *McGinley v United Kingdom* (1999) 27 EHRR 1 at [107] and following; P Hirvelä and S Heikkilä, *Right to a Fair Trial* (Intersentia, 2022) at 104.

[6] *Harmony Shipping Co SA v Davies* [1979] 1 WLR 1380 at 1385; *Davies v Eli Lilley & Co* [1087] 1 WLR 428 at 431.

[7] J H Wigmore, *Evidence in Trials at Common Law* (Chadbourn Revision, 1976) Vol 6, at 490–492; *Preston v Carr* (1826) 1 Y & J 175 at 179; Evidence Act 1851, s 6; Common Law Procedure Act 1854, ss 51, 52.

[8] N Andrews, *Andrews on Civil Processes* (Intersentia, 2019) at 245.

promotes efficient trial preparation and management, which in turn facilitates procedural economy and proportionality.

5. Evidential access also plays a crucial role in promoting consensual settlement as well as adjudicative accuracy.[9] Parties are better able to assess the merits of their and their opponent's respective positions where they have access to relevant evidence. Equally, from the perspective of adjudicative accuracy, courts plainly cannot reach substantively accurate decisions unless they can determine right fact.[10] That also requires evidence to be available to the parties, which they can assess and, where appropriate, adduce and test in court.
6. Evidential access is not only important for the parties and their interest in securing a fair process and resolution of their dispute; it is also important in the wider public interest. Zuckerman identifies that public interest by reference to the publicity principle. As he puts it, if the public were to gain the impression that disputes were determined by courts on the basis of partial or incomplete evidence because one of the parties was unable to access it, it would undermine confidence in the judicial process.[11] Judgments would thus lose their credibility for the public. Equally, it could be said that such judgments would, where the losing party was the one who was unable to secure evidence, lose their credibility in the eyes of that party. In turn that could be expected to reduce their sense of having received a fair hearing and of having been able to participate effectively in it. Where that is the case, the risk would arise that they would refuse to comply with the judgment, again undermining public confidence in the judicial process. That both parties and the public are able to see that equal access to evidence is available, that judgments are based on probative evidence that parties wish to adduce, through publicly accessible proceedings is an essential part of the educational aspect of the publicity principle.
7. To help give effect to these various principles, this Part is intended to enable parties to ensure that they and the court have access to the broadest range of relevant, probative evidence.[12] To further facilitate this, exchange of evidence is also encouraged during the pre-action phase of dispute management. Care must, however, be taken where access to evidence is concerned. Both the CPR and, particularly its predecessors, suffered from providing too generous access to and submission of evidence: access to documentary evidence and to expert evidence are two longstanding sources of excessive litigation cost and delay.[13] This Part thus maintains the approach taken under the CPR and seeks to control and limit the use of evidence by reference to procedural economy, efficiency, and, particularly, proportionality.[14]

[9] J Langbein, 'The Disappearance of Civil Trial In the United States' (2012) 122 Yale LJ 522 at 565–566; W Brazil, 'The Adversary Character of Civil Discovery' (1978) 31 Vand LR 1296 at 1302.

[10] J Bentham, 'Rationale of Judicial Evidence', in *The Works of Jeremy Bentham* (*Rationale*) (ed Bowring) (1843) (William Tait, Edinburgh) Vol 6 at 212; *Tweed v Parades Commission for Northern Ireland* [2006] UKHL 53; [2007] 1 AC 650 at [2].

[11] A Zuckerman (2021) at 182.

[12] *Rex v Hardy* (1794) 24 State Tr 199 at 808; *Marks v Beyfus* (1890) 25 QBD 494; *Rogers v Home Secretary* [1973] AC 388 at 407.

[13] S Rosenbaum, *The Rule-making Authority in the English Supreme Court* (Boston, 1917) at 74, citing the Report of the Lord Chancellor's Legal Procedure Committee 1881; H Woolf, *Access to Justice: Interim Report to the Lord Chancellor on the Civil Justice System in England and Wales* (HMSO) (1995) at 181.

[14] CPR rr 31.6, 35.1; CPR PD57AC.

## RULE 2.—THE COURT'S ROLE IN DETERMINING ISSUES OF FACT

**(1) The court is the tribunal of fact. It is responsible for determining any matters of fact that are in dispute in the proceedings.**

**(2) In determining factual matters, the court will evaluate the reliability, credibility, and weight to be given to all the admissible evidence. Evaluation will be carried out by reference to all the evidence. Evaluation is subject to any applicable rule of law.**

*Sources: ALI/UNIDROIT Principles, principle 16.6; ALI/UNIDROIT Reporters' Study, r 28.2; ELI-UNIDROIT Model Rules, r 98.*

## COMMENTARY

1. The court, consistently with the independence and accuracy principles, is responsible for determining all factual issues in dispute. With the decline and now virtual extinction of the civil jury, this generally means a judge is the tribunal of fact. In those rare cases where jury trial takes place, it is the tribunal of fact. It is not for the parties to determine contested matters, nor is it for third parties to do so. Courts cannot delegate or outsource fact-finding.[15]
2. Courts must evaluate all the admissible evidence, and must do so as it relates to particular issues.[16] They must do so to reach correct findings of fact. To do so they must determine whether evidence is credible and, if so, what weight is to be given to it. The latter is a '*matter of common sense*'[17] carried out by reference to several factors.[18] In English and Welsh civil procedure,[19] the evaluation of evidence is subject, in some cases, to rules governing the weight to be given to specific types of evidence. For instance, sealed documents are deemed to be authentic because they are sealed due to section 132 of the Senior Courts Act 1981. In assessing evidence, the court is also not bound to accept as true evidence given by an expert witness in preference to a lay witness.[20] Evaluation must take place when all evidence is before the court and not when specific evidence is adduced.[21] In all circumstances the court must give sufficient reasons justifying its assessment of, and conclusions concerning, evidence.[22]
3. One particular problem that can arise where evidence evaluation is concerned is that of judicial bias; particularly conscious or, more perniciously, unconscious

[15] J Jolowicz, 'Fact-finding', in J Jolowicz, *On Civil Procedure* (CUP, 2000) at 211; *Armstrong v First York* [2005] EWCA Civ 277; [2005] 1 WLR 2751 at [28].

[16] H Hodge and M Malek, *Phipson on Evidence* (Sweet & Maxwell, 2021) at [45–02].

[17] A Keane and P McKeown, *The Modern Law of Evidence* (11th edn) (OUP, 2016) at 33.

[18] A Keane and P McKeown (2016) at 33.

[19] As is also the case in other countries, eg in France small claims may, generally, only be proved by documentary evidence: M Stürner, 'Evaluation of Evidence and Standard of Proof in the ELI/UNIDROIT European Rules of Civil Procedure', in L Tichy, *Standard of Proof in Europe* (Mohr Siebeck, 2019) at 279. J Sladicˇ and A Uzelac, 'Assessment of Evidence', in V Rijavec, T Keresteš, and T Ivanc, *Dimensions of Evidence in European Civil Procedure* (Wolters Kluwer, 2015); M Damaska, 'Free Proof and its Detractors' (1995) 43 Am J Comp L 343; D Dwyer, 'What Does It Mean To Be Free? The Concept of "Free Proof" in the Western Legal Tradition' (2005) 3(1) International Commentary on Evidence: Article 6.

[20] *Armstrong v First York* [2005] EWCA Civ 277; [2005] 1 WLR 2751 at [25]–[30].

[21] *ASK v The Secretary of State for the Home Department* [2017] EWHC 196 (Admin) at [70]–[79]; *BR (Proof of Facts)* [2015] EWFC 41 at [8], '*Each piece of evidence must be considered in the context of the whole.*'

[22] *Flannery v Halifax Estate Agencies Ltd* [2000] 1 WLR 377.

bias. Such problems have been noted in several studies.[23] This Code provides a basis for counteracting such biases, and thus improving judicial impartiality and adjudicative accuracy, by promoting judicial training through the use of AI.[24]

## RULE 3.—STANDARD OF PROOF

**(1) Civil courts are required to decide disputed issues of fact according to the civil standard of proof, except where a rule of law requires it to apply the standard of proof to the criminal standard. Courts are not required to take active steps to find the truth.**

**(2) The civil standard requires a court to be reasonably and objectively satisfied that it is more probable than not, on the evidence before it, that a disputed factual issue occurred.**

**(3) The criminal standard requires a court to be reasonably and objectively satisfied beyond a reasonable doubt that a disputed factual issue occurred.**

*Sources: ALI/UNIDROIT Principles, principle 21; ALI/UNIDROIT Reporters' Study, r 28.2; ELI-UNIDROIT Model Rules, rr 87, 88.*

## COMMENTARY

1. The standard and burden of proof are not set out in the CPR. They are viewed as forming part of the law of evidence,[25] and are matters of substantive not procedural law.[26] They are codified here due to the central importance that they have to the prosecution, defence, and adjudication of proceedings.[27]
2. Whether a party is likely to be able to satisfy the standard of proof is an important consideration before and after proceedings are commenced for all parties. It plays a part in any assessment of the prospects of success, and hence is an important factor for consideration in the promotion and conclusion of any settlement process; it shapes parties' litigation and settlement strategy.[28] It is equally a factor that the court must consider when managing the dispute, eg when considering whether to strike out a claim as well as considering the management of the evidence-gathering process; it thus also shapes the dispute management process.
3. There are two standards of proof: the civil and criminal standard. The civil standard applies in all cases, except where a rule of law requires application of the criminal standard. The civil standard is one that requires a court to be reasonably and objectively satisfied that a disputed factual matter's occurrence was more probable than not.[29] The standard applicable does not differ depending on the nature of

[23] Part 1, r 13.
[24] Part 1, r 24(5).
[25] H Hodge and M Malek (2021), Part 6.
[26] A Zuckerman (2021) at 1106–1107, noting that they form part of the substantive law due to the fact they allocate risk between the parties.
[27] ELI-UNIDROIT Model Rules, r 87, comment 1.
[28] A Zuckerman (2021) at 1106–1107.
[29] *Miller v Minister of Pensions* [1947] 2 All ER 372 at 374; *Re H (minors)* [1996] AC 563 at [73].

the disputed issue.[30] The court considering whether the evidence before it meets the standard must do so by carrying out a general, ie an overall, assessment of the evidence and considering '*whether the case for believing that the suggested event happened is more compelling than the case for not reaching that belief*'.[31] This is not an exercise in probability theory or statistical analysis.

4. Implicit in the standard of proof, and made explicit in rule 3(1), is that civil courts are not under a duty to actively find the truth.[32] Their role is to adjudicate on the evidence put before them. Judges are arbiters not investigators. They are not to '*seek their own forms of information or evidence*'.[33] If parties fail to adduce relevant and probative evidence, or choose not to do so, that is a matter for them. This is the case even if a court is otherwise aware of the existence of such evidence. It is confined to adjudicate solely on the evidence before it, and thus may in some cases determine proceedings on the balance of probabilities based on evidence that does not reflect the truth.[34] In some cases the court may well be aware of the possibility, probability, or reality of that fact.[35] As long as it has discharged its responsibility to adjudicate to the civil standard on the evidence adduced in the proceedings, it has secured justice according to the law.
5. The criminal standard is applicable in a limited range of civil proceedings.[36] The most common situation where this arises is in proceedings for criminal contempt of court.[37] The criminal standard requires the court to be satisfied beyond a reasonable doubt.[38]

## RULE 4.—THE BURDEN OF PROOF

**(1) The burden of proving their case or a disputed factual issue lies on the party that asserts it affirmatively.**

**(2) Where a fact is admitted or not disputed, the party asserting it need not prove it. The court may also take notice of facts and matters that are well-known.**

**(3) Where the court is unable, on the evidence before it, to determine disputed issues in proceedings by reference to the standard of proof, it may decide them by reference to the burden of proof.**

*Sources: ALI/UNIDROIT Principles, principle 21; ALI/UNIDROIT Reporters' Study, r 28.1; ELI-UNIDROIT Model Rules, r 88.*

30 M Redmayne, 'Standards of Proof in Civil Litigation' (1999) 62 MLR 167; E McBride, 'Is the Civil "Higher Standard of Proof" a Coherent Concept?' (2009) 8 Law Prob & Risk 323; *Secretary of the Home Department v Rehman* (2001) [2001] UKHL 47; [2003] 1 AC 153 at [55]; *Re B (Children) (Care Proceedings: Standard of Proof)* [2008] UKHL 35; [2009] AC 11 at [13]; *Re J (Children)* [2013] UKSC 9; [2013] 1 AC 680 at [35]–[36].

31 *Nulty v Milton Keynes Borough Council* [2013] EWCA Civ 15; [2013] 1 WLR 1183 at [35]–[37].

32 J Jolowicz, 'Procedural Reform' in J Jolowicz (2000) at 384, 390–391; *Loveridge and Loveridge v Healey* [2004] EWCA Civ 173 at [23].

33 *Official Solicitor v K* [1965] AC 201 at 239 and 241.

34 *Harmony Shipping Co SA v Davies* [1979] 1 WLR 1380 at 1285; *Air v Secretary of State for Trade* [1983] 2 AC 394 at 438–439; *Ball v Ball* [2017] EWHC 1750 (Ch) at [17]–[19].

35 *GB v Stoke City Football Club Ltd* [2015] EWHC 2862 (QB) at [141].

36 A Keane and P McKeown (2016) at 115.

37 *Seldon v Wilde* [1911] 1 KB 701; *Re Bramblevale Ltd* [1970] Ch 128.

38 *Woolmington v DPP* [1935] AC 462; *Miller v Minister of Pensions* [1947] 2 All ER 372 at 373–374; *Walters v R* [1969] 2 AC 26; *R v Ching* (1976) 63 Cr App Rep 7; *R v Hunt* [1987] AC 352; H Hodge and M Malek (2021) at [6.51]–[6.55].

## COMMENTARY

1. The burden of proof is '*the duty which lies on one or other the parties, either to establish a case or to establish the facts upon a particular issue*'.[39] This duty lies upon the party asserting a proposition. Those who assert must generally prove.[40]
2. Not all facts need to be proved. Party autonomy enables parties to admit facts or agree them. In such cases requiring parties to prove them would serve no positive purpose. On the contrary, it would result in a waste of party and court time and resources. The court may also, for instance, take judicial notice of notorious facts, ie that the earth revolves round the Sun or that water is wet.[41]
3. Where the party on whom the burden of proof lies is unable to satisfy the court to the civil standard, the burden of proof may then be determinative. Failure to discharge the burden will result in a claim failing, where the burden lies on the claimant.[42] While it is rare in civil proceedings for disputes to be determined by reference to the burden of proof,[43] such an approach ensures that proceedings are brought to an end. The alternative, where a party failed to discharge the burden, would be to permit them further opportunities to pursue the cause of action in fresh proceedings. Such an approach would be contrary to the proportionality, concentration, and, particularly, finality principles; each of which rule 4(3) serves.

# SECTION 2: EVIDENCE-GATHERING

## RULE 5.—THE GENERAL RIGHT TO EVIDENCE AND INFORMATION

**(1) Parties have a general right to access and rely upon evidence and information that is necessary to enable the court to give effect to the purposive principle and which is relevant and proportionate to matters of fact that are in dispute in the proceedings. This includes the right to rely upon lay witness and expert evidence.**
**(2) The right may be subject to any restriction or limitation imposed by a rule of law or court order.**

*Sources: ALI/UNIDROIT Principles, principle 16.1; ALI/UNIDROIT Reporters' Study, r 25; ELI-UNIDROIT Model Rules, rr 89, 100.*

## COMMENTARY

1. Parties have a general right to access and rely upon evidence and information as a consequence of the evidential access principle. This applies to both lay witness evidence and expert evidence. It is, however, subject to important qualifications. Access is limited to evidence that is necessary to secure the purposive principle, ie to

[39] H Hodge and M Malek (2021) at [6.01].
[40] *Robins v National Trust Co Ltd* [1927] AC 515 at 520.
[41] H Hodge and M Malek (2021), Parts 3 and 4.
[42] *Wakelin v L & S W Railway* (1886) 12 App Cas 41 at 45; *Ball v Ball* [2017] EWHC 1750 (Ch) at [18]; H Hodge and M Malek (2021) at [6.07].
[43] *Re B (Children) (Care Proceedings: Standard of Proof)* [2008] UKHL 35; [2009] AC 11 at [32].

secure a fair procedure and a fair result. It is thus 'necessity' as defined by reference to accuracy as well as other the procedural principles, such as economy, efficiency, and effective dispute management. Access and reliance are also limited by what is relevant to the proceedings. Relevance is a function of the nature of the dispute, as that is defined by the parties' case statements.

2. Access and reliance are also, specifically, limited by proportionality. One of the main problems with documentary and expert evidence has, historically, been the cost and delay associated with it. Both problems arose due to an absence of proper court management of the evidentiary access process married to an ostensible overriding objective of securing justice on its substantive merits. The two led to parties having, to all intents and purposes, free reign over the extent of documentary disclosure and the appointment of expert witnesses. The evidentiary process was consequently a significant factor in the development of disproportionate litigation cost to the parties and the court.[44]
3. Imposing a proportionality requirement on evidentiary access and reliance is thus particularly important. Such an approach was introduced by the CPR in 1999 due to the application of its overriding objective. Where documentary evidence was concerned this was less than successful, particularly in complex, high value litigation.[45] Ultimately, this led to the introduction of a discrete documentary disclosure process applicable in the Business and Property Courts in 2022.[46] That process was explicitly intended to effect a new procedural culture of party co-operation and proportionality in documentary disclosure.[47] This rule, and the overall approach in this Part, are intended to be consistent with that approach; see rule 14.
4. Specific reference to proportionality in rule 5(1), when necessity is already defined by reference to the purposive principle, is intended to ensure that proportionality is embedded into the rule. This is to ensure its importance and centrality to the evidentiary process cannot be minimised when it is carried out.
5. Access and reliance on evidence may also be limited even where it is otherwise admissible, eg where an evidentiary privilege applies or a party is barred from adducing evidence as a sanction for procedural non-compliance.

## RULE 6.—PARTY SUBMISSION OF EVIDENCE

**(1) Parties must co-operate with each other and the court in ensuring that evidence is identified, obtained, exchanged, and relied upon in proceedings consistently with the purposive principle.**

**(2) Parties may agree to limit or restrict evidence to be submitted in proceedings. Any such agreement must be in writing and filed with the court.**

*Sources: ELI-UNIDROIT Model Rules, rr 2, 99.*

[44] H Woolf, *Access to Justice: Final Report to the Lord Chancellor on the Civil Justice System in England and Wales* (HMSO) (1996) at 124.

[45] R Aikens et al, *Report and Recommendations of the Commercial Court Long Trials Working Party* (Judicial Office, 2007) at 58; R Jackson, *Review of Civil Litigation Costs: Preliminary Report* (May 2009) Vol 1 at 368; Disclosure Working Party, *Disclosure Pilot Briefing Note* (Judicial Office, November 2017).

[46] CPR PD57AD.

[47] *UTB LLC v Sheffield United Ltd* [2019] EWHC 914 (Ch); [2019] 3 All ER 698, at [75].

## COMMENTARY

1. This rule complements rule 5. It gives concrete effect to the co-operation principle where evidence-gathering and exchange is concerned. The importance of party co-operation in this area was latterly stressed under the CPR. It is a central feature of the innovative disclosure regime introduced into the CPR by PD57AD.[48] It places particular emphasis on party co-operation in agreeing the scope of documentary disclosure as a means to promote proportionality.[49] As with rule 5 this rule is also of general application.
2. Parties may, further to party autonomy, restrict or limit evidence to be adduced in proceedings. This may cover specific items or categories of evidence, eg evidence may be limited to documentary evidence or expert evidence. Evidence may also be limited to specific issues, eg liability or damage. Such agreements amount to a waiver of the right to evidentiary access and reliance. They must therefore be set out in a freely made, express agreement made on an informed and prospective basis.[50] Where parties agree to such restrictions or limits the court ought to give effect to them.[51]

## RULE 7.—THE COURT'S POWER TO RESTRICT OR EXCLUDE EVIDENCE

**(1) The court may restrict or exclude access to or reliance upon evidence and information that is not relevant or necessary to matters of fact in dispute or where access or reliance would be contrary to the purposive principle.**
**(2) Before the court excludes or restricts access to or reliance upon evidence it must provide the parties with an opportunity to make representations to it.**

*Sources: ELI-UNIDROIT Model Rules, r 90; CPR r 32.1.*

## COMMENTARY

1. This rule limits party control over the evidentiary process by placing the right to access under the court's control. It thus enables the court to give effect to its duty to ensure that parties exercise this right consistently with the purposive principle. The central aim here is to ensure that the evidentiary process is carried out efficiently, economically, and, most importantly, proportionately.
2. English and Welsh civil procedure has, subject to one exception, never adopted the position that evidence that was obtained illegally is inadmissible.[52] Hence evidence that was stolen, obtained through hacking a computer, or via an illegal recording if

[48] The PD was introduced following a successful pilot scheme run under PD51U; G Vos, *Chancellor of the High Court and Master of the Rolls welcome the Disclosure Working Pilot being approved* (Judicial Office, 15 July 2022).

[49] *McParland & Partners Ltd v Whitehead* [2020] EWHC 298 (Ch) at [4], [53]–[54] and [58]; *Obaid v Al-Hezaimi* [2019] EWHC 1953 (Ch) at [43]–[44].

[50] *Smith v Kvaerner Cementation Foundations Ltd* [2006] EWCA Civ 242; [2007] 1 WLR 370; Part 1, r 13.

[51] CPR r 31.6.

[52] *Ras Al Khaimah Investment Authority v Azima* [2021] EWCA Civ 349; [2021] 1 CLC 715 at [41]–[50].

relevant is generally admissible subject to it being necessary, proportionate, etc.[53] The exception is evidence obtained by torture.[54] The common law has prohibited reliance on such evidence since '*its earliest days*'.[55]

3. Where evidence has been obtained illegally, it may be excluded under this rule.[56] The appropriate test, which would fall under the purposive principle limb of rule 7(1), requires the court to balance two competing public interests: that of promoting the rule of law, eg 'observance of the law' and that of securing a fair trial. Where it is not excluded the court may, under its general dispute management powers or under its discretion concerning costs, impose adverse consequences on the party that seeks to adduce illegally obtained evidence. It may do so to indicate its disapproval of the methods employed to obtain the evidence and to discourage such methods being adopted by others.[57]

## RULE 8.—THE COURT'S POWER TO CALL AND IDENTIFY EVIDENCE

**(1) The court may not call evidence of its own initiative without the consent of the parties. This general rule does not apply to the appointment of court-appointed experts. It also does not apply to contempt proceedings brought under Part 11.**

**(2) Where a party is not represented by a lawyer the court may, consistently with the purposive principle,**

**(a) identify categories of evidence relevant to the proceedings, which that party may wish to rely upon; and**

**(b) if necessary, appoint a court-appointed expert witness.**

**(3) All parties must be notified of any identified categories of evidence.**

**(4) Identification may be carried out by a judge, court officer, or via the use of artificial intelligence through the digital procedure.**

**(5) A lawyerless party is under no obligation to act on the court's identification of potential evidence.**

*Sources: ELI-UNIDROIT Model Rules, r 92; CPR r 3.1A(5); German Code of Civil Procedure, s 139.*

## COMMENTARY

1. The court has no general power to call evidence on its own initiative. Exceptionally, it may do so in three circumstances. First, it may do so where parties consent.[58] Secondly, it may do so, without party consent, where contempt proceedings are

[53] *R v Kuruma* [1955] AC 197; *Helliwell v Piggott-Sims* [1980] FSR 356; *Bell Cablemedia Plc v Simmons* [2002] FSR 34 at [42].

[54] *A v Secretary of State for the Home Department (No 2)* [2005] UKHL 71; [2006] 2 AC 221 at [51]–[52]; *Shagang Shipping Company Ltd v HNA Group Company Ltd* [2020] UKSC 34; [2020] 1 WLR 3549.

[55] *A v Secretary of State for the Home Department (No 2)* [2005] UKHL 71; [2006] 2 AC 221 at [11].

[56] CPR r 32.1; *Khan v United Kingdom* (2001) 31 EHRR 45; [2000] Crim LR 684 at [34]–[40]. Evidence obtained in breach of a fundamental right might be properly excluded under this rule.

[57] *Jones v University of Warwick* [2003] EWCA Civ 151; [2003] 1 WLR 954 at [30].

[58] *In re Enoch and Zaretzky, Bock & Co's Arbitration* [1910] 1 KB 327 at 332–334; *Fallon v Calvert* [1960] 2 QB 201 at 205; *Harmony Shipping Co SA v Davies* [1979] 1 WLR 1380 at 1385.

concerned.[59] Thirdly, it may do so when it appoints a court-appointed expert witness. Rule 8(1) codifies the general rule and its exceptions.

2. Rule 8(2) also enables the court to assist a lawyerless party in identifying categories of evidence that may be relevant to matters in dispute. The court's role is intended to be facilitative. It is not to identify specific items of evidence. The limit here is intended to ensure that the court does not, in assisting the party, stray beyond the role of an independent arbiter. It remains to the party to determine whether to act in the light of the court's help, to determine what evidence to obtain, and whether to rely upon it. In this way, the potential for a court that assists a party to develop any form of bias is minimised if not eliminated. The rule also acknowledges the court's power to appoint a court-appointed expert. This may be necessary in circumstances where one or more parties are unrepresented if they are unable to identify and appoint suitable party-appointed experts.
3. The evidence identification process under rule 8(4) may be carried out by a judge or court officer. It may also, as a consequence of the parties having to submit their case statements via the digital dispute management system, be provided by the application of a court-based artificial intelligence programme. This last alternative would be the most cost-effective and efficient mechanism to assist lawyerless parties in this respect, where it can do so properly. It also is the most effective means to minimise the potential for the development of judicial bias. However the identification process is carried out, all parties must be informed of it and the categories of evidence identified. This is to secure procedural equality and due notice.
4. Rule 8(2) to (5) mark a departure for English and Welsh civil procedure. Historically, the court had no role in assisting parties on such matters. Substantive case or dispute management has, unlike in other European jurisdictions,[60] played no part in English and Welsh procedure. This difference in approach can be explained in a number of ways. Substantive dispute management is contrary to the adversarial process historically adopted in England and Wales, which saw the court as an essentially passive recipient of materials and submissions from the parties; the idea of the judge as an impartial arbiter.[61] It can also be explained by the idea that judicial involvement may promote the development of judicial bias, which is avoided by the approach here.[62] Finally, it can be explained by reference to the theoretical argument that English and Welsh proceedings were simply concerned with enabling parties to resolve their disputes, whereas some European jurisdictions understood the civil process as being concerned with the promotion of social welfare. The former could be achieved without judicial assistance on the substance of the dispute, the latter could not.[63]
5. The rationale for the introduction of this form of substantive dispute management was originally identified in the Hickinbottom Report, which led to the introduction of CPR r 3.1A. It is that court assistance via a 'more inquisitorial' form of process is necessary for the civil courts properly to give effect to the general access right where lawyerless parties are concerned.[64] Given the overarching structure of this Code, and particularly its approach to litigation funding, this new discretion ought not to be used widely.

[59] *Fallon v Calvert* [1960] 2 QB 201 at 205; *Yianni v Yianni* [1966] 1 WLR 120 at 124.

[60] R Stürner and P Murphy, *German Civil Justice* (Carolina, 2004) at 171–178; German Code of Civil Procedure, s 139.

[61] F Pollock and F W Maitland, *History of English Law* (Cambridge, 1895) at 667.

[62] J Jolowicz, 'Adversarial and Inquisitorial Approaches to Civil Litigation', in J Jolowicz (2000).

[63] M Damaska, *The Faces of Justice and State Authority* (Yale, 1986).

[64] *The Judicial Working Group on Litigants in Person*, Report (The Hickinbottom Report) (Judicial Office, 2013) at 24.

## RULE 9.—EVIDENCE MANAGEMENT

**(1) The court shall actively manage the process of party identification of evidence and the provision by parties, non-parties, and witnesses of such evidence. It shall do so as part of post-issue dispute management.**
**(2) Parties, non-parties, and witnesses shall co-operate with the court in evidence management.**
**(3) Generally, the provision of documents by parties to each other and to the court shall be carried out through the digital procedure. Where evidence cannot be provided digitally, physical copies may be provided to the court and other parties.**
**(4) Active management includes the use of artificial intelligence to assist the court in determining the nature and scope of any orders concerning evidence in proceedings. Parties shall be provided with, and given an opportunity to respond to, any such assistance.**
**(5) Parties should endeavour to make any application concerning evidence at the earliest reasonable time during pre-action and post-issue dispute management. Applications may be made during a trial or appeal hearing, where necessary in the interests of justice.**
**(6) Sanctions for non-compliance with evidence management may be imposed by the court. Sanctions include the court directing that a party may not rely on evidence in whole or in part.**

*Sources: ELI-UNIDROIT Model Rules, r 92.*

## COMMENTARY

1. Rule 9 complements Pt 11. It makes specific provision for the effective management by the court of the evidence-gathering process. It should be read consistently with rules 5, 6, and 7. It is intended to stress the importance of party co-operation with the court in managing evidence-gathering so that that process is economic, efficient, and proportionate. It is not sufficient for parties to ensure that they limit evidence-gathering to evidence that is proportionate. The manner in which that process is managed must itself also be carried out so as not to have a negative impact on the cost, time, and proportionality of proceedings.
2. To promote economy, efficiency, and proportionality in evidence management, rule 9(3) provides for the provision of documents to be carried out via the court's digital procedure. Documentary evidence, witness statements, etc must therefore be uploaded to the parties' digital dispute management file. The intention here is to reduce court costs in managing the documents, eg by removing the need to process, store, and provide judges with physical copies of parties' documents.
3. Additionally, provision is made for the use of artificial intelligence, whether by the use of predicative analytics or otherwise, to assist the court in determining the nature and scope of any orders relating to evidence and procedural time limits for compliance with such orders. Such procedures could be used, for instance, to help determine which issues require which categories of evidence or the order in which evidence could be obtained. Any use of artificial intelligence must be notified to the parties who, consistently with the due notice principle, must be afforded an opportunity to challenge any recommendations or proposed directions that arise from its use. To assist both legally represented and unrepresented parties the digital

procedure should also make available to parties e-disclosure systems that could assist them in carrying out any necessary documentary disclosure process.

4. To promote effective dispute management, rule 9(5) requires parties to make applications for evidence at the earliest possible opportunity. This enables the court to properly set and manage the procedural timetable. It also ensures that all parties are able to plan their approach to proceedings effectively. Late applications for evidence also tend to pose problems for other litigants' right to effective access as they generate satellite litigation and may result in hearings being postponed or adjourned to enable evidence to be obtained. That is not to say that late applications should not be made where they are necessary. If, for instance, an issue comes to light late in proceedings or, due to developments in the course of proceedings or at trial, an issue takes on greater importance than was previously appreciated by the parties and the court, a late application for further evidence on the point may well be justified by reference to the purposive principle notwithstanding the adverse effect it might have on procedural economy, efficiency, and proportionality.
5. Where parties fail to comply with any evidence management order the court may impose sanctions. Sanctions ought, as they ought generally, to be proportionate to the nature of the non-compliance. In some circumstances, where non-compliance is particularly serious, a party may be barred from relying on evidence.[65] That such a sanction may increase the prospect that the court would not be able to make an accurate finding of fact, ie that it reduces adjudicative accuracy, is justified by reference to the public interest in promoting systemic proportionality.[66]

## RULE 10.—PROHIBITION ON FURTHER USE OF EVIDENCE AND INFORMATION

**(1) Witness statements, documentary evidence, information derived from such evidence, and any other document or information that was provided under compulsion to a party in proceedings may not be used for any purpose other than the proceedings for which it was provided except where**
**(a) and to the extent, that it was adduced at a hearing held in public;**
**(b) the party whose evidence it is agrees to its further use; or**
**(c) the court grants permission for its further use where there is good reason justifying such use and it is just to do so.**

**(2) Exceptionally, the court may grant permission for further use retrospectively where it is just to do so.**

**(3) Where further use is permitted under sub-rules 1(a) or (b), the court may prohibit or restrict such use as it considers just.**

**(4) Any hearing to determine whether to permit, prohibit, or restrict further use should be held in private.**

**(5) Non-compliance with any prohibition or restriction on further use may result in the imposition of measures by the court to protect the administration of justice.**

*Sources: CPR rr 31.22, 32.12(1).*

[65] *Beachley Property Ltd v Edgar* (CA 21 June 1996, unreported) at 6.
[66] Part 1, r 5.

## COMMENTARY

1. Rule 10 restates the approach taken at common law and under CPR r 31.22 to prohibit the subsequent use of information that was subject to compulsory disclosure or derived from such information during proceedings.[67] It does not apply, however, to enforcement proceedings brought under Part 16.[68]
2. The rationale for the prohibition is to ensure that the invasion of a party's privacy and confidentiality, which results from compulsory disclosure of evidence, is kept to a minimum.[69] Hence documents and information derived from them within proceedings should, generally, only be used within those proceedings. They should not be capable of being freely used in, for instance, other unrelated proceedings. The same protection is also extended to witness statements. The rationale for the extension beyond the protection of information subject to compulsory process is to promote the administration of justice. As Zuckerman explains it, the protection is intended to encourage witnesses to come forward and give evidence by protecting the use to which their information can be put.[70] The prohibition is protected through the application of proceedings for contempt of court should it be breached.
3. Rule 10(1) restates the three bases on which exceptions to the prohibition may arise. Where information was referred to in open court,[71] the publicity principle weighs heavily against prohibiting or restricting further use. What has entered into the public domain ought generally to be available to the parties and non-parties to utilise for their own purposes.[72] Where the parties agree to further use by either or both of them, or by a third party, the court should also hesitate to place restrictions on it.[73] Party autonomy ought, generally, to prevail. The court does, however, retain a discretion to override these two exceptions and prohibit or restrict further use where it is just to maintain the prohibition, ie where, for instance, the public interest in the administration of justice required it. Where rule 10(1)(a) and (b) do not apply, the court retains a discretion to permit further use. That discretion must only be exercised where it is just to do so. It is also for the applicant seeking permission to demonstrate that there is good reason to release the document or information from the prohibition.[74] Rule 10(1)(c) thus provides an effective balance between a party's right to a private life, guaranteed by article 8 of the European Convention on Human Rights, and the right to a fair trial, guaranteed by article 6 of the Convention.[75]

[67] *Crest Homes plc v Marks* [1987] 1 AC 829 at 854; *IG Index Plc v Cloete* [2013] EWHC 3789 (QB) at [31]. The prohibition thus applies more widely than documents that were subject to documentary disclosure. It thus applies, for instance, to: affidavits (*Medway v Doublelock Ltd* [1978] 1 All ER 126) and witness summons (*Sybron Corp v Barclays Bank Plc* [1985] 1 Ch 299).

[68] *Vitol SA v Capri Marine Ltd* [2010] EWHC 458 (Comm); [2011] 1 All ER (Comm) 366; *Grosvenor Chemicals Ltd v UPL Europe Ltd* [2017] EWHC 1893 (Ch).

[69] *Home Office v Harman* [1982] 1 All ER 352 at 534 and 540; *Derby v Weldon (No 2)*, The Times, 20 October 1988, on the prohibition not applying to information disclosed or put into evidence voluntarily.

[70] A Zuckerman (2021) at 1047.

[71] This includes hearings to obtain information under Part 16, r 5: *Slade v Abbhi* [2020] EWHC 2181 (Comm).

[72] *NAB v Serco Ltd* [2014] EWHC 1225 (QB) at [28]–[38].

[73] *International Game Technology Plc v The Gambling Commission* [2023] EWHC 1420 (TCC).

[74] *Official Receiver v Skeene* [2020] EWHC 1252 (Ch); [2020] Lloyd's Rep FC 391.

[75] A Zuckerman (2021) at 868.

4. Applications for permission to use information for further purposes outside the immediate proceedings ought generally to be prospective. Exceptionally, the court may grant permission retrospectively where it is just to do so. In determining such an application, the court should consider if it would have granted permission if the application had been made prospectively. It should also consider what prejudice would be caused to the party whose information was used, whether breach of the prohibition was deliberate or not, whether the application was made promptly, and the proportionality of refusing permission.[76] Any application, whether dealing with the question of permission to use or a restriction or prohibition on use should be held in private to protect the party whose information it is from its further exposure, ie to protect confidentiality in the information in so far as possible.[77]

## RULE 11.—LANGUAGE, INTERPRETATION, AND TRANSLATION

**(1) Evidence may be given in English or Welsh.**
**(2) Where evidence cannot be given in English or Welsh, it may be given in another language. A translation of any such evidence must be provided to the parties and the court and made public, except where restrictions on publicity are imposed by the court.**
**(3) Where a party or witness requires the assistance of an interpreter to give their evidence, the court may direct the appointment of an interpreter.**
**(4) The court may restrict or limit the translation of evidence, particularly documentary evidence where necessary to ensure compliance with the purposive principle. It may also limit the use of interpretation.**
**(5) The cost of translation or interpretation shall be costs in the proceedings.**

*Sources: ALI/UNIDROIT Principles, principle 6; ALI/UNIDROIT Reporters' Study, r 8; ELI-UNIDROIT Model Rules, rr 19, 116.*

## COMMENTARY

1. Rule 10(1) applies the general rule that proceedings should be conducted in either English or Welsh to evidence. It also provides that where that is not possible evidence may be given in another language. A party's access to the court should not be prejudiced by the fact that they or witnesses on their behalf are unable to give evidence in either of these languages. Moreover, procedural equality requires the court to take steps to ensure that parties are not prejudiced in this way. Where a party or a witness is therefore unable to give their evidence in either English or Welsh, the court may permit them to do so in any other language. To enable the court to adjudicate properly on the evidence and to maintain the public nature of the proceedings, any such evidence must be accompanied by a translation. The translation must be made public, except where the evidence itself is subject to any derogations from the publicity principle.

[76] *Miller v Scorey* [1996] 1 WLR 1122 at 1133; *Shlaimoun v Mining Technologies International Inc* [2011] EWHC 3278 (QB); [2012] 1 WLR 1276; *The ECU Group Plc v HSBC Bank Plc* [2018] EWHC 3045 (Comm); *Lakatamia Shipping Co Ltd v Su* [2020] EWHC 3201 (Comm); [2021] 1 WLR 1097.

[77] *The ECU Group Plc v HSBC Bank Plc* [2018] EWHC 3045 (Comm) at [3].

2. Article 6 of the European Convention on Human Rights does not provide for the right to an interpreter. The furthest it goes is to accept that in some instances access to an interpreter may be required for a trial to be fair.[78] The same approach is taken under the CPR, where the court has a wide discretion to require provision of an interpreter where that is necessary to secure a properly effective adversarial process.[79] Rule 10(3) codifies this approach to ensure that where an interpreter is needed to render a trial fair, and thus provide effective access and procedural equality, the court shall appoint one. Again, this also promotes adjudicative accuracy as it enables the court to have relevant evidence put before it, while also helping the parties present their evidence and test such evidence effectively, ie it also helps secure an effective adversarial process.
3. Rule 10(4) gives effect to the purposive principle, and specifically the proportionality principle by enabling the court to restrict or limit evidence translation where it would otherwise adversely affect dispute and trial management. This may form the basis of the court requiring translation or interpretation be provided by the court digitally, ie through use of court-based AI.
4. Parties who require translation or interpretation to prosecute or defend proceedings effectively should not be penalised, nor should the opposing party. Such an approach would run counter to the general access principle. Rule 10(5) provides that any translation or interpretation costs should be costs in the proceedings. They will therefore be borne by the losing party as tariff costs.[80] This ensures that cost is allocated according to the substantive merits of the dispute.

# SECTION 3: DOCUMENTARY EVIDENCE

## RULE 12.—PRESERVATION OF DOCUMENTARY EVIDENCE

**(1) Parties, and persons who are reasonably likely to be parties to proceedings, shall take reasonable steps to secure the preservation of documents and, where necessary, copies of documents that are in their control and which are likely to be relevant to a matter in dispute in proceedings.**
**(2) A party's lawyer must take all reasonable steps to secure the preservation of documents. This includes taking steps to ensure compliance by the party instructing them with their duty to preserve documents.**
**(3) Non-compliance with the duty to preserve documents may be punishable by proceedings for contempt of court.**
**(4) A document is any record, physical, electronic, or digital, that contains information. A copy of a document is anything in which, directly or indirectly, information from a document has been replicated or otherwise recorded.**

*Sources: ALI/UNIDROIT Principles, principle 16.1; ELI-UNIDROIT Model Rules, r 95; CPR r 31.4 PD31B paras 1, 5(3), 7, PD57AD paras 3, 4; Civil Evidence Act 1995, s 13.*

[78] *Sahar Shuker v Inspecs Limited* [2022] EWHC 2668 (Ch); Part 1, r 15.
[79] *Re Trepca Mines Ltd* [1960] 1 WLR 24; *Re Fuld* [1965] 1 WLR 1336 at 1340–1341; *Citibank NA v Ercole Ltd* [2001] EWCA Civ 1562 at [20]. The discretion also applies to provision of an interpreter to enable a party to understand proceedings and to give their evidence or submissions.
[80] *Santiago v Motor Insurers' Bureau* [2023] EWCA Civ 838.

## COMMENTARY

1. This rule places a duty on parties, persons who are likely to be parties to proceedings, and their lawyers to take active steps to preserve documents and copies of documents that are likely to be relevant to proceedings.[81] This duty is of fundamental importance. Access to documentary evidence is, in many cases, essential if parties are to properly understand the nature and strength of claims or defences, and support them at trial. It is thus an essential element in the promotion of consensual settlement as well as accurate adjudication and an important pre-requisite of a fair process and the achievement of a fair resolution.
2. The duty to preserve documents applies to those documents and copies that are in an individual's control. Control is a question of fact. It does not require a party to have possession of a document or a right to possession of one held by a third party.[82]
3. The definition of document and copy is derived from CPR r 31.4, which in turn replicates statutory definitions set out in, for instance, the Civil Evidence Act 1995. A document as a medium within which information is contained[83] and which may be in any form; it thus encompasses electronic documents. It covers information contained in audio and video recordings, emails, text messages, databases, floppy disks, hard drives, flash drives, the blockchain, metadata,[84] and so on.
4. A party's lawyer's duty goes further than the party's duty to preserve. They are also required to take necessary steps, at the earliest possible opportunity, to ensure that their client understands the nature of the party's duty and complies with it.[85] This is particularly important where the client is unfamiliar with proceedings in England and Wales. Given the difference in approach between such proceedings and, for instance, proceedings in civil law jurisdictions in Europe where documentary evidence is subject to markedly different approaches to those in England and Wales, the need to take such steps cannot be underestimated.[86]
5. Non-compliance with this rule, as an interference with the proper administration of justice, may result in the non-compliant party or lawyer being held in contempt of court.
6. On the court's power to issue, and a party's ability to apply for, orders requiring the preservation of documents, see Part 13, section 2.

## RULE 13.—PRE-ISSUE DOCUMENTARY DISCLOSURE

**(1) The court may order on application by a party to potential proceedings the identification of specified documents and the provision of those documents or copies to that party. An application must be supported by evidence. The court may make an order where**

[81] *Infabrics Ltd v Jaytex Ltd* [1985] FSR 75.

[82] *North Shore Ventures Ltd v Anstead Holdings Inc* [2012] EWCA Civ 11 at [40].

[83] *Hill v The King* [1945] KB 329 at 334.

[84] *Tinkler v Stobart Group Ltd* [2021] EWHC 3035 (Ch) at [65]–[66].

[85] *Rockwell Machine Tool Co Ltd v EP Barrus (Concessionaires) Ltd* [1968] 2 All ER 98.

[86] O Chase, H Hershkoff, L Silberman, J Sorabji, R Stürner, Y Taniguchi, and V Varano, *Civil Litigation in Comparative Context* (West Academic, 2017), chap 5; *Provimi France SAS v Stour Bay Co Ltd* [2022] EWHC 218 (Comm) at [32]–[33].

**(a) the applicant and respondent to the application are likely to be parties in potential proceedings that have a real prospect of success;**
**(b) the documents subject to the application would, if proceedings had commenced, come within the scope of Initial Disclosure;**
**(c) pre-issue disclosure is desirable as it would further the purposive principle, promote potential settlement, and would save costs; and**
**(d) the order is justified by reference to the nature of the potential dispute, the clarity and identification of the issues in the potential dispute, the nature of the documents, compliance with pre-action dispute management, and the extent to which the applicant is able to establish the claim or defence without the order being made.**

**(2) Where the application is granted and a document is no longer in the control of a respondent, the respondent must inform the applicant of that fact and explain what happened to it.**

*Sources: ELI-UNIDROIT Model Rules, r 101; CPR r 31.16; Senior Courts Act 1981, s 33; County Courts Act 1984, s 52.*

## COMMENTARY

1. This rule restates CPR r 31.16 and its approach to pre-issue disclosure. While it applies to private and public law disputes, in practice, it is rare for such an order to be made in support of the latter.[87] The power to order such disclosure is a statute-based exception to the general rule that the court's jurisdiction commences when proceedings themselves commence.[88] It is maintained here as part of the wider pre-action jurisdiction provided in Part 5. It is a power that can only be used pre-action.[89]
2. The jurisdiction to order pre-issue disclosure was introduced in 1969, at which time it was limited to potential proceedings that concerned personal injury or death.[90] Since 1999 it has applied to all types of dispute.[91] The reason for this was, and remains, the utility of pre-issue disclosure to promote effective co-operation between parties during the pre-action phase of a dispute and to enable them to better understand the merits of their, and their opponent's, positions as a means to promote pre-issue settlement.[92] By promoting pre-issue settlement the jurisdiction is an important mechanism through which both individual and systemic proportionality can be promoted.
3. There is, however, scope for the jurisdiction to be misused. Were courts to adopt a liberal approach to the grant of orders for pre-issue disclosure they could be used by parties to engage in 'fishing expeditions', ie to engage potential defendants in costly disclosure exercises as a means to ascertain if there was an arguable claim

[87] *British Union for the Abolition of Vivisection (BUAV) v Secretary of State for the Home Department* [2014] EWHC 43 (Admin); [2014] ACD 69 at [32]–[34].

[88] Senior Courts Act 1981, s 33; County Courts Act 1984, s 52; *Snowstar Shipping Co Ltd v Graig Shipping Plc* [2003] EWHC 1367 (Comm) at [35]; *Hutchison 3G UK Ltd v O2 (UK) Ltd* [2008] EWHC 55 (Comm) at [40].

[89] *Personal Management Solutions Ltd v Gee 7 Group Wealth Ltd* [2015] EWHC 3859 (Ch); [2016] 1 WLR 2132 at [14]–[21].

[90] Administration of Justice Act 1969, s 21(1).

[91] Civil Procedure Act 1997, s 8.

[92] H Woolf (1996) at 127.

against them. They could also be used to harass potential defendants.[93] This problem was minimised under the CPR through the development of a series of threshold, jurisdictional, tests and, if they are satisfied, through the court retaining a discretion whether to grant the order. It was further minimised by requiring an applicant to support their application with cogent evidence.[94]

4. The jurisdictional tests are codified in rule 13(1)(a)–(c).[95] Assuming they are satisfied the court must then consider whether to exercise its discretion to grant the order. Non-exhaustive criteria, again drawn from the authorities, are codified in rule 13(1)(d).[96] The discretion is the most important aspect of the overall approach. The jurisdictional tests set a low threshold. The requirement, where the discretion is concerned, that the court consider the nature of the potential proceedings heightens the bar that must be satisfied, and does so in a flexible way. It ensures that, generally, the normal rule concerning disclosure will be observed, ie that it is to be ordered once proceedings have commenced. This is particularly the case in contract or commercial disputes, where pre-issue disclosure is rare. In other circumstances, such as disputes relating to personal injury, pre-issue access to medical records is more readily available under this discretionary power. In the latter cases, such materials are generally going to be only in the control of potential defendants. Thus, there is a greater necessity for potential claimants to have pre-issue access to them to assess their potential claim.[97]
5. Where a party subject to an order for pre-issue disclosure no longer has control of a document, they must inform the applicant of that fact and explain what happened to it.[98] The practical benefit of this requirement is that, where the document is now under the control of another party or non-party, it may enable the applicant to take steps to secure the document from the person who has control over it (rule 16).

## RULE 14.—INITIAL DISCLOSURE OF DOCUMENTARY EVIDENCE

**(1) Parties should identify, and where they have not already been exchanged during pre-action dispute management, provide other parties, as Initial Disclosure, a list of documents that support their claim or defence and the key documents, which**
**(a) they intend to rely upon in proceedings; and**
**(b) are necessary to understand the nature of their claim or defence.**
**(2) Initial Disclosure shall be effected by a party annexing documents to their first case statement.**

93 H Woolf (1996) at 127.

94 CPR r 31.16(2).

95 *Black v Sumitomo* [2001] EWCA Civ 1819; [2002] 1 WLR 1562 at [71]–[73]; *Assetco Plc v Grant Thornton UK LLP* [2013] EWHC 1215 (Comm) at [17]; *Carillion Plc v KPMG LLP* [2020] EWHC 1416 (Comm) at [66]; *Bermuda International Securities Ltd v KPMG* [2001] EWCA Civ 269; [2001] Lloyd's Rep PN 392 at [26].

96 *Black v Sumitomo* [2001] EWCA Civ 1819; [2002] 1 WLR 1562 at [88].

97 *Black v Sumitomo* [2001] EWCA Civ 1819; [2002] 1 WLR 1562 at [83]; *Phoenix Natural Gas Ltd v British gas Trading Ltd* [2004] EWHC 451 (Comm) at [2]; *Hands v Morrison Construction Services Ltd* [2006] EWHC 2018 (Ch) at [38]; *Assetco Plc v Grant Thornton UK LLP* [2013] EWHC 1215 (Comm) at [17]; *Carillion Plc v KPMG LLP* [2020] EWHC 1416 (Comm) at [15].

98 CPR r 31.16(5).

**(3) Any subsequent identification, and/or provision, of documents shall be governed by the rules concerning Subsequent Disclosure.**

**(4) Parties may agree to dispense with or limit Initial Disclosure. Where agreement cannot be reached a party may also apply to the court for an order dispensing with, limiting, or restricting Initial Disclosure. The court may grant such an order where Initial Disclosure would be disproportionate.**

**(5) Disclosure of documents in low value proceedings is limited to Initial Disclosure only.**

*Sources: ALI/UNIDROIT Principles, principle 16.2; ALI/UNIDROIT Reporters' Study, rr 21, 22; ELI-UNIDROIT Model Rules, rr 94, 101, 102; CPR PD27, Appendix B, CPR Pt 31, CPR PD57AD.*

## COMMENTARY

1. The process for documentary disclosure has proved to be problematic since it became available generally in English and Welsh civil procedure following the Judicature Act reforms. Its role is to ensure that all relevant and necessary documentary evidence is placed in the hands of parties to litigation. In that way it not only gives effect to the procedural equality and adversariality principles, but most significantly to the accuracy principle.[99] To facilitate adjudicative accuracy, discovery was, historically, not limited by reference to, for instance, the cost and time it generated. On the contrary, following *Compagnie Financiere du Pacifique v Peruvian Guano Company* (1882), it was '*virtually unlimited*' in its scope.[100] From the RSC's introduction and, notwithstanding attempts to limit disclosure (as it became known in 1999) consistently with the economy, efficiency, and proportionality principles under the CPR, it was a process that generated excess litigation cost and delay due to this lack of effective control.[101] As a consequence it was a major factor undermining effective access to justice.
2. The position concerning disclosure reached under the CPR is one that provides three separate regimes: limited disclosure in small claims, so that parties only disclose documents they intend to rely upon to support their claim or defence;[102] a range of disclosure options otherwise applicable generally;[103] and a specialist disclosure regime applicable to proceedings in the Business and Property Courts,[104] which is specifically intended to ensure that disclosure is proportionate.[105] That this last approach is limited to those courts and that it differs from the generally applicable regime is problematic. There is no good principled reason to depart from a trans-substantive approach, not least where it is one that promotes procedural proportionality.

99 A point stressed in connection with the US Federal Rules of Civil Procedure but equally applicable to the approach in England and Wales, W Brazil, 'The Adversary Character of Civil Discovery' (1978) 31 Vand LR 1296; *Tweed v Parades Commission for Northern Ireland* [2006] UKHL 53; [2007] 1 AC 650 at [2].

100 *Compagnie Financiere du Pacifique v Peruvian Guano Company* (1882) 11 QBD 55; H Woolf (1995) at 167.

101 H Woolf (1995) at 8, 165–166; R Aikens et al (2007) at 58 and following; R Jackson (May 2009) Vol II, chap 41.

102 CPR PD27A, Appendix B.

103 CPR Pt 31.

104 CPR PD57AD.

105 *UTB LLC v Sheffield United Ltd* [2019] EWHC 914 (Ch); [2019] 3 All ER 698 at [75].

3. This rule and rule 15 adapt the approach taken in the CPR to small claims and to proceedings in the Business and Property Courts. It thus does not adopt the generally applicable approach taken in CPR Pt 31. This is intended to avoid what Andrews identified as the three ignoble functions of the disclosure process: the facilitation of profit-seeking by lawyers; the promotion of delay by parties who seek to avoid the provision of documentary evidence to other parties; and, the creation of a disincentive to litigate (or the promotion of under-settlement) of document heavy cases.[106] It is also intended to generalise the benefits of the Business and Property Courts' approach.
4. Initial Disclosure only seeks to give effect to the positive functions of the disclosure process. It aims to secure a fair balance between disclosure's primary purpose, the promotion of adjudicative accuracy through bringing to light relevant evidence,[107] and the need to secure a cost-effective, efficient, and proportionate process. Equally, it is intended to promote procedural equality and due notice through enabling all parties to have equal access to evidence that is in their possession. Consequently, it promotes consensual settlement. Too little disclosure can adversely affect these latter principles, just as too much disclosure or too great a delay in effecting disclosure can generate disproportionate cost and delay, while undermining adjudicative accuracy and effective enforcement.[108]
5. To give effect to disclosure's various positive functions, the general rule for all proceedings, except those classified as low value proceedings, is that Initial Disclosure must be effected by parties annexing documents that they intend to rely upon to their case statements. Subsequently they may also apply for Subsequent Disclosure. To maintain proportionality, low value proceedings are limited to Initial Disclosure.
6. Given that the majority of parties will already have taken part in the pre-action dispute management process, Initial Disclosure ought not to be either time-consuming or costly. Documents ought already to have been identified and may have been exchanged. Where it is necessary, it will be limited not least to promote economy and proportionality.[109] Hence it will be limited to only those key documents a party intends to rely upon and which are necessary to understand the nature of their claim or defence.[110]
7. Initial Disclosure may be dispensed with entirely or limited by party agreement consistently with party autonomy[111] and proportionality. Parties should particularly consider this when determining whether and how to narrow the issues in dispute.

[106] N Andrews, *English Civil Procedure: Fundamentals of the New Civil Justice System* (OUP, 2003) at 597.

[107] J Jacob, *The Fabric of English Civil Justice* (Stevens & Sons, 1987) at 93.

[108] N Andrews (2003) at 597.

[109] *Qatar v Banque Havilland SA* [2020] EWHC 1248 (Comm) at [16]; *Patisserie Holdings Plc (In Liquidation) v Grant Thornton UK LLP* [2021] EWHC 3022 (Comm) at [30].

[110] CPR PD57AD, para 5; *Breitenbach v Canaccord Genuity Financial Planning Ltd* [2020] EWHC 1355 (Ch).

[111] CPR PD 31, para 1.4.

They may properly do so where evidence has been disclosed during pre-action dispute management.

## RULE 15.—SUBSEQUENT DISCLOSURE OF DOCUMENTARY EVIDENCE

**(1) Subsequent Disclosure is the provision of any documents by a party following either Initial Disclosure or an agreement or order limiting or dispensing with Initial Disclosure. This includes the provision of documents following any amendment to a case statement. It shall not take place until after the closure of case statements.**

**(2) The scope of Subsequent Disclosure shall be no more than necessary to secure compliance with the purposive principle. It must therefore be no more than proportionate.**

**(3) In considering whether Subsequent Disclosure is necessary and no more than proportionate, the court shall take into account all the circumstances including**

**(a) the nature and complexity of the issues;**

**(b) the importance of the case, including any non-monetary relief sought;**

**(c) the number and likelihood of documents existing that have probative value;**

**(d) the ease and expense of searching for and retrieval of each document;**

**(e) the financial position of each party;**

**(f) the need to ensure the case is dealt with economically and efficiently; and**

**(g) the interests of parties to other proceedings in securing a fair share of the court's time and resources.**

**(4) Parties should, initially, seek to agree the scope of Subsequent Disclosure, consistently with the factors identified in sub-rule (3), by agreeing a Disclosure Plan. Where they cannot agree a Disclosure Plan or otherwise need guidance in respect of it, they should seek the court's guidance.**

**(5) The Disclosure Plan should identify whether the provision of documents is to be limited to specific types or categories of documents, including being limited to documents to be relied upon and/or which are adverse to a party. It should also specify if it encompasses documents that may lead to a direct or indirect train of inquiry, which is likely to result in the identification of documents that may be relied upon and/or which are adverse to a party.**

**(6) The Disclosure Plan should also identify whether, and if so to what extent, the provision of documents is limited to specific documents, or categories of documents, relating to specific issues.**

**(7) The Disclosure Plan should also make provision, where relevant, for the provision of documents to be carried out at specific times during the proceedings.**

**(8) Where parties cannot agree a Disclosure Plan having sought the court's guidance, any party may seek an order for Subsequent Disclosure.**

**(9) An order for Subsequent Disclosure shall contain such matters as would otherwise be in a Disclosure Plan. Only exceptionally, where justified by the circumstances of particular proceedings, will such an order include provision for the provision of train of inquiry documents.**

*Sources: ELI-UNIDROIT Model Rules, rr 101, 102; CPR PD57AD.*

## COMMENTARY

1. Subsequent Disclosure is based on Extended Disclosure, which is provided for in CPR PD57AD.[112] As with Initial Disclosure, consistently with party autonomy, it may be limited or dispensed with by the parties. Unlike with Initial Disclosure this is achieved by the fact that Subsequent Disclosure requires an active choice by the parties, ie they can choose to dispense with it by taking no steps to secure it. It is also subject to limit as it requires parties to co-operate with each other to identify documents that are to fall within its scope and to then draw up a plan setting out how it is to be effected.
2. The basic premise of Subsequent Disclosure is that it should be targeted. Its scope is limited by what is necessary to secure a just resolution of the proceedings. This will require it to be focused on what is necessary to determine the key issues in the dispute. It also requires disclosure to be both proportionate to the individual dispute and generally. The parties when considering Subsequent Disclosure, and devising their Disclosure Plan, must therefore have in the forefront of their minds the need to ensure that documents subject to such an order are both necessary and proportionate. The court must ensure that that is the case. To achieve this when considering whether to grant an order for Subsequent Disclosure the court must consider all the circumstances, including those set out at rule 15(3). Those factors are based on the factors to be considered for an order for Extended Disclosure under PD57AD, para 6.4. They are also to be taken into consideration by the parties in devising their Disclosure Plan.
3. Different approaches can be taken to ensure Subsequent Disclosure is necessary and proportionate. The parties may, for instance, be able to reach an appropriate Disclosure Plan without reference to the court. They may, however, need to seek the court's advice. The court is thus intended to play a significantly more active role in managing the substance of the proceedings than was permissible under the RSC or the CPR prior to the introduction of CPR PD57AD. It is to do so by working with the parties, advising them, and offering suggestions as to how they can formulate an effective plan that it can then approve. This is to be a co-operative process. Judicial continuity is essential if this is to work effectively: the judge offering guidance and then approving the Disclosure Plan will need to be one who is familiar with the proceedings and thus best placed to understand the issues and offer constructive comment on draft plans.[113]
4. Disclosure plans may provide for different approaches to be taken to disclosure by different parties. A claimant, for instance, may be required to disclose a wider range of documents than a defendant, and vice versa. Disclosure may be ordered to take place in stages. An issue-based approach may be taken. Exceptionally, train of inquiry disclosure may be ordered, although even then it must be limited by reference to proportionality. The greater the extent of Subsequent Disclosure the stronger the justification will be needed to demonstrate it is necessary, and the greater the prospect will be that it will be disproportionate. The key factor with this, as with Initial Disclosure, is to ensure that the disclosure process is kept within bounds that promote rather than undermine its positive functions and do not give rise to the negative consequences that disclosure created historically.

[112] CPR PD57AD, para 6.

[113] Part 11, r 14.

## RULE 16.—DISCLOSURE OF DOCUMENTARY EVIDENCE BY NON-PARTIES

**(1) A party may apply for an order requiring a non-party to provide them with specified documents. An application must be supported by evidence.**

**(2) The court may, exceptionally, make such an order. It may do so where**

**(a) the documents are extant and relevant to the applicant's claim or defence;**

**(b) the documents may well support the applicant's case or be adverse to the case of another party;**

**(c) provision of the documents to the applicant will, in all the circumstances, give effect to the purposive principle and would not harm the public interest.**

**(3) The court must apply the test in sub-rule 2(a)–(c) in respect of each document specified in the application.**

*Sources: CPR r 31.17; Bankers' Books Evidence Act 1879; Evidence (Proceedings in other Jurisdictions) Act 1975; Senior Courts Act 1981, s 34; County Courts Act 1984, s 53.*

## COMMENTARY

1. This rule restates CPR r 31.17. It enables parties to apply for an order requiring a non-party to provide them with specific documents in their control. The application cannot therefore be wide-ranging or general. It must particularly respect the non-party's right to property or to privacy.[114] Due to fact that such orders tend to be intrusive, the court will only exercise its discretion exceptionally.[115] Where disclosure is ordered, it may be limited to disclosure to the applicant's lawyers, medical, or other professional advisers.[116]

2. Rule 16(2)(a)–(c) codifies the approach under CPR r 31.17 taken by the authorities. It thus requires the applicant to demonstrate that the documents sought are extant and are relevant to their claim. Relevance is determined by: reference to the case statements in the proceedings;[117] whether they support the applicant's case or are adverse to another parties' case;[118] and, whether it is necessary to give effect to the purposive principle. In assessing whether an order would further the purposive principle, and save cost, time, and promote proportionality, the court shall consider all the circumstances.[119]

3. An application must be supported by evidence. This ensures the court is in an appropriate position to determine whether the tests of relevance, necessity, and fairness have been made out.[120] The tests of relevance, necessity, and fairness must be applied to each document specified in the application. This minimises the intrusion into non-party's rights.[121]

[114] *Flood v Times Newspapers Ltd* [2009] EWHC 411 (QB); [2009] EMLR 18 at [29].

[115] *Frankson v Secretary of State for the Home Department* [2003] EWCA Civ 655; [2003] 1 WLR 1952 at [10].

[116] Senior Courts Act 1981, s 34(2)(b); County Courts Act 1984, s 53(2)(b).

[117] *American Home Products Corpn v Novartis Pharmaceuticals UK Ltd* [2001] FSR 784; *Flood v Times Newspapers Ltd* [2009] EWHC 411 (QB); [2009] EMLR 18 at [36].

[118] *Three Rivers DC v Bank of England (No 4)* [2002] EWCA Civ 1182; [2003] 1 WLR 210.

[119] *Sarayiah v Royal & Sun Alliance Plc* [2018] EWHC 3437 (Ch) at [56].

[120] *Commissioner of Police of the Metropolis v The Times Newspapers Ltd* [2011] EWHC 1566 (QB) at [29]–[30].

[121] *Three Rivers DC v Bank of England (No 4)* [2002] EWCA Civ 1182; [2003] 1 WLR 210.

# SECTION 4: WITNESS EVIDENCE

## RULE 17.—WITNESS EVIDENCE

**A party may rely on the evidence of witnesses of fact in proceedings. Witness evidence, whether oral or written, must be given on oath or affirmation.**

*Sources: ALI/UNIDROIT Principles, principle 16.1; ALI/UNIDROIT Reporters' Study, r 25.4; ELI-UNIDROIT Model Rules, r 114.*

## COMMENTARY

1. Parties may adduce admissible evidence from witnesses of fact to support their claims and defences. Such evidence may be given orally or via witness statement. A fact concerns the state of the world, eg whether or not a defendant actually carried out an act; whether a car was being driven at 30 mph; whether a vendor knew of a defect in the product they sold; and so on.[122] Witnesses of fact cannot give opinion evidence.[123]
2. Generally, witnesses of fact give evidence as to what they observed or of which they are otherwise aware. They must give their evidence on either oath or affirmation.[124] This requirement emphasises the importance of providing truthful evidence. It is intended to promote adjudicative accuracy. It also acts as a disincentive to give untruthful evidence, supportive as it is of proceedings for perjury and for proceedings for contempt of court where false evidence is given.[125]
3. In certain circumstances evidence of fact can only be given by an expert witness: rule 21(5).

## RULE 18.—PROVISION OF WITNESS EVIDENCE

**(1) Parties should provide each other and the court, at the earliest opportunity during pre-action or post-issue dispute management, information concerning the witnesses of fact whose evidence they intend to rely upon in proceedings. Information should identify the witness and the issues on which they are to give evidence.**
**(2) Parties are not entitled to the provision of witness evidence in advance of trial. Nor may they cross-examine a witness prior to trial, except where the court grants permission for a deposition to be taken.**
**(3) Witness evidence may be given by a written witness statement. Such a statement must be concise, confined to evidence concerning matters of fact in dispute of which the witness has personal knowledge, written in the witness's own words and in the language of the witness. It must be verified by a statement of truth signed by the witness, and accompanied by a certified translation where it is written in a foreign language. The witness must confirm that the statement is in their own words.**
**(4) Witness statements must not contain extracts from documents. They may refer, by list in an annex, to documents referred to in the statement.**

[122] H Hodge and M Malek (2021) at [1.41]–[1.42]; S Gross, 'Expert Evidence' (1991) Wis L Rev 1113 at 1126 and following.
[123] *Adams v Canon* (1621) Ley's KB Rep 68.
[124] Oaths Act 1978.
[125] Perjury Act 1911, s 1; Part 10, r 41.

**(5) Sanctions may be imposed for non-compliance with sub-rules (3) and (4).**

**(6) Where a witness statement is not verified by a statement of truth, the court may direct that it is inadmissible as evidence. Where a court does not direct that the witness statement is inadmissible, a party may rely upon it although the court may consider it to be less credible and of less weight than evidence verified by a statement of truth or, where given orally, on oath.**

**(7) If a party intends to call a witness to give evidence at trial, they must provide other parties with the witness's witness statement prior to trial, unless the court directs otherwise.**

**(8) Where permission to obtain a deposition is granted the witness's evidence shall be taken on oath before a judge, examiner of the court appointed by the Lord Chancellor, or other person authorised by the court. The witness may be cross-examined by any other party. A transcript or video-recording of the deposition shall be put in evidence at trial.**

**(9) Permission to obtain a deposition may be granted where**

**(a) a witness is within the jurisdiction and is unable to attend trial;**

**(b) the evidence is necessary for the just determination of a pre-trial hearing and the witness is unwilling to attend the hearing to give their evidence voluntarily; or**

**(c) the deposition is in support of proceedings taking place outside the jurisdiction.**

*Sources: ALI/UNIDROIT Principles, principle 16.4; ALI/UNIDROIT Reporters' Study, r 23; ELI-UNIDROIT Model Rules, rr 114, 115; CPR Pts 33, 34, PD32, PD57AC.*

## COMMENTARY

1. Witness evidence was historically given orally at trial.[126] Witness statements are now the main means through which witness evidence-in-chief is given. They were originally introduced in 1978 and were intended to provide a concise indication—as '*epitomes of evidence of fact*'[127]—of the evidence a witness was to give at trial. They were thus not intended to stand as the witness's evidence, but rather were originally to provide a degree of advance notice of the likely evidence. They were formalised in 1986 and now stand as the witness's evidence-in-chief at trial.[128] Advance notice was intended to assist the development of court-based case management, and to enable parties to more fully consider the merits of their respective cases. This was to render proceedings, and specifically trials, more economical and efficient, while also promoting pre-trial settlement.[129]

2. Since their introduction, the use of witness statements has confounded their original intention. They have grown in length and strayed beyond evidence on matters of fact, and have come, wrongly, to include opinion evidence and evidence on matters of law.[130] They have been repeatedly criticised for unnecessarily increasing the cost of proceedings. Both the Woolf and Jackson reforms sought to tackle

[126] J Jacob (1987) at 19–20, 163.

[127] Donaldson J made an order to that effect in *Philadelphia Manufacturers Mutual Insurance Co Ltd* (3 July 1978, unreported). The order was subsequently confirmed by Parker J in the same proceedings on 2 December 1978: A Colman, *The Practice and Procedure of the Commercial Court* (1983) at 62.

[128] RSC Ord 38, r 2A; CPR r 32.5(2); A Zuckerman (2021) at 1029; although see r 19.

[129] *Mercer v Chief Constable of the Lancashire Constabulary* [1991] 1 WLR 367 at 373.

[130] *JD Wetherspoon Plc v Harris* [2013] EWHC 1088 (Ch); [2013] 1 WLR 3296 at [38]–[41].

these problems. Both failed to do so.[131] Further reform was introduced in 2021 via CPR PD57AC. It provided a specialist regime for witness statements used in trials in the Business & Property Courts. There is, again, no principled reason why that reform should be targeted at specific proceedings. This rule generalises that specialist regime.

3. As with CPR PD57AC the intention behind this rule is to ensure that witness statements are tightly focused on factual issues and that they are written in the witness's own words; as a consequence they cannot be drafted with the assistance of artificial intelligence. The rationale here is to ensure that the process is economical and efficient. To ensure a culture of compliance develops in respect of this, the court should be astute to manage this aspect of the pre-trial process particularly closely. That would include imposing relevant sanctions on non-compliant parties, including striking out witness statements where there has been egregious non-compliance with procedural obligations.[132]
4. To ensure that a witness who is unable to provide a witness statement in either English, or where appropriate Welsh, gives their evidence in their own words, their witness statement must be provided in their own language. It cannot be translated for them, as that would raise a doubt as to whether the statement actually sets out their evidence. To enable the court, other parties, and the public to understand their evidence a certified translation must accompany the witness statement.[133]
5. Witness statements are required to be verified by a statement of truth, in that they mirror evidence given orally on oath.[134] Where one is not verified by a statement of truth, a party may still rely on it, subject to the court's discretion to direct that it is inadmissible. Should it be relied on, as it is not verified by a statement of truth, a court is likely to view it as less credible than a verified statement and place less weight on it. As, inevitably, the witness will not be present in court when an unverified statement is adduced, it is also likely to be considered to be less credible and of less weight as the witness will not be available for cross-examination.
6. Rules 18(7) and (8) make provision for depositions. Unlike depositions in the United States of America, which provide a general process for examining witnesses under oath prior to trial, this procedure is not generally available.[135] It is only used where a witness is unable to attend a trial hearing. It thus replicates the taking of evidence that would occur at a trial, ie it is carried out before an adjudicator and the witness gives both evidence-in-chief and is cross-examined. The written transcript of evidence or, as under this rule a video-recording of the deposition, is then put before the court at trial. The witness does not, as in the US, also give evidence at trial. Permission to obtain a deposition may only be granted in three circumstances, each of which is

[131] H Woolf (1996) at 176; R Jackson, *Review of Civil Litigation Costs: Final Report* (December 2009) at 375; Witness Evidence Working Group, *Report of The Witness Evidence Working Group—Factual Witness Evidence in Trials before the Business & Property Courts* (Judicial Office, 2019).

[132] *Curtiss v Zurich Insurance Plc* [2022] EWHC 1514 (TCC); *Mansion Place Ltd v Fox Industrial Services Ltd* [2021] EWHC 2747 (TCC) at [38]; *Blue Manchester Ltd v Bug-Alu Technic GmbH* [2021 EWHC 3095 (TCC).

[133] *Correia v Williams* [2022] EWHC 2824 (KB).

[134] Oaths Act 1978; Judicial College, *Equality Treatment Benchbook* (Judicial College, 2021), Appendix D.

[135] E Sunderland, 'Scope and Method of Discovery Before Trial' (1932–1933) 42 Yale LJ 863 at 874. A proposal to introduce the US approach was rejected by the Witness Evidence Working Group ( 2019) at [34].

intended to promote adjudicative accuracy. In the first instance, a deposition may be ordered where a witness is not able to attend a trial because they are unwell.[136] Secondly, and exceptionally, where a witness refuses to attend a pre-trial hearing and their evidence is necessary for the court to properly determine an application at that hearing the court may direct that a deposition be taken.[137] Depositions may also be taken in support of proceedings outside the jurisdiction.[138]

## RULE 19.—WITNESS EVIDENCE AT A HEARING

**(1) A party may rely on a witness statement at any hearing.**

**(2) Witness evidence whether at trial or otherwise will, generally, be given by written witness statement. Oral evidence in low or moderate value proceedings may be given where to do so is proportionate.**

**(3) The court may permit a witness to amplify matters set out in their witness statement orally at a hearing. It may also permit a witness to raise matters orally at a hearing that have arisen since the witness statement was prepared. It may only do so for good reason.**

**(4) If a witness gives evidence at trial, they may be subject to oral cross-examination by any other party and re-examination by the party on whose behalf they give evidence.**

**(5) The court may ask clarificatory questions of witnesses. In asking questions it may not act as an advocate for either party.**

**(6) Where a witness fails to attend a hearing where they were to give evidence, their witness statement may only be relied upon with the court's permission.**

**(7) Where a witness is unable to provide a witness statement, a party may with the court's permission rely upon a summary of their evidence. Permission may be granted where doing so will further the purposive principle and**

**(a) the party has been unable to obtain a witness statement;**

**(b) the witness's proposed evidence is relevant to an issue in the proceedings; and**

**(c) is adequate.**

**(8) The court may, on application of a party, order a witness to attend a hearing to give evidence or to produce specific documents at the hearing. Non-compliance with such an order may result in proceedings for committal for contempt of court.**

**(9) Exceptionally, the court may with the consent of the parties order the attendance of a witness, who is not to be called to give evidence by a party, to give evidence. The court may examine the witness and any party may cross-examine the witness.**

*Sources: ALI/UNIDROIT Principles, principle 16.4; ALI/UNIDROIT Reporters' Study, r 23; ELI-UNIDROIT Model Rules, rr 114, 115; CPR r 32.9, 34.2.*

## COMMENTARY

1. This rule supplements rule 18. It gives effect to a party's right to give evidence, as limited by the court's power to control evidence.

[136] *Re Bradbrook, ex parte Hawkins* (1889) 23 QBD 226.

[137] *Barratt & Shaw v Ashton* [2001] EWCA Civ 137; [2001] CR Rep 57; *Charman v Charman* [2005] EWCA Civ 1606; [2006] 1 WLR 1053.

[138] The Evidence (Proceedings in Other Jurisdictions) Act 1975.

2. Witness evidence, when given, should generally be given by witness statement. Oral evidence-in-chief is the exception. The move to written witness evidence is intended to improve hearing management. Pre-reading of such evidence by the court and all parties reduces the time spent on the provision of such evidence during a hearing.[139] It also enables parties to prepare more effectively for cross-examination, which again reduces the time and expense of hearings.[140] In low or moderate value proceedings, witness evidence need not to be given by witness statement where the time and expense of preparation of such statements may be disproportionate.
3. That witness evidence is to be given by witness statement does not entail that a witness may not raise matters for the first time orally at a hearing. The court retains a discretion, which is to be exercised only for a good reason, to permit a witness to amplify matters set out in their witness statement at a hearing or to raise matters that have arisen since it was made.[141] This narrow exception is intended to ensure that sufficient weight is given to the accuracy principle, notwithstanding the important role that witness statements play in promoting economy, efficiency, and proportionality.
4. Rule 19(4) gives effect to the adversariality principle.[142] It is of fundamental importance to any procedural system that aims to promote accuracy and a fair process. It is the basis on which parties may test the evidence presented by opposing parties and is thus one aspect of the minimum irreducible core of a fair trial.[143]
5. Where a witness fails to attend a hearing where they are to give evidence, and hence will not be available for cross-examination, their evidence may only be relied upon with the court's permission. Where permission is granted, the weight and credibility of the evidence will be a matter for the court to assess in the light of it not being subject to adversarial, forensic, scrutiny.
6. Rule 19(6) restates the general rule that the court under its inherent jurisdiction may also question witnesses. When doing so the court should ensure its questioning is clarificatory. It must take care not to descend into the arena and act, or give the impression that it is acting as an advocate for one of the parties and hence that it is no longer impartial. Nor should it carry out the conduct of the questioning in an improper, ie aggressive or hectoring, manner.[144]
7. Rules 19(7) enables a party to provide a summary of evidence that an intended witness is or was expected to give at a hearing. This rule applies to a situation where a party is to call a witness at trial or intends to summon them to give evidence, under rule 19(8), and they are unable to obtain a witness statement from them. Resort to a witness summary should only be made where a witness statement cannot be obtained because, for instance, an individual has been asked to act as a witness and has refused; hence a witness statement is obtainable. This sub-rule codifies the test for the grant of permission.[145] Evidence contained in a witness summary adduced

[139] Part 14, r 4.

[140] *Blue v Ashley* [2017] EWHC 1553 (Comm) at [13].

[141] CPR r 32.5(3).

[142] *Khouj v Acropolis Capital Partners Ltd* [2021] EWHC 1667 (Comm) at [45].

[143] *Tariq v The Home Office* [2011] UKSC 35; [2012] 1 AC 452 at [119] and [124]; *Al-Rawi v The Security Services* [2011] UKSC 34; [2012] 1 AC 531 at [89]–[90].

[144] *Yuill v Yuill* [1945] P 156; *Jones v National Coal Board* [1957] 2 QB 55; *Serafin v Malkiewicz* [2020] UKSC 23; [2020] 1 WLR 2455.

[145] *Otuo v Watch Tower Bible & Tract Society of Britain* [2019] EWHC 346 (QB); *Morley (t/a Morley Estates) v Royal Bank of Scotland Plc* [2019] EWHC 2865 (Ch).

at trial will, inevitably, be given little weight as it is neither verified by a statement of truth nor will have been tested during cross-examination.

8. Rule 19(8) restates CPR r 34.2, which itself replaced the *subpoena ad testificandum* and the *subpoena duces tecum*.[146] It provides the means to compel a witness's attendance at a hearing or the production of specific documents. The latter is not, however, to be used as a means to evade any limits on documentary disclosure.[147] Non-compliance with such orders may result in the individual against whom they are directed being held in contempt of court.[148] Where committal proceedings are concerned, the court may on its own initiative issue a witness summons to compel an individual to attend court to either give witness evidence or produce documents.[149]
9. Rule 19(9) enables the court to order the attendance of a witness on its own initiative. This marks an exception to the general rule that it is a matter for parties to adduce evidence. It is thus an exception to the adversariality principle and can be seen as a quasi-inquisitorial power. This power arises under the court's inherent jurisdiction. It is, however and again exceptionally, subject to consent of the parties.[150] It should only be exercised exceptionally given that it is primarily a matter for the parties to determine what evidence is to be adduced, and that it may result in the imposition of unnecessary cost and delay to any hearing.

## RULE 20.—THE COURT'S POWER TO ASSIST UNREPRESENTED PARTIES IN RESPECT OF WITNESS EVIDENCE

**(1) Where a party is not represented by a lawyer, the court may at a hearing identify issues on which that party may want to question witnesses.**
**(2) An unrepresented party is under no obligation to act on the court's identification of those issues.**
**(3) Where a party is not represented by a lawyer at a hearing where witness evidence is to be presented, the court may, consistently with the purposive principle and with the consent of the lawyerless party**
  **(a) to the extent it had not already done so, help the lawyerless party to identify the issues in respect of which they would like to question the witness. This must be done in the presence of all other parties;**
  **(b) ask the witness such questions in respect of any identified issues as the court sees fit consistently with the independence and impartiality principles.**
**(4) Where the court asks questions on behalf of a lawyerless party that does not preclude that party from asking further or additional questions.**
**(5) In asking questions the court is not cross-examining a witness on behalf of the lawyerless party nor does the asking of such questions preclude that party from cross-examining the witness.**

*Sources: CPR r 3.1A*

[146] *Re Howglen* [2001] 1 All ER 376 at 384.
[147] *South Tyneside Metropolitan Borough Council v Wickes Building Supplies Ltd* [2017] EWHC 2428 (Comm) at [23].
[148] *Tajik Aluminium Plant v Hydro Aluminium AS* [2005] EWCA Civ 1218; [2006] 1 WLR 767.
[149] *Yianni v Yianni* [1966] 1 WLR 120.
[150] *Coulson v Disborough* [1894] 2 QB 316; *Re Enoch & Zaretzky Bock & Co's Arbitration* [1910] 1 KB 327.

## COMMENTARY

1. This rule restates CPR r 3.1A(5). It complements rule 8. As with that rule it is intended to facilitate effective access to justice for lawyerless parties. While rule 8 aids identification of relevant evidence, this rule provides assistance during hearings through enabling the court to help a lawyerless party to identify issues on which they may wish to question witnesses. It also provides assistance by enabling the court to put questions to witnesses on behalf of that party. This will facilitate economy, efficiency, and proportionality. In the absence of court assistance, a lawyerless party might fail through no fault of their own to put questions to the other party or witnesses in a speedy or effective manner. Were that to occur hearings might take longer than necessary, thus adversely affecting the court's ability to properly manage its timetable contrary to the requirements of systemic proportionality.
2. In identifying issues and putting questions on a lawyerless party's behalf, the court must ensure that it does not descend into the arena and start to act, or give the impression that it is acting, as an advocate for that party. The court must therefore exercise this power so that it remains impartial and is seen to be so.[151] The court must be astute to ensure that it is providing no more than assistance, particularly when it puts questions on behalf of a lawyerless party. Putting questions is not cross-examination and the court must ensure that it does not cross-examine parties or witnesses when exercising the power under this rule.[152] Moreover, the fact that a court has put questions on behalf of a lawyerless party does not preclude that party putting questions themselves or cross-examining on their own behalf.

# SECTION 5: EXPERT EVIDENCE AND ASSESSORS

## RULE 21.—APPOINTMENT OF EXPERTS

**(1) The court may appoint an expert to provide opinion evidence or expert evidence of fact on any matter in dispute in proceedings. Parties may object to the appointment of a specific court-appointed expert on the basis of bias or the existence of a conflict of interest.**

**(2) A party, with the court's permission, may adduce evidence from an expert on any matter in dispute in proceedings. Permission may be granted where it would further the purposive principle.**

**(3) Where it would further the purposive principle, the court may direct that any expert evidence to be given shall be given by a single expert jointly instructed by the parties.**

**(4) Any application for permission should be made at the earliest reasonable time. The court may, exceptionally, grant permission at a later stage of proceedings.**

**(5) An expert may be appointed by the court or given permission to adduce evidence where the provision of expert evidence is proportionate and**

**(a) their evidence is within a recognised area of knowledge, which is governed by recognised rules and standards, relevant to the matter in dispute;**

[151] *Drysdale v Department of Transport (Maritime and Coastguard Agency)* [2014] EWCA Civ 1083; [2014] CP Rep 43 at [49].

[152] *Rea v Rea* [2022] EWCA Civ 195 at [76].

**(b) the issue on which they are to give evidence is one that can only properly be provided by an individual with specialist knowledge or experience within the recognised area of knowledge; and**

**(c) it is necessary for the court to receive such evidence on the relevant matter in dispute in order for it to determine the matter or, if it is not necessary, it would reasonably assist the court in determining the matter.**

**(6) In determining whether expert evidence would reasonably assist the court in determining a matter, the court should take account of the nature and value of the claim, any cost to the parties arising from such evidence, any effect on the time taken to final resolution if permission is granted, the likely effect on the judgment if permission is granted, and proportionality.**

*Sources: ALI/UNIDROIT Principles, principle 16.4; ALI/UNIDROIT Reporters' Study, r 26; ELI-UNIDROIT Model Rules, rr 119, 120; CPR Pt 35; RSC Ord 40.*

## COMMENTARY

1. Generally, opinion evidence may not be adduced in English and Welsh civil proceedings.[153] Evidence ought generally to be confined to evidence of fact. It is, however, well-established that opinion evidence on matters concerning, for instance, scientific or technical matters may be submitted.[154] This has been the case since at least the 16th century.[155] The rationale for this was aptly summarised by Jolowicz when he noted that the justice system cannot operate on the assumption that '*judges ... have knowledge of every branch of science, of every art and of the mysteries of every profession*'.[156]
2. Evidence of fact may also come within the ambit of expert evidence. It will do so where only an expert is capable of giving it. This may include evidence that explains technical subjects or terminology or matters that are observable, comprehensible, or only capable of being described by experts, eg observations taken during clinical trials or matters only observable using specialist scientific equipment.[157] Other areas where evidence of fact may be given by an expert under this rule are: evidence drawn from the expert's own knowledge, such as evidence of historical knowledge; an expert's summary of knowledge drawn from other experts' knowledge or knowledge generally within their field of expertise; or, evidence concerning foreign law.[158]
3. As with evidence generally, expert evidence may only be permitted with the court's permission, consistently with the purposive principle.[159] It will therefore be limited to what is reasonably necessary to determine issues in dispute and will be proportionate.[160] To promote effective dispute management applications to rely on expert evidence should be made as early as possible in the proceedings.

[153] *Kennedy v Cordia (Services) LLP (Scotland)* [2016] UKSC 6; [2016] 1 WLR 597.

[154] *Adams v Canon* (1621) Ley's KB Rep 68; *Griffiths v TUI UK Ltd* [2023] UKSC 48; [2023] 3 WLR 1204 at [36].

[155] *Buckley v Rice Thomas* (1554) 1 Plowden 118 at 124; *Folkes v Chadd* (1782) 3 Doug 157.

[156] J Jolowicz (2000) at 22.

[157] *Kennedy v Cordia (Services) LLP (Scotland)* [2016] UKSC 6; [2016] 1 WLR 597 at [41]–[44].

[158] *Declan Colgan Music Ltd v UMG Recordings, Inc* [2023] EWHC 4 (Ch) at [93] and [132].

[159] *Grobbelaar v Sun Newspapers*, The Times, 12 August 1999.

[160] *Re RBS (Rights Issue Litigation)* [2015] EWHC 3433 (Ch) at [11].

4. Expert evidence may be adduced either by an expert appointed by a party, by an expert appointed jointly by parties to proceedings, or by an expert appointed by the court. Normally, experts are appointed by parties individually, ie each party will appoint their own expert to give evidence. The court will then have to determine which, if any, expert's evidence is to be preferred.[161]
5. Jointly instructed experts may be appointed in lower value proceedings to promote proportionality.[162] Care should be taken in appointing such experts, however, where the issue in question is particularly contentious or the area of expertise is one where there is a broad range of differing professional opinion. In such situations their appointment could pose a real risk to the court's adjudicative function.[163]
6. The power to appoint a court-appointed expert is a departure from the CPR. It reintroduces the power to do so that was previously set out in RSC Ord 40, but which was little used as it was broadly inconsistent with its more full-blooded commitment to party autonomy, adversarial process, and limited court responsibility for case management.[164] It is reintroduced here for three reasons. First, proceedings are no longer carried out consistently with the overarching approach taken under the RSC. Party autonomy is, particularly, more limited. Secondly, procedure now operates in an adversarial system consistently with the purposive principle (under the CPR, its overriding objective). And, thirdly, the court is now firmly established as having responsibility for the proper management of disputes. The reasons, such as they were, for the court's failure to use this power thus no longer exist. Positively, the benefit of a court-appointed expert has also long been recognised. Such an expert is less likely to succumb to personal bias and is likely to give careful, objective evidence that may promote settlement as much as it may promote adjudicative accuracy.[165] Given that there is nevertheless a risk that a court-appointed expert may be subject to personal bias or to a conflict of interest, a party may object to their appointment.
7. To ensure that expert evidence is only given when it is appropriate, an expert may only be appointed where their evidence relates to a recognised specialist area. Permissible opinion evidence is thus limited to areas of recognised expertise. It may also only be adduced where the individual to give the evidence is themselves an expert in that specialist area and their evidence is reasonably necessary for the court to determine a matter in dispute,[166] or it would reasonably assist the court in doing so.[167] Expert evidence cannot therefore be given by anybody or on any issue. Nor can it be given unless it will promote adjudicative accuracy. Rule 21(6) sets out a non-exhaustive list of factors to be considered when approaching the question whether to grant permission to adduce expert evidence.

[161] *Armstrong v First York* [2005] EWCA Civ 227; [2005] 1 WLR 2751.

[162] CPR r 35.7.

[163] *MP v Mid Kent Healthcare NHS Trust* [2001] EWCA Civ 1703; [2002] 1 WLR 210 at [14].

[164] T Bingham, *The Rule of Law* (Penguin, 2010) at 23.

[165] *Abbey Mortgages Plc v Key Surgeons Nationwide Ltd* [1996] 1 WLR 1534.

[166] Civil Evidence Act 1972, s 3(3); *Barings Plc (In Liquidation) v Coopers & Lybrand* [2001] Lloyd's Rep Bank 85 at [54]; *Liddell v Middleton* [1996] PIQR P36 at 43.

[167] *Re RBS (Rights Issue Litigation)* [2015] EWHC 3433 (Ch) at [13]–[14], [17]; *GM v Carmarthenshire County Council* [2018] EWFC 36; [2018] 3 FCR 170 at [14]; *British Airways Plc v Spencer* [2015] EWHC 2477 (Ch); [2015] Pens LR 519 at [68].

## RULE 22.—EXPERTS' DUTIES

**(1) A court or party-appointed expert owes a continuing and overriding duty to the court. That duty is to provide the court with**

**(a) objective, independent, impartial, and unbiased evidence that identifies its sources;**

**(b) evidence within their field of expertise and on the matter in dispute in respect of which they were instructed only;**

**(c) an explanation of any reservations or qualifications the expert may have concerning their evidence;**

**(d) information concerning any assistance the expert may have had in preparing their evidence, and from whom and what they had such assistance;**

**(e) evidence in a reasonable time following their appointment or the grant of permission to adduce evidence; and**

**(f) not to act as an advocate for any party.**

**(2) An expert must also inform the court and all parties at the earliest opportunity, as part of their overriding duty to the court, of any actual or potential conflicts of interest that exist or may arise in connection with the evidence they are to give.**

**(3) An expert may apply to the court for directions concerning how they comply with their overriding duty to the court in carrying out their instructions in the proceedings. Any such request and the court's response must be disclosed to the parties.**

**(4) Non-compliance with the overriding duty may result in the imposition of sanctions on a party instructing the expert and/or on the expert. Sanctions include: exclusion of the expert's evidence; adverse costs orders against the expert; referral to the expert's representative or regulatory body; proceedings for contempt of court; or referral for proceedings for perjury.**

*Sources: ALI/UNIDROIT Reporters' Study, rr 26.3; ELI-UNIDROIT Model Rules, r 122; CPR r 35.3; PD35 paras 3.2, 3.3.*

## COMMENTARY

1. Expert evidence is an exception to the general rule that witnesses are witnesses of fact. Unlike such witnesses, who will of necessity be limited in number, a party may—in principle—choose any available expert to give evidence on their behalf.
2. This freedom to instruct creates a potential problem: expert witness bias.[168] The reason for this, historically, was that experts were not fully independent of the parties. They would be chosen because they were more likely to support their instructing party's case.[169] If not explicitly or implicitly instructed because they would or were expected to support their instructing party's case, the risk always existed that once instructed and paid for they would identify with their instructing party and either consciously or subconsciously tailor their evidence to support them.[170] As Langbein put it, '*The more measured and impartial an expert is, the less likely he is to be used by either side*' and conversely, once instructed, '*the subtle pressure to join the team*'[171]

[168] S Gross, 'Expert Evidence' (1991) Wis L Rev 1113 at 1116.

[169] *The Tracy Peerage* (1843) 10 CL & F 154; 8 ER at 700; *Thorne v Worthing Skating Rink* (1877) 6 Ch D 415; *Abbey Mortgages Plc v Key Surgeons Nationwide Ltd* [1996] 1 WLR 1534; H Woolf (1995) at 182.

[170] *Lord Abinger v Ashton* (1873) 17 LR Eq 358 at 373–374; S Gross (1991) at 1139.

[171] J Langbein, 'German Advantage in Civil Procedure' (1985) 52 University of Chicago LR 823 at 835.

would be likely to lead an expert to identify with their instructing party and structure their evidence accordingly. That subtle pressure could be compounded where, as is not uncommon, an expert is instructed routinely by the same solicitors' firm or solicitor and works through issues with them and their clients in ways that a lay witness would not. Thus they are more likely over time to consider themselves as being a claimant expert or defendant expert or, more broadly, part of the solicitor's team.[172] At worst, the subtle pressure could lead to an expert becoming an advocate for the party instructing them.[173]

3. Dwyer has cogently argued that these problems can be summarised in two ways. First, that expert evidence is at risk of structural bias: '*... the expert genuinely holds his or her opinion in the case, which he or she has formed without subconscious error, and he or she is involved in the case because his or her opinion supports the case of his or her instructing party.*'[174] Secondly, that the expert is at risk of personal bias: they either have a personal animus to the opposing party or favours their instructing party, or both. This can arise either consciously or subconsciously.[175] Court-appointed experts, as they are not chosen or instructed by the parties are likely to be less susceptible to personal bias, albeit the risk of structural bias remains.[176] Moreover, where the only expert is a court-appointed one, a similar risk arises as it does for single-joint experts: that the court will only have before it an expert who suffers from structural bias. There is thus a risk with court-appointed experts (as there is for single-joint experts), where they are the only expert, that the court's ability to adjudicate accurately is impaired.

4. The common law and CPR both adopted approaches that sought to reduce both forms of bias. The former attempted to do this by imposing a series of duties on experts aimed at emphasising their independence, impartiality, and that the evidence should not be tainted by bias.[177] It particularly emphasised that experts' evidence should be objective and uninfluenced either by any personal feelings they may have concerning the parties or the perceived needs of those instructing them.[178] It also stressed that they should not act as advocates for the party instructing them.[179] The latter attempted to reduce both forms of bias by imposing an overriding duty to the court on experts.[180] Furthermore, by requiring experts to draw attention to any advice they had obtained in preparing their evidence,[181] to their assumptions, or any qualifications on their evidence, the CPR took additional steps to bring to light any potential structural bias.

5. To further promote impartiality and protect against bias, or at the least alert opposing parties and the court to the possibility of it, the common law further imposed a

[172] S Gross (1991) at 1138–1142.

[173] *The Ritz Hotel Casino Ltd v Mr Safa Abdulla al Geabury* [2015] EWHC 2294 (QB) at [98]–[103].

[174] D Dwyer, 'The Effective Management of Bias in Civil Expert Evidence' (2007) 26 CJQ 57 at 57 and following.

[175] D Dwyer, 'The Causes and Manifestations of Bias in Civil Expert Evidence' (2007) 26 CJQ 425.

[176] J Langbein (1985) at 836–840.

[177] *National Justice Compania Naviera SA v Prudential Assurance Co Ltd (The Ikarian Reefer)* [1993] 2 Lloyd's Rep 68 (Comm) at 81–82; *Kennedy v Cordia (Services) LLP* [2016] UKSC 6; [2016] 1 WLR 597 at [50].

[178] *Phillips v Symes (A Bankrupt) (Mental Capacity)* [2004] EWHC 1887 (Ch); *Re C (A Child) (Immunisation: Parental Rights)* [2003] EWCA Civ 1148; [2003] 2 FLR 1095.

[179] *Franks v Towse* [2001] EWCA Civ 9; [2002] RVR 15; *Stagecoach South Western Trains Ltd v Hind* [2014] EWHC 1891 (TCC); [2014] 3 EGLR 59 (TCC).

[180] CPR r 35.3; N Andrews, *The Three Paths to Justice* (Springer, 2012) at 82.

[181] *R v Pabon* [2018] EWCA Crim 420; [2018] Lloyd's Rep FC 258 (CACD) at [52].

continuing duty upon parties to give notice at the first possible opportunity of any actual or potential conflict of interest they may have. This would enable opposing parties to consider whether and how to challenge such evidence. It also enables the court to consider whether an expert in such circumstances should be permitted to give evidence and, if so, what credibility or weight should be attached to it given the conflict. It also, importantly, gives the party instructing the expert time to consider whether to instruct another expert; one whose evidence is not likely to be either excluded or given limited weight due to the conflict.[182] To give effect to this duty parties should ensure that the court is able to assess the question of conflict effectively. They must therefore ensure that sufficient evidence is put before the court, preferably at the earliest possible dispute management hearing, to determine the issue.[183]

6. The approaches taken at common law and under the CPR to reduce the potential for both personal and structural bias are not, however, unproblematic. It can be said that duties to the court cannot overcome the subtle pressure to join the team that flows from party-instruction of experts within an adversarial process. Independence and impartiality could, on this view, only genuinely be achieved through moving to an approach that only permits court-appointed experts.[184] Dwyer has also argued that the scope of the duties is not clear.[185] Lack of clarity thus undermines any potential positive effect that the duties could have. More broadly, it has been argued that the duties cannot deal effectively with structural bias, a problem that is arguably compounded where there is only one single jointly instructed expert or a court-appointed expert.
7. Notwithstanding those criticisms, this rule does not adopt Langbein's preferred approach to cure them, which is to adopt a court-appointed expert only approach. That would, as he acknowledges, require further fundamental changes in the civil justice system, not least the adoption of court-control over the fact-finding process and, subsequently, the introduction of a career judiciary. That new judiciary would need to be one which had greater numbers than at present given the necessary transfer of responsibility and workload from parties and their lawyers to the court. It would also place much greater weight on ensuring that single, court-appointed experts were both of a high standard and not subject to structural bias. There is no prospect of such structural changes to the judiciary or the transfer of fact-finding responsibility to the judiciary in England and Wales, not least due to the increased cost to the justice system that that would entail.
8. Nor does this rule accept that the clarity of the duties is questionable. The requirements to be objective, independent, impartial, and to ensure that evidence is not tainted by bias are not difficult to understand. Lawyers are well able to explain the nature of those duties to experts and, where necessary an expert can seek guidance from the court as to their application in any particular case. Understanding conflicts of interest is also a common feature of professional life in many fields, particularly those from which experts are drawn regularly, eg medical, and scientific experts. And, again, the nature of such conflicts can be explained properly by parties' lawyers. That the duties are supported by significant sanctions and also the potential for

[182] *Toth v Jarman* [2006] EWCA Civ 1028 at [20]; *EXP v Barker* [2015] EWHC 1289 (QB); *EXP v Barker* [2017] EWCA Civ 63; [2017] Med LR 121.

[183] *Helical Bar Plc v Armchair Passenger Transport Ltd* [2003] EWHC 367 (QB) at [29].

[184] J Langbein (1985).

[185] D Dwyer (2007) 26 CJQ 57; A Edis, 'Privilege and Immunity: Problems of Expert Evidence' (2007) 26 CJQ 40.

professional negligence proceedings to be brought against an expert who fails to act consistently with their duties to the standard expected of a reasonable expert, incentivises both compliance with and active steps by experts to ascertain the nature and scope of the duty to the court.[186]

9. Rule 22 thus codifies the approach taken under the common law and CPR. In doing so though, it accepts that the greatest focus of the duties is the reduction in personal bias. While, through requiring experts to explain their assumptions and qualifications, it does go some way to expose any potential structural bias, the duty to the court can only go so far to reduce it. The real means by which structural bias can be exposed is through the various application of: court-appointed experts in those cases that justify the expense and time of their appointment; party experts being required to meet and discuss their evidence prior to trial; the adversarial process at trial; and, particularly the use of concurrent evidence processes.

## RULE 23.—EXPERT REPORTS

**(1) Expert evidence shall, generally, be given by written report. The report must contain**

**(a) details of the expert's qualifications and experience;**

**(b) the expert's confirmation that the report is prepared for the court and that they understand and have complied with their overriding duty to the court;**

**(c) the expert's instructions in so far as they are material to the report;**

**(d) a summary of relevant facts;**

**(e) detail of all facts within the expert's own knowledge and any assumptions upon which their conclusions are based;**

**(f) detail of any experiments or other tests carried out by the expert or other individuals or processes, including the use of artificial intelligence, on their behalf in preparing their report, and details of any such individuals or processes;**

**(g) their conclusions, and any relevant qualifications on them, on the matters in dispute in respect of which they were given permission to provide evidence; and**

**(h) where there is a range of opinion, detail of that range of opinion.**

**(2) An expert's report must be verified by a statement of truth, which also confirms that the expert understands and has complied with their duty to the court. An unverified report cannot be relied upon in proceedings.**

**(3) A party given permission to adduce expert evidence by written report may only rely upon it if it is disclosed to other parties in proceedings. Any such written report must also be disclosed where a party is given permission, for good reason, to replace an expert who has been given permission to adduce evidence on their behalf with another expert.**

**(4) Where expert evidence is to be given by written report only, questions may be put to the expert by any party. Answers to those questions are deemed to form part of the expert's report. The court may impose sanctions on the expert and/or the party instructing them if the expert fails to provide answers either within a reasonable**

[186] *Phillips v Symes* [2004] EWHC 2330 (Ch); [2005] 1 WLR 2043 (adverse costs orders); *Pearce v Ove Arup* [2001] EWHC Ch 481 and *Meadow v General Medical Council* [2006] EWCA Civ 1390; [2007] QB 462 (report to professional body); *Hussein v William Hill Group* [2004] EWHC 208 (QB) (referral to Director of Public Prosecutions for consideration of perjury proceedings); *Jones v Kaney* [2011] UKSC 13; [2011] 2 AC 398, *Radia v Marks* [2022] EWHC 145 (QB); [2022] PNLR 12 (professional negligence liability).

**period of time or at all. Sanctions include the withdrawal of permission to adduce the expert's evidence.**

**(5) An expert may ask the court to provide them with directions concerning the carrying out of their duties as experts.**

**(6) Where multiple experts are to give evidence in the same field of expertise, the court may direct that, prior to finalising their reports, the experts discuss them with each other to identify any areas of agreement or disagreement they may have on the matters on which they are to give evidence.**

**(7) The court may direct that experts file a joint statement with the court setting out any matters, arising from their discussion, on which the experts agreed or disagreed. The experts' discussions concerning a joint statement are, however, subject to without-prejudice privilege.**

*Sources: CPR rr 35.5, 35.6, 35.10, 35.12, 35.13, 35.14; CPR PD 35, paras 3, 6, 9.*

## COMMENTARY

1. This rule consolidates a range of provisions contained within CPR Pt 35 and its Practice Direction concerning expert reports. It is not intended to diverge from the approach taken by them.
2. Written expert reports, which should be brief,[187] are the means by which experts provide the court with their opinion on matters within their expertise.[188] That they should be brief does not mean that they should not set out the expert's reasoning. They must do so if they are to enable their evidence to be tested effectively and for it to assist the court.[189] Reports may only be relied upon if disclosed in advance of a relevant hearing, ordinarily the trial hearing. The use and disclosure of reports is intended to promote not only effective dispute management, but also economy, efficiency and proportionality.[190] As they are the functional equivalent of oral evidence they must be verified by a modified statement of truth, which must also confirm that the expert has both understood and complied with their duty to the court.[191] This requirement is intended to promote rule compliance and minimise the prospect that the evidence will be tainted by personal or structural bias.
3. Where a party wishes to change expert, they may be permitted to do so for good reason. Permission may only be granted on condition that the original expert's report is, however, disclosed. This is to prevent expert-shopping, and the attendant costs that are incurred by it.[192] By reducing the scope for expert shopping, ie searching for a favourable expert, it helps reduce personal bias. The non-reliance sanction is intended to promote rule-compliance as a means to promote effective and cost and time-efficient dispute and, particularly, trial management.[193]

[187] *Harman (A Child) v East Kent Hospitals NHS Foundation Trust* [2015] EWHC 1662 (QB); [2015] PIQR Q4 at [32].

[188] *Pacific Biosciences of California, Inc v Oxford Nanopore Technologies Ltd* [2018] EWHC 806 (Ch) at [46].

[189] *Griffiths v TUI UK Ltd* [2023] UKSC 48; [2023] 3 WLR 1204 at [38]–[39].

[190] H Woolf (1996) at 37.

[191] CPR r 35.10(2).

[192] *Beck v Ministry of Defence* [2003] EWCA Civ 1043; [2005] 1 WLR 2206; *Vasiliou v Hajigeorgiou* [2005] EWCA Civ 236; [2005] 1 WLR 2195.

[193] H Woolf (1996) at 35 and 72; *Baron v Lovell* [1999] CPLR 630.

4. Rules 23(1)(a)–(h) are intended to promote compliance with experts' duties and ensure that parties and the court have sufficient information to understand and, where necessary, challenge an expert's report. Rule 23(1)(g) goes beyond the CPR. It acknowledges the possibility that in future experts may be assisted by the use of artificial intelligence in preparing their reports. This sub-rule ensures that such assistance is brought to the attention of the court and other parties and their experts.
5. Rule 23(4) focuses on clarifying and where necessary raising issues that could have been but were not dealt with in an expert's report.[194] Non-compliance by an expert with this sub-rule is particularly problematic as it undermines the adversarial process and the right to test their written evidence.
6. Experts may find themselves unsure as to how to comply with their duties when drafting their reports. They may also be unsure whether their instructions, either from the party instructing them or their lawyers, are consistent with their duties to the court. Moreover, they may have difficulty in complying with dispute management directions. To enable them to obtain clarity on such issues, and thus further rule compliance and the purposive principle, rule 23(5) enables them to request directions from the court on such matters (also see rule 22(3)).
7. Rules 23(6) and (7) focus on compliance with the accuracy and proportionality principles. They are intended to help experts identify matters on which they agree and disagree. This is intended to enable the real issues to be identified and dealt with.[195] They are not intended to provide a forum for cross-examination.[196] Any joint statement prepared must, consistently with the experts' duties to the court, be their own work and opinion. Parties must not therefore attempt to guide the drafting of any joint statement.[197] To promote candour during experts' discussions, their content is covered by without prejudice privilege.[198]

## RULE 24.—EXPERTS—ORAL EVIDENCE

**(1) The court may permit a court-appointed or party-appointed expert to give evidence orally at a hearing. The court may summon an expert to attend a hearing.**

**(2) Permission may be granted where oral evidence would further the purposive principle.**

**(3) Where, however, proceedings are classified as low value, permission to give oral evidence shall only be granted exceptionally and only if the proceedings cannot otherwise be resolved justly.**

**(4) Where more than one expert in the same area of expertise is given permission to give evidence orally, the court may order that they give their evidence concurrently through a party-led process.**

*Sources: ALI/UNIDROIT Reporters' Study, rr 26.2, 26.4; ELI-UNIDROIT Model Rules, r 124; CPR r 35.5, PD35 para 11.*

194 *Mutch v Allen* [2001] EWCA Civ 76; [2001] CP Rep 77.
195 *H v Lambeth, Southwark and Lewisham HA* [2001] EWCA Civ 1455; [2001] CP Rep 117.
196 *Aderounmu v Colvin* [2021] EWHC 2293 (QB).
197 *BDW Trading Ltd v Integral Geotechnique (Wales) Ltd* [2018] EWHC 1915 (TCC); [2019] TCLR 1 at [18].
198 CPR r 35.12(4).

## COMMENTARY

1. To promote proportionality, this rule together with rule 23 restates the position under the CPR, which limits the form in which expert evidence may be adduced.[199] While rule 23 sets out the general rule that it should be given by written report, this one provides that the court may give an expert permission to give evidence orally at a hearing. It may do so to further the purposive principle.[200] Where permission is granted, the court and parties must ensure that the oral evidence itself is proportionate. The court may also order an expert to attend a hearing to enable oral evidence to be given.[201]
2. The position is different in low value proceedings. Ordinarily, a written report only will be the most cost-effective and proportionate approach. Exceptionally, oral evidence may be given in such proceedings where that is necessary for the court to resolve the dispute justly.
3. This rule also makes provision for the court to direct that oral expert witness evidence be given concurrently. The facility to give concurrent evidence, colloquially known as hot-tubbing was introduced following the Jackson Costs reforms.[202] It is, however, long established in Australia and in international arbitration.[203] The essence of concurrent evidence is that rather than experts giving their evidence sequentially during a trial, they give their evidence at the same time after all the lay witness evidence has been given. Each of the parties' experts on a specific issue is sworn at the same time, and they then go on to give their evidence together. Starting with the claimant's expert, each expert should provide a brief summary of their evidence. After each has done so, they may be questioned by the other parties' experts. Once completed the experts summarise their points and can then be cross-examined by counsel. There are variations on this outline. The one adopted under the CPR following reforms in 2017 has the judge lead the experts through their evidence.[204]
4. Four distinct benefits are said to flow from the use of a concurrent evidence process. As Heerey put it, it enables experts to give evidence at a point during a trial when all the real issues have been identified and explored. Expert evidence can thus be narrowed to those issues. It also enables judges to hear the experts' evidence at the same time, ensuring that they do not view each expert's evidence at a temporal distance and after its basic, factual assumptions may have been qualified or displaced. It is also said to reduce the possibility that each expert will identify with the party instructing them, giving them a more neutral and detached approach to their evidence due to their giving evidence in close proximity to other experts from their field. It is said to thus reduce partisanship or personal bias. Finally, Heerey notes the process is said to reduce the time spent on dealing with expert evidence at trial.[205] The process is thus expected (intended) to promote economy, efficiency, and proportionality by

[199] CPR r 35.5.

[200] *Homebase Ltd v Jeyakanthan Rengasamy* [2015] EWHC 618 (QB).

[201] *Society of Lloyds v Clemenston (No 2)* [1996] CLC 1205 at [1].

[202] A Clarke, 'The Role of the Expert After Woolf' (2008) 14(3) Clinical Risk 85; R Jackson (May 2009), Vol II at 593; R Jackson (December 2009) at 384; H Genn, 'Getting to the Truth: Experts and Judges in the "Hot Tub"' (2013) 32(2) CJQ 275.

[203] W Peter, 'Witness Conferencing' (2002) 18 Arbitration International, Issue 1, 47.

[204] Civil Justice Council, *Concurrent Expert Evidence and 'Hot-Tubbing' in English Litigation since the 'Jackson Reforms'* (2016). The revised approach was introduced via CPR PD Update 93 (2017).

[205] P Heerey, 'Recent Australian Developments' (2004) 23 CJQ 386 at 391.

reducing the time, and hence cost,[206] of expert evidence at trial. It is also expected to improve the quality of evidence and adjudicative accuracy through reducing the effect of any personal bias by an expert. Arguably, it also exposes more effectively any structural bias in an expert's evidence, as it is a process designed to bring to light any professional assumptions, theories, or divergent theoretical standpoints and enable them to be challenged and tested by the experts themselves.[207]

5. A cogent argument has been developed that the use of judge-led concurrent evidence is a significant in-road into the adversarial process; one that moves civil procedure, unreflectively, to an inquisitorial form of process. Such a move is said to undermine the court's ability to maintain judicial impartiality; concurrent evidence is said to be a process that encourages judges to descend into the arena and act as an advocate, which leads to cognitive bias.[208] Thus, by attempting to reduce expert witness bias, the process introduces a risk of judicial bias. There is a good deal of force in this argument.
6. Concurrent evidence need not, however, be a judge-led process. To avoid the risk that this approach could give rise to potential problems concerning judicial impartiality, rule 24(4) prohibits judges from leading the process. Under that rule concurrent evidence must give effect to both the party autonomy and adversariality principles. It must be party-led,[209] albeit as with the proper management of disputes generally, management of the trial process remains for the court. The rule is thus intended to secure the benefits of the concurrent evidence process without running the risk of introducing new problems into procedure.

## RULE 25.—DISCLOSURE OF AND RELIANCE ON EXPERT REPORTS

**(1) A court-appointed expert's report may be relied on by any party. A party-appointed expert's report may be relied on by any party to proceedings if the report is disclosed by the party that appointed the expert.**

**(2) Where a party intends to rely upon another party's expert's report they should inform the court and that party of that fact and how they intend to rely upon it at the earliest opportunity.**

**(3) Where an expert's report is not disclosed, it may not be relied on at any hearing nor may the expert give oral evidence except where the court grants permission to do so.**

*Sources: ALI/UNIDROIT Reporters' Study, rr 26.2, 26.4; ELI-UNIDROIT Model Rules, r 124; CPR rr 35.11, 35.13.*

[206] *Harrison v Shephard Homes* [2011] EWHC 1811 (TCC); [2011] 27 Const LJ 709, at [26].

[207] G Edmond, 'Secrets of the "Hot Tub": Expert Witnesses, Concurrent Evidence and Judge-led Reform in Australia' (2008) 27 CJQ 51. Administrative Appeals Tribunal, *An Evaluation of the Use of Concurrent Evidence in the Administrative Appeals Tribunal* (November 2005) at 5; Civil Justice Council (2016); S Rares, 'Using the "Hot Tub"—How Concurrent Expert Evidence Aids Understanding Issues' (2012) 31(1) CJQ 30.

[208] G Edmond, A Plenderleith Ferguson, and T Ward, 'Assessing Concurrent Expert Evidence' (2018) 37 CJQ 344.

[209] A Clarke (2008); Civil Justice Council (2016) at 16.

## COMMENTARY

1. This rule restates, in consolidated form, CPR rr 35.11 and 35.13. It expands those rules to apply to court-appointed experts.
2. Rule 25(1) makes explicit that any party may rely upon a court-appointed expert's report. Any such report is automatically to be made available to all parties and the court and any evidence in it may be relied upon (or challenged) by any party. Where party-appointed experts are concerned, their reports may only be relied upon if they are disclosed by the party appointing the expert. This gives effect to party-control over their evidence. A party may instruct an expert but choose not to put their report in evidence. Only if they choose to rely on their expert's evidence, and hence must disclose it, may another party rely upon it.
3. Where a party-expert's report is disclosed and another party intends to rely upon it, effective dispute management and due notice requires the party relying upon it to inform the court and the party who instructed the expert of that fact.[210] They must also inform them of the purpose for which they intend to rely upon it. This enables the court to consider how best to manage the trial process. It also enables the party who instructed the expert to consider, further to the adversarial principle, whether they may need to obtain evidence to rebut any point to be made through such use of their expert's evidence.
4. Rule 25(3) replicates the approach taken in CPR r 35.13. It restricts a party's ability to rely upon an undisclosed expert's report. This rule, as does CPR r 35.13, applies irrespective of whether the party has chosen not to disclose the report or has failed to do so having been ordered to disclose it. This restriction on use is not a procedural sanction. It is a rule of procedural fairness that gives effect to the due notice, adversarial, and procedural equality principles. If a party is to rely on evidence, the other party needs to have effective notice of it so as to prepare their case accordingly. In considering whether to grant permission to enable a non-disclosing party to rely upon an expert's report the court will thus need to consider the purposive principle, and particularly how its decision can give effect to those specific procedural principles noted above.

## RULE 26.—EXPERTS' COSTS AND REMUNERATION

**(1) Costs incurred by party and court-appointed experts shall be costs in the proceedings.**
**(2) No expert appointed to or granted permission to adduce evidence in proceedings may be remunerated through a contingency funding agreement.**

*Sources: ELI-UNIDROIT Model Rules, r 125; CPR r 35.4(4); Civil Justice Council, Guidance for the Instruction of Experts in Civil Claims 2014, para 88.*

[210] *Shepherd & Neame v EDF Energy Networks (SPN) Plc* [2008] EWHC 123 (TCC); [2008] Bus LR D43 (TCC) at [11]–[14]; *Jarman v Brighton and Sussex University Hospitals NHS Trust* [2020] EWHC 3238 (QB) at [8]–[10].

## COMMENTARY

1. This rule restates the general principle that costs of experts are costs in the proceedings. Recoverability of such costs from the losing party is thus subject to the same controls as provided for in respect of cost recoverability generally. Hence expert costs should, as with other costs, be proportionate.[211]
2. Under the CPR, experts have been able to be instructed on the basis that they will be remunerated on a contingency basis where that does not harm the proper administration of justice, ie they would only be paid if the party instructing them succeeded in their claim. The rationale for this is that it is said to increase access to justice.[212] Rule 25(2) rejects that approach. It does so, as it is doubtful that permitting experts to act on a contingency basis does, to any real degree, increase access to experts and, hence, access to justice. There is an absence of an evidential basis for that claim. There are in fact few decisions where it is reported that experts have acted on such a basis.[213] The approach is also rejected on principled grounds. Permitting experts to act on a contingency basis creates a clear conflict of interest between them and their duty to the court. They give experts a financial interest in the outcome of litigation. As experts are required to act with impartiality and independence, creating such a conflict of interest fundamentally undermines the appearance that they are doing. It also creates the risk that that appearance may be reality. It thus calls into question the credibility and weight to be given to an expert's evidence where they are acting on such a basis.
3. In *Davis v Stena Line* (2005) it was, however, suggested that questions concerning bias arising from expert entry into contingency funding agreements could be dealt with via cross-examination at trial.[214] That is entirely unsatisfactory. It introduces an unnecessary, additional, and hence time-consuming and costly process into trials. Were it to show bias, justice would not be served as the expert's evidence would either have to be set aside or given little weight. It would thus do a disservice to the party instructing the expert. It would also undermine the court's ability to adjudicate accurately and proportionately as it would, absent an adjournment to permit a new expert to be instructed (which itself would be expensive, time-consuming, and contrary to the proportionate management of disputes), lead to the court having to determine the claim in the absence of potentially probative evidence. The means by which potential bias could be policed is thus contrary to the proper, proportionate, administration of justice. It is a cure that poses more problems than the disease.
4. Given the risk of conflicts of interest arising, the doubtful benefit of such an approach in the first instance, and the problems that arise from policing it effectively, the possibility of experts acting on a contingency basis is prohibited.

[211] *Kranidiotes v Paschali* [2001] EWCA Civ 357; [2001] CP Rep 81.

[212] *R (Factortame) v Secretary of State for Transport, Environment & The Regions* (*Ex parte Factortame (No 8)*) [2002] EWCA Civ 932; [2003] QB 381 at [70]–[73].

[213] *Davis v Stena Line* [2005] EWHC 420 (QB); [2005] Lloyd's Rep 13.

[214] *Davis v Stena Line* [2005] EWHC 420 (QB); [2005] Lloyd's Rep 13 at [28].

## RULE 27.—ASSESSORS

**(1) The court, on its own initiative or on application of a party, may appoint an assessor to assist it with any matter in dispute. It may direct how and in what manner the assessor is to provide assistance.**
**(2) In considering whether to appoint an assessor, the court shall take into account whether**
**(a) the subject matter of the proceedings is either technically complex or concerns a subject with which the court is unfamiliar; and**
**(b) an appointment would further the purposive principle.**
**(3) An individual, including a judge, may be appointed as an assessor to assist a court in a matter in which they have skill and expertise.**
**(4) Any assistance provided by an assessor to the court must be disclosed to the parties, who shall be given an opportunity to make representations to the court in respect of it.**
**(5) Assessors may only assist the court on matters within their field of expertise. They may not give evidence.**
**(6) Any costs incurred by an assessor shall be costs in the proceedings, except where a judge is appointed as an assessor.**

*Sources: ALI/UNIDROIT Principles, principle 16.4; ALI/UNIDROIT Reporters' Study, r 26; ELI-UNIDROIT Model Rules, r 120; Senior Courts Act 1981, s 70; County Courts Act 1984, s 63; CPR rr 35.15, 63.13, CPR PD 35 para 10, PD52C para 26.*

## COMMENTARY

1. Assessors may be appointed by any civil court.[215] They are a form of '*statutory court-appointed expert*'.[216] Unlike expert witnesses, however, they do not act for or take instructions from the parties to proceedings. They are individuals who, like an expert, have specific expertise on complex or technical matters. Their role is to help the court carry out its adjudicative function in as properly and informed a way as possible.[217] Once appointed they provide the court with assistance on matters within the scope of their expertise, including suggesting possible questions for the court to ask parties or witnesses in order to clarify issues in the proceedings.[218] As they are not witnesses they may not give evidence or, as a necessary corollary, be subject to any form of cross-examination.
2. The use of assessors is longstanding.[219] It is an exception to the general approach taken, historically, by English and Welsh procedure that understood the judge's role to be passive. The historic reason for this inroad into judicial passivity and the

[215] D Dwyer, *The Judicial Assessment of Expert Evidence* (CUP, 2008) at 315.

[216] *Owners of the Bow Spring v Owners of the Manzanillo II* [2004] EWCA Civ 1007; [2005] 1 WLR 144 at [60].

[217] *Richardson v Redpath Brown & Co Ltd* [1944] AC 62 at 70–71; *Owners of the Bow Spring v Owners of the Manzanillo II* [2004] EWCA Civ 1007; [2005] 1 WLR 144 at [59]; *Ahmed v University of Oxford* [2002] EWCA Civ 1907; [2003] 1 WLR 995 at [29].

[218] *Watson v General Medical Council* [2005] EWHC 1896 (Admin); [2006] ICR 113 at [71].

[219] *Swyny v N E Railway Co* 74 LT 88 noted in W Blake Odgers, *The Principles of Pleading and Practice in Civil Actions in the High Court of Justice* (Stevens & Sons, 1912) at 306; J Østergaard, 'An Assessor on the Tribunal: How a Court is to Decide When Experts Disagree' (2016) 35 CJQ 319.

adversarial nature of procedure stems from the basis of this jurisdiction prior to the Judicature Act reforms, and particularly its origin within the Admiralty Court, a civilian court that contained quasi-inquisitorial elements.[220] Hence, the most common historic use arose in admiralty claims, where Trinity House Brethren were typically appointed as assessors to assist judges dealing with shipping disputes.[221] That remains the case today. The Judicature Act reforms incorporated this feature of admiralty practice into the procedure available to the post-1873 civil courts.[222] The power is now used widely, albeit still relatively rarely, across the civil courts. Assessors have, for instance, been appointed to assist the court in respect to employment practices[223] and, increasingly under the CPR, where complex issues concerning litigation costs arise in proceedings. In this latter case, the assessors are generally expert costs judges.[224]

3. Rule 26(2) codifies the approach to the appointment of assessors developed in *Balcombe Group plc v London Development Agency* (2008).[225] The first question is whether the subject matter that the assessor is to provide assistance on is of a nature that justifies an appointment. This requires the court to consider the specialist or technical nature of the issue on which the assessor is to provide assistance and the court's familiarity, or lack of familiarity, with it. Typically, assistance would be justified where issues raise particularly complex scientific matters and the parties are adducing expert evidence. An assessor could assist the court, in such circumstances, to gain a proper understanding of the science.[226] This would then enable them to consider the expert evidence properly. The second question for the court to determine is whether such an appointment would further the purposive principle. Relevant considerations will therefore be whether an appointment will assist the court in carrying out its adjudicative function effectively, whether it and any costs arising from it are proportionate and can properly be borne by the parties.
4. Where an assessor is appointed, it is essential that any advice they provide to the court is also shared with the parties. This is required by the due notice principle. For there to be an effective adversarial and fair process, parties must also be put in a position where they can make submissions to the court in respect of an assessor's advice or assistance. To facilitate this, the court ought to discuss the issues and any questions it intends to put to the assessor with the parties before it raises them with the assessor.[227] It should do so at as early a stage as possible, and preferably at a dispute management hearing.

[220] J Baker, *An Introduction to English Legal History* (OUP, 2019) at 132–133; W Senior, *Doctors' Commons and the Old Court of Admiralty: A Short History of the Civilians in England* (Longmans, 1922).

[221] The Corporation of Trinity House.

[222] Judicature Act 1873, s 56.

[223] *Cary v Commissioner of Police for the Metropolis* [2014] EWCA Civ 987; [2004] CP Rep 42 at [61]–[70].

[224] *Diag Human SE v Volterra Fietta (A Firm)* [2022] EWHC 2054 (QB).

[225] *Balcombe Group plc v London Development Agency* [2008] EWHC 1392 (TCC); [2008] TCLR 8 (TCC) at [6].

[226] *Electromagnetic Geoservices ASA v Petroleum Geo-Services ASA* [2016] EWHC 27 (Pat); [2016] 1 WLR 2353.

[227] *Global Mariner v Atlantic Crusader* [2005] EWHC 380 (Admlty); [2005] 2 All ER (Comm) 389 at [14]–[17].

# SECTION 6: SPECIAL CASES

## RULE 28.—SECURING EVIDENCE OF IDENTITY OF WRONGDOER

**(1) The court, on application, may order a person to provide relevant documents and other information concerning any individual, including their identity, alleged to have committed a tortious act or other civil wrong.**

**(2) The court may, exceptionally, grant such an order where the following threshold criteria are satisfied**

**(a) there is a good arguable case of wrongdoing by an individual;**

**(b) the respondent had facilitated, participated in, or otherwise been involved in the wrongdoing;**

**(c) the applicant intends to take some legitimate action, whether through proceedings or otherwise, in response to the wrongdoing;**

**(d) the application serves a legitimate purpose; and**

**(e) in all the circumstances, provision of the documents or information is necessary and proportionate to enable the applicant to take the intended legitimate action.**

**(3) Where the threshold criteria are satisfied the court may exercise its discretion to grant an order where it is in the interests of justice to do so.**

**(4) The court may not grant such an order where doing so would be contrary to any rule of law, privilege, or immunity.**

*Sources: CPR r 31.18.*

## COMMENTARY

1. The court has an inherent jurisdiction to order the disclosure of information from individuals who, while they have not themselves committed any wrong,[228] have become involved innocently and even unknowingly with the wrongdoing of others.[229] This includes disclosure of evidence as to the alleged wrongdoer's identity. Involvement may arise where the innocent individual has facilitated, participated, or otherwise been involved in the wrongdoing. Involvement is thus given a broad meaning.[230] The jurisdiction exists to enable a party to potential proceedings to discover the identity of an individual against whom proceedings can be pursued, ie it promotes the general access principle.
2. This jurisdiction was first identified in *Norwich Pharmacal v Customs & Excise Commissioners* (1974).[231] It is not codified in the CPR. It is, however, acknowledged in it and preserved by CPR r 31.18.[232] Rule 28 codifies the jurisdiction. Rule 28(2)

[228] *Orb ARL v Fiddler* [2016] EWHC 361 (Comm) at [82].

[229] *Norwich Pharmacal v Customs & Excise Commissioners* [1974] AC 133.

[230] R (*Omar*) *v Secretary of State for Foreign & Commonwealth Affairs* [2013] EWCA Civ 118; [2014] QB 112 at [36]–[40].

[231] *Norwich Pharmacal v Customs & Excise Commissioners* [1974] AC 133; *Ramilos Trading Ltd v Buyanovsky* [2016] EWHC 3175 (Comm); [2016] 2 CLC 896.

[232] *Mitsui & Co Ltd v Nexen Petroleum UK Ltd* [2005] EWHC 625 (Ch); [2005] 3 All ER 511.

and (3) specifically codifies the threshold criteria that must be satisfied for the court to consider whether to exercise its discretion to grant such an order.[233]

3. The authorities have identified a wide range of factors that can be considered when a court is assessing whether it is in the interests of justice to make an order. They have been summarised as follows:

> *... (i) the strength of the possible cause of action contemplated by the applicant for the order:... (ii) the strong public interest in allowing an applicant to vindicate his legal rights:... (iii) whether the making of the order will deter similar wrongdoing in the future: ... (iv) whether the information could be obtained from another source: ... (v) whether the respondent to the application knew or ought to have known that he was facilitating arguable wrongdoing: ... (vi) whether the order might reveal the names of innocent persons as well as wrongdoers, and if so whether such innocent persons will suffer any harm as a result: ... (vii) the degree of confidentiality of the information sought: ... (viii) the privacy rights under article 8 of the European Convention for the Protection of Human Rights and Fundamental Freedoms of the individuals whose identity is to be disclosed: ... (ix) the rights and freedoms under the EU data protection regime of the individuals whose identity is to be disclosed: ... (x) the public interest in maintaining the confidentiality of journalistic sources . . .*[234]

4. Such an order may not be granted in several circumstances. It may not, for instance, be granted where statute limits its application.[235] The privilege against self-incrimination also provides a basis for an individual to resist an application under this rule as that privilege stands at the common law.[236] Under the privilege as modified under rule 32, it would not do so.

## RULE 29.—SECURING EVIDENCE FROM OUTSIDE THE COURT'S JURISDICTION

**(1) Evidence may be obtained from outside the court's jurisdiction further to any rule of law, international convention, or treaty to which the UK is signatory.**
**(2) A party may apply to the court for permission to obtain witness evidence by deposition outside the court's jurisdiction.**
**(3) The court may appoint an examiner to secure evidence from outside the jurisdiction. An examiner must either be a barrister or solicitor-advocate who has been in active practice for at least three years.**
**(4) The court may conduct a hearing outside its jurisdiction in order to receive or view physical evidence.**

*Sources: ELI-UNIDROIT Model Rules, r 129; CPR Pt 34.*

[233] Traditionally the threshold criteria are set out as three conditions: *Orb ARL v Fiddler* [2016] EWHC 361 (Comm) at [83]–[89]; *Ashworth Hospital Authority v MGN Ltd* [2002] UKHL 29; [2002] 1 WLR 2033 at [57]. The better approach is that adopted in *R (Omar) v Secretary of State for Foreign & Commonwealth Affairs* [2013] EWCA Civ 118; [2014] QB 112 at [36]–[40] and elaborated in *Green v CT Group Holdings Ltd* [2023] EWHC 3168 (Comm) at [18], [44]–[46], and [54] as they identify four and then five clear criteria respectively.

[234] *Rugby Football Union v Consolidated Information Services Limited (formerly Viagogo Limited) (in liquidation)* [2012] UKSC 55; [2012] 1 WLR 3333 at [17].

[235] *Ramilos Trading Ltd v Buyanovsky* [2016] EWHC 3175 (Comm); [2016] 2 CLC 896; *Green v CT Group Holdings Ltd* [2023] EWHC 3168 (Comm) (Evidence (Proceedings in Other Jurisdictions) Act 1975); *Koo Golden East Mongolia v Bank of Nova Scotia* [2007] EWCA Civ 1443; [2008] QB 717 (State Immunity Act 1978); Justice and Security Act 2013, s 17.

[236] P Coulson (ed), *Civil Procedure 2024* (Sweet & Maxwell, 2024) Vol 1 at 31.18.7.

### COMMENTARY

1. Evidence will not always be located within the jurisdiction. Parties may therefore require the court's assistance to obtain it from parties or non-parties who are outside the jurisdiction.
2. This rule acknowledges the court's jurisdiction to secure evidence where provision arises under a rule of law, eg statute, an international convention, or treaty, eg The Hague Evidence Convention.[237] It also makes provision for witness evidence to be taken by deposition outside the jurisdiction by an examiner appointed by the court.[238]
3. Rule 29(4) should be read with Part 14, rule 2(3).

## SECTION 7: EVIDENTIARY IMMUNITY AND INADMISSIBILITY

### RULE 30.—EVIDENTIAL IMMUNITY AND INADMISSIBILITY

**(1) The court shall give effect to any relevant rule of law that**
**(a) protects any person from the compulsory provision of information in whatever form (oral, written, electronic) to a party in proceedings;**
**(b) renders any such information inadmissible in proceedings.**
**(2) Relevant rules of law include**
**(a) legal professional privilege, including its application to information concerning settlement negotiations;**
**(b) the privilege against self-incrimination;**
**(c) settlement privilege;**
**(d) without-prejudice privilege; and**
**(e) public interest immunity.**

*Sources: ALI/UNIDROIT Principles, principle 18; ALI/UNIDROIT Reporters' Study, r 27.1; ELI-UNIDROIT Model Rules, r 91.*

### COMMENTARY

1. English civil procedure has not, historically, contained rules relating to what are generally referred to as privileges from the compulsory provision of documentary or witness evidence. This is not to say that English law, uniquely, makes no provision for such rules.[239] They are to be found in the common law[240] and, in some cases, are modified by legislation.[241]

[237] Convention on the Taking of Evidence Abroad in Civil or Commercial Matters (18 March 1970); S Cockerill, *The Law and Practice of Compelled Evidence in Civil Proceedings* (OUP, 2011), albeit the provisions it refers to concerning evidence-taking in the European Union no longer apply following the UK's withdrawal from the EU; *Nix v Emerdata Ltd* [2022] EWHC 718 (Comm); *Gorbachev v Guriev* [2022] EWCA Civ 1270.

[238] CPR rr 34.8, 31.15. Exceptionally, a judge may be appointed as an examiner, *Peer International Corporation v Termidor Music Publishers Ltd* [2005] EWHC 1048; [2006] CP Rep 2.

[239] ALI/UNIDROIT Principles, P-18A.

[240] Eg legal professional privilege, without-prejudice privilege.

[241] Eg the privilege against self-incrimination; Senior Courts Act 1981, s 72.

2. This rule, and the following ones, are not intended to codify the various established privileges. They acknowledge their existence and that the court must give effect to them. This is to enable them to continue, as they have done historically, to be subject to common law development as that is necessary to meet new conditions and situations.
3. Where the privilege against self-incrimination is concerned, however, rule 32 modifies its operation. A general settlement privilege is also introduced due to the increased emphasis within the Code on the promotion of consensual settlement.

## RULE 31.—LEGAL PROFESSIONAL PRIVILEGE

**(1) The court shall give effect to legal professional privilege, which is a fundamental constitutional and human right.**
**(2) Legal professional privilege is a single, integrated privilege that applies to legal advice generally (legal advice privilege) and to legal advice given for the purpose of preparing for contemplated or ongoing proceedings, including the settlement of such proceedings (litigation privilege).**
**(3) Information subject to the privilege is immune from compulsory disclosure. It is also inadmissible.**
**(4) The privilege may be subject to such exceptions as are provided for by law.**
**(5) The party in whose favour the privilege exists may waive the privilege.**

*Sources: ALI/UNIDROIT Principles, principle 18; ALI/UNIDROIT Reporters' Study, r 27.1.1; ELI-UNIDROIT Model Rules, r 91(2)(c); Police and Criminal Evidence Act 1984, s 10(1).*

## COMMENTARY

1. Legal professional privilege forms part of substantive law. It is a common law constitutional right.[242] It is also a fundamental human right,[243] and one that belongs not to lawyers but to their clients, ie parties.[244] It is recognised as such throughout common law and civil law systems.[245] Its origins in England and Wales can be traced back to the 16th century, although it developed mainly during the 19th and 20th centuries.[246] This rule does not, subject to one point considered below, seek to revise or amend legal professional privilege. Rather—as a procedural code—it acknowledges it and specifies that the court is under a duty to give effect to it.
2. The privilege exists to protect the due administration of justice.[247] It does so as it renders confidential communications between parties and their lawyers or third parties where litigation is contemplated or ongoing, including related settlement

[242] *R v Derby Magistrates' Court, ex parte B* [1996] 1 AC 487. A Zuckerman (2021) chap 16.

[243] *R (Morgan Grenfell & Co Ltd) v Special Commissioner of Income Tax* [2002] UKHL 21; [2003] 1 AC 563 at [7]–[9].

[244] *Craig v Earl of Angelsea* (1743) 17 How St Tr 1139 at 1223–1234; *Wisden v Wisden* (1849) 6 Hare 549; *Ventouris v Mountain* [1991] 1 WLR 607 at 611; *R (Prudential) v Special Commissioners* [2013] UKSC 1; [2013] 2 AC 185 at [22] and [114]. Litigation privilege can also apply to non-parties to proceedings: *Al Sadeq v Dechert LLP* [2023] EWHC 795 (KB).

[245] *Lavallee, Rackel & Heintz v Canada* [2002] 3 SCR 209; R Stürner and P Murray (2004) at 301, in respect of the broader 'professionals privilege' in Germany, which applies to a wide range of professionals eg lawyers, judges, doctors, etc.

[246] H Lai, 'History and Judicial Theories of Legal Professional Privilege' (1995) Sing J L Studies 558.

[247] *Glazebrook Ltd v Wallens* [1973] ICR 256 at 258.

processes, immune from compulsory disclosure.[248] Several rationales are advanced to justify its existence and effect.[249] The predominant rationale is that it enables individuals to obtain '*skilled advice about the law*' through enabling them to place all matters before their lawyers without fearing they may then be used against them due to the application of compulsory disclosure.[250] It thus promotes candour.[251] And it enables lawyers therefore to give effective advice. Underpinning this rationale, it is apparent several procedural principles are engaged.[252] The general access principle is inherent in the need for individuals to be able to be candid with their lawyers,[253] as is procedural equality—all parties should be able to obtain advice as a means to secure access to justice whether that is preventive, consensual, or adjudicative justice.

3. By protecting communications with lawyers, the privilege further enables individuals to obtain effective legal representation, which would otherwise be hampered if there was a fear that communications with lawyers could be subject to compulsory disclosure.[254] The accuracy and consensual settlement principles are specifically engaged here: the privilege enables lawyers to give clear advice on the merits of disputes. The adversarial and participation principles are also engaged as by providing a secure zone within which advice can be sought and given, both lawyer and client can prepare effectively for proceedings. Inherent in all these procedural principles is that the privilege secures a fair process. It is thus also inherent in the purposive principle. And, taken together, each of these principles point to the privilege ultimately being justified as a means to secure the rule of law.[255]
4. The privilege is not, however, absolute. It is subject to statutory and common law exceptions, which are intended to ensure that it is not used abusively. It does not, therefore apply where advice is sought for an illegal or improper purpose, eg to further crime or fraud (the iniquity exception).[256] It is also, for instance, subject to statutory anti-money laundering provisions.[257]
5. Rule 31(4) clarifies one point concerning the privilege's effect. This makes clear that information subject to the privilege is inadmissible as well as immune from compulsory disclosure. Inadvertent disclosure of privileged information cannot therefore, unless the court agrees to set the privilege aside, render it admissible. This follows from the rationales that justify the existence of the privilege. Admissibility undermines the idea that the privilege creates a secure area within which an individual can be candid with their lawyer. It thus undermines each of the procedural principles that the privilege promotes.[258]

[248] *Three Rivers District Council v Bank of England (No 6)* [2005] 1 AC 610 at [105].

[249] H Lai (1995) for a discussion of the various rationales.

[250] *R (Morgan Grenfell & Co Ltd) v Special Commissioner of Income Tax* [2002] UKHL 21; [2003] 1 AC 563 at [7]–[9].

[251] *R v Derby Magistrates' Court, ex parte B* [1996] 1 AC 487 at 507; *Campbell and Fell v UK* (1983) 5 EHRR 207 at [158].

[252] *Three Rivers District Council v Bank of England (No 5)* [2003] QB 1556 at [26].

[253] *Oxfordshire County Council v M* [1994] 2 All ER 269 at 280.

[254] *D v National Society for the Prevention of Cruelty to Children* [1978] AC 171 at 231.

[255] *Three Rivers District Council v Bank of England (No 6)* [2005] 1 AC 610 at [34].

[256] *Craig v Earl of Angelsea* (1743) 17 How St Tr 1139 at 1240; *R v Cox and Railton* (1884) 14 QBD 153; *Kuwait Airways Corp v Iraqi Airways Co (No 6)* [2005] EWCA Civ 286; [2005] 1 WLR 2734 at [42]; *Al Sadeq v Dechert LLP* [2024] EWCA Civ 28 at [60]–[63] and [223].

[257] Money Laundering, Terrorist Financing and Transfer of Fund (Information on the Payer) Regulations 2017 (SI 2017/692); Regulation of Investigatory Powers Act 2000.

[258] A Zuckerman (2021) at 893–897.

## RULE 32.—PRIVILEGE AGAINST SELF-INCRIMINATION

**(1) The right of any person in proceedings other than criminal proceedings to refuse to answer any question or produce any document or thing if doing so would tend to expose them to proceedings for an offence or to a penalty does not apply to proceedings subject to this Code.**

**(2) Subject to rule 32(3), no evidence, howsoever given, by a person in proceedings subject to this Code that would tend to expose them either to proceedings for an offence or to a penalty shall be admissible for such purposes against that person, their spouse, or civil partner.**

**(3) Evidence given by a person in proceedings shall be admissible as evidence in proceedings for perjury or contempt of court.**

*Sources: Criminal Evidence Act 1968, s 14; Theft Act 1968, s 31; Civil Evidence Act 1981, s 14; Senior Courts Act 1981, s 72; ALI/UNIDROIT Principles, principle 18; ELI-UNIDROIT Model Rules, r 91(2)(b).*

## COMMENTARY

1. The privilege against self-incrimination is the '*right of a person in any legal proceedings other than criminal proceedings to refuse to answer any question or produce any document or thing if to do so would tend to expose that person to proceedings for an offence or for the recovery of a penalty . . .*'[259] It can be traced back to the 18th and 19th centuries.[260] It is recognised as an aspect of the right to fair trial within article 6 of the European Convention on Human Rights.[261] It has also long been accepted to be a rule that could only be abrogated or otherwise limited by legislation.[262] This remains the case notwithstanding significant criticism of its continued existence by the House of Lords and UK Supreme Court,[263] law reform bodies throughout the common law world,[264] and academic commentators.[265]

2. This rule, as part of a legislative code, abrogates the privilege against self-incrimination in proceedings to which this Code applies. It replaces it with a use-immunity, ie an immunity that prohibits the use, in criminal proceedings or in proceedings that might result in the imposition of a penalty on the person who gave the evidence, of

[259] Civil Evidence Act 1981, s 14; *Blunt v Park Lane Hotel* [1942] 2 KB 253 at 257.

[260] J Langbein, 'The Historical Origins of the Privilege against Self-Incrimination at Common Law' (1994) 92 Michigan Law Review 1047; M Macnair, 'The Early Development of the Privilege Against Self-Incrimination' (1990) 10 OJLS 66; *Brown v Walker* (1896) 161 US 591 at 596–597.

[261] *Saunders v United Kingdom* (1996) 23 EHRR 313 at [69]; *Brown v Stott* [2003] 1 AC 681 at 703–704; ALI-UNIDROIT Principles at P-18A; German Code of Civil Procedure, s 384, on its wider acceptance. And see *Pyneboard Pty Ltd v Trade Practices Commission* [1983] HCA 9; (1983) 152 CLR 328 at [24].

[262] *Parry-Jones v The Law Society* [1969] 1 Ch 1 at 9.

[263] *AT & T Istel v Tully* [1993] AC 45; *C Plc v P* [2007] 3 WLR 437 at [59]–[65]; *Coogan v News Group Newspapers* [2012] EWCA Civ 48; [2012] 2 All ER 74 at [17].

[264] *Queensland Law Reform Commission*, 'Abrogation of the Privilege Against Self-incrimination' (1994) QLRC R 59; *New Zealand Law Commission*, 'The Privilege Against Self-Incrimination' (1996) NZLC PP25. It was also subject to review in England and Wales in 1992, Lord Chancellor's Department, *The Privilege against Self-Incrimination in Civil Proceedings* (Consultation Paper, July 1992).

[265] D Dripps, 'Self-Incrimination and Self-Preservation: A Skeptical View' (1991) 2 University of Illinois Law Review 329; N Andrews (2003) at 690; M Redmayne, 'Rethinking the Privilege Against Self-incrimination' (2007) 29(2) OJLS 209.

any self-incriminatory evidence given in civil proceedings.[266] Rule 32(1)'s wording is derived from the Criminal Evidence Act 1968, s 14(1). The wording of rule 32(2) and (3) is derived from the Senior Court's Act 1981, s 72(3) and (4). By taking this approach, rule 32 adopts the approach endorsed by Lord Neuberger PSC in *Coogan v News Group Newspapers & Mulcaire, Phillips v News Group Newspapers & Mulcaire* (2012), ie that the privilege be abolished subject to its replacement with a use-immunity[267] as is the case now in, for instance, Canada.[268]

3. Seven rationales are traditionally deployed to justify the existence of this privilege.[269] The classic formulation of them is set out in US rather than English and Welsh jurisprudence. In *Murphy v Waterfront Commission* (1964)[270] they were summarised as follows.

> *"The privilege against self-incrimination "registers an important advance in the development of our liberty—one of the great landmarks in man's struggle to make himself civilized." It reflects many of our fundamental values and most noble aspirations: our unwillingness to subject those suspected of crime to the cruel trilemma of self-accusation, perjury or contempt; our preference for an accusatorial rather than an inquisitorial system of criminal justice; our fear that self-incriminating statements will be elicited by inhumane treatment and abuses; our sense of fair play which dictates "a fair state-individual balance by requiring the government to leave the individual alone until good cause is shown for disturbing him and requiring the government in its contest with the individual to shoulder the entire load"; our respect for the inviolability of the human personality and of the right of each individual "to a private enclave where he may lead a private life"; our distrust of self-deprecatory statements; and our realization that the privilege, while sometimes "a shelter to the guilty", is often a protection to the innocent".*[271]

4. Various criticisms can be raised against each of the rationales. It is specifically a question for criminal procedure whether or not they are valid where it is concerned. From a functional perspective the rationales can be protected, in so far as criminal proceedings are concerned, by a use-immunity. By creating a zone of security around evidence given in civil proceedings the objectives that the rationales seek to achieve are secured: a use-immunity is the functional equivalent to the privilege where criminal proceedings are concerned. For instance, a use-immunity maintains protection from the 'cruel trilemma', while maintaining a preference for accusatorial criminal process as it does not affect either of them. It maintains fair play in criminal proceedings, while being consistent with the general approach in civil proceedings that permits compulsory disclosure as a means, for instance, to promote procedural equality. It protects individuals' personal dignity from oppression by the state by maintaining the privilege in so far as criminal proceedings are concerned, while

[266] Penalties include civil ones, such as fines and imprisonment for contempt, *Dadourian Group Ltd v Simms* [2006] EWCA Civ 1745; [2007] 1 WLR 2967 at [13].

[267] *Coogan v News Group Newspapers* [2012] EWCA Civ 48; [2012] 2 All ER 74 at [18].

[268] Criminal Evidence Act 1985 (Canada), s 5(1) abrogates the privilege, while s 5(2) provides for a use-immunity in those circumstances where the privilege would have previously applied.

[269] The existence of the rationales was not, however, acknowledged in *AT & T Istel v Tully* [1993] AC 45 at 53.

[270] *Murphy v Waterfront Commission* 378 US 52 (1964); L Lauden, *Truth, Error, and Criminal Law* (CUP, 2006) at 150–155.

[271] *Murphy v Waterfront Commission* (1964) 378 US 52 at 55. For criticism see, for instance, Queensland Law Reform Commission (1994).

minimising the possibility that the state could misuse civil proceedings as a means to secure evidence that could then be used in criminal proceedings.

5. Importantly, a use-immunity has the clear advantage over the privilege against self-incrimination as it currently stands as it promotes accuracy and consensual settlement in civil proceedings. It enables relevant evidence to be obtained, which in promoting those civil procedural principles further promote effective dispute management and via that proportionality. This is particularly the case where compelled evidence that would otherwise have been protected by the privilege facilitates narrowing of issues, as much as it does to the extent it promotes settlement.[272] Maintaining the benefits of the privilege in criminal proceedings, while securing the benefits of its abolition in civil proceedings thus underpins the approach taken in this rule.

## RULE 33.—WITHOUT-PREJUDICE PRIVILEGE

**(1) The court shall give effect to without-prejudice privilege.**

**(2) Without-prejudice privilege applies to any oral or written communication genuinely made for the purpose of settling a dispute where the communication is made during negotiations entered into**

**(a) by parties where proceedings are contemplated or might reasonably be contemplated were settlement not to be reached; or**

**(b) by parties to proceedings.**

**(3) Where the privilege applies, communications are both immune from compulsory disclosure and are inadmissible in proceedings.**

**(4) The privilege may be disapplied in circumstances where its application is limited by agreement of the parties, where necessary to resolve any dispute concerning settlement, or where necessary to protect the public interest in the proper administration of justice.**

**(5) Parties may by mutual agreement waive the privilege.**

*Sources: ALI/UNIDROIT Principles, principle 18; ALI/UNIDROIT Reporters' Study, r 27.1.2; ELI-UNIDROIT Model Rules, r 91(2)(d).*

## COMMENTARY

1. Without-prejudice privilege has been recognised since, at least, the 1700s.[273] It is a rule that renders statements, whether written or oral, made by parties during the course of settlement negotiations inadmissible as evidence where they are genuinely intended to promote settlement.[274] It is thus an exception to the general rule that admissions made by parties may be adduced against them in evidence.[275] The rule also renders such statements immune from compulsory disclosure, ie where that is sought by third parties.[276] Such negotiations may take place either prior to proceedings commencing where they are contemplated or where they might reasonably be contemplated by the

[272] Maintaining a use-immunity is the price to be paid for promoting the public interest in the proper administration of civil justice that comes with abolishing the privilege's application to such proceedings: *R v Nedelecu* 2012 SCC 59; [2012] 3 SCR 311 at [6]–[8].

[273] *Bradford v Kennison* (1794) 1 Esp 142; D Foskett, *Foskett on Compromise* (Sweet & Maxwell, 2024) chap 19.

[274] *Rush v Tomkins Ltd v GLC* [1989] AC 1280 at 1299–1301 and 1305.

[275] *Muller v Linsley & Mortimer* (1996) 1 PNLR 74 at 79–80.

[276] *Rush v Tomkins Ltd v GLC* [1989] AC 1280 at 1299.

parties in the event that settlement is not reached.[277] They may also take place during the course of proceedings.

2. Two rationales underpin the privilege. The most important one is that it encourages parties to settle their disputes through free and frank discussions.[278] It is thus a specific application of the consensual settlement principle. The second rationale is that the rule rests on the implied or express agreement of the parties that such statements be inadmissible.[279] Given this, parties may agree to limit or waive the privilege.
3. The most common limitation placed on the privilege is where parties limit its application so that statements subject to it may be referred to in costs proceedings.[280] Limitation and waiver must however be based on agreement. One party may not unilaterally limit or waive the privilege. Particularly where the latter is concerned to permit unilateral waiver would undermine the primary rationale: no party could have confidence in the privilege if their opponent could waive its affect unilaterally.[281]
4. The privilege may be disapplied by the court in a limited number of circumstances summarised by the Court of Appeal in *Unilever v The Proctor & Gamble Co* (2000).[282] Rather than articulate each of them within rule 33, which could be taken to restrict the potential development of further exceptions by the courts as they develop the privilege, three broad categories of exception are set out. These are intended to encompass the established exceptions and leave room for future common law development. Care should, however, be taken not to unnecessarily expand these circumstances as that would tend to undermine the primary, public policy, rationale underpinning the privilege.
5. Rule 33(4) thus provides that the privilege may be disapplied where there is agreement by the parties, eg where the privilege's application is limited so as not to apply to issues concerning costs. It disapplies it where that is necessary to resolve disputes concerning any settlement reached by negotiation, ie to determine whether: statements to which the privilege applies resulted in settlement; a party has acted reasonably to mitigate their loss through the negotiation process; to explain delay or apparent acquiescence by a party to the settlement; or, to determine whether a statement to which the privilege applies gave rise to an estoppel. It also disapplies the privilege where that would protect the public interest in the administration of justice, ie where that is necessary to enable the court to determine whether to set aside a settlement on the basis of fraud, misrepresentation, or undue influence or where maintaining the privilege would protect wrongful behaviour (perjury, blackmail, threats, and other such unambiguous impropriety)[283] from being investigated properly.

[277] *Barnetson v Framlington Group Ltd* [2007] EWCA Civ 502; [2007] 1 WLR 2443 at [30]–[36].

[278] *Cutts v Head* [1984] Ch 290 at 306; *Muller v Linsley & Mortimer* (1996) 1 PNLR 74 at 77; *Unilever v The Proctor & Gamble Co* [2000] 1 WLR 2436 at 2442; *Rush v Tomkins Ltd v GLC* [1989] AC 1280 at 1299; *Ofulue v Bossert* [2009] UKHL 16; [2009] 1 AC 990 at [85]; *Willers v Joyce* [2019] EWHC 937 (Ch) at [32].

[279] E Bray, *The Principles and Practice of Discovery* (Reeves & Turner, 1885) at 308 cited in A Zuckerman (2021) at 951; *Ofulue v Bossert* [2009] UKHL 16; [2009] 1 AC 990 at [85]; *Oceanbulk Shipping & Trading SA v TMT Asia Ltd* [2010] UKSC 44; [2011] 1 AC 662 at [24].

[280] *Computer Machinery Co Ltd v Drescher* [1983] 1 WLR 1379 at 1382; *Sternberg Reed Solicitors v Harrison* [2019] EWHC 2065 (Ch) at [28]–[30].

[281] *Walker v Wilsher* (1889) 23 QBD 335; *Somatra Ltd v Touche Roche & Temperley (No 1)* [2000] 1 WLR 2453 at 2465–2467; *Avonwick Holdings Ltd v Webinvest Ltd* [2014] EWCA Civ 1436 at [21].

[282] *Unilever v The Proctor & Gamble Co* [2000] 1 WLR 2436 at 2444. It also notes a hybrid exception, which has developed into a separate privilege in matrimonial proceedings known as conciliation privilege; A Zuckerman (2021) at 972.

[283] *Forster v Friedland* (1992) CAT 1052.

## RULE 34.—SETTLEMENT PRIVILEGE

**(1) The court shall give effect to settlement privilege.**

**(2) Settlement privilege applies to all communications, oral or written the aim of which is to settle a dispute and/or to settle issues in dispute where they are made in a settlement process.**

**(3) Settlement processes are forms of facilitated negotiation including but not limited to: mediation; early-neutral evaluation; collaborative law.**

**(4) Participants in settlement processes include: parties to proceedings or contemplated proceedings; mediators; and any other third party involved in the process.**

**(5) Where the privilege applies, communications are both immune from compulsory disclosure and are inadmissible in proceedings.**

**(6) The privilege may be disapplied in circumstances where its application is limited by agreement of the parties, where necessary to resolve any dispute concerning settlement, or where necessary to protect the public interest in the proper administration of justice.**

**(7) Parties may, by mutual agreement, waive the privilege.**

*Sources: ALI/UNIDROIT Principles, principle 18; ALI/UNIDROIT Reporters' Study, r 27.1.2; ELI-UNIDROIT Model Rules, r 91(2)(d); Mediation Directive, art 7.*

## COMMENTARY

1. English and Welsh civil procedure does not acknowledge a general form of settlement privilege. There has, however, long been an argument that it ought to recognise a general form of mediation privilege, which would protect all communications that arise within a mediation process.[284] It does not yet do so.[285] The furthest developments have gone is for a general form of 'conciliation' privilege in family disputes[286] and for a limited form of mediation confidentiality where civil and commercial disputes are concerned (due to the application of European Union law) to be recognised.[287]
2. The rationale for the creation of mediation privilege is the need to provide effective protection for communications to and from mediators; the third party in the process. Such protection is said to be necessary for the same reason negotiation communications between parties are protected under without-prejudice privilege. By securing the integrity of the process within which parties and third party settlement facilitators can communicate, the privilege promotes their ability to do so freely and frankly.[288] It thereby promotes the public interest in settlement.[289]

[284] H Brown and A Marriott, *ADR: Principles and Practice* (Sweet & Maxwell, 2019) at 329–332.

[285] *Farm Assist Ltd v Secretary of State for the Environment, Food & Rural Affairs (No 2)* [2009] EWHC 1102 (TCC); 125 Con LR 154 at [43]. M Briggs, 'Mediation Privilege?' (2009) 159 NLJ 506 and 550.

[286] *McTaggart v McTaggart* [1984] 2 All ER 754; *Mole v Mole* [1950] 2 All ER 328; *Re D (Minors) (Conciliation: Disclosure of Information)* [1993] Fam 231 at 238.

[287] Directive 2008/52/EC of *The European* Parliament and of The Council of 21 May 2008 on certain aspects of mediation in civil and commercial matters (The Mediation Directive), art 7; The Cross-Border Mediation (EU Directive) Regulations 2011, regs 9 and 10; and see CPR r 78.26 as it was prior to the UK's withdrawal from the European Union.

[288] *Cutts v Head* [1984] Ch 290 at 306.

[289] *Mionis v Democratic Press SA* [2017] EWCA Civ 1194; [2018] QB 662 at [89].

3. This rule does not simply introduce mediation privilege to further the public interest. Consistently with the general approach of promoting consensual settlement it broadens it out into a general settlement privilege that applies to all forms of facilitated negotiation that involve third parties. It thus also applies to early neutral evaluation (ENE) and collaborative law, both of which involve or may involve third parties. The former does so through the third-party neutral who provides an opinion on the merits of the parties' positions. The latter does so via its interdisciplinary team approach where professionals from a range of disciplines assist the parties to resolve their dispute.[290] It will also apply, by necessary implication, to hybrid forms of such processes, eg where ENE is used as part of a broader mediation process. The rationale for the extension of what has been promoted as mediation privilege to these other processes rests on their comparable involvement of third parties.
4. The extension of mediation privilege to these other processes also builds on the approaches endorsed by both the best practice seen in the ALI/UNIDROIT Reporters' Study and the ELI-UNIDROIT Model Rules. Both adopt the position that settlement processes generally ought to be protected by a specific privilege. In the latter case, that is one instance of the general duty to settle which those Model Rules introduce. This Code adopts a comparable approach to settlement through its incorporation of the consensual settlement principle endorsed in Part 1, rule 8. Adopting a more general form of settlement privilege here is thus also consistent with the best practice rationale that rests on the increasing emphasis placed on settlement as a fundamental procedural principle.
5. Disapplication and waiver may occur on the same basis as they may for without-prejudice privilege.

## RULE 35.—PUBLIC INTEREST IMMUNITY

**(1) Any person may object to the disclosure of information, including the existence of information, to a party to proceedings.**

**(2) Where an objection is raised, or the court acts on its own initiative, the court must consider whether the public interest in maintaining confidentiality in the information outweighs the public interest in the administration of justice.**

**(3) Where the public interest in maintaining confidentiality in the information outweighs the public interest in the administration of justice, the court must determine that the information is both immune from compulsory disclosure and inadmissible in proceedings.**

**(4) Immunity from compulsory disclosure and inadmissibility cannot be waived either deliberately or inadvertently.**

**(5) The court may vary or set aside immunity and inadmissibility where the public interest in maintaining confidentiality no longer outweighs the public interest in the administration of justice.**

*Sources: ALI/UNIDROIT Principles, principle 18; ELI-UNIDROIT Model Rules, r 91(2)(e).*

[290] P Tesler, 'Collaborative Family Law' (2004) 4(3) Pepperdine Dispute Resolution Law Journal 317. The interdisciplinary team approach can also be adapted to apply to mediation.

## COMMENTARY

1. Certain documentary and other information, including the existence of such information, may be of such a sensitive nature that its disclosure would adversely affect the public interest. Typically, information concerning natural security, defence, police operations, eg the identity of confidential informants for the police, falls into this category.[291] To protect the public interest any person may object to the disclosure of such information. The court may also raise the issue whether information needs to be protected on its own initiative.[292]
2. Where an objection is raised, the court must consider if departure from the general rule that the administration of justice requires it to have '*the fullest possible access to all relevant evidence*'[293] should be set aside to protect the public interest. Where it does, the information subject to protection is both immune from compulsory disclosure and inadmissible in proceedings. This is known as Public Interest Immunity (PII).
3. Where PII arises, it imposes a duty on parties not to disclose information. Duties cannot be waived.[294] It is thus for the court and not the parties to determine both whether information is subject to the immunity and whether it can properly be released from it.[295] PII can only be set aside by the court determining that it is no longer in the public interest to render information immune from compulsory disclosure. Consequently, inadvertent disclosure of material subject to PII does not render it admissible. Where there has been inadvertent disclosure, it may not be adduced in evidence unless the court determines that protecting the relevant public interest no longer outweighs the public interest in the administration of justice.[296]

## RULE 36.—PROTECTION OF CONFIDENTIALITY

**(1) Confidential information is not generally immune from compulsory disclosure nor is it generally inadmissible.**

**(2) Confidential information may be protected where it is necessary to protect a party or non-party's rights, commercial confidentiality, or technical secrets.**

**(3) The court may restrict the provision of confidential information, including such information contained in or relied on in an expert's report, by ordering that**

**(a) if contained in a document, in whatever form, the document be redacted to protect the information from disclosure or use in the proceedings;**

**(b) if it be disclosed to a party's lawyers or other named individuals only, that it shall not be disclosed to any other person without the court's prior permission, and may only be used for the purpose for which it was disclosed.**

*Sources: ALI/UNIDROIT Principles, principles, 16.5, 18; ALI/UNIDROIT Reporters' Study, r 27.1.1; ELI-UNIDROIT Model Rules, rr 91(1), 103, 104.*

291 *Duncan v Cammell Laird & Co* [1942] AC 624; *Conway v Rimmer* [1968] AC 910; *D v National Society for the Prevention of Cruelty to Children* [1978] AC 171; *Chief Constable of Greater Manchester v McNally* [2002] EWCA Civ 14; [2002] 2 Cr App R 37.

292 *Rogers v Home Secretary* [1973] AC 388 at 406.

293 *Rogers v Home Secretary* [1973] AC 388 at 407.

294 *R v Lewes Justices, Ex parte Secretary of State for Home Department* [1973] AC 388 at 407; *Science Research Council v Nasse* [1980] AC 1028 at 1073; *Marks v Beyfus* (1890) 25 QBD 494; *Rogers v Home Secretary* [1973] AC 388 at 407.

295 *Makanjuola v Commissioner of Police of the Metropolis* [1992] 3 All ER 617 at 623; *R v Chief Constable of the West Midlands, ex parte Wiley* [1995] 1 AC 274 at 296 and following.

296 *Tchenguiz v Director of the Serious Fraud Office* [2014] EWCA Civ 1129; [2015] 1 WLR 797 at [32]–[35].

## COMMENTARY

1. Confidential information is not immune from compulsory disclosure.[297] In this the English and Welsh approach differs from other jurisdictions, such as Germany where professional privilege applies, for instance, to clerics, journalists, and other professionals as it does to lawyers.[298]
2. Confidentiality is not, however, entirely without protection. Where compulsory disclosure or the admission of confidential evidence would, for instance, breach fundamental human rights it may be protected. Compulsory disclosure of information could, for instance, breach a non-party's right to a private life. It may harm a party's or non-party's right to life. It may harm freedom of expression, where the protection of journalistic sources is concerned.[299] It may also be protected where its disclosure may result in commercially sensitive information or scientific and other technical secrets coming into the public domain.[300]
3. In determining if it is necessary to take steps to protect confidentiality, the court must consider if any steps can properly be taken to enable the information to be adduced in proceedings while preserving, as far as possible, confidentiality. Such steps could include derogating from the publicity principle, eg by determining that those aspects of the proceedings or any hearing where the confidential information is deployed should be private. They could also include redacting information in documents, including expert's reports,[301] so that only non-confidential information is made available.[302] It could also include limiting access to the information to a party's lawyers subject to conditions on its use and disclosure.[303]

## *RULE 37.—CLOSED MATERIAL PROCEEDINGS*

***(1) Where authorised by legislation, the court may order proceedings or part of proceedings to be conducted as a closed material proceeding.***
***(2) A closed material proceeding is one that, as authorised by legislation, is inconsistent with the purposive, accuracy, general access, representation, due notice and evidential access, adversarial, publicity, and reasoned judgment principles.***
***(3) A closed material proceeding is one where***
***(a) His Majesty's Government, as a party to proceedings, rely on matters pleaded in a case statement and may adduce evidence that are not made available to any other party to proceedings (closed material);***
***(b) closed material cannot be tested by any other party to proceedings, other than by a Special Advocate to the extent provided for by legislation;***
***(c) the court may rely on closed material in reaching its decision;***

[297] *The Trial of the Duchess of Kingston* (1776) 20 How St Tr 355 at 572–573.

[298] German Code of Civil Procedure, s 383; The French Penal Code, art 226-13; *R (Prudential) v Special Commissioners* [2013] UKSC 1; [2013] 2 AC 185 at [115].

[299] *R v Local Authority in the Midlands, Ex parte LM* [2000] 1 FLR 612; *Goodwin v The UK* (1996) 22 EHRR 123; *Gaskin v The UK* (1990) 12 EHRR 36.

[300] *Warner-Lambert Co v Glaxo Laboratories Ltd* [1975] RPC 354.

[301] *Zverev v Ace Group International Ltd* [2020] EWHC 3513 (Ch).

[302] *Croft House Care Ltd v Durham County Council* [2010] EWHC 909 (TCC); [2011] PTSR 363 at [38]–[39].

[303] Such limitations are generally referred to as creating 'confidentiality rings', ie disclosure is limited to a small number of people, each of whom is under a duty to maintain confidentiality in the disclosed information. *Unwired Planet International Ltd v Huawei Technologies Co Ltd* [2017] EWHC 711 (Pat) at [25]; *Infederation Ltd v Google LLC* [2020] EWHC 657 (Ch) at [42].

***(d) any judgment, to the extent that it refers to or incorporates closed material, may not be disclosed to any party, other than His Majesty's Government, or to any non-party. Any judgment published shall not contain any closed material.***

*Sources: Justice and Security Act 2013; CPR Pt 82.*

## COMMENTARY

1. This rule does not form part of the Code, as signified by its inclusion here in italics. It is only included here to indicate how such a rule could be set out in the Code. It is a form of process that '*negates the judicial function*'.[304] It is '*inherently and irremediably unfair*'.[305]
2. Closed material proceedings were formally introduced into English and Welsh civil procedure by the Justice and Security Act 2013.[306] This followed the UK Supreme Court's conclusion that such a process was contrary to the right to fair trial at common law and thus could only be authorised by statute.[307] It is a form of procedure where one party, invariably the government, is permitted to rely on case statements and documentary and oral evidence that is not disclosed to other parties. The rationale for non-disclosure is that the material, if disclosed, would prejudice the public interest, ie national security, international relations of the United Kingdom, or the detection and prevention of crime.[308] The court has access to the material and may adjudicate upon it. While the material is not provided to the other party, a summary of it is provided to a special advocate, appointed by the Attorney-General. Special advocates may test the evidence in so far as they have access to it.[309] They are not, however, permitted to communicate to the other party once they have had access to any such material. The basis for this approach is that without being able to rely on such material the government would not be able to defend claims, ie they would not be able to secure a fair trial. They would thus either have to allow judgment to be entered against them or settle proceedings. To resolve this conundrum, the closed material proceeding permits the government to rely on the material without it being provided to the other party or coming into the public domain generally.
3. The difficulty is that while this approach may enable one party (the government) to secure, for themselves, a fair trial, in doing so it fails to recognise that it also amounts to an absolute denial of the other party's ability to be afforded a fair trial. By denying access to case statements that concern closed material, it is a denial of due notice.[310] By denying access to evidence in support of those pleadings, it denies access to evidence. By denying the other party the ability to take part in that part of the proceedings that concern the closed material, it is a denial of the adversarial and participatory

[304] *Secretary of State for the Home Office v AF* [2009] UKHL 28; [2010] 2 AC 269 at [84].

[305] *R (Sarkandi) v Secretary of State for Foreign & Commonwealth Affairs* [2015] EWCA Civ 687 at [52].

[306] J Ip, 'Al Rawi, Tariq and the Future of Closed Material Procedures and Special Advocates' (2012) 75(4) Modern Law Review 60.

[307] *Al-Rawi v The Security Services* [2011] UKSC 34; [2012] 1 AC 531; *Tariq v The Home Office* [2011] UKSC 35; [2012] 1 AC 452. The judgments provide a comprehensive analysis of the multiple procedural principles that the closed material procedure breaches.

[308] *Al-Rawi v The Security Services* [2011] UKSC 34; [2012] 1 AC 531 at 539.

[309] CPR r 82.10.

[310] *Tariq v The Home Office* [2011] UKSC 35; [2012] 1 AC 452 at [102]–[105]; *Al-Rawi v The Security Services* [2011] UKSC 34; [2012] 1 AC 531 at [89]–[94].

principles. By restricting access to the closed material to special advocates who the non-government party does not instruct, it is a denial of the right to have a lawyer of their choice. Consequently, it is also a denial of the accuracy principle: untested evidence is evidence that cannot be said, with any confidence, to lead to an accurate decision. At its heart though it is a process that denies both aspects of '*the minimum irreducible core of a fair trial*': due notice and an adversarial hearing.[311] That denial is furthermore a denial of procedural equality: the process is heavily weighted in favour of one party rather than the other.[312] It is also a process that runs counter to the accountability and state-checking functions of the reasoned judgment and publicity principles.[313] It has no place in any procedural code that is consistent with the rule of law.[314]

[311] *Tariq v The Home Office* [2011] UKSC 35; [2012] 1 AC 452 at [119] and [124]; *Al-Rawi v The Security Services* [2011] UKSC 34; [2012] 1 AC 531 at [89]–[90]; L Graham, 'Statutory Secret Trials: The Judicial Approach to Closed Material Procedures Under the Justice and Security Act 2013' (2019) 38 CJQ 189 at 200.

[312] *Tariq v The Home Office* [2011] UKSC 35; [2012] 1 AC 452 at [105].

[313] A Zuckerman (2021) at 1025–1026.

[314] O J Settem, *Applications of the 'Fair Hearing' Norm in ECHR Article 6(1) to Civil Proceedings* (Springer, 2016) at 111.

# PART 13

# PROVISIONAL MEASURES

## SECTION 1: GENERAL

1. This Part concerns provisional or interim measures, eg interim injunctive relief, civil search orders, freezing injunctions, orders to preserve evidence, interim payments. It deals with the various statutory, common law, and equitable measures gathered together in CPR Pt 25. It adopts a different approach to that taken in the CPR, which is to provide a non-exhaustive list of the most commonly known and used measures and then set out specific rules relating to them throughout the rest of Pt 25.[1] Rather than follow that approach, this Part adopts one that looks to systemise the various measures by looking to their function, ie one that focuses their classification on how they protect and promote the court's ability to do justice pending a dispute being finally determined and enforced effectively.
2. A functional approach to this aspect of procedure is well-known outside England and Wales. It has also been canvassed by Zuckerman in respect of English and Welsh civil procedure. Where the former is concerned, since 1968 it has underpinned its treatment in the Brussels Convention, which classifies the various measures as provisional or protective ones.[2] The same classification system was also adopted by the Storme Report in 1994;[3] the *Helsinki Principles on Provisional and Protective Measures in International Litigation* in 1998;[4] the ALI-UNIDROIT Principles;[5] and the ELI-UNIDROIT Model Rules.[6] Comparably, Zuckerman has categorised these measures as either protective orders, ie those that protect substantive rights on a provisional basis, or process orders, ie those that promote access to evidence or the effective regulation of proceedings.[7] Common to all these approaches is an intention to make clear the underlying purpose or function of the various type of interim order a court can make.

[1] RSC Ord 29 and to a limited extent CCR Ord 13, rr 6, 7, and 12; R Scott, *Supreme Court Practice 1999* (Sweet & Maxwell, 1999) Vol 1 at C13/6 and following.

[2] 1968 Brussels Convention on jurisdiction and the enforcement of judgments in civil and commercial matters (consolidated version), art 24.

[3] M Storme (ed), *Rapprochement du Droit Judiciaire de L'Union européenne/Approximation of Judiciary Law in the European Union* (Martinus Nijhoff, 1994) art 10. X E Kramer, 'Harmonisation of Provisional and Protective Measures in Europe', in M Storme (ed), *Procedural Laws in Europe. Towards Harmonisation* (Maklu, 2003).

[4] International Law Association, *The Helsinki Principles on Provisional and Protective Measures in International Litigation*, Rabels Zeitschrift für ausländisches und internationals Privatrecht, Januar 1998, Bd 62, H 1 (January 1998) 128, Principle 1.

[5] ALI/UNIDROIT Principles, principle 8.

[6] ELI-UNIDROIT Model Rules, Pt X, esp Introduction, comment 3.

[7] A Zuckerman, *Zuckerman on Civil Procedure—Principles of Practice* (Sweet & Maxwell, 2021) at 431.

*A Model Civil Procedure Code for England and Wales*. John Sorabji, Oxford University Press. © John Sorabji 2024.
DOI: 10.1093/oso/9780192848680.003.0014

3. This Part adopts the classification scheme more commonly known in European civil procedure, albeit it identifies three rather than two different types of provisional and protective measure: preservation measures; regulatory measures; and anticipatory measures.[8] This is intended to emphasise more clearly than the historic approach taken in England and Wales their nature and underlying rationale. This ought to assist with a more principled development of them and their application. It ought also, consistently with the promotion of procedural accessibility and intelligibility, make their nature and application more readily comprehensible to the public. Increased comprehensibility will also be particularly important to help give effect to the digital accountability principle. Computer programmers and coders will need to understand the nature of these measures if they are to design the digital procedure to give effect to practice and procedure concerning them. It will also be necessary to ensure that the Civil Courts Rule Committee and Parliament through the rule approval process are able to assess if the digital procedure makes proper provision for them. Hence functional classification ought also to promote democratic accountability of the Code.

## RULE 1.—SCOPE AND PURPOSE

**(1) This Part concerns provisional measures, which are either: preservative; regulatory; or anticipatory.**

**(2) Provisional measures are ancillary to proceedings. They protect the integrity of intended and commenced proceedings by preserving evidence and protecting rights pending their conclusion including, where necessary, enforcement. They further the procedural equality, accuracy, consensual settlement, effective enforcement, and finality principles.**

**(3) Provisional measures may be granted as provided for by the court's inherent jurisdiction, equity, the common law or by statute. They may be granted subject to such terms or conditions as are just in all the circumstances.**

**(4) Provisional measures must be proportionate to the purpose for which they are granted.**

*Sources: ALI/UNIDROIT Principles, principle 8; ALI/UNIDROIT Reporters' Study, r 17; ELI-UNIDROIT Model Rules, rr 184, 185, 190; The Helsinki Principles on Provisional and Protective Measures in International Litigation, Principles 1, 2; CPR Pt 25.*

## COMMENTARY

1. The general purpose of all provisional measures is the same. It is to protect the integrity of substantive, including intended substantive, proceedings. They are thus ancillary to such proceedings.[9] Within the ambit of that general purpose, three distinct functional categories of measure are identifiable, which are specified in rule 1(2). The categories are intended to encompass the various interim measures identified in CPR Pt 25. Like Pt 25, rule 1 is not intended to limit provisional measures to those

[8] X E Kramer in M Storme (ed) (2003) at 306; ELI-UNIDROIT Model Rules, r 184.

[9] *The Helsinki Principles on Provisional and Protective Measures in International Litigation*, Principles 10 to 15; *Smith v Peters* (1875) LR Eq 511 at 513.

that have been recognised previously.[10] New forms of provisional measure and new applications of existing measures may arise in the future within the three categories.

2. The three different categories of provisional measure all give effect to the same procedural principles. The most important of those are identified in rule 1(2). Ensuring that evidence or information is preserved, inspected, subject to examination or experiment places parties to proceedings on an equal footing. In that way all parties can assess evidence and information both in the context of trial preparation and the promotion of consensual settlement. Where the latter is not achieved, adjudicative accuracy is promoted as parties can ensure that necessary evidence or information is before the court and capable of robust examination and testing. Other forms of preservation measure, such as asset preservation orders (freezing injunctions) help promote effective enforcement by preventing assets subject to judgment being placed outside the court's jurisdiction. A necessary corollary of this is that they promote finality of litigation. Regulatory orders, such as interim injunctions, most obviously help the achievement of a fair process and effective enforcement through ensuring that the court is able to secure effective adjudication and enforcement. Similarly, anticipatory orders, by enabling claimants to receive interim payments of damages pending final judgment, help promote effective enforcement in a reasonable time. They also promote finality by prompting early and cost-effective resolution of disputes.
3. Rule 1(2) also highlights a further and obvious aspect of the functionality of provisional measures: their provisionality. They are interim measures and are not intended to nor should they finally determine proceedings (see rules 3(2) and 10(2)). That they are provisional in this way emphasises their role is intended to assist with the proper administration of justice, ie with the process through which effective dispute resolution is carried out.
4. Providing a three-fold, functional, categorisation of provisional measures does, however, obscure the different jurisprudential bases of the various types of measure. Some have their basis in equity.[11] Others arise under, or are now codified in, statute.[12] Others are and remain a product of the court's inherent jurisdiction, which is unlimited and broad in application.[13] Others again are solely the product of rules of court.[14] It is not for rules of court to prescribe the lawful basis for provisional measures. However, consistently with an approach that is intended to provide clarity and procedural accessibility, there is a strong argument for codifying in statute the court's jurisdiction to issue provisional measures and its power to develop new measures capable of application to novel situations.
5. Codification could also, in the interests of clarity and accessibility, draw together the different extant statutory bases for these measures within a single statute; thereby enhancing statutory transparency and accessibility. There is no specific reason, for instance, why the statutory basis for civil search orders should be in the Civil Procedure Act 1997 and the power to grant interim injunctions and freezing

[10] CPR r 25.1(1).

[11] *Hogg v Kirby* (1803) 8 Ves Jr 215 at 225.

[12] *Nippon Yusen Kaisha v Karageorgis* [1975] 1 WLR 1093; *Mareva Compania Naviera SA v International Bulkcarriers SA* [1975] 2 Lloyd's Rep 509; *Anton Piller KG v Manufacturing Processes* [1976] Ch 55; Senior Courts Act 1981, s 37(1) and (3) and Civil Procedure Act 1997, s 7; Administration of Justice Act 1969, s 20; Senior Courts Act 1981, s 32 and County Courts Act 1984, s 50.

[13] *Smith v Peters* (1875) LR Eq 511 at 513.

[14] Within the CPR security of costs is provided for within CPR Pt 25 Pt II. Here it is provided for within Pt 3.

injunctions should be in the Senior Courts Act 1981. Nor, consistently with the approach to court structure in Part 2, is there any necessity for the County Courts Act 1984 to maintain separate statutory provision to that in the Senior Courts Act 1981 for orders providing for inspection of property.[15] Any statutory codification could properly be set out by reference to the threefold categorisation of provisional measures set out within this rule. Absent such reform, Rule 1(3), however, identifies by reference the current variegated basis on which provisional measures may be granted.

6. Rule 1(3) not only acknowledges the different lawful bases on which provisional measures may be granted, it also acknowledges that such measures are discretionary; a point given effect by the criteria for the grant of such orders in this Part.[16] It also acknowledges that any provisional measure may be issued subject to such terms or conditions as are just in the circumstances. Typically, these might include a requirement that an applicant give an undertaking in damages to the subject of the order, fortify that undertaking with a requirement that security is given by the applicant, or that where the order is issued before proceedings are commenced that the applicant issue proceedings within a specified period of time absent which the order will lapse. Imposing, where necessary, such conditions is a matter of basic procedural fairness.[17] It is a means by which an effective balance is struck between applicants seeking such orders and those subject to them. This is particularly obvious where a measure requires property, information, or assets to be subject to preservation, detention, or custody. In each such case, the party subject to the order's substantive rights are, pending final determination, interfered with due to the order. Requiring an applicant to commit to make good any damage or loss sustained as a result of such interference, if it ultimately transpires that the provisional measure ought not to have been granted, is a basic aspect of procedural fairness.
7. Finally, rule 1(4) articulates a limitation on the grant of provisional measures. They must be proportionate. This is to ensure that they interfere with the exercise of the respondent's substantive rights in a way that is no more than necessary to achieve their purpose.

## RULE 2.—APPLICATION FOR PROVISIONAL MEASURES

**(1) The court may make an order for provisional measures on the application of a party to intended proceedings or proceedings. It may not make an order of its own initiative. Part 11, rule 8 applies to such applications, except as provided for in this Part.**

**(2) Applications for provisional measures may generally, and subject to any specific provisions in this Part, be made at any time before or after proceedings have commenced. They shall be heard with-notice, except as provided for by Part 14, rule 6.**

**(3) A party may apply for disclosure where it would facilitate the enforcement of a provisional measure. Disclosure may be ordered where**

**(a) the applicant has, on the face of it, an extremely strong case on the merits;**

15 Senior Courts Act 1981, s 34(3) and County Courts Act 1984, s 53(3). The approach taken in Part 2 would see the repeal of the 1984 Act.

16 The discretionary nature of such measures is also recognised internationally, *The Helsinki Principles on Provisional and Protective Measures in International Litigation*, Principle 4.

17 *SmithKline Beecham Plc v Apotex Europe Ltd* [2005] EWHC 1655; [2006] 1 WLR 872 at [41]; ALI/UNIDROIT Principles, principle 8.3; ELI-UNIDROIT Model Rules, r 190.

**(b) damage or potential damage to the applicant were there to be non-compliance with the provisional measure is likely to be serious;**

**(c) there is clear evidence that the person subject to the provisional measure has incriminating evidence and there is a real risk that they will destroy it; and**

**(d) any harm caused by the order must be neither disproportionate nor excessive.**

**(4) In considering whether to grant any form of provisional measure the court shall take into account whether the applicant is willing and able to give an undertaking in damages to the court. Such an undertaking should provide an indemnity to the respondent, and where appropriate any non-party adversely effected by the order, if it is subsequently determined that it was granted improperly.**

*Sources: ALI/UNIDROIT Principles, principle 8.2; ALI/UNIDROIT Reporters' Study, r 17; ELI-UNIDROIT Model Rules, rr 184, 186; The Helsinki Principles on Provisional and Protective Measures in International Litigation, Principles 1, 2; CPR Pt 25.*

## COMMENTARY

1. Provisional measures, consistently with the principle of party autonomy, may only be granted on the application of a party to proceedings or intended proceedings.

2. The general rules governing applications to the court apply to such applications. Consequently, applications should be made at as early a stage in the dispute as possible either before or after proceedings have commenced, ie when it is reasonably apparent that the measure sought is either necessary or desirable.[18] Any delay in making an application may undermine the justification for the order. It may undermine the credibility of the applicant's case, eg if made too late it may undermine the credibility of a claim that such an order is needed urgently. A late application, even if granted, may equally come too late for it to be effective.

3. Applications must, generally, be with-notice to parties and non-parties who are likely to be effected by any order granted. There are, however, a number of circumstances where a provisional measure can, exceptionally,[19] be made on a without-notice basis. The most common reasons are: urgency, ie a hearing must take place immediately such that reasonable notice could not be given, or that notice would frustrate the purpose of the application.[20]

4. Effective enforcement requires the court to have, and where appropriate, to take such steps as will enable a party in whose favour provisional measures have been granted to give effect to the order. Rule 2(3) codifies the inherent jurisdiction and gives effect to the power under section 37(1) of the Senior Courts Act 1981 to require disclosure from those who are subject to such measures where that would assist enforcement.[21] Disclosure orders in support of provisional measures are more likely to be granted post-judgment, not least to support asset preservation orders. This gives effect to the enforcement principle, as it helps secure effective compliance with judgments.[22]

5. All provisional measures may, if granted, potentially cause loss and damage to the party subject to them as well as to non-parties. This is particularly the case where

[18] Part 11, r 8.
[19] *Moat Housing Group South Ltd v Harris* [2005] EWCA Civ 287; [2006] QB 606 at [71].
[20] Part 14, r 6.
[21] *Lakatamia Shipping Co Ltd v Su* [2020] EWHC 865 (Comm); [2020] 1 WLR 2852 at [16]–[33].
[22] *Lakatamia Shipping Co Ltd v Su* [2020] EWHC 865 (Comm); [2020] 1 WLR 2852 at [27].

preservation and regulatory orders are concerned. An asset preservation order, if wrongly granted, may cause damage to the respondent through their not being able to utilise their assets freely. Orders detaining items of evidence may result in a respondent not being in a position to use or sell them; circumstances that could, again, cause them loss and damage. Interim injunctions may cause damage to both parties and non-parties bound by them, particularly where it is ultimately determined that the applicant's substantive claim fails. Given this, while assessing whether to grant an order a court must consider the extent to which an applicant is willing and able to give an undertaking in damages, which could form the basis of compensation for any loss or damage caused by the grant of an order if it later transpires it was improperly granted.[23]

## RULE 3.—VARIATION AND DISCHARGE OF PROVISIONAL MEASURES

**(1) The court may vary or discharge an order for provisional measures of its own initiative or on the application of any party or person affected by the order.**

**(2) All orders for provisional measures must contain a date at which the measure must be reconsidered by the court absent which it will be discharged automatically and without further order. Any party or person subject to the order may apply to vary that date.**

**(3) An application to vary or discharge an order for provisional measures made at a with-notice hearing, other than to vary the date at which it must be reconsidered or automatically discharged, may not be brought on the basis of the same evidence as was before the court at the original hearing.**

**(4) Where an order for provisional measures is made in proposed proceedings, the order must specify the date by which proceedings must be commenced. Failure to commence proceedings by that date shall, unless the court orders otherwise either on its own initiative or on the application of a party, automatically discharge the provisional measure without further order.**

*Sources: ELI-UNIDROIT Model Rules, rr 188, 189; CPR Pt 25, rr 25.2(3), 25.2(4), PD25 para 5.1.*

## COMMENTARY

1. Provisional measures may be varied by either the court of its own initiative or on application of any person subject to or affected by the order.[24] They may be discharged on the same basis, not least to maintain their provisional nature.
2. There is, however, a risk with preservation and regulatory orders, that they could, as a matter of fact, finally determine the proceedings.[25] This risk is particularly acute where interim injunctions are concerned. Most recently, the development of so-called super-injunctions, ie interim injunctions that enjoined disclosure of the fact of the injunction as well as of its content, saw parties treat them as finally determining proceedings. This arose, amongst other things, because these orders tended not

[23] S Gee, 'The Undertaking in Damages' [2006] LMCLQ 181; *Z Ltd v A-Z* [1982] QB 558; *Birch v Birch* [2017] UKSC 53; [2017] 1 WLR 2959 at [5].

[24] Part 15, r 13(5).

[25] *British Air Line Pilots Association v British Airways Cityflyer Ltd* [2018] EWHC 1889 (QB) at [24].

specify a date when the matter had to come back before the court.[26] This was particularly problematic as treating these injunctions as finally determining proceedings enabled parties to side-step a substantive limitation on interim injunctions. Interim injunctions do not bind non-parties where proceedings are concluded.[27] As the parties treated the order as finally determining the matter, they placed non-parties under a form of restraint that would not arise under a genuine final order. Hence, by rendering the interim injunction practically permanent, applicants gained a procedural advantage prohibited by the substantive law. The Practice Guidance on Interim Non-Disclosure Orders (2012) put a stop to this impermissible practice.[28] It did so by requiring the inclusion of a specified date (a return date) in any such orders requiring the matter to come back before the court.[29]

3. Rule 3(2) codifies the requirement to include a return date in any order granting a provisional measure. It does so to ensure that such measures cannot become permanent by default. Compliance with this requirement is incentivised as the rule mandates that absent compliance with it the provisional measure will be discharged automatically. This also promotes effective dispute management as it is a means by which the court can ensure that it can monitor progress of the substantive proceedings that underlie the provisional measure effectively.[30] Within the digital procedure it ought to be straightforward to enable automated reminders of upcoming return dates and to schedule dispute management conferences to consider the order and the progress of the underlying proceedings. As with other requirements in orders, the return date may be varied on application. Such an application will itself provide the court with the opportunity to scrutinise whether the variation is justified or whether it may tend to transform the provisional measure into a permanent order.

4. Any application to vary or discharge a provisional measure, which was made at a with-notice hearing, must only be made on the basis of fresh evidence or a material change in position that calls into question the basis on which the order was granted. This limitation is consistent with the general approach to subsequent and further applications for the same relief or to vary or discharge orders.[31] This approach does not apply where the application to vary or discharge forms part of a with-notice rehearing of an order granted on a without-notice basis. It also does not apply to an application to vary the return date.

5. Finally, rule 3(4) provides that where a provisional measure is granted before proceedings are commenced, it must specify the date by which substantive proceedings must be commenced. Unless the court directs otherwise or a party applies to vary the order, absent commencement the order is automatically discharged. This ensures such orders are only obtained where proceedings are genuinely in contemplation, ie they are not sought abusively to harass respondents. It also ensures that such measures do not become final by default.

[26] D Neuberger et al, *Report of the Committee on Super-Injunctions: Super-Injunctions, Anonymised Injunctions and Open Justice* (Judicial Office, 2011) at 28–31.

[27] *Jockey Club v Buffham* [2003] QB 462.

[28] *Practice Guidance: Interim Non-Disclosure Orders* [2012] 1 WLR 1003.

[29] *Practice Guidance: Interim Non-Disclosure Orders* [2012] 1 WLR 1003 at [37]–[41].

[30] *G & G v Wikimedia* [2010] EMLR 14 at [21]–[27]; *Terry v Persons Unknown* [2010] 1 FCR 659 at [37]–[41].

[31] Part 11, r 8 and Part 15, r 13.

# SECTION 2: PRESERVATION ORDERS

## RULE 4.—PRESERVATION ORDERS

**(1) The court may make an interim order preserving, securing, or detaining evidence, property, or financial assets for the purpose of protecting the effective administration of justice. It may also make an interim order, for the same purpose, securing access to, experiments on, or information about, evidence, property, or financial assets.**
**(2) A preservation order may be granted against a party or a non-party to proceedings. An order may be granted before or after proceedings have commenced where permitted by statute.**
**(3) A preservation order that requires property to be transferred to the applicant from the person subject to it must provide that the property be held, on behalf of the applicant, by their lawyers or a custodian authorised by the court.**

*Sources: ELI-UNIDROIT Model Rules, rr 192, 198; Torts (Interference with Goods) Act 1977, s 4; Senior Courts Act 1981, ss 32, 34; County Courts Act 1984, ss 52, 53; Civil Procedure Act 1997, s 7; Council Directive (EC) 2004/48, art 9; CPR r 25.1(1)(c), (d), (e), (f), (g), (h), (i), (j), (k), (l), (m), (n), (o), and (p).*

## COMMENTARY

1. Preservation orders encompass all the forms of interim order specified in CPR Pt 25 other than interim injunctions, interim declarations, and interim payments. Consistently with the court's jurisdiction to develop new forms of provisional measure, rule 4(1) is not drafted in prescriptive terms.[32]
2. Preservation orders can be divided into two categories. The first can be conceived of, in Zuckerman's terms, as process orders. They are concerned with facilitating the proper administration of justice. Thus, they operate to expedite access to evidence, and secure, detain, or preserve it from destruction. In this way they make evidence, including samples of evidence or property, available for inspection or examination by the parties, or expert witnesses. They also ensure that it will be available, where necessary, for trial. Thus, they promote procedural equality by ensuring all parties have equivalent access to evidence, which in turn helps secure effective participation and a properly adversarial process. Ultimately, they also thereby promote consensual settlement as the parties, through access to evidence, may properly evaluate their prospects of success in the proceedings. Absent settlement these orders promote adjudicative accuracy at trial.
3. The second category could be conceived of, again following Zuckerman, as a protective order. It is a form of injunctive relief. Unlike interim injunctions, which are categorised here as regulatory orders, the form of injunctive relief—a freezing injunction—is categorised here as a preservation order; an asset preservation order. Unlike regulatory orders, which regulate the exercise of substantive rights in dispute in proceedings pending final judgment, an asset preservation order protects the proper administration of justice through ensuring that a defendant's assets are not improperly dissipated or moved out of the jurisdiction in order to frustrate effective

[32] Rule 4(1), above.

enforcement of a final judgment. Such orders, in contrast to regulatory orders, are thus primarily intended to secure effective judgment and enforcement.

4. Preservation orders may be granted against either parties or non-parties.[33] Where preservation orders require property to be transferred from a party or non-party to the applicant, it must be held on the applicant's behalf by their lawyer or by a custodian authorised by the court.[34] This is to ensure that the property's integrity is maintained while the proceedings are ongoing and the interference with any substantive rights of the party or non-party required to transfer the property is no more than necessary.

## RULE 5.—CRITERIA FOR AWARD OF PRESERVATION ORDERS—GENERAL

**(1) The court may grant a preservation order, other than those specifically provided for in this Part, when**
  **(a) the applicant has an arguable case on the merits of their claim;**
  **(b) any property or information to be subject to the order is clearly identifiable and is or may become the subject matter of proceedings or is relevant to an issue in dispute in the proceedings; and**
  **(c) in all the circumstances it is necessary for the proper administration of justice.**

**(2) Evidence, property, or assets subject to a preservation order may only be used by the person in whose favour the order is made for the purpose specified in the order.**

*Sources: ELI-UNIDROIT Model Rules, r 199; Torts (Interference with Goods) Act 1977, s 4; Senior Courts Act 1981, ss 32, 34; County Courts Act 1984, ss 52, 53; Civil Procedure Act 1997, s 7; Council Directive (EC) 2004/ 48, art 9; CPR r 25.1(1)(c), (d), (e), (f), (g), (h), (i), (j), (k), (l), (m), (n), (o), and (p), r 25.5.*

## COMMENTARY

1. The court should not grant a preservation order, other than an access to premises or asset preservation order, unless it is just to do so. In determining whether it is just to do so the court must take account of all the circumstances. If such an order is granted the evidence, property, information, or asset subject to the order must only be used by the applicant in whose favour the order was made. It must also only be used for the purpose specified in the order.

2. If, for instance, property is subject to an order for delivery-up to the applicant to preserve it pending trial and judgment or it is subject to an order requiring access to enable specific experiments to be carried out on it by an expert witness, it may not be used for any other purpose. This restriction helps ensure the order is proportionate, ie the interference with the respondent's substantive rights is kept to a minimum.

3. This rule adopts a similar approach to the test set out within the ELI-UNIDROIT Model rules for asset and evidence preservation orders. It does not

[33] Where a preservation order relates to the inspection, preservation, custody etc of property it may only be granted against a non-party after proceedings have commenced if the statutory basis of the order is either s 34(3) of the Senior Courts Act 1981, ss 33(1), 34(3), and 53(3) or County Courts Act 1984, ss 52(1) and 53(3).

[34] *CBS United Kingdom Ltd v Lambert* [1983] Ch 37 at 45.

therefore seek to replicate or codify the various different approaches to such orders developed in England and Wales either within statute,[35] the CPR,[36] or common law.[37] The intention behind the approach adopted is to set out a principled approach, which is intended to give effect to the procedural principles set out in Part 1.

4. The first limb of the test is intended to balance a claimant's right to a fair process, and particularly one that can give effect to the accuracy, consensual settlement,[38] and effective enforcement principles with a defendant's or non-party's right to exercise their substantive rights over their property or information without improper interference. It thus requires the applicant to demonstrate that their claim in proceedings or proposed proceedings is not fanciful: that they have an arguable case. Absent that, there is no justification for interfering with defendant or non-party's substantive rights. This particular requirement is, for instance, evident in the test applicable to orders for delivery-up of property under the Torts (Interference with Goods) Act 1977.[39] This rule generalises and codifies it.
5. The second limb of the test is intended to ensure that any order made is both necessary and proportionate. Necessity, in the sense that the property or information subject to the order must be necessary for the court to determine issues in the proceedings, is long-established as an underpinning of the grant of provisional orders.[40] The second limb also requires the applicant to identify with certainty the subject matter of the proposed order. Property must therefore be properly identifiable.[41] Absent this an order could become a means by which the applicant could engage in a wide-ranging fishing expedition for evidence or property.[42]
6. The third limb requires the court to consider whether, in all the circumstances, an order is necessary for the proper administration of justice. This enables the court to consider a range of factors, some of which will be generally applicable to all types of preservation order. It enables, for instance, the court to take account of whether it is likely that the subject matter of the order, absent the order, is likely to be disposed of or otherwise put outside the court's jurisdiction before trial, judgment, or effective enforcement. Where there is no risk of that, it is difficult to see how granting an order would promote the proper administration of justice. This limb also enables the court to consider whether and to what extent an order may be oppressive as against the defendant or a non-party, and hence whether it ought properly to be granted.
7. The third limb also enables the court to consider a range of factors, which may and inevitably will be tailored to specific types of preservation order. In claims currently dealt with under the Torts (Interference with Goods) Act 1977, for instance, whether an order is necessary for the proper administration of justice could also, as it does currently, require consideration of the question whether there was clear

[35] Senior Courts Act 1981, ss 33(1) and 34(3); County Courts Act 1984, ss 52(1) and 53(3).
[36] CPR r 25.5.
[37] Eg orders under the Torts (Interference with Goods) Act 1977; *CBS United Kingdom Ltd v Lambert* [1983] Ch 37 at 44.
[38] *Boehringer Ingelheim Pharma GmbH v Generics (UK) Ltd* [2019] EWHC 584; [2019] FSR 21.
[39] *CBS United Kingdom Ltd v Lambert* [1983] Ch 37 at 44.
[40] *Smith v Peters* (1875) LR Eq 511 at 513.
[41] Senior Courts Act 1981, ss 33(1) and 34(3); County Courts Act 1984, ss 52(1) and 53(3); CPR r 25.5.
[42] *Tudor Accumulator Co Ltd v China Mutual Steam Navigation Co Ltd* [1930] WN 200 at 201.

evidence that the defendant had acquired the property wrongfully, ie whether it is likely that the claimant would succeed at trial and hence there is a justification for not permitting the defendant to maintain possession of the property pending final determination.[43]

8. None of the limbs, however, codify or otherwise give effect to a criterion applicable to orders made under CPR r 25.1(1)(c) and (d).[44] Under the CPR, these orders concerned the detention, custody, preservation, and inspection of property, taking samples, carrying out experiments or selling property (where it is perishable), requiring the payment of income from such property pending judgment and the entry into land or property to carry out the foregoing. The orders all required the subject matter of the order to be physical in nature. Such a limitation, in a digital age, is no longer justifiable. As the courts have accepted that digital assets, such as non-fungible tokens and various crypto-assets, are a form of property, preservation orders ought to be capable of being applied to them. To enable preservation orders to be able to operate effectively in a digital age, the criteria in rule 5 does not therefore replicate the restriction to physical property.
9. Finally, rule 5(3) gives effect to the proposition that property or information subject to a preservation order may not be used for any purpose other than that provided for in the order. It thus prohibits collateral use of any property or information subject to the order. This further, protects the substantive rights of the defendant or any non-party subject to an order.[45]

## RULE 6.—AWARD AND EFFECT OF ACCESS AND PRESERVATION ORDERS (SEARCH ORDERS)

**(1) The purpose of an access and preservation order is to enable the applicant to obtain access to premises to preserve: evidence relevant or potentially relevant to proceedings; or property that is or may be the subject matter of proceedings or in respect of which any question has or may arise in proceedings.**
**(2) An application may be made before proceedings have commenced and after judgment. An order may be granted on a without-notice basis.**
**(3) The court may grant an order against a specified person when**
  **(a) the party seeking the order has, on the face of it, a strong case on the merits in the proceedings or proposed proceedings;**
  **(b) there is a serious risk of harm to the interests of the party seeking the order;**
  **(c) there is clear evidence that incriminating evidence is in the possession of the person against whom the order is to be made;**
  **(d) there is a real risk that the incriminating evidence will be destroyed or otherwise dealt with so as to prejudice the administration of justice if the order is not made on a without-notice basis; and**
  **(e) any harm caused by execution of the order is not disproportionate.**

*Sources: ELI-UNIDROIT Model Rules, r 198; Civil Procedure Act 1997, s 7; CPR r 25.1(1)(h), PD25A, standard form search order.*

[43] *CBS United Kingdom Ltd v Lambert* [1983] Ch 37 at 44.
[44] *Tudor Accumulator Co Ltd v China Mutual Steam Navigation Co Ltd* [1930] WN 200.
[45] *Boehringer Ingelheim Pharma GmbH v Generics (UK) Ltd* [2019] EWHC 584; [2019] FSR 21.

## COMMENTARY

1. Access to premises orders were developed in English and Welsh civil procedure during the 1970s.[46] They were first recognised by the Court of Appeal in *Anton Piller KG v Manufacturing Processes Ltd* (1976),[47] which affirmed that the High Court could grant an interim injunction that enabled an applicant to gain access to a respondent's premises to secure evidence relevant to proceedings, which, absent the order, was likely to be destroyed.[48] The order, then known as an *Anton Piller* order, was thus intended to facilitate the administration of justice and specifically the accuracy principle by enabling relevant evidence to be identified and preserved for trial.[49] The High Court's inherent jurisdiction was subsequently codified in section 7 of the Civil Procedure Act 1997[50] and the order renamed as a *search order*.
2. Neither its original nor subsequent name fully capture the order's purpose or application, which is to secure access to premises and the preservation of evidence or property relevant to proceedings or proposed proceedings. Hence the order is renamed here as an 'access and preservation order'. Nor is access secured as if the order was the civil equivalent of a search warrant in a criminal investigation. It does not authorise the applicant to enter a respondent's premises absent their consent. It is more nuanced than that. It directs the respondent to give their consent to entry on pain of being found in contempt of court.[51]
3. Access and preservation orders can and in most cases will be granted on a without-notice basis. Advance notice would, for instance, enable a respondent to destroy the evidence or property that is to be secured by the order.[52] An order may also be granted before proceedings commence to protect evidence or property for proposed proceedings.[53] One may also be granted after judgment against either a party or non-party to the proceedings to promote effective enforcement.[54]
4. Rule 6(3) sets out the criteria for granting such an order. In doing so it recognises that an access and preservation order acts *in personam*.[55] Hence it must be granted in respect of a specified individual. The criteria to be applied are intended to ensure that these orders are only issued when necessary to protect evidence or property from destruction, and thus protect the proper administration of justice. They are also intended to protect respondents. As this type of order is a significant interference with their property rights[56] care must be taken to ensure that they are not granted by the court lightly. Nor should they amount to a disproportionate interference with the respondent's substantive rights.[57] To protect the respondent's rights, the five criteria,

[46] *EMI Ltd v Pandit* [1975] 1 WLR 302.

[47] *Anton Piller KG v Manufacturing Processes Ltd* [1976] Ch 55; *TBD (Owen Holland) Ltd v Simons* [2020] EWCA Civ 1182; [2021] 1 WLR 992 at [127] and following.

[48] *Anton Piller KG v Manufacturing Processes Ltd* [1976] Ch 55 at 60.

[49] *TBD (Owen Holland) Ltd v Simons* [2020] EWCA Civ 1182; [2021] 1 WLR 992 at [175].

[50] Derived from Civil Procedure Act 1997, s 7.

[51] *Anton Piller KG v Manufacturing Processes Ltd* [1976] Ch 55 at 60.

[52] *Anton Piller KG v Manufacturing Processes Ltd* [1976] Ch 55 at 61.

[53] Civil Procedure Act 1997, s 7(1).

[54] *Distributori Automatici Italia SpA v Holford General Trading Co Ltd* [1985] 1 WLR 1066; *Abdela v Baadarani (No 2)* [2017] EWHC 269 (Ch); [2018] 1 WLR 89.

[55] *Anton Piller KG v Manufacturing Processes Ltd* [1976] Ch 55 at 62.

[56] *Bank Mellat v Nikpour* (1985) 2 FSR 87 at 92.

[57] The grant of an order is subject to any applicable privilege.

which codify those established in the authorities,[58] create a high bar for an applicant to surmount before the court may exercise its discretion to grant the order. Given its draconian nature, it would also ordinarily be expected that the grant of such an order would be conditional on the applicant providing an undertaking in damages (rules 1(3) and 4(2)).[59]

5. Preservation of evidence may now, and in the future is likely to, focus on digital material. Access and preservation orders can, as a consequence, encompass such evidence. Preservation may in such circumstances take the form of digital imaging.[60] Once evidence is secured and preserved it may then be subject to an order for disclosure.[61]

## RULE 7.—AWARD AND EFFECT OF ASSET PRESERVATION ORDERS (FREEZING INJUNCTIONS)

**(1) The court may grant an asset preservation order. This is an interim order to preserve the existence of assets within or outside the jurisdiction pending final judgment or enforcement of a final judgment. Assets subject to the order may either be within or outside the jurisdiction. The order may be granted on a without-notice basis.**

**(2) An order may be granted over assets within the jurisdiction when**
- **(a) the applicant has a good arguable case in the proceedings before the court or the order is sought to support enforcement in proceedings brought outside England and Wales;**
- **(b) the party against whom the order is sought has assets within the jurisdiction;**
- **(c) the judgment in the proceedings would otherwise go unsatisfied because there is a real risk of dissipation of or unjustified dealing with the assets; and**
- **(d) it is just and convenient in all the circumstances to make the order.**

**(3) An order may be granted over assets outside the jurisdiction when**
- **(a) the conditions for the grant of an order over assets within the jurisdiction are satisfied; and**
- **(b) the party against whom the order is sought has insufficient assets within the jurisdiction to satisfy a final judgment in the proceedings and has assets outside the jurisdiction.**

**Such an order will not, however, bind non-parties who are outside the jurisdiction.**

**(4) An order granted in respect of assets outside the jurisdiction may only be enforced with the court's permission. Permission will generally only be granted at a with-notice hearing. Where it is just to do so in cases of urgency, permission may be granted at a without-notice hearing.**

**(5) Permission to enforce an order outside the jurisdiction will only be granted when it is just and convenient to do so. In considering whether it is just and convenient to do so the court shall consider**
- **(a) all the relevant circumstances and options available, including any terms or conditions such as undertakings to non-parties and the proportionality of any steps taken outside the jurisdiction;**

[58] *Indichii Salus Ltd (In Receivership) v Chandrasekaran* [2006] EWHC 521 (Ch) at [85] and *MX1 Ltd v F* [2018] EWHC 717 (Ch) at [40]–[41].

[59] *Anton Piller KG v Manufacturing Processes Ltd* [1976] Ch 55 at 61.

[60] *TBD (Owen Holland) Ltd v Simons* [2020] EWCA Civ 1182; [2021] 1 WLR 992.

[61] *EMI Ltd v Pandit* [1975] 1 WLR 302; *TBD (Owen Holland) Ltd v Simons* [2020] EWCA Civ 1182; [2021] 1 WLR 992 at [135].

**(b) the applicant's interests balanced against those of other parties, and any likely new parties, to any relevant proceedings outside the jurisdiction;**

**(c) the nature of any relief available in foreign proceedings concerning the assets. Permission should not, normally, be granted in terms that would enable the applicant to obtain superior relief in foreign proceedings than that given by the asset preservation order;**

**(d) all relevant evidence in support of the application, including evidence concerning the law and practice of any relevant foreign court and any proposed proceedings in the foreign court's jurisdiction;**

**(e) evidence that there is a real risk of dissipation of the assets subject to the order; and**

**(f) that there must be a real prospect that the assets in question are within the jurisdiction of a relevant foreign court.**

**(6) An order ought, generally, to apply to an amount in value of no more than the amount specified in the judgment subject to enforcement.**

**(7) Where an order is made and an undertaking to the court is given by the applicant, the court may order the applicant to provide security for the undertaking. The giving of security includes making a payment into court. The court may make such an order where the respondent can demonstrate**

**(a) the likely loss to them resulting from the grant of the order can reasonably be assessed;**

**(b) there is a good arguable case that there is a risk that loss will occur as a result of the order being granted; and**

**(c) such loss either has been or is likely to be caused by the order.**

**(8) An order takes effect once it is announced. It may be varied or set aside where it is in the interests of justice to do so.**

**(9) A party may be required, by order, to provide an applicant with information concerning the location of property or assets that are or may be subject to an asset preservation order. Where property or assets may be subject to such an order, the provision of information can only be ordered where there is credible evidence that the assets would be subject to an asset preservation order if one were to be made.**

*Sources: ELI-UNIDROIT Model Rules, rr 192, 193; Senior Courts Act 1981, s 37(3); CPR rr 25.1(1) (f), (g), PD25A, standard form freezing injunction.*

## COMMENTARY

1. Rule 7 makes provision for specific interim injunctions, which were originally known as *Mareva* injunctions[62] before being renamed under the CPR as freezing injunctions.[63] Consistently with the categorisation of provisional measures in this Part and their primary function, which is to stop a respondent from frustrating enforcement of a final judgment by dissipating their assets,[64] hiding them, or moving them outside the jurisdiction,[65] they are renamed here as asset preservation orders.

[62] *Mareva Compania Naviera SA v International Carriers SA (The Mareva)* [1975] 2 Lloyd's Rep 509; *Nippon Yusen Kaisha v Karageorgis* [1975] 1 WLR 1093.

[63] Senior Courts Act 1981, s 37.

[64] *Lakatamia Shipping Company Ltd v Morimoto* [2019] EWCA Civ 2203; [2020] 2 All ER (Comm) 359 at [34] for the approach to be taken to determining the risk of dissipation.

[65] A Zuckerman (2021) at 529; *Parbulk II AS v PT Humpuss Intermoda Transportasi TBK* [2011] EWHC 3143 (Comm) at [38]; *Broad Idea International Ltd v Conway Collateral Ltd* [2021] UKPC 24; [2022] 2 WLR

Consistently with this they neither provide security for judgment[66] nor do they create a proprietary interest in any of the respondent's assets.[67] To minimise the risk that advance notice might enable a respondent to frustrate their purpose before an order is made, they are generally made without-notice to the respondent. For the same reasons they take effect immediately upon being made.[68]

2. Asset preservation orders are draconian orders.[69] By their very nature they amount to a significant interference with the substantive rights of parties who are subject to them. They also amount to a significant interference with non-party rights. They typically require bank accounts to be frozen, thus limiting a bank's ability to deal with assets subject to them. To protect the rights of parties and non-parties who may become subject to such orders, while protecting an applicant's right to a fair process a high, four-part, threshold test has developed governing the exercise of the court's discretion to grant them. Rule 7(2)(a) to (d) codifies that test as it has developed within the case law.[70]
3. The threshold test's most significant limb is set out in rule 7(2)(c): that there is a real risk of dissipation, of unjustified dealing with the assets. This criterion goes to the primary function of asset preservation orders as it focuses on the question whether there is a need to enjoin a respondent from dealing with their assets in a way that frustrates effective enforcement.[71]
4. An asset preservation order's reach is not limited to assets within the jurisdiction. They may be applied to assets outside the jurisdiction where the respondent has insufficient assets within the jurisdiction.[72] Such extra-territorial asset preservation orders (worldwide freezing injunctions) do not, however, bind non-parties who are otherwise outside the jurisdiction.[73] They may, furthermore, only be enforced with the court's permission, which should only be granted where it is just to do so. These limitations ensure that extra-territorial orders are neither an oppressive nor too exorbitant an exercise of the courts' jurisdiction.[74]
5. The test for enforcement outside the jurisdiction in rule 7(4) codifies the applicable guidelines developed in *Dadourian Group International v Simms* (2006).[75]

703. They act *in personam*, ie against a specific person: *JSC Mezhdunarodniy Promyshlenniy Bank v Pugachev* [2015] EWCA Civ 139; [2016] 1 WLR 160 at [14].

[66] *Mills v Northern Railway of Buenos Ayres Co* [1870] 5 Ch App 621; *Z Ltd v A-Z* [1982] QB 558 at 571, 585.

[67] Asset preservation orders must be distinguished from interim proprietary injunctions granted where the applicant has a proprietary claim in the proceedings to the asset in question. *Mercedes Benz AG v Leiduck* [1996] 1 AC 284; *Capital Cameras Ltd v Harold Lines Ltd* [1991] 1 WLR 54.

[68] *Z Ltd v A-Z* [1982] QB 558 at 572.

[69] *Bank Mellat v Nikpour* (1985) 2 FSR 87 at 92.

[70] See for instance, *Unitel SA v Unitel International Holdings BV* [2023] EWHC 3231 (Comm) affirming the 'good arguable case' criterion.

[71] *JSC BTA Bank v Ablyasov* [2013] EWCA Civ 928; [2014] 1 WLR 1414 at [34].

[72] *Babanaft International Co SA v Bassatne* [1990] Ch 13.

[73] *Ashtiani v Kashi* [1987] QB 888; *Derby & Co v Weldon (No 1)* [1990] Ch 48; *Babanaft International Co SA v Bassatne* [1990] Ch 13.

[74] *In re Bank of Credit and Commerce International SA* [1994] 1 WLR 708; *Dadourian Group International v Simms* [2006] EWCA Civ 399; [2006] 1 WLR 2499.

[75] *Dadourian Group International v Simms* [2006] EWCA Civ 399; [2006] 1 WLR 2499 at [25].

6. The amount specified to be subject to an asset preservation order must ordinarily be no more than the maximum amount that is to be enforced.[76] This limitation is intended to ensure that the order granted is one that makes no more than necessary provision to promote effective enforcement. In certain circumstances, where for instance the value of assets subject to the order is uncertain or may fluctuate, an order for a higher amount than that specified in the judgment to be enforced may justifiably be made.
7. Asset preservation orders should generally be granted on condition that the applicant gives an undertaking in damages to the court.[77] Due to their draconian nature and the manner in which they interfere with a respondent's substantive rights,[78] this should be done in all but exceptional circumstances.[79] Rule 7(7) codifies the applicable test for the giving of security for any undertaking provided.[80]
8. Finally, rule 7(13) gives effect to what is currently CPR r 25.1(g): the power to order a party to provide information concerning the location of property or assets that may be subject to an asset preservation order. Where property or assets are subject to an asset preservation order, this form of ancillary provisional measure may be granted consequent upon the grant of the order. Where there is a doubt whether the property or assets falls under an asset preservation order, this ancillary order may only be granted where the applicant can adduce credible evidence that they would do so. This stops them from becoming fishing expeditions.[81]

## RULE 8.—RESTRICTIONS ON THE SCOPE OF ASSET PRESERVATION ORDERS

**(1) An asset preservation order must make reasonable provision for the party subject to the order to receive and use assets in good faith for**
**(a) their and their family's ordinary living expenses;**
**(b) where necessary, legitimate work or business expenses;**
**(c) legal fees concerning the conduct of the proceedings in which the order was made.**
**(2) The court may impose restrictions or limitations on the order as are just in all the circumstances.**
**(3) An order may require the party subject to it give the applicant prior notice of any specific expenditure for a permitted use.**

*Sources: ELI-UNIDROIT Model Rules, r 194.*

[76] *Z Ltd v A-Z* [1982] QB 558 at 574–575.

[77] *Banco Nacional de Comercio Exterior SNC v Empresa de Telecomunicationes de Cuba SA* [2007] EWCA Civ 662; [2008] 1 WLR 1936.

[78] Including non-parties: *SmithKline Beecham Plc v Apotex Europe Ltd* [2005] EWHC 1655; [2006] 1 WLR 872.

[79] *RBG (Resources) Plc v Rastogi* [2002] BPIR 1028.

[80] *Energy Venture Partners Ltd v Malabu Oil & Gas Ltd* [2014] EWCA Civ 1295; [2015] 1 WLR 2309 at [53]–[54].

[81] *Parker v Structured Credit Fund Ltd* [2003] EWHC 391 (Ch); [2003] 1 WLR 1680 at [22]–[25].

## COMMENTARY

1. An asset preservation order should be proportionate in its effect, ie it should do no more than ensure a respondent's assets are not improperly dissipated. This rule codifies the three main limitations on such orders, which promote proportionality and ensure they do not become oppressive[82] or amount to security for judgment.[83]
2. The three limitations are also intended to balance the need to secure the proper administration of justice and the applicant's ability to access a fair process with the respondent's right to family life[84] and property,[85] as well as their own right of effective access to a fair process.[86] In addition to these three specific limitations, the court retains a general discretion to impose such restrictions or limitations on an order as are just in all the circumstances.[87]
3. To maintain proportionality and particularly ensure an order does not amount to security for judgment, provision must be made within it for a specified amount of their assets, which the respondent, in good faith,[88] is able to use for their ordinary living expenses,[89] necessary and legitimate work or ordinary business expenses whether they are legally due or not,[90] and sums incurred for legal fees relating to the immediate proceedings in the absence of other forms of funding.[91] Existing debts come within the scope of such expenses.[92] The order must specify the amount provided for under this provision.[93]
4. Where reasonable provision for the receipt and proportionate use of assets is provided for in an order, the court may require the respondent to give prior notice to the applicant of any specific use of their assets. An order could, for instance, provide for a specific amount of expenditure on living or legal expenses, but require notice to be given prior to spending over a certain limit or for all such expenditure.[94] Notice would enable an applicant to take steps to stop a respondent spending money that was arguably outside the scope of reasonable provision.

[82] *Babanaft International Co SA v Bassatne* [1990] Ch 13 at 42; ELI-UNIDROIT Model Rules, r 194, comment 1.

[83] *Derby & Co Ltd v Weldon (Nos 3 and 4)* [1990] Ch 65; *Halifax Plc v Chandler* [2001] EWCA Civ 1750; [2002] CPLR 41 at [18]–[20].

[84] European Convention on Human Rights, art 8; *R (K) v Her Majesty's Treasury* [2009] EWHC 1643 (Admin).

[85] European Convention on Human Rights, art 1, protocol 1.

[86] European Convention on Human Rights, art 6.

[87] *Atlas Maritime Co SA v Avalon Maritime Ltd (The Coral Rose) (No 3)* [1991] 1 WLR 917 at 928.

[88] On the good faith requirement see, for instance, *Iraqi Ministry of Defence v Arcepey Shipping Co SA (The Angel Bell)* [1981] QB 65 at 70–71; *Atlas Maritime Co SA v Avalon Maritime Ltd (The Coral Rose) (No 3)* [1991] 1 WLR 917 at 928.

[89] *TDK Tape Distributor (UK) Ltd v Videochoice Ltd* [1986] 1 WLR 141 at 146. Ordinary living expenses do not include one-off exceptional or extraordinary purchases.

[90] *Iraqi Ministry of Defence v Arcepey Shipping Co SA (The Angel Bell)* [1981] QB 65; *Halifax Plc v Chandler* [2001] EWCA Civ 1750; [2002] CPLR 41; *Abbey Forwarding Ltd v Hone* [2010] EWHC 1532 at [19].

[91] *Derby & Co Ltd v Weldon (Nos 3 and 4)* [1990] Ch 65 at 76; *Atlas Maritime Co SA v Avalon Maritime Ltd (The Coral Rose) (No 3)* [1991] 1 WLR 917.

[92] *Atlas Maritime Co SA v Avalon Maritime Ltd (The Coral Rose) (No 1)* [1991] 1 Lloyd's Rep 563.

[93] *Z Ltd v A-Z* [1982] QB 558 at 576–577.

[94] *Halifax Plc v Chandler* [2001] EWCA Civ 1750; [2002] CPLR 41 at [4].

# SECTION 3: REGULATORY ORDERS

## RULE 9.—INTERIM INJUNCTIONS AND INTERIM DECLARATIONS

**(1) The court may make an interim order regulating the conduct of parties or third parties. Such an order may take the form of an interim injunction or interim declaration.**
**(2) An interim injunction is a regulatory order that protects the effective administration of justice by requiring a person to act or prohibiting a person from acting in a manner specified in the order.**
**(3) An interim declaration determines, on a provisional basis, a state of fact or law or a person's rights.**

*Sources: ALI/UNIDROIT Principles, principles 5.8, 8.2; ALI/UNIDROIT Reporters' Study, r 17; ELI-UNIDROIT Model Rules, r 196; Crown Proceedings Act 1947, s 21; Senior Courts Act 1981, ss 19, 31, 37; CPR rr 25.1(1)(a), (b).*

## COMMENTARY

1. This rule makes provision for two types of regulatory order: interim injunctions and interim declarations. It defines the scope and effect of each of them.
2. Interim injunctions enjoin those who are subject to or have notice of them to either refrain from acting or to carry out an act.[95] The court's power to grant such orders is unlimited.[96] They may therefore be granted in aid of substantive legal or equitable rights that are the subject matter of proceedings, ie where the right is in issue in the claim. It may also be granted in the absence of such a contested right, eg a post-judgment freezing injunction, disclosure orders, costs orders.[97] There is, however, no absolute requirement that the injunction is in support of a substantive right.[98]
3. The fundamental aim of this type of order is to promote the administration of justice through ensuring that the court is able to secure accurate decisions, promote settlement, or secure effective enforcement. It is not, as has repeatedly and misleadingly been said, to maintain the '*status quo*'[99] pending the final determination of a claim.[100] As Lord Hoffmann rightly put it, the purpose of such interim injunctions

[95] Interim injunctions bind all those who have notice of them, ie they apply to non-parties as well as to parties to proceedings: *Attorney-General v Newspaper Publishing Plc* [1988] Ch 333 at 375 at 380. Included within interim injunctions are newcomer injunctions, which were recognised as a new form of injunction in *Wolverhampton City Council v London Gypsies and Travellers* [2023] UKSC 47; [2024] 2 WLR 45. They are included here as they regulate party or third party conduct.

[96] *Broad Idea International Ltd v Conway Collateral Ltd* [2021] UKPC 24; [2022] 2 WLR 70.

[97] *Stewart Chartering Ltd v C & O Managements SA* [1980] 1 WLR 460; *Norwich Pharmacal Co v Commissioners for Customs & Excise* [1974] AC 133; *Bankers Trust Co v Shapira* [1980] 1 WLR 1274; *Jet West Ltd v Haddison* [1992] 1 WLR 487, respectively.

[98] *Broad Idea International Ltd v Conway Collateral Ltd* [2021] UKPC 24; [2022] 2 WLR 70; *Linemile Properties Ltd v Plater* [2023] EWHC 810 (Ch).

[99] *Preston v Luck* (1884) 27 ChD 497; *Siskina v Distos Compania Naviera SA* [1979] AC 210 at 259; *American Cyanamid v Ethicon* [1975] AC 396 at 408; J Leubsdorf, 'The Standard for Preliminary Injunctions' (1978) 91 Harv LR 525.

[100] Note the absence of any reference to maintaining the status quo in the ELI-UNIDROIT Model Rules, rr 196 and 197 in contrast to such reference in the ALI/UNIDROIT Principles, principle 8.1. Criticism of

is '*to improve the chances of the court being able to do justice after a determination of the merits at the trial*'.[101] Through the grant of such an order the court regulates party, and in some cases non-party conduct, for a specified time.[102]

4. The second form of regulatory order is an interim declaration.[103] A declaration is an order by which the court determines (declares) the nature of legal rights, facts, or principles of law.[104] An interim declaration thereby regulates party conduct by making such a declaration on a provisional basis pending final determination of proceedings.

## RULE 10.—CRITERIA FOR AWARD OF AN INTERIM INJUNCTION

**(1) The court may grant an interim injunction where it is just and equitable to do so.**
**(2) In considering whether it is just and equitable to do so, the court shall consider**
  **(a) the prospect of success at trial of the parties;**
  **(b) the probable, irreparable, harm to the parties if the court's view of the prospects of success at trial turns out to be wrong;**
  **(c) whether the applicant is willing and able to provide an undertaking in damages if the interim injunction is granted.**
**(3) Where proceedings in which an interim injunction is made are stayed or discontinued, the interim injunction is automatically discharged unless the court directs otherwise.**

*Sources: ELI-UNIDROIT Model Rules, r 197; Senior Courts Act 1981, s 37; CPR rr 25.1(1)(a).*

## COMMENTARY

1. The fundamental criterion for determining whether to grant an interim injunction over an individual over whom the court has personal jurisdiction, is whether it is just and equitable to do so.[105]
2. Up to the 1970s, the courts took a broad-brush approach to this test. Originally it required the court to assess all the circumstances of the case and determine whether the '*justice of the case*' justified the court granting such an order.[106] The rationale underpinning this approach was to try to ensure that the court protected substantive rights as best as it could pending final determination, while minimising the prospect of harm. This necessarily, however, required the court—in taking account of all the

reference to the status quo can be found in, for instance, A. Zuckerman (2021) at 437–441 and Lord Hoffmann's opinion in *National Commercial Bank of Jamaica Ltd v Olint Corp Ltd* [2009] WLR 1405 at [16].

[101] *National Commercial Bank of Jamaica Ltd v Olint Corp Ltd* [2009] WLR 1405 at [16].

[102] ALI/UNIDROIT Principles, principles 5.8, 8.2; *ALI/UNIDROIT Reporters' Study*, r 17; ELI-UNIDROIT Model Rules, r 196.

[103] *The NHS Trust v Ms T* [2004] EWHC 1279 (Fam); [2005] 1 All ER 387 at [35]–[38]; *British Air Line Pilots Association v British Airways Cityflyer Ltd* [2018] EWHC 1889 (QB) at [24].

[104] *Financial Services Authority v Rourke* [2002] CP Rep 14.

[105] *Fourie v Le Roux* [2007] UKHL 1; [2007] 1 WLR 320; *Broad Idea International Ltd v Conway Collateral Ltd* [2021] UKPC 24; [2022] 2 WLR 70; *Wolverhampton City Council v London Gypsies and Travellers* [2023] UKSC 47; [2024] 2 WLR 45; *Re G (Court of Protection: Injunction)* [2022] EWCA Civ 1312; [2022] 3 WLR 1339; Senior Courts Act 1981, s 37.

[106] *Saunders v Smith* (1883) 3 My & Cr 711; 40 ER 1023; *Munro v Wivenhoe* (1865) 12 LT 655.

circumstances to see where the justice of the case lay—to consider the merits.[107] Hence up to the 1970s, applicants where required to demonstrate that, on the face of it, they had a case on the merits.[108]

3. This approach was misapplied during the 1970s, however due to the manner in which Megarry VC and parties approached applications for such injunctions. Application hearings were used as a form of truncated mini-trial, which parties, either by tacit or express agreement, treated as a low cost, proportionate, expedited means of finally determining their dispute. Assessing the case on the merits became an ersatz form of final determination.[109] By permitting the process to be misused in this way, the court was essentially conniving in an abuse of its process by permitting interim applications and orders to be deliberately and systematically used as final determinations. It also undermined procedural equality. Those parties who could legitimately apply for an interim injunction could, in effect, jump the queue[110] and have their disputes resolved quicker and more economically than those litigants who could not do so. A necessary corollary was that this increased delay within the system for other litigants.[111] This development, and misuse of the process, was effectively ended by *American Cyanamid* through its replacement of the merits-test.[112] In a single judgment, which has rightly been criticised by Andrews as an unjustifiable form of judicial legislation,[113] it established a multi-stage test for the grant of interim injunctions that purported to avoid a consideration of the merits.
4. The *American Cyanamid* test first requires an applicant to pass a basic and low threshold test: they have to show there is a serious issue to be tried. If there is, then the court should consider, if the application were to be refused, if damages would be an adequate remedy to compensate the applicant for an infringement of their substantive rights if, at trial, their claim is upheld and, if so, could the respondent pay any such damages. If damages were an adequate remedy and a respondent could pay them the application should be refused. If, however, damages would not be an adequate remedy to the applicant, the court should then consider whether the respondent could be compensated adequately for any harm caused to it if the application were to be granted and, at trial, the claim were to be dismissed. If the respondent could be compensated and the applicant could not, then the injunction should be granted. In those cases where there was a doubt as to the adequacy of damages to either applicant or respondent the court should assess the balance of convenience. That required the court to consider, for instance, the need to preserve the '*status quo*', the extent of any uncompensatable harm, and the relative strengths of the merits of each party's case. This test remains in place under the CPR, albeit it has been subject to significant qualification and explanation.[114]

[107] J Leubsdorf (1978).

[108] *Hubbard v Vosper* [1972] 2 QB 84.

[109] See above, r 3, and P Prescott, 'Note' (1975) 91 LQR 161; I R Scott, 'Re-assessing American Cyanamid' (2002) 21 CJQ 190; A Swarup, 'Rethinking American Cyanamid: Procedural and Timely Justice' (2012) 31(4) CJQ 475 at 477.

[110] N Andrews, *Principles of Civil Procedure* (Sweet & Maxwell, 1994) at 226.

[111] I R Scott, 'Re-assessing American Cyanamid' (2002) 21 CJQ 190 at 192; G Hammond, 'Interlocutory Injunctions; Time for a New Model?' (1980) 30 Univ of Toronto L Jour 240, 251.

[112] *American Cyanamid v Ethicon* [1975] AC 396.

[113] N Andrews (1994) at 224.

[114] A Zuckerman (2021) at 448 and following.

5. This rule rejects the approach taken in *American Cyanamid*. It prefers that which it rejected, albeit it draws out more clearly the role that merits assessment ought to play. It does so for several reasons that have convincingly been articulated by Prescott, Andrews and Zuckerman.[115]
6. The first argument raised against the *American Cyanamid* test is that developed by Prescott. It was simply that the test is unnecessary as there was no problem with the application of the previous merits-test. On the contrary, it cured a problem arising from the misuse of the test by parties and Megarry VC. The better approach would have been to put a stop to that, rather than changing the test. Moreover, as both Scott and Andrews have suggested rather than reject the merits-test, the need for a truncated form of trial process through which parties could obtain timely and proportionate justice should have been met by the introduction of effective case management and procedure that matched process to the nature of the dispute.[116] The CPR would, twenty-four years after *American Cyanamid*, introduce a case managed, proportionate form of procedure and later still the Shorter and Flexible Trials Schemes.[117] Both of those approaches would have cured the cause of the problem that led to *American Cyanamid*. If they had been adopted the misuse of interim injunction applications would have been brought to an end without the need to set aside the merits-test.
7. That point, however, goes to the justification for replacing the merits-test. It could, nevertheless, be argued in defence of *American Cyanamid* that it sets a more appropriate or effective test for the grant of interim injunctions. Such a stance has also been cogently doubted. Zuckerman, has for instance, noted how it is logically incoherent. It rejects an assessment of the merits on the basis that the court, at the interim stage, is unable to properly assess them. However, it also accepts that, at the same stage, it can properly assess the magnitude of harm to each party. The court can either do both or do neither. It cannot do one, but not the other.[118] Moreover, the test accepts that the court has no difficulty in assessing the merits at this stage where summary judgment is concerned or where other forms of interim order are concerned; removing the merits test here was thus incoherent and unprincipled.[119] This is particularly evident from the fact that *American Cyanamid* accepted that merits could be considered as part of the balance of convenience, that Lord Diplock accepted that merits could be taken account of where the interim injunction could finally determine proceedings[120]—which in principle is any interim injunction –, and that the courts have consistently continued to take account of the merits either via multiple exceptions to *American Cyanamid* or otherwise.[121] In essence, as both

[115] P Prescott, 'Note' (1975) 91 LQR 161 at 168–171; N Andrews (1994) at 226 and following; A Zuckerman (2021) at 448 and following. Zuckerman has repeated these points consistently in each of the editions of his commentary since its first publication in 2003.

[116] N Andrews (1994) at 227; I R Scott, 'Re-assessing American Cyanamid' (2002) 21 CJQ 190.

[117] CPR PD 57AB.

[118] A Zuckerman (2021) at 447.

[119] N Andrews (1994) at 227.

[120] *NWL Ltd v Woods* [1979] 1 WLR 1294.

[121] *Office Overload Ltd v Gunn* [1977] FSR 39; *Cayne v Global Natural Resources Plc* [1984] 1 All ER 912; *The Seahawk* [1986] 1 WLR 657; *National Commercial Bank of Jamaica Ltd v Olint Corp Ltd* [2009] WLR 1405; *R v Secretary of State for Transport, ex. parte Factortame (No 2)* [1991] 1 AC 603; *Series 5 Software v Clarke* [1996] 1 ALL ER 853; A Key, 'Whither American Cyanamid?: Interim Injunctions in the 21st Century' (2004) 23 CJQ 133; A Zuckerman (2021) at 450–452.

Andrews and Zuckerman have concluded the authorities lead to the view that *the American Cyanamid* test is in reality an unprincipled exception masquerading as a principled general rule.[122] It is thus no better, and in fact worse, than the merits-test it replaced.

8. Rather than adopt the *American Cyanamid* test therefore this rule adopts a version of the previous merits-test. It does so by clarifying the role that the merits play in determining whether it is just and equitable to grant an interim injunction. It also clarifies the role that an assessment of harm and the need to minimise harm play. It takes as its basis the point Leubsdorf has made about any general test for interim injunctions: that the grant of such an order ought to '*inflict the smallest probable irreparable loss of rights*'.[123] This type of approach would more effectively implement the view expressed by Hoffmann J in *Management Publications Ltd v Blenheim Exhibitions Group Plc* (1991), that the court should chart a course of action that carries with it the '*least risk of causing injustice*' in the sense of irreparable harm to either applicant or respondent.[124] To achieve this, rule 10(2) requires the court to assess the merits, ie who is most likely to succeed at trial, and the likely loss or damage to each party if its view of the merits turns out to be wrong.[125] Such an assessment would enable the court to determine whether granting or refusing the application is likely to lead to the smallest, probable, irreparable loss of rights. It thus adopts Leubsdorf's approach to the test.
9. Unlike other forms of provisional measure, the grant of an interim injunction is predicated upon the applicant giving an undertaking in damages. This requirement, as a basic requirement of justice, is longstanding.[126] An innocent party or non-party[127] who has suffered loss due to their substantive rights having been interfered with by the injunctive relief ought not to bear such loss. It is loss that the applicant ought to bear. Hence rule 10(2) also requires the applicant, as a means to minimise loss to a respondent or non-party affected by an interim injunction that ultimately is found to have been wrongly granted, to give an undertaking as a pre-condition for granting the injunction.[128]
10. To ensure that interim injunctions remain no more than provisional should proceedings in which one is granted be stayed or discontinued they will stand automatically discharged in such an eventuality.[129] A court may order otherwise. If it were to do so, it would have to ensure that directions were given to manage the dispute, not least through the provision of an appropriate return date in the order (rule 3(2)).

[122] N Andrews (1994) at 227; A Zuckerman (2021) at 448–450.
[123] J Leubsdorf (1978) at 541.
[124] *Management Publications Ltd v Blenheim Exhibitions Group Plc* [1991] FSR 348 at 352.
[125] J Leubsdorf (1978) at 541; A Zuckerman (2021) at 442 and following.
[126] *Graham v Campbell* (1878) 7 ChD 490 at 494.
[127] *Miller Brewing Co v Rushi Enterprises Ltd* [2003] EWHC 1606 (Ch); [2004] FSR 5.
[128] ELI-UNIDROIT Model Rules, r 197.
[129] CPR r 25.10.

## RULE 11.—CRITERIA FOR AWARD OF AN INTERIM DECLARATION

**(1) Where it is just and equitable to do so, the court may exceptionally grant an interim declaration in private or public law proceedings in which it could, as a final order, grant a declaration.**

**(2) In considering whether it is just and equitable to do so, the court shall consider whether**

**(a) the applicant, on the face of it, has a strong case on the merits;**

**(b) the applicant is willing and able to provide an undertaking in damages if the interim declaration is granted; and consider**

**(c) all the circumstances of the case.**

*Sources: Crown Proceedings Act 1947, s 21; Senior Courts Act 1981, ss 19, 31; CPR r 25.1(1)(b).*

## COMMENTARY

1. Until they were introduced by the CPR, via CPR r 25.1(1)(b), the courts did not have jurisdiction to issue interim declarations. The power was introduced as a consequence of positive recommendations by the Law Commission in 1994.[130] No guidance is provided within the CPR, however, concerning the criteria to be applied when the question of whether to grant such a declaration is being considered.[131] There remains scant authority on the criteria to apply. It is apparent, however, that both in public and private law proceedings the grant of an interim declaration is understood to be exceptional. It has, particularly, been noted that there are no reported judgments where such a declaration has been granted in a private law case.[132] Rule 11(1) emphasises this feature of the authorities, one which reflects a continued caution over the grant of such a remedy.

2. To ensure that an interim declaration is only awarded exceptionally, one may only be granted if it is just and equitable for the court to do so. In considering whether that is the case, the court must ascertain whether the applicant has, on the face of it, a strong case on the merits. This heightened threshold test is intended to ensure an order is only granted where there is a high degree of assurance that a final declaration would be granted.[133] It will thus be necessary to persuade the court that a declaration is likely to be granted as a final order.[134] Thus consideration must be given to the test for the grant of declarations as part of the merits criterion.[135] Only such a high degree of assurance can satisfy the evidential threshold necessary to enable the court to give a '*close consideration of the merits*'[136] of granting interim declarations.

3. To minimise the risk of harm to a respondent, it is likely that an applicant will be required to give an undertaking in damages.

[130] Law Commission, *Administrative Law: Judicial Review and Statutory Appeals* (1994) (Law Com No 226) (Cmnd 669) at 6.21.

[131] The Law Commission had suggested that they be awarded on the same basis as interim injunctions: *N v Royal Bank of Scotland plc* [2017] EWCA Civ 253; [2017] 1 WLR 3938 at 89.

[132] *British Airline Pilots' Association v British Airways Cityflyer Limited* [2018] EWHC 1889 (QB) at [25].

[133] *N v Royal Bank of Scotland plc* [2017] EWCA Civ 253; [2017] 1 WLR 3938 at [89].

[134] *Financial Services Authority v Rourke* [2002] CP Rep 14.

[135] *Nokia Corporation v Interdigital Technology Corporation* [2006] EWCA Civ 1618; [2007] FSR 23.

[136] *N v Royal Bank of Scotland plc* [2017] EWCA Civ 253; [2017] 1 WLR 3938 at [89].

## RULE 12.—JURISDICTION ORDERS

**(1) The court may grant an order to promote the effective administration of justice by requiring a defendant or proposed defendant to surrender their passport to the court (a jurisdiction order).**
**(2) A jurisdiction order may be granted before or after judgment.**

*Sources: Senior Courts Act 1981, s 37(1).*

## COMMENTARY

1. This rule codifies what are colloquially known as '*passport orders*' made under section 37(1) of the Senior Courts Act 1981. They are intended to support the court's ability to secure a fair process by stopping a respondent to the order seeking to frustrate the proper administration of justice by leaving the jurisdiction.
2. No specific provision is provided for them within the CPR. The order was initially developed as a means to help give effect to freezing injunctions and civil search orders.[137] It is not limited to such circumstances and may be granted to help give effect to any of the court's processes.[138] It is particularly effective a means to support enforcement through restricting a respondent's ability to leave the jurisdiction where they seek to do so to frustrate the court's ability to give effect to its judgment.[139]

## RULE 13.—CRITERIA FOR GRANTING JURISDICTION ORDERS

**(1) The court may grant a jurisdiction order for no more than a very short period of time**
**(a) when another form of provisional measure has been granted, the effect of which would be undermined if the person against whom it were made were to leave the jurisdiction; and**
**(b) it is just and reasonable to do so.**
**(2) In considering whether it is just and reasonable to do so, the court must, at the least, be satisfied that**
**(a) the applicant has a good cause of action for a substantive award;**
**(b) there is good reason to conclude that the respondent is likely to leave the jurisdiction unless restrained from doing so; and,**
**(c) the proceedings will not be properly resolved if the respondent is outside the jurisdiction.**

*Sources: Senior Courts Act 1981, s 37(1).*

[137] *Bayer AG v Winter* [1986] 1 WLR 497; *Young v Young* [2012] EWHC 138 (Fam); [2012] Fam 198. N Andrews (2019) at 628.
[138] *B v B (Injunction Jurisdiction)* [1998] 1 WLR 329 at 334; *Robinson v Robinson* [2003] EWHC 2473 (Ch); [2004] 1 P & CR DG7.
[139] *B v B (Injunction Jurisdiction)* [1998] 1 WLR 329 at 334.

## COMMENTARY

1. Rule 13 codifies the criteria for the grant of a jurisdiction order, the object of which is to keep the person subject to it within England and Wales. As an ancillary form of order, it may only be granted in support of another form of provisional measure. Thus, it may, for instance, be granted to ensure that injunctive relief or an asset preservation order is not frustrated by a respondent leaving the jurisdiction.[140]
2. A court must be careful when considering an application for this form of order as it interferes with an individual's liberty. Two criteria give effect to this requirement. An order must only be granted for a very short period of time. Where therefore an order is made in support of an asset preservation or civil search order it should last for no longer than the time taken to serve the order.[141] An order may also be granted where a hearing is shortly to take place.[142] The second criterion is that it must be just and reasonable to grant the order.[143]
3. In considering whether it is just and reasonable to grant such an order the court must, at the least, be satisfied of three matters. These are derived from section 6 of the Debtors Act 1869 and were applied to jurisdiction orders in *Young v Young* (2012).[144] They require the court to be satisfied that the applicant has a good cause of action for a substantive award. This criterion is most obviously to be satisfied where the order is intended to support an asset preservation order. It must also be satisfied that there is good reason to conclude the respondent is likely to leave the jurisdiction absent any restraint. And, it must be satisfied that the respondent needs to be within the jurisdiction to enable the proceedings to be properly resolved. If, for instance, there was no danger of effective enforcement being frustrated by the respondent being abroad, there could be no real justification for interfering with their liberty.[145] The intention behind these three specific criteria is to ensure that jurisdiction orders are not used to sidestep the statutory limitations imposed on writs of ne exeat regno by the 1869 Act (see rule 14).

## RULE 14.—ATTENDANCE ORDER

**(1) To facilitate the effective administration of justice, the court may require a court officer to secure the attendance at court of a specified individual who owes a sum of money.**
**(2) An attendance order may not be granted after judgment or to secure enforcement of a judgment.**

*Sources: Writ of ne exeat regno; Debtors Act 1869, s 6.*

[140] *B v B (Injunction Jurisdiction)* [1998] 1 WLR 329; *Robinson v Robinson* [2003] EWHC 2473 (Ch); [2004] 1 P & CR DG7 at 334.
[141] *Bayer AG v Winter* [1986] 1 WLR 497 at 503.
[142] *B v B (Injunction Jurisdiction)* [1998] 1 WLR 329 at 334.
[143] *Bayer AG v Winter* [1986] 1 WLR 497 at 502.
[144] *Young v Young* [2012] EWHC 138 (Fam); [2012] Fam 198.
[145] *Young v Young* [2012] EWHC 138 (Fam); [2012] Fam 198 at [16]–[22].

## COMMENTARY

1. Rule 14 replaces the writ of ne exeat regno.[146] It makes provision for what is colloquially known as a 'tipstaff order'. The Tipstaff is the High Court's enforcement officer. It is the means by which an individual's attendance at court can be secured where that is necessary to enable proceedings for sums of money to be secured effectively. It is thus a means to secure a fair process.
2. The court's power to issue a writ of ne exeat regno was limited by section 6 of the Debtors Act 1869 (see rule 15). One consequence of that limitation is that the writ could only be issued in support of substantive proceedings. It cannot therefore be issued post-judgment to support enforcement, including post-judgment freezing injunctions (asset preservation orders).[147] That statutory limitation is maintained here.

## RULE 15.—CRITERIA FOR GRANTING AN ATTENDANCE ORDER

**(1) The court may grant an attendance order where the person against whom it is to be made**
  **(a) would have been subject to arrest at law under the former process for arrest as an interim (mesne) process;**
  **(b) the applicant has a good cause of action for a substantive award;**
  **(c) there is good reason to conclude the respondent is likely to leave the jurisdiction unless they are arrested; and**
  **(d) the proceedings will not be resolved properly if the respondent is outside the jurisdiction.**

**(2) The court may exercise its discretion to grant an order only where one is necessary to facilitate the administration of justice.**

*Sources: Writ of ne exeat regno; Debtors Act 1869, s 6.*

## COMMENTARY

1. This rule codifies the statutory criteria for granting a writ of ne exeat regno, as limited by section 6 of the Debtors Act 1869.[148]
2. Rule 15(a) refers to the need to demonstrate that the respondent to the application would have been liable to arrest at law as the law stood prior to the introduction of the Debtors Act 1869, ie but for that Act would the respondent have been liable to arrest. As a consequence, this criterion will only be satisfied if '*there exists the equitable equivalent of an action in which the [claimant] would previously have been liable to arrest at law*', ie the debt must be an equitable one.[149]

[146] In English, the '*writ of let him not leave the Kingdom*'.
[147] *Allied Arab Bank Ltd v Hajjar* [1988] QB 787 at 794.
[148] *Felton v Callis* [1969] 1 QB 200.
[149] *Felton v Callis* [1969] 1 QB 200 at 210–211.

3. Rule 15(d) codifies the statutory requirement that an applicant demonstrate that they have a good cause of action for £50 or more. It does so consistently with the modern interpretation of that requirement, which reads it as requiring there to be a good cause of action for a '*substantive award*'.[150]
4. To grant an order it is not sufficient that the four criteria are satisfied. The court must also be convinced that the grant of such relief is necessary in the interests of the administration of justice.[151]

## SECTION 4: ANTICIPATORY ORDERS

### RULE 16.—INTERIM PAYMENT ORDERS

**(1) Where a claimant pursues a claim for monetary relief or for possession of land for which a defendant or defendants may be liable to pay the claimant a sum of money, the court may make an interim payment order. Payment is made on account of monetary relief that the court may award the claimant in any final judgment.**

**(2) An interim payment order is a payment of such a sum as is just in all the circumstances to a claimant from another party to proceedings. In determining what is just in all the circumstances the court must**

**(a) determine the amount, excluding litigation costs, the claimant is likely to receive in the final judgment under rule 18 and identify a reasonable proportion of that amount; and**

**(b) take account of any relevant matter.**

**(3) When taking account of any relevant matter, the court must not require a claimant to demonstrate that they have a specific or particular need for an interim payment when assessing whether to exercise its discretion to order an interim payment.**

**(4) An interim payment order may require any interim payment to be paid in instalments.**

**(5) An interim payment order may be varied or set aside. Where an order is set aside or varied the court may order repayment of part or all of any sum paid. The court may require a claimant to pay the defendant interest on any sum repaid. It may also require a defendant to reimburse any other defendant in respect of any sum paid as an interim payment.**

**(6) The fact that any interim payment has been made must not be disclosed prior to determination of all issues of liability and quantum. A trial judge who becomes aware of an interim payment before determination of such issues may only continue to deal with the proceedings if they satisfy the test for impartiality or the parties waive the right to impartiality (Part 1, rule 13(2) and (4)). Exceptionally, the fact of an interim payment may be disclosed prior to trial when it is in the public interest to do so.**

*Sources: ELI-UNIDROIT Model Rules, r 200; Senior Courts Act, 1981, s 32; County Courts Act 1984, s 50; CPR rr 25.1(1)(k), 25.6, 25.7. 25.8, 25.9.*

[150] *Young v Young* [2012] EWHC 138 (Fam); [2012] Fam 198 at [21].
[151] *Felton v Callis* [1969] 1 QB 200 at 212.

## COMMENTARY

1. An interim payment is a form of anticipatory order. By providing the means by which a claimant can receive payment of a monetary sum on account of the sum they expect to receive at the conclusion of proceedings, the order anticipates the final judgment. Such orders are not a general feature of procedural codes.[152] The Helsinki Principles, for instance, exclude interim payments from international litigation.[153] They were also excluded from the ALI/UNIDROIT Principles. One rationale for such an exclusion is that they do not maintain the '*status quo*' pending final determination.[154] Where a putative final judgment is concerned there is no status quo to maintain as it has not, at the time any interim payment could be granted, been made. Thus there is therefore no judgment to maintain. The broader rationale for the inclusion of interim payments into a procedural code, and the one accepted here, is that they promote the administration of justice.
2. Moving away from the misnomer that provisional and protective measures maintain the status quo and are more properly understand as a means to promote and protect the effective administration of justice identifies more clearly the justification for the inclusion of interim payments. This is particularly apparent where the basis on which they were introduced into English and Welsh civil procedure is noted. They were initially introduced by the Administration of Justice Act 1969[155] to implement recommendations made by the Winn Committee, which examined personal injury litigation. It recommended that such payments be introduced in such litigation to promote procedural equality and help secure settlement: '*to produce a greater measure of equality of bargaining position of the parties which may lead to a settlement* ... '.[156] By enabling a claimant to obtain an interim payment, any incentive that a defendant may have to prolong litigation or refuse to take part in settlement processes, which today would be viewed as contrary to the economy, efficient and proportionality principles, is reduced. In this way the administration of justice, both for the immediate parties and for litigants in other proceedings, is promoted. For the immediate parties, this arises through either the promotion of settlement or through promoting the efficient and proportionate conduct of proceedings. Through that being achieved court resources can be more effectively targeted to other proceedings. Looked at in this way, and by acknowledging that the underlying rationale of all provisional and protective measures is to promote the effective administration of justice, it ought to be apparent that interim payments can properly be classified as an anticipatory form of such measures.
3. A second rationale that justifies the inclusion of a power to grant interim payments as a form of anticipatory provisional and protective measure was highlighted in *Ricci Burns Ltd v Toole* (1989).[157] In that case Ralph Gibson LJ stated that the

[152] ELI-UNIDROIT Model Rules, comment 1 to rule 200.

[153] *The Helsinki Principles on Provisional and Protective Measures in International Litigation*, Principle 22.

[154] X E Kramer in M Storme (ed) (2003).

[155] Administration of Justice Act 1969, s 20. They are now provided for by Senior Courts Act 1981, s 32 and County Courts Act 1984, s 50. Originally the power applied only to personal injury litigation and fatal accident claims. Following the introduction of Senior Courts Act 1981, s 32 it applied generally: see *Associated Bulk Carriers Ltd v Koch Shipping Inc* [1978] 2 All ER 254 for criticism of the original limitation and for confirmation that absent the statutory authorisation to make interim payment orders the court has no jurisdiction to do so.

[156] R Winn et al, *Report of the Committee on Personal Injuries Litigation* (HMSO, 1968) (Cmnd Paper 3691) at 81.

[157] *Ricci Burns Ltd v Toole* [1989] 1 WLR 993.

underlying rationale of such orders was to mitigate a claimant's hardship or any prejudice to them that might arise between the commencement of proceedings and judgment.[158] Ensuring that a claimant is able to obtain such a payment where one of the three criteria for making an interim payment has been met, eg liability is admitted, judgment on liability has been given, or a favourable judgment on liability is substantially likely, is consistent with the accuracy and effective enforcement principles. The former because of the fact it anticipates what the court will award by way of vindication of the claimant's rights. The latter because it ensures that damages, as a measure of such vindication, are put into effect in a timely manner, eg there is no delay in effective enforcement. The promotion of both principles is an inherent aspect of what it means to secure the proper administration of justice for claimants, who obtain a proportion of what they are due or substantially likely to be due, and for defendants. It does so for the latter because the vindication of rights for them, through requiring such payments, is a means by which they are provided with a measure of finality and certainty in litigation; that coming from the fact that payment is made.

4. The wording of this rule is derived from section 32 of the Senior Courts Act 1981, which creates the rule-making power.[159] Monetary relief does not include costs.[160] It relates to monetary relief sought by way of the claimant's claim, ie as it arises from their cause of action. This includes any sum of money that may arise from possession of land.[161] The criteria for ordering an interim payment are set out in rule 18. Interim payments may be made by way of instalment.[162] The total sum paid by way of interim payment must be just in all the circumstances. This requires the court to balance the claimant's interest in receiving such a payment and a defendant's interest in not paying more than they are likely to be liable to pay at the conclusion of the proceedings. It is therefore essential for the court to determine the likely amount that the claimant will receive by way of final judgment.[163] Once it has done that it must identify a reasonable proportion of that amount. It must then consider any other relevant matter that arises in the circumstances of the case.[164] Rule 16(3) codifies the position made clear in the case law that the claimant need not demonstrate that they would suffer any specific or particular hardship or prejudice if an order is not made.[165] The claimant need only demonstrate that there is a need for payment. Taking account of any counterclaim or reduction by way of contributory negligence in calculating the amount of any payment serves to protect the defendant's interest.[166] Taking account of any potential hardship, as indicated in *Ricci Burns Ltd v Toole* (1989),[167] serves to ensure the claimant's interest is protected. By taking account of these steps, both

[158] *Ricci Burns Ltd v Toole* [1989] 1 WLR 993 at 1003.

[159] *Deutsche Bank AG v Unitech Global Ltd* [2016] EWCA Civ 119; [2016] 1 WLR 3598.

[160] Senior Courts Act 1982, s 32(5).

[161] R Scott (1999) Vol 1 at 29/12/3; RSC Ord 29, r 12; CPR r 25.7(1)(d).

[162] CPR r 25.6(7)

[163] *Eeles v Cobham Hire Services Ltd* [2009] EWCA Civ 204; [2010] 1 WLR 409 at [34]–[38].

[164] *Schott Kem Ltd v Bentley* [1991] 1 QB 61.

[165] *Schott Kem Ltd v Bentley* [1991] 1 QB 61; *Brown v Emery* [2010] EWHC 388 (QB) at 12 citing *Eeles v Cobham Hire Services Ltd* [2009] EWCA Civ 204; [2010] 1 WLR 409. Compare ELI-UNIDROIT Model Rules, r 201.

[166] *Shanning International Ltd v George Wimpey International Ltd* [1988] 1 WLR 981; *Spillman v Bradfield Riding Centre* [2007] EWHC 89 (QB) at [12].

[167] *Ricci Burns Ltd v Toole* [1989] 1 WLR 993.

interests can be given effect. They particularly ensure that the court does not act beyond its jurisdiction and make an order for payment of a sum greater than the claimant would ultimately be awarded.[168]

5. Interim payment orders may, in certain circumstances, be varied or set aside. It may, for instance, become apparent that the sum awarded is more than a reasonable amount because evidence comes to light to call into question the likely quantum to be awarded. Where the order was made on the basis that it was likely that the claimant would secure judgment in their favour evidence may come to light to also undermine that conclusion. In extreme cases, a claimant may abandon their claim and discontinue proceedings. To ensure justice is done to the defendant in such and similar cases, the court may require any payment made to be repaid; depending on the circumstances it also may not order repayment. The court may also, again to do justice to the defendant, require in appropriate circumstances the claimant to pay the defendant interest on the sum repaid.[169] The payment of interest here serves to recognise and mitigate the fact that the defendant has been improperly deprived of their funds.
6. Interim payments may be ordered where there are multiple defendants. Where one defendant is ordered to make such a payment, the court may in appropriate circumstances order them to be reimbursed for part or all of the amount paid by one or more of the other defendants. Specific circumstances where this may arise are where there is, for instance, a successful claim for contribution or indemnity between the defendants.[170]
7. The fact that an interim payment order has been made must not be disclosed to the trial judge. As with non-disclosure of any offer to settle, the rationale for this is to ensure that the fact that payment has been made and the amount of any such payment does not prejudice the trial judge's determination of the monetary sum ultimately held to be due.[171] Where a trial judge becomes aware of an interim payment, whether paid voluntarily or by court order, they must not continue to deal with the proceedings unless they can satisfy the test for impartiality, ie a fair-minded and informed observer would conclude that there was no real possibility that they were biased as a result of their becoming aware of the payment.[172] The parties may, however, waive the question of bias.[173]
8. Notwithstanding the general non-disclosure rule, the court may exceptionally make public the fact of an interim payment before trial. It may only do so if it is in the public interest to do so. An example where this was the case was *British Commonwealth Holdings plc v Quadrex Holdings Inc* (1989), where the reasons for making an interim payment order were made public in order to ensure that non-disclosure did not have an adverse and improper effect on the market in the parties' shares.[174]

[168] *Eeles v Cobham Hire Services Ltd* [2009] EWCA Civ 204; [2010] 1 WLR 409 at [30].

[169] CPR r 25.8(5); *Wardens and Commonalty of The Mystery of Mercers of The City of London v New Hampshire Insurance Co* [1991] 1 WLR 1173.

[170] CPR r 25.8(3).

[171] Part 11, r 17(4).

[172] Part 1, r 13(2); *Berg v IML London Ltd* [2002] 1 WLR 3271.

[173] Part 1, r 13(4).

[174] *British Commonwealth Holdings plc v Quadrex Holdings Inc* [1989] QB 842; noted to that effect in R Scott (1999) Vol 1 at 29/15/1/.

## RULE 17.—APPLICATION PROCEDURE FOR INTERIM PAYMENT ORDERS

**(1) An application for an interim payment order may not be made before the defendant against whom it is sought has served an admission or their substantive defence or the court has dispensed with the need for the defendant to provide a substantive defence.**

**(2) An applicant may make multiple applications for an interim payment order. They may only do so where there is a material change in circumstance or where the basis on which the original application was refused was obviously mistaken.**

*Sources: CPR r 25.6(1) and (2).*

## COMMENTARY

1. A claimant ought to seek an interim payment at the earliest opportunity after an admission or substantive defence has been served or after the court has dispensed with the need for such a defence to be served. At that point there is no issue as to jurisdiction, and the court will, in principle, be in a position to determine whether it should order payment.
2. Where there has been either a material change in circumstance or an adjudicative error by the court in determining the original application, further applications for interim payments may be made. This is a specific application of the general approach to renewed or successive applications for the same relief and serves the same purpose, ie to ensure that the court's resources are not unnecessarily and disproportionately expended on repetitive applications.

## RULE 18.—CRITERIA FOR AWARD OF INTERIM PAYMENT ORDERS

**(1) An Interim Payment Order may only be granted**
- **(a) where the defendant against whom it is to be made has admitted liability for a sum of money to the claimant;**
- **(b) the claimant has obtained a judgment on liability for a sum of money; or**
- **(c) it is likely that in proceedings of intermediate or high value, judgment for a substantial sum of money, exclusive of costs, would be obtained at trial. The burden of proof lies on the claimant to establish that they are likely to secure such a judgment at trial.**

**(2) Where the claimant applies for an order in proceedings against multiple defendants, the criteria in rule 18(1)(c) must be satisfied against one of the defendants.**

*Sources: CPR r 25.7.*

## COMMENTARY

1. This rule restates the criteria for determining whether the court may make an interim payment. It sets out the three key criteria, each of which focuses on the fact that a claimant must establish that they are likely to obtain an award of damages at the conclusion of the proceedings. That is obviously the case where a defendant has

either admitted liability or judgment on liability has been entered. It is less certain to be the case otherwise. Hence, the third criterion requires the court to be satisfied that it is likely that judgment for a substantial sum will be obtained at trial in proceedings of intermediate or higher value, eg proceedings for a monetary claim of at least £25,000.[175] The burden of proof is the civil standard of proof.[176]

2. Rule 18(2) ensures that where there are multiple defendants, the claimant must be likely to succeed at trial against at least one of them where they apply for an interim payment order against one or more of them under rule 18(1)(c).

175 A Zuckerman (2021) at 572.

176 *Ricci Burns Ltd v Toole* [1989] 1 WLR 993 at 1002.

# PART 14

# HEARINGS

## SECTION 1: GENERAL

1. This Part concerns hearings within proceedings. Historically, in English and Welsh civil proceedings they have been conducted as single, concentrated, and oral events.[1] The basis of this can be traced to the needs of the common law civil jury trial as jurors could not be repeatedly drawn away from their occupations to consider matters over a long period of time.
2. Two particular trends have, however, effected the approach taken to hearings. There has been a shift away from orality, not least since the introduction of the CPR and the introduction of witness statements and written legal submissions. Most recently and in limited circumstances, the oral hearing has also been replaced by entirely written proceedings either as a result of European cross-border procedure[2] or to promote economy, efficiency, and proportionality.[3] Additionally, there has been a move away from hearings being physical, single, concentrated events. Digitisation of procedure, and particularly the effects of the Covid-19 pandemic, have seen a shift away from physical hearings to 'online' or 'digital' hearings, as well as experiments with discontinuous, multi-event hearings.[4] This Part sets out an approach to hearings that takes account of both these developmental trends.

### RULE 1.—SCOPE AND PURPOSE

**(1) This Part concerns hearings, the process through which applications, claims and defences are presented and tested. Hearings, particularly, promote the due notice, participatory and adversariality, accuracy, settlement, and publicity principles. In so far as possible they must also be consistent with the procedural equality principle.**
**(2) Hearings should, consistently with the purposive principle be facilitated through the digital procedure and accountability, artificial intelligence, and digital access principles.**

*Sources: Senior Courts Act 1981, s 67.*

[1] J Jacob, *The Fabric of English Civil Justice* (Stevens & Sons, 1987) at 19–21; J Langbein, 'The Disappearance of Civil Trial in the United States' (2012) 122 Yale LJ 522 at 529.

[2] European Small Claims Procedure: Regulation (EC) 861/2007) of the European Parliament and of the European Commission of 11 July 2007 establishing a European Small Claims Procedure; CPR Pt 78, prior to the UK's withdrawal from the European Union.

[3] The development of presumptively written-only permission to appeal proceedings, eg, under CPR r 52.5 and the pilot scheme for written determination of small claims proceedings under CPR PD51ZC highlight this trend.

[4] N Byrom, S Beardon, and A Kendrick, *The Impact of COVID-19 Measures on the Civil Justice System* (Civil Justice Council, 2020).

*A Model Civil Procedure Code for England and Wales.* John Sorabji, Oxford University Press. © John Sorabji 2024.
DOI: 10.1093/oso/9780192848680.003.0015

## COMMENTARY

1. Hearings are the forum in which the court adjudicates or promotes settlement. Rule 1(1) identifies the main purposes they serve, the most important of which is to enable the parties to present their respective cases and test their opponent's case before the court. It is for this reason that a fair, adversarial hearing is understood to be one of the most fundamental aspects of the right to fair trial.[5] Hearings are also one of the main means through which parties, and where relevant non-parties, are able to participate effectively in dispute resolution. In this way, where they have had due notice, a hearing can particularly give effect to individual dignity, ie enabling parties to take part in the decision-making process effectively facilitates individual autonomy and self-respect, and through that trust and confidence in the process is promoted.[6] A fair hearing is thus also a means to secure judicial legitimacy.
2. Effective participation also, and independently of the promotion of individual dignity, helps promote adjudicative accuracy and, where possible, settlement. Where adjudicative accuracy is concerned it does so through what is known as the principle of immediacy. That is the idea that the judge who presides at a final, trial hearing may properly determine the dispute.[7] Hearings, and particularly oral hearings, are also one of the fundamental means by which the publicity principle is given effect.[8] That parties set out their cases in a public forum in which the public and the media are able to scrutinise, report and debate what goes on in the courts. Hearings are, in this way, an important means by which democratic accountability is imposed on the civil justice system.[9] Again, this promotes judicial legitimacy.
3. These various principles can be understood to have informed the development of oral hearings within English and Welsh civil procedure.[10] It should not, however, be thought that they entail that hearings may only be held following effective notice to all parties and any relevant non-party, that they are only effective if parties can take part in the hearing (or take part on an equal footing further to the equality principle), or that they must be held in public. It must also not be thought that hearings must be oral hearings.
4. Hearings may properly be held without notice being given to a party, particularly where such notice would undermine the proper administration of justice. A party may be stopped from taking part in a hearing personally if, for instance, their conduct within the hearing is abusive. And a hearing may take place partially[11] or entirely via a written procedure, as was not uncommon under the pre-1873 equity-based

[5] *Al-Rawi v The Security Services* [2011] UKSC 34; [2012] 1 AC 531: the right to a fair hearing lives, for instance, within the due notice, adversariality, and equality principles identified in the judgments of Lords Dyson, Brown, Hope, and Kerr.

[6] J Mashaw, 'Administrative Due Process: The Quest for a Dignitary Theory' (1981) 61 Boston University Law Review 885, esp 886–887.

[7] J Jacob (1987) at 19–21; ELI-UNIDROIT Principles, r 164, comment 2.

[8] P Hirvelä and S Heikkilä, *Right to a Fair Trial* (Intersentia, 2022) at 172; *Jussila v Finland* [2006] ECHR 996; (2007) 45 EHRR 39 at [40]–[42].

[9] *Al-Rawi v The Security Services* [2011] UKSC 34; [2012] 1 AC 531 at 543.

[10] J Jacob (1987) at 19–21.

[11] J Jacob (1987) at 150 citing *R v Local Government Board, ex p Arlidge* [1914] 1 KB 160 at 191.

procedure in the Court of Chancery,[12] and was and is permitted in specified circumstances under the CPR.[13]

5. While this Part is intended to give effect to the established principles that underpin hearings, it also recognises that in future further principles will shape them. Digital technology now means that hearings need not take place in a physical space, ie a court room. They may take place partially or wholly online via the use of online video-conferencing platforms. They also need not necessarily be single, concentrated events; albeit with the effective elimination of the civil jury after the 1940s,[14] the necessity of trial hearings being carried out in such a way had long passed before the advent of digital technology. This Part therefore also develops rules concerning hearings that are influenced by the newer procedural principles concerning digital procedure and accountability, artificial intelligence, and digital access. Any such developments, and their use, must not however compromise the court's ability to give effect to the other procedural principles provided for in Part 1, not least the purposive principle. Technology is a servant not a master of those principles.

## RULE 2.—HEARING TYPES

**(1) Hearings include procedural and adjudicative hearings. Procedural hearings include dispute management and application hearings. An adjudicative hearing is one that involves the determination of a claim for relief or substantive issue in dispute.**
**(2) A hearing is either a single, concentrated event, a continuous digital process, or a wholly written process. A jury trial must be a single, concentrated event.**
**(3) Except where a hearing is a written one (a written hearing), a hearing may take place in a physical place (a physical hearing), via a non-physical medium (a non-physical hearing), or any combination of physical and non-physical hearings (a hybrid hearing).**
**(4) Hearings must be carried out consistently with the publicity principle. The court must take reasonable steps to secure public access to hearings, including written hearings. Access to a non-physical or hybrid hearing must be equivalent to access provided for physical hearings.**
**(5) Public access to a written hearing may be facilitated by the provision of public access, before the hearing takes place, to statements of case, any evidence and legal submissions relied upon by the parties.**
**(6) Any hearing may be held in private consistently with exceptions to the publicity principle.**

*Sources: ALI/UNIDROIT Reporters' Study, rr 18.4, 29.1; ELI-UNIDROIT Model Rules, r 64(1); Senior Courts Act 1981, s 67; County Courts Act 1984, s 67; CPR Pt 39.*

## COMMENTARY

1. Hearings are the means within proceedings through which the court is able to '*conduct the kind of direct, immediate and dialectical investigation into the relevant*

[12] A Kessler, 'Our Inquisitorial Inheritance' (2004–2005) 90 Cornell L Rev 1181.
[13] CPR Pt 78, before it was revoked. CPR PD51ZC and r 52.5.
[14] *Gregory v Commissioner of Police for the Metropolis* [2014] EWHC 3922 (QB); [2015] 1 WLR 4253 at [12]–[26].

*facts and the applicable law and by this process of "cross fertilisation," they promote the ascertainment of the truth and the production of the correct decision.*'[15] They take several forms.

2. The majority of hearings in any dispute will be procedural. Their focus will be to ensure the dispute is conducted by the parties and managed by the court consistently with the purposive principle. They will also deal with applications, not least those concerning evidentiary management, provisional measures and, where necessary, management of the enforcement process.
3. Separate from procedural hearings are adjudicative hearings, which involve the determination of substantive issues in dispute on their substantive merits.[16] The primary aim of such hearings is to give effect to the accuracy principle, again consistently with the purposive principle. They may, however, promote settlement where they, for instance, resolve specific issues in the dispute, which can then lead the parties to reconsider the merits of their respective cases. Adjudicative hearings also take several forms. They can be short hearings that take place during the dispute management phase of proceedings, the aim of which is to finally determine the dispute, eg, hearings for strike out, summary judgment, or permission to appeal. They can also be full trials, which depending on the nature of the dispute may take the form of short, truncated trials or lengthy processes. The pursuit of adjudicative accuracy here, as throughout procedure, is leavened by the commitment to procedural proportionality.
4. The other feature of hearings highlighted by this rule is that they are as much a process as they are an event. Historically, it might have been correct, to a certain degree, to characterise hearings as events. Procedural hearings took place as short, concentrated events before a single judge. Adjudicative hearings took place in the same manner due to the need to empanel a civil jury, which had to be kept together and sequestered until the trial was completed. That, at least, was the position in common law procedure, maintained under the RSC, and more recently the CPR, after the Judicature Act 1873–1875 reforms. Hearings in pre-1873 equity process differed from this approach to a certain extent. Equity included a greater emphasis on written procedure, which meant proceedings did not have to be and were not necessarily resolved by hearings as single, concentrated events. Equity hearings were very much more of a process than an event.[17] Rule 2(2) acknowledges that hearings in the future will be a greater blend of event and process than has been the case since the 1873–1875 Act reforms. It thus identifies three forms of hearing: the single, concentrated event, the continuous digital process, and the wholly written process.
5. The rationale behind rule 2(2)'s tripartite classification of hearings rests on the economy, efficiency, proportionality, and digitisation principles. Taken together they justify the use of wholly written hearings. Digitisation enables them to take place with greater ease, economy, and efficiency, than via a traditional paper-based written process, which itself offered a more economical, efficient, and proportionate process than an oral hearing, particularly for low value proceedings. Digitisation also provides the basis for introducing continuous, digital hearings that were

[15] J Jacob (1987) at 20; L Fuller, 'The Forms and Limits of Adjudication' (1978–1979) 92 Harv L Rev 353, at 366.

[16] *Pozzoli Spa v BDMO Spa* [2007] EWCA Civ 588 at [8].

[17] A Kessler, 'Our Inquisitorial Inheritance' (2004–2005) 90 Cornell L Rev 1181; J Jacob (1987) at 20–21.

initially introduced as '*continuous online resolution*' in proceedings in the Tribunals justice system as part of the HMCTS modernisation programme.[18] This form of hearing is in one sense well-known; its continuous, iterative nature is broadly comparable to the pre-1873 equity process and is typical of processes in some civil law jurisdictions.[19] Its novel feature is that it is facilitated by the move to digital procedure. Its use in this Code is limited. It may be used where one or more parties do not have legal representation as it may assist the court in taking a more active role in managing proceedings. It may also be used to promote settlement through facilitating online dispute resolution processes, such as online negotiation, ENE, or mediation.[20]

6. Linked to the tripartite classification of hearings, rule 2(3) identifies different mediums through which hearings can take place. In addition to the traditional venue for a hearing, a physical court room (including a judge's chambers) or similar venue (a physical hearing),[21] hearings may now take place via the use of various forms of technology. This development builds on the long-standing availability of audio- and video-conferencing technology, which has been used to permit parties or witnesses to give evidence and lawyers to make submissions in traditional, physical hearings remotely.[22] Digitisation has simply generalised that longstanding practice and enabled it to be applied to trial hearings, rather than previously where it was limited to short case management hearings or the taking of evidence where a witness was, for instance, outside the jurisdiction. Technology-neutral terminology is adopted to describe this type of hearing (a non-physical hearing).[23] Finally, the rule makes provision for hybrid hearings. These are a combination of physical and non-physical hearings. They could, for instance, involve the judge taking part physically from a court room, with the parties and their lawyers taking part via a video-conferencing platform or vice versa. It could equally involve some parties taking part via such a platform and other parties taking part via audio technology, with further parties taking part physically in a court and so on.
7. Rule 2(4) gives concrete effect to the requirement that, generally, hearings must take place in public consistently with the publicity principle.[24] This requires all hearings to be held in public, except where a derogation to that principle applies.

[18] E Ryder, 'The Modernisation of Access to Justice in Times of Austerity', in J Cooper (ed), *Being a Judge in the Modern World* (OUP, 2017) at 141–142.

[19] On the problems caused by an iterative process see, R Caponi, 'The Performance of the Italian Civil Justice System: An Empirical Assessment' (2016) 2(1) The Italian Law Journal 15 at 26–27; R Thomas and J Tomlinson, 'Remodelling Social Security Appeals (Again): The Advent of Online Tribunals' (2018) 25(2) Journal of Social Security Law 84 at 9 and following.

[20] Senior President of Tribunals, *The Modernisation of Tribunals—Innovation Plan for 2019/2020* at 4.

[21] Part 1, r 26.

[22] CPR rr 1.4(2)(k), 3.1(2)(d), 32.3, PD32, Annex 3; *Heyward v Plymouth Hospital NHS Trust* [2005] EWCA Civ 939; [2006] CP Rep 4; *Babbings v Kirklees Metropolitan Borough Council* (2004) 101 (45) LSG 32; *Black v Pastouma* [2005] EWCA Civ 1389; [2006] CP Rep 11.

[23] Within the CPR, reference is made to 'use of technology' and the use of 'direct oral communication' to avoid drawing a distinction between audio and digital formats: CPR rr 1.4(2)(k), 3.1(2)(d). On the use of audio technology in a hybrid hearing see: *Jankowski v Regional Court of Torun, Poland* [2020] EWHC 826 (Admin) at [2]–[3].

[24] Part 1, r 20.

8. The development of written, non-physical, or hybrid hearings cannot properly be viewed, or permitted, to create default exceptions to that principle. A positive obligation is thus imposed on the court, and through it its administration, to take reasonable steps to ensure that all hearings, irrespective of their format, are properly accessible to the public. Access to each medium must be equivalent to that provided for others. As such access to non-physical or hybrid hearings must not require advance notice of attendance by a member of the public or media or any requirement to provide personal information by them to obtain access. Such requirements do not, and have never, formed part of the right to access physical hearings and would amount to an impermissible intrusion into the public's ability to exercise their right to scrutinise and hold the courts accountable. Further steps to secure access may include: the provision of material from the court record via online links before the hearing takes place where the hearing is non-physical or written; the provision of access to a non-physical hearing via online links; or the hearing being broadcast via the Internet or on the court's website. Where written hearings are concerned such access can be secured through public access to all the written materials via online links or the provision of paper copies.

## SECTION 2: HEARING MANAGEMENT

### RULE 3.—PHYSICAL, NON-PHYSICAL, HYBRID, AND WRITTEN HEARINGS

**(1) The court either on its own initiative or on application of the parties shall determine the form a hearing is to take.**

**(2) A physical hearing shall take place at the court centre nearest to the defendant's residential or business address, unless otherwise directed. Physical hearings in the High Court's Upper Tier and the Court of Appeal will take place in the Royal Courts of Justice (including the Rolls Building), unless provided for in the digital procedure consistently with the purposive principle or otherwise directed.**

**(3) Physical hearings, and the physical part of a hybrid hearing, may take place anywhere in England and Wales. They cannot take place outside England and Wales, except where the court is to view evidence that is located outside England and Wales.**

**(4) Where a non-physical hearing takes place, including the non-physical aspect of a hybrid hearing, participants may take part from within or outside England and Wales. Where a judge takes part in such a hearing from within England and Wales they should, generally, do so from a court building. Where they do so from outside England and Wales they are deemed to be within the precincts of the court in England and Wales.**

*Sources: Senior Courts Act 1981, s 57(1); CPR r 2.7.*

### COMMENTARY

1. This rule provides that it is the court's responsibility to determine the appropriate medium in which hearings take place. The discretion shall be exercised consistently with the provisions in this rule and in rules 4 and 5.

2. If the hearing is to be a physical one, rule 3(2) generally requires it to take place at the court centre closest to the defendant's residential or business address. This gives precedence to the defendant's convenience to reflect the fact that they have not chosen to take part in the proceedings. It is thus intended to provide a degree of procedural equality through redressing the imbalance that necessarily flows from the claimant's election to pursue proceedings. The general rule does not, however apply to the Court of Appeal or generally to the High Court's Upper Tier. Physical hearings in proceedings in the former are generally required to take place in the Royal Courts of Justice in London. Such hearings in the High Court's Upper Tier will generally take place there too. The digital procedure will, however, provide for Upper Tier hearings to take place elsewhere, eg in court centres around England and Wales (located in what are currently the High Court's District Registries) where it is convenient, eg cost-effective and proportionate, for them to be heard outside London. Additionally, the court may direct a physical hearing take place at any other place. Rule 3(3) further provides that should the court direct that a physical hearing take place elsewhere than the default venue provided for in rule 3(2), it may take place anywhere within England and Wales.[25]
3. Physical hearings may not, however, take place outside England and Wales,[26] except for the purposes of site visits to view evidence that is located outside the jurisdiction.[27] This reflects the fact that historically judges were not able to sit or exercise their authority outside the court's territorial jurisdiction. Courts exercise the judicial power of the State. International comity between courts and respect for the jurisdiction and sovereignty of other countries has historically required States not to exercise their judicial power within the jurisdiction of other countries. For these reasons judges were not permitted at common law to sit outside England and Wales.[28]
4. Rule 2(4) might appear to infringe that common law rule as it permits any participant in a non-physical or hybrid hearing to take part in it from anywhere in the world. They need not be in England and Wales.[29] In so far as this rule permits a judge to take part in a physical hearing from outside England and Wales it is a departure from the common law.[30] It is, however, consistent with developments in British Columbia in *Endean v British Columbia* (2014)[31] and, most recently, with the Privy Council's decision in *Attorney-General of the Turk & Caicos Islands v Misick* (2020).[32]
5. The former is authority for the proposition that the common law, via the court's inherent jurisdiction to administer its own processes, could deem a judge to be within a physical court room within the jurisdiction even though they were connected to it from outside the jurisdiction via digital technology. It is also authority for the proposition that such an approach does not offend against procedural principle.

[25] *Re Blackfriars* [2020] EWHC 845 (Ch) at [23]–[24] and [37]; *Teesside Gas Transportation Ltd v Cats North Sea Ltd* [2020] EWCA Civ 503 at [93]–[96].

[26] *Endean v British Columbia* [2014] BCCA 61, esp, at [43] and [47]; *Endean v British Columbia* [2016] SCC 42; [2016] 2 SCR 16; *Attorney-General of the Turk & Caicos Islands v Misick* [2020] UKPC 30.

[27] *Tito v Waddell* [1975] 1 WLR 1303.

[28] *Attorney-General of the Turk & Caicos Islands v Misick* [2020] UKPC 30 at [61].

[29] *Polanski v Conde Nast Publications Ltd* [2005] 1 WLR 637.

[30] *Huber v X-Yachts (GB) Ltd* [2020] EWHC 3082 (TCC) at [29].

[31] *Endean v British Columbia* [2014] BCCA 61 at [78]–[80].

[32] *Attorney-General of the Turk & Caicos Islands v Misick* [2020] UKPC 30 at [61].

Such hearings are equivalent to well-established telephone hearings and, for instance, just as such hearings do not, they do not offend against the publicity principle. The latter is authority for the proposition that, by Regulation, it is permissible to deem a judge's participation in a non-physical hearing from outside the jurisdiction to be taking place from within the jurisdiction, ie from within a courtroom situated within the jurisdiction. Rule 2(4) is intended to codify both the common law inherent jurisdiction, acknowledged in Canada, and to be an equivalent statutory power to that upheld by the Privy Council.

## RULE 4.—HEARING DETERMINATION

**(1) In determining the type of hearing that is to take place, the court must give effect to the purposive principle. In particular, it must consider the impact a specific form of hearing is likely to have on**
- **(a) the parties' ability to properly and effectively present their respective cases, and particularly to present and test evidence;**
- **(b) the court's ability to properly assess evidence;**
- **(c) the health and well-being of the participants; and**
- **(d) the proper administration of justice.**

**(2) A physical hearing is presumed to give effect to the purposive principle where the hearing is**
- **(a) scheduled to last more than a day;**
- **(b) involves complex issues of law or fact that cannot properly be tested in a non-physical or hybrid hearing; or**
- **(c) involves issues of fraud or dishonesty.**

**(3) A jury trial may only take place as a either a physical hearing or a hybrid hearing. A continuous, digital hearing may only be a non-physical or hybrid process.**

**(4) A non-physical hearing is presumed to give effect to the purposive principle where the hearing is**
- **(a) uncontested;**
- **(b) a dispute management hearing;**
- **(c) an application hearing that is scheduled to last no more than a day;**
- **(d) an adjudicative hearing that is scheduled to last no more than a day;**
- **(e) an application for permission to bring judicial review proceedings; or**
- **(f) a costs hearing.**

**(5) The court, consistently with the purposive principle, may direct a hybrid hearing take place where it would otherwise direct a physical hearing take place and a participant is unable to attend such a hearing.**

**(6) When assessing whether or not to hold a physical hearing the court must take account of**
- **(a) the extent to which such a hearing is necessary to give effect to the procedural equality principle;**
- **(b) the extent to which such a hearing is necessary to enable effective cross-examination of witnesses;**
- **(c) any characteristic of the parties or witnesses that may affect their ability to take part in proceedings effectively;**
- **(d) the cost to parties and witnesses of attendance at a physical hearing;**
- **(e) the time taken by parties and witnesses to attend a physical hearing; and**
- **(f) the needs of other litigants to have their proceedings dealt with in a timely and cost-effective manner.**

**(7) The court may direct that a hearing is a written hearing, which is one determined entirely on the papers whether they are in digital or physical form. Such a hearing may only take place where**
  **(a) the hearing is an application for permission to bring judicial review proceedings;**
  **(b) the court derogates from the right to an oral hearing because such a hearing is either unnecessary or the derogation is in the interests of justice;**
  **(c) the parties waive their right to an oral hearing. Any waiver must be fully-informed and given of the waiving party's free will; or**
  **(d) a specific rule provides for a written hearing.**

**(8) Where a written hearing is to take place the court shall where necessary direct a procedure through which parties and any non-party likely to be affected by the application, may make written submissions prior to the court's determination of the matter.**

*Sources: ELI-UNIDROIT Model Rules, r 64(1); CPR rr 1.4(2)(k), 3.1(2)(d) and (m), 54.11A, PD54, para 7.3.*

## COMMENTARY

1. The court determines the nature of any hearing. Historically, this would have meant no more than the court determining whether to accept that a small claim be disposed of, with the parties' consent, without an oral hearing, whether an application for permission to appeal be determined at an oral hearing instead of on the papers, or whether part of a hearing may take place via video-link or video-conferencing facilities.[33]
2. The development of audio and, more recently, video-conferencing, and digital online platforms has, however, expanded the possibilities. Hearings may now take place in a myriad of ways. They may be wholly physical in a court room. They may take place via telephone, via video-link, or a video-conferencing platform.[34] Or, they may take place via a combination of the different methods in hybrid form.
3. This rule is intended, in the light of experience gained through the use of such technology during the Covid-19 pandemic, to guide the court in exercising its discretion to determine which type of hearing will further the purposive principle.[35]
4. Physical hearings remain the gold standard and the default approach, except in limited circumstances where a non-physical hearing is presumed to be a more effective way to give effect to the purposive principle.[36] Such circumstances include where a physical hearing is unnecessary because matters are not contested or where the hearing would be sufficiently short that it would be a disproportionate use of court and party time and expense to hold such a hearing. As is noted rightly in the

[33] CPR rr 27.10, 52.5, and PD32, Annex 3.

[34] CPR PD51V—The Video Hearings Pilot Scheme; M Briggs, *Civil Courts Structure Review—Interim Report* (2015) at 2.20; T Etherton, *The Civil Court of the Future* (Judicial Office, 2017) at [33]–[42]. The use of such technology was significantly expanded due to the effect of the Covid-19 pandemic; N Byrom, S Beardon, and A Kendrick (2020). For an overview of the uptake, and issues raised by non-physical hearings, see: The Standing International Forum of Commercial Courts, *SIFoCC Covid-19 Memorandum, SIFoCC Covid-19 Annex A* (May 2020), and the *Second SIFoCC COVID-19 Memorandum* (March 2021).

[35] Chancery Guide (2022), Appendix Z.

[36] *Rahbarpoor v Said* [2021] EWHC 3319 (Ch).

ELI-UNIDROIT Model Rules, use of digital technology to, particularly, hear small claims, which are usually heard at short hearings, will generally be lower than the costs of attending a physical hearing.[37] Thus their use ought to be promoted in such circumstances. Rule 4(4) identifies the circumstances where a non-physical hearing is presumed to give effect to the purposive principle. Conversely, where a hearing involves those matters identified in rule 4(2) the presumption is that it will be a physical hearing.

5. When considering whether to rebut a presumption or whether to hold a hybrid hearing, the court is required to consider the factors identified in rule 4(1). These are intended to ensure that the nature of the hearing does not adversely affect the court's ability to give effect to the purposive principle. They are also intended to ensure that they respect the health and well-being of the participants. One factor that became apparent during the Covid-19 pandemic is that hearings that use digital technology can adversely affect parties and judges' ability to concentrate. It is now more widely apparent that they can adversely affect participants' health more generally. Moreover, they generally appear to be more tiring than physical hearings and may, as a consequence, require greater breaks during the hearing than physical hearings.[38] Care needs therefore to be taken to ensure that non-physical or hybrid hearings do not cause short or long-term adverse health effects, nor that they result in a hearing being longer, and hence more expensive, than it would have been if held as a physical hearing.
6. Care also needs to be taken to ensure that non-physical and hybrid hearings do not undermine the court's ability to secure adjudicative accuracy. It must therefore consider the affect that each option might have on the judge's ability to assess evidence, such as witness credibility as well as the parties' ability to adduce and test evidence.[39] Here the effect specific types of hearing may have on procedural equality must also be considered. While it should be borne in mind that this will not necessarily be infringed where some but not all participants in a hearing take part non-physically, it may do so.[40] Careful assessment is required on a case-by-case basis.
7. Care should also be taken to ensure that the choice of hearing type does not undermine the court's ability to promote settlement. One question then that the court must consider when considering whether a specific type of hearing promotes the proper administration of justice is the effect that a hearing type may have on the promotion of effective settlement. It is often the case that informal discussions between parties while they wait at court for a hearing to commence can result in last minute

[37] ELI-UNIDROIT MODEL Rules, r 97, comment 6.

[38] N Byrom, S Beardon, and A Kendrick (2020) at 56 noting eye strain, screen fatigue, and headaches as a consequence of non-physical hearings. There is also evidence that prolonged use of video-conferencing platforms may increase cortisol levels, which may adversely affect long term health. There is thus a need to study the effect of the use of non-physical hearings particularly on lawyers and judges; UNODC, *Exploring Linkages between Judicial Well-Being and Judicial Integrity* (2022); A Bullock, A Colvin, and M Jackson, 'Zoom Fatigue in the Age of COVID-19' (2022) 7(1) Journal of Social Work in the Global Community 1–9.

[39] *Navigator Equities Ltd v Deripaska* [2020] EWHC 1798 (Comm) at [9]; *Re A (Children) (Remote Hearing: Care and Placement Orders)* [2020] EWCA Civ 583 at [7]–[9] and *A Local Authority v Mother* [2020] EWHC 1086 (Fam) at [27]: guidance when to hold a remote hearing where witness evidence is to be tested and on assessing witness credibility. R Susskind, Evidence to House of Lords' Constitution Select Committee, 3 June 2020, at (10)–(11) and A Reed and M Adler, *Virtual Hearings Put Children, Abuse Victims at Ease in Court*, Bloomberg Law News, 23 July 2020 on the claim that non-physical hearings improve assessment of witness evidence.

[40] *Re C (Children) (Covid-19 Representation)* [2020] EWCA Civ 734 at [22]–[25].

settlement. Such discussions may also result in issues being narrowed, which can either promote a more proportionate process or lead to settlement. The ability to meet informally before and during breaks in hearings when they are held in a court does not exist to the same degree in a hybrid hearing. It does not exist at all in a non-physical hearing. This is because hybrid and non-physical hearings introduce a degree of formality into the time before hearings commence and during breaks in hearings that simply does not exist where a physical hearing takes place. It will therefore be necessary, if such hearings are to operate consistently with the settlement principle, that formal opportunities for informal discussions be introduced into such hearings. This could be done by providing for 'break out rooms' which are commonly available via, for instance, MS Teams and Zoom to be set up before and during hybrid and non-physical hearings and which all parties and their representatives can join at any time. While there is a degree of artificiality about such formal processes for informal meetings, it should be anticipated that given time lawyers will become familiar with them and that they therefore become a means to promote settlement at the 'non-physical' door of the court.

8. Civil jury trials, where they take place,[41] must either take place via a physical hearing or, where a party or witness needs to take part remotely, as a hybrid hearing. The latter situation may arise where a party or witness is vulnerable due, for instance, to their past relationship with the other party.

9. Finally, rule 4(7) makes provision for written hearings. While it is generally thought that parties are entitled to their 'day in court', there is no absolute right to an oral, physical hearing.[42] The right to such a hearing may be subject to derogations. Three bases are set out under which a written hearing, rather than a physical, non-physical or hybrid one may take place. Reference to 'written' encompasses both digital and paper-based formats for such a hearing.

10. The first situation where a matter could be determined by way of a written hearing is, as it is under the CPR, where an application is issued seeking permission to bring judicial review proceedings.[43] The court retains a discretion to order such applications to be dealt with via an oral hearing, in which case it would ordinarily be dealt with at a non-physical hearing.

11. The second situation is where the court determines that it is permissible to derogate from an oral hearing in proceedings where one is unnecessary, or it is in the interests of justice to do so. The former could occur where, for instance, a hearing required determination of a technical issue that did not require oral evidence or justify the need for oral submissions.[44] The latter could arise where a written hearing is necessary to protect the court's processes from abuse or where, for instance, the applicant or a respondent has acted abusively and is subject to a restriction order (Part 11, rule 37).[45] A written hearing may also be justified on grounds of economy, efficiency and/or proportionality.[46] On applications being determined via a written hearing, also see Part 11, rule 8.

[41] *Phillips v Commissioner of Police of the Metropolis* [2003] EWCA Civ 382 at [17]; *Armstrong v Times Newspapers Ltd* [2005] EWHC 2816 (QB); [2006] EMLR 166.

[42] *Jussila v Finland* [2006] ECHR 996; (2007) 45 EHRR 39 at [40]–[42].

[43] CPR PD54 para 7.3.

[44] *Martinie v France* [2006] ECHR 392 at [41].

[45] *Bhamjee v Forsdick (No 2)* [2003] EWCA 1113; [2004] 1 WLR 88.

[46] Part 17, r 20(5).

12. The third situation is where a party, consistently with the party autonomy principle, waives the right to an oral hearing in favour of a written hearing. While the European Court of Human Rights has held that implied waiver in such a situation is permissible,[47] for the court and opposing parties to be properly and reasonably confident that waiver has occurred this rule requires it to be express (as well as fully-informed and of the parties' own free will). This enables the court, if necessary, to satisfy itself by questioning the party either in writing or at a dispute management hearing if they understand that they are waiving the right and that they do so of their own free will.[48] Express waiver thus promotes finality of litigation, and with it the proportionality principle, as it ensures that a party cannot, at a later date, raise a challenge to any decision taken at a written hearing on the basis that they ought not to have been taken to have impliedly waived the right. Finally, specific rules may make provision for applications and other matters to be dealt with by way of a written process, such as an application to reopen appeal proceedings.
13. This rule does not adopt the approach, considered under the CPR, which permits a class-based derogation from the right to an oral hearing.[49] It rejects the idea that very low value proceedings should, as a general rule, be determined via a written process.[50] That approach may be viewed as an economical, efficient, and proportionate way to deal with such claims. It may be so in some cases, and particularly where such claims do not involve oral evidence. In other cases, oral evidence may be necessary, and an oral hearing may be a more effective and economical way of proceeding than requiring the production of witness statements and submissions based on, and in response to, them. The better approach, taken here, is to provide the discretion to order a written process under rule 7(b) rather than take the CPR's class-based approach.
14. Rule 4(8) requires the court to consider if any necessary steps are required to ensure that, where a written hearing is to be held, parties or non-parties who may be affected by the outcome of the application are given sufficient notice of it consistently with the due notice principle.

## RULE 5.—CONTINUOUS DIGITAL HEARINGS

**(1) The court may direct that the settlement management process be managed as a continuous digital hearing. The continuous digital hearing will be an asynchronous process.**

**(2) Exceptionally, and only where at least one party is unrepresented, may the court otherwise direct proceedings be managed as a continuous digital hearing. Where a direction is made in such circumstances, no temporal distinction is made between procedural and adjudicative hearings. The court must, however, specify**

**(a) when it is dealing with procedural and adjudicative matters; and**

**(b) when it will provide the parties with a final opportunity to submit and respond to evidence, legal submissions, and argument.**

[47] *Le Compte v Belgium* [1981] ECHR 3; (1982) 4 EHRR 1 at [59].

[48] *Albert & Le Compte v Belgium* [1983] ECHR 1; (1983) 5 EHRR 533 at [35].

[49] P Hirvelä and S Heikkilä (2022) at 174–175; *Martinie v France* [2006] ECHR 392 at [42]; *R (Siddiqui) v Lord Chancellor* [2019] EWCA Civ 1040.

[50] PD51Z—The Small Claims Paper Determination Pilot.

**(3) When the court directs a continuous digital hearing, it must specify a date by which it must be concluded. That date may only be varied for good reason.**

**(4) All communications between the court and parties made during a continuous digital hearing, except those which take place as part of a consensual settlement process, shall be made available to the public consistently with the publicity principle.**

*Sources: The HMCTS Modernisation Programme; The Civil Resolution Tribunal (British Columbia), Phase 2 (Negotiation), Phase 3 (Facilitation).*

## COMMENTARY

1. This rule makes provision for continuous digital hearings. This type of hearing was piloted as 'continuous online resolution' in the Tribunals justice system as part of the HMCTS reform programme.[51] That was a process through which parties and the judge made submissions and statements via a digital format at different times, eg asynchronously, rather than, as in a traditional hearing process, at the same time. In this way the process was, broadly, a digital analogue of the approach taken to the evidence-gathering phase of proceedings in Italian civil procedure, albeit that process is carried out synchronously.[52] The fundamental problem with the approach when piloted was that it was more expensive than traditional hearings, contrary to what was believed to be the unsupported assumption on which the pilot was based.[53] In the light of this, work on continuous online resolution was abandoned by the reform programme.[54]

2. It might be thought therefore that there was accordingly no justifiable basis for including such a form of hearing process within this Code. The pilot scheme would seem to suggest that it would undermine the economy, efficiency, and proportionality principles. It is, however, incorporated here for two limited purposes.

3. First, and primarily, it is included as a means to facilitate settlement where proceedings are allocated to the settlement dispute management track. Asynchronous hearings, particularly digital ones, are a well-established means to carry out settlement processes. This rule would thus help to embed this into post-issue dispute management.[55] Its particular focus here is on enabling parties, and any mediator (including one provided by AI), to communicate with each other digitally over a defined period of time to carry out e-negotiation or e-mediation.

4. It is also, albeit only exceptionally, to be used where at least one party is unrepresented. Under this Code, this ought to be rare due to the basis on which litigation funding

[51] R Thomas and J Tomlinson (2018).

[52] R Caponi (2016).

[53] J Tomlinson, *Justice in the Digital State* (Bristol University Press, 2019) at 49.

[54] M Fouzder, *Digital appeals system 'cost six times more' than going to court, The Law Gazette* (21 December 2020).

[55] N Ebner, 'E-Mediation', in M Abdul Wahab, E Katsh, and D Rainey, *Online Dispute resolution: Theory and Practice* (Eleven Publishing, 2012), at 365; A Sela, 'The Effect of Online Technologies on Dispute Resolution System Design: Antecedents, Current Trends, and Future Directions' (2017) 21 Lewis & Clark L Rev 635 at 668. S Salter and D Thompson, 'Public-Centred Civil Justice Redesign: a case study of the British Columbia Civil Resolution Tribunal' (2016–2017) 3 McGill Journal of Dispute Resolution 113 at 132–134. This type of approach was also endorsed by M. Briggs (2015) at 51 and M. Briggs, *Civil Courts Structure Review—Final Report* (2016) at 36ff.

is to be generally available under Part 4. Where, however, in an exceptional case a party is not funded or is otherwise unable to obtain legal representation or chooses not to do so, rule 5(2) provides the court with a discretion to direct a continuous digital hearing. This may be done when the court is exercising substantive dispute management functions under Part 12, rule 8. It would thus enable the court to satisfy itself that, through questioning the parties via a digital medium, the issues in dispute and evidence had been identified effectively. It would also enable it to ensure through such questioning that any relevant evidence and submissions, wherever possible, had been uploaded to the digital dispute management account and file. By ensuring that this type of managerial use of the process is limited to disputes where a party is unrepresented, any increase in court resource use will be minimised. This rule will thus lessen any adverse effect on the implementation of the economy, efficiency, and proportionality principles. By ensuring that an unrepresented party has an appropriate opportunity to participate effectively in proceedings through being able to consider and respond to questioning over a period of time, it also helps to promote their effective access to and participation in the proceedings. Assistance via this form of process, albeit it may be more resource intensive than a traditional hearing process, may then reduce consequential resource use that may adversely affect the proper administration of justice were an unrepresented party to otherwise conclude, rightly or wrongly, that they had not been afforded a fair process and appeal from any decisions made in a traditional hearing process.

5. Rule 5(2) and (3) make provision for the effective management of a continuous digital process. They specifically require the court to take steps to identify when it will deal with procedural and adjudicative issues during a continuous digital hearing and to set a date by which the process shall conclude. The former is intended to ensure that the parties, at least one of whom will be unrepresented, and any member of the public accessing the hearing will clearly understand the nature of the process and the stage it has reached. It thus improves both effective party participation and the educative function of the publicity principle, which is itself further implemented by rule 5(4). The latter is intended to further effective dispute management by focusing the minds of parties and the court on the fact that the process is not an indefinite one; hence steps within the process while they may be taken asynchronously may not be taken at the pace and leisure of the parties and the court. It is a process that must also be carried out consistently with the purposive principle.

## SECTION 3: SPECIAL CASES

### RULE 6.—WITH-NOTICE AND WITHOUT-NOTICE HEARINGS

**(1) A with-notice hearing is one that takes place after reasonable notice has been given to all parties, including non-parties likely to be affected by any judgment or order made at it.**

**(2) A without-notice hearing is one that takes place with no or no reasonable notice having been given to parties, including non-parties likely to be affected by any judgment or order made at it.**

**(3) Hearings shall, generally, be heard with-notice to all parties. The following hearings must be held with-notice**

**(a) trials;**
**(b) application hearings that may finally determine proceedings;**
**(c) application hearings that concern a party or non-party's liberty;**
**(d) application hearings to compel compliance with a rule, practice direction or court order;**
**(e) those specified by a rule, practice direction or court order.**

**(4) A hearing may be held without-notice where there is clear and cogent evidence that it is in the interests of the proper administration of justice to do so. Matters considered at a without-notice hearing will be subject to intense scrutiny by the court.**

**(5) It may be in the interests of the proper administration of justice to hold a hearing without-notice where**
**(a) the hearing needs to be held urgently and reasonable notice cannot be given before the hearing is to be held; or**
**(b) notice would defeat the purpose of the hearing.**

**(6) Where reasonable notice cannot be given in the interests of the proper administration of justice, such notice as is possible must be given.**

**(7) A party seeking an order at a without-notice hearing is under a continuing duty to give full and frank disclosure. They must provide the court with all relevant information relating to legal, factual, and procedural issues, which both supports and is adverse to the grant of the order sought.**

**(8) A material breach of the duty to give full and frank disclosure may result in any order made at the without-notice hearing being varied or discharged where doing so would, in all the circumstances, promote the purposive principle.**

**(9) A lawyer present at a without-notice hearing of an application is under a duty to prepare and provide a note of the hearing to parties and non-parties affected by any provisional measure granted at the hearing. Where the applicant is not represented by a lawyer at the hearing, the court must make available its digital transcript of the hearing.**

**(10) Where an order is made at a without-notice hearing**
**(a) the subject of the order must be given notice of it as soon as reasonably possible;**
**(b) the application shall be reheard as soon as reasonably possible at a with-notice hearing. The date by which the with-notice hearing must be heard must be specified in the court order made at the without-notice hearing. The subject of the order may waive their right to have the application reheard.**

*Sources: ALI/UNIDROIT Principles, principles 5.8, 8.2; ALI/UNIDROIT Reporters' Study, r 17; ELI-UNIDROIT Model Rules, rr 50, 184, 186; CPR rr 23.4, 23.9, 25.3, 81.5.*

## COMMENTARY

1. As a general rule notice of a hearing must be given to all parties to proceedings and any non-party that is likely to be affected by any judgment or order that may be made it. This is an aspect of the due notice and general access principles. Equally, it gives effect to the effective participation, adversarial and accuracy and settlement principles. Without notice of a hearing a party or relevant non-party cannot contribute effectively to the court's decision-making process nor will they, or the public more generally, be in a position to maintain trust and confidence in the civil process. A system that fails to provide effective notice of hearings is one that is more akin to that described in Kafka's *The Trial* than one committed to securing a fair process.

2. Rule 6(3) gives effect to this general rule. It applies without qualification where trial hearings are concerned: adjudicative justice cannot be achieved in the absence of notice. Applications that have the same effect as trials, eg strike out or summary judgment applications that finally determine proceedings, are treated in the same way.[56] The same approach also applies to hearings that have a significant impact on an individual's rights, eg those that may result in imprisonment for contempt of court or those that seek to compel compliance with any rule, practice direction or court order on pain of sanctions for non-compliance that would debar the party from adducing evidence or continuing with the proceedings. It also applies as required by a rule, practice direction or court order.[57]
3. Under rule 6(4), the general rule can, however, be displaced in limited circumstances. As a derogation from a number of fundamental fair process principles, the court will need to be satisfied that holding a hearing on a without-notice basis is justified. It ought therefore to be satisfied on '*clear and cogent evidence*'[58] that there are compelling reasons to do so.
4. Rule 6(4) provides that such hearings may be held where it is in the interests of the proper administration of justice to do so. Rule 6(5) specifies the two, alternative, bases on which that may be the case: urgency;[59] and, where notice would defeat the purpose of the hearing. The former may arise where, for instance, an interim injunction is sought to enjoin a party from carrying out an action which, if reasonable notice were to be given, would have occurred by the time the hearing had taken place. Urgency does not arise where it is self-created by the party seeking an order.[60] Where reasonable notice cannot be given on this basis, to ensure the derogation from the due notice and other relevant principles is kept to a minimum, the party seeking the hearing must give such notice as they possibly can.[61] This enables the other to take part in the without-notice hearing, albeit to a lesser extent than normal. Such participation does not transform the hearing into a with-notice hearing.
5. The second basis on which hearings can be held without-notice arises where it would defeat the hearing's purpose. No notice is given where this applies. Advance notice of an asset preservation order, for instance, would tip-off the respondent and enable them to take steps to frustrate the order itself. Notice could, for instance, enable them to dispose of their assets before the order enjoining them from doing so were granted. Similar considerations may also arise where an interim injunction is aimed at enjoining publication of information. Notice would provide the opportunity to publish the information prior to the injunction being granted.[62] Where secrecy is required as a means to ensure that the hearing's purpose is not frustrated prior to any order being granted that justifies it being held on a without-notice basis.[63]

[56] *Irwin Mitchell Solicitors v Patel* [2003] EWCA Civ 633.

[57] Part 15, r 13(5): consideration must be given to holding a hearing to consider varying or setting aside an order made at a without-notice hearing on a with-notice basis.

[58] *Practice Guidance: Interim Non-Disclosure Orders* [2012] 1 WLR 1003 at [21]; *X & Y v Persons Unknown* [2007] EMLR 290 at [10]–[12].

[59] *National Commercial Bank Jamaica Ltd v Olint Corp Ltd* [2009] UKPC 16; [2009] 1 WLR 1405.

[60] *Bates v Lord Hailsham of St Marylebone* [1972] 1 WLR 1383.

[61] CPR PD23A para 4.2.

[62] *Terry v Persons Unknown* [2010] EWHC 119 (QB); [2010] 1 FCR 659 at [138].

[63] *DFT v TFD* [2010] EWHC 2335 (QB); *RST v UVW* [2009] EWHC 24 at [7]; ELI-UNIDROIT Model Rules, r 186(1).

6. Where a hearing is dealt with, initially, on a without-notice basis, the applicant at such a hearing is under a continuing duty to give full and frank disclosure.[64] They must disclose to the court all relevant, material facts, both in favour of and against granting any order that the court could reasonably be expected to consider.[65] They must also set out any relevant legal and procedural issues in a neutral manner.[66] These requirements are particularly intended to give effect to procedural equality and fair access for all affected parties pending the with-notice hearing.[67] It also helps to minimise the risk that the application will be granted on a false basis. It thus protects the integrity of the court process.[68] It also helps to minimise the risk that the rights of those individuals subject to any order granted would be interfered with improperly.[69]
7. Where an order is obtained in material breach of the continuing duty, it may be varied or discharged where doing so would further the purposive, and particularly, the proportionality principles.[70] Where the without-notice hearing concerned the grant of provisional measures, breach may also result in any undertaking in damages that had been given being enforced against the applicant.[71] This is the case even where the court concludes that there was a proper basis for granting or otherwise continuing the order.[72]
8. The rationale for discharging an order where there was a material breach of the duty is to both ensure that the applicant does not secure the benefit of the order improperly, but also—and more importantly—to deter applicants from seeking and obtaining orders on a false basis. Both rationale help promote the purposive principle, not least because they help the court to secure a fair process while promoting the accuracy principle.[73]
9. To promote procedural equality and enable all those affected by any order granted at a without-notice hearing to understand the basis on which an order was granted and consider whether they may wish to challenge it, the applicant's lawyers are under a duty to prepare and provide a note of the hearing to anyone affected by any order made at it.[74] It should also secure effective due notice of both the applicant's

[64] *JSC BTA Bank v Ablyazov* [2018] EWHC 259 (Comm).

[65] *Siporex Trade SA v Comdel Commodities Ltd* [1986] 2 Lloyd's Rep 428 at 437; *Brink's Mat Ltd v Elcombe* [1988] 1 WLR 1350 at 1356.

[66] *Memory Corporation Plc v Sidhu (No 2)* [2000] 1 WLR 1443 at 1459–1460; *Re OJSC ANK Yugraneft* [2008] EWHC 2614 (Ch); [2010] BCC 475 at 72 citing *The Arena Corporation Limited v Schroeder* [2003] EWHC 1089 (Ch) at [117].

[67] *Fitzgerald v Williams* [1996] QB 657 at 667; *Memory Corporation Plc v Sidhu (No 2)* [2000] 1 WLR 1443 at 1459–1460; *Hunt v Ubhi* [2023] EWCA Civ 417; [2023] Bus LR 1827 at [41].

[68] *Re OJSC ANK Yugraneft* [2008] EWHC 2614 (Ch); [2010] BCC 475 at [72] citing *Chafoor v Cliff* [2006] EWHC 825 (Ch); [2006] 1 WLR 3020.

[69] *Thane Investments Ltd v Tomlinson* [2003] EWCA Civ 1272 at [21].

[70] *Memory Corporation Plc v Sidhu (No 2)* [2000] 1 WLR 1443 at 1455.

[71] *Dadourian Group International v Simms* [2007] EWHC 1673 at [29]–[32]; *Dadourian Group International v Simms* [2009] EWCA Civ 169; [2009] 1 Lloyd's Rep 601 at [167]–[210], on which see Part 13, r 7.

[72] *R v Kensington Income Tax Commissioners, ex parte de Polignac* [1917] 1 KB 486 at 514.

[73] *Brink's-MAT Ltd v Elcombe* [1988] 1 WLR 1350 at 1358; *Lloyds Bowmaker Ltd v Britannia Arrow Holdings* [1988] 1 WLR 1337.

[74] *Interoute Telecommunications (UK) Ltd v Fashion Gossip Ltd*, The Times, 10 November 1999, cited in D Neuberger et al, *Report of the Committee on Super-Injunctions: Super-Injunctions, Anonymised Injunctions and Open Justice* (Judicial Office, 2011) at 39–40.

submissions and any matters raised by the judge hearing the application.[75] This also complements the requirement to give full and frank disclosure as it is should enable the party affected by an order to ascertain if there was a breach of that duty. Where an applicant is not represented by a lawyer, the court must make its digital transcript of the hearing available to affected parties.

10. An order granted on a without-notice basis must last for no more than a short period. Compliance with the due notice, effective participation and adversarial process principles require any orders made at such hearings to be heard on a with-notice basis as soon as reasonably possible after an order is granted on a without-notice basis.[76] This minimises the departure from fundamental principle. It also, as with-notice hearings are rehearings, secures procedural equality; a review hearing or a hearing where the affected parties had to persuade the court to depart from the order previously granted would place them at a procedural disadvantage vis a vis the applicant. As with other departures from procedural principle, the right to a rehearing may be waived, consistently with party autonomy and proportionality, by those who are subject to a provisional order.

## RULE 7.—ABSENCE OR NON-PARTICIPATION OF A PARTY OR WITNESS

**(1) Hearings may be held in the absence of or without the participation of any party or witness.**

**(2) Non-attendance or non-participation in an adjudicative hearing may result in the court striking out the proceedings, including any defences, counterclaims, and defences to counterclaims.**

**(3) An order made in the absence or non-participation of a party may be set aside or varied and any matter struck out may be restored by the court on application of that party. The rules concerning relief from sanction apply to such applications.**

**(4) Where a trial is held in the absence or with the non-participation of a party who has not been served with actual notice of the hearing, any judgment or order made at that hearing may, on the party's application, be set aside as of right.**

**(5) Where an absent or non-participating party chooses to appeal from an order or judgment made in their absence, they waive their right to make an application to vary, set aside or restore under this rule.**

*Sources: CPR rr 3.1(2)(m), 3.10, 23.11, 39.3.*

[75] *G v Wikimedia Foundation Inc* [2009] EWHC 3148 (QB); [2010] EMLR 14 at [31].

[76] CPR PD 25, para 5.1 currently gives effect to this requirement where interim injunctions are concerned. And see CPR PD 23A 4.2 on its general application.

## COMMENTARY

1. This rule consolidates the established approach under the CPR, which confirms that hearings may take place in the absence, or without the participation, of a party.[77] Its rationale ought to be self-evident. Effective, and particularly proportionate, management of court resources would be undermined if parties were effectively able to dictate when and if hearings took place through failing or refusing to attend them.[78] Any approach that permitted a party to unilaterally dictate the pace of proceedings or deny their opponent a hearing would not only breach the procedural equality principle, it would also be fundamentally at odds with their opponent's general right of access and right to receive judgment in a reasonable time.[79]
2. The power to proceed where a party does not attend or participate in proceedings is a discretionary one, which must be exercised consistently with the purposive principle. Where, for instance, a party cannot attend due to ill-health or other good reason, the court may and in some cases ought to adjourn a hearing to a later date.
3. Where a court has held or concluded a hearing in the absence or with the non-participation of a party, there is one circumstance where, on application, any judgment or order made at it should be set aside as of right.[80] That is when it is shown that that party did not receive actual, due notice of a trial hearing. In all other circumstances, any judgment or order may be varied, set aside or restored following a successful application for relief from sanction.[81] In considering under that test whether, in all the circumstances, the grant of relief would further the purposive principle the court will inevitably have to consider whether the party seeking relief has a real prospect of succeeding on their claim or defence or whether in the absence of such a prospect there is another compelling reason to grant relief. Were they not to have such a prospect of success, the grant of relief would give rise to unnecessary and disproportionate cost and court resource use.[82] Satisfaction of the test for relief requires the court to grant the relief sought.[83]
4. An absent or non-participating party may, rather than apply to set aside, vary, or restore under this rule, elect to appeal from the substantive order or judgment made in their absence. If they do so, however, they are deemed to accept the validity of the court having proceeded in their absence. Under the CPR it was possible for an absent party to pursue both an application to vary and an appeal.[84] Rule 7(5) does not adopt this approach. In order to promote proportionality, it requires the absent party to elect which approach to take.

[77] Absence or non-participation is determined by failure to attend the hearing by a time after its commencement as determined by the judge: *Akita v Governor & Company of the Bank of Ireland* [2019] EWHC 1712 (QB). It is also determined by reference to whether the party or witness has been ordered to attend in person or to attend a physical hearing. In such circumstances, attendance by lawyer or via a digital medium has been held to be non-attendance: *Falmouth House Ltd v Abou-Hamdan* [2017] EWHC 799 (Ch). Ordinarily, attendance via lawyer is sufficient for there to be attendance: *Owen v Black Horse Ltd* [2023] EWCA Civ 325.

[78] *Leave.EU Group Ltd v Information Commissioner* [2022] EWCA Civ 109 at [18]–[21].

[79] A Zuckerman, *Zuckerman on Civil Procedure—Principles of Practice* (Sweet & Maxwell, 2021) at 397.

[80] *Nelson v Clearsprings (Management) Ltd* [2006] EWCA Civ 1252; [2007] 1 WLR 962.

[81] *Probst v Germany* No 19913/92, 11 January 1995, unrep, EComHR.

[82] This incorporates and broadens CPR r 39.3(5) to include the alternative requirement applicable to setting aside default judgment and granting permission to bring a first appeal: CPR r 13.3. Also see CPR r 52.6. See Part 15, r 11(3)(b), Part 17, r 6(2).

[83] Under the CPR the court retained a discretion, exercisable exceptionally, not to grant relief: *Sir John Fitzgerald Ltd v MacArthur* [2009] EWHC 2659 (QB).

[84] *Bank of Scotland v Pereira* [2011] EWCA Civ 241; [2011] 1 WLR 3926.

## SECTION 4: PUBLICITY

### RULE 8.—BROADCASTING AND RECORDING HEARINGS

**(1) The court may authorise the recording and/or broadcast of any hearing via any electronic medium. Authorisation may be subject to conditions that protect the administration of justice.**
**(2) Unauthorised recording or broadcasting of any hearing is prohibited. Breaches of this rule may be subject to the court's powers to protect the administration of justice.**
**(3) Live text-based communications and their equivalent are not a form of unauthorised recording or broadcasting. They may be prohibited by the court to protect the administration of justice.**
**(4) All hearings shall be audio-recorded unless the court directs otherwise. Non-physical and hybrid hearings may also be video-recorded. Recordings may only be made by the court or a body or individual authorised by the court to do so.**
**(5) Recordings of hearings form part of the court record.**

*Sources: ALI/UNIDROIT Principles, principle 20.1; ALI/UNIDROIT Reporters' Study, r 23.1; ELI-UNIDROIT Model Rules, r 17; Criminal Justice Act 1925, s 41; Contempt of Court Act 1981, s 9; Practice Direction (Tape Recorders) [1981] 1 WLR 1546; Crime and Courts Act 2013, s 32; The Court of Appeal (Recording and Broadcasting) Order 2013 (SI 2013/2786); Courts Act 2003, s 85A to 85D; Remote Observation and Recording (Courts and Tribunals) Regulations 2022 (SI 2022/705); CPR r 39.9; Practice Guidance (Court Proceedings: Live Text-Based Communications) (No 2) [2012] 1 WLR 12; Practice Direction (Audio Recordings: Access) [2014] 1 WLR 632.*

### COMMENTARY

1. The power to permit hearings to be broadcast is currently contained within legislation and, where proceedings are to be broadcast within a court building or an area designated as being within the court, by the common law.[85] The prohibition on unauthorised recording, whether audio or video, is set out in both statute and the CPR.[86] It would otherwise arise under the court's inherent common law jurisdiction to protect its processes from abuse. The power to derogate from the publicity principle would also provide a basis to restrict unauthorised recording.
2. Rule 8(1) and (2) provide a simplified scheme to control the recording and broadcasting of proceedings.[87] It places responsibility for decisions of this kind in the hands of the court. This reflects both separation of powers and judicial independence, ie that it is a matter for the court how its processes generally and in any specific proceeding are carried out consistently with the publicity principle. That hearings can now be recorded and/or broadcast particularly helps promote the educative and accountability roles played by that principle as they enable

[85] Crime and Courts Act 2013, s 32; Courts Act 2003, s 85A to 85D; *R (Spurrier) v Secretary of State for Transport* [2019] EWHC 528 (Admin); [2019 EMLR 2016 at [21]; *Re One Blackfriars* Ltd [2020] EWHC 845 (Ch) at [24].

[86] Criminal Justice Act 1925, s 41; Contempt of Court Act 1981, s 9; CPR r 39.9(2); *Practice Direction (Tape Recorders)* [1981] 1 WLR 1546.

[87] Courts Act 2003, s 85A and Crime and Courts Act 2013, s 32.

increased access to hearings by the public and the media.[88] Care should be taken to ensure that broadcasting hearings does not undermine the administration of justice, eg by prejudicing a fair trial through exposing witnesses, parties or judges to particular notoriety (not least over the Internet) and/or intimidation, through tending to trivialise the purpose of proceedings, or enabling them to be used for collateral purposes.[89]

3. To maintain consistency with the publicity principle, there is an expectation under rule 8(1) that access to a non-physical hearing should be facilitated through the provision of an online access link on the court listing, which is to be made available through the digital portal. This is to be the means through which the public may access a hearing in an equivalent way to that which they could access a physical hearing by attending court. Where a hearing is likely to involve significant or important issues of public importance, the court may also direct that it is live-streamed via the Internet.
4. Rule 8(2) maintains the prohibition on unauthorised recording or broadcasting of hearings.[90] This is not to maintain the 'dignity' of court proceedings. It is to protect the proper administration of justice. An unauthorised recording could, for instance, be doctored so as to insert oral evidence that was not given, to delete evidence or submissions or, to alter what a judge said during proceedings or in their judgment. An unauthorised broadcast could also undermine the administration of justice for the same reasons as noted in respect of authorised broadcasts. The prohibition also protects the integrity of the publicity principle where derogations from it are in place.
5. Rule 8(2) consolidates the approach taken currently to the prohibition on unauthorised recording or broadcasting. It thus renders such conduct punishable by imprisonment on conviction (unauthorised broadcasting includes publication of photographs of proceedings)[91] or under the court's powers to commit for contempt of court (unauthorised broadcasting and unauthorised recording).[92] As both the statutory criminal sanction imposed on unauthorised broadcasting and the sanction that arises under the court's power to commit are intended to protect the administration of justice, a single regime that serves that purpose is as effective as, and simpler than, the current multi-stranded approach.[93]
6. Live text-based communication, eg text messages, tweets, or their equivalent, which can make generally available over the Internet what is taking place within a hearing, does not fall within the scope of unauthorised recording or broadcasting. It is a technological instance of the public's right to take written notes during hearings.[94]

[88] The Court of Appeal (Recording and Broadcasting) Order 2013 (SI 2013/2786); The Court of Appeal's YouTube page <https://www.youtube.com/channel/UCi3XytDJY8a3I9_vL7A_5SQ>; *National Bank of Kazakhstan v The Bank of New York Mellon* (Claim No FL-2018-000007) in the Financial List (QBD) on 27 March 2020, where live-streaming of proceedings added to the immediacy of such public scrutiny.

[89] Collateral purposes might be, for instance, the misuse of proceedings as a vehicle for a party or witness to advance a political, campaigning, or self-serving agenda unconnected to or unnecessary for the resolution of the dispute.

[90] Recording includes both audio and video recording.

[91] Criminal Justice Act 1925, s 41; Courts Act 2003, s 85B.

[92] Contempt of Court Act 1981, s 9; the court's inherent jurisdiction.

[93] *Gubarev v Orbis Business Intelligence Ltd* [2020] EWHC 2167 (QB); [2020] 4 WLR 122.

[94] *Practice Guidance (Court Proceedings: Live Text-Based Communications) (No 2)* [2012] 1 WLR 12. The right to take notes is a manifestation of both the publicity principle and the right to freedom of expression; A Zuckerman (2021) at 142.

Like that right, it is, however, subject to the court's power to restrict or otherwise limit it to protect the administration of justice.[95]

7. Rule 8(4) provides for hearings to be recorded. Recording preserves a record of the hearing, enabling the parties—if necessary—to refer to it if they wish to challenge any decision made by the court.[96] An appeal may be brought, for instance, on the grounds of judicial bias or other misconduct that is evidenced in the recording. A recording of an oral judgment given at the conclusion of a hearing can be the basis of a written transcript of judgment and can, if necessary form the basis of scrutiny of it for accuracy.[97] Recording also facilitates accurate reporting of proceedings and oral judgments as they can be accessed by the media and, particularly, court reporters. They may refer to them to check the accuracy of their reports.[98] Recordings, and access to them, are therefore an additional means of promoting the educative and accountability purposes of the publicity principle.

8. To facilitate these purposes, rule 8(4) adopts the current approach that all hearings are to be audio-recorded unless otherwise directed by the court.[99] The discretion takes account of the fact that in some circumstances it may not, for instance, be possible to record a hearing due to technological problems or due to the hearing taking place outside a court building where recording facilities either do not exist or are not able to work, eg a site visit. In exceptional circumstances derogations from the publicity principle may also justify such a direction, eg, to minimise the risk of a recording being subject to a data security breach, which could expose very sensitive information that might, for instance, pose a risk to life or national security.

9. Non-physical and hybrid hearings may also be video-recorded. The default position is that such recordings be made by the court and under its control. The court may, however, authorise other bodies or individuals to record a hearing, eg a company acting on its or the court administration's behalf or a party to proceedings. The rule does not specify the medium through which the audio or video recording is to be effected. It is technology-neutral.

10. Recordings of hearings form part of the court record. Consequently, access to them is governed by Part 2, rule 8.

[95] *Ewing v Crown Court sitting at Cardiff and Newport* [2016] EWHC 183 (Admin); [2016] 4 WLR 21.

[96] *JR & B farming Ltd v Hewitt* [2021] EWHC 1704 (Comm); *Business Mortgage Finance 4 plc v Hussain* [2021] EWHC 2766 (Ch).

[97] *Bath v Escott* [2017] EWHC 1101 (Ch); Part 15, r 9.

[98] *Practice Direction (Audio Recordings: Access)* [2014] 1 WLR 632 at [6].

[99] CPR r 39.9(1) and (2).

# PART 15
# JUDGMENTS AND ORDERS

## SECTION 1: GENERAL

1. Judgments and orders are '*the vehicle through which the judicial power of the state is exercised*'.[1] They are one of the four main ways in which disputes are brought to an end; the other three being: withdrawal from the dispute; consensual settlement; and, overbearing of one party by another.[2]
2. This Part provides the rules through which judgments and orders are formulated, served on parties, and made available to the public. It also makes provision for their procedural consequences. In doing so it draws a simple distinction between procedural judgments and orders and those that determine disputes on their substantive merits, whether they do so as a result of a summary process or following a full-blown trial. It also provides rules concerned with judgments and orders that give effect to settlement, including settlement of representative proceedings.

### RULE 1.—SCOPE AND PURPOSE

**(1) This Part concerns court judgments and orders, which are the means through which proceedings are managed effectively and disputes are resolved on their substantive merits.**

**(2) Judgments and orders primarily give effect to the purposive, accuracy, publicity, reasoned decision, finality, and effective enforcement principles. They also underpin the effectiveness of the consensual settlement principle, and through that they promote the economy, efficiency, proportionality, and artificial intelligence principles. Through the transmission of information from them to Ombudsman schemes they also further the digital integration principle.**

*Sources: ALI/UNIDROIT Principles, principle 23; ALI/UNIDROIT Reporters' Study, r 31; ELI-UNIDROIT Model Rules, Part VIII; CPR Pt 40.*

### COMMENTARY

1. Courts may issue judgments and orders. Prior to the CPR's introduction the distinction between the two was a product of the historic development of different forms of civil process. As explained in the *White Book*, 'judgment' was the term used to describe the decision that finally determined proceedings that were 'actions'.[3]

[1] A Zuckerman, *Zuckerman on Civil Procedure – Principles of Practice* (Sweet & Maxwell, 2021) at 1146.

[2] W Ury, J Brett, and S Goldberg, *Getting Disputes Resolved* (PON, 1993).

[3] *Ex parte Chinery* (1884) 12 QBD 342; *Onslow v Commissioners of Inland Revenue* (1890) 25 QBD 465; P Coulson (ed), *Civil Procedure 2024* (Sweet & Maxwell, 2024) Vol 1 at 40.1.1.

*A Model Civil Procedure Code for England and Wales*. John Sorabji, Oxford University Press. © John Sorabji 2024.
DOI: 10.1093/oso/9780192848680.003.0016

Orders, on the other hand, referred to the decision that finally determined proceedings that were 'matters'. Orders also referred to any procedural decision that did not finally determine actions or matters. Whether proceedings were actions or matters depended on the mechanism through which they were commenced. Under the CPR the distinction between actions and matters no longer exists. However, there remains under it a certain lack of clarity as to the distinction between judgments and orders. Again, as the *White Book* puts it, '*In modern parlance, judgment is most commonly used in relation to the reasons leading to an order . . . consequent upon it.*'[4]

2. This Part builds on, but goes further than, the CPR's approach. A clear, functional, distinction is drawn between judgments and orders. Judgment refers to a court decision that sets out sufficient details concerning the parties, the nature of the proceedings, and reasons for the decision.
3. The main function that judgments serve is an explanatory one. They explain to the parties and to the public the nature of the decision being made. Where parties are concerned this is of importance as it enables them to understand why the court has reached its decision. It demonstrates to them that their case and arguments were heard and considered. It thus helps to promote party confidence in the judicial process, particularly amongst losing parties. Judgments also have a disciplinary function. By requiring reasons to be given, judges must ensure that they deal properly with the arguments raised before them. It thus reduces the potential for arbitrary decision-making, while promoting a fair process and adjudicative accuracy. Where the public are concerned, the explanatory nature of judgments is an integral aspect of the publicity principle. It is educative. Reasoned judgments promote understanding of the judicial process and of the nature of the law. They are also the main means to secure democratic accountability of the judicial process.
4. Orders are functionally distinct from judgments. They are directive and specify what must be done to comply with the court's decision as explained in its judgment.[5] They are therefore the means through which rights and obligations are vindicated. Where there is non-compliance, they form the basis of enforcement proceedings, ie they prescribe what is to be enforced and thus determine which enforcement methods are available to the party seeking to enforce the court's judgment by giving effect to its order.
5. The effect of both judgments, particularly the reasons justifying the court's decision, and orders goes beyond the immediate parties to any proceedings. Through their publication they play a key role in the development of the shadow of the law. As Galanter noted, '*Courts produce not only decisions but also messages. These messages are resources which parties use in envisioning, devising, negotiating and vindicating claims (and in avoiding, defending and defeating them).*'[6] Those messages are integral to dispute formation and prevention, which could through the use of artificial intelligence, both predictive and generative, help individuals order their affairs so as to minimise the prospect that disputes would arise. They are similarly integral to

[4] P Coulson (ed) (2024) Vol 1 at 40.1.1.

[5] ELI-UNIDROIT Model Rules, r 131, comment 6.

[6] M Galanter, 'Justice in Many Rooms', in M Capelletti (ed), *Access to Justice and the Welfare State* (Sijthoff, 1981) at 158.

dispute resolution, as they form the backdrop to negotiated or mediated settlements; to consent-based settlement generally. Judgments, rather than orders then, are not only the means by which the accuracy principle is given expression in individual proceedings, but through their publication they give effect to both preventive justice and consensual settlement.

6. As judgments play a role in dispute formation, they ought also to play a role in the promotion of the systemic aspect of preventive justice further to the digital integration principle. Through extracting anonymised information from judgments and providing that to Ombudsman schemes etc, they should be able to contribute to the development and potential implementation of systemic reforms that could reduce the potential for future disputes to arise.

## RULE 2.—JUDGMENTS AND ORDERS

**(1) A court may give the following types of judgment**
  **(a) a procedural judgment, which includes a judgment in default;**
  **(b) a final judgment, which includes a summary judgment, whether on a specific matter in dispute or on the dispute as a whole.**

**(2) A procedural judgment does not finally determine substantive matters in dispute. A final judgment determines substantive matters in dispute.**

**(3) An order gives effect to a judgment. Orders may be procedural or final.**

**(4) Judgments and orders may grant or refuse such relief, including declaratory relief, as determined by the case statements. Where monetary relief is claimed, the judgment and order may be given in pounds sterling or a foreign currency.**

**(5) Judgments must be issued within a reasonable time. Wherever possible, judgment should be given no later than three months after the conclusion of a hearing.**

**(6) Judgments and orders take effect when they are given or issued, except where the court specifies that it shall come into effect on another date. Its effect may be antedated in exceptional circumstances. Judgments and orders are valid unless and until they are stayed, varied or set aside.**

**(7) Judgments and orders must be complied with by those subject to their terms within 14 days of their being given or issued unless the court directs otherwise, a different time limit is provided for in this Code, or the proceedings are subject to a stay.**

*Sources: ALI/UNIDROIT Principles, principle 23; ALI/UNIDROIT Reporters' Study, rr 31.2, 31.3; ELI-UNIDROIT Model Rules, r 130; Senior Courts Act 1981, s 19; CPR rr 40.2, 40.7, 40.11, 40.20.*

## COMMENTARY

1. The civil court's primary constitutional function is to give effect to the rule of law. Historically, it has done so through adjudicating individual disputes. This remains the case. Integrated dispute resolution's success depends upon adjudication to provide the framework within which consensual settlement, and the various processes that facilitate it operate effectively. Adjudication also provides the most important information to facilitate the promotion of preventive justice. Judgments and orders are the basis on which both these forms of justice rest.

2. Rule 2(1) identifies the various types of judgments and orders that a court may deliver. Of the former there are two distinct types: procedural judgments, which

include judgments in default of defending proceedings; and final judgments, which include summary judgments. Final judgments may be given on specific issues or on all claims disputed in proceedings.[7] Where the court directs, as part of effective dispute management, that a specific issue of fact or law is determined as a preliminary issue,[8] the court's decision at the hearing of that issue will result in a final judgment.

3. Rule 2(3) gives effect to the functional distinction between orders and judgments by specifying that it is the court's order that gives effect to its judgment: it is the operative part of the court's decision.[9] It further elaborates what is a necessary corollary of the distinction between procedural and final judgments: orders will also either be procedural or final. The former are those that do not finally determine proceedings on their substantive merits; the latter, conversely being those that do so.
4. Rule 2(4) identifies and places an important limit on the nature of judgments and orders. It makes explicit that civil courts may only grant or refuse the relief specified by the parties' case statements. Consistently with its jurisdiction as determined by Part 7, rule 6, a court cannot grant relief on matters not raised by the parties. The court may also grant relief in either pounds sterling or any foreign currency.[10]
5. Rule 2(5) is intended to give effect to that aspect of the reasoned decision principle, as well as the principle of efficiency, which requires judgments to be given in a reasonable time. Undue delay may undermine party and public confidence in the judicial process, and specifically the judgment itself. It may lead them to believe that the judge was not properly able to recall the evidence and argument given at trial, thus calling into question the judge's assessment and judgement concerning the issues. It may lead to crucial material being lost, which would also frustrate the court's ability to deliver a properly considered judgment.[11] Delay equally frustrates the requirement that judgment and enforcement is given in reasonable time. Ultimately, unreasonable delay undermines the rule of law.[12] To guide the court, and set reasonable party expectations, this rule codifies and generalises the judiciary's unofficial time limit within which judgments should be given.[13] This is not an absolute time limit. Greater time may reasonably be taken to deliver a judgment where, for instance, special circumstances arise which take the proceedings and judgment-writing out of the ordinary.[14] It is important to note that delay in itself is not sufficient to justify the court setting aside a judgment and ordering a rehearing or retrial.[15]
6. Rule 2(6) should be read consistently with rules 3 and 5. Judgments and orders take effect from the moment they are given or issued.[16] It is essential therefore that the court specifies when that occurs. Consistently with the principle of

[7] *Sangha v Amicus Finance Plc* [2020] EWHC 1074 (Ch) at [6].

[8] *McLoughlin v Grovers* [2001] EWCA Civ 1743 at [66]; *Steele v Steele* [2001] CP Rep 106.

[9] ELI-UNIDROIT Model Rules, r 131, comment 6.

[10] *Miliangos v George Frank (Textiles) Ltd* [1976] AC 443; *Barclays Bank International Ltd v Levin Brothers (Bradford) Ltd* [1977] QB 270; *Services Europe Atlantique Sud SEAS v Stockholms Rederiaktiebolog SVEA (The Folias)* [1979] AC 685; *Carnegie v Giessen* [2005] EWCA Civ 191; [2005] 1 WLR 2510. *Practice Direction (Judgment: Foreign Currency) (No 1)* [1976] 1 WLR 83.

[11] *Goose v Wilson Sandford & Co (No 1)*, The Times, 19 February 1998; *Bond v Dunster Properties Ltd* [2011] EWCA Civ 455; (2011) 108(19) LSG 21.

[12] *Goose v Wilson Sandford & Co (No 1)*, The Times, 19 February 1998 cited in *Bank St Petersburg PJSC v Arkhangelsky* [2020] EWCA Civ 408; [2020] 4 WLR 55 at [78].

[13] Part 1, r 21; *Bank St Petersburg PJSC v Arkhangelsky* [2020] EWCA Civ 408; [2020] 4 WLR 55 at [78].

[14] *Bank St Petersburg PJSC v Arkhangelsky* [2020] EWCA Civ 408; [2020] 4 WLR 55 at [84].

[15] Part 1, r 20; *Bank St Petersburg PJSC v Arkhangelsky* [2020] EWCA Civ 408; [2020] 4 WLR 55 at [78].

[16] *Shelley's Case* [1581] 1 Co Rep 93.

finality, they are valid and hence enforceable unless and until they are stayed, varied, or set aside.[17] Under rule 5(2) the court may issue its judgment after the conclusion of a hearing. It is not uncommon for a written judgment in those circumstances to be circulated to the parties before it is issued formally. Where this occurs the date of issue is that provided for under rule 2(6) not the date when it was circulated to the parties.[18] The same approach is taken to orders. The court does, however, retain discretion to vary the date on which judgments or orders take effect. Under the RSC, this discretion could both ante-date and post-date the effect of judgments and orders.[19] It was well-established that ante-dating could only be carried out in exceptional circumstances[20] and that it could not be used to confer on the court jurisdiction, ie to side-step an expired limitation period.[21] The CPR takes a more restrictive approach, only permitting the discretion to be exercised to post-date.[22] No reason was given for this change in approach. Rule 2(6) reinstates the full extent of the court's jurisdiction as provided for under the RSC. While, it may only be exercised rarely, it may be necessary to use the power to further the purposive principle. It may, for instance, be necessary exceptionally for a court to direct that its judgment take effect from the date of a previous hearing, and of a previous judgment or order, when due to a procedural error on the part of the court it failed to refer to a matter in the earlier judgment that was raised before it and which it intended to deal with at that earlier time but inadvertently failed to do so.

7. Finally, rule 2(7) restates CPR r 40.11. It sets the default time period for compliance with judgments and orders. That period may be varied by the court where a greater period of time is necessary to enable a party or non-party subject to the terms of the judgment or order to comply. It may, for instance, be necessary to provide a longer period of time for a defendant to pay any damages or costs due to the claimant.[23]

## RULE 3.—CONTENT OF JUDGMENTS AND ORDERS

**(1) All judgments shall contain**
- **(a) the means to identify the court, judge, the parties to the dispute, and any lawyer or person providing the parties with reasonable assistance;**
- **(b) the court's decision, sufficient reasons justifying that decision, including reference to relevant legal principles, matters of fact as found by the court, the parties' arguments and evidence, and the relief claimed;**
- **(c) the neutral identification code or citation for the judgment;**
- **(d) the dates on which the court heard the matter and judgment was given;**
- **(e) any other matter, including costs, relevant to the proceedings; and,**
- **(f) it may also contain the court's order.**

[17] *KW v Rochdale Metropolitan Borough Council (Rev 3)* [2015] EWCA Civ 1054; [2016] 1 WLR 198 at [22].
[18] *Prudential Assurance Co Ltd v McBains Cooper* [2000] 1 WLR 2000.
[19] RSC Ord 42, r 3(2).
[20] *Belgian Grain Produce v Cox & Co* [1919] WN 317.
[21] *Re Keystone Knitting Mills' Trade Mark* [1929] 1 Ch 92 at 98–99.
[22] CPR r 40.7; *Rowan Companies Inc v Lambert Eggink Offshore Transport Consultants vof (The Gilbert Rowe) (No 2)* [1999] 2 Lloyd's Rep 443.
[23] *Gipping Construction Ltd v Eaves* [2008] EWHC 3134 (TCC) at [11].

**(2) All orders shall contain**
- **(a) the means to identify the court, judge, and the parties to the dispute;**
- **(b) the neutral identification code or citation for the judgment to which the order gives effect;**
- **(c) the order made by the court, including whether a claim, defence, application, or response to an application was dismissed as being totally without merit;**
- **(d) the date of the order and the date by which anyone subject to its terms must comply with them;**
- **(e) the date, if any, by which an application for permission to appeal from the order should be made; and**
- **(f) any other matter, including costs, relevant to the proceedings.**

**(3) The court may anonymise a judgment or order where that is justified by an exception to the publicity principle. Anonymisation may apply to any person, other than members of the judiciary, referred to in the judgment or order. A copy of the de-anonymised judgment or order must be kept by the court.**

**(4) All judgments and orders shall be sealed by the court.**

*Sources: ELI-UNIDROIT Model Rules, r 131; CPR rr 40.2, 40.8, 40.11, 40.12.*

## COMMENTARY

1. Court judgments and orders must satisfy a minimum number of formal requirements. These are set out in rule 5(1) and (2).[24]
2. Clear identification of the judge giving the judgment or order is a fundamental requirement. It is essential that the parties and the public know who has exercised the judicial power of the State, which is both mandatory and coercive. Such knowledge is a means by which courts and judges are made democratically accountable. Were these matters to be kept secret it would undermine the integrity of the judicial process and public confidence in the courts and the rule of law. As the ELI-UNIDROIT Model Rules note, rightly, a '*justice system in which the judge remains an anonymous figure may lead to a lack of moral responsibility or the abuse of power by the judiciary.*'[25] To ensure that this does not arise the court and judge who gave the judgment or order must be identified. Their details must always be known, even if this leads to unfair, unjust, or ill-founded party, public or media criticism, or abuse of the judiciary.[26]
3. Parties, their lawyers, and anyone providing them with reasonable assistance must also be identified for several reasons. Parties require identification so that the public may know who is calling upon the State's power to vindicate their rights, and who is subject to the effect of the judgment or order. It is thus required by reference to the publicity and finality principles, and is a means to identify the scope of any preclusionary effect of the judgment. Information about lawyers and those providing reasonable assistance to parties is necessary to enable the court administration to communicate with them effectively, eg where they are responsible for uploading documents to the digital dispute management system, where they are responsible for drawing-up court orders, or where there are questions about their conduct or alleged

[24] *Practice Direction (Judgments: Form and Content)* [2001] 1 WLR 194; *Practice Direction (Judgments: Neutral Citations)* [2002] 1 WLR 346.

[25] ELI-UNIDROIT Model Rules, r 131, comment 2.

[26] *Attorney-General v Ebert* [2001] EWHC 695 (Admin) at [28].

misconduct during proceedings.[27] Such information is thus required for effective dispute management as well as to promote the proper administration of justice.

4. Rule 3(1)(b) gives specific effect to the reasoned decision and publicity principles. To do so it prescribes that judgments must, at a minimum, contain sufficient reasons enabling the parties and the public to understand the legal principles and the findings of fact that the judge has, respectively, applied and made. They should also contain sufficient detail concerning the parties' arguments and the evidence adduced before the court, including the judge's assessment of them. Finally, the judgment should identify the relief sought and either granted or denied. Consistently, with the reasoned decision principle, the judgment should be proportionate to the nature of the matter that it determines. It would be a waste of court time and resources to provide a lengthy judgment on a short, factual dispute or a short, interim application. Reasons given must thus be commensurate to the matter before the court so that they enable the parties and the public to understand what has been determined and how the judge reached their decision.[28]

5. Judgments and orders must also contain any other relevant matter, including costs under rule 3(1)(e). This is a wide-ranging, situation-specific requirement. It may, for instance, require the court to record if an individual providing reasonable assistance to a party was barred from doing so at the commencement of or during a hearing. It could require the court to set out if an application or proceedings was dismissed as totally without merit. More broadly, where a non-party is likely to be or is to be subject to or affected by the decision, this should be recorded as a relevant matter. Questions concerning interest on damages and when interest on damages runs should also be set out under this requirement. A judgment may, but need not, also contain the court's order. Where it does so it will generally be set out at the end of the judgment and should be clearly identified as such.

6. Court orders must set out similar matters. One particularly important element they must contain is information about any applicable appeal process, including the date by which an application for permission to appeal should be made. A fair process requires this not only because it gives effect to the general access principle, but also because it helps promote, in appropriate cases, accurate decision-making by promoting access to appeals. Providing the date by which such an application must be made also promotes effective dispute management and proportionality by prompting parties to make any application before the expiry of the applicable time limit.

7. Judgments and orders may, subject to the point made above concerning the identification of judges, be anonymised where that is permissible as a derogation from the publicity principle. Parties, witnesses, experts, and non-parties may therefore be anonymised. Notwithstanding anonymisation, or any other derogation from the publicity principle, a copy of the full, unredacted, judgment and order must be kept by the court as part of the court record. Thus, an authoritative record should be maintained, not least so that it can be referred to where any issues of, for instance, enforcement, appeal, or preclusion arise. That a judgment or order is subject to anonymisation or other redactions does not mean that it is so indefinitely. The court either on its own initiative or on application may set aside any such derogations. Before doing so, to protect the interests protected by the derogation, it must give

[27] *Gubarev v Orbis Business Intelligence Ltd* [2020] EWHC 2167 (QB).

[28] Part 1, r 21.

any affected party or non-party notice of its intention to do so and hear them on the issue.

8. Rule 3(4) requires judgments and orders to be sealed. This is an explicit application to judgments and orders of the general rule concerning sealing documents. It provides proof of their authenticity. It also marks the point where the judgment or order is perfected.

## RULE 4.—CIRCULATION OF DRAFT JUDGMENTS

**(1) To promote the proper administration of justice, the court may provide, in confidence, a copy of a draft written judgment to the parties, any non-party reasonably likely to be affected by the judgment, and their lawyers before it is issued. Any further circulation without the court's prior and express permission is contrary to the proper administration of justice and may result in sanctions being imposed under Pt 11.**

**(2) Draft judgments are provided for the following purposes only**

**(a) to facilitate the identification of typographical or factual errors in the judgment and their correction by the court;**

**(b) to enable parties to consider and make applications and/or submissions to the court;**

**(c) to enable parties to consider and prepare any draft orders.**

**(3) Draft judgments are not provided to enable parties to reargue any matter or raise new matters to be determined. Nor are they provided as a means to facilitate settlement.**

*Sources: CPR r 40.2, PD 40E.*

## COMMENTARY

1. Where the court intends to give a written judgment, it may provide a copy of its judgment in draft to the parties, relevant non-parties, and their lawyers. This is intended to promote the efficient administration of justice and effective dispute management.[29]

2. Advance notice enables parties' lawyers to check the draft judgment for any accidental typographical or factual errors, which could then be corrected before the judgment is issued.[30] This reduces the prospect that they would have to be corrected under rule 3(5) after the judgment is issued. It also enables parties to consider what, if any applications or submissions, they may want to make when the judgment is issued. They may wish to seek permission to appeal or make submissions concerning costs or, if the judgment is a procedural one, on the future management of the dispute.[31] Advance notice thus enables proper planning of those applications. In doing so it promotes procedural efficiency, and through that effective dispute management. Where a draft judgment is to be subject to anonymisation or where parts of it are to be made private, circulation in draft also enables parties to check or suggest proposed

[29] *Prudential Assurance Co Ltd v McBains Cooper* [2000] 1 WLR 2000 at 2008.

[30] *Robinson v Fernsby* [2003] EWCA Civ 1820; [2004] WTLR 257 at [95].

[31] *Egan v Motor Services (Bath) Ltd* [2007] EWCA Civ 1002; [2008] 1 WLR 1589 at [50].

derogations from the publicity principle.[32] Advance notice further enables parties to draft, and seek to agree where appropriate, draft orders. Again, this is more efficient, and hence cost-effective, both for the parties and the court than the situation where the terms of any orders are considered and are potentially subject to argument at the time the judgment is issued.

3. Advance notice also plays an important role where non-parties are concerned. Where they are to be subject to criticism or adverse comment in the judgment, it gives them the opportunity to obtain legal advice and where appropriate make submissions or applications to the court before the judgment is perfected.[33] This is particularly important as a means to ensure that non-parties are provided with an opportunity to be heard on matters that may affect their rights.
4. Advance notice may, however, be subject to potential misuse. This can occur in either of two ways. By providing the parties with the draft judgment, they and their lawyers may seek to reargue points dealt with in it. They may also seek to raise new arguments. While the court retains jurisdiction to alter its decision, and hence its judgment and any order, before it is perfected, were parties able to use the provision of draft judgments in this way, it would make significant in-roads into the principle of finality. Parties could come to routinely view circulation of a draft judgment as an opportunity to further argue their case, to which their opponent would then have to be afforded an opportunity to respond, ie it would require additional hearings contrary to effective dispute management. Potentially this could lead parties to holding back arguments for deployment post-circulation of the draft judgment. The courts have clearly and strongly deprecated this type of approach and it is prohibited here under rule 4(3), except where the court could properly reconsider a judgment or order prior to their being perfected (rule 7).[34]
5. Misuse may also occur if parties or their lawyers circulate or use the draft judgment for purposes not specified in rule 4(2). Circulation is purely to promote the administration of justice and must only be to those lawyers who are engaged in the immediate proceedings.[35] Where parties are legal persons this means circulation should be restricted to, for instance, directors or employees who have a genuine need to see it.[36] They are confidential to them.[37] Nor are they circulated to enable lawyers to prepare their own media releases concerning, for instance, their involvement in proceedings. Most obviously, draft judgments must not be made public.
6. Rule 4(1) is intended to ensure that the risk of misuse is minimised. It makes clear that any misuse may result in the application of sanctions, which would include proceedings for contempt of court.

[32] *R (Mohamed) v Secretary of State for Foreign and Commonwealth Affairs* [2010] EWCA Civ 158; [2011] QB 218 at [259].

[33] *ISTIL Group Inc v Zahoor* [2003] EWHC 165 (Ch); [2003] 2 All ER 252.

[34] *Royal Brompton Hospital NHS Trust v Hammond (No 8)* [2001] EWCA Civ 778; [2001] CP Rep 90 at [11]; *R (Edwards) v Environment Agency* [2008] UKHL 22; [2008] 1 WLR 1587 at [66].

[35] *Crown Prosecution Service v P* [2007] EWHC 1144 (Admin); [2008] 1 WLR 1024; *R (Counsel General for Wales) v Secretary of State for Business, Energy and Industrial Strategy* [2022] EWCA Civ 181; [2022] 1 WLR 1915; *Public Institution for Social Security v Banque Pictet & Cie SA* [2022] EWCA Civ 368 at [18]; *HM Attorney General v Crosland* [2021] UKSC 58 at [63] and [77].

[36] *R (Counsel General for Wales) v Secretary of State for Business, Energy and Industrial Strategy* [2022] EWCA Civ 181; [2022] 1 WLR 1915 at [23].

[37] *Baigent v Random House Group Ltd* [2006] EWHC 1131 (Ch); *Crown Prosecution Service v P* [2007] EWHC 1144 (Admin); [2008] 1 WLR 1024.

7. It is also important to note that while draft judgments may prompt settlement, and an application to the court to refrain from issuing its judgment, circulation of draft judgments is not carried out as means to facilitate settlement. Rule 4(3) codifies the case law on this purposive limitation.[38] Were parties to view draft judgments as a means to facilitate settlement, they would start to take on the quality of an assessment of the merits such as those provided by an ENE process. This would not only undermine effective dispute management, but it would also conflate the trial process with that of a settlement process. It would tend to call the proper administration of justice into question.

## RULE 5.—ISSUING AND SERVING JUDGMENTS AND ORDERS

**(1) Subject to rule 5(6), a judgment must be given formally in open court. It may be given orally or in writing. An oral judgment may only be given at the conclusion of a hearing. A written judgment may be given after the conclusion of a hearing, where that is appropriate. In considering whether it is appropriate to do so the court should consider all the circumstances, including**
**(a) the nature and complexity of the hearing;**
**(b) the nature of the written and oral evidence; and**
**(c) the need to consider the overall probabilities of the arguments advanced by the parties in a reflective, structured manner.**
**(2) Where judgment is not given at the conclusion of a hearing, the court will issue a written judgment either at a later hearing or by making it available publicly. Public availability may be effected digitally.**
**(3) Where judgment is given at a hearing at which not all parties are present, the court must serve the judgment on the parties not present.**
**(4) Orders may be formally issued in open court. They must be served on the parties to proceedings.**
**(5) Judgments and orders should be served on any non-party affected by them.**
**(6) Judgments and orders may be formally given or issued at a private hearing where that is justified by reference to an exception to the publicity principle.**
**(7) Service shall be affected under Part 10.**

*Sources: ALI/UNIDROIT Reporters' Study, r 31.3; ELI-UNIDROIT Model Rules, r 134; CPR r 40.2(2)(a), 40.4, 40.5, 40.7.*

## COMMENTARY

1. Subject to one exception, judgments must be given formally in open court.[39] This may be carried out in either of two ways. They may be given formally at the conclusion of a hearing orally (an ex tempore judgment). They may also be given formally at a later date in written form (a reserved judgment). This gives effect to both the due notice and participation principles. A sufficiently reasoned judgment demonstrates that the court has heard the parties and that their participation, in principle, was effective.[40] Unless the court delivers its judgment and order to them, it is not evident

[38] *R (S) v General Teaching Council for England* [2013] EWHC 2779 (Admin) at [26]–[27].
[39] *Owusu v Jackson* [2002] EWCA Civ 877.
[40] ELI-UNIDROIT Model Rules, r 134, comment 1.

that this has taken place. Judgments and orders are also a necessary prerequisite for the parties to consider whether they have valid grounds for appeal. Their delivery is therefore also necessary to give effect to the appellate principle. The giving of a judgment in open court also satisfies the publicity principle.

2. Oral judgments are most likely to be given in straightforward matters. Procedural and dispute management applications and judgments in low and moderate value proceedings will generally result in oral judgments being given. The court may depart from this general rule where justice is better served by the judge taking a period of time to reflect before issuing their judgment. Rule 5(1)(a) to (c) codifies the guidance set out in *Gow v Harker* (2003)[41] on the considerations the court should take into account when considering whether to issue a written judgment after the conclusion of a hearing. The three criteria draw attention to the need for the court to consider if it is possible to give an oral judgment that takes proper account of the issues raised and evidence adduced in the hearing. The more important the issues, higher the value of any claim for relief, greater the complexity of the issues and evidence, and the more difficult any assessment whether a claimant or applicant has made out their case to the requisite standard the greater the rationale for reserving the judgment to a later date. Time provides the means for the court to consider those matters in a structured, reflective way.[42]
3. Written judgments may be given in different ways. They may be given at a hearing. They may be given by being made available to the parties digitally via the digital dispute management system or, where one or more parties are not present in court when it is given at a hearing, by ensuring it is served on them via Part 10. Where judgments are made available to the parties other than at a hearing, public notice may be effected by publication on The National Archives judgment database. Judgments given in this way must include sufficient information specifying the date and time when they were given.[43] This is essential for the purposes of rule 2(5).
4. An oral judgment does not need to be served or otherwise provided to the parties. They receive notice of it and its contents when it is delivered orally in court. The public, in principle, receives notice similarly as it is delivered in open court. Actual public access to an oral judgment may in practice, however, only be effected through later publication of a written version of the judgment or through a request to the court for access to a written transcript or digital recording of the judgment.
5. Orders, as the operative part of the court's decision, must be served on all parties to proceedings. They (and judgments) must also be served on non-parties affected by the court's decision. Service here is again a basic principle of a fair procedure as it ensures that the non-party is aware of the judgment or order and may then take such steps as they conclude are necessary to comply with or challenge it. Service may not, however, be required to give effect to an order in all circumstances, ie notice of interim injunctions is sufficient for them to bind non-parties.[44] As a general rule, judgments and orders will be served digitally under Part 10.

[41] *Gow v Harker* [2003] EWCA Civ 1160.

[42] *Gow v Harker* [2003] EWCA Civ 1160 at [52]–[55].

[43] The approach adopted under the Covid-19 Protocol for this purpose was: '*Covid-19 Protocol: This judgment was handed down remotely by circulation to the parties' representatives by email, release to BAILII and publication on the Courts and Tribunals Judiciary website. The date and time for hand down is deemed to be [insert time] on [insert date].*'

[44] *Attorney-General v Newspaper Publishing Plc* [1988] Ch 333; *Attorney-General v The Times Newspaper Ltd* [1992] 1 AC 191.

6. Rule 5(6) confirms that judgments and orders may be given in private where a derogation from the publicity principle applies.

## RULE 6.—PUBLICATION OF JUDGMENTS AND ORDERS

**(1) All judgments and orders of the civil courts shall be made available publicly when issued, except and to the extent that they are subject to an exception to the publicity principle. Judgments or orders that commit a person to prison must, however, be made available publicly.**

**(2) All written judgments of the Upper Tier of the High Court and Court of Appeal (Civil Division) that finally determine proceedings shall be made available through publication by The National Archives in machine readable form. They may be made available by publication on the digital portal. Other judgments shall be made available**

**(a) to any person on request to the court;**

**(b) to The National Archives for publication where they are of legal significance;**

**(c) for research purposes that seek to promote the effective administration of justice or law reform.**

**(3) Judgments of legal significance**

**(a) create a new precedent;**

**(b) clarify the law or its application;**

**(c) depart from or do not follow previous authority;**

**(d) decline to extend the law.**

**(4) To facilitate public access to judgments, the High Court and Court of Appeal (Civil Division) shall make available, via the digital portal, a publicly searchable register of all judgments and orders. The Register shall include**

**(a) a digital link to a publicly accessible version of any judgment available via The National Archives;**

**(b) the means to request a copy of the judgment where it is not available via The National Archives.**

*Sources: Public Records Act 1958, s 5; County Courts Act 1984, s 73 (pre-2006); CPR r 81.8, CPR PD5A, para 4.2; Practice Direction (Committal for Contempt: Open Court) [2018] 1 WLR 2195; Practice Guidance: Committal for Contempt of Court—Open Court) (24 June 2015).*

## COMMENTARY

1. Public access to judgments and orders is necessary for the court to give effect to the publicity principle. This rule articulates how that is to be done. Rule 6(1) sets out the general rule: judgments and orders are to be issued publicly, subject to any applicable exception to the publicity principle. The power to derogate from the publicity principle is, however, subject to one fundamental limitation. It may not be used to commit any person to prison without that fact being made known publicly.[45] That limitation gives effect to the wider public interest in securing the liberty of the person, the proper administration of justice, and the rule of law. Public knowledge

[45] *Practice Direction (Committal for Contempt: Open Court)* [2015] 1 WLR 2195 at [13]–[15]; *Practice Guidance: Committal for Contempt of Court—Open Court)* (24 June 2015) at [2]; *Practice Guidance: Publication of Privacy and Anonymity Orders* (16 April 2019).

of imprisonment is a fundamental prerequisite for challenges to imprisonment to be brought, for habeas corpus applications to be made, and for public scrutiny to be brought to bear on the use of the civil courts and their processes to imprison individuals. Liberal democracies do not imprison people in secret.

2. Rules 6(2) to (4) set out how judgments and orders are to be made publicly available. The general approach is to ensure that all final decisions of the High Court's Upper Tier and Court of Appeal (Civil Division) are published via The National Archives in machine readable form. That the judgments should be in machine readable form is to facilitate publication and judgment analysis by, eg the judiciary, lawyers, the media, academic research bodies, legal publishers, and LawTech companies. This is particularly to facilitate the application of AI to the information contained in them for the purposes of dispute prevention and consensual settlement.
3. Rule 6(2) does not provide that all judgments and orders be published on The National Archives.[46] Its focus is on publication of all judgments that are likely to have precedential value, ie that either are binding on lower courts or ought generally to be followed according to the doctrine of precedent. Procedural judgments and orders will not ordinarily therefore be published; they do not normally have precedential value. They should nevertheless be made publicly available consistently with the publicity and accountability principles. To facilitate the former, they should be made available on request to any person (rule 6(4)(b)). Requests are to be facilitated through the provision of a searchable database of all judgments and orders provided via the digital portal. It is also to be facilitated through the provision to and publication by The National Archive of such judgments where they are of legal significance (rule 6(2)(b)). Rule 6(3) defines legal significance. It is derived from Practice Direction (Citation of Authorities) (2001).[47]
4. Rule 6(2)(c) provides a further basis on which judgments and orders may be made available. It does so to give effect to the digital procedure and accountability principle. It is intended to enable research to be carried out independently of any carried out by the Civil Dispute Resolution Council, judiciary, or government. It is, particularly, intended to facilitate academic scrutiny of the operation and accessibility of the civil justice system as well as of judicial decision-making. It is thus intended to facilitate, for instance, academic scrutiny of how accessible the system is for the public generally, whether it is more or less accessible for specific sectors of, or groups in, society, and whether it operates proportionately and fairly.[48] Access in this way should thus promote the effective administration of justice. It may also be used for independent research on the question whether judgments are bringing to light systemic legal problems that might be cured by regulatory or remedial reform. In this it complements the provision of such information by the court to Ombudsman, regulators etc, and thus further assists the promotion of preventive justice. Where access is sought for reasons that cannot properly be said to promote these aims, it must be refused.

[46] The National Archives has, since April 2022, provided such a database: <https://caselaw.nationalarchives.gov.uk>.

[47] *Practice Direction (Citation of Authorities)* [2001] 1 WLR 1001 at [6.1]–[6.2].

[48] N Byrom, *Digital Justice: HMCTS data strategy and delivering access to justice—Report and recommendations* (Legal Education Foundation, 2019).

## RULE 7.—PERFECTION, RECALL, RECONSIDERATION, AND ALTERATION OF A JUDGMENT OR ORDER

**(1) The court, on its own initiative or on application, may recall, reconsider and, where necessary, alter a judgment or order at any time until it is perfected. Judgments and orders are perfected when they are sealed by the court.**

**(2) The court may only recall, reconsider, and alter its judgment when that will further the purposive principle. In determining this the court must consider the weight to be given to the finality principle in the context of the particular judgment or order.**

**(3) The court may direct that a judgment or order not be sealed for a specified period of time to provide a party with the opportunity to take such steps, as may be justified in the circumstances, which would provide the court with good reason to alter its judgment or order.**

**(4) An administrative or clerical error or defect in a judgment or order whether caused by the court or a party may be corrected at any time after it is perfected by the court of its own initiative or on the request or application of a party. A correction to a judgment or order takes effect from the date of the judgment or order unless otherwise directed by the court.**

**(5) Except as provided in rule 7(4), the court may not correct any error or defect in a perfected judgment or order, other than where it may properly vary, set aside, or allow an appeal from the judgment or order.**

*Sources: CPR r 40.12, CPR PD 40B para 4.2.*

## COMMENTARY

1. It might be thought that once a judgment or order is given or issued, that is the end of the matter and that the court no longer had any jurisdiction to revisit it. This line of thought, as Zuckerman suggests, might be supported by the fact that judgments and orders take effect immediately upon being given or issued.[49] They can, however, be revisited, reconsidered, and altered at any time prior to being perfected, ie sealed by the court.[50] This means that finality in litigation takes effect as soon as a judgment or order is issued, albeit it only becomes absolute when it is perfected.[51]
2. The fact that the court retains jurisdiction until a judgment or order is perfected illustrates a careful balance struck between the finality principle and the accuracy principle, which is intended to promote a fair and proportionate process. By providing a short period of time for parties to raise concerns or issues with the court that cast doubt on its judgment or order, English and Welsh procedure enables the court to correct any error without the need for either a formal application to vary its order or judgment or an appeal.[52] Proportionality's promotion here stems from the potential avoidance of those, more formal, time-consuming, and expensive remedial processes.

[49] A Zuckerman (2021) at 1156.

[50] *R v Cripps, ex p Muldoon* [1984] QB 686 at 695; *Carleton (Earl of Malmesbury) v Strutt & Parker* [2007] EWHC 2199 (QB). Also see *Galliani v Sartori* [2023] EWHC 3306 (Comm) at [33]–[34] noting that 'entry of judgment' is another way of referring to perfecting a judgment.

[51] *AIC Ltd v Federal Airports Authority of Nigeria* [2022] UKSC 16; [2022] 1 WLR 3223 at [35].

[52] See rr 12 and 13.

3. Rule 7(1) restates the power to recall, reconsider and revise judgments and orders prior to their being perfected. Along with rule 8 it provides the means through which the court can ensure that its judgments and orders accurately reflect its intentions. This power may be used to correct errors in the judgment.[53] It may also be used to alter judgments substantially, even to the extent that the court reverses its original decision. This power, known under the CPR as the *Barrell* jurisdiction, arises at common law.[54] It is codified here. Its exercise was authoritatively restated in *AIC Ltd v Federal Airports Authority of Nigeria* (2022).[55] It affirmed, as here, that the appropriate question for the court to ask is whether recall etc furthered the purposive principle; exceptional circumstances are not required to justify exercise of the power.
4. *AIC Ltd v Federal Airports Authority of Nigeria* (2022) further stressed that the finality principle was inherent in the purposive principle. Were the court to too readily accede to applications under the jurisdiction, the finality principle would be undermined and, consequently, so would other aspects of the purposive principle, including the proportionality and compliance principles.[56] The discretion is thus not to be used to such an extent that it would, where trials are concerned, turn them into dress rehearsals.[57] To ensure that the court gives appropriate weight to the finality principle it must take as its starting point the need to give it effect. Specific weight to be given to it is, however, context-dependent. Where procedural judgments or orders are concerned it may be afforded less weight. Where final judgments or orders, particularly those issued following a trial, are concerned it may be afforded greater weight.[58] Rule 7(2) codifies this approach.
5. Rule 7(2) also enables the court to make more routine changes to a judgment. Where, for instance, a judgment is given orally, a judge may wish to correct any typographical mistakes or make other amendments to make their intention clear before the transcript of the judgment is perfected.[59]
6. Rule 7(3) provides the court with a degree of flexibility in circumstances where it considers that there is a reasonable possibility that matters may come to light that may justify reconsideration of its judgment or order. It therefore codifies the practice of courts directing that orders should not be sealed for a specified period of time.[60] It makes explicit that it may also make such a direction where judgments are concerned.
7. Judges and court administrators are not infallible. They make mistakes. Where documents are concerned typographical mistakes, with the best will in the world and focused proof-reading, are commonplace. Judgments and orders as official documents ought not to contain such mistakes. Rule 7(4) codifies the court's inherent

[53] *Space Airconditioning Plc v Guy* [2012] EWCA Civ 1664; [2013] 1 WLR 1293: judgments should accurately record the decision reached and should be corrected to do so unless there is good reason to the contrary.

[54] *Holtby v Hodgson* (1890) LR 24 QBD 103; *Re Barrell Enterprises* [1973] 1 WLR 19; *Re L-B (Children) (Preliminary Finding: Power to Reverse)* [2013] UKSC 8; [2013] 1 WLR 634.

[55] *AIC Ltd v Federal Airports Authority of Nigeria* [2022] UKSC 16; [2022] 1 WLR 3223.

[56] *AIC Ltd v Federal Airports Authority of Nigeria* [2022] UKSC 16; [2022] 1 WLR 3223 at [30]–[31], [36]–[40].

[57] *FAGE UK Ltd v Chobani UK Ltd* [2014] EWCA Civ 5; [2014] FSR 29 at [114], 'The trial is not a dress rehearsal. It is the first and last night of the show.'

[58] *AIC Ltd v Federal Airports Authority of Nigeria* [2022] UKSC 16; [2022] 1 WLR 3223 at [32]–[34].

[59] *Bath v Escott* [2017] EWHC 1101 (Ch).

[60] *Anglo-Eastern Trust Ltd v Kermanshahchi* [2002] EWCA Civ 198 at [71].

jurisdiction to correct such typographical, grammatical, spelling, and similar accidental mistakes and omissions after judgments or orders have been perfected.[61] It may not, however, be relied upon to correct substantive errors, such as where the court makes an error of law,[62] nor does it provide a judge an opportunity to have second thoughts about their decision.[63] Typical examples of its proper use are where a party's name has been misspelt, a party has been misidentified as a claimant when they were a defendant or vice versa, or documents or dates have been accidentally misstated. It may also be relied upon to correct an omission or error that arose due to a mistake by the party or their lawyers in drawing up the order.[64] It may not however be relied upon where the order was drawn up by a party and the alleged mistake or error arose because it was deliberately incorporated into the order by the party or resulted from such an omission on their part.[65]

8. Where a party seeks to rely upon rule 7(4) they need not make a formal application. They may simply make an informal request that the error be corrected. A formal application and hearing may, however, be required where the request is contested or where the court is concerned that it does not involve the correction of a genuinely accidental error or omission. Finally, rule 7(5) makes explicit that where the finality principle applies absolutely, a judgment or order is only capable of being varied where the court has made explicit provision in an order for the parties to apply to vary it, where an application to vary the order is made under rule 12 or 13 or an appeal is pursued.[66]

## RULE 8.—CLARIFICATION OF JUDGMENTS AND ORDERS

**(1) A party, or non-party affected by a judgment or order, may apply to the court**

**(a) to amplify or clarify the reasons justifying its decision where that is necessary to enable the unsuccessful party to understand why they did not succeed in their claim or defence; or**

**(b) clarify the meaning or intention of an order.**

**(2) Where a judgment or order is circulated to a party or non-party in draft, any application to amplify or clarify should be made by request before the judgment or order is issued. An application must otherwise be made promptly after the judgment or order is issued.**

**(3) An appeal court considering whether to grant permission to appeal under Part 17 on the ground that a judgment was insufficiently reasoned may request amplification or clarification of the judgment. The judge who gave the judgment in question should, where possible, comply with the request.**

*Sources: CPR PD 40B para 4.5.*

[61] *Ainsworth v Wilding* [1896] 1 Ch 673; The discretion exists to enable the court to correct 'slips' of the pen; *Adam & Harvey Ltd v International Maritime Supplies Co Ltd* [1967] 1 WLR 445.

[62] *Bright v Sellar* [1904] 1 KB 6; *Markos v Goodfellow* [2002] EWCA Civ 1542; (2002) 146 SJLB 231 at [13]–[17].

[63] *R v Cripps, ex p Muldoon* [1984] QB 686; *Bristol-Myers Squibb v Baker Norton Pharmaceuticals Inc* [2001] EWCA Civ 414; [2001] RPC 414 at [25].

[64] RSC Ord 28, r 11.

[65] *Leo Pharma A/S v Sandoz Ltd* [2010] EWHC 1911 (Pat); [2010] FSR 41 at [17]–[28].

[66] *AIC Ltd v Federal Airports Authority of Nigeria* [2022] UKSC 16; [2022] 1 WLR 3223 at [35].

## COMMENTARY

1. Judgments must set out the court's reasons for reaching its decision. Judges are, however, free to draft their judgments as they wish. This flows from the principle of judicial independence. It is required by individual independence as judges must be free to make their own decisions based on their assessment of the facts and law. It is also an aspect of institutional independence. Judges cannot be directed as to the substantive content of their judgments by other judges, members of the government or Parliament. Their reasons are an expression of their independence.
2. Reasons must, however, enable the parties and the public to understand the judge's reasoning process. This is required by the reasoned judgment and publicity principles.[67] A balance must, consequently, be struck between judicial independence and these principles. That is achieved initially by requiring judges to give sufficient reasons for their decisions, ie sufficient to be understood. Where they fail to meet that standard a party or non-party affected by the judgment may apply to the court to clarify or expand its reasoning. Where possible they should do so by request before the judgment is finalised. A request at that time should enable the court to resolve the issue more speedily and cost-effectively than if a formal application were made after the judgment had been finalised.
3. Where a judgment has been perfected a party dissatisfied with the reasons may appeal from the decision.[68] Insufficient reasons may suggest that the judge concerned did not consider all the evidence or arguments set out by the parties, or did not consider key issues in the proceedings. They may suggest that the judge did not pay sufficient attention to such matters.[69] In extreme situations reasons may be so insufficient that the judgment fails to provide confidence to the parties and the public that justice has been done, not least because it cannot be seen to have been done. In such circumstances, rather than moving to give permission to appeal, the appeal court could itself request amplification or clarification. Such a step may avoid the need for an appeal, as well as the time and expense it would generate.
4. Where they can properly do so, a judge should comply with a request for clarification or amplification. It may not however be appropriate for a party of the appeal court to make such a request. It may, for instance, be some considerable time after the judge gave their judgment, such that any clarification might then be the product of after-the-fact rationalisation or reconstruction.[70] The delay itself in giving the judgment initially may be of such a duration that a request would, given the further delay it would cause, be inappropriate.[71] It may also be evident due to the paucity of reasons given that no amplification or clarification is reasonably possible. In such circumstances the appeal court should go straight on to consider the application for permission to appeal without making a request.

[67] *English v Emery Reimbold & Strick Ltd* [2002] 1 WLR 2409; *Ruiz Torija v Spain* (1994) 19 EHRR 553 at [29]; *Van de Hurk v The Netherlands* (1994) 18 EHRR 481 at [59].

[68] *Flannery v Halifax Estate Agencies Ltd (trading as Colleys Professional Services)* [2000] 1 WLR 377.

[69] *English v Emery Reimbold & Strick Ltd* [2002] 1 WLR 2409 at [26].

[70] *Adami v The Ethical Standards Officer of the Standards Board for England* [2005] EWCA Civ 1754; [2006] BLGR 397 at [24]; *Aerospace Publishing Limited v Thames Water Utilities Ltd* [2006] EWCA Civ 717.

[71] *Michael Hyde & Associates Ltd v J D Williams & Co Ltd* [2001] PNLR 8 at 20; *English v Emery Reimbold & Strick Ltd* [2002] 1 WLR 2409 at [26].

5. Orders may also be clarified where that is necessary to ensure their meaning and the court's intention is fully understandable. This jurisdiction is inherent in the court's power to administer justice effectively.

## SECTION 2: DEFAULT JUDGMENT

### RULE 9.—JUDGMENT IN DEFAULT

**(1) A judgment in default is a procedural judgment that determines a claim administratively. It does not determine the dispute on its substantive merits.**
**(2) Judgment in default may only be granted for such relief as the claimant is entitled to as defined by their particulars of claim.**
**(3) Except where a rule of law prohibits the grant of one, the court, on the application of a claimant, may issue a judgment in default where**
**(a) the time limit to respond to the particulars of claim has expired;**
**(b) the defendant has failed to respond to the particulars of claim;**
**(c) the defendant has not applied to strike out or sought summary judgment on the claim; and**
**(d) the defendant has not satisfied the claim, including any applicable costs.**
**Where judgment in default is granted, the order shall indicate that each of these conditions is satisfied. No separate judgment will be issued.**
**(4) Except where the court directs otherwise,**
**(a) an application for judgment in default may be made on a without-notice basis;**
**(b) evidence in support of the application need not be served on the defendant.**
**(5) Where proceedings are brought against multiple defendants, judgment in default may be obtained against one or more defendants. Where judgment in default is obtained against some but not all defendants, the proceedings shall continue against those defendants against whom judgment in default was not obtained.**
**(6) Where a claim seeks relief other than by way of a specified sum of money, including interest or tariff costs, judgment in default shall be granted on liability only. On granting judgment in default on liability, the court shall give directions for determining the outstanding issues on the claim.**
**(7) Judgment in default shall be granted by a court officer, except where proceedings are brought against the Crown, a minor or a protected party, in which case the application must be determined by a judge. Evidence in support of such an application must be provided to the court with the application for judgment in default.**
**(8) A defendant may not appeal from a judgment in default.**

*Sources: ALI/UNIDROIT Principles, principle 15; ALI/UNIDROIT Reporters' Study, r 15; ELI-UNIDROIT Model Rules, rr 135, 136, 137, 138; CPR Pt 12.*

### COMMENTARY

1. Defendants are under no duty to take part in proceedings. It is perfectly permissible for a defendant when served with particulars of claim to take no steps to respond to them. Equally, a defendant could seek to frustrate the civil process by actively refusing to respond. In either case, if the claimant could take no further steps in the proceedings and the court had no power to make any judgment or order in the face of such conduct, it would render the exercise of the judicial power of the State subject to defendant consent.

2. The ability to obtain judgment in default of a defence is the means by which the court can ensure that its power is exercisable effectively and without defendant consent. It is also the means by which a claimant can secure an efficient and economical resolution of their dispute. Moreover, it is, importantly, the means by which a defendant who does not want to go to the time and expense of submitting an admission may waive their right to contest the claim through being non-responsive.[72]
3. Where a defendant waives their right to defend proceedings brought against them through failing to respond to particulars of claim, a claimant is entitled to seek judgment in default of such a defence. This is not an adjudicative judgment as no assessment of the claim's substantive merits takes place. Nor could one properly be given as an adversarial process involving the submission and scrutiny of contested issues and evidence is not possible. Judgment in default is thus a procedural rather than a final judgment. It is also an administrative judgment that can, generally, be effected by a member of the court administration. The exception to this is that a judge is required to determine whether to grant judgment in default where the defendant is either the Crown or a minor or protected party.[73] In the former case, judicial scrutiny is required to ascertain whether service on the Crown was properly effected further to the Crown Proceedings Act 1947. It is required in the latter cases, so the court can ascertain if the minor or protected party requires and, if so, has a litigation friend and, hence, be satisfied that they have chosen not to respond. If none had been appointed the court may need to consider the appointment of one prior to dealing with the application.[74]
4. If a claimant intends to seek judgment in default they must make an application to the court. Under the CPR two different approaches can be taken. Where judgment in default is sought for a fixed sum, for the delivery of goods or fixed costs, an informal request may be made.[75] In other circumstances, a formal application must be made.[76] Under the digital procedure as there ought to be no practical difference between an informal request and a formal application, procedural simplicity justifies adopting one form of process, which can then be tailored to the specific information relevant to the application.
5. There are several procedural limitations on the grant of judgment in default.[77] These are intended to ensure that the court is satisfied that the defendant has been afforded a fair process. Thus, such a judgment is limited to what is claimed within the particulars of claim.[78] It may only be granted when the defendant has been served with the particulars of claim and the time to respond to them has expired. The principle of due notice must therefore be respected. Additionally, judgment may not be given unless the defendant has failed to respond to the particulars of claim. It may also not be entered where the defendant has sought to bring proceedings to an end through a truncated form of response, ie by seeking a strike out or summary judgment on the particulars of claim. In this way, the adversarial, participation, and accuracy principles are respected. It may also not be entered where the defendant has satisfied the claimant's claim. A defendant who has done so ought not be subject

[72] A Zuckerman (2021) at 396–398.
[73] CPR r 12.4(5).
[74] CPR r 12.12(4).
[75] CPR rr 12.4(1), 12.10.
[76] CPR r 12.4(3).
[77] A Zuckerman (2021) at 397. The safeguards set out in r 9(3) are derived from CPR rr 12.2 and 12.3.
[78] CPR r 12.12(1).

to the court's coercive authority. Moreover, they ought not to subject to any adverse consequences that might otherwise follow from having had an adverse judgment entered against them, eg a reduction in their credit rating. This last restriction is justified by reference to the purposive principle. A fair process does not visit adverse consequences on defendants who have taken steps to settle their dispute.

6. In addition to the procedural limitations on the grant of judgment in default rule 9 also imposes a substantive limit on its availability to claimants. It may not be granted where a rule of law prohibits that being done. This may arise where a statutory provision excludes the possibility of obtaining judgment in default.[79]
7. Where judgment in default is granted, no reasoned decision is given. All that is issued is the order granting judgment in default, which will indicate that the conditions for the grant of the order have been satisfied. A reasoned judgment cannot be given as the judgment is administrative and not adjudicative. As an administrative, procedural judgment arrived at in this way, it is also not appropriate for an appeal to lie from a default judgment.[80] This does not mean that no challenge is available to such a judgment. A defendant may apply to vary or set aside such a judgment.
8. Rule 9(4) sets out further procedural requirements concerning applications for judgment in default. As a general rule, there is no reason to give notice to a non-responsive defendant. A defendant will be aware of the possibility of default judgment being made as service of particulars of claim will include such information. It also provides that evidence is not generally required to support an application for judgment in default. Evidence may, however, be required where the application is made against a State.[81]
9. Rule 9(5) clarifies that judgment in default can be pursued against one or more defendants as well as the effect of doing so. Rule 9(6) further clarifies that judgment in default may be obtained solely on the question of liability. This leaves questions of quantum for determination on their merits. These two rules enable claimants to truncate proceedings. They therefore provide the means by which disputes can be managed more cost-effectively and efficiently. They also promote proportionality. Wherever reasonably possible a claimant should consider whether to seek the benefit of these rules further to its duty to co-operate with the court to promote the purposive principle.

## RULE 10.—VARYING OR SETTING ASIDE JUDGMENT IN DEFAULT

**(1) A defendant, or non-party, may apply to vary or set aside a judgment in default.**

**(2) A judgment in default must be set aside as of right by the court where it was granted improperly. A judgment in default is granted improperly if any of the conditions specified in rule 9 (2) or (3) were not satisfied at the time it was granted.**

**(3) In all other circumstances, the court may vary or set aside a judgment in default where the defendant had good reason for failing to respond to the particulars of claim and**

**(a) the application is made promptly;**

[79] Consumer Credit Act 1974; Justice and Security Act 2013, s 6.

[80] A Zuckerman (2021) at 404.

[81] CPR r 12.12(9).

**(b) the defendant's response to the claim has a real prospect of success; or**

**(c) there is some other good reason why the defendant should be permitted to defend the claim.**

**(4) Where an application under rule 10(3) is not made promptly the defendant must obtain relief from sanction.**

**(5) An application to set aside or vary must be supported by evidence.**

**(6) Where a judgment in default is set aside or varied, the claimant's claim shall be as it was before the application for default judgment was made.**

**(7) Once an application to set aside or vary a judgment in default is determined no further applications to set aside or vary may be made. The judgment or order on the application may be subject to appeal.**

*Sources: ALI/UNIDROIT Principles, principle 15.5; ALI/UNIDROIT Reporters' Study, r 15.7; ELI-UNIDROIT Model Rules, rr 139, 140; CPR Pt 13.*

## COMMENTARY

1. A defendant may challenge the grant of judgment in default. They may apply to vary the judgment or set it aside. Two different tests apply to such applications: one requires the court to set aside the judgment as of right; the other provides a discretion to vary or set aside the judgment. Applications must be supported by evidence to enable the claimant to contest the application effectively and the court to ascertain if the tests have been met.
2. Where an application is made on the basis that one of the pre-conditions set out in rules 9(2) or (3) have not been made the judgment must be set aside as of right. This secures a fair process for defendants. It may be, for instance, that the defendant did not respond because they had no actual knowledge of the proceedings. Despite service being effected in accordance with the rules in Part 10, the proceedings may not have actually come to the defendant's attention. Under the CPR this would not justify setting aside as of right under rule 10(2), but rather a discretionary application under rule 10(3).[82] The CPR's approach to this is wrong in principle as it fails to give proper weight to the due notice principle, which is as Denning LJ rightly put it a '*fundamental principle of our law*'.[83] Any suggestion that due notice here can be limited by reference to, for instance, the purposive principle (under the CPR, its overriding objective) and the need to give effect to proportionality is misconceived. An application to set aside judgment in default raises no issues concerning proportionality as it arises before any steps by the defendant have been taken in proceedings.
3. Rule 10(3) restates the approach to setting aside or varying provided for by CPR r 13.3. Such an application ought to be made promptly. This is required both to afford a fair process to the claimant and finality in litigation. A claimant who has secured a judgment ought to expect that it can be and will be complied with and, if not, enforced. Delay in seeking to set aside the judgment undermines that legitimate expectation. This is not to say that delay, even a lengthy delay, would justify the court

[82] *Akram v Adam* [2004] EWCA Civ 1720; *Nelson v Clearsprings* [2006] EWCA Civ 1252; [2007] 1 WLR 962; *Execuzen Ltd v De Ferranti* [2013] EWCA Civ 592 at [48]–[49]; A Zuckerman (2021) at 406–407.

[83] *R v London Quarterly Sessions Appeal Committee, ex parte Rossi* [1951] 1 QB 682 at 691.

refusing to entertain an application. It may be, for instance, that delay arose due to the defendant being unaware of proceedings or the judgment through no fault of their own for a considerable period of time.[84] Delay may also be justified given the nature and importance of the issues in dispute, eg where they relate to dishonesty or fraud.[85] Any such potential justifications must, however, be approached by way of an application for relief from sanction.[86] The requirement to act promptly imposes a procedural obligation on a defendant. Both the purposive and compliance principles require defendants to act according to its terms.

4. Relief from sanction only applies to the requirement to apply promptly (rule 10(3)(a)). It does not apply to the other elements of rule 10(3).[87] This is because the other elements of the test to set aside or vary are not concerned with breach of a procedural obligation. Under the other criteria in this sub-rule, the defendant must first demonstrate that there was a good reason why they failed to respond to the particulars of claim. A negligent defendant or one who deliberately chose not to engage with the process ought not to, generally, be permitted to set aside or vary the judgment. It may, however, be permissible to grant such an application where a defendant had been negligent or deliberately failed to respond if the nature of the dispute is such as to provide a good reason for doing so. It may be that the proceedings involve a dispute of general public importance or, alternatively, are of significant importance to the parties as they raise allegations of fraud or serious dishonesty. Such reasons may satisfy the 'good reason' criterion.
5. Where there is good reason for the failure to respond, a defendant must then show that their defence has a good prospect of success. There is no justification for permitting the defendant to set aside a regular judgment against them if doing so would present no prospect of a different result, notwithstanding that it would be reached on an assessment of the substantive merits. Alternatively, the application may be granted where there is some other good reason for permitting the defendant to defend the claim. The approach here is that taken to summary judgment applications, albeit the test is good reason rather than compelling reason.
6. Rule 10(6) and (7) provide for the consequences of a successful application. The former establishes that a successful application places the claimant in the position they would have been in before the application was made. This ensures they are not prejudiced in any way by having obtained and lost the benefit of judgment in default.[88] The latter makes explicit that a judgment given on an application to set

[84] *Estate Acquisition & Development Ltd v Wiltshire* [2006] EWCA Civ 533.

[85] *Barons Bridging Finance Plc v Nnadiekwe* [2012] EWHC 2817 (Comm).

[86] This is the only application of the test for relief from sanction where this rule is concerned. An application to set aside a default judgment is not itself an application for relief from sanction. Default judgment is not a sanction; *Attorney General for Trinidad and Tobago v Matthews* [2011] UKPC 38 and *Cunico Resources NV v Daskalakis* [2018] EWHC 3382 (Comm); [2019] 1 WLR 2881 preferred to the approach taken in *FXF v English Karate Federation Ltd* [2023] EWCA Civ 891. The latter's emphasis on the application of relief from sanction to apply to help promote effective compliance is met by the application of the tests set out in rule 10(3) as is, properly, the case under CPR r 13.3.

[87] *Samara v MBI & Partners UK Ltd* [2014] EWHC 563 (QB) at [34]–[39]; *Blackmores LDP v Scott* [2015] EWCA Civ 999; [2016] CP Rep 1 at [56]–[61].

[88] Where for, instance, a claimant abandoned a claim for relief in order to obtain judgment in default; CPR r 13.6.

aside or vary judgment is a final judgment. Further applications cannot be pursued. However, as the court's decision on such an application is an adjudicative one based on an assessment of evidence it is subject to appeal.[89]

## SECTION 3: SUMMARY JUDGMENT

### RULE 11.—SUMMARY JUDGMENT

**(1) A party may apply for summary judgment on a claim or defence, in part or in whole. Where an application is made before service of the defendant's response to the particulars of claim, it may only be made with the court's permission. The court may also commence summary judgment proceedings on its own initiative.**

**(2) An application for summary judgment against the Crown may only be made after service of a defence.**

**(3) The court may grant summary judgment where**

**(a) a claim, defence, or issue in the proceedings has no real prospect of success;**

**(b) there is no other compelling reason why the claim, defence or issue in the proceedings should be determined at trial.**

**(4) A real prospect of success is one that is realistic rather than fanciful. It is more than merely arguable.**

**(5) The burden of proof lies on the party applying for summary judgment. Where the applicant presents sufficient, credible, evidence to the court in support of their application, the burden of proof shifts to the respondent to adduce sufficient, credible, evidence that the claim, defence, or issue has a real prospect of success or that there is another compelling reason to permit it to be determined at trial.**

**(6) In determining a summary judgment application, the court must not conduct a mini-trial. It must, however, take into consideration the evidence adduced by the parties on the application and the evidence that could reasonably be expected to be presented at trial.**

**(7) Summary judgment may not be granted against a defendant in proceedings for possession of residential property against mortgagors or protected tenants, in admiralty claims in rem or where an application for summary disposal has been made under section 8 of the Defamation Act 1996.**

**(8) Summary judgment is a final judgment. Where the court grants summary judgment on part of a claim or defence or refuses to grant summary judgment, it must give dispute management directions.**

*Sources: ELI-UNIDROIT Model Rules, r 65, CPR Pt 24.*

### COMMENTARY

1. Economy, efficiency, and proportionality all support the facility for a claimant or defendant to bring proceedings to an end prior to the application of a full dispute management process and trial. Summary judgment is one means by which they can do so by enabling a party to apply to the court for an adjudication on the substantive

[89] *Samara v MBI & Partners UK Ltd* [2016] EWHC 441(QB).

merits of the dispute following a truncated or streamlined process.[90] The underlying rationale is straightforward. Where a claim or defence has no real prospect of succeeding at trial and there is no other justification for the dispute to proceed to trial, the parties should not be put to the time and expense of the full litigation process. Nor should the court be put to the time and expense of managing and conducting a trial of such a dispute to the detriment of other litigants, upon whom its resources could more properly be expended.[91] Summary judgment thus benefits individual litigants and the effective administration of justice as a whole. To further this, it may be granted on either the whole of a claim or defence, or part of one.

2. To secure the benefits that flow from it an application for summary judgment may be made at any time, including at a trial.[92] It may be commenced by a party or the court; the latter doing so as part of effective and proportionate dispute management.[93] Where a defendant wishes to make such an application before it has served its response to particulars of claim the court's permission is required.[94] This is to enable the court to manage the dispute effectively, not least to give directions varying time limits for responding to the particulars of claim, if necessary. More importantly, it enables it to ensure that only meritorious applications are made prior to the defendant joining issue with the claim in its substantive defence.[95]
3. This rule codifies the approach to summary judgment set out in CPR Pt 24 as that has been interpreted by the courts. It adopts the test for summary judgment from CPR r 24.2, ie that only those claims and defences that have a real prospect of succeeding at trial or those that raise another compelling reason to justify a trial should be permitted to access the full nature of the civil process.[96] It also codifies the principles applicable to the application of that test, which were approved by the Court of Appeal in *AC Ward & Sons Ltd v Catlin (Five) Ltd* (2009).[97] It further codifies the principle articulated in *ED & F Man Liquid Products v Patel* (2003),[98] that the burden lies on the applicant to satisfy the court that summary judgment should be granted. Finally, it codifies the current approach to summary judgment against the Crown and in respect of residential property disputes.[99] It also makes explicit the position where section 8 of the Defamation Act 1996 applies.[100]
4. As a judgment on the substantive merits of the dispute, summary judgment is a final judgment.

[90] J Bauman, 'The Evolution of the Summary Judgment Procedure: An Essay Commemorating the Centennial Anniversary of Keating' (1956) 31(3) Indiana Law Journal 329; N Andrews, *Andrews on Civil Processes* (Intersentia, 2019) at 221.

[91] H Woolf, *Access to Justice: Final Report to the Lord Chancellor on the Civil Justice System in England and Wales* (HMSO) (1996) at 123.

[92] *Alexander v Arts Council of Wales* [2001] EWCA Civ 514.

[93] *Clark v University of Lincolnshire* [2000] 1 WLR 1998 at [27].

[94] CPR r 24.4.

[95] *Clark v University of Lincolnshire* [2000] 1 WLR 1998 at [39].

[96] Compelling reasons could, for instance, arise where trial by jury is required by law: Senior Courts Act 1981, s 69; *Commerz Real Investmentgesellschaft MBH v TFS Stores Ltd* [2021] EWHC 863 (Ch) at [14]–[17].

[97] *AC Ward & Sons Ltd v Catlin (Five) Ltd* [2009] EWCA Civ 1098; [2010] Lloyd's Rep IR 301 at [24], approving *Easyair Ltd v Opal Telecom Ltd* [2009] EWHC 339 (Ch) at [15]. *Swain v Hillman* [2001] 1 All ER 91 at 92.

[98] *ED & F Man Liquid Products v Patel* [2003] EWCA Civ 472.

[99] CPR r 24.4(1A).

[100] Defamation Act 1996, s 8 provides a statutory summary procedure for such claims.

# SECTION 4: PROCEDURAL AND FINAL JUDGMENTS AND ORDERS

## RULE 12.—PROCEDURAL JUDGMENTS AND ORDERS

**(1) The court, on its own initiative or on the application of a party or non-party, may give a procedural judgment or order.**

**(2) Procedural judgments and orders should only be made on the court's own initiative when the court has sufficient information to determine the matter consistently with the purposive principle.**

**(3) A procedural judgment or order made on the court's own initiative may be made without a hearing or the parties or any interested non-party having made representations to the court. A party or interested non-party may apply to set aside or vary any such judgment or order. Such an application must be made promptly. It will be determined at a hearing, unless the parties consent to a written hearing. The hearing, however held, will be a rehearing not a review.**

**(4) A procedural judgment or order made in circumstances other than those specified in rule 12(3) or made under Part 14, rule 6(10) may be varied or set aside on the application of a party or a non-party whose interests are directly affected by it. Such an application will be heard by way of review, unless otherwise directed by the court. The judgment or order may be varied or set aside where**

**(a) the application is made promptly; and**

**(b) there has been a material change in circumstance since the judgment or order was given; or**

**(c) the judgment or order was based on facts that were misstated.**

**(5) A procedural judgment or order may be challenged by way of an appeal.**

*Sources: CPR rr 3.1(1), 3.1(7), 3.3(1).*

## COMMENTARY

1. This rule elaborates procedural judgments and orders, the majority of which concern case statements, service, dispute management, including provisional and protective measures, and hearings. They may be given by the court on its own initiative or on application of the parties and do not finally determine issues within proceedings or proceedings as a whole.[101] They are what were known, respectively, under the CPR and its predecessors as interim or interlocutory orders.

2. Where the court intends to make a judgment or order on its own initiative it must ensure that it has sufficient information to determine the matter fairly. This is required by the purposive principle.[102] Decisions made in the absence of such information are likely to be partial, which may result in either an unfair process or an unjust result. Sufficient information is also necessary for reasons of economy, efficiency, and proportionality. Were decisions to routinely be made by the court on its own initiative absent sufficient information to determine the matter fairly, they would routinely be challenged by either or both parties. Poor quality decision-making would consequently lead to the waste of court, and party, resources.

[101] *Prestney v Colchester Corp* (1883) 24 Ch D 376 at 384.

[102] *Shawton Engineering Ltd v DGP International Ltd* [2003] EWCA Civ 1956; [2004] CP Rep 23 at [16].

3. The court retains a broad jurisdiction to revisit procedural judgments and orders. It is particularly important that it can do so where it makes decisions on its own initiative in the absence of a party or interested non-party.[103] In such situations, the absent party or non-party must be afforded the possibility of challenging the decision before the court at a rehearing.[104] That is a basic consequence of the due notice and general access principles. It is required for there to be a fair process.[105] It, of course, remains entirely permissible for them not to challenge such decisions. Whether they do so or not flows from party autonomy. In some cases, particularly those where the court makes a dispute management decision of its own initiative, absent parties should consider carefully, further to the co-operation principle, whether to bring a challenge. In some cases, for instance, it would be disproportionate to do so, not least where the decision is one that the court would reasonably be expected to affirm at a further hearing. The parties may, however, agree to such a hearing being held by way of a written hearing to reduce the cost and time involved.[106]
4. Where a procedural judgment or order is made in other circumstances, the court retains a broad discretion to set aside them aside or vary them. The discretion must be exercised consistently with the purposive principle, and particularly by reference to the proportionality principle. It may therefore only be exercised where a number of criteria a met.[107]
5. First, an application to set aside or vary must be made promptly. If not, both the court and other parties may expend unnecessary and disproportionate resources based on the judgment or order. The application must also demonstrate that there has been a material change in circumstance since the judgment or order was made. Thus, the court on such an application is considering new circumstances and not simply revisiting its previous decision on the same material as was previously before it. The discretion is not one that should enable parties to simply have further attempts to reargue the same points or to rely upon evidence or arguments that could and should have been set out at the initial hearing; to permit that would be to provide an unfair and unequal process as one party would be afforded more and more time to argue the same points.[108] Alternatively, where there has been no material change of circumstances, an application may be granted where the judgment or order was based on a misstatement of fact by one of the parties. The public interest in accuracy justifies variation or setting aside in this last circumstance. As the power to vary or set aside is discretionary, the court retains jurisdiction to refuse an application even where these conditions are met. This test also applies to multiple applications for the same relief.[109]
6. Where procedural judgments and orders are made at without-notice hearings, the procedure set out in Part 14, rule 6(10) applies.

[103] *R (MD) (Afghanistan) v Secretary of State for the Home Department* [2012] EWCA Civ 194; [2012] 1 WLR 2422 at [21].

[104] *Al-Zahra (Pvt) Hospital v DDM* [2019] EWCA Civ 1103 at [64].

[105] One consequence of this is that a judgment or order made without notice is not capable of being set aside as of right. Whether it is set aside (or varied) depends on the outcome of the rehearing: *Nelson v Clearsprings* [2006] EWCA Civ 1252; [2007] 1 WLR 962; *Execuzen Ltd v De Ferranti* [2013] EWCA Civ 592 at [48]–[49]. Although note the rejection of this approach where judgment in default is concerned: r 10.

[106] *Collier v Williams* [2006] EWCA Civ 20; [2006] 1 WLR 1945.

[107] *Tibbles v SIG Plc* [2012] EWCA Civ 518; [2012] 1 WLR 2591 at [39]; *Roult v North West Strategic Health Authority* [2009] EWCA Civ 444; [2010] 1 WLR 487.

[108] *Woodhouse v Consignia* [2002] EWCA Civ 275; [2002] 1 WLR 2558.

[109] Part 11, r 8.

## RULE 13.—FINAL JUDGMENTS AND ORDERS

**(1) A final judgment, including an appellate judgment, is one that conclusively determines the rights of the parties to proceedings. A final order gives effect to a final judgment.**

**(2) A final judgment or order may be varied or set aside in exceptional circumstances, which include where the judgment or order was**

**(a) obtained by fraud;**

**(b) made in the absence of a party and that party applies to vary or set it aside;**

**(c) made following an admission by a party and the court has granted permission for its withdrawal.**

**(3) A final judgment or order may only be varied or set aside when made in the absence of a party where**

**(a) that party had not consented to it being made in their absence;**

**(b) the judgment or order was not made within a digital continuous procedure in which the court had previously directed that judgments or orders could be given or issued in the absence of the parties; and**

**(c) the absent party applies to vary or set aside the judgment or order promptly, they were absent with good reason from the hearing where the judgment or order was given or issued, and their claim or defence has a real prospect of success.**

**(4) A non-party whose interests are directly affected by a final judgment or order may apply to have it varied or set aside.**

**(5) Except as provided for in Part 16, a final judgment may be challenged by way of an appeal.**

**(6) Where proceedings are determined by a final judgment, anonymised information shall be provided to Ombudsman, regulators, and the government.**

*Sources: CPR rr 3.1(1), 3.1(7), 3.3(1), 39.3.*

## COMMENTARY

1. This rule elaborates final judgments and orders. These are orders that resolve a matter on its substantive merits and once perfected have a preclusionary effect (rule 14). Given the importance of the finality principle, they may only be challenged in limited circumstances. Generally, they should be challenged by way of appeal, however, they may also (as an exception to the general principle that once a judgment or order has been perfected the court no longer has jurisdiction over the proceedings[110]) vary or set aside final judgments or orders.[111] Both parties and any non-party whose interests are directly affected by the judgment may seek to do so.

2. The power to vary or set aside final judgments and orders, as a significant in-road into the finality principle, is one that may only be exercised exceptionally.[112] Any other approach would tend to undermine not only that principle, but also the purposive and proportionality principles for the same reason as too ready resort to the discretion to vary or set aside procedural judgments would do so.

[110] *R v Cripps, ex parte Muldoon* [1984] QB 686 at 695; *Carleton (Earl of Malmesbury) v Strutt & Parker* [2007] EWHC 2199 QB.

[111] *Lloyds Investment (Scandinavia) Limited v Christen Ager-Hanssen* [2003] EWHC 1740 (Ch) at [7].

[112] *BCS Corporate Acceptances Ltd v Terry* [2018] EWCA Civ 2422 at [75].

3. The authorities demonstrate that there are three bases on which a final judgment or order may be varied or set aside. They are codified in rule 13(2)(a) to (c). In each case the in-road into finality rests on greater weight needing to be given to other procedural principles.
4. Rule 13(2)(a),[113] rests on the purposive, accuracy and procedural equality principles. Parties should not, by their deceit, take improper advantage of their opponent. Neither should they render the process unfair nor the result inaccurate through such conduct. Most significantly, they should not be permitted to subvert the proper administration of justice and thereby undermine the public interest in the rule of law. The judicial power of the State should not be used to commit fraud or wrongdoing, nor should the court once it is aware that a judgment has been obtained by fraud connive in the maintenance of that act by failing to rectify the situation.
5. Rules 13(2)(b) and (c), again, protect the integrity of the court process and justify overriding the finality principle due to the need to afford parties a fair process. Where a party failed to attend a hearing, there may be good reason to exercise the discretion and vary or set aside any final judgment or order made.[114] The basis on which the court may do so is, however, circumscribed. It requires that the judgment or order was not properly made in the absence of a party, eg because they had not consented to that course of action or the court had not previously directed that decisions could be made in the party's absence. It also requires, where those criteria are satisfied, that the absent party acts promptly in applying to vary or set aside, that they have a good reason for being absent, and their claim or defence has a real prospect of success. Promptness is, again, required to ensure that the judgment or order is not relied upon by other parties.[115] On good reason and the need to demonstrate a real prospect of success, see the commentary to rule 10(3).
6. Where a party has satisfied the requirements for the withdrawal of an admission, the basis on which any final judgment or order was made may fall away. Both the procedural equality and the accuracy principles may justify reconsideration by the court of any final judgment or order it made based on the, now, withdrawn admission.[116]
7. Rule 13(6) gives effect to the digital integration principle. It is intended to facilitate the development and promotion of pre-action forms of preventive justice.

## RULE 14.—EFFECT OF JUDGMENTS

**(1) A cause of action or an issue in proceedings that is determined by a final judgment cannot form the subject matter in those proceedings or in any future proceedings between the parties and their successors. Nor can a claim for relief that ought to have been pursued in proceedings that have been finally determined be pursued in future proceedings.**

**(2) A final judgment, other than a declaratory judgment, extinguishes parties' rights and liabilities arising from the cause of action determined by the judgment. Those**

[113] *Salekipour v Parmar* [2017] EWCA Civ 214; [2018] QB 833; *BCS Corporate Acceptances Ltd v Terry* [2018] EWCA Civ 2422.

[114] *Forcelux Ltd v Binnie* [2009] EWCA Civ 854; [2010] HLR 20.

[115] See r 12, comment 4.

[116] *Madison CF UK v Various* [2018] EWHC 2786 (Ch).

**rights and liabilities are replaced with the rights and liabilities that arise under the judgment.**

**(3) Where parties may waive the effect of rule 14(1), they may only do so with the court's permission.**

*Sources: ALI/UNIDROIT Principles, principle 28; ELI-UNIDROIT Model Rules, rr 147, 148, 149, 150.*

## COMMENTARY

1. This rule concerns what are generally referred to as res judicata and the doctrine of merger.[117] Neither are provided for within the CPR. They are included here to make clear a limit on both the court's powers and on party autonomy.

2. Rule 14(1) encompasses three related concepts, each of which gives effect to the parties' legitimate expectations that once proceedings have been finally determined '*that is the end of the matter*'.[118] First, it encompasses cause of action estoppel. This gives effect to the finality principle by providing that where a cause of action is finally determined in proceedings, the court's decision may not be relitigated in further proceedings by the parties or their successors[119] Secondly, it encompasses a concept related to cause of action estoppel, which although not forming part of cause of action estoppel gives rise to a form a res judicata that operates in a similar fashion. This precludes a claimant from bringing further proceedings arising from the same cause of action. A claimant may not, for instance, pursue a claim seeking one form of relief and then, at the conclusion of those proceedings, initiate new proceedings seeking another form of relief arising from the same claim.[120] In *Virgin Atlantic Airways Ltd v Zodiac Seats UK Ltd* (2013), Lord Sumption noted that it was difficult to refer to this concept as a form of estoppel. It could, however, be construed as a 'claim for relief estoppel', as its focus is on limiting a claimant's ability to seek different forms of relief in multiple proceedings arising from the same cause of action. As cause of action estoppel promotes the finality principle so does claim for relief estoppel. In both cases they promote the general policy objective that flows from the concentration principle, ie that parties ought to raise all their claims and defences in a single set of proceedings.[121]

3. The final concept within the ambit of rule 14(1) is that of issue estoppel.[122] It also gives effect to the finality principle. It is more targeted than the first two concepts. It provides that where a specific issue in proceedings has been finally determined it may not be relitigated by the parties or their successors.[123] This applies where

[117] G Spencer Bower and K Handley, *Res Judicata* (LexisNexis, 2019). The principle derives from the Latin: *nemo debet bis vexari pro una et eadem causa*; and *interest reipublicae ut sit finis litium*.

[118] *Smith v Brough* [2005] EWCA Civ 261; [2006] CP Rep 17 at [25].

[119] *Ord v Ord* [1923] 2 KB 423 at 439; *Virgin Atlantic Airways Ltd v Zodiac Seats UK Ltd* [2013] UKSC 46; [2014] AC 160 at [17]. Res judicata only binds the parties to proceedings and their successors. It does not bind other persons not party to the proceedings: *Townsend v Bishop* [1939] 1 All ER 805. Decisions should not bind those who have not been heard: *C (a minor) v Hackney London Borough Council* [1996] 1 WLR 789 at 793; *Yat Tung Investment Co Ltd v Dao Heng Bank* Ltd [1975] AC 581.

[120] *Conquer v Boot* [1928] 2 KB 336; *Virgin Atlantic Airways Ltd v Zodiac Seats UK Ltd* [2013] UKSC 46; [2014] AC 160 at [17].

[121] *Henderson v Henderson* (1843) 3 Hare 100.

[122] *Fidelitas Shipping Co Ltd v V/O Exportchleb* [1966] 1 QB 630 at 643; *Arnold v National Westminster Bank Plc* [1991] 2 AC 93 at 106.

[123] *Orji v Nagra* [2023] EWCA Civ 1289 at [46]–[47].

proceedings are pursued, which arise from a different cause of action than the one in which the issue estoppel arose. The decision on the issue is binding on the parties notwithstanding the different bases of the two causes of action. As with the first two concepts, finality is achieved as the preclusionary effect of the estoppel is to prevent the same, in this case, issue being relitigated. Related to the concepts given effect in rule 14(1) are those that preclude a party from pursuing matters, as an abuse of process, in subsequent proceedings that ought to have been pursued in previous ones and the prohibition on pursuing abusive proceedings.[124]

4. Rule 14(2) sets out what is known as the doctrine of merger.[125] This is a rule of substantive law rather than procedure.[126] It is included here to make explicit its place within the approach to judgments. It concerns the concept of a cause of action ceasing to exist when it is finally determined. Once final judgment is given on it the cause of action ceases to exist; it merges with the judgment. Hence cause of action estoppel arises because once there has been a final determination there is no cause of action that continues to exist capable of forming the basis of future proceedings.[127] Thus a final judgment replaces or supersedes[128] the rights and obligations that arose from the cause of action with those that arise from the judgment. This doctrine, and rule 14(2), do not apply to declaratory judgments. This was made clear by the Court of Appeal in *Zavarco Plc v Nasir* (2021).[129] This is because a declaratory judgment does not extinguish a right. On the contrary, it simply confirms that a right or obligation exists.[130]
5. At common law, parties could waive an estoppel (albeit not cause of action estoppel given the doctrine of merger).[131] Rule 14(3) modifies this position to require court consent to waiver. It does so as waiver could result in the court having to expend its time and resources on the same issue multiple times. This could undermine the finality principle, as well as the proportionality principle. The importance of these two principles in the present context can be seen by reference to the longstanding rationales for the development of res judicata identified in *Lockyer v Ferryman* (1877). It explained that there were two bases on which it rested

> *... that it is the interest of the State that there should be an end of litigation, and ..., the hardship on the individual, that he should be vexed twice for the same cause.*[132]

6. Bringing an end to litigation helps promote the proper allocation of the court's resources consistently with systemic proportionality. It stops some litigants receiving more than their fair share of those resources through litigating the same matter

[124] *Virgin Atlantic Airways Ltd v Zodiac Seats UK Ltd* [2013] UKSC 46; [2014] AC 160 at [17], see the fifth and sixth principles identified there.

[125] Civil Jurisdiction and Judgments Act 1982, s 34.

[126] *Zavarco Plc v Nasir* [2021] EWCA Civ 121; [2022] Ch 105 at [27].

[127] *Clark v In Focus Asset Management and Tax Solutions Ltd* [2014] EWCA Civ 118; [2014] 1 WLR 2502 at [5].

[128] *Brown v Wootton* (1604) SC Cro Jac 73; *King v Hoare* (1844) 13 M & W 494 at 504, '*... the cause of action is changed into a matter of record, which is of a higher nature, and the inferior remedy is merged in the higher.*'; *Kendall v Hamilton* (1879) 4 App Cas 504 at 506.

[129] *Zavarco Plc v Nasir* [2021] EWCA Civ 121; [2022] Ch 105.

[130] *Zavarco Plc v Nasir* [2021] EWCA Civ 121; [2022] Ch 105 at [37].

[131] *Vooght v Winch* (1819) 106 ER 507; (1819) 2 B & Ald 662; *Morrison Rose & Partners v Hillman* [1961] 2 QB 266 at 276 and following.

[132] *Lockyer v Ferryman* (1877) 2 App Cas 519 at 530.

multiple times. It also promotes this by helping to bring about early resolution of disputes, ie their resolution the first time round rather than following multiple attempts.[133] By restricting party ability to relitigate the same matter multiple times it also helps reduce the cost and time—the hardship—to individual litigants. More broadly, were parties to be afforded the ability to relitigate the same issues in multiple proceedings that could lead to different courts giving different judgments on the same point. The potential for and growth of such conflicting judgments would, as it did in the 19th century when in some circumstances the same claim could be litigated in both the common law and equity courts, undermine confidence in the courts. As it would lead to uncertainty over rights it would also undermine the rule of law. This in turn could lead to increasing amounts of litigation by parties seeking to secure clarity in the law so they could order their affairs effectively. To protect these various interests, permission to waive an estoppel is thus required under this rule. Before granting permission, the court must consider whether to do so carefully.[134] Parties, further to the co-operation principle, must also consider whether any proposed waiver is consistent with the proportionality principle before seeking the court's permission.

## RULE 15.—EFFECT OF JUDGMENTS AND ORDERS IN GROUP AND REPRESENTATIVE PROCEEDINGS

**(1) Procedural and final judgments or orders in group proceedings bind all those parties who are registered on the digital register. In representative proceedings they bind the representative party and any other parties.**

**(2) Represented class members are bound by any procedural or final judgment or order in the proceedings, unless the court directs otherwise where there are special circumstances justifying such a direction.**

*Sources: ELI-UNIDROIT Model Rules, r 227, CPR rr 19.8(4), 19.23.*

## COMMENTARY

1. Rule 15 specifies the effect of judgments and orders in group and representative proceedings. It makes clear that they bind the parties to such proceedings. It also clarifies the effect they have in representative proceedings on represented class members. They are also bound by such judgments and orders.[135] It does, however, provide that the court may order otherwise where they are concerned. It may do so, for instance, where the represented class member can demonstrate that the order or judgment was procured by fraud, collusion, or similar special circumstances.[136]

2. This rule is an important means to clarify the preclusionary effect of such orders and judgments. By clarifying that represented class members, who are not parties

[133] *Talbot v Berkshire County Council* [1994] QB 290 at 301.

[134] A Zuckerman (2021) at 1347–1348; r 18(3).

[135] *Markt & Co Limited v Knight Steamship Company Limited* [1910] 2 QB 1021 at 1039; *Moon v Atherton* [1972] 2 QB 435; *Lloyd v Google LLC* [2021] UKSC 50; [2021] 3 WLR 1268 at [34].

[136] *Commissioners of Sewers of the City of London v Gellatly* [1871] 3 ChD 610; *Howells v Dominion Insurance Company Ltd* [2005] EWHC 552 (QB) at [10].

to the proceedings, are bound by orders and judgments in the proceedings it means that they cannot bring future proceedings concerning the same cause of action. Without this rule, only the representative party (if they are a claimant) and defendants would be bound. In principle therefore without it there would be nothing to stop, as rightly emphasised by the commentary to the ELI-UNIDROIT Model Rules,[137] a represented class member from seeking to commence fresh representative proceedings concerning the same matter. While it would be very unlikely that any court would grant permission for such a claim to be authorised as fresh representative proceedings (and it is more than likely that any such proceedings would be struck out as an abuse of process), this rule plays an important role. By giving effect to the finality principle in so far as represented class members are concerned, it ensures that defendants and the court are not put to the unnecessary and unreasonable expense and time of applying to strike them out or contest applications to authorise further proceedings as representative proceedings. Rule 15(2) thus not only promotes the finality principle, it also promotes proportionality.

## SECTION 5: JUDGMENTS, ORDERS, AND SETTLEMENT

### RULE 16.—CONSENT ORDERS AND JUDGMENTS AND ORDERS THAT GIVE EFFECT TO SETTLEMENT

**(1) Parties may agree the terms by which judgment may be given. They may also agree the terms of any order.**
**(2) The court's consent to any judgment or order made by party agreement is required where**
**(a) a party is represented by a litigation friend; or**
**(b) the judgment or order involves the settlement of proceedings, including an appeal.**
**(3) Except where an order seeks to give effect to the settlement of representative proceedings, the court may give consent where it has the power to make such an order and where it is just and reasonable to do so.**
**(4) The court may order proceedings be stayed where parties have agreed the terms of settlement and those terms are annexed as a schedule to the court's order. Where the court makes such an order**
**(a) it must not consider or review the terms of the settlement other than at the request of all the parties;**
**(b) it has no jurisdiction to amend or otherwise vary the terms of the settlement;**
**(c) the schedule, which does not form part of the order, shall be confidential and not subject to the publicity principle;**
**(d) the stay may be lifted by the court, on application of a party, in order to give effect to the terms of the settlement.**

*Sources: ELI-UNIDROIT Model Rules, r 141, CPR rr 19.8(4), 23.8, 40.6, CPR PD 52A, para 6.*

[137] ELI-UNIDROIT Model Rules, r 227, comment 2.

## COMMENTARY

1. This covers two situations. It gives effect to the longstanding approach taken under the CPR and its predecessors that enables parties to consent to judgments and orders. It also codifies, in rule 16(4), what are known as *Tomlin Orders*. Both rules promote the settlement principle, and by doing so the proportionality principle. They are also a means by which party autonomy is given effect.
2. Rule 16(1) states the general rule that parties may agree the terms of a judgment or order.[138] To do so they must demonstrate to the court that their agreement is intended to bind them. They must also confirm that they have provided each other with all relevant information and evidence relevant to the matters on which they have reached agreement.[139] These requirements are intended to ensure that the agreement is one that will bring finality to proceedings. Where, however, an agreed judgment or order concerns either a person represented by a litigation friend or settles proceedings, the court must approve the order. It is primarily intended to ensure that the court is satisfied that the order is one that is made in the best interests of the party. Court consent is also required to ensure that the terms agreed are such as the court could order. It is essential that the terms of agreed final judgments and orders are within the court's power as party consent cannot extend the judicial power of the State.
3. Rule 16(4) codifies *Tomlin Orders*, which are orders derived from *Dashwood v Dashwood* (1927).[140] They are orders made where the parties agree the terms of settlement of their dispute and those terms are not included in the body of the court's order.[141] Rather they are set out in a confidential schedule, annexed to the order. The order, which is by consent, contains two terms: that the proceedings are stayed except for the purpose of giving effect to the terms agreed in the schedule; and, that the parties have permission to apply to the court to carry out the terms set out in the schedule. As the terms of settlement do not form part of the court order, they do not fall under the publicity principle. They are confidential to the parties. Moreover, as they are not part of the court order, they do not form part of the court process or the court record.[142] Several consequences flow from this. First, it means that, as a matter of principle, the court has no power to review the terms of the schedule and should not purport to do so other than with party consent.[143] Secondly, as the terms do not form part of a court order, the court has no jurisdiction to vary or set them aside. They form an agreement between the parties and any variation is governed by the law of contract.[144]

[138] Part 11, r 8.

[139] *R (Compton) v Wiltshire Primary Care Trust* [2008] EWCA Civ 749; [2009] 1 WLR 1436.

[140] *Dashwood v Dashwood* (1927) 71 SJ 911; Practice Note [1927] WN 290; *Horizon Technologies International v Lucky Wealth Consultants Ltd* [1992] 1 WLR 24.

[141] D Foskett, *Foskett on Compromise* (Sweet & Maxwell, 2024) at 149: Tomlin Order precedent.

[142] *Zenith Logistics Services (UK) Ltd v Coury* [2020] EWHC 774 (QB) at [65]–[66].

[143] *Zenith Logistics Services (UK) Ltd v Coury* [2020] EWHC 774 (QB) at [57] notes a practice in the Commercial Court to review such terms. The approach taken here rejects this, except where the parties request that the court do so.

[144] For a detailed account of *Tomlin Orders,* D Foskett (2024) at 149–155.

## RULE 17.—SETTLEMENT OF REPRESENTATIVE PROCEEDINGS

**(1) Where a representative party intends to settle its own dispute in representative proceedings, it must inform the court of that fact promptly so that it may make any necessary consequential directions to manage the proceedings.**

**(2) Where the parties to opt-in representative proceedings intend to settle the dispute**

**(a) they should notify the court of that fact promptly; and**

**(b) settlement may not take effect until the date by which class members may opt-in to the proceedings has expired.**

**(3) Where the parties to opt-out representative proceedings intend to settle the dispute, they must jointly apply to the court for approval of the proposed settlement. The application must**

**(a) identify the parties to the proposed collective settlement;**

**(b) provide details of the claims for relief to be settled by the proposed collective settlement;**

**(c) provide a description of the class (including any who may be outside the jurisdiction) to be bound by the settlement, an estimate of the number of class members and the basis of that estimate;**

**(d) specify why the proposed collective settlement is in the best interests of the represented class;**

**(e) identify the party to be responsible for administering the settlement and how it will be administered; and**

**(f) include a draft collective settlement order.**

**(4) The court may approve a proposed settlement where it is in best interests of the represented class. The court may appoint an assessor to assist its determination of this issue.**

**(5) An approved settlement will bind the parties and the represented class members, unless the court directs otherwise.**

*Sources: Competition Act 1998, s 49A; Competition Appeal Tribunal Rules (2015), rr 94, 95; ELI-UNIDROIT Model Rules, rr 221 to 226.*

## COMMENTARY

1. As with any other form of proceedings, representative proceedings may conclude with a consensual settlement. This may occur in any of three ways. In each situation the court must be informed.

2. The representative party may settle their individual dispute with the defendant. In such a situation, it will no longer share a common interest with the represented class. They may therefore no longer be able to fairly and adequately act in the represented class's interests. The court must therefore consider whether it should set aside that party's authorisation to act as a representative and appoint a new representative party. To facilitate the effective management of that process, rule 17(1) requires the representative party to notify the court of any intended settlement.

3. Where parties to opt-in representative proceedings settle two requirements must be satisfied. Again, the court must be notified promptly so that it can take steps to manage the settlement and its effect on the management of proceedings. The settlement must also not take effect until the date by which class members may join the proceedings has expired. This provision is derived from rule 95 of the Competition Appeal

Tribunal Rules (CAT) (2015). As the Guide to CAT Rules explains, this ensures that the class is properly constituted; that it is clear who is within the represented class, and that the class representative can consult the class effectively in respect of the proposed settlement.[145]

4. The final situation is where a settlement is agreed in opt-out proceedings. Here consideration must be given to safeguarding the interests and rights of the represented class members, many of whom may be unaware of the proceedings. There is thus a need to ensure that the settlement reached is one that is fair to them. The court may only approve the settlement if it concludes that it is in the best interests of the represented class members. This requires the court to scrutinise the proposed settlement, its terms, and how they affect the class members, carefully.[146] To enable it to carry out this exercise effectively, the parties, who must apply for approval jointly, must provide the court with the detail specified in rule 17(3). This requirement is derived from rule 94(3) of the CAT Rules 2015.[147] The party responsible for administering the settlement will ordinarily be the representative party, although the actual administration is likely to be carried out by their lawyers.
5. In considering whether settlement is in the best interests of the represented class, the court will also need to consider the nature, complexity and value of their individual claims and the costs incurred to date and the potential future costs of the litigation as that will impinge upon the value of any potential damages award. Where consideration of costs is concerned, any private funding mechanism will need to be considered, eg if funding was provided via a form of contingency fee agreement or funding arrangement that may have an impact on the quantum of any financial settlement that might ultimately be distributed to the represented class members. The court may appoint an assessor to assist it in determining whether the proposed settlement is in the best interests of the represented class.

## RULE 18.—THE COURT'S POWER TO ISSUE JUDGMENT AFTER SETTLEMENT

**(1) The court may issue a judgment in any proceedings after the parties settle their dispute where it is in the public interest to do so. It may do so whether or not the parties consent to the judgment being issued.**

**(2) In considering whether it is in the public interest to hand down a judgment after settlement the court may take account of all the circumstances, including**

**(a) the fact of the parties' agreement to settle their dispute;**

**(b) whether the judgment would vindicate the honesty or conduct of a party or non-party that had been subject to criticism during the proceedings;**

**(c) whether the judgment deals with a point of law or matters of fact of general public interest;**

**(d) whether the judgment departs from previous authority or develops the law; and**

**(e) the extent to which handing down judgment would promote the purposive principle.**

[145] The rationale is as set out in Competition Appeal Tribunal, *Guide to Proceedings (2015)*, at 6.95.

[146] Competition Appeal Tribunal, *Guide to Proceedings (2015)*, at 6.124.

[147] Competition Appeal Tribunal, *Guide to Proceedings (2015)*, at 6.96–6.101, 6.123–6.129.

## COMMENTARY

1. The judicial process serves both the private interests of the party and the wider public interest. This is most clearly seen in the application of the proportionality principle to dispute management so that the court's resources are equitably distributed to all proceedings. It is also apparent in the appellate process where it gives effect to both the parties' private interest in accurate adjudication and the public interest in, for instance, the development of the law. In both cases, the public interest can outweigh the parties' private interest. Proportionality, by rationing access to procedure, places greater weight on the need to secure the proper administration of justice for all those who need to access the court than it does on securing the private interest of accurate adjudication in any individual proceeding. The public interest in developing the law, as the underpinning of second appeals, prioritises that interest over the parties' private interest in correcting judicial error that may have occurred up to and including at a first appeal.
2. The power to hand down judgment, with and particularly without the parties' consent, after they have settled their dispute is another instance where giving effect to the parties' private interests must be balanced against the wider public interest.[148] Rule 18(1) gives effect to the court's inherent jurisdiction in this respect. This applies to any proceedings, irrespective of whether they are private or public law proceedings.[149] The jurisdiction enables the court to set aside the normal position that where parties settle their dispute they take it out of the public realm. It does not, however, provide a power to disturb the settlement itself. It does not in that respect, therefore, adversely affect party autonomy.
3. Exercise of the jurisdiction requires the court to consider both private and public interest factors. This is intended to enable the court to balance them properly. The factors set out in rule 18(2) codify the approach developed by the authorities.[150] Private interest factors include the fact that the parties have reached a settlement, which on its own points towards not issuing a judgment. However, that must be balanced against other private interest factors. Where proceedings have placed in the public realm criticism of parties or non-parties, it may be necessary to issue the judgment to enable their conduct to be vindicated. This is particularly important where, for instance, a party or non-party has been accused of dishonesty during the course of proceedings.
4. There are several public interest factors that must be weighed against the parties' private interest. Those that weigh heavily in favour of issuing the judgment include that it will give authoritative guidance on an important issue of law or fact, or that it is likely to develop, alter, or clarify the law. Whether or not issuing the judgment will further the purposive principle must also be considered. Consequently, the court must consider factors such as whether issuing the judgment furthers the proportionality principle.

[148] *R (Mohamed) v Secretary of State for Foreign and Commonwealth Affairs* [2010] EWCA Civ 65; [2011] QB 218 at [179].

[149] *Jabbar v Aviva Insurance UK Ltd* [2022] EWHC 912 (QB); [2022] 4 WLR 68.

[150] *Prudential Assurance Co Ltd v McBains Cooper* [2000] 1 WLR 2000 at 2008–2009; *Barclays Bank Plc v Nylon Capital* LLP [2011] EWCA Civ 826; [2012] 1 All ER (Comm) 912 at [74]–[75]; *F&C Alternative Investments (Holdings) Ltd v Barthelemy* [2011] EWHC 1851 (Ch); [2012] Bus LR 884, at [7].

5. The court may be more likely to exercise its discretion not to issue a judgment if settlement is reached before judgment drafting has started. Similarly, it is more likely not to issue a judgment if settlement is reached before a draft judgment is circulated.[151] Such approaches further the proportionality principle as they conserve judicial time. Proportionality may itself be outweighed by other factors, not least the need to vindicate a party or non-party who has been subject to criticism during the proceedings. Consideration of all the factors, which are non-exhaustive, will therefore be case-sensitive.

[151] *Gurney Consulting Engineers v Gleeds Health & Safety Ltd (No 2)* [2006] EWHC 536 (TCC); 108 Con LR 58.

# PART 16
# ENFORCEMENT

## SECTION 1: GENERAL

1. This Part concerns the enforcement of judgments and orders where that is necessary to secure compliance with their terms. It is primarily concerned with the enforcement of monetary judgments.[1] Debt enforcement and personal injury claims form a significant proportion of litigation.
2. Kennett identifies three broad types of enforcement model that could be adopted: an administrative model; a judicial officer model; and a court-centred model. The first type places responsibility for enforcement in the hands of an administrative agency that forms part of the executive. The second places responsibility in the hands of a specific branch of the legal profession. The third places it in the hands of the court. Sweden and Finland favour the first model. France, Belgium, Portugal, and countries in Eastern Europe favour the second. Common law jurisdictions, such as England and Wales, as well as civil law jurisdictions, such as Austria, Germany, Slovenia, and Spain, to varying degrees, favour the third.[2] This Part maintains the court-centred model.
3. Historically, enforcement was '*an unplanned, unsystematic, haphazard, complex system*', which was '*ineffective, inefficient, somewhat random and sometimes oppressive*'.[3] It was the product of several common law writs, eg the writ of fieri facias (now a writ of control or warrant of execution),[4] and various statutes, eg the Debtors Act 1869, the Attachment of Earnings Act 1971, the Charging Orders Act 1979. A degree of rationalisation was, however, achieved via the Tribunals, Courts and Enforcement Act 2007, albeit not all of its reforms have as yet been brought into force.[5] This Part is not intended to codify the various legislative provisions that exist. That should be done via a complete review, modernisation, and codification of the substantive law concerning enforcement. It does, however, seek to simplify the procedural approach to enforcement.

[1] W Kennett, *Civil Enforcement in a Comparative Perspective* (Intersentia, 2021) at 7. Judgments such as those that are declaratory or constitutive (eg an order dissolving a partnership) do not generally require the parties to do anything and, hence, do not engage the enforcement process.

[2] W Kennett (2021) at 9–10. The historic approach to enforcement can be seen in W Blake Odgers, *The Principles of Pleading and Practice in Civil Actions in the High Court of Justice* (Stevens & Sons, 1912) at 339.

[3] J Jacob, *The Fabric of English Civil Justice* (Stevens & Sons, 1987) at 188.

[4] Tribunals, Courts and Enforcement Act 2007, s 62.

[5] Tribunals, Courts and Enforcement Act 2007, Pt 4.

*A Model Civil Procedure Code for England and Wales*. John Sorabji, Oxford University Press. © John Sorabji 2024.
DOI: 10.1093/oso/9780192848680.003.0017

## RULE 1.—SCOPE AND PURPOSE

**(1) This Part concerns the enforcement of orders and judgments.**
**(2) Enforcement processes give effect to the general access, effective enforcement, and finality principles. They should also, where necessary, take account of the substantive rights of third parties.**
**(3) To promote the economy, efficiency and proportionality principles, effective enforcement also incorporates the promotion of settlement.**

*Sources: ALI/UNIDROIT Principles, principle 29; CPR Pts 69 to 74, 84 to 89.*

## COMMENTARY

1. Effective enforcement is an essential element of any civil process that purports to vindicate rights and obligations.[6] It serves two fundamental purposes.
2. First, an effective enforcement system is a means to promote the effective shadow of the law.[7] That individuals and businesses understand that, just as the dispute resolution system is easily accessible, enforcement is cost-effective, efficient, and easily accessible is a means to promote dispute prevention and consensual resolution prior to judgment.[8] Secondly, where proceedings result in a final judgment, enforcement ensures that the substantive law is given effect. It is thus an additional means to ensure the general access right is practical and effective and not merely a theoretical paper exercise.[9]
3. Specific forms of enforcement may impinge on the substantive rights of third parties. Enforcement against property may, for instance, have an impact on the rights of a judgment debtor's spouse or children.[10] A fair enforcement process is one that respects such rights in so far as they are not over-ridden by the rights of the judgment creditor.[11] By doing so it would provide an additional means to give effect to the finality principle (and proportionality principle) by reducing the prospect that the enforcement process may itself be a source of further proceedings.
4. This Part moves beyond the CPR in one particular way. It does so by incorporating an explicit commitment to, and process for, the promotion of settlement within the enforcement process. This brings it in line with international better practice developments, which recognise settlement as both a practical reality within enforcement generally and as something that can and should properly be facilitated. Its incorporation is also consistent with the general approach taken in this Code to the full integration of consensual settlement into its processes.
5. As with the rest of the Code, enforcement processes are to be provided for and accessible via the court's digital procedure.[12]

[6] J Bentham, *Rationale of Judicial Evidence*, in *The Works of Jeremy Bentham* (*Rationale*) (ed Bowring) (1843) (William Tait, Edinburgh) at 7; J Bentham, *The Works of Jeremy Bentham* (ed Bowring) (1843) (William Tait, Edinburgh) (1843) 9, *The Constitutional Code* at 25–26.

[7] Part 1, r 1.

[8] Part 1, r 8.

[9] *Tolstoy-Miloslavksy v The United Kingdom* (1995) 20 EHRR 442; *Hornsby v Greece* (1997) 24 EHRR 250 at [40].

[10] See the effect of '*Mesher orders*', which postpone enforcement orders for the sale of property until children reach the age of 18 years old or conclude their education: *Mesher v Mesher* [1980] 1 All ER 126; S Allinson, *Enforcement of a Judgment* (Sweet & Maxwell, 2016) at 148–151.

[11] *Austin-Fell v Austin-Fell* [1990] Fam 172.

[12] Enforcement and Information hearings may therefore be held as non-physical or hybrid hearings: Part 14; *Just Digital Marketplace Ltd v High Court Enforcement Officers Association* [2021] EWHC 15 (QB).

## RULE 2.—GENERAL

**(1) A judgment creditor is the party, including representative party, entitled to enforce a court order or judgment.**

**(2) In representative proceedings, a represented party may apply for permission to enforce a court order or judgment. Where permission is granted they are a judgment creditor for the purposes of enforcement.**

**(3) A judgment debtor is the party against whom a court order or judgment can be enforced.**

**(4) In this Part 'order' or 'judgment' includes reference to orders and judgments of the courts and tribunals, including those relating to the costs of litigation. It also includes reference to any order or judgment that is enforceable further to any international treaty or agreement.**

**(5) An order to pay money into court cannot be enforced under this Part, except by sequestration proceedings.**

*Sources: ALI/UNIDROIT Principles, principle 29; ALI/UNIDROIT Reporters' Study, r 35; ELI-UNIDROIT Model Rules, r 227(3); CPR rr 19.8(4)(b), 46.2, 70.1, 70.4.*

## COMMENTARY

1. Rule 2 defines judgment creditors and judgment debtors; the parties who seek to enforce orders or judgments and those parties or non-parties against whom enforcement is sought.[13] There is no principled reason to treat parties and non-parties differently where enforcement of orders or judgments is concerned.[14] The rule further defines 'order' and 'judgment' for the purposes of this Part. The approach here is consistent with that taken by CPR r 70(1).
2. Where representative proceedings take place represented class members are not parties to the proceedings. Ordinarily therefore they would not be able to enforce any order or judgment. They may, however, apply for permission to do so. This may arise where the representative party has failed, or refuses, to take enforcement action (rule 4).
3. Reference to orders or judgments that are enforceable further to an international treaty or agreement serves two purposes.[15] From the perspective of procedural accessibility, it ensures that this rule clearly covers any relevant treaty or agreement. Technical detail concerning such matters can properly be incorporated into the digital procedure under this rule (and see rules 15 and 16). This approach also promotes simplicity as it means the rule will not need to be amended whenever a new treaty or agreement is entered into or an extant one is no longer applicable. Substantively, it ensures that foreign judgments are capable of enforcement under this Code; in this it restates the effect of CPR r 70.1(2)(c) and (ca).

[13] Typically, enforcement against a non-party will arise in respect of non-party costs orders and wasted costs orders.

[14] CPR r 70.4. And see r 2 above.

[15] The United Nations Convention on the Recognition and Enforcement of Foreign Arbitral Awards (New York, 10 June 1958) (The New York Convention), The Convention of 2 July 2019 on the Recognition and Enforcement of Foreign Judgments in Civil or Commercial Matters (The Hague Judgments Convention), The United Nations Convention on International Settlement Agreements Resulting from Mediation (The Singapore Convention).

4. Finally, rule 2(5) makes clear that orders to pay money into court are outside the scope of enforcement, except as they may be enforced through sequestration.[16] Such matters should be enforced through applications for the imposition of sanctions as part of effective dispute management, however sequestration as a form of contempt proceeding may be used to bring pressure to bear on a party to make a payment into court.[17]

## RULE 3.—COURTS OF ENFORCEMENT

**(1) All enforcement proceedings must be issued in the First-tier of the High Court.**
**(2) United Kingdom Supreme Court and Court of Appeal (Civil Division) orders and judgments shall be enforced as if they are judgments of the High Court.**
**(3) Enforcement proceedings shall generally be heard by a judge of the First-tier of the High Court. They may be heard by a judge of the Upper Tier of the High Court where it is in the interests of the administration of justice to do so due to the nature and complexity of the issues involved in enforcement.**

*Sources: Senior Courts Act 1981, s 15(4); County Courts Act 1984, s 76; CPR rr 30.4(3), 70.3, 83.19, CPR PD40B, para 13, PD70A.*

## COMMENTARY

1. The current approach to enforcement is spread across the High Court and the County Court. Broadly parallel enforcement mechanisms exist in both courts, with judgments of the Court of Appeal and UK Supreme Court enforced as judgments of the High Court.[18] This approach was heavily criticised by the Briggs Review in 2015 and 2016. It recommended legislative reform, which would have resulted in enforcement being the responsibility of a single court.[19] That recommendation has, unfortunately, not been implemented.
2. This Code is predicated upon the long overdue unification of the County and High Court into a single civil court, albeit one divided into two Tiers (Part 2). Unification of the enforcement process follows from that policy choice. Even if unification were not to take place, there are good reasons to reform enforcement so that a single court is responsible for it. Duplication of process across two courts is inefficient, not least for the court administration that has to run two parallel systems. This inefficiency is compounded by the need to transfer, in some cases, enforcement proceedings between different County Court hearing centres.[20] Furthermore, it is confusing for litigants. They must choose the correct court and/or court hearing centre within which to issue enforcement process. In some cases, proceedings may or must be transferred between courts.[21] Transfer involves what would otherwise be

[16] *Ward v Shakeshaft* 1 Dr & Sm 269; *Pratt v Inman* (1889) 43 Ch D 175 at 177.
[17] See r 14.
[18] Senior Courts Act 1981, s 15(4); *Ager v Ager* [1998] 1 WLR 1074.
[19] M Briggs, *Civil Courts Structure Review—Interim Report* (December 2015) chap 5; M Briggs, *Civil Courts Structure Review—Final Report* (July 2016) at [10.3]–[10.33].
[20] CPR r 70.3; S Allinson (2016) chap 5.
[21] High Court and County Courts Jurisdiction Order 1991 (SI 1991/724) (as amended); CPR r 70.3, PD 70A, r 83.19.

unnecessary time and cost for both courts and parties. The present situation cannot but generate unnecessary and disproportionate cost and delay.

3. This rule gives effect to the Briggs Review's proposal. It introduces a more cost-effective, efficient, and proportionate enforcement process. It provides that the First-tier of the High Court (the successor to the County Court) shall be the court of enforcement. Hence all enforcement proceedings must be issued, administered, and heard in it (rule 3(1)). This is irrespective of which court issued the order to be enforced (rule 3(2) and (3)). Moreover, the new process shall be administered through a streamlined, simple digital procedure; all of which would require significant legislative reform.[22]
4. A residual discretion is provided to enable proceedings to be heard by a judge of the Upper Tier (rule 3(3)). That may be necessary, for instance, where enforcement out of the jurisdiction is involved. In such a circumstance, given the unification of the civil courts, and the use of a single digital procedure within the High Court and Court of Appeal there will be no need to engage in any transfer of proceedings. The Upper Tier judge would simply need to deal with the matter in the First-tier.

## RULE 4.—ENFORCEMENT METHODS

**(1) Enforcement may be executed by one or more enforcement methods. Where more than one method is used, they may be used simultaneously or sequentially.**

**(2) Enforcement may be effected by a judgment creditor against one or more judgment debtors or third parties.**

**(3) The means of enforcement will be effected either by a court enforcement officer or an individual otherwise authorised to effect enforcement.**

**(4) Enforcement may be carried out through**

**(a) a financial payment order, which provides for the payment of a sum of money out of the judgment debtor's earnings, assets, goods, or debts due to them;**

**(b) a control order, which restricts the judgment debtor's use of land, securities, funds in court, dividends and interest, or an interest in a trust. It may be further enforced by way of sale and financial payment order;**

**(c) a possession order, which provides for the recovery of possession of land;**

**(d) receivership, which provides for payment of rents, profits or other money receivable by a custodian who has power to apply those funds to satisfy a money judgment;**

**(e) a punitive order, which provides for committal to prison under the Debtors Act 1869;**

**(f) an order under rule 12 of this Part, which requires a non-party to give effect to a mandatory injunction or which requires specific performance; or**

**(g) via any effective digital method approved by the court.**

**(5) Enforcement by way of a control order or a financial payment order may either be interim or final. An application for an interim order is a without-notice application and will be considered without a hearing.**

**(6) Enforcement may be supported through the application of asset preservation orders made under Part 13 or through a sequestration order under rule 13 of this Part.**

*Sources: ALI/UNIDROIT Principles, principle 29; ALI/UNIDROIT Reporters' Study, r 35; CPR Pts 69, 70, 72, 73, 74, 81, 83, 84, 85, 89; County Court Rules, Ord 28.*

[22] M Briggs (2015) at [10.05].

## COMMENTARY

1. A judgment creditor can utilise a wide-range of enforcement methods. They may use any method provided for by law[23] and may do so sequentially or simultaneously.[24] They may also do so against multiple judgment debtors.[25] The choice of which and how to seek enforcement should be an informed one. The judgment creditor should utilise the method or methods most likely to give effect,[26] in the most economical, efficient, and proportionate manner, to the judgment or order in their favour.
2. Enforcement is not, however, effected by the judgment creditor personally. It will be effected by court enforcement officers or an individual authorised by the court to carry out enforcement. Such authorisation may be provided by the court on a case-by-case basis[27] or by the government further to regulations, as is currently the case.[28]
3. Where an order or judgment in representative proceedings is to be enforced, ordinarily the representative party is the judgment creditor. The decision whether and how to enforce will be theirs to take (Part 11, rule 27(3) and (4)). Exceptionally, the court may permit a class member to act as the judgment creditor by substituting them for the representative party (rule 2(2); Part 11, rule 28(5)). This may occur where it is evident that the representative party is unable to or does not intend to commence or complete enforcement proceedings and the court is satisfied that it is appropriate to substitute the class member as representative party. Valid circumstances for substitution could arise where, for instance, the representative party is unable to commence or complete enforcement proceedings due to a lack of funds and the class member has sufficient funds to do so, or the representative party has no good reason for failing to commence or complete such proceedings.
4. Rule 4(4) identifies the seven main forms of enforcement method available under this Part.[29] They encompass the methods available under the CPR. Financial payment orders, so-called because they make provision for the payment of money judgments, replace orders for the attachment of goods (CPR Pts 73, 89), the delivery and control of goods (Tribunal, Courts and Enforcement Act 2007, s 62, Sch 13; CPR Pts 83, 84; warrants or writs of control), third party debt orders (CPR Pt 72), and administration orders (County Courts Act 1984, s 112;[30] CCR Ord 39). Possession orders succeed orders for the possession of land (CPR Pt 83; warrants or writs of possession). Control orders replace charging orders, stop orders, and stop notices (CPR Pt 73). Financial payment and control orders may be interim or final.[31]

[23] Enforcement methods can be found in the Debtors Acts 1869 and 1878, the County Courts Act 1984, s 119, the Tribunals, Courts and Enforcement Act 2007, and (which is outside the scope of this Code) Insolvency legislation.

[24] CPR r 70.2.

[25] *Land Credit Company of Ireland v Lord Fermoy, ex p Munster* (1869–70) LR 5 Ch App 323.

[26] *Re Overseas Aviation Engineering (GB) Ltd* [1963] Ch 24 at 39.

[27] Eg where a warrant or writ is issued and that contains the individual's authority to enforce.

[28] Courts Act 2003, Sch 7, para 2; High Court Enforcement Officers Regulations 2004 (SI/2004/400); Tribunals, Courts and Enforcement Act 2007, ss 63 and 64, Sch 12; The Certification of Enforcement Agents Regulations 2014 (SI 2014/421).

[29] Contempt of court may also assist with enforcement where a judgment debtor has failed to obey a court order (Part 11, r 41).

[30] Tribunals, Courts and Enforcement Act 2007, s 106 is intended to bring into effect a new scheme for administration orders. It has not, as yet, been brought into force.

[31] As with interim injunctions, interim financial payment and control orders are intended to promote the proper administration of justice pending final determination of the issue, and particularly in respect of enforcement the rights of any interested third party.

Receivership encompasses receivership and equitable receivership (Senior Courts Act 1981, s 37(1); County Courts Act 1984, ss 38 and 107; CPR Pt 69). Punitive orders replace judgment summons (Debtors Act 1869, s 5; CCR Ord 28). Rule 4(4) describes the nature of these orders. Any specific process required to give effect to them shall be set out in the digital procedure.

5. Enforcement may also, and will likely increasingly, take place via digital methods. This will be particularly relevant where enforcement is to be effected against crypto or digital assets. As rightly identified by the Union Internationale des Huissiers de Justice, determination of the most effective and efficient form of enforcement may, in future, be facilitated through the use of AI.[32]
6. Finally, rule 4(6) provides a cross-reference to Part 13. It does so to draw attention to the fact that the enforcement process may be supported by the grant of an asset preservation order, which will preserve a judgment debtor's assets from dissipation or removal from the jurisdiction (Part 13, rules 4 and 7). It thus helps to ensure that enforcement is not frustrated. Enforcement is also supported by sequestration orders under rule 13, which replace writs of sequestration (CPR Pt 70).

## RULE 5.—SETTLEMENT WITHIN ENFORCEMENT

**(1) A judgment creditor and judgment debtor may enter into a co-operative enforcement process at any stage during enforcement proceedings.**
**(2) A co-operative enforcement process is one carried out through negotiation or mediation between the judgment creditor and debtor, the aim of which is to enable the parties to reach agreement on the nature, amount, or timing of enforcement.**
**(3) The court shall provide access to its enforcement negotiation or mediation scheme, which may be facilitated through the use of AI, as part of the co-operative enforcement process.**
**(4) The court enforcement negotiation or mediation scheme shall provide e-negotiation, e-mediation or telephone-facilitated negotiation or mediation. This shall be provided by the court or a third party.**

*Sources: Recommendation Rec (2003)17 of the Committee of Ministers of the Council of Europe to member states on enforcement; International Union of Judicial Officers, Global Code of Enforcement.*

## COMMENTARY

1. It is not uncommon that a judgment creditor is often willing (grudgingly or otherwise) to compromise their claim even at the enforcement stage. Enforcement may be costly and time-consuming. The judgment debtor may not be able to satisfy the judgment debt in full. Equally, it may be necessary to agree a payment schedule either for the whole or part-satisfaction of the judgment debt. Such considerations may lead a judgment creditor to seek to compromise satisfaction of their judgment. Practical reality may mean that consensual settlement of a judgment debt may be preferable

[32] International Union of Judicial Officers, *Global Code of Digital Enforcement* (2021).

in so far as it enables the judgment creditor to receive some financial value for their judgment. Equally, a judgment debtor may seek to compromise a judgment debt where they are unable to satisfy it in full. For both parties, enforcement generating further cost and time may result in the incurrence of further irrecoverable cost (from the judgment creditor's perspective) and wasted cost (from the judgment debtor's perspective). Questions of protracted enforcement cost and time, from the court's perspective, also raise considerations of systemic proportionality and the need to ensure that all proceedings are able to secure access to a proportionate share of the court's resources.

2. To reflect this practical reality and promote the means by which parties can take active steps with the court's assistance to reach settlement within enforcement, this rule introduces an explicit enforcement settlement process, ie 'co-operative enforcement'.[33] Co-operative because the parties, further to their duty to co-operate, can seek to work together collaboratively to negotiate or mediate a settlement of what would otherwise be subject to enforcement. Moreover, this rule is included to give expression to the general incorporation of consensual settlement as an integral part of this Code.

3. This rule also seeks to ensure that English and Welsh civil procedure keeps proper pace with the development of enforcement, and its inclusion of settlement processes, as better practice in other jurisdictions. This wider development can be seen in several ways. Implicitly, it is apparent from the promotion of the general principle of party co-operation in enforcement to ensure that it is carried out as efficiently and effectively as possible, which the State is required to facilitate. The promotion of this idea is set out within the Council of Europe's Recommendation Rec (2003) 17, article III(1)(c).[34] The Council of Europe here can be seen to be relying on what, in this Code, are the economy, efficiency and proportionality, and dispute management principles to promote settlement. The implicit promotion of consensual settlement contained within the Council of Europe Recommendation is now also given explicit effect in article 10 of the International Union of Judicial Officers' *Global Code of Enforcement*.[35] This mandates the availability of consensual settlement processes, at a judgment debtor's request.

4. Where a co-operative enforcement process commences, the court may stay enforcement proceedings pending its conclusion. As with any other form of negotiation or mediation, the co-operative process does not require settlement to occur; it is a forum to promote settlement not mandate it. Further to the AI principle negotiation or mediation process may be facilitated by AI. It may, otherwise, be facilitated consistently with the approach to negotiation and mediation taken during the dispute management process.

[33] The CPR does not provide an explicit process for the settlement of enforcement proceedings. It is, arguably, implicit in CPR rr 1.1 and 1.4(2)(e).

[34] It is thus consistent with the economy, efficiency and proportionality and co-operation principles; European Commission for the Efficiency of Justice (CEPEJ), *Guidelines for a better implementation of the existing recommendation concerning family mediation and mediation in civil matters* (2007).

[35] International Union of Judicial Officers, *Global Code of Enforcement* (May 2015) <https://www.uihj.com/downloads-2/global-code-of-enforcement/>.

# SECTION 2: PROCESS TO ASSIST ENFORCEMENT

## RULE 6.—APPLICATION FOR INFORMATION FROM JUDGMENT DEBTOR

**(1) A judgment creditor may make an application for information.**

**(2) An application for information does not form part of enforcement proceedings. It is an aid to effective enforcement. It is intended to enable a judgment creditor to assess whether, and if so how best, to seek enforcement.**

**(3) An application may be granted where it contains the following information**

**(a) the judgment debtor's name and address;**

**(b) where the judgment debtor is a legal person, the name and address of a natural person who is one of its officers;**

**(c) details of the judgment or order entered against the judgment debtor relevant to the application, including the date on which it became enforceable;**

**(d) details of any relevant information sought;**

**(e) details of any documents the judgment debtor is to produce at the Information Hearing;**

**(f) if the judgment creditor wishes the Information Hearing to be conducted by a judge and, if so, why.**

**(4) Relevant information is information concerning prospective or pending enforcement proceedings. It may include information concerning the judgment debtor's finances, assets (both those within and outside the jurisdiction), financial obligations and any other matter relevant to enforcement.**

**(5) An application may be granted by a court officer. Where the court officer considers that the application may not comply with the requirements of rule 6(3), they may refer the application to a judge.**[36]

**(6) Where an application is granted, the court will order the judgment debtor to provide relevant information, including documents in their control, at an Information Hearing. Where the judgment debtor is a legal person, information shall be provided by one of its officers.**

**(7) The Information Hearing will, generally, be conducted before a court officer. Exceptionally where there are compelling reasons, it may be conducted before a judge. The judgment creditor may attend where the hearing is conducted by a court officer. They must attend when it is conducted by a judge.**

**(8) The judgment debtor shall give their evidence orally and on oath at the Information Hearing. They shall be questioned by the court officer or judge. Where the judgment creditor attends the hearing, they may cross-examine the judgment debtor.**

**(9) Except for the reasonable travel expenses of any person required to attend an Information Hearing to provide evidence, which are payable by the judgment creditor, the costs of an application for information shall be paid by the judgment debtor. Such costs shall be tariff costs.**

**(10) Failure to comply with an order to attend an Information Hearing may be subject to proceedings for contempt of court.**

*Sources: CPR Pt 71.*

[36] *White Son & Pill v Stebbings* [1911] 2 KB 418, where a judgment is not enforceable, enforcement proceedings cannot be commenced.

## COMMENTARY

1. When a party to proceedings obtains judgment in their favour, they may not be in a position to determine properly whether they wish to commence enforcement proceedings should it be necessary. They may not know the judgment debtor's financial circumstances. They may not know what assets they have or where they are located. Enforcement against an impecunious judgment debtor or one whose main assets are outside the jurisdiction may be a fruitless exercise. If not fruitless, it may be time-consuming and expensive. This rule, which substantively restates CPR Pt 71, enables a judgment creditor to apply to the court to secure information from the judgment debtor to enable them to form a reasoned decision whether to pursue enforcement through one of the methods provided for in rule 4.
2. The process is intended to be a simple,[37] speedy and inexpensive means to secure all relevant information necessary to enable the judgment creditor to assess their enforcement options.[38] The judgment creditor is thus required to specify in their application the issues on which they require information and any documents required to assist their evaluation of whether to pursue enforcement.[39]
3. The Information Hearing, where the judgment debtor[40] will be questioned on the issues raised in the application and required to produce relevant documents that are in their control,[41] will ordinarily be conducted by a court officer. It may be conducted by a judge on request. A judge will only accede to such a request where there is a compelling reason for doing so,[42] eg the judgment debtor has a history of non-compliance with court orders, is unlikely to respond to questions put by a court officer, or the judgment creditor intends to attend the hearing to cross-examine the judgment debtor.
4. The hearing is intended to be a robust inquisitorial process.[43] That in itself is intended to minimise the cost and time involved. Judgment creditors, who choose to attend Information Hearings, may cross-examine the judgment debtor following questioning by the court. To both discourage unnecessary attendance and cross-examination and to maintain the economical and efficient nature of the process, only tariff costs are recoverable by judgment creditors where they attend a hearing.

[37] One aspect of its simplicity here is that rule 6 does not adopt the approach to service of the application taken under CPR r 71.3(1).

[38] *Interpool Ltd v Galani* [1988] QB 738 at 741–743 (information required on assets outside the jurisdiction).

[39] *White Son & Pill v Stebbings* [1911] 2 KB 418 (on the court officer's discretion); *Vale SA v BSG Resources Ltd (In Administration)* [2020] EWHC 2021 (Comm) (general right to the grant of the application).

[40] Ordinarily this will be the judgment debtor themselves. Where the judgment debtor is a legal person, eg a company, the rule provides for a company officer, which includes a former company officer, to attend the hearing: *Societé Générale du Commerce et de L'industrie en France v Johann Maria Farina & Co* [1904] 1 KB 794; *Vitoil SA v Capri Marine Ltd* [2008] EWHC 378 (Comm); [2009] Bus LR 271; the officer in question must, however, be within the jurisdiction at the time the application for an Information Hearing is made: *CIMC Raffles Offshore (Singapore) Pte Ltd v Schahin Holdings SA* [2014] EWHC 1742 (Comm) explaining *Masri v Consolidated Contractors International (UK) Ltd (No 4)* [2009] UKHL 43; [2010] 1 AC 90.

[41] Control is not the same as possession: *North Shore Ventures Ltd v Anstead Holdings Ltd* [2012] EWCA Civ 11; [2012] WTLR 1241.

[42] CPR PD 71, para 2.2.

[43] *Republic of Costa Rica v Strousberg (No 2)* [1880] 16 Ch D 8 at 12–13, '*The examination is not only intended to be an examination, but to be a cross-examination, and that of the severest kind.*'

5. Non-compliance with an order to attend court for an Information Hearing may amount to an interference with the proper administration of justice. Where there is no good reason for non-attendance, it may, therefore, be subject to contempt of court proceedings. Where there is good reason, that ought properly to be communicated to the court before the hearing with an application to adjourn and reschedule the hearing. A refusal or failure to answer questions put at an Information Hearing may also amount to a contempt of court. As with any other form of application, multiple applications for information may be made.

## SECTION 3: GENERAL ENFORCEMENT PROVISIONS

### RULE 7.—STARTING AND COMPLETING ENFORCEMENT PROCEEDINGS

**(1) A judgment creditor may take steps to give effect to any order or judgment by starting enforcement proceedings under this Part.**

**(2) Enforcement proceedings must be commenced within six years of the date of the order or judgment. Thereafter they may be commenced with the court's permission where the judgment creditor demonstrates, in all the circumstances, it is just to do so.**

**(3) The enforcement process is complete when the judgment creditor receives that which they are due under the terms of the court order or judgment.**

*Sources: Limitation Act 1980, s 24; CPR r 83.2.*

### COMMENTARY

1. Enforcement is a choice; an aspect of party autonomy. A judgment creditor may choose whether or not to take steps to enforce any order or judgment in their favour. That can also be said of any settlement agreement, albeit there the means of enforcement will be contractual.
2. Where a party chooses to enforce a judgment two options present themselves. They may seek to bring fresh proceedings based on the judgment.[44] The objective of such proceedings is to obtain a further judgment.[45] The second method is to execute, ie ensure that effect is given to the existing order or judgment. That is done by commencing enforcement proceedings under this Part. Where the judgment creditor chooses to pursue enforcement proceedings, there is a strong presumption that the court will facilitate enforcement.[46] That presumption flows from the court's role in giving effect to the rule of law.[47]
3. Under the CPR the relevant procedural time period for commencing the enforcement process is six years for writs and warrants of control, writs of execution (including writs of possession, writs of delivery, writs of sequestration and writs of fieri facias

[44] Limitation Act 1980, s 24.

[45] *Ridgeway Motors (Isleworth) Ltd v ALTS Ltd* [2005] EWCA Civ 92; [2005] 1 WLR 2871 at [10]–[14] citing *WT Lamb & Sons v Rider* [1948] 2 KB 331.

[46] *Roberts Petroleum v Bernard Kenny Ltd* [1983] 2 AC 192 at 207.

[47] J Bentham, *Rationale*, at 7.

de bonis ecclesiasticis), warrants of delivery and warrants of possession.[48] There is no procedural time period for seeking a third-party debt order or a charging order.[49] A uniform approach is, however, taken in rule 7(2). It requires any form of enforcement proceedings to be commenced within six years of the date of the order or judgment. The general procedural time limit is thus the same as that applicable to bringing proceedings that seek a judgment on the original order or judgment.[50] That time limit may also be extended with the court's permission, as the limitation period for further proceedings may also be extended with the court's permission.[51] The rule also places the onus on the judgment creditor to justify the extension.[52]

4. A uniform approach, which places the onus on the judgment creditor to justify the grant of permission to commence enforcement proceedings after six years have elapsed, is a principled one to take. It is also consistent with the approach taken in the Limitation Act 1980. This is justifiable as both procedural and statutory time limits serve the same purpose. They both promote finality in litigation: that is their function and it is one that does not differ depending on the means of enforcement. They both ensure that a judgment debtor knows with reasonable certainty when they will no longer be troubled by the order or judgment that has been entered against them. A consistent approach across the two mechanisms thus creates a single point in time when judgment debtors are certain as to their obligations.
5. That permission to extent the procedural time limit may only be granted where it is just in all the circumstances ensures that a judgment creditor cannot simply sit on their hands and do nothing to enforce an order or judgment in their favour until after the six-year period has elapsed. There must be good reason to justify an extension of time; particularly strong reasons given finality in litigation and the presumption that enforcement should be effected within the six year period, ie that a judgment creditor should get on with the process of enforcement with alacrity.[53] The reason or reasons explaining the delay given must take the case '*out of the ordinary*' and demonstrate that the grant of permission will further the purposive principle.[54]
6. Finally, rule 7(3) makes explicit that the end point of the enforcement process is when the judgment creditor receives what they are due under the order or judgment enforced. When that occurs the enforcement process (and the proceedings as a whole) will have finally concluded.[55]

[48] CPR r 83.2.

[49] CPR Pts 72, 73; *Fellows v Thornton* [1884] QBD 335; *Patel v Singh* [2002] EWCA Civ 1938; [2003] CPLR 149; *Westacre Investments Inc. (a company incorporated under the laws of Panama) v The State-Owned Company Yugoimport SDPR (also known as Jugoimport-SDPR)* [2008] EWHC 801 (Comm); [2009] 1 All ER (Comm) 780 at [22]–[24].

[50] *National Westminster Bank Plc v Powney* [1991] Ch 339; *Lowlsey v Forbes (T/A LE Design Services)* [1999] 1 AC 329 for consideration of the historic development of the difference between bringing fresh proceedings and taking procedural steps to enforce a judgment; *Ridgeway Motors (Isleworth) Ltd v ALTS Ltd* [2005] EWCA Civ 92; [2005] 1 WLR 2871 at [14].

[51] Limitation Act 1980, s 32.

[52] Note the different approach taken by the CPR: *Westacre Investments Inc (a company incorporated under the laws of Panama) v The State-Owned Company Yugoimport SDPR (also known as Jugoimport-SDPR)* [2008] EWHC 801 (Comm); [2009] 1 All ER (Comm) 780 at [23].

[53] *Patel v Singh* [2002] EWCA Civ 1938; [2003] CPLR 149 at [19].

[54] *Duer v Frazer* [2001] 1 WLR 919; *Patel v Singh* [2002] EWCA Civ 1938; [2003] CPLR 149 at [21]–[22]; *Society of Lloyd's v Longtin* [2005] EWHC 2491 (Comm); [2005] 2 CLC 774 at [23].

[55] *Re Overseas Aviation Engineering (GB) Ltd* [1963] Ch 24 at 39.

## RULE 8.—STAY OF ENFORCEMENT PROCEEDINGS

**The court under its dispute management power may stay processes to assist enforcement and enforcement proceedings either on its own initiative or on application of a party to the proceedings.**

*Sources: Senior Courts Act 1981, s 49(3); County Courts Act 1984, s 88; Tribunals, Courts and Enforcement Act 2007, s 70; CPR rr 3.1(2)(f), 40.8A, 83.7.*

## COMMENTARY

1. The general power to stay proceedings applies to enforcement and enforcement.[56] This rule thus gives specific effect to legislative powers to stay or suspend enforcement of financial payment orders, eg to stay enforcement processes to secure the payment of sums of money,[57] as well as the general statutory power to stay proceedings contained in section 49(3) of the Senior Courts Act 1981.
2. Stays may be issued in a wide range of circumstances. They may be granted, for instance, where it is difficult to enforce a judgment out of the jurisdiction, where the judgment debtor demonstrates a genuine need for time to satisfy the judgment, or to facilitate settlement. They may be granted subject to conditions. As Allinson notes, the imposition of conditions can maintain appropriate pressure, ie incentivise, the judgment debtor to maintain repayment where a repayment schedule has been agreed with the judgment creditor or ordered by the court as part of the stay.[58]

## RULE 9.—EFFECT OF ORDER OR JUDGMENT SUBJECT TO ENFORCEMENT BEING SET ASIDE

**(1) Where an order or judgment is set aside or is otherwise rendered unenforceable any application for information or enforcement proceedings shall stand dismissed unless the court orders otherwise.**

**(2) Costs consequent on the dismissal of the information or enforcement process shall, unless the court orders otherwise, be awarded as follows:**

**(a) where the order or judgment was a regular one, the costs shall be paid by the judgment debtor;**

**(b) where the order or judgment was an irregular one, the costs shall be paid by the judgment creditor.**

*Sources: CPR r 70.6.*

## COMMENTARY

1. Where an order or judgment becomes unenforceable the enforcement process cannot but fall away. In such circumstances there is also no basis on which a party can properly make an application for information (rule 5). This rule gives effect to

[56] In this it goes beyond the CPR; *Sucden Financial Ltd v Fluxo-Cane Overseas Ltd* [2009] EWHC 3555 (QB) at [14].

[57] County Courts Act 1984, s 88; Tribunals, Courts and Enforcement Act 2007, s 70.

[58] S Allinson (2016) at 58.

the consequences of the underlying judgment or order becoming unenforceable through being set aside. It restates the approach set out under CPR r 70.6. Its effect is to dismiss the information or enforcement process, absent an order to the contrary by the court. That the court may order otherwise enables it to stay the information or enforcement process. This may be appropriate where the judgment creditor has or indicates an intention to appeal from the order setting aside the order or judgment that was subject to either processes.

2. Cost allocation, generally, depends upon the basis on which the substantive order or judgment being enforced was set aside. If the order or judgment was properly obtained—it was regular order or judgment—the costs ought to fall upon the judgment debtor. Until the order or judgment was set aside the judgment creditor had a right to receive the fruits of the order or judgment. If the order or judgment was not properly obtained—it was an irregular order or judgment –, such as a default judgment obtained contrary to the requirements set out in Part 15, rule 10(3), the costs should fall on the judgment creditor. Rule 9(2) also maintains the court's general discretion over costs, enabling it to depart from the general approach set out in rules 9(2)(a) and (b) in appropriate circumstances. It may, for instance, be appropriate to order that the costs be costs in the ongoing proceedings and thus fall for determination at the overall conclusion of the dispute or enforcement process.

## RULE 10.—THIRD PARTY CHALLENGE TO ENFORCEMENT

**(1) Where a third party's rights are affected by a possession or control order, they may apply to the court for a remedial order. A remedial order may**
- **(a) set aside the order giving effect to enforcement in so far as it applies to the third party;**
- **(b) direct the delivery-up of any goods or property of the third party that were wrongly made subject to enforcement.**

**(2) Where the court awards costs, the costs of any application for a remedial order, shall be tariff costs to be paid to the third party. The court shall award costs where it is just to do so in all the circumstances.**

*Sources: Tribunals, Courts and Enforcement Act 2007, Sch 12; Taking Control of Goods Regulations 2013 (SI 2013/894); CPR Pt 85.*

## COMMENTARY

1. A judgment creditor who takes possession or control of property to enforce a judgment or order in their favour may only do so in respect of the judgment debtor's property. It is not uncommon, in practice, for a third party's property to become subject to such orders inadvertently, eg because an enforcement officer takes possession or control of a third party's property by mistake when taking possession or control of the judgment debtor's property. In such circumstances, there has been an inadvertent but unlawful interference with the third party's property rights. This rule protects those substantive rights.

2. Where a dispute arises concerning whether property subject to enforcement is a third party's property, it would be expected—consistently with the settlement and co-operation principles—that the third party and judgment creditor would initially attempt to resolve it without resort to court process. The most obvious way for this to be done, as it is now, is for the third party to approach the enforcement officer who executed the enforcement process. Where informal approaches do not resolve the issue, the third party may apply for a remedial order under this rule. Where granted, the court may then order the return of the property to the third party.
3. Any costs awarded shall be tariff costs. They may be awarded where it is just to do so. There may be circumstances where it will not be just to award costs, eg where the third party failed to take any steps to resolve the question of ownership of the property prior to issuing an application for a remedial order.

### RULE 11.—COSTS OF ENFORCEMENT PROCEEDINGS

**The costs of enforcement shall be borne by the judgment debtor. Such costs shall be tariff costs, except where the order or judgment enforced was made in proceedings in which proportionate cost recovery was available.**

*Sources: Courts and Legal Services Act 1990, s 15(3); CPR r 45.8.*

### COMMENTARY

1. Rule 11 requires the judgment debtor to pay the costs of enforcement.[59] A judgment creditor ought not to be out-of-pocket for costs incurred in ensuring compliance by a judgment debtor with orders made against them. As with costs generally, this is subject to the proportionality principle.

## SECTION 4: SPECIFIC PROVISIONS

### RULE 12.—ENFORCEMENT OF MANDATORY INJUNCTION OR ORDER FOR SPECIFIC PERFORMANCE

**(1) The court may direct execution of a mandatory injunction or order for specific performance to be carried out, in so far as it reasonably can, by a person other than the party against whom the injunction or order is made. Any costs incurred by that person, in giving effect to that direction, may be enforced against the judgment debtor.**

**(2) This rule does not affect the court's power to direct a person to execute any conveyance, contract, or other document, or to indorse any negotiable instrument or to exercise its powers relating to contempt of court.**

*Sources: Senior Courts Act 1981, s 39; RSC Ord 45, r 8; CPR r 70.1A.*

[59] It thus does not apply to the costs of Information Hearings, see r 6.

## COMMENTARY

1. This rule restates CPR r 70.1A. It enables the court to secure the enforcement of mandatory injunctions or specific enforcement where the person against whom those orders have been made fails or refuses to comply with them. It does so by providing the means to direct a third party to carry out the injunction or order where they can reasonably do so.
2. The rule thus provides a practical power, additional to the court's contempt powers and its statutory power to direct the execution of conveyances, contracts etc, to secure effective enforcement of orders that require a person subject to them to take positive steps. It may also be used to support the completion of other enforcement processes.

## RULE 13.—SEQUESTRATION

**(1) A judgment creditor may seek permission to issue proceedings to sequestrate the assets of any person (the contemnor) who has failed to comply with a court order or judgment.**
**(2) Permission may be granted where an order or judgment (the underlying order) requires a person to either undertake an act within a specified time or refrain from acting in a specified way and they have wilfully failed to do so.**
**(3) If permission to issue sequestration proceedings is granted the court will appoint sequestrators, nominated by the applicant, to take control of the contemnor's assets, including land.**
**(4) Where sequestration proceedings are brought against a legal person, the court may fine the legal person rather than make a sequestration order.**
**(5) Sequestration remains in force until the contemnor complies with the underlying order.**

*Sources: CPR Pt 83.*

## COMMENTARY

1. Sequestration places the assets of the contemnor in the possession of sequestrators,[60] who are officers of the court. While they owe a duty of care to the contemnor, as owner of the property subject to sequestration,[61] until the contemnor's contempt is discharged or the underlying order is otherwise complied with, they must keep the property in their possession.[62]
2. Sequestration, as a means to compel compliance with a court order may only be carried out with the court's permission (Part 11, rule 41(4)).[63] Permission may be granted where there has been wilful non-compliance with an order of the court,[64]

[60] The County Court's jurisdiction arose under County Court's Act 1984, s 38: *Rose v Laskington Ltd* [1990] 1 QB 562 at 566. Under Part 2 of this Code sequestration would arise solely under the High Court's jurisdiction concerning contempt of court and its inherent jurisdiction.

[61] *Inland Revenue Commissioners v Hoogstraten* [1985] QB 1077.

[62] On the use to which sequestrated assets can be put for the benefit of judgment creditors, S. Allinson (2016) at 487 and following.

[63] *Pratt v Inman* (1889) 43 Ch D 175 at 177; *Re Pollard* [1903] 2 KB 41 at 47.

[64] *Steiner Products Ltd v Willer Steiner Ltd* [1966] 1 WLR 986 at 991; *Webster v Southwark London Borough Council* [1983] QB 698.

such as an order to pay a sum of money or to transfer property to a judgment creditor. Sequestration may also be used to promote payment of a money into court.[65]

3. Where sequestration is pursued against a company or other form of legal person, the court may issue a fine in place of sequestration. This may be particularly pertinent where sequestration would adversely affect innocent third parties.[66]

## SECTION 5: ENFORCEMENT OF ORDERS WITHIN AND OUTSIDE ENGLAND AND WALES

### RULE 14.—ENFORCEMENT OF FOREIGN ORDERS AND JUDGMENTS IN ENGLAND AND WALES

**(1) A judgment creditor may apply to the High Court to enforce an order or judgment made outside the jurisdiction within England and Wales.**

**(2) Where the order or judgment to be enforced was made in Scotland or Northern Ireland, it must first be registered, by application, by the judgment creditor with the High Court under the Civil Jurisdiction and Judgments Act 1982. An application to register a judgment must include the following information**

**(a) the name and address of the judgment creditor and debtor;**

**(b) full details of the judgment to be enforced, and if a money judgment the amount, including any interest, due under the judgment;**

**(c) that the judgment is not subject to a stay or appeal;**

**(d) that the time to seek permission to appeal has expired.**

**(3) Where the order or judgment to be enforced was made in a jurisdiction with which the UK has entered into a reciprocal treaty, it must first be registered by the judgment creditor with the High Court under the terms of relevant legislation. Relevant legislation includes**

**(a) The Administration of Justice Act 1920;**

**(b) The Foreign Judgments (Reciprocal Enforcement) Act 1933;**

**(c) The Civil Jurisdiction and Judgments Act 1982;**

**(d) Article 11 of the Protection Measures Regulation.**

**(4) The application for registration under a reciprocal treaty must contain the following**

**(a) a certified copy of the judgment and a certified translation of it into English or Welsh;**

**(b) the name and address for service within England and Wales of the judgment creditor and debtor;**

**(c) full details of the judgment to be enforced, and if a money judgment the amount, including any interest, due under the judgment; and**

**(d) where the application is made under the 1920 Act, that the judgment to be enforced is not one to which section 9 of that Act or section 5 of the Protection of Trading Interests Act 1980 applies; or**

**(e) where the application is made under the 1933 Act, confirmation that the judgment to be enforced is for a sum of money and that it can be enforced in the jurisdiction that issued the judgment. Where some but not all aspects of**

[65] *Pratt v Inman* (1889) 43 Ch D 175 at 179.

[66] *Steiner Products Ltd v Willer Steiner Ltd* [1966] 1 WLR 986 at 992.

**the judgment can be registered those to be registered must be identified and evidence given in respect of them to demonstrate that they are enforceable in the jurisdiction that issued the judgment. Evidence of the applicable law from that jurisdiction that provides for the payment of interest under the judgment should also be set out; or**

**(f) where the application is brought under the 1982 Act, evidence that the judgment is enforceable in the jurisdiction that issued the judgment and that it had been served on the judgment debtor and, if the judgment to be enforced is a judgment in default, that the judgment debtor was served with the process that commenced the proceedings in which that judgment was given and, where relevant, evidence concerning any legal aid or assistance that the judgment creditor was in receipt of in the jurisdiction in which the proceedings were conducted.**

**(5) Registration may be without-notice to the judgment debtor.**

**(6) Where the High Court registers a judgment, a Registration Order must be served on the judgment debtor. Service is to be effected as if the Registration Order is a case statement. Permission to serve outside the jurisdiction is not required.**

**(7) Upon registration an order or judgment registered is deemed to be an order or judgment of the High Court.**

**(8) Where the order or judgment to be enforced was made in a jurisdiction with which the UK has not entered into a reciprocal treaty, the judgment creditor must commence proceedings, without taking part in pre-dispute management, based on the judgment. Those proceedings may be determined by way of summary judgment.**

*Sources: CPR Pt 74.*

## COMMENTARY

1. This rule deals with the enforcement of orders or judgments issued outside England and Wales within the jurisdiction. The approach taken in CPR Pt 74 is restated. Enforcement may arise in the following three ways.
2. Enforcement of judgments from Scotland and Northern Ireland fall under the provisions of section 18 and schedules 6 and 7 of the Civil Jurisdiction and Judgments Act 1982. This requires a judgment creditor to register the judgment, and thereafter enforce it as a judgment of the High Court, in England and Wales.
3. Enforcement under a reciprocal treaty may be effected further to either section 9 of the Administration of Justice Act 1920, section 2 of the Foreign Judgments (Reciprocal Enforcement) Act 1933, section 4 of the Civil Jurisdiction Act 1982; or article 11 of the Protection Measures Regulation.[67] Rather than adopt the detailed approach taken by the CPR, this rule only sets out essential requirements. Technical matters should be set out in the digital procedure.
4. Finally, where there is no reciprocal treaty in place, the judgment creditor must issue proceedings in England and Wales for enforcement of the judgment. They may do so without taking part in any pre-dispute management, which is otiose. To facilitate the economical, efficient, and proportionate resolution of enforcement, the judgment creditor may apply for summary judgment.

[67] CPR r 74.46. This Regulation continues in force following the UK's withdrawal from the European Union: Mutual Recognition of Protection Measures in Civil Matters (Amendment) (EU) Exit) Regulations 2019 (SI 2019/493).

5. As with other orders, where registration is granted, application may be made to set them aside.[68]

## RULE 15.—ENFORCEMENT OF ORDERS AND JUDGMENTS OUTSIDE ENGLAND AND WALES

**(1) A judgment creditor may apply for an order or judgment made in England and Wales to be enforced outside the jurisdiction.**

**(2) To enforce an order or judgment in Scotland or Northern Ireland, a judgment creditor must apply to the High Court for a certified copy of the order or judgment to be enforced. If a certified copy is issued by the court, it may then be registered by the judgment creditor in Scotland or Northern Ireland.**

**(3) To enforce an order or judgment in a jurisdiction with which the UK has entered into a reciprocal treaty, the judgment creditor must apply, under the terms of relevant legislation, to the court which made the judgment for a certified copy of the order or judgment to be enforced. Relevant legislation includes**

**(a) The Administration of Justice Act 1920;**

**(b) The Foreign Judgments (Reciprocal Enforcement) Act 1933;**

**(c) The Civil Jurisdiction and Judgments Act 1982.**

**(4) An application for a certified copy may be without-notice to the judgment debtor. Where the High Court issues a certified copy, the judgment creditor may register it outside the jurisdiction according to the terms of the relevant legislation.**

**(5) An application for a certified copy to enforce in Scotland, Northern Ireland or under a reciprocal treaty must contain the following information**

**(a) the name and address for service of the judgment creditor and debtor;**

**(b) full details of the judgment to be enforced, and if a money judgment the amount, including any interest, due under the judgment;**

**(c) that the judgment is not subject to a stay or appeal;**

**(d) that the time to seek permission to appeal has expired; and**

**(e) where the application is made under a reciprocal treaty the statements of case, evidence of service of the particulars of claim on the defendant in the proceedings, and details of any applicable legal aid funding.**

**(6) Where the order or judgment is to be enforced in a jurisdiction with which the UK has not entered into a reciprocal treaty, the judgment creditor may**

**(a) seek to enforce the order or judgment within the jurisdiction, where possible;**

**(b) seek enforcement in that jurisdiction according to its laws; or**

**(c) refer the order or judgment to an arbitral centre in England and Wales to transform the order or judgment into an arbitral award and, consequently, seek enforcement of that award under the New York Convention 1958.**

**(7) A judgment creditor may only refer the order or judgment to an arbitral centre, and commence arbitral proceedings, where**

**(a) the order or judgment is for payment of a monetary sum; and**

**(b) the parties to the proceedings have agreed to refer any dispute concerning any final order or judgment in the proceedings to arbitration.**

*Sources: CPR Pt 74.*

[68] CPR r 74.7.

## COMMENTARY

1. This rule complements rule 15. Just as orders and judgments from outside England and Wales may need to be enforced in the jurisdiction, those from England and Wales may need to be enforced in other jurisdictions. With the ever-increasing development of e-commerce, there is likely to be an increasing need for effective enforcement against judgment debtors who are outside England and Wales. Enforcement out of the jurisdiction may arise in the following three ways.
2. First, it may be done in Scotland and Northern Ireland. This is governed by the Civil Jurisdiction and Judgments Act 1982, particularly its schedule 2. The approach to this taken in CPR rr.74.17 and 74.18 is straightforward and is restated here in rules 15(2) and (4). It requires a judgment creditor to apply for a certified copy of the order or judgment to be enforced, which if issued may then be registered and enforced in Scotland or Northern Ireland.
3. Secondly, it may be achieved via a reciprocal treaty further to either section 10 of the Administration of Justice Act 1920, section 10 of the Foreign Judgments (Reciprocal Enforcement) Act 1933, or section 12 of the Civil Jurisdiction Act 1982. The CPR sets out detailed provisions concerning the approach to such applications in CPR rr 74.12 and 74.13. The essential procedural requirements derived from those rules are set out in rule 15(3) and (4). Allinson notes that under the CPR the question can potentially arise whether a judgment is capable of enforcement under a reciprocal treaty where the judgment to be enforced was issued by the County Court.[69] This potential problem does not arise under this Code as all orders and judgments issued are either judgments of the High Court or enforceable as such (rule 3).
4. Finally, where there is no reciprocal enforcement treaty a judgment debtor has three options. They may try to enforce the judgment in England and Wales. They may seek to enforce the judgment within the specific jurisdiction according to its enforcement regime. Or, they may seek to take advantage of an innovative aspect of this Code. Rule 15(5)(c) incorporates into English and Welsh procedure an approach to enforcement pioneered in Dubai.[70] This permits, where parties to proceedings have agreed to it, an order or judgment to be transformed into an arbitral award, which can then be enforced outside the jurisdiction under the New York Convention 1958. This may be particularly useful where the initial proceedings concerned a commercial dispute between contract parties. The utility of this rule, given the relative ease of enforcement or arbitral awards under the Convention, may promote the development of standard contractual clauses in commercial contracts making provision for use of this procedure.

[69] S Allinson (2016) at 214.

[70] M Hwang, 'Commercial Courts and International Arbitration—Competitors or Partners?' (2015) 31 Arbitration International 193, at 203 reprinted in M Hwang, *Selected Essays on Dispute Resolution* (SIAC, 2018) at 55–56.

# PART 17

# APPEALS

## SECTION 1: GENERAL

1. English and Welsh civil justice has provided a generally available appellate process since the creation of the Court of Appeal in 1873. This Part maintains that position and is functionally equivalent to CPR Pt 52. It thus contains a semi-discrete code of procedure as the appellate process is separate from, and to a large extent mirrors, first instance process. It sets out rules that are specific to appellate procedure and those where a differential approach from that at first instance needs to be taken at the appellate level. Where it does not provide a specific rule, such as in respect of appellate dispute management, the rules set out in other Parts of the Code apply.

### RULE 1.—SCOPE AND PURPOSE

**(1) This Part concerns the appeal process in the High Court and Court of Appeal (Civil Division). Its principal purposes are, by giving effect to the appellate principle, to protect the private interest of parties and the public interest.**

**(1) The private interest of parties refers to their interest in securing a final judgment as free from judicial error as reasonably possible. The public interest refers to the need to secure**

**(a) the proper administration of justice and public confidence in it;**

**(b) consistency in the law and its application; and**

**(c) authoritative statements of the law.**

**(2) Taken together the private and public interest in appeals justify its operation as an exception to the finality principle. They do so through promoting a fair and proportionate process and, particularly, the accuracy, settlement, and general access principles.**

*Sources: ALI/UNIDROIT Principles, principle 27; ALI/UNIDROIT Reporters' Study, r 33; ELI-UNIDROIT Model Rules, Part IX; CPR Pt 52.*

### COMMENTARY

1. Appellate process promotes the private interest in securing a fair procedure and accurate results in individual proceedings. It also promotes the broader public interest, which encompasses securing the proper administration of justice and public confidence in it. It seeks to achieve both the private and public interest by helping to promote good standards in dispute management and adjudication in first instance proceedings: appellate accountability, via the appeal process, is a vehicle

*A Model Civil Procedure Code for England and Wales*. John Sorabji, Oxford University Press. © John Sorabji 2024.
DOI: 10.1093/oso/9780192848680.003.0018

to promote judicial competence and diligence.[1] The public interest goes further than that, however. It also encompasses the promotion of consistency in the law and its application through appellate courts correcting judicial error or inconsistent applications of the law by first instance courts. Linked to this, the public interest further includes the giving of authoritative statements of the law: correcting it; developing it; and, in certain cases, creating it through novel departures. In this, it promotes preventive and consensual justice as much as it does adjudicative justice.

2. Each one of the public purposes is only capable of being secured through the achievement of appeal's private purpose. Underpinning this, therefore, is another example of how English and Welsh civil procedure is shaped primarily by the party autonomy and adversarial principles as parties determine whether to bring and defend appeals, determine their scope, and which arguments to advance. The extent to which appellate courts can secure appeal's public purposes is, consequently, limited by the way in which parties seek to give effect to its private purpose. Except on those rare occasions where an academic or hypothetical appeal is permitted to go forward, the appeal process is not one that gives greater precedence to its public purposes.
3. In identifying the scope of the rule's private purpose as being to secure '*a final judgment as free from judicial error as reasonably possible*' rule 1(2) takes a pragmatic approach. An idealist position would have been to state the private purpose as being to secure a final judgment free from judicial error. The rule, however, recognises that no justice system can guarantee that its decisions are free from error.[2] The appeal process, like that at first instance, thus adopts an approach and rules that seek to minimise procedural error.[3] In doing so it also reflects the balance struck between adjudicative accuracy in individual proceedings and the need to secure an economic, efficient and, most importantly, proportionate process. It thus balances accuracy's achievement against these other procedural principles in limiting access to and the scope of the appellate process.

## RULE 2.—GENERAL

**In this part 'court' includes reference to any tribunal or other decision-maker from which a right of appeal lies to the High Court or Court of Appeal.**

*Sources: Senior Courts Act 1981, ss 15, 18; Tribunals, Courts and Enforcement Act 2007, s 13; CPR r 52.1, PD52B, PD52C, PD52D, and PD52E.*

## COMMENTARY

1. Appeals may arise from civil proceedings. They may lie from the High Court's First-tier to its Upper Tier and from the High Court to the Court of Appeal.[4] Statutory

[1] Part 1, r 23.

[2] J Rawls, *A Theory of Justice* (Harvard, 1999, rev) at 75; L Solum, 'Procedural Justice' (2004) 78 Southern California Law Review 181; A Zuckerman, 'The Second Great English Reform of Civil Justice: A Triumph of Hope over Experience' (2000) 1 Hibernian LJ 178 at 179; L Wittgenstein, *Philosophical Investigations* (Blackwells, 1989), s 265.

[3] J Nash and F Pardo, 'An Empirical Investigation into Appellate Structure and the Perceived Quality of Appellate Review' (2008) 61(6) Vanderbilt Law Review 1746.

[4] In analogous manner to appeals from the County Court to the High Court and from the High Court to the County Court under the CPR: CPR PD52B, 52C, and 52D.

provisions may also provide for appeals to lie from other courts[5] and tribunals[6] to these courts. Legislation may also provide for appeals from non-judicial bodies, such as housing authorities or the Solicitors Disciplinary Tribunal to the High Court.[7] All such appeals, consistently with the approach under the CPR and as provided for in primary legislation, are governed by the rules in this Part of the Code.

## RULE 3.—THE COURT'S POWERS ON APPEAL

**(1) An appellate court when hearing an appeal from an order or a judgment of another court has, subject to any legislation to the contrary, all the powers of that other court.**
**(2) Subject to any legislative restriction, an appellate court may hear an appeal on a point of fact or a point of law. It may do so in the absence of any party to the appeal.**
**(3) At the conclusion of an appeal, the appellate court may**
**(a) allow the appeal in whole or in part;**
**(b) affirm, set aside, or vary the order or judgment subject to the appeal;**
**(c) make any award, including awards of costs or interest, or order that the court whose order or judgment was subject to appeal could make;**
**(d) refer, either before the appeal is held or after it is determined, the matter back to the court whose order or judgment was subject to the appeal for consideration or reconsideration;**
**(e) direct a new trial be held;**
**(f) dismiss the appeal in whole or in part;**
**(g) make any consequential order necessary to do justice on the appeal.**
**(4) The appellate court will allow an appeal where it determines that the order or judgment subject to the appeal**
**(a) was wrong because no reasonable court could have made such an order or reached such a judgment; or**
**(b) was subject to a serious procedural irregularity that rendered it unjust.**
**(5) An appellate court may dismiss an appeal by adopting the reasoning set out in the judgment under appeal.**

*Sources: ELI-UNIDROIT Model Rules, rr 170, 171, 175, 176; Senior Courts Act 1981, ss 15(3), 19; CPR r 52.20, 52.21(3).*

## COMMENTARY

1. This rule codifies the powers available to an appellate court when dealing with an appeal. It also sets out the test for determining the outcome of an appeal. Unlike appeals to the UK Supreme Court and some civilian legal systems, where forms of appellate review (cassation appeals) are limited to points of law,[8] appeals may be brought on questions of fact or of law. Specific legislation may, however, limit the scope of particular appeals to questions of law only.[9]

[5] The Access to Justice Act 1999 (Destination of Appeals) (Family Proceedings) (Amendment) Order 2014 (SI 2014/602) (as amended by The Access to Justice Act 1999 (Destination of Appeals) (Family Proceedings) (Amendment) Order 2016 (SI/2016 891)); Mental Capacity Act 2005, s 53.
[6] Tribunals, Courts and Enforcement Act 2007, s 13; Employment Tribunals Act 1996, s 37.
[7] Housing Act 1996, s 204; Solicitors Act 1974, s 49; CPR PD52D.
[8] J Nieva-Fenoll, 'The English Origin of French Cassation' (2022) 41(1) CJQ 78.
[9] Arbitration Act 1996, s 69.

2. Appellate courts have full power to determine any appeal,[10] including wide powers to make any necessary order consequent on the appeal to enable them to do justice on the appeal.[11] To facilitate this they have all the powers of the court whose judgment is subject to appeal in addition to their own powers as appellate courts. If that were not the case, an appellate court would have to refer an appeal back to the court below for it to manage appellate disputes, consider and determine applications concerning appeals, and fully and finally dispose of proceedings. If, for instance, an appeal was brought from a first instance court's exercise of discretion, if the appellate court could not exercise that discretion itself on a successful appeal, it would have to refer the matter back for re-determination. Such an approach is neither efficient nor proportionate. This is not to say that in all cases it will be appropriate for an appellate court to exercise its jurisdiction. It may be necessary, having allowed an appeal, for the matter to be referred back to the first instance court for re-determination or rehearing.
3. The power to refer a matter back to the first instance court may be exercised before or after an appeal takes place. The latter use will be more common, however referral back prior to the appeal may be beneficial where, for instance, there are issues that could be ruled on contingently pending the outcome of the appeal.[12] For instance, it may be that if an appeal succeeds further findings may be needed to enable an award of damages to be made. Such findings may not have been made at first instance due to the judge dismissing the claim. If an appeal court grants permission to appeal, there is at least a real prospect that the dismissal of the damages claim may be set aside and an award of damages made. If the trial judge heard the evidence on the point and is in a position to rule on it, it may be in the interests of procedural economy, efficiency, and proportionality for those findings to be made and placed before the Court of Appeal so that it could make any necessary damages award should the appeal succeed.[13] The alternative would be to refer the matter back to the trial judge after the appeal court has finally determined the matter. That may be the better option where evidence was not taken on the point during the trial. The power may otherwise be used to refer a matter back for reconsideration by the court below consequent upon the appellate court setting aside the judgment or order subject to appeal.[14]
4. The most commonly used of an appellate court's powers will be those to allow or dismiss an appeal, either in whole or in part. Consequently, an appellate court may affirm, set aside, or vary any order or judgment under appeal. It may also need to refer the matter back for a fresh trial to be heard. Where, for instance, it held that a trial was tainted by judicial bias or that significant evidence had not been properly taken into account, the most appropriate course of action would be to refer the matter back for a fresh trial before either a new judge or the same judge who dealt with the original trial, as appropriate.[15] In neither case should an appellate court conduct a fresh trial; it is neither equipped to do so nor would such an approach provide the parties with adequate access to the first instance and appellate process. Trial by an appellate court would rob the parties of the same level of access to the appellate process as afforded to other litigants, contrary to the procedural equality principle.

[10] Senior Courts Act 1981, ss 15(3), 19.
[11] *SP v Hewson* [2020] EWHC 499 (QB).
[12] P Coulson (ed), *Civil Procedure 2024* (Sweet & Maxwell, 2024) Vol 1 at 52.20.2.
[13] *Hicks v Russell Jones & Walker* [2007] EWCA Civ 844; [2009] 1 WLR 487.
[14] *MVF3 APS v Bestnet Europe Ltd* [2011] EWHC 477 (Ch).
[15] *Serafin v Malkiewicz* [2020] UKSC 23; [2020] 1 WLR 2455 at [49].

5. Where settlement is concerned, it forms as integral a part of appellate proceedings as it does first instance proceedings and enforcement. An appellate court is under the same duties to manage appeals so as to promote settlement as parties are to co-operate with each other and the court in seeking to secure settlement. Due to the more limited nature of appellate proceedings, the appeal process does not contain a discrete settlement management track. The digital appellate procedure ought, however, to have built into it similar settlement prompts as those present in first instance procedure. Equally, it should provide access to the same range of consensual settlement processes as are available at first instance.
6. Appeals may succeed where the appellate court concludes that the judgment or order subject to the appeal was wrong because it was substantively wrong. It may also do so where it concludes the judgment or order was unjust because it involved a serious procedural irregularity.[16] How these tests are applied depends upon the supervisory role that appellate courts have over lower courts, which flows from the private and public purposes of appeals.[17] Given this role appellate courts should not ordinarily defer to the decisions or reasoning of first instance courts.[18] There may be situations, however, where a degree of deference is required and an appellate court should be cautious in concluding that the lower court's decision was substantively wrong, ie outside the bounds of reasonable decision-making. This is particularly the case where the lower court's decision concerns the exercise of a discretion. In such situations, the lower court judge will be better placed to weigh up both the application of the purposive principle to the circumstances of the individual case and the balance to be struck between any of the specific factors relevant to the discretion.[19] Similar considerations arise where an appeal concerns an issue of fact that called for an assessment of oral witness evidence, particularly their credibility.[20] Where, for instance, the credibility of witnesses is in issue on an appeal, the appellate court should not conclude the judgment or order under appeal was wrong unless the first instance court's decision on the point cannot be reasonably justified.[21] A similar approach should be taken to appeals concerning the evaluation of evidence.[22] Less deference is, however, called for when the appellate court is in as good a position as the lower court to determine matters, eg where the assessment of documentary evidence is concerned.[23]
7. The question of whether to allow an appeal on the 'unjust' ground goes further than whether the judgment is wrong. The two grounds for allowing an appeal, while they may overlap, are distinct. A judgment may be entirely justifiable such that it could not be said to be wrong in so far as its substance is concerned. It could, however, properly be set aside and an appeal allowed on the basis that it is otherwise unjust to allow it to stand. Where, for instance, the judgment was reached by a fundamentally flawed or tainted procedure, eg one party was deliberately and improperly not given notice of the trial, was wrongly not permitted to give evidence,[24] or was led

[16] *Tanfern Ltd v Cameron-MacDonald* [2000] 1 WLR 1311 at [31]–[33].
[17] R Noble and D Schiff, 'The Right to Appeal and Workable Systems of Justice' (2002) 65 MLR 676.
[18] A Zuckerman, *Zuckerman on Civil Procedure—Principles of Practice* (Sweet & Maxwell, 2021) at 1213.
[19] *Stuart v Goldberg* [2008] EWCA Civ 2; [2008] 1 WLR 823 at [76]–[81].
[20] *Assicurazioni Generali SpA v Arab Insurance Group* [2002] EWCA Civ 1642; [2003] 1 WLR 577 at [6]–[23].
[21] *Chen v Ng (BVI)* [2017] UKPC 27; [2018] 1 P & CR DG2 at [54]–[55].
[22] *Re Sprintroom Ltd* [2019] EWCA Civ 932; [2019] BCC 1031 at [72]–[78].
[23] *Haringey London Borough Council v Ahmed* [2017] EWCA Civ 1861 at [29]–[31].
[24] *Labrouche v Frey* [2012] EWCA Civ 881; [2012] 1 WLR 3160.

to believe by the judge that the proceedings had been determined prior to their making any submissions,[25] it would be unjust to let it stand even if the decision was, in its substance correct. Not to allow an appeal in such circumstances would tend to undermine public confidence in the proper administration of justice. It would also undermine the appellate court's supervisory jurisdiction, one aim of which is to promote high standards in first instance adjudication.[26]

8. An appeal court may proceed to hear and determine, including dismiss, an appeal in the absence of one of the parties.[27] The jurisdiction ought, however, to be exercised sparingly further to the purposive principle. It should, generally, only be exercised where it is apparent that the absent party had effective notice of the hearing date. In determining whether to proceed in the absence of a party, the court should consider any reasons for their absence, any application for an adjournment, and whether it is in a proper position to determine the matter in the party's absence. Questions of proportionality, particularly systemic proportionality, will need to be considered in assessing whether or not to adjourn a hearing where a party is absent.[28] Equally, the question whether hearing an appeal in the absence of a party is in the public interest will need to be considered. If, for instance, the issue in the appeal is one of wider public interest it may be beneficial for the court to proceed in the party's absence if it has full written argument such as to enable it to consider the issue properly. On the other hand, if it is unable to obtain full argument except via the attendance of both parties, the general public interest may require the court to either adjourn the hearing or determine it without dealing with that issue in substantive terms.[29]

9. Finally, the rule codifies an approach, which is commonly accepted in European civil procedure and has been endorsed by the European Court of Human Rights as consistent with article 6 of the European Convention on Human Rights.[30] It is underused in England and Wales. It specifies that when an appeal court dismisses an appeal it can do so by adopting the reasons given in the judgment under appeal.[31] As long as the appeal court makes it clear that it has given proper consideration to the issues raised on appeal and that it is rejecting them on the basis that it affirms the reasoning of the judge below, there is nothing objectionable about this approach. It enables parties and the public to understand why the appeal has been dismissed and it promotes an efficient and proportionate use of judicial resources, as time is not unnecessarily expended in restating the findings in the judgment under appeal in new words.

## RULE 4.—RIGHT OF APPEAL

**(1) A party and, exceptionally, a non-party to proceedings has, except as restricted by legislation or this Code, a right to appeal from any order made in those proceedings**

[25] *Roberts v Earley* [2006] EWCA Civ 1064 at [23].

[26] Part 1, r 23.

[27] *In Leave.EU Group Ltd v Information Commissioner* [2022] EWCA Civ 1099; [2022] 1 WLR 1909 at [18]–[21]; *General Medical Council v Theodoropolous (Rev 1)* [2017] EWHC 1984 (Admin).

[28] *In Leave.EU Group Ltd v Information Commissioner* [2022] EWCA Civ 1099; [2022] 1 WLR 1909 at [21].

[29] *General Medical Council v Adeogou* [2016] EWCA Civ 162; [2016] 1 WLR 3867; *In Leave.EU Group Ltd v Information Commissioner* [2022] EWCA Civ 1099; [2022] 1 WLR 1909 at [19]–[21].

[30] *Garcia Ruiz v Spain* (2001) 31 EHRR 589 at [26]; *North Range Shipping Ltd v Seatrans Shipping Corp* [2002] EWCA Civ 405; [2002] 1 WLR 2397 at [20].

[31] *Re Portsmouth Football Club* [2013] EWCA Civ 916; [2014] 1 All ER 12.

**or a finding in a judgment. A non-party's right to appeal only arises where their rights are affected by an order or finding in a judgment.**

**(2) In representative proceedings only the parties have a right of appeal.**

**(3) A party or non-party may, at any time, waive their right to appeal. Waiver must be fully informed and express.**

**(4) Except as provided by legislation, the right to appeal may only be exercised with the court's permission. Permission to bring a second appeal may only be granted by the Court of Appeal (Civil Division). A second appeal is an appeal from any decision that was itself made on a first appeal.**

**(5) A decision to grant or refuse permission to appeal cannot be subject to appeal.**

**(6) An appeal hearing is by way of review and not rehearing, except where a rehearing is required by legislation or by order of the court where it is in the interests of justice.**

*Sources: Council of Europe Recommendation No R (95) 5, Introduction and Improvement of the functioning of appeal systems and procedures in civil and commercial cases, chapter 1, art 3(b); ALI/UNIDROIT Principles, principle 27; ALI/UNIDROIT Reporters' Study, r 33; ELI-UNIDROIT Model Rules, rr 153, 154, 166, 167, 172, 173; Administration of Justice Act 1960, s 13; Access to Justice Act 1999, s 54(4); CPR r 52.21(1).*

## COMMENTARY

1. This rule concerns the right of appeal. It articulates the basic principle that parties to proceedings have a right to appeal from any order or any finding in a judgment. There is, conversely, no right to appeal from the reasoning that lies behind any finding within a judgment. A successful party cannot, therefore, appeal from an order or judgment in their favour in order to challenge the judge's reasoning. The right to appeal is a right to challenge decisions that determine rights and obligations against a party.[32]
2. The right to appeal is not limited to parties to proceedings. The Court of Appeal has acknowledged that the outcome of proceedings may have an impact on the rights of non-parties. Judgments, for instance, may include adverse comment on witnesses, which effect their rights guaranteed by the European Convention on Human Rights.[33] Orders may also affect other substantive rights.[34] In such situations, non-parties are afforded, exceptionally, a right of appeal. They are provided this right both to give effect to their substantive rights and also, further to the concentration principle, to ensure that all rights are capable of resolution within a single set of proceedings. Where representative proceedings are pursued, however, only the representative party may bring or defend appeals. Represented class members may not exercise a non-party right of appeal. If they were to do so they would undermine the rationale of representative proceedings.
3. The right to appeal is subject to party autonomy. It can, therefore, be waived by a party or non-party to proceedings.[35] Most obviously, it can be waived simply by not being exercised. Parties may, however, wish to expressly waive the right of appeal.

[32] P Coulson (ed) (2024) Vol 1 at 52.0.6.

[33] *George Wimpey UK Ltd v Tewkesbury BC* [2008] EWCA Civ 12; [2008] 1 WLR 1649.

[34] *Re W (A child) (Care Proceedings: Non Party Appeal)* [2016] EWCA Civ 1140; [2017] 1 WLR 2415; *Popely v Ayton Ltd* [2022] EWHC 3217 (Ch).

[35] ELI-UNIDROIT Model Rules, r 154.

They may, for instance, seek to do so contractually before a dispute arises or after a dispute has arisen. Such an agreement may be entered into to promote economical and proportionate dispute resolution by confining any dispute to first instance proceedings.[36] Waiver is, however, subject to court approval. Approval is required to ensure it is fully informed and express. It may be given straightforwardly during the initial dispute management process when proceedings commence through the parties seeking dispute management directions on the point.

4. The right of appeal is not unfettered, except where, as in the case of appeals from committals for contempt where an individual's liberty is at stake,[37] legislation provides otherwise. Exercise of the right to appeal, whether a first or second appeal,[38] is thus generally subject to the court granting permission to appeal.[39] The permission requirement acts as an effective filter the aim of which is to ensure that parties do not expend their, their opponent's, and the court's time and resources challenging orders or judgments that could not even arguably be said to be wrongly decided. A permission filter thus promotes the effective, economical, and proportionate distribution of party and court resources. It is also justified as neither the private interest in adjudicative accuracy nor the public interest in promoting confidence in the administration of justice are engaged where there is no arguable case for saying that a first instance judgment or order was wrongly determined or was otherwise unjust.[40]
5. From a broader perspective, if there were no means to limit the right to appeal, there would be a real risk that first instance proceedings would become no more than a dress rehearsal; that parties would use them to test their arguments with the appeal stage becoming the phase of proceedings where they set out their final and fully considered arguments and evidence. It would turn appeal proceedings into an ersatz form of first instance proceedings, which may equally lead the public to view first instance proceedings as generally being decided wrongly to the detriment of public confidence in the administration of justice.[41] Were this to happen there would be a significant expansion of the use of an appellate court's resources, while effectively wasting the first instance court's time and resources. It would also increase appellate delay as appellate courts tend to have fewer judges than first instance courts and would thus not be able to cope with a level of appeal hearings equivalent to hearings dealt with by first instance courts.[42] Such increased cost and delay would, inevitably, call into question public confidence in the administration of justice. Increased cost may equally lead to respondents having to abandon their claims for financial reasons or settle appeals at an undervalue. Increased delay may itself, for no good reason, also postpone and be a device for postponing compliance with, and enforcement of, first instance judgments. It would thus also be contrary to procedural equality; a generally unfettered right of appeal might thus adversely

[36] Arbitration Act 1996, s 69.

[37] Administration of Justice Act 1960, s 13.

[38] *Reddy v The General Medical Council* [2012] EWCA Civ 310 at [13]–[19].

[39] Council of Europe Recommendation No R (95) 5, *Introduction and Improvement of the functioning of appeal systems and procedures in civil and commercial cases*, chapter 1, art 3(b).

[40] *Colley v Council for Licensed Conveyancers* [2001] EWCA Civ 1137 at [31]; *Pozzoli Spa v BDMO Spa* [2007] EWCA Civ 588 at [8].

[41] N Andrews, *Principles of Civil Procedure* (Sweet & Maxwell, 1994) at 489.

[42] N Trocker and G. Pailli, *Basic Features of Civil Procedure*, in A DeLuca and A Simoni, *Fundamentals of Italian Law* (Giuffrè, 2014) 175–177.

and unjustifiably affect one party to proceedings to a greater extent than the other party.[43]

6. An unfettered right of appeal would also bring with it further substantive problems. Were there to be a significant number of appeals, the risk would increase that appellate decisions on the same point would be inconsistent. This would undermine certainty in the law, contrary to the public interest in appellate courts giving authoritative statements of the law. It could also lead to more appellate decisions being decided in ignorance of others on the same point, which would lead to the need for further appellate proceedings in other disputes to clarify and correct the law. In turn this could lead to the doctrine of precedent being called into disrepute. Finally, were the appellate process to be too readily accessible it would undermine the principle of finality. Rather than being a limited and carefully constrained exception to that principle, an unfettered right of appeal would run a coach and horses through it.[44]
7. To ensure that the permission to appeal requirement does not itself become the subject of satellite litigation, a grant or refusal of permission to appeal cannot itself be subject to appeal.[45] The grant of permission may, in limited, circumstances be set aside by an appellate court. A refusal of permission to bring a final appeal may, however, be reopened.
8. Finally, this rule gives effect to the approach to appeals taken since the introduction of the CPR: that an appeal is by way of review and not rehearing. Again, this provides a degree of deference to the first instance decision-maker.[46] A rehearing may, however, be ordered where it is in the interests of justice to do so or specific legislation provides for one. A rehearing may be in the interests of justice where there has been a serious procedural irregularity in the proceedings subject to appeal, eg where a party was denied a fair hearing because, for instance, the court refused to hear a party on an issue.[47] Where inadequate or no reasons where given by the first instance court a rehearing may be necessary; a review not being possible.[48]

## RULE 5.—EFFECT OF EXERCISING THE RIGHT OF APPEAL

**(1) The status or enforceability of an order or judgment is not affected by the right of appeal being exercised.**

**(2) A court, on application, may stay the enforcement of an order or judgment or part of an order or judgment**

**(a) until such time as a right of appeal may no longer be exercised; or**

**(b) while a right to appeal is exercised.**

**(3) A stay may be granted where, in all the circumstances, there is a risk of injustice to one or more of the parties to the appeal if a stay is refused.**

[43] R Sharpe, 'Judicial Discretion' [1998] Advocates Society J (Canada) 4 at 8 cited in N Andrews, *English Civil Procedure: Fundamentals of the New Civil Justice System* (OUP, 2003) at 901.

[44] N Andrews (1994) at 489.

[45] Access to Justice Act 1999, s 54(4); *Clark v Perks* [2001] 1 WLR 525.

[46] *Tanfern Ltd v Cameron-MacDonald* [2000] 1 WLR 1311 at [31]; *Assicurazioni Generali SpA v Arab Insurance Group* [2002] EWCA Civ 1642; [2003] 1 WLR 577; *Dupont de Nemours (EI) & Co v ST Dupont* [2003] EWCA Civ 1368; [2006] 1 WLR 2793 at [97].

[47] *Audergon v La Baguette Ltd* [2002] EWCA Civ 10; [2002] CP Rep 27 at [83].

[48] *Ansari v Puffin Investment Co Ltd* [2002] EWHC 1243 (QB); [2002] CPLR 257.

**(4) Where a stay application has been refused by the court, further applications for a stay may only be brought where there is a material change in circumstance or where the basis on which the original application was refused was obviously mistaken.**

*Sources: Council of Europe Recommendation No R (95) 5, Introduction and Improvement of the functioning of appeal systems and procedures in civil and commercial cases, chapter 1, art 4 (c); ALI/UNIDROIT Reporters' Study, r 33.2; ELI-UNIDROIT Model Rules, r 162; CPR rr 3.1(2)(f), 52.16.*

## COMMENTARY

1. Judgments and orders are generally enforceable from the date on which they are given, or otherwise ordered by the court. Except as provided by legislation,[49] neither an application for permission to appeal nor the grant of permission effects the status or enforceability of any judgment or order. A party in whose favour judgment has been given may, ordinarily, therefore take steps to enforce it where an application for permission to appeal or an appeal is pending. This is because until and unless an appeal succeeds, the party in whose favour judgment was given has a valid and enforceable right.[50]
2. Where a party enforces a judgment or order pending an appeal and the appeal succeeds, the effect of enforcement will inevitably however have to be set aside. This may require repayment of damages paid, return of property, the lifting of a charge or release of security over property. In some cases, it may be difficult, expensive, or time-consuming to undo the enforcement process. In other, more extreme cases, it may not be possible to do so, eg where the respondent to the appeal dissipates damages paid further to a judgment that was later subject to a successful appeal.[51] It may, therefore, be in the interests of justice for the effect of a judgment or order to be suspended pending the outcome of an application for permission to appeal or an appeal. This rule thus codifies the common law jurisdiction to impose a stay on enforcement to achieve that end.[52]
3. The applicable test for the grant of a stay is well-established. It requires the court to determine, by reference to all the circumstances of the case, if there is a '*risk of injustice to one or other or both parties if it grants or refuses a stay*'.[53] Injustice to an appellant may arise if enforcement pending the outcome of the appeal may not be capable of being reversed. Injustice to the respondent may arise where an appeal may enable the appellant to take steps to avoid enforcement. In assessing the risk of injustice, where the relative balance between the appellant and defendant is difficult to determine, the court may properly consider the appeal's prospects of success: the greater the prospects, the greater the balance would fall in favour of granting a stay and vice versa. It is the risk of injustice and the need to redress that, which justifies the court displacing the general rule and placing a temporary restriction on the respondent's substantive right to enforce the judgment or order subject to the appeal process.[54]

[49] Asylum and Immigration Act 1993, s 9.

[50] A Zuckerman (2021) at 1307.

[51] ELI-UNIDROIT Model Rules, r 162, comment 2; *Department for Environment, Food and Rural Affairs v Downs* [2009] EWCA Civ 257 at [9].

[52] *Bibby v Partap* [1996] 1 WLR 931 at 934.

[53] *Hammond Suddards Solicitors v Agrichem International Holdings Ltd* [2001] EWCA Civ 2065; [2002] CP Rep 21 at [22]; *Mahtani v Sippy* [2013] EWCA Civ 1820 at [13]–[14].

[54] *Leicester Circuits Ltd v Coates Brothers Plc* [2002] EWCA Civ 474 at [12]–[13].

Moreover, as with the rationale underpinning interim injunctions, where there is a risk of injustice, the grant of a stay protects the integrity of the administration of justice. Here it does so through protecting the integrity of the appellate process pending its conclusion by ensuring that any judgment or order made at the end of that process can be enforced effectively. In this way, the power to stay enforcement can be seen as giving effect to a fair process, further to the purposive principle, through helping to ensure the general access right and enforcement principles are given practical effect and are not frustrated by enforcement or non-enforcement, as applicable, during the appellate process.

4. The rule also codifies the approach taken to repeated applications for stays made during the appellate process. Thus, where an application for a stay of enforcement is refused any further application for one may only be made if there has been either a material change in circumstance since the first, failed, application or some obvious mistake was made on the first application.[55] Both limbs of the test reduce the prospect that repeated applications would needlessly and disproportionately expend the court and parties' resources. The first limb enables justice to be done by enabling the court to take account of a change in circumstances, which if material, would justify a different outcome. The second limb also does so by enabling the court to correct an adjudicative error. Both limbs thus promote adjudicative accuracy as much as they do proportionality.

## SECTION 2: PERMISSION TO APPEAL AND TRANSFER OF APPEALS

### RULE 6.—TEST FOR THE GRANT OF PERMISSION TO BRING A FIRST APPEAL

**(1) A first appeal is an appeal from an order or judgment given in first instance proceedings.**
**(2) Permission to bring a first appeal may only be granted where**
**(a) the appeal would have a real prospect of success on the merits; or**
**(b) there is another compelling reason for permission to be granted.**
**(3) Permission may be refused where an appeal process would, in all the circumstances, be a disproportionate use of the parties' or court's resources.**

*Sources: Council of Europe Recommendation No R (95) 5, Introduction and Improvement of the functioning of appeal systems and procedures in civil and commercial cases, art 5; ELI-UNIDROIT Model Rules, r 166; CPR r 52.6.*

### COMMENTARY

1. Permission to bring a first appeal, that is an appeal from an order or judgment made by a first instance court, is subject to a relatively low threshold test. It requires the

[55] *Hall v Elia* [2016] EWHC 1023 (Ch) at [12]–[18] citing *Thevarajah v Riordan* [2015] UKSC 78; [2016] 1 WLR 76 and *Papanicola v Humphreys* [2005] All ER 418 at [35].

appellant to demonstrate that the proposed appeal has a real prospect of success.[56] It must show that there is a genuine case that the matter subject to the proposed appeal was wrongly decided and thus inconsistent with the accuracy principle. This test focuses primarily on the private interest in appeals, ie their corrective function. Through focusing on that the test gives effect to the public interest in promoting the proper administration of justice and confidence on it.

2. The second, and alternative, basis on which permission may be granted is that there is a compelling reason to do so. This limb of the test can be relied upon where an appeal cannot be said to have a real prospect of success. It can, therefore, be relied upon when a judgment or order challenged may have resulted from a serious procedural irregularity, albeit one that does not necessarily call into question the merits of the decision made. It thus enables justice to be seen to be done by enabling an appellate court to correct a procedural defect that would otherwise leave the losing party and the public with the reasonable belief that the decision had not been the product of a fair first instance process. Thus permission to appeal can be given where the public interest in maintaining the proper administration of justice, and public confidence in it, is in issue.[57] Equally, permission may be granted to enable an appellate court to clarify or develop the law where, for instance, there are conflicting first instance decisions on the point in issue albeit the fact of the conflict does not, itself, give rise to an appeal having a real prospect of success.[58]
3. The CPR does not restrict access to first appeals other than through the test restated here.[59] The Civil Justice Council has, however, recommended that there ought to be a restricted right of appeal in very small claims. It has suggested that permission in such cases should only be granted where, the threshold test for a first or second appeal is met, and the appeal concerns either a serious procedural irregularity or a mistake of law.[60] This rule adopts a similar approach, albeit one that does not restrict appeals from very low value claims. It rather provides that permission to appeal may be refused where access to the appellate process would be a disproportionate use of the parties' or the courts' resources. This would enable an appellate court to consider whether the public interest function of appeals justifies the grant of permission to appeal where the intrinsic value of the claim for relief is very low. It would therefore achieve the Civil Justice Council's aim without adopting a blanket restriction on appeals that may be brought from very low value claims. In that way it strikes a more effective balance between the private interest, the public interest, and the need to ensure systemic proportionality in the appellate process.

## RULE 7.—TEST FOR THE GRANT OF PERMISSION TO BRING A SECOND APPEAL

**(1) Permission to bring a second appeal may only be granted by the Court of Appeal. Permission granted by any other court is a nullity and of no effect.**
**(2) Permission to bring a second appeal may only be granted where the appeal**

[56] *Tanfern Ltd v Cameron-MacDonald* [2000] 1 WLR 1311 at [21]; *R (A Child)* [2019] EWCA Civ 895 at [29]–[31].
[57] *Smith v Cosworth* [1997] 1 WLR 1538.
[58] *Shared network Services Ltd v Nextiroane UK Ltd* [2012] EWCA Civ 1171.
[59] CPR r 52.6.
[60] Civil Justice Council, *The Resolution of Small Claims – Final Report* (January 2022) at 35.

(a) **raises an important point of principle or practice; or**

(b) **there is another compelling reason for permission to be granted. A compelling reason will not generally arise unless the prospects of success of the appeal are very high.**

(3) **Permission may be refused where an appeal process would, in all the circumstances, be a disproportionate use of the parties' and court's resources.**

*Sources: Council of Europe Recommendation No R (95) 5, Introduction and Improvement of the functioning of appeal systems and procedures in civil and commercial cases, art 5; ELI-UNIDROIT Model Rules, r 172; CPR r 52.7.*

## COMMENTARY

1. Permission to bring a second appeal, that is one brought from an appeal judgment, is focused firmly on the public interest functions of the appellate process. Such appeals are only capable of being heard in the Court of Appeal and permission can only be granted by that court. If another court purports to give permission to bring a second appeal that decision is a nullity.[61] The general aim of the second appeal test is to limit second appeals to matters that concern the public interest in appeals and, in that way, help focus the Court of Appeal's limited resources on those cases that as a consequence ought properly be considered by it.[62] The appeal test thus seeks to give effect to the proportionality principle, and particularly systemic proportionality, through limiting access to the Court of Appeal.
2. Focus on the public interest underscores the first limb of the second appeal test. It requires a second appeal to concern matters that go beyond the immediate interests of the parties. Rule 7(1)(a) differs, however, from the approach taken under CPR r 52.7(2), which requires, in addition to the second appeal raising an important point of principle or practice, that it has a real prospect of success. This additional criterion, introduced in 2016, is otiose. If a second appeal raises an important point of principle or practice, it is difficult to conceive of how it could not properly be said to also have a real prospect of success. If it did not, the issue would not stand in need of clarification or development. Even if it could be said that an important issue did not have a real prospect of success, the introduction of this first appeal test into second appeals is unprincipled. Second appeals focus on the public interest function of appeals, not the private interest. A real prospect of success test focuses on the private interest, ie on correcting arguable adjudicative error for the benefit of the parties. The private interest is a secondary consideration at the second appeal stage. It is only relevant in so far as it promotes the public interest in the proper administration of justice and confidence in it. The test here therefore maintains the focus on the public interest and does not seek to cut it down by reference to the first appeal test and its focus on the private interest of litigants.
3. The second limb of the test mirrors, albeit by way of a narrower test, the second limb of the first appeal test. It does so by giving effect to the requirement, acknowledged by the Court of Appeal in *Uphill v BRB (Residuary) Ltd* (2005),[63] that generally for

[61] Access to Justice Act 1999, s 55; *Clark (Inspector of Taxes) v Perks* [2001] 1 WLR 17 at [16].

[62] *Tanfern Ltd v Cameron-MacDonald* [2000] 1 WLR 1311; J Bowman, *Review of the Court of Appeal—Report to the Lord Chancellor* (HMSO, 1997) at 23–26.

[63] *Uphill v BRB (Residuary) Ltd* [2005] EWCA Civ 60; [2005] 1 WLR 2070 at [24].

there to be a compelling reason to grant a second appeal there must be, at least, very high prospects of success. The merits can properly be taken account of here as this limb places greater weight on the public interest in maintaining confidence in the judiciary, and hence the need to secure the private interest. Exceptionally, permission may be granted where the prospects of success are not that high, not least where the first appeal was the first time when the proceedings were considered by a civil court.[64] This residuary power may be relied upon where there was a serious procedural irregularity in the first appeal that would render it unfair. A lack of fair process, such as an appeal judge failing to exercise their appellate authority appropriately,[65] may not give rise a very high prospect of success. Nevertheless, if there were to have been a fundamental lack of a fair process, that may justify the grant of permission on its own.

4. Given the public interest focus of second appeals it will rarely be the case that they will be disproportionate. Rule 7(3) provides a safety valve applicable to those exceptional cases where it would be disproportionate for the parties to pursue a second appeal.

## RULE 8.—PERMISSION TO BRING AN ACADEMIC OR HYPOTHETICAL APPEAL

**(1) The appeal process does not generally involve the determination of academic or hypothetical issues.**

**(2) Permission to appeal may only, exceptionally, be given to bring an appeal on an academic or hypothetical issue where the first or second appeal test for the grant of permission to appeal is satisfied and**

**(a) the issue is one of general public importance and can be fully argued on appeal or the appeal court is otherwise able to determine it;**

**(b) the grant of permission will further the purposive principle; and**

**(c) the issue cannot reasonably be determined otherwise.**

## COMMENTARY

1. As a general principle, courts will only hear appeals where there is a live dispute between parties.[66] Generally, if parties wish to obtain authoritative guidance they should do so through proceedings against a party where there is a live dispute. Where there is no dispute, if a court were to give judgment it would simply be '*expressing its view on a legal conundrum*'.[67]

2. There are, however, exceptions to the general principle, which are justified by reference to the purposive principle and, particularly the economy, efficiency, and proportionality principles.[68] An academic or hypothetical appeal may not promote the private interest of the parties to proceedings given there is no live dispute

[64] *Cramp v Hastings BC* [2005] EWCA Civ 1005; [2005] 4 ALL ER 1014 at [64]–[67].

[65] *esure Insurance Ltd v Direct Line Insurance Plc* [2008] EWCA Civ 842; [2009] Bus LR 438.

[66] *Ainsley v Millington* [1987] 1 WLR 379 at 381.

[67] *Sun Life Assurance Co of Canada v Jervis* [1944] AC 111 at 113–114.

[68] A Zuckerman (2021) at 1300.

between them, however, such an appeal could be heard in a similar manner to the ability of courts, under Part 7, rule 5, to hear proceedings where there is no live dispute between the parties. Where, for instance, an academic or hypothetical appeal concerned an issue that was relevant to other proceedings that involved a live dispute, or where it involved a point of public or private law that would have widespread general effect,[69] the public interest could justify a departure from the general principle.[70] It could do this by helping to sharpen the shadow of law. Clarification or development of the law could, for instance, provide a sounder basis for individuals to understand their legal rights and obligations. It could thus help to promote preventive and consensual justice's achievement. Again, that would not only help secure benefits to parties and potential parties to proceedings through promoting dispute avoidance or early settlement, but it would also promote systemic proportionality by reducing the number of potential proceedings brought before the civil courts.

3. To give effect to both the general principle and its exception, this rule codifies the approach adopted under the CPR, but not given expression in it. It requires an academic or hypothetical issue on appeal to be one that engages the wider public interest, including the purposive principle. It also requires the issue to be subject to fully argued submissions either by both parties to the proceedings, by the appellant and a properly interested third party, by properly interested third parties who take opposing positions on the issue under appeal, or by reference to, for instance, written submissions from the proceedings at first instance or on the first appeal. Furthering the purposive principle will also require consideration of whether a respondent can be indemnified in costs by the appellant in circumstances where the latter but not the former would benefit from any determination of the academic or hypothetical issue. In other words, whether it is necessary to compensate them for taking an active part in the appeal to enable the issues to be fully argued. Permission will also only be granted if there is no other reasonable alternative that would enable the court to resolve the issue on the proposed appeal.[71] Given the difference between the likely wider impact of decisions in private and public law disputes, the grant of permission to appeal will be more exceptional in the former.[72]
4. Care needs to be taken where this jurisdiction is concerned. Too great a willingness to hear and determine such appeals would tend to result in appellate courts expending too great a share of their limited resources on academic or hypothetical disputes to the detriment of parties whose appeals concern a live dispute. Those latter cases ought, generally, to take precedence where access to the court's resources is concerned as they further both the private interests of the parties and the wider public interest.

[69] *Bowman v Fels* [2005] EWCA Civ 226; [2005] 1 WLR 3083 at [12]–[13].

[70] *National Coal Board v Ridgeway* [1987] 3 All ER 582; *R (MD (Afghanistan)) v Secretary of State for the Home Department* [2012] EWCA Civ 194; [2012] 1 WLR 2422; *Al-Rawi v The Security Service* [2011] UKSC 34; [2012] 1 AC 531.

[71] *Bowman v Fels* [2005] EWCA Civ 226; [2005] 1 WLR 3083 at [13]; *Rolls-Royce plc v Unite the Union* [2009] EWCA Civ 387; [2010] 1 WLR 318; *Hutcheson v Popdog Ltd* [2011] EWCA Civ 1580; [2012] 1 WLR 782 at [13], [15], and [27]; Part 7, r 5.

[72] *Gawlor v Raetigg* [2007] EWCA Civ 1560 at [36]–[37].

## RULE 9.—TRANSFER OF PERMISSION TO APPEAL OR APPEAL TO THE COURT OF APPEAL

**(1) The High Court may transfer, either on its own initiative or on application, an application for permission to bring a first appeal or a first appeal to the Court of Appeal. Any such transfer must be confirmed by the Court of Appeal. Where the Court of Appeal declines to accept the transfer, the application for permission to appeal or appeal will be remitted back to the High Court.**

**(2) The Court of Appeal may, either on its own initiative, on application, or referral by the court that would otherwise have jurisdiction, direct that an appeal be transferred to it from the High Court.**

**(3) No application for permission to appeal or appeal may be transferred to the Court of Appeal unless it**

**(a) raises an important point of principle or practice; or**

**(b) there is another compelling reason for the Court of Appeal to hear the appeal.**

**(4) The power under this rule cannot be exercised where permission to appeal has been refused by the High Court.**

*Sources: Access to Justice Act 1999, s 57; CPR r 52.23.*

## COMMENTARY

1. A statutory procedure exists under the Access to Justice Act 1999, which provides the Master of the Rolls with a power to require an appeal that would be heard in another civil court to be heard by the Court of Appeal. A comparable power is provided to the High Court, which enables it to direct the transfer of an application for permission to appeal or an appeal that it would hear to the Court of Appeal. This rule consolidates the two powers. It also codifies the restriction, acknowledged by the Court of Appeal, that the power to transfer an application for permission to appeal or appeal cannot be exercised where the High Court has refused permission to appeal.[73]
2. The rule differs from the approach taken by the Access to Justice Act 1999. Rather than the Master of the Rolls directing the transfer of an appeal to the Court of Appeal, the power is vested in the Court of Appeal itself. It thereby renders that power consistent with the Court of Appeal's jurisdiction to confirm, or not, transfers to it effected by the High Court, which both CPR r 52.23(2) and this rule provide. This variation is intended to promote administrative efficiency as it enables all Court of Appeal judges to make such directions.
3. The transfer power should only be used rarely or exceptionally.[74] A compelling reason for transferring an appeal to the Court of Appeal may arise '*(1) where there appear to be conflicting authorities requiring resolution by the Court of Appeal; (2) in relation to points of practice or procedure where there is no guidance at present and the point is of significant importance for the practice or procedure of the courts; (3) where the issue is one of general principle and importance in the development of the substantive law; or (4) the issue is one where there are a number of appeals on*

[73] *7E Communications Ltd v Vertex Antennentechnik GmbH* [2007] EWCA Civ 140; [2007] 1 WLR 2175 at [13].

[74] *Clark (Inspector of Taxes) v Perks* [2001] 1 WLR 17 at [9].

*similar points so as to suggest that a theme or trend is developing which the Court of Appeal needs to consider.'*[75]

4. The rationale underpinning each of these examples is to promote both the efficient and proportionate use of court and party resources and the wider public interest. It facilitates the former by minimising the number of appeal stages to resolve the issue at hand. Where the latter is concerned, it facilitates early clarification or development of the law. This obviously helps the immediate parties achieve an accurate determination of their dispute without having to go through an intermediate appeal before the High Court. It also provides benefits for the public generally. Through its clarificatory or developmental effect on the law it helps promote dispute prevention and, where necessary, early consensual resolution of disputes. Where the issue on appeal is a procedural one, as the Court of Appeal has the primary role for developing procedural law and its interpretation,[76] this is particularly important: early definitive guidance helps promote the effective administration and management of civil proceedings generally. Use of the power in respect of procedural matters can also, therefore, be seen to promote the purposive principle.

## RULE 10.—APPEALS TO THE UNITED KINGDOM SUPREME COURT

**(1) Subject to any legislative restriction, the Court of Appeal may grant permission to appeal from its own orders or judgments to the United Kingdom Supreme Court.**
**(2) When considering whether to grant permission to appeal, the Court of Appeal must apply the same test for the grant of permission that the United Kingdom Supreme Court would apply to an application for permission to appeal.**
**(3) An appeal, where legislation permits, may be transferred by the High Court to the United Kingdom Supreme Court.**

*Sources: Administration of Justice Act 1969, Part II; Supreme Court Practice Direction 3, para 3.3.3.*

## COMMENTARY

1. The United Kingdom is constituted of three separate legal jurisdictions: England and Wales; Scotland; and Northern Ireland. Each jurisdiction has its own, independent, civil justice systems. This Code, like the CPR and its predecessors, applies to England and Wales only.[77] The United Kingdom Supreme Court sits outside those three legal jurisdictions. It is not, therefore, a court in England and Wales and is consequently subject to its own procedural rules: The Supreme Court Rules 2009 and their associated Practice Directions.[78]
2. Civil proceedings from any of the three UK legal jurisdictions may be appealed to the UK Supreme Court.[79] Permission to appeal to it from England and Wales can only

[75] H Brooke, D di Mambro, L di Mambro, D Gladwell, B Keith, *Manual of Civil Appeals* (Tottel, 2nd edn, 2008) at 119 per Lord Woolf MR.

[76] *Callery v Gray* [2002] UKHL 28; [2002] WLR 2000 at [17].

[77] Part 1, r 1(1).

[78] SI 2009/1603.

[79] Constitutional Reform Act 2005, ss 40(1), (2), and (6) and Access to Justice Act 1999, s 54(4); Supreme Court Practice Direction 1, paras 1.2.7 and 1.2.21.

be granted by the Court of Appeal or UK Supreme Court itself.[80] An application for permission to appeal must be made to the former court first. That requirement is not, however, set out in the CPR, which does not in fact make any provision for appeals to the UK Supreme Court. It is, however, set out in the Supreme Court Rules.[81] The CPR also does not specify the nature of the test for the grant of permission to appeal to the UK Supreme Court. Supreme Court Practice Direction 3, para 3.3.3 does so. It provides that permission may only be granted where the proposed appeal raises an '*arguable point of law of general public importance ...* '[82] The Court of Appeal, as a matter of practice and logic, applies the same test when it considers whether to grant permission to appeal to the UK Supreme Court. Rule 10(2) incorporates by reference the test for the grant of permission to appeal applied by the UK Supreme Court. In that way it makes the test more transparent while respecting the fact that it sits outside the Code's jurisdiction. Any appellate digital procedure should straightforwardly provide a link to the relevant Supreme Court Practice Direction, which would facilitate further transparency. It should also facilitate the digital transfer of the matter to the UK Supreme Court's digital procedure.

3. This rule also acknowledges that, exceptionally, appeals may be transferred from the High Court direct to the UK Supreme Court; a so-called 'leapfrog appeal'.[83] The procedure for the grant of permission to appeal in such matters is set out in the Administration of Justice Act 1969. It provides that permission to proceed direct to the UK Supreme Court may be granted if the High Court certifies that the proposed appeal raises a point of law of general public importance and either that: the point concerns a matter of statutory construction that has been fully argued before it; it is one where there is prior binding Court of Appeal or Supreme Court authority; or, alternatively the point of law raises a matter of national importance or consideration. The result of such an appeal should also be of such significance that it warranted adjudication by the UK Supreme Court and the benefits of such adjudication outweighed prior Court of Appeal consideration.[84]

4. If the High Court certifies the matter, it is then for the UK Supreme Court to consider if permission should be granted.[85] Again, the digital procedure ought to articulate the relevant threshold requirements for the grant of a certificate from the High Court so that a party may easily be guided through the process for such an application. An application seeking transfer to the UK Supreme Court should typically be made at or after the hand down of the judgment to be subject to the proposed appeal. Again the digital procedure should facilitate transfer to the UK Supreme Court.

5. The rationale for a means to appeal directly to the Supreme Court is based on the economy, efficiency, and proportionality principles. It ensures that parties are not required to fruitlessly expend their and the Court of Appeal's time and resources on appeals that would be more appropriately determined by the Supreme Court. This is particularly pertinent where the Court of Appeal is bound by authority and an appeal to it would be a pointlessly expensive, time-consuming formality that undermined the effective administration and distribution of the Court of Appeal's resources.[86] It

[80] Constitutional Reform Act 2005, s 40(6).

[81] Supreme Court Rules 2009, r 10(2).

[82] Supreme Court Practice Direction 3, para 3.3.3.

[83] Administration of Justice Act 1969, ss 12–16; Supreme Court Practice Direction 1, para 1.2.17.

[84] Administration of Justice Act 1969, s 12(3) and (3A); *Beedel v West Ferry Printers Ltd* [2001] EWCA Civ 400; [2001] CP Rep 83.

[85] Supreme Court Practice Direction 1, para 1.2.17.

[86] *R (Jones) v Ceredigion County Council* [2007] UKHL 24; [2007] 1 WLR 1400 at [19].

also, in those cases where the Court of Appeal is not bound by precedent, enables an issue to be resolved more efficiently and in a more timely manner where there is a need to provide for early, definitive, and authoritative guidance on a point of law: thus promoting the wider public interest in the rule of law, and via that effective dispute prevention, settlement, and adjudicative accuracy.

## SECTION 3: SCOPE OF AN APPEAL

### RULE 11.—SCOPE OF AN APPEAL

**(1) An appeal's scope is defined by the appellant's notice of appeal and any response to it made by a respondent.**
**(2) Neither the appellant nor respondent may rely on matters at an appeal hearing that is not within the scope of the appeal, except with the court's permission. The court may require an application to amend either the notice of appeal or response to be made where an appellant or respondent wishes to rely on such matters.**

*Sources: ELI-UNIDROIT Model Rules, rr 167, 173. Senior Courts Act 1981, s 15.*

### COMMENTARY

1. The notice of appeal and respondent's response are the functional equivalent of case statements and serve the same purpose. They define and inform the court, parties to the appeal, and public of the scope of appellate proceedings. They define the appellate court's jurisdiction.
2. As the notice of appeal and response define the scope of the court's jurisdiction, should either the appellant or respondent wish to go beyond it they will need the court's permission to do so. Such permission should ordinarily only be granted upon an application to amend the notice of appeal or response. In that way, the court, parties, and the public will have a clear understanding of the issues before the court. This is particularly important where appellate proceedings are concerned because of the public interest function of appeals and the need for transparency and accountability to the public where important legal issues of principle or practice are being determined.

### RULE 12.—APPEAL ON A MATTER NOT RAISED AT FIRST INSTANCE OR ON NEW EVIDENCE

**(1) The scope of an appeal is generally limited to the matters raised before and determined by the court whose order or judgment is subject to appeal.**
**(2) An appellate court may permit new matters to be raised on an appeal. It will be cautious in its approach to granting permission for a new matter to be raised.**
**(3) Where the new matter raises a pure question of law, permission will not be granted where the other party**
**(a) does not have sufficient time to deal with the point;**
**(b) has acted to their detriment in reliance on the fact that the point had not been raised earlier; and**
**(c) cannot be compensated in costs.**

**(4) Where the new matter raises a question of fact, permission will not generally be granted**

**(a) where it would require new evidence to be adduced; or**

**(b) had any such new evidence been adduced before the court whose order or judgment is subject to appeal, a different approach to the evidence before that court at trial would have been taken.**

**(5) Where permission is granted to raise a new matter, an appellate court may also permit a party to amend a case statement, notice of appeal or response.**

**(6) An appellate court may also permit an appellant or respondent to rely on evidence in the appeal that was not adduced before the court whose order or judgment is subject to appeal. Permission to adduce such new evidence may be granted where it will further the purposive principle. In determining whether to grant permission the court may consider whether the new evidence**

**(a) could not reasonably have been obtained before trial in the court whose order or judgment is subject to appeal;**

**(b) if adduced, is likely to have an important, albeit not necessarily decisive, influence on the determination of the dispute; and**

**(c) is apparently credible.**

*Sources: ELI-UNIDROIT Model Rules, rr 167; 168, 173; CPR r 52.21.*

## COMMENTARY

1. Appeals are ordinarily limited to the facts and issues contested in the proceedings appealed from. This is an aspect of the concentration principle: parties ought to bring and defend all relevant matters in a single proceeding. It is also an important aspect of the finality principle.[87] Parties ought not, therefore, hold matters back for deployment on an appeal.[88] They should also ensure that, in so far as possible, they properly investigate matters so that they are able to deploy at first instance all the evidence that can properly be adduced. That such an approach also furthers procedural economy, efficiency, and proportionality ought to be self-evident. For these reasons and consistently with appeals being carried out by way of review not rehearing,[89] appeals are, ordinarily, limited to the issues raised and determined by the order or judgment under appeal.

2. It may, however, be necessary for a party to an appeal to raise novel issues on an appeal or seek to adduce new evidence. English and Welsh civil procedure has always permitted parties, with the court's permission, to do so to enable justice to be done and to be seen to be done. This rule codifies the approach to both issues. It thereby maintains the balance struck between concentration, finality, economy, efficiency, and proportionality on the one hand, and the need to ensure that adjudicative accuracy and a fair process to all parties are also achieved.

3. The approach to raising new matters is long-settled. Given the importance of giving effect to the concentration principle, appellate courts have always subjected applications to raise such issues to intense scrutiny.[90] Rules 12(2) to (5) codify the test as summarised in *Singh v Das* (2019).[91]

[87] *Hertfordshire Investments Ltd v Bubb* [2000] 1 WLR 2318 at [25].

[88] ELI-UNIDROIT Model Rules, r 168, comment 2.

[89] ELI-UNIDROIT Model Rules, r 168, comment 1.

[90] *The Tasmania* (1890) 15 App Cas 223 at 225.

[91] *Singh v Dass* [2019] EWCA Civ 1337 at [16]–[18]; *Notting Hill Finance Ltd v Sheikh* [2019] EWCA Civ 1337 at [23]–[26].

4. Permitting new matters to be raised may require the amendment of a notice of appeal, response, or of a case statement from the first instance proceedings. To ensure that a proper record of the proceedings exists to secure proper dispute management, to ensure that the scope of the court's jurisdiction is clearly defined and understood,[92] and that there is effective public transparency and accountability concerning the nature of the proceedings, such consequential amendments should be effected by the appellate court.[93]
5. The approach to adducing fresh evidence was until the CPR's introduction governed by rules of court. RSC Ord 59, r 10(2) set out the test for permitting such matters to be adduced on appeal. It did so by codifying the approach set out in *Ladd v Marshall* (1954).[94] The CPR has, however, provided a general discretion, which it has tended to apply consistently with that approach.[95] In that way it sought to give effect to the CPR's overriding objective.[96] Rule 12(6) codifies the approach taken under the CPR.

## SECTION 4: APPEAL PROCEDURE

### RULE 13.—NOTICE OF APPEAL—STARTING AN APPEAL

**(1) Appeal proceedings start when a party (the appellant) gives notice of appeal. Notice of appeal means that the appellant has informed the court that they are exercising their right to appeal or to seek permission to appeal. Notice of appeal must identify**
- **(a) the order or part of a judgment subject to appeal;**
- **(b) the respondent or respondents and any interested parties to the appeal;**
- **(c) the reasons for the appeal; and**
- **(d) the relief sought.**

**(2) Except as provided in this Part, notice of appeal may be given to either the court whose order or judgment forms the subject matter of the appeal or to the appellate court. The appellate court is the court that will hear the appeal.**

**(3) Where an order or judgment is formally issued at a hearing, notice of appeal may be given orally at that hearing. Where permission to appeal is granted at such a hearing, a written notice of appeal, noting the grant of permission, must be filed with the appellate court within 14 days of the hearing.**

**(4) Except where notice of appeal is given orally, it must be given by the appellant filing a written notice of appeal with the appellate court within 28 days of the order or judgment being appealed having been issued formally. Service of the written notice is to be effected according to Part 10.**

**(5) The digital procedure may make provision, applicable to specific categories of appeal, for a shorter time limit to apply to the giving of notice.**

92 Rule 12(1); *Gover v Propertycare Ltd* [2006] EWCA Civ 286; [2006] ICR 1073 at [10].

93 *Islington London Borough Council v UCKAC* [2006] EWCA Civ 340; [2006] 1 WLR 1303.

94 *Ladd v Marshall* [1954] 1 WLR 1489 at 1491.

95 *Hamilton v Al-Fayed (Joined Party)* [2001] EMLR 15 at [11].

96 *Terluk v Berezovsky* [2011] EWCA Civ 1534 at [32]; *Hertfordshire Investments Ltd v Bubb* [2000] 1 WLR 2318 at [35]; *Sharab v Al-Sud* [2009] EWCA Civ 353 at [52]; *Fixsler v Manchester University NHS Foundation Trust* [2021] EWCA Civ 1018; [2021] 4 WLR 123 at [52].

**(6) The court to which notice of appeal is to be given may, on application and for good reason, vary the time limit to give notice.**
**(7) Notice of appeal may include any application incidental or consequential to the application for permission to appeal. This includes an application to stay enforcement.**
**(8) Where an appellant fails to give notice of appeal within the specified time limit they are barred from doing so unless the appellate court, on application, grants relief from sanction.**
**(9) An appellant must elaborate their reasons for appeal and response in a concise skeleton argument submitted to the appellate court before the appeal hearing.**

*Sources: ELI-UNIDROIT Model Rules, rr 155; 158, 173; CPR rr 52.3, 52.12, 52.15.*

## COMMENTARY

1. The appeal process commences when a party gives notice to the court that they seek permission to appeal from an order or part of a judgment. Notice may be given to the court whose order or judgment is subject to the application. Such notice must be given immediately upon the order or judgment being given. That may mean therefore that the application is made orally at the conclusion of a hearing where the order or judgment is given. Where that occurs, and permission is granted, a formal written notice of appeal must be submitted to the appellate court. This is to ensure that the appellate court has proper notice of the appeal and its basis. From a practical perspective this is essential for effective appellate dispute management.
2. Where an application is made directly to the appellate court, it must be made via a written notice of appeal. Notice must be given within the time limit specified to maintain consistency with the finality principle. The time limit may be varied generally through the digital procedure for specific categories of appeal. It may also be varied on a case-by-case basis by the appellate court. The former may be necessary to give effect to shorter time limits required for appeals in, for instance, judicial review proceedings or statutory appeals.[97] The latter may be justified where an appellant is outside the jurisdiction and more time is needed to enable them to prepare their notice of appeal. It may also be necessary where there are a large number of grounds of appeal and greater time is needed to properly articulate them in the notice of appeal. Where an appellant considers that they may need more time to file their notice of appeal they ought, consistently with the co-operation and proportionality principles, to apply prospectively for an extension of time to file their notice. This will use less court and party resources on the application than if one for relief from sanction had to be made following a failure to comply with the time limit.
3. The notice of appeal is the primary document that defines the scope of an appeal. For that reason, the appellant must clearly specify the order or part of a judgment that is subject to the application for permission to appeal, the other parties, including interested parties, to the appeal, the reasons or grounds for the appeal, and the relief sought. The notice of appeal may also include any other information or applications incidental or consequential to the application for permission to appeal. The appellant

[97] CPR rr 52.8–52.11.

may, for instance, seek a stay of enforcement of the order or judgment subject to the application. Applications may, additionally, be made throughout the course of appellate proceedings.

4. As with case statements, the exact content of the information set out in a notice of appeal is, as a consequence of party autonomy, a matter for the appellant. An appellant may, therefore, limit their reasons for seeking permission to appeal to a small number even though other, valid, reasons exist. In considering their reasons for appeal, appellants should, consistently with the co-operation principle, look to limit their reasons by reference to proportionality. Appellants may therefore need to consider whether to limit their reasons of appeal to several of their strongest challenges to the order or judgment under appeal.
5. The process by which permission to appeal is granted is intended to be a unilateral process. Respondents are not generally required to take part in it. As a consequence and to give effect, as far as possible, to procedural equality and fair access for all parties to a proposed appeal, appellants are under a duty to make full and frank disclosure in their notice of appeal. Failure to do so may result in the imposition of sanctions for non-compliance, including permission being set aside under rule 19.[98]
6. The reasons for appeal and any response to them ensure that due notice is given of the basis on which the appeal is brought. Those reasons and any arguments to rebut the respondent's arguments on the appeal must be set out by the appellant where permission is granted in their written skeleton arguments. Skeleton arguments play the same role in appellate proceedings as they do in first instance proceedings.[99]

## RULE 14.—RESPONDING TO A NOTICE OF APPEAL

**(1) Any respondent to an appeal may reply to the notice of appeal (the response).**

**(2) Generally, a response need only be filed within 14 days of deemed service on the respondent of the order granting permission to appeal.**

**(3) Where a respondent wishes to make submissions concerning whether permission to appeal should be granted, the response must be filed with the court within 14 days of deemed service of the notice of appeal. The response must then be served on the appellant in accordance with Part 10 of this Code. Such a response should only be made to bring to the appellate court's attention**

**(a) reasons why the appeal would not meet the relevant threshold test; or**

**(b) any material inaccuracy in the matters raised in the appeal notice, which could lead to permission to appeal being granted where it would otherwise not be granted.**

**(4) Permission to extend the time for service may be granted on application. Where a respondent fails to respond to a notice of appeal within the specified time limit, they are barred from doing so unless the appellate court, on application, grants relief from sanction.**

**(5) A response to a notice of appeal must identify, as applicable, the reason or reasons why permission to appeal should not be granted, the appeal should be dismissed or the order or part of the judgment subject to appeal should be upheld.**

[98] *Obsession Hair and Day Spa Ltd v Hi-Lite Electrical Ltd* [2011] EWCA Civ 1148.

[99] *Philosophy Inc v Ferretti Studio SRL* [2002] EWCA Civ 921; [2003] ETMR 8 at [30].

**(6) The reasons why an order or part of the judgment subject to appeal should be upheld may be different from those given by the court whose order or judgment is subject to appeal.**

**(7) Where a respondent does not respond to a notice of appeal they are deemed to join issue with the appellant on all matters for which permission to appeal was granted.**

**(8) Where a respondent also wishes to appeal from the order or part of the judgment subject to an appeal they must do so by issuing a notice of appeal. They may set out their notice of appeal in their response.**

**(9) A respondent must elaborate their reasons for appeal and response in a concise skeleton argument submitted to the appellate court before the appeal hearing.**

*Sources: ELI-UNIDROIT Model Rules, rr 159, 160; CPR r 52.13.*

## COMMENTARY

1. A respondent to an appeal may set out their reply to the notice of appeal in their 'response' to it. The response serves several purposes.
2. Its primary purpose is to set out the respondent's position concerning the grounds of appeal. It is thus functionally equivalent to a defence to particulars of claim. It is the means by which a respondent joins issue, or not, with the points raised by the appellant. This can be done in two ways. First, a respondent may wish to bring to the court and the appellant's notice a matter that tells against permission to appeal being granted. It is a means by which arguments can be set out why the test for permission to appeal is said to not be met. It may also inform the court about any inaccuracy in the notice of appeal or supporting documents that might lead to permission to appeal being granted on a false basis.[100] In this way it can, if served at the permission to appeal stage, help the appeal court determine more accurately whether permission should be granted. It thus also promotes proportionality by helping to ensure that only those matters that properly meet the permission threshold go forward as appeals. Secondly, and more usually, it is done through the respondent setting out their arguments why an appeal should be rejected after permission to appeal has been granted. In both cases, the provision of this information by the respondent satisfies the due notice principle, enabling the appellate court to carry out its dispute management function effectively. It particularly facilitates the latter as it helps the court determine the length of time needed to hear the appeal, what additional materials may be needed, and whether permission to intervene may justifiably be granted and, if so, on what issues.
3. Submission of a response before permission to appeal is granted is optional. The permission to appeal process is intended to be a unilateral process.[101] In many cases, responding prior to the grant of permission would result in both the respondent and the court incurring unnecessary time and expense; an early response would be disproportionate. This is particularly the case because the appellate court in considering whether to grant permission is simply determining if the jurisdictional threshold for there to be an appeal on the merits has been reached. Hence, if a respondent intends to submit their response before permission is granted, they

[100] H Brooke, D di Mambro, L di Mambro, D Gladwell, B Keith (2008) at 92, relying upon *Jolly v Jay* [2002] EWCA Civ 277 at [42]–[48].

[101] *Jolly v Jay* [2002] EWCA Civ 277 at [46].

should confine themselves to identifying matters that go to the question whether permission should be granted.

4. Where permission is granted, matters are different. It is necessary then to inform the appellant and the court what positive stance is taken to the grounds on which permission has been granted. This can be achieved either through provision of a response to the notice of appeal or if the respondent wishes to join issue on all matters by not filing a response. In the latter case, the respondent is deemed to join issue on all such matters. The latter course of action in many cases will be the most economical and proportionate.
5. Where a respondent wishes to argue that the judgment appealed should be upheld for reasons other than those set out in the judgment, they will need to file a response. This is to give both the appellant and the court effective notice of the argument to be raised so both can take it into account in considering how the appeal should be managed effectively. Early notice of such additional grounds to support the order or judgment under appeal may, however rare that may be in practice, also help to promote settlement of the appeal or lead to its withdrawal upon consideration by the appellant. As such, early notice via the response of such a ground is an important means to promote effective appellate management, and through it, proportionality. Moreover, notice is necessary if the respondent wishes to adduce evidence or other material on the appeal. This might be of particular importance where an appeal challenges an exercise of discretion. If such an appeal succeeded, the appellate court is likely to re-exercise the discretion rather than refer the matter back to the lower court. If the respondent wishes to rely on such evidence or material, as may be relevant to the exercise of the discretion, it is necessary to put the appellant and court formally on notice of it.[102]
6. Effective management of appellate proceedings, just as with first instance proceedings, requires compliance with procedural time limits. This rule recognises that respondents may need longer than the prescribed time limits to provide the appellant and the court with their response. A respondent complying with the co-operation principle will ensure that they seek any extension before the time limit expires. Breach of that principle will result in them being subject to the regime for relief from sanction if they later seek an extension of time.[103] Late applications may also prejudice the appellant's preparations for the appeal and the court's ability to manage the appeal proportionately.
7. Where a respondent also wishes to appeal from the order or judgment that is subject to appeal, they must do so by issuing their own notice of appeal.[104] As with a defence and counterclaim, if they wish to issue their notice of appeal at the same time as they issue a response, they may combine the two documents into a response and notice of appeal, which is equivalent to a defence and counterclaim.
8. The requirement to elaborate a respondent's arguments in a skeleton argument ensures the appellate process is an adversarial one and also, where necessary, ensures the appellant and the court are provided with due notice of the respondent's case on the appeal.

[102] *Sahota v Singh* [2018] EWHC 1685 (Ch) at [18]–[19].

[103] *Salford Estates (No 2) Ltd v Altomart Ltd* [2014] EWCA Civ 1408; [2015] 1 WLR 1825.

[104] CPR PD52C para 8.

## RULE 15.—AMENDMENT OF NOTICE OF APPEAL AND RESPONSE

**(1) A notice of appeal may only be amended with permission of the appellate court.**
**(2) Where permission is granted, the respondent may, with the appellate court's consent, respond to any amendments made to the notice of appeal.**
**(3) The court shall exercise its discretion to grant or refuse permission consistently with the general approach to amendment.**

*Sources: CPR r 52.17.*

## COMMENTARY

1. This rule mirrors the approach to amending case statements set out in Part 9. It thus provides for notices of appeal and responses to be amended consistently with the approach taken to amendment of case statements. It serves the same purpose as amendment generally: to enable errors or mistakes to be corrected and to enable appellate courts to determine the real issues in dispute.
2. The main difference between amendment of notices of appeal and responses and of case statements is that the former may only be amended with the appellate court's consent. Appellate courts tend to have more limited resources than first instance courts. There is, therefore, a greater need for appellate courts to control amendment so that parties do not bring about disproportionate use of their resources by, for instance, widening the issues on appeal unnecessarily.[105]
3. Where a party wishes to raise new grounds of appeal by way of amendment the application to amend should also include an application for permission to appeal. Further to the co-operation principle, the party seeking to raise a new ground of appeal ought to obtain, and provide the court with, the respondent's view on whether permission should be granted.[106] This places the appeal court in a better position to consider whether or not granting permission would further the purposive principle. Whether or not permission is granted to raise a new ground will, however, depend upon whether it satisfies the relevant permission to appeal test.

## RULE 16.—DETERMINATION OF APPLICATION FOR PERMISSION TO APPEAL

**(1) Except where an application for permission to appeal is made orally to the court whose order or judgment is subject to the application, all applications for permission to appeal shall be determined in writing without a hearing unless the court directs otherwise.**
**(2) Where an application for permission to appeal is made orally to the court whose order or judgment is subject to the application the court should determine the application at that time. Exceptionally, the court may adjourn the application to be determined either in writing or at a hearing following submission of a notice of appeal and any response.**

[105] *Clark (Inspector of Taxes) v Perks* [2001] 1 WLR 17 at [17].
[106] *Shire v Secretary of State for Work and Pensions* [2003] EWCA Civ 1465; [2004] CP Rep 11 at [6]–[7].

**(3) The court may direct that an application for permission to appeal is determined at a hearing where it is in the interests of justice to do so.**
**(4) Where an application for permission to appeal is made to an appellate court, the application will be determined by a single judge of that court.**
**(5) Before determining an application, the appellate court may request the judge whose order or judgment is subject to challenge to clarify or amplify their judgment. It may only do so where clarification or amplification of the judgment would reasonably assist it in determining the permission to appeal application.**
**(6) Permission to appeal may be granted generally or it may be limited to specific issues.**
**(7) A respondent is not required to take an active part in the application for permission to appeal process.**

*Sources: CPR rr 52.3, 52.4, 52.5.*

## COMMENTARY

1. The process by which an application for permission to appeal is considered is primarily written. Except where an oral application is made to the court whose order or judgment is subject to the application, it will be made via a notice of appeal submitted through the digital procedure and considered by a judge of the appellate court. This reflects the fact that the permission process is one that ordinarily does not involve the respondent. It also enables appellate court resources to be targeted towards substantive appeals. Thus, it helps facilitate systemic proportionality where use of those resources is concerned. Such an approach is consistent with the general access principle.[107]
2. Generally, it ought to be evident from the notice of appeal and supporting documentation whether the proposed appeal meets the requisite threshold for the grant of permission. There may, however, be circumstances when the nature of the application or the underlying proceedings mean that a judge is unable to determine whether permission should be granted without there being an oral hearing. To avoid injustice, the rule thus provides a discretion to direct an oral hearing in an appropriate case.
3. The rule also states the approach to be taken to oral applications for permission made at the conclusion of a hearing when an order or judgment is handed down. Such applications should be heard immediately. Exceptionally, they may be adjourned to give the appellant time to marshal their grounds of appeal. Applications to adjourn ought to be exceptional as they involve increased use of party and court resources; the expense of a written application ought to be limited to applications made to the appellate court.[108] The court whose order or judgment is subject to challenge has no jurisdiction to grant permission to appeal except as provided for in this rule.[109]
4. Rule 16(5) provides a general discretion for the appellate court to request further reasons or clarification from the court whose order or judgment is subject to challenge. This is to put it in the best position to determine the application where material before it is unclear or there is a gap in, for instance, the judgment's reasoning.[110]

[107] *R (Siddiqui) v Lord Chancellor* [2019] EWCA Civ 1040 at [19].
[108] *McDonald v Rose* [2019] EWCA Civ 4 at [21].
[109] *Lisle-Mainwairing v Associated Newspapers Ltd* [2018] EWCA Civ 1470; [2018] 1 WLR 4766 at [15].
[110] *Flannery v Halifax Estate Agencies Ltd* [2000] 1 WLR 377.

This power should be used carefully. Generally, an appellate court should be capable of determining an application for permission on the basis of the order and judgment as given by the court below. The power should not, therefore, be used routinely. It ought, consistently with the economy, efficiency, and proportionality principles, only be relied upon where clarification or amplification is necessary to enable the appellate court to determine the application for permission properly. Routine use of the power would amount to an unnecessary drain on judicial resources.

5. Finally, the rule makes clear that power to grant permission to appeal is unfettered. The court granting permission may do so generally. It may grant permission in respect of some grounds for appeal, while refusing permission on others.

## RULE 17.—EXERCISE OF THE RIGHT TO APPEAL MAY BE SUBJECT TO CONDITIONS

**(1) Permission to appeal may be granted subject to conditions. The court may also impose conditions after permission to appeal has been granted.**
**(2) Conditions may be imposed where and in so far as it is in the interests of justice to do so. Compelling reasons are required to justify their imposition. Conditions may be varied or set aside. Conditions imposed must be proportionate.**

*Sources: Council of Europe Recommendation No R (95) 5, Introduction and Improvement of the functioning of appeal systems and procedures in civil and commercial cases, chapter 1, art 4(d), (e); CPR rr 52.6, 52.18.*

## COMMENTARY

1. Within the CPR, the power to impose conditions is contained in CPR r 52.6, which concerns permission to bring first appeals. It provides that the power applies to both first appeals and second appeals. CPR r 52.18 then makes provision for conditions to be imposed after permission to appeal has been granted. Three situations are thus governed by two rules. This rule differs in approach as it provides a single, compendious power to impose conditions on the exercise of the right to appeal. This is intended to further procedural simplicity and accessibility.
2. Conditions may be imposed on permission to appeal or on an appeal where it is in the interests of justice to do so and there are compelling reasons to support that conclusion.[111] Conditions must be proportionate and must not stifle an appellant's ability to access the appellate process.[112] For that reason, as under the CPR, financial conditions, such as those related to the payment of costs of the appeal should not be imposed in low value claims.[113]

[111] *Days Medical Aids Ltd v Pihsiang Machinery Manufacturing Co Ltd* [2004] EWCA Civ 993 at [4]–[5].
[112] *Dumford Trading Ag v OAO Atlantrybflot* [2004] EWCA Civ 1265; *Hammond Suddards Solicitors v Agrichem International Holdings Ltd* [2001] EWCA Civ 2065; [2002] CP Rep 21.
[113] *Smith v Royal Bank of Scotland Plc* [2021] EWCA Civ 977; [2021] Costs LR 677.

3. A wide range of conditions could be justified in the interests of justice. Appellants could be required, as noted above, to pay the respondent's appeal costs.[114] They could be required to give security for costs.[115] They could be required to comply with any rules or court orders in respect of which they are in breach.[116] They could also be required to satisfy the judgment subject to appeal, any outstanding costs orders or give security for judgment.[117] Underpinning each of these possibilities are considerations arising from the overarching procedural principles. Procedural fairness, for instance, justifies requiring an appellant to pay the respondent's costs where it is a business and the respondent is a consumer and where any benefit from the appeal to it goes beyond the immediate case. Equally, procedural fairness, procedural equality, and the compliance principles justify requiring an appellant to comply with court orders as a condition precedent to being able to appeal. Security for judgment is justifiable as a condition to protect the integrity of the appellate process further to the general access principle, eg to counter the possibility that an appeal is being pursued to delay enforcement of a judgment in circumstances where there is a real risk that the appellant will dissipate their assets or move them out of the jurisdiction. Applying the interests of justice test by reference to the various procedural principles, thus enables the court to take account of a wide range of factors and circumstances in determining the nature of any conditions and whether to impose them.
4. Under the CPR where conditions are imposed by the court whose judgment is subject to appeal when it gave permission to appeal, the appellant is put to their election.[118] They have to either proceed to appeal subject to the conditions imposed or treat the permission subject to conditions as a refusal of permission to appeal. In the latter case they have to then seek permission to appeal from the appellate court. This rule does not codify that approach. As a matter of principle, the appellate court ought to give effect to the lower court's order and the appellant ought to abide by it, unless and until it is subject to a successful challenge. The election approach of the CPR is disproportionate as it multiplies applications to the court, while undermining the value of the first application. Equally, it can be seen to be unfair in that it enables an appellant, if permission is granted without conditions, to take the benefit of that, while they can, if permission is granted subject to conditions, treat it as a consequence-free dress rehearsal and discard it. The better and fairer approach is to hold an appellant to the nature of permission they have been granted, ie to subject them to the benefit or burden of the application irrespective of the outcome, which may, should the circumstances warrant it, be subject to variation, on application, by the appellate court.

[114] *Jones v T-Mobile (UK) Ltd* [2003] EWCA Civ 1162; [2003] 1 EGLR 55 at [26].

[115] *Merchant International Co Ltd v Natsionalna Aktsionerna Kompaniia Naftogaz Ukrainy* [2016] EWCA Civ 710.

[116] *Days Medical Aids Ltd v Pihsiang Machinery Manufacturering Co Ltd* [2004] EWCA Civ 993.

[117] *Bell Electric Ltd v Aweco Appliance Systems GmbH & Co KG* [2002] EWCA Civ 1501; [2003] 1 All ER 344; *Hammond Suddards Solicitors v Agrichem International Holdings Ltd* [2001] EWCA Civ 2065; [2002] CP Rep 21; *Golstrail Travel Ltd v Onur Air Tasimacilik AS* [2017] UKSC 57; [2017] 1 WLR 3014; *Onur Air Tasimacilik AS v Golstrail Travel Ltd* [2017] EWCA Civ 1830.

[118] *R (Medical Justice) v Secretary of State for the Home Department* [2011] EWCA Civ 269; [2011] 1 WLR 2852.

## RULE 18.—DISCONTINUANCE OF PERMISSION TO APPEAL APPLICATION OR APPEAL

**(1) An application for permission to appeal may be discontinued without consent.**

**(2) An appellant may discontinue their application for permission to appeal or appeal, in whole or in part. Discontinuance of an appeal by either an appellant or respondent may only be effected with the court's consent.**

**(3) A respondent discontinues the appeal process by consenting to the appeal being allowed. The court will only grant such an order where there are good and sufficient reasons for so doing.**

**(4) Unless the court exceptionally orders otherwise, where an application for permission to appeal or an appeal is discontinued, the party discontinuing shall pay any costs incurred by the other party arising from the appeal process. The court may not order otherwise unless the party discontinuing demonstrates that there is good reason for it to do so.**

**(5) Where discontinuance results from the parties settling the proceedings, they should inform the court of the fact of the settlement promptly upon settlement being reached. Failure to do so may result in an adverse costs award.**

*Sources: ELI-UNIDROIT Model Rules, r 163; CPR PD52A, Section VI.*

## COMMENTARY

1. This rule is similar in effect to that which governs the ability of a party to withdraw proceedings generally. It also therefore gives effect to the party autonomy principle by enabling an appellant or respondent to bring an application for permission to appeal or an appeal to an end prior to its determination by an appellate court.
2. Discontinuance may be effected by either an appellant or respondent. The former discontinues by either withdrawing or abandoning their application for permission to appeal or appeal. The latter does so by consenting to an appeal being allowed. Consent to an appeal being allowed will, at the least, require the parties to provide the court with plausible reasons why the lower court's decision was wrong. Party consent must also be on legal advice.[119] Such an approach promotes economy, efficiency, and proportionality. A respondent cannot discontinue until permission to appeal has been granted, as until that time there are no appeal proceedings to discontinue. If, however, a respondent intends not to contest an appeal, they may indicate that intention in a response to the notice of appeal, which should be submitted prior to the determination of the permission application. The respondent's indication can then be considered by the appellate court in determining whether the prospect of success threshold for granting permission is met or not. The indication does not, however, go to the question of whether or not permission to bring a second appeal should be granted as that requires there to be more than simply a real prospect of success.
3. The main difference between this rule and withdrawal of first instance proceedings is that in all appeals withdrawal may only be effected with the appellate court's consent. Where permission to appeal has been granted, there may be reasons why the appeal should not be withdrawn. The appeal may raise an issue of general or public importance, or it may be capable of being continued by an intervenor. In such circumstances, there is a strong public interest in the appeal continuing that overrides a party's interest

[119] *KW v Rochdale Metropolitan Borough Council (Rev 3)* [2015] EWCA Civ 1054; [2016] 1 WLR 198.

in discontinuing. Consent is not, however, needed to discontinue an application for permission to appeal. Prior to permission being granted there are no extant appeal proceedings that would give rise to any public interest in their continuance, and which would outweigh the appellant's interest in withdrawing their putative appeal.

4. Where an application for permission to appeal or appeal is discontinued, the party discontinuing is required to compensate the other party in costs for any costs incurred prior to discontinuance. Exceptionally, the court may for good reason order otherwise. This mirrors the approach at first instance. It is as much of a basic aspect of procedural fairness at the appellate level as it is at first instance.[120] Ordinarily, where discontinuance concerns an application for permission to appeal the respondent will have incurred or ought to have incurred no compensatable costs. Where, however, they submitted a response to the notice of appeal to, for instance, draw to the appellate court's attention an inaccuracy in the notice, their costs ought to be recoverable on discontinuance of the permission application.
5. Where discontinuance is a consequence of settlement, the parties ought to inform the court of their agreement to discontinue the appeal promptly. This will minimise the use of judicial and administrative resources managing the appeal. Where settlement occurs after the appeal hearing it will particularly help minimise the use of judicial time that would otherwise have been expended on judgment writing. Failure to keep the appellate court promptly and properly informed of settlement, as a breach of the compliance and co-operation principles, may result in the imposition of an adverse costs award.[121] Discontinuance following settlement, as with other bases on which discontinuance arises, is subject to court consent.

## RULE 19.—SETTING ASIDE PERMISSION TO APPEAL

**The court may, on the application of a respondent to an appeal, set aside permission to appeal where there is a compelling reason to do so. Such an application must be made promptly after permission is granted.**

*Sources: CPR r 52.18; RSC Ord 59, r 14.*

## COMMENTARY

1. This rule promotes the proper administration of justice at the appellate level as it is intended to protect the appellate process from abuse.[122] Thus permission may be set aside where the judge granting permission had been misled by the appellant[123] or where the appellant has breached their duty to the court to make full and frank disclosure of all matters relevant to the permission application.[124] It is also intended to protect the proper administration of justice by enabling a respondent to have permission set aside where it was granted in ignorance of the fact the appellate court had no jurisdiction to hear the appeal.[125]

[120] Part 7, r 7.

[121] *Red River UK Ltd v Sheikh* [2009] EWCA Civ 643 at [34]–[37].

[122] *Barings Bank Plc v Coopers & Lybrand* [2002] EWCA Civ 1155; [2003] CP Rep 2 at [43]; *Obsession Hair and Day Spa Ltd v Hi -Lite Electrical Ltd* [2011] EWCA Civ 1148 at [28].

[123] *Nathan v Smilovitch* [2002] EWCA Civ 759 at [9].

[124] *Obsession Hair and Day Spa Ltd v Hi-Lite Electrical Ltd* [2011] EWCA Civ 1148 at [28].

[125] *Athletic Union of Constantinople v National Basketball Association (No 2)* [2002] EWCA Civ 830; [2002] 1 WLR 2863.

2. Cogent reasons must be shown to justify setting aside permission.[126] It is not enough to demonstrate, for instance, that the grant of permission was made in ignorance of a relevant statutory provision or precedent. The statute or precedent must be such as to '*plainly and unarguably*' demonstrate that the appeal cannot succeed and thus there is a compelling reason to set aside permission. The strictness of the test is intended to ensure that it is not itself abused, ie that it does not become a source of tactical or satellite litigation that would be wasteful of the appellate court's resources or those of appellants.[127]
3. To save the appellate court and the appellant time and expense, an application to set aside should be made promptly after permission is granted.[128] By doing so, the respondent will further the purposive principle by helping to minimise work done by the court administratively to list the appeal, by the appellate judiciary in managing the appeal or preparing for an appeal hearing, and by the appellant in preparing for the appeal.

## RULE 20.—REOPENING AN APPEAL

**(1) An appeal court may reopen an application for permission to bring a final appeal or a final appeal. It may do so on the application of a party or of a non-party affected by the appellate court's order or judgment.**
**(2) A final appeal is an appeal determined by either the High Court or Court of Appeal (Civil Division) that cannot be subject to a further appeal.**
**(3) An application for permission to bring a final appeal or a final appeal may only be reopened where**
**(a) it is necessary in the interests of justice;**
**(b) there are exceptional circumstances that undermine the integrity of the court process;**
**(c) there is a strong probability that the court would have reached a different decision on the application for permission to appeal or appeal in the absence of the exceptional circumstances; and**
**(d) there are no other available remedies.**
**(4) Exceptional circumstances may arise where the integrity of the court process has been critically undermined by fraud, corruption, bias, or gross maladministration by the court.**
**(5) An application to reopen shall, unless the court orders otherwise, be considered in writing without a hearing.**
**(6) A decision whether to reopen an application for permission to bring a final appeal or a final appeal cannot be challenged.**

*Sources: ELI-UNIDROIT Model Rules, rr 181, 182, 183; CPR r 52.30.*

[126] *The Iran Nabuvat* [1990] 1 WLR 1115 at 1117–1118; *Nathan v Smilovitch* [2002] EWCA Civ 759 at [9]; *Barings Bank Plc v Coopers & Lybrand* [2002] EWCA Civ 1155; [2003] CP Rep 2 at [43].

[127] *Nathan v Smilovitch* [2002] EWCA Civ 759 at [8].

[128] *Mamidoil-Jetoil Greek Petroleum Co SA v Okta Crude Oil Refinery AD (No 4)* [2003] EWCA Civ 617; [2003] 2 Lloyd's Rep 645 at [10]–[11]; *Tradigrain SA v Intertek Testing Services (ITS) Canada Ltd* [2007] EWCA Civ 154; [2007] Bus LR D32.

## COMMENTARY

1. The ability to reopen a final appeal or an application for permission to bring a final appeal is a significant departure from the finality principle. Ordinarily, where proceedings have concluded in such a manner all parties and the public have a strong, legitimate expectation that the dispute has come to an end and that the parties' respective rights and obligations have been finally determined.[129] Notwithstanding this, many civil procedural systems provide mechanisms where, exceptionally, final decisions can be subject to challenge.[130] In England and Wales, for instance, actions to set aside final judgments where they are said to have been procured by fraud by a party can typically be brought.[131]
2. This rule is justified by reference to the appellate process's private and public purposes. It serves to correct error, thus promoting the parties' private interest in adjudicative accuracy. It also serves to maintain high standards in adjudication, and through that the rule of law and public confidence in the civil justice system. If it were, otherwise, to become well-known that final appellate decisions procured by fraud, subject to judicial bias etc were not capable of being corrected, confidence in the appellate courts would, inevitably, be harmed. This power acts as a safety valve to protect the integrity of the appellate process and is a means by which the courts are able to ensure that does not occur.
3. The existence of a jurisdiction to reopen appellate decisions is not a longstanding one. It was not recognised by the Court of Appeal until 2002, when it accepted that, in addition to an action for fraud brought by one of the parties to challenge a final decision, an appellate court had an inherent power to reopen applications for permission to appeal and final appeals.[132] In the same year it also recognised that the High Court had an equivalent power where it dealt with such a permission application or final appeal.[133] The impetus for this development was the House of Lords' decision in *Ex parte Pinochet (No 2)* (2000), which accepted that it, as a final appeal court, had an inherent jurisdiction to reopen one of its decisions where its procedure had been tainted by apparent bias.[134] This inherent jurisdiction was codified originally as CPR r 52.17 and then as r 52.30.[135]
4. This rule provides, as did the CPR, that the jurisdiction should only be exercisable where it is in the interests of justice to do so because exceptional circumstances exist that show the court's process was corrupted, that the effect of the corruption was such that without it there was a strong probability that a different decision would have been reached, and no alternative remedy exists.[136] It is thus only exercisable to avoid a '*real injustice*'.[137] In many cases, this will mean that the power will be used

[129] *The Ampthill Peerage* [1977] AC 547 at 569.

[130] German Code of Civil Procedure, s 578.

[131] *Jonesco v Beard* [1930] AC 298; *Salekipour v Parmar* [2017] EWCA Civ 2141; [2018] QB 833; *Royal Bank of Scotland plc v Highland Financial Partners LP* [2013] EWCA Civ 328; [2013] 1 CLC 596; *Takhar v Gracefield Developments Ltd* [2019] UKSC 13; [2020] AC 450; *Tinkler v Esken Ltd* [2023] EWCA Civ 655.

[132] *Taylor v Lawrence* [2002] EWCA Civ 90; [2003] QB 528 at [17] at [52]–[53]; *Lawal v Circle 33 Housing Trust* [2014] EWCA Civ 1514; [2015] HLR 9 at [65].

[133] *Seray-Wurie v Hackney LBC* [2002] EWCA Civ 909; [2003] 1 WLR 257.

[134] *R v Bow Street Metropolitan Stipendiary Magistrate Ex p Pinochet Ugarte (No 2)* [2000] 1 AC 119.

[135] Civil Procedure (Amendment No 3) Rules 2006 (SI 2016/798); *Ceredigion Recycling and Furniture Team v Pope* [2022] EWCA Civ 22.

[136] Examples of alternative remedies are, in addition to actions for fraud, the possibility to vary or set aside the judgment or order.

[137] *Taylor v Lawrence* [2002] EWCA Civ 90; [2003] QB 528 at [55].

where the integrity of the process was undermined by some action on the part of the court, eg bias on the part of a judge[138] or that the judge read the wrong material in considering the application or appeal (an example of gross maladministration by the court).[139] It may also arise where: a fraud has been perpetrated on the Court of Appeal or High Court acting as an appellate court;[140] or, the court had been seriously misled by evidence submitted to it that was untrue,[141] an approach taken both under the CPR, albeit not unequivocally, and by the ELI-UNIDROIT Model Rules.[142] In many cases, the existence of an action for fraud will, however, mean that an effective alternative remedy exists: the jurisdiction should thus not generally be exercised where there has been a fraud on the court.[143] It will not, however, be exercisable where the integrity of the process has been adversely effected by errors by the parties or their lawyers.[144]

5. To promote procedural proportionality, applications to reopen should be dealt with in writing without a hearing. A decision whether to reopen or not is final. It is not subject to any possibility of challenge or review or reopening.[145] This ensures that the jurisdiction remains one that does not itself become a basis for satellite litigation contrary to the finality principle. The process by which an application to reopen is considered is, thus, itself one that gives—as far as possible—significant weight to that principle.

138 *Taylor v Lawrence* [2002] EWCA Civ 90; [2003] QB 528 at [8].

139 *Municipio De Mariana v BHP Group Plc* [2021] EWCA Civ 1156; [2022] 1 WLR 919 at [60].

140 *Taylor v Lawrence* [2002] EWCA Civ 90; [2003] QB 528 at [34] and following.

141 *Feakins v Department for Environment, Food & Rural Affairs* [2006] EWCA Civ 699.

142 *Couwenbergh v Valkova* [2004] EWCA Civ 676; [2004] CP Rep 38; *Re Uddin (A Child)* [2005] EWCA Civ 52; [2005] 1 WLR 2398; *Jaffray v Society of Lloyd's* [2007] EWCA Civ 586; [2008] 1 WLR 75; ELI-UNIDROIT Model Rules, r 182.

143 P Coulson (ed) (2024) Vol 1 at 52.30.2.

144 *R (Nicholas) v Upper Tribunal (Administrative Appeal Chamber)* [2013] EWCA Civ 799.

145 Truly exceptionally further applications to reopen can be made where an initial application has failed: *UCP plc v Nectrus Ltd* [2022] EWCA Civ 949.

# INDEX

*For the benefit of digital users, indexed terms that span two pages (e.g., 52–53) may, on occasion, appear on only one of those pages.*